IMPORTANT:

HERE IS YOUR REGISTRATION CODE TO ACCESS
YOUR PREMIUM McGRAW-HILL ONLINE RESOURCES.

For key premium online resources you need THIS CODE to gain access. Once the code is entered, you will be able to use the Web resources for the length of your course.

If your course is using **WebCT** or **Blackboard**, you'll be able to use this code to access the McGraw-Hill content within your instructor's online course.

Access is provided if you have purchased a new book. If the registration code is missing from this book, the registration screen on our Website, and within your WebCT or Blackboard course, will tell you how to obtain your new code.

Registering for McGraw-Hill Online Resources

TO gain access to your McGraw-Hill web resources simply follow the steps below:

1. USE YOUR WEB BROWSER TO GO TO: **www.mhhe.com/magill7e**

2. CLICK ON **FIRST TIME USER**.

3. ENTER THE REGISTRATION CODE* PRINTED ON THE TEAR-OFF BOOKMARK ON THE RIGHT.

4. AFTER YOU HAVE ENTERED YOUR REGISTRATION CODE, CLICK **REGISTER**.

5. FOLLOW THE INSTRUCTIONS TO SET-UP YOUR PERSONAL UserID AND PASSWORD.

6. WRITE YOUR UserID AND PASSWORD DOWN FOR FUTURE REFERENCE.
   KEEP IT IN A SAFE PLACE.

TO GAIN ACCESS to the McGraw-Hill content in your instructor's **WebCT** or **Blackboard** course simply log in to the course with the UserID and Password provided by your instructor. Enter the registration code exactly as it appears in the box to the right when prompted by the system. You will only need to use the code the first time you click on McGraw-Hill content.

Thank you, and welcome to your McGraw-Hill online Resources!

* YOUR REGISTRATION CODE CAN BE USED ONLY ONCE TO ESTABLISH ACCESS. IT IS NOT TRANSFERABLE.

0-07-292176-5 T/A MAGILL: MOTOR LEARNING AND CONTROL

MCGRAW-HILL
ONLINE RESOURCES

REGISTRATION CODE

PMIR-8142-UALD-GANT-T46A

Higher Education

MOTOR LEARNING AND CONTROL
CONCEPTS AND APPLICATIONS

SEVENTH EDITION

Richard A. Magill

Louisiana State University

Boston Burr Ridge, IL Dubuque, IA Madison, WI New York San Francisco St. Louis
Bangkok Bogotá Caracas Kuala Lumpur Lisbon London Madrid Mexico City
Milan Montreal New Delhi Santiago Seoul Singapore Sydney Taipei Toronto

Higher Education

MOTOR LEARNING AND CONTROL: CONCEPTS AND APPLICATIONS, SEVENTH EDITION

Published by McGraw-Hill, a business unit of The McGraw-Hill Companies, Inc., 1221 Avenue of the Americas, New York, NY 10020. Copyright © 2004 by the The McGraw-Hill Companies, Inc. All rights reserved. Previous edition(s) 2001, 1998, 1993, 1989, 1985, 1980. All rights reserved. No part of this publication may be reproduced or distributed in any form or by any means, or stored in a database or retrieval system, without the prior written consent of The McGraw-Hill Companies, Inc., including, but not limited to, in any network or other electronic storage or transmission, or broadcast for distance learning.

Some ancillaries, including electronic and print components, may not be available to customers outside the United States.

This book is printed on acid-free paper containing 10% postconsumer waste.

3 4 5 6 7 8 9 0 DOC/DOC 0 9 8 7 6 5 4

ISBN 0-07-255722-2

Vice president and editor-in-chief: *Thalia Dorwick*
Publisher: *Jane E. Karpacz*
Executive editor: *Vicki Malinee*
Developmental editor: *Carlotta Seely*
Senior marketing manager: *Pamela S. Cooper*
Production supervisor: *Enboge Chong*
Media technology producer: *Lance Gerhart*
Senior designer: *Violeta Diaz*
Cover designer: *Glenda King*
Interior designer: *Seilah Barrett*
Cover image: *© David Madison Sports Image, Inc.*
Art editor: *Emma Ghiselli*
Manager, photo research: *Brian J. Pecko*
Senior supplement producer: *David A. Welsh*
Compositor: *Thompson Type*
Typeface: *10/12 Times*
Printer: *R. R. Donnelley/Crawfordsville, IN*

PHOTO CREDITS Pages 5, 146, 174, 108, 337, 354: © Royalty-Free/Corbis; **Page 28:** Courtesy of the author; **Page 51:** Steve Mason/Getty Images/PhotoDisc; **Pages 80a, 333:** Ryan McVay/Getty Images/PhotoDisc; **Pages 80b, 106:** Jules Frazier/Getty Images/PhotoDisc; **Page 125:** Jeff Maloney/Getty Images/PhotoDisc; **Pages 201, 319:** Karl Weatherly/Getty Images/PhotoDisc; **Pages 235, 278:** Photolink/Getty Images/PhotoDisc

Library of Congress Cataloging-in-Publication Data

Magill, Richard A.
    Motor learning and control : concepts and applications/Richard A. Magill.—7th ed.
        p. cm.
    Includes bibliographical references and index.
    ISBN 0-07-255722-2 (hard cover : alk. paper)
    1. Motor learning and control. I. Title

BF295.M36 2004
152.3´34—dc21

2003051309

www.mhhe.com

DETAILED CONTENTS

PREFACE

The goal of this text continues in the path of earlier editions: to offer an introduction to motor learning and motor control for students who aspire to become practitioners in a variety of professions. In some of these professions, individuals will work with people who perform motor skills very well, such as elite athletes; in others, they will work with people who have difficulty performing motor skills, such as those with physical disabilities. Regardless of the characteristics and needs of the people with whom the practitioner works, he or she will need a solid understanding of the concepts and applications of motor learning and motor control. With this understanding as a foundation, the practitioner can adapt to the specific demands of each professional setting.

This edition includes specific changes designed to enhance the quality of the book as well as the educational experience of the student. The changes are the result of welcomed comments from instructors who use the book in their classes and from the reviewers of the previous edition.

NEW TO THIS EDITION

New Title

This new edition features the term *motor control* added to the title. The incentive to add this term came from reviewers of the text, who indicated they were not aware that motor control issues are included in the book. However, a comparison of the chapter titles in this seventh edition with the titles in previous editions shows that motor control issues such as motor control theories, motor control of complex skills, the roles of proprioception and vision in the control of motor skills, and action preparation, have consistently been included in previous editions. It is important for users of previous editions of this book to understand that the title change does not mean that the emphasis of this edition has changed; only the title has been changed to reflect the content of the book more accurately.

Chapter Restructuring

Reviewers of the sixth edition expressed their concern that the book contained more chapters than could be covered in a typical one-semester course. Although it is difficult to write a textbook that would be an exact fit for every user's semester or instructional term, I have addressed this issue by reducing the number of chapters. The seventh edition includes 18 chapters, rather than 23 chapters, as in the sixth edition. This reduction was achieved by combining several of the sixth-edition chapters:

- Chapter 8 (Attention) combines the separate chapters on attention and visual selective attention.
- Chapter 11 (The Stages of Learning) combines the sixth edition's chapters on the stages of learning and predicting performance for later learning stages.
- Chapter 14 (Augmented Feedback) combines the three chapters that formerly addressed this topic.

- Chapter 16 (Amount and Distribution of Practice) combines the sixth edition's chapters on the amount of practice and the distribution of practice.

In addition to the combining of several sixth-edition chapters, this new edition reverses the order of two chapters in the first unit: Chapter 2 (The Measurement of Motor Performance) was Chapter 3 in the sixth edition, and Chapter 3 (Motor Abilities) was Chapter 2 in that edition.

New Research

One of the exciting aspects of the study of motor learning and motor control is the amount of research activity that takes place throughout the world. In fact, this activity appears to be increasing every year. Therefore it becomes especially important to regularly update this textbook in order to offer the students the most current information. Each chapter in the seventh edition includes an updating of research in the text, the A Closer Look boxes, and the Related Readings section.

Greater Emphasis on Motor Skills Applications

As in previous editions, numerous types of motor skills are used as examples throughout the book to allow students to apply the various motor learning and control concepts to specific motor skills with which they are familiar. However, the number of practical applications has been increased to demonstrate how teachers, coaches, physical and occupational therapists, and athletic trainers can use motor learning and control in their fields.

My own teaching experience with undergraduates has convinced me that students acquire a better understanding of the concepts discussed in this book when they can relate them to their own skill performance or learning experiences. Because of the variety of backgrounds, interests, and professional aspirations of students who use this book, the specific skills included throughout the book relate to a wide range of types of motor skills, including activities of daily living, physical education, fitness activities, sports, and dance.

Chapter Objectives

Each chapter now begins with a list of chapter objectives. This new feature encourages students to focus on the key topics, making it easier for them to learn and review the content of each chapter.

Lab Links

The Online Learning Center developed for this book includes a laboratory manual that features laboratory experiences designed for most chapters in this text. To direct students' attention to these activities, this edition includes a Lab Links box that highlights a specific online laboratory activity that corresponds to a particular chapter topic. Most of the chapters have one Lab Links box, and some have more than one.

NEW OR EXPANDED TOPICS

This new edition has undergone a thorough revision that includes updating in all chapters. Each chapter features topics that are either new to this revision or covered in greater depth than in the last edition. Following is a sampling of these new or expanded topics:

Chapter 1: The Classification of Motor Skills

- New figure to illustrate examples of skills associated with the three motor skill classification systems based on one dimension of motor skills
- Revised table presenting skill categories of Gentile's taxonomy to include examples of motor skills
- New A Closer Look box to offer examples of use of Gentile's taxonomy to evaluate movement capabilities in physical therapy and physical education

Chapter 2: The Measurement of Motor Performance

- New A Closer Look box to present example of calculation and use of absolute error, constant error, and variable error
- New figure to illustrate calculation of radial error

- Revised figure showing displacement, velocity, and acceleration with examples based on wrist movement in dart throwing
- Expanded discussion of kinetics
- Expanded discussion of EMG

Chapter 3: Motor Abilities
- Expanded discussion of specificity view of motor abilities
- Expanded intercorrelation table (Drowatzky and Zuccato experiment) with added descriptions of balance tests
- Added section on balance and timing as motor abilities
- New A Closer Look box presenting Henry's 1961 study of the relationship between reaction time and movement time
- New table focusing on definitions, tests, and motor skill examples of the perceptual–motor abilities categories of Fleishman's taxonomy

Chapter 4: Motor Control Theories
- Expanded discussion of the definition of *coordination*
- New A Closer Look box presenting a demonstration used by Bernstein to demonstrate the degrees-of-freedom problem
- Added discussion of the relationship between invariant features and parameters of a generalized motor program
- Revised figure showing the results of a study by Shapiro and colleagues to illustrate the differences between relative time characteristics of walking and running
- Added discussion concerning intrinsic coordinative structures
- Expanded discussion of perception-action coupling
- Revised discussion of the present state of the control theory issue

Chapter 5: Performance Characteristics of Complex Skills
- Revised figure of examples of tasks with different indexes of difficulty to show approximate movement times

- New A Closer Look box to describe a study investigating initial difficulties people have trying to control upper-extremity prostheses when performing a prehension task
- New section on head stability and locomotion

Chapter 6: Proprioception and Vision
- Expanded discussion of the role of proprioception in control of human movement
- New A Closer Look box featuring the use of eye tracking in the study of eye and hand movements
- Expanded discussion of the roles of central (foveal) and peripheral vision in control of human movement
- Added discussion on maintaining of postural balance and the role of optical flow
- New A Closer Look box describing an experiment that demonstrates how skilled gymnasts use vision on the balance beam
- New A Closer Look box highlighting research evidence concerning the information that vision provides people during stair climbing
- New A Closer Look box describing mathematical models that answer the question, What control strategy does a person use to catch a ball that requires running some distance to catch it?
- New A Closer Look box featuring conclusions derived from research concerning the question, Do general vision training programs for athletes improve sports performance?

Chapter 7: Action Preparation
- New A Closer Look box presenting a historical look at the use of reaction time to study action preparation
- Added discussion of the Stroop effect in the section on stimulus-response compatibility
- Expanded discussion of postural preparation
- Added discussion of setting of the amount of force in preparation for manipulating an object

- Added discussion of preparation of sequences of simple movements

Chapter 8: Attention as a Limited Capacity Resource

- New A Closer Look box featuring a recent research study on attention and cell-phone use while driving a vehicle
- New A Closer Look box describing a physical therapy study that demonstrates the use of dual-task procedure to investigate attention demands of gait for people with Parkinson's disease
- New discussion of a comparison of focusing attention on movements versus movement effects
- Added discussion of visual search and intended actions
- New A Closer Look box about a study concerning the influence of distractors on prehension and implications for physical rehabilitation treatment protocols

Chapter 9: Memory Components, Forgetting, and Strategies

- New A Closer Look box to describe a series of studies concerning the influence of proactive interference on gymnastic judges
- Expanded discussion of the use of visual imagery and verbal labels to aid motor skill learning
- Chapter content revised and reduced for clarity

Chapter 10: Defining and Assessing Learning

- Clarification of examples of performance curves for kinematic measures
- Expanded discussion of assessing learning based on coordination dynamics

Chapter 11: The Stages of Learning

- Expanded and updated terminology in the discussion of Gentile's model
- Expanded discussion of the relationship between the degrees-of-freedom problem (Chapter 4) and the freezing of degrees

of freedom as an early stage of learning strategy
- Revised and expanded discussion of changes in energy cost
- Expanded discussion of changes in visual selective attention
- Expanded discussion of changes in error detection and correction capability
- New discussion of specificity of use of sources of feedback as a performer characteristic that does not change across stages of learning
- New A Closer Look box presenting views of researchers and practitioners about the use of mirrors in dance studios and weight training rooms

Chapter 12: Transfer of Learning

- Expanded discussion on assessing effectiveness of practice conditions
- New discussion concerning what constitutes "component part" of a skill
- New A Closer Look box describing research study concerning use of bilateral transfer as occupational therapy treatment strategy

Chapter 13: Demonstration and Verbal Instructions

- Expanded discussion of frequency and timing of demonstrations
- Revised and expanded discussion of auditory modeling
- Expanded discussions of cognitive mediation theory and dynamic view
- New discussion of the action effect hypothesis in relation to verbal instructions
- New A Closer Look box describing a research study concerning the use of implicit learning-based instructional strategy to train anticipatory skills in tennis
- New A Closer Look box focusing on potential instruction-related problems experts may expect with beginners

Chapter 14: Augmented Feedback
- Expanded discussion of types of augmented feedback
- New A Closer Look box featuring a research study that describes the stages skilled athletes progress through in learning to use videotape replays as augmented feedback
- New A Closer Look box to describe some forms that concurrent augmented feedback can take, with examples
- Expanded discussion of self-selected augmented feedback
- Revised discussion of summary technique to include average augmented feedback technique

Chapter 15: Practice Variability
- Expanded discussion of future performance benefits of practice variability
- New A Closer Look box to describe an experiment comparing constant and variable practice for learning to shoot free throws in basketball
- New A Closer Look box to describe an experiment demonstrating the application of the contextual interference effect for physical therapy for stroke patients
- Expanded discussion of explanations for the contextual interference effect
- New A Closer Look box to discuss the relationship of practice variability to practice specificity and contextual interference

Chapter 16: The Amount and Distribution of Practice
- Expanded discussion of how overlearning strategy can lead to poor test performance
- New section on explanations for distributed practice benefit in relation to distribution of practice sessions across days

Chapter 17: Whole and Part Practice
- More motor skill examples in discussion of practicing skills involving asymmetric limb coordination

- Expanded discussion of methods for reducing task difficulty as practice strategy

Chapter 18: Mental Practice
- Expanded definition of the term *mental practice*
- New A Closer Look box to describe an experiment demonstrating the use of mental practice in a physical therapy treatment program
- Expanded discussion of mental practice and imagery ability

SUCCESSFUL FEATURES

Motor Learning and Control: Concepts and Applications offers the following helpful features to enhance student learning.

Definition Boxes
Key terms, which are highlighted in the text in boldface type, are defined in corresponding boxes for easy reference. Other important terms in the text appear in italics for emphasis.

Applications
Each chapter begins with an Applications section that explains the chapter concept in practical terms. This feature helps students understand the relevance of the concept to professional practice.

Discussion
This section explains how the chapter concept will be presented. It gives students the rationale for this presentation, making the concept easier to understand at the outset.

Summary
Each chapter concludes with a summary that presents the main ideas and their significance. Using this tool, students can return easily to a chapter topic for clarification or study.

Related Readings
For students who want to know more about a particular topic, this list at the end of each chapter offers carefully selected journal articles and books for exploration.

Study Questions

A set of questions appears at the end of each chapter to encourage students to review and analyze the chapter content.

Glossary

At the end of the text, all terms that are defined in the definition boxes are included in a comprehensive glossary. This glossary is useful for quick reference and helpful for review in preparation for examinations.

Name Index

In addition to the regular subject index, this book features a name index, which highlights important names in the field of motor learning and control—both past and present.

SUPPLEMENTS

Computerized Test Bank CD-ROM
ISBN: 0–07–255724–9

Brownstone's Computerized Testing is the most flexible, powerful, easy-to-use electronic testing program available in higher education. The Diploma system (for Windows users) allows the test maker to create a print version, an online version (to be delivered to a computer lab), or an Internet version of each test. Diploma includes a built-in instructor gradebook, into which student rosters and files can be imported. The CD-ROM includes a separate testing program, Exam VI, for Macintosh users.

Health and Human Performance Website
www.mhhe.com/hhp

McGraw-Hill's Health and Human Performance website provides a wide variety of information for both instructors and students, including monthly articles about current issues, downloadable supplements for instructors, a "how to" technology guide, study tips, and exam preparation materials. It includes information about professional organizations, conventions, and careers.

Online Learning Center
www.mhhe.com/magill7e

The Online Learning Center to accompany this text offers a number of additional resources for both students and instructors. Visit this website to find useful materials such as the following:

For the instructor:
- Downloadable PowerPoint presentations
- Lecture outlines
- Links to professional resources

For the student:
- Self-scoring chapter quizzes and online study guides
- Flashcards for learning key terms and their definitions
- Online laboratory manual
- Web links for study and exploration of topics in the text
- Information on careers in this field

PageOut: The Course Website Development Center
www.pageout.net

PageOut, free to instructors who use a McGraw-Hill textbook, is an online program you can use to create your own course web site. PageOut offers the following features:

- A course home page
- An instructor home page
- A syllabus (interactive and customizable, including quizzing, instructor notes, and links to the text's Online Learning Center)
- Web links
- Discussions (multiple discussion areas per class)
- An online gradebook
- Links to student web pages

Contact your McGraw-Hill sales representative to obtain a password.

PowerWeb
www.dushkin.com/online

The PowerWeb website is a reservoir of course-specific articles and current events. Students can visit PowerWeb to take a self-scoring quiz, complete an interactive exercise, click through an interactive glossary, or check the daily news. An expert in each discipline analyzes the day's news to show students how it relates to their field of study.

PowerWeb is packaged with many McGraw-Hill textbooks. Students are also granted full access to Dushkin/McGraw-Hill's Student Site, where they can read study tips, conduct web research, learn about different career paths, and follow fun links on the web.

Primis Online
www.mhhe.com /primis /online

Primis Online is a database-driven publishing system that allows instructors to create content-rich textbooks, lab manuals, or readers for their courses directly from the Primis website. The customized text can be delivered in print or electronic (eBook) form. A Primis eBook is a digital version of the customized text (sold directly to students as a file downloadable to their computer or accessed online by a password).

ACKNOWLEDGMENTS

No new edition of a textbook could be accomplished without the support of colleagues, friends, and loved ones. In particular, I want to acknowledge the level of support I continue to receive from Amelia Lee, my department chair in the Department of Kinesiology at Louisiana State University. Without support and encouragement from her, as well as from others in the department, this new edition would not have been possible. I also want to recognize colleagues from around the world who have regularly sent me their ideas and suggestions concerning ways to make the book work better for them in the classes they teach.

On a personal level, I want to publicly acknowledge and thank Susan Koff, to whom I dedicate this new edition and to whom I was recently married, for both her patience and her efforts as "taskmaster" throughout my work on this revision.

I am pleased to have had the same developmental editor and project manager who worked on the sixth edition. I thank them both for their direction, suggestions, patience, and other qualities that made the revision experience a smooth process.

Finally, as I have in each of the previous editions, I wish to thank the many undergraduate and graduate students who have been in my motor learning classes. Few of them will ever know how much I have learned from them and how they have influenced much of the content of this book.

The publisher's reviewers made especially helpful comments and suggestions to guide my revision of this textbook. I greatly appreciate these contributions from the following reviewers:

For the seventh edition

Diane Hurlbut
Central Connecticut State University

Gerard G. Lyons
Idaho State University

Larry W. McDaniel
Chadron State College

Erin McLaughlin Hall
California State University

Dawn L. Patel
University of Indianapolis

Geraldine L. Pellecchia
University of Hartford

Shannon D. Robertson
Arizona State University

Marco Santello
Arizona State University

Tina Stoeckmann
Marquette University

Richard A. Magill
Baton Rouge, Louisiana

———— ■ ————

TO MY LOVELY WIFE

SUSAN RUTH KOFF

———— ■ ————

UNIT

I

INTRODUCTION TO MOTOR SKILLS AND ABILITIES

The Classification
of Motor Skills

*Concept: Motor skills can be classified
into general categories*

After completing this chapter, you will be able to

- Define and distinguish the terms *action* and *movement*, and give examples of each

- Describe the one common motor skill characteristic for each of three motor skill classification systems, the two categories of skills in each system, and examples of motor skills in each category of each system

- Describe the two dimensions used to classify skills in the Gentile taxonomy of motor skills and the classification characteristic included within each dimension

- Discuss ways to use the Gentile taxonomy of motor skills in physical rehabilitation or physical education and sport contexts

Application

When people run, walk with an artificial limb, throw a baseball, hit a tennis ball, play the piano, dance, or operate a wood lathe, they are engaged in the performance of a type of human behavior called *motor skills.* In this book, the focus is on helping you understand how people learn, and how you can help people learn, motor skills such as these.

As you engage in this study, you will find it useful to draw general conclusions, applying what you learn to a broad range of motor skills, rather than making many specific statements about many skills. The starting point for doing this is the classification of motor skills into broad categories that emphasize the similarities rather than the differences among skills.

For example, the skill of maneuvering a wheelchair through a crowded hallway and that of hitting a pitched baseball seem quite distinct. However, both skills have one characteristic in common. People must perform both skills in an "open" environment. This means that to perform the skill successfully, a person must adapt certain aspects of his or her movements to changing characteristics in the performance environment. For the wheelchair skill, this means that the person must be able to maneuver successfully through a crowded hallway in which people are walking. For the baseball-hitting skill, the changing environment involves the ball itself as it moves toward the person. For both of these skills, performance success requires the performer to adapt quickly and accurately to changing conditions. When we view them in terms of this common characteristic, we can see that these two seemingly diverse skills are related.

Discussion

To begin your study of motor learning, you should understand some things about the skills that are at the heart of this study. To enhance this understanding, two important points about motor skills will be discussed. First, we will define motor skills, considering what distinguishes them from other skills; as we do so, we will define some other commonly used terms related to the term *motor skill*. Second, we will discuss four different approaches to classifying motor skills into categories that identify common characteristics of various skills. The benefit of classifying skills is that it can provide you with an appropriate basis for establishing generalizations, or principles, about how we perform and learn motor skills. These generalizations will enable you in turn to develop theories about skill performance and learning. Additionally, they help establish guidelines for instructors, coaches, and therapists who must develop effective strategies that will enhance motor skill learning and rehabilitation.

SKILLS, ACTIONS, AND MOVEMENTS

Several terms in the motor learning literature are related to the term *motor skills*. These are *skills, actions,* and *movements.* Each term is used in a specific way you should understand and use correctly.

Skills and Actions
The term **skill** is a commonly used word that you will see in this text denotes *a task that has a specific goal to achieve.* For example, we commonly say that "multiplication is a fundamental skill of mathematics," or "playing the piano is a skill that takes practice." Of these two examples, the skill of

piano playing includes a **motor skill** because it is *a skill that requires voluntary body, head, and/or limb movement to achieve its goal,* which is to play the piano. Looked at this way, the skill of piano playing involves the goal of striking the correct keys in the proper sequence and at the appropriate time, and it requires finger and hand movement to achieve that goal.

In the motor learning and control research literature, a term that has become increasingly more common to designate a specific motor skill is the term *actions.* For our purposes, we can consider this term as synonymous and interchangeable with the term *motor skills.* That is, **actions** are *goal-directed activities that consist of body, head, and/or limb movements.*

Note several characteristics that are common to motor skills. First, there is *a goal to achieve.* This means that motor skills have a purpose. Sometimes you will see the term *action goal* used to refer to the goal of a motor skill. Second, the types of motor skills of interest in this text are *performed voluntarily;* in other words, we are not considering reflexes as skills. Although an eye blink may have a purpose and involve movement, it occurs involuntarily and is therefore not a skill in the sense in which we are using the term. Third, a motor skill *requires body, head, and/or limb movement* to accomplish the goal of the task. This characteristic is especially important because it is the basis for distinguishing motor skills from other types of human skills. For example, although solving math problems is a skill, it does not *require* body and/or limb movement to achieve its goal. We commonly refer

---

skill   (a) an action or task that has a specific goal to achieve; (b) an indicator of quality of performance.

motor skill   a skill that requires voluntary body and/or limb movement to achieve its goal.

action   a goal-directed activity that consists of body and/or limb movements.

A CLOSER LOOK

Examples of Skills, Actions, Goals, and Movements

The following examples illustrate how a skill or action can have various goals, which would require movements that differ according to the action goal. For each of the goals within a skill/action, consider how the movements would differ to allow the person to achieve the goal while carrying out the same skill/action.

Skills/Actions	Goal
1. Walking	a. To walk from the front of an empty room to the back of the room
	b. To walk from one store to another store in a crowded mall
	c. To walk several blocks on a sidewalk
2. Throwing	a. To accurately throw a small round ball at a target on the wall
	b. To throw a small round ball as far as possible
	c. To throw a beach ball to a friend to catch
3. Reaching and grasping an object	a. To pick up a full coffee mug from a table and drink from it
	b. To pick up a bowl of soup to move it from one location on a table to another location on the table
	c. To pick up a can of juice and shake it

---

to the solving of math problems as a cognitive skill.

One additional characteristic further identifies the types of motor skills of interest in this text: they *need to be learned, or relearned,* in order for a person to achieve the goal of the skill. In our example, the piano playing clearly must be learned. But consider a skill like walking. Although walking may seem to be something that humans do "naturally," it must be learned by the infant who is attempting to move in his or her environment by this new and exciting means of locomotion. And walking is a skill some people may need to relearn. Examples are people who have had strokes, or hip or knee joint replacements, as well as people who must learn to walk with artificial legs.

Movements

In the motor learning and control research literature, the term **movements** indicates *behavioral characteristics of the body, the head, and/or a specific limb or combination of limbs.* This means that movements are the component parts of motor skills and actions. A variety of body, head, and limb behavior characteristics can occur that enable a person to walk successfully. For example, our arms and legs move in different and distinct ways when we walk on a concrete sidewalk and when we walk on an icy sidewalk—or on a sandy beach. However, although the actual movements may differ, the motor skill we perform in each of these different situations is walking.

The important point here is that a variety of movements can produce the same action and thereby accomplish the same goal. For example, walking up a set of stairs is an action. The goal is to get to the top of the stairs. However, to achieve this goal a person can use a variety of different movements. A person can take one step at a time very slowly, or take each step very quickly, or take two steps at a time, and so on. In each situation, the action is the same but the movements the person produces to achieve the goal of the action are different.

Why distinguish movements from skills and actions? There are three reasons why it is important, and useful, to consider movements as distinct from motor skills and actions. First, people learn motor skills and actions. Although people must produce movements to perform a motor skill or action, different people may produce different movement characteristics to achieve the same action goal. For example, how many golfers swing a golf club exactly alike? All golfers must learn the action of hitting a golf ball with a golf club, but each person will likely have some unique movement characteristics.

Second, people adapt movement characteristics to achieve a common action goal. Why do golfers have different swing characteristics but yet achieve the same action goal? People differ in physical features that limit the movement characteristics they can produce to perform a skill. This physical feature limitation is an especially critical concern to take into account when working with people in physical rehabilitation settings. Although there may be a "preferred" way for people to walk, certain sensory or motor impairments may not allow a person to walk in that way. But people can make movement characteristic adjustments and still be able to successfully walk. Even though their gait pattern may look different from the nondisabled pattern, they can successfully achieve the action goal.

Third, as you will see in chapter 2, people evaluate actions and movements with different types of measures. We typically evaluate actions in terms of measures that relate to the outcome of the action, such as the distance a person walked, the length of time it took a person to run a certain distance, or the number of points a basketball shot was worth. Movements, on the other hand, are evaluated by measures that relate to specific characteristics of body, head, limb, and/or muscle activity, such as kinematic, kinetic, and electromyographic (EMG) measures. (These measures of movement characteristics will be defined and discussed in chapter 2.)

ONE-DIMENSION CLASSIFICATION SYSTEMS

We can classify motor skills by determining which skill characteristics are similar to those of other skills. The most prevalent approach has been to categorize skills according to one common characteristic. This common characteristic is divided into two categories, which represent extreme ends of a continuum rather than dichotomous categories. This continuum approach allows a skill to be classified in terms of which category the skill charac-

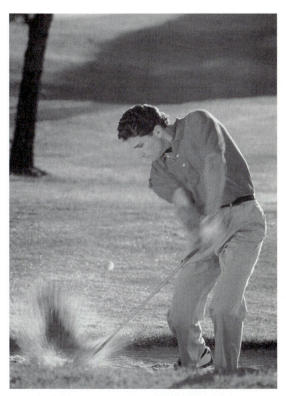

The action of hitting a golf ball typically involves different movement characteristics from one shot to the next.

teristic is more like, rather than requiring that the characteristic fit one category exclusively.

Consider an analogy. The concepts "hot" and "cold" represent two categories of temperatures. Although we typically consider them as distinct categories, we also can view hot and cold as words describing opposite ends of a temperature continuum, because there are degrees of hot or cold that do not fit exclusively into one or the other category. By considering hot and cold as anchor points on a continuum, we can maintain the category distinctions, while at the same time we can more accurately

---

movements   behavioral characteristics of specific limbs or a combination of limbs that are component parts of an action or motor skill.

1. Size of primary musculature required

2. Specificity of where actions begin and end

3. Stability of the environmental context

FIGURE 1.1   Three one-dimension motor skill classification systems.   Each is illustrated as a continuum of the two skill classification categories for the dimension on which the system is based. Also shown are some examples of motor skills for each of the two categories. For the first two classification systems, skills are also shown that best fit on the continuum between the two categories.

classify various temperature levels that do not fit into only one or the other category.

We will consider three motor skill classification systems that use the one-dimension approach to categorize skills. These classification systems are summarized in figure 1.1.

Size of Primary Musculature Required

One characteristic that distinguishes categories of motor skills is the size of muscle groups required to perform the skill. Skills like walking and hopping do not require as the prime movers muscle groups of the same size as those used for skills like piano playing and eating with chopsticks. By distinguishing skills based on the size of the muscle groups required to accomplish the actions, researchers have established a motor skill classification system in which there are two categories, known as gross and fine motor skills.

To achieve the goals of **gross motor skills,** people need to use *large musculature* to produce the actions. These skills need less movement precision than fine motor skills do. We classify skills such as the so-called *fundamental motor skills*—walking, jumping, throwing, leaping, etc.—as gross motor skills.

Fine motor skills fall at the other end of this classification continuum. Fine motor skills require greater control of the *small muscles,* especially those involved in hand-eye coordination, and require a high degree of precision in hand and finger movement. Handwriting, typing, drawing, sewing, and fastening a button are examples of motor skills that are on the fine motor skill end of the continuum in the muscle size classification system. Note that whereas large muscles may be involved in the action of a fine motor skill, the small muscles are the primary muscles involved to achieve the goal of the skill.

Some motor skills involve both large and small muscles as the primary muscles required to achieve the action goal. We cannot categorize these types of skills as gross or fine, but, as shown in figure 1.1, these skills would be located along the continuum between these two categories. For example, to shoot an arrow at a target in archery requires the precision in hand and finger control of fine motor skills, and the involvement of the larger arm and shoulder muscles that characterizes gross motor skills. Although many fine motor skills may also involve the arm and shoulder muscles (e.g., the three examples in figure 1.1), these do not constitute the primary musculature required. A person could achieve the action goals of these skills with the arms restricted in such a way that he or she would have to use hand and finger movements only.

The use of the gross/fine distinction for motor skills is popular in a number of settings. In education settings, special education and adapted physical education curricula and tests commonly distinguish skills on this basis. We also find this classification system in rehabilitation environments. Physical therapists typically work with patients who need to rehabilitate gross motor skills such as walking, whereas occupational therapists more commonly deal with patients who need to learn fine motor skills. People who are involved in early childhood development also find the gross/ fine categorization useful and have developed tests of motor development along the gross/fine dimension. Also, industrial and military aptitude tests commonly use the gross and fine motor skill distinction.

The Specificity of Where Actions Begin and End
Another way to classify motor skills is on the basis of how specific the beginning and end locations are for an action. If a skill requires a specified beginning and end location, we categorize the skill as a **discrete motor skill.** Discrete skills include flipping a light switch, depressing the clutch of an automobile, and hitting a piano key. Each of these skills involves a specified place to begin and end the action. Also, note from the examples that discrete skills typically are simple, one-movement skills.

At the opposite end of this classification system continuum fall **continuous motor skills,** which are skills with arbitrary beginning and end locations. In addition, continuous skills usually contain repetitive movements. We can classify skills such as steering an automobile, tracking a moving cursor

---

gross motor skill   a motor skill that requires the use of large musculature to achieve the goal of the skill.

fine motor skill   a motor skill that requires control of small muscles to achieve the goal of the skill; typically involves eye-hand coordination and requires a high degree of precision of hand and finger movement.

discrete motor skill   a motor skill with clearly defined beginning and end points, usually requiring a simple movement.

continuous motor skill   a motor skill with arbitrary beginning and end points. These skills usually involve repetitive movements.

on a computer monitor with a joystick, swimming, and walking as continuous skills. Although some continuous skills, such as walking and swimming, have distinct beginning locations, the end location is arbitrary, and the movements are repetitive.

Sometimes a skill requires a series or sequence of discrete movements, such as shifting gears in a standard shift car, or playing a piece on a piano. We refer to these types of skills as **serial motor skills.** As figure 1.1 indicates, these skills include the repetitive movements characteristic of continuous skills and the specified beginning and end points of each movement that characterize discrete skills. As a result, it is best to locate serial motor skills on the continuum between the continuous and discrete skills categories. The gear shifting example is a good illustration. To shift gears in a car, the driver must perform a sequence of discrete movements. To shift from second to third gear, the driver performs a sequence of seven discrete movements. First he or she lifts a foot off the accelerator, then depresses the clutch with the other foot, then moves the gear shift forward to neutral, then to the right, then forward again to third gear, then releases the clutch, and finally depresses the accelerator.

This classification system has been especially prevalent in motor skills research literature when authors are focusing on the control of movement. Researchers have found, for example, that certain phenomena about how we control movement are applicable to discrete skills but not to continuous skills, and vice versa. The distinction between discrete and continuous skills is especially popular in the research literature of those who view motor skill performance from the perspectives of human engineering and human factors.

The Stability of the Environmental Context

One classification system has its roots in industrial as well as educational and rehabilitation settings. Researchers base this system on the stability of the environmental context in which the skill is performed (Gentile, 2000). For this classification system, the term *environmental context* refers to the supporting surface on which the person performs the skill, objects involved in performing the skill,

and/or other people involved in the performance situation. For example, if a person is hitting a ball, the relevant feature of the environmental context is the ball. For the skill of walking, the relevant environmental features are the surface on which the person must walk and the characteristics of the environment in which the person must walk.

According to this classification scheme, the term *stability* refers to whether the relevant environmental context features are stationary (i.e., stable) or in motion (i.e., not stable). When the supporting surface, object, or other people involved in the performance of a skill are stationary, the skill is a **closed motor skill.** For these skills, *the relevant environmental context features are stationary, which means they do not change locations during the performance of a skill.* For example, picking up a cup from a table while you are sitting on a chair is a closed motor skill; the chair (i.e., supporting surface) and the cup (i.e., object) do not move between the time you decide to pick up the cup and the moment you pick it up. Walking in a room full of furniture is also a closed motor skill, because nothing in the environmental context moves or changes location while you are walking. Other examples of closed motor skills are shooting an arrow at a stationary target, buttoning a shirt, climbing a flight of stairs, and hitting a ball off a tee. For each of these skills, the performer initiates the movements involved in performing the skill when he or she is ready to do so. Because of this timing of movement initiation characteristic, some motor learning and control researchers have referred to these types of skills as *self-paced.*

Conversely, an **open motor skill** is *a skill that a person performs in an environment in which objects, other people, and/or supporting surfaces are in motion while the person performs the skill.* To perform this type of skill successfully, the performer must act according to the movement of an object, other people, and/or supporting surfaces. Accordingly, some motor learning and control researchers have referred to these types of skills as *externally paced.* This means that for open motor skills, the relevant environmental context features determine when people can initiate the movements required to perform a skill. Some examples of open motor skills that involve the performer's supporting surface in motion include driving a car and stepping onto a moving escalator; skills that involve objects in motion include striking a moving ball and catching a thrown ball; and skills that involve other people in motion include walking on a sidewalk crowded with people walking and running a distance race with other runners.

Notice that in the last two paragraphs, we have classified the skill of walking as *both an open and a closed skill*. The distinguishing characteristics concern whether or not there are objects or other people in the environmental context, and, when there are objects or other people, whether they are stationary or in motion. Also taken into consideration for this distinction is whether the supporting surface on which a person walks is stationary or in motion. This means that when walking occurs in a hallway with no objects or other people, walking is a closed skill. Walking is also a closed skill if objects and/or other people are in the hallway, but stationary. However, if the objects and/or other people are in motion, walking becomes an open skill. Similarly, walking is an open skill when a person walks on a treadmill, which means the supporting surface is in motion. We can make the same distinction for several other motor skills. For example, hitting a ball from a tee is a closed skill, whereas hitting a pitched ball is an open skill. And, throwing a ball is a closed skill when throwing to a stationary person, but an open skill when throwing to a person who is moving.

Consider how closed and open skills differ in terms of the performance demands placed on the person. A person can initiate his or her movements at will when performing a closed skill. In addition, the person does not need to adjust the movements to changing conditions while the performance is in progress. For example, to climb a set of stairs, a person can initiate his or her first step at will. However, quite the opposite is the case when someone performs open skills. To perform an open skill successfully, a person must time the initiation of movement to conform to the movement of the supporting surface, other people, and/or object involved in the action. If, for example, the person

must step onto a moving escalator, the timing or when the first step can be initiated must conform to the speed and position of the escalator. And for many open skills, changes can occur while an action is in progress that will require the person to make movement adjustments to conform to these environmental changes. For example, the spin of a tennis ball will influence the direction and height of its bounce, which may require the tennis player to adjust his or her planned movements to return a serve after the ball hits the ground.

The open/closed classification system has achieved a large degree of popularity in instructional methodology contexts and increasing popularity in rehabilitation contexts. A likely reason for this is that the closed and open skill categories relate so easily to the types of motor skills involved in these settings. Skills in each of these categories follow common principles of instruction that instructors and therapists can readily apply to specific situations. The closed and open distinction between motor skills also has become increasingly common in the motor learning research literature, undoubtedly because of its simplicity and its ability to accommodate both complex "real-world" skills and laboratory skills.

GENTILE'S TWO-DIMENSIONS TAXONOMY

A problem with the one-dimension basis for the classification of motor skills is that it does not always capture the complexity of many skills that a

---

serial motor skill   a motor skill involving a series of discrete skills.

closed motor skill   a motor skill performed in a stable or predictable environment where the performer determines when to begin the action.

open motor skill   a motor skill that involves a nonstable, unpredictable environment where an object or environmental context is in motion and determines when to begin the action.

practitioner must take into account when making decisions about instruction or practice routines. To overcome this limitation, Gentile (2000) broadened the one-dimension approach by considering two general characteristics of all skills: (1) the *environmental context* in which the person performs the skill and (2) the *function of the action* characterizing the skill. She then subdivided these two characteristics to create an expansive taxonomy that yields sixteen skill categories, depicted in table 1.1. A **taxonomy** is a classification system that is organized according to relationships among the component characteristics of whatever is being classified. For example, taxonomies have been developed in biology to provide systematic classification systems for plants and animals. Gentile's taxonomy presents a similar approach to the classification of motor skills.

In addition to providing a classification system for motor skills, Gentile proposed this taxonomy as a functional guide for physical therapists to assist them in determining the movement problems characterizing patients and selecting functionally appropriate activities for patients. However, the taxonomy is not limited to the physical therapy context. It provides an excellent basis for understanding the performer demands for a wide variety of motor skills. Everyone who is involved in teaching motor skills should appreciate this taxonomy. It is an excellent means of becoming aware of the skill characteristics that make skills distinct from, as well as related to, other skills, and is an excellent guide for establishing practice or training routines.

Environmental Context

The first dimension of Gentile's taxonomy can be seen in the first column of table 1.1. This dimension is the *environmental context* in which a person performs a skill. Two characteristics are involved in this dimension. We see these in the category labels in the first column in table 1.1.

The first environmental characteristic concerns regulatory conditions. This is the term Gentile used to describe the "relevant environmental context features," which we discussed previously in this chapter in the section concerning the motor skills classification scheme based on the stability of the environmental context. The term **regulatory conditions** refers to those features of the environmental context that specify the movement characteristics a person must implement to successfully perform an action. Recall from our earlier discussion about open and closed motor skills that the environmental context features include the surface that supports performer or object, and any objects or other people that may be involved during the performance of an action.

The following skill performance situation that involves walking presents some examples of regulatory conditions. If a person's action goal is to walk from one location to another, the surface on which the person walks is a regulatory condition that determines the movement characteristics the person must use to achieve the action goal on that surface. The surface may be soft or hard, rough or smooth, flat or inclined, among other possible characteristics. To walk on a sandy beach, you would very likely move your body, legs, and feet differently from the way you would walk on a concrete sidewalk. Similarly, you would use different movements as you walked on a flat surface compared to a steep incline. Objects and other people may also be regulatory conditions in the walking environmental context. For example, how would your walking movements differ if a child's tricycle were in the pathway from a situation in which no object was there? And how would your walking movements compare when another person walked beside you, behind you, or in front of you?

We can see additional examples of regulatory conditions in the environmental context when a person must manipulate an object. If a person's action goal is to throw a ball to another person, or to catch a ball thrown by another person, important regulatory conditions relate to certain characteristics of the ball, such as size, shape, and weight. For example, throwing a baseball and throwing a basketball would require distinctly different arm, hand, and finger movements to achieve the throwing action goal. Similarly, a person could catch a tennis ball with one hand, but may need to use two hands to catch a beach ball.

A CLOSER LOOK

Examples of Stationary and In-Motion Regulatory Conditions

Stationary Environmental Context
spatial features of the environment control spatial movement characteristics of an action; the *timing* of the initiation of an action is controlled by the performer

e.g. picking up a cup

walking up a flight of stairs

hitting a ball from a tee

throwing a dart at a target

In-Motion Environmental Context
spatial and timing features of the environment control spatial movement characteristics and timing of the initiation of an action

e.g. stepping onto an escalator

standing in a moving bus

hitting a pitched ball

catching a batted ball

In Gentile's taxonomy, an important distinction for differentiating motor skills is whether the regulatory conditions during performance are *stationary* or *in motion.* Sometimes the regulatory conditions are stationary; this is the case when you walk on a sidewalk or hit a ball off a tee. Sometimes the regulatory conditions are in motion; this occurs when you must step onto an escalator or hit a pitched ball. It is important to note that in this part of Gentile's taxonomy, you can see the application of the closed and open motor skills categories. Skills for which the regulatory conditions are stationary are closed skills, whereas those for which they are in motion are open skills. However, this closed/open distinction is too limiting to capture the wide range of skills that people perform every day. Because of this limitation, Gentile added another environmental context characteristic.

The second environmental characteristic in the taxonomy is **intertrial variability,** which refers to *whether the regulatory conditions during performance are the same or different from one attempt to perform the skill to another.* We can distinguish motor skills according to whether intertrial variability is *absent* or *present.* For example, when a person walks through an uncluttered room, intertrial variability is absent, because the regulatory conditions do not change each time the person walks across the room. On the other hand, intertrial

variability is present when someone walks through different rooms in which various objects are located in different places, because each room requires the person to walk with different movements to avoid colliding with the objects.

The Function of the Action
The *function of the action* is the second dimension on which the taxonomy is based. This dimension is presented in the top row of table 1.1. Gentile specified that we can determine the function of an action by deciding whether or not performing a

taxonomy   a classification system organized according to relationships among the component characteristics of the group of items or objects being classified.

regulatory conditions   characteristics of the environmental context that determine (i.e., "regulate") the movement characteristics needed to perform an action.

intertrial variability   an environmental characteristic in Gentile's taxonomy of motor skills. The term refers to whether the regulatory conditions that exist for the performance of a skill in one situation or for one trial are present or absent in the next situation or trial.

TABLE 1.1   Gentile's Taxonomy of Motor Skills

Environmental ↓ Context	Action Function			
	Body Stability		**Body Transport**	
	No Object Manipulation	**Object Manipulation**	**No Object Manipulation**	**Object Manipulation**
Stationary Regulatory Conditions and No Intertrial Variability	**1A** Body stability No object Stationary regulatory conditions No intertrial variability • *Standing alone in a room* • *Practicing a basketball free-throw shot without a ball*	**1B** Body stability Object Stationary regulatory conditions No intertrial variability • *Brushing teeth standing alone at a sink* • *Shooting basketball free-throws*	**1C** Body transport No object Stationary regulatory conditions No intertrial variability • *Climbing stairs* • *Running through a basketball play several times without a ball*	**1D** Body transport Object Stationary regulatory conditions No intertrial variability • *Climbing stairs while holding a book* • *Running through a basketball play several times with a ball*
Stationary Regulatory Conditions and Intertrial Variability	**2A** Body stability No object Stationary regulatory conditions Intertrial variability • *Standing on different surfaces* • *Swinging a baseball bat at different ball locations without a bat or ball*	**2B** Body stability Object Stationary regulatory conditions Intertrial variability • *Standing on different surfaces while holding a bag of groceries* • *Hitting baseballs off a batting tee; varying ball locations for each swing*	**2C** Body transport No object Stationary regulatory conditions Intertrial variability • *Walking on different surfaces* • *Running through several basketball plays without a ball*	**2D** Body transport Object Stationary regulatory conditions Intertrial variability • *Walking on different surfaces while carrying a bag of groceries* • *Running through several basketball plays with a ball*
In-Motion Regulatory Conditions and No Intertrial Variability	**3A** Body stability No object Regulatory conditions in motion No intertrial variability • *Sitting in a wheelchair being pushed along an empty hallway* • *Passing basketballs to a moving player running the same pattern several times, without a ball*	**3B** Body stability Object Regulatory conditions in motion No intertrial variability • *Wheeling a wheelchair along an empty hallway* • *Catching a series of softballs thrown at the same speed by a pitching machine*	**3C** Body transport No object Regulatory conditions in motion No intertrial variability • *Walking on a treadmill at a constant speed* • *Running through a basketball play without a ball but with moving defenders*	**3D** Body transport Object Regulatory conditions in motion No intertrial variability • *Walking on a treadmill at a constant speed while holding a cup of water* • *Running through a basketball play with a ball and moving defenders*
In-Motion Regulatory Conditions and Intertrial Variability	**4A** Body stability No object Regulatory conditions in motion Intertrial variability • *Sitting in a moving car* • *Passing basketballs to a moving player running different patterns, without a ball*	**4B** Body stability Object Regulatory conditions in motion Intertrial variability • *Sitting in a moving car holding a baby* • *Catching softballs thrown at various speeds by a pitching machine*	**4C** Body transport No object Regulatory conditions in motion Intertrial variability • *Walking in a crowded mall* • *Practicing several soccer plays without a ball but with defenders*	**4D** Body transport Object Regulatory conditions in motion Intertrial variability • *Walking in a crowded mall carrying a baby* • *Practicing several soccer plays with a ball and defenders*

Note: (1) The number/letter labels for each skill category were not included in Gentile's original presentation of the taxonomy, but are included here to provide an easy reference to each skill category. The numbers 1–4 represent the four environmental context subdimensions; the letters A–D represent the four action function subdimensions. (2) The two examples of skills for each of the 16 categories include an example of a daily activity skill and one of a sport/physical education skill.

given skill involves moving the body, and whether or not performance involves manipulating an object. She viewed these characteristics as parts of two broad action functions: body orientation and manipulation.

Body orientation refers to the changing or maintaining of body location. Two body orientation roles are important for classifying motor skills. *Body stability* is the orientation role for skills that involve no change in body location during the performance of the skill, such as standing, drinking from a cup, and shooting an arrow in archery. For skills that require the body to move from one place to another, the orientation role is *body transport.* Skills such as walking, running, and swimming involve body transport. It is important to note that body transport role for motor skills includes active and passive changes of body locations. This means that both walking, which involves the active changing of body location, and standing in a moving bus, which involves the passive changing of body location, serve body transport roles.

The second type of action function concerns *object manipulation.* Some motor skills require us to *change or maintain the position of an object,* such as a ball, a tool, or another person. We perform other skills with *no object manipulation.* It is important to note that when a person must manipulate an object, the skill increases in complexity and difficulty, because the person must do two things at once. First, the person must manipulate the object correctly, and second, he or she must adjust body posture to accommodate for the imbalance created by the object.

The sixteen skill categories. The interaction of the four environmental context characteristics and the four action function characteristics creates sixteen skill categories. Table 1.1 shows the critical characteristics of these sixteen categories, along with two examples of skills in each category. Gentile specified that each skill category poses different demands on the performer in terms of the characteristics and number of variables the performer needs to pay attention to and control to achieve the action goals. Skills that demand the least of the performer

LAB LINKS

Lab 1 in the Online Learning Center Lab Manual for chapter 1 provides an opportunity for you to become more familiar with Gentile's Taxonomy of Motor Skills by applying it to sports skills or to motor skills we experience in the everyday world.

are the simplest; those that demand the most are the most complex. Accordingly, the skill categories in table 1.1 are organized in terms of increasing complexity, beginning at the top leftmost category with the simplest skills and progressing to the most complex skills in the bottom rightmost category.

Gentile (2000) based the taxonomy on the view that any motor skill must be considered in terms of the environmental context in which it is performed and the functional role it plays when performed. As a result, these two dimensions form the basis for creating sixteen categories of motor skills. The *environmental context dimension* includes the regulatory conditions to which the performer of a skill must conform, and whether these conditions change from one performance attempt to the next. The *action function dimension* establishes that all motor skills are performed to serve a specific purpose, or function. The action function may require the maintaining or changing of the performer's body location, and/or the maintaining or changing of the position of objects.

A closer inspection of table 1.1 reveals that the skill categories in each row of the environmental context dimension can be considered in terms of the closed and open skills categories discussed earlier in this chapter. When these two categories include whether intertrial variability is present or absent in the skill performance situation, it is possible to create a four-skill continuum, which you can see in figure 1.2. At the extreme left end of this continuum are completely closed skills (stationary regulatory conditions with no intertribal variability); completely open skills (regulatory conditions in motion with intertribal variability) are located at the extreme right end. In between are closed skills with intertrial variability and open skills with no

A CLOSER LOOK

A Practical Application of the Closed/Open Motor Skills Continuum to Organizing Instruction for Teaching Open Skills [1]

Those who teach motor skills can apply Gentile's taxonomy to the teaching of open skills by applying the closed/open skills continuum in figure 1.2 to develop a logical progression from totally closed to totally open skills from these components. Consider the following example of a practice sequence when the performance goal of a person is to hit a baseball thrown by a pitcher under game conditions.

1. Practice begins with a closed version of the open skill; the instructor or coach keeps the regulatory conditions "stationary" and has intertrial variability "absent."
   ➡ the learner bats the ball from a batting tee at the same height on each practice attempt
2. Next, the instructor or coach keeps the regulatory conditions "stationary" but has intertrial variability "present."
   ➡ the learner bats the ball from a batting tee, but from different heights on each practice attempt
3. Next, practice proceeds to an open version of the skill; the instructor or coach has the regulatory

conditions "in motion" but intertrial variability "absent."
   ➡ a pitching machine that can keep the speed and location of each pitch constant puts the ball in motion
4. Finally, the instructor or coach has the learner practice the completely open skill itself; the regulatory conditions are "in motion" and intertrial variability is "present."
   ➡ a live pitcher pitches the ball using different speeds and locations on each practice attempt.

[1] For research evidence supporting the effectiveness of this progression for helping people learn an open skill, see Hautala and Conn (1993).

intertrial variability. When we relate this continuum of skill characteristics to the action function dimension of Gentile's taxonomy, each of the four skill categories expands by including the stability or transport body orientation function of the skill, and by involving or not involving an object that the person must manipulate in some way.

Practical Application of the Taxonomy
Gentile proposed that the taxonomy has practical value for professionals. First, it can be a useful guide for *evaluation of movement capabilities and limitations.* The professional can determine deficiencies by systematically altering environmental contexts and/or action functions to identify skill

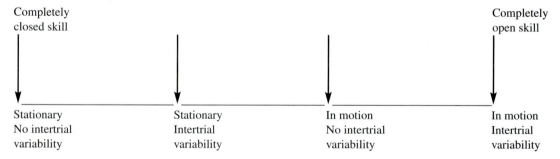

Completely
closed skill

Completely
open skill

Stationary	Stationary	In motion	In motion
No intertrial	Intertrial	No intertrial	Intertrial
variability	variability	variability	variability

FIGURE 1.2   A skill category continuum for open and closed motor skills.   The four subdimensions of the Environmental Context dimension of Gentile's Taxonomy of Motor Skills on a continuum from the most closed to most open skills.

A CLOSER LOOK

Examples of Using the Gentile Taxonomy to Evaluate Movement Capabilities and Limitations

Physical Therapy

An evaluation of the static and dynamic standing posture capabilities and limitations of a neurologic or orthopedic patient could follow the sequence of taxonomy categories by progressing across the top row of categories. The patient

1. stands without assistance (category 1A)
2. stands without assistance while holding a book (category 1B)
3. walks without assistance a specified distance in an uncluttered walkway (category 1C)
4. walks without assistance a specified distance in an uncluttered walkway while holding a book (category 1D)

Further assessments could then include standing and walking activities that would follow the progression of skill requirements in the three other rows of skill categories in the taxonomy.

Physical Education

An evaluation of a student's ball-catching capabilities and limitations could use the following sequence of taxonomy categories. The student

1. catches a ball thrown from the same distance at the same speed for several trials (category 3B)
2. catches a ball thrown from various distances at the same speed for several trials (category 4B)
3. catches a ball while running along a line parallel to the thrower for several trails. The ball should be thrown the same distance and at the same speed in each trial, and the student should run at the same speed in each trial (category 3D)
4. catches a ball while running along a line parallel to the thrower for several trials. The ball should be thrown the same distance but at various heights, and the student should run at the same speed in each trial (category 4D).

---

performance characteristics that pose difficulty for an individual. For example, a physical therapist could evaluate a neurological patient for static and dynamic standing posture capabilities. The assessment could follow the taxonomy by beginning with the simplest skill situation (category 1A) and then systematically progress to include more complex skill requirements of categories 1B, 1C, and 1D. Similarly, a physical education teacher could use the taxonomy to evaluate a student's ball-catching capabilities and limitations. Because this skill involves in-motion regulatory conditions and the manipulation of an object, the evaluation would include only those taxonomy categories that involve these characteristics (i.e., categories 3B, 3D, 4B, and 4D). And to evaluate the simpler skills before the more complex skills, the teacher should begin with the body stability action function categories (3B and 4B), and then progress to those involving body transport (3D and 4D). By identifying the specific characteristics limiting performance, the therapist or teacher can determine what

he or she needs to do to help the person improve his or her performance capabilities.

After the professional assesses performance problems, the taxonomy then becomes a valuable tool for systematically *selecting a progression of functionally appropriate activities* to help the person overcome his or her deficits and increase his or her skill performance capabilities. This is an important feature of the taxonomy, because it emphasizes the complementary part of the rehabilitation or skill training process. To assess skill deficits is important, but the effectiveness of any rehabilitation or training protocol depends on the implementation of appropriate activities to achieve functional goals for the patient or student. In the activity selection process, the therapist or teacher begins selecting activities related to the taxonomy category in which the person is not capable at first of handling the demands of the skill. Then, the professional can develop a program of rehabilitation or instruction by systematically increasing the complexity of the skills included in the program. A third practical use of the taxonomy is as a means of *charting the individual progress* of patients or students as they work to attain their rehabilitation or physical activity performance goals. Gentile emphasized the benefit of using the taxonomy to create a "profile of competencies" that can aid the therapist or teacher in the assessment of the effectiveness of the rehabilitation or instructional program he or she developed for the patient or student. Because the taxonomy follows a simple-to-complex progression of skills, it provides an objective basis for determining progress in overcoming skill performance deficits and increasing skill performance capabilities. When used in this way, the taxonomy provides an effective way for the therapist or teacher to establish a record that can satisfy demands for accountability of his or her time and effectiveness.

SUMMARY

- *Motor skills* and *actions* are terms that were defined similarly, in that both refer to goal-directed activities that involve voluntary body, head, and/or limb movements. The term *movements* refers to the behavioral characteristics of the body, head, and/or specific limb or combination of limbs that serve as components of actins and motor skills.

- Motor skills are often classified according to common characteristics. One-dimension classification systems place skills into categories based on one common characteristic; two-dimension classification systems place skills into categories based on two common characteristics.

- Three one-dimension classification systems distinguish skills on the basis of (a) the size of the primary musculature required to perform the skill, classifying skills as gross or fine; (b) the specificity of where performance of the skill begins, classifying skills as continuous or discrete; and (c) the stability of the environmental context in which the skill is performed, classifying skills as open or closed.

- Gentile's taxonomy of motor skills is a two-dimension classification system that describes sixteen categories of skills that are created from characteristics associated with the environmental context in which the skill is performed and the function of the action. The taxonomy provides a means of understanding the factors that influence motor skill complexity and the unique requirements placed on a person when he or she performs skills of different complexity. The taxonomy can serve as (1) a useful guide for the evaluation of movement capabilities and limitations, (2) a valuable tool for selecting a progression of functionally appropriate activities to help a person overcome his or her skill performance deficits and increase performance capabilities, and (3) a means of charting the individual progress of physical rehabilitation patients and students as they work to attain specific physical activity performance goals.

RELATED READINGS

Kincaid, A. E., Duncan, S., Scott, S. A. (2002). Assessments of fine motor skill in musicians and nonmusicians: Differences in timing versus sequence accuracy in a bimanual fingering task. *Perceptual and Motor Skills, 95,* 245–257.

Maraj, B., Allard, F., & Elliott, D. (1998). The effect of nonregulatory stimuli on the triple-jump approach run. *Research Quarterly for Exercise and Sport, 69,* 129–135.

Mulder, T., & Geurts, S. (1991). The assessment of motor dysfunctions: Preliminaries to a disability-oriented approach. *Human Movement Science, 10,* 565–574.

STUDY QUESTIONS

1. Discuss how the terms *actions* and *movements* are related to motor skills. Give an example that illustrates this relationship.

2. What are three reasons for distinguishing between actions and movements?

3. Describe the one dimension that distinguishes the two categories in each of the following skill classification schemes, and give three examples

of motor skills for each category: (a) gross vs. fine motor skills; (b) discrete vs. continuous motor skills; (c) closed vs. open motor skills.

4. (a) What are the two dimensions used to classify skills in the Gentile taxonomy? (b) Describe the four classification characteristics included under each of these two dimensions.

5. (a) What does the term regulatory conditions refer to in Gentile's skill classification system? (b) Why are regulatory conditions important to consider when categorizing skills?

6. Discuss how you would implement the three practical uses Gentile described for her taxonomy of motor skills.

CHAPTER

The Measurement
of Motor Performance

*Concept: The measurement of motor performance
is critical to understanding motor learning*

After completing this chapter, you will be able to

- Describe the differences between and give examples of performance outcome measures and performance production measures

- Describe the differences among simple, choice, and discrimination RT situations

- Describe three measures for measuring performance outcome accuracy for skills that require discrete spatial and/or temporal accuracy in one and two dimensions, and for continuous skills that require spatial and temporal accuracy

- Define three kinematic measures of motion and describe one way to calculate each measure for a specific movement

- Describe ways that EMG can be used to provide information about human movement

- Describe how angle-angle diagrams provide useful information about the coordination characteristics of limbs or limb segments

Application

Suppose that you are a physical educator teaching your students a tennis serve. What characteristic of performance will you measure to assess students' progress? Consider a few possibilities. You could count the number of serves that land in and out of the proper service court. Or you could mark the service court in some way so that the "better" serves, in terms of where they land, are scored higher than others. Or you could develop a measure that is concerned with the students' serving form.

Now, imagine that you are a physical therapist helping a stroke patient learning to walk again. How will you measure your patient's progress to determine if what you are doing is beneficial to his or her rehabilitation? You have several possible walking characteristics to choose from. For example, you could count the number of steps made or the distance walked on each walking attempt; these measures could give you some general indicators of progress. If you wanted to know more about some specific walking-related characteristics, you could measure the balance and postural stability of the person as he or she walked. Or you could assess the biomechanical progress the person was making by analyzing the kinematic characteristics of the movements of the legs, trunk, and arms. Each of these measurements can be valuable, and will tell you something different about the person's walking performance.

In both of these performance assessment situations, your important concern as an educator or therapist is using a performance measure, or measures, to make an assessment. As a first step in addressing this problem, you must determine which aspects of performance you should measure to make a valid performance assessment. Then, you must determine how to measure those aspects of performance. The following discussion will help you to know how to accomplish this two-step measurement process by describing several different motor skill performance measures. Throughout this text, we will refer to the various measures introduced in this section, especially as researchers use these measures to investigate various concepts.

Discussion

There are a variety of ways to measure motor skill performance. A useful way to organize the many types of motor performance measures is by creating two categories related to different levels of performance observation. We will call the first category **performance outcome measures.** Included in this category are measures that indicate the outcome or result of performing a motor skill. For example, measures of how far a person walked, how fast a person ran a certain distance, and how many degrees a person flexed his or her knee all are based on the outcome of the person's performance.

Notice that performance outcome measures do not tell us anything about the behavior of the limbs or body that led to the observed outcome. Nor do these measures provide any information about the activity of the various muscles involved in each action. To know something about these types of characteristics, we must use measures in the category called **performance production measures.**

These measures relate to performance characteristics that produced the outcome. As a result, they can tell us such things as how the nervous system is functioning, how the muscular system is operating, and how the limbs or joints are acting before, during, or after a person performs a skill.

Although additional categories of performance measures could exist, these two represent the motor skill performance measures found in this text. Table 2.1 presents examples of these two categories of measures. For the remainder of this discussion, we will discuss several of the more common performance measures found in the motor learning research literature.

REACTION TIME

The common measure indicating how long it takes a person to prepare and initiate a movement is **reaction time (RT).** Figure 2.1 shows that RT is the interval of time between the onset of a signal (stimulus) that indicates the required action and the *initiation* of the action. Note that RT does not

---

performance outcome measures   a category of motor skill performance measures that indicates the outcome or result of performing a motor skill (e.g., how far a person walked, how fast a person ran a certain distance, or how many degrees a person flexed a knee).

performance production measures   a category of motor skill performance measures that indicates the performance of specific aspects of the motor control system during the performance of an action (e.g., limb kinematics, force, EEG, EMG, etc.).

reaction time (RT)   the interval of time between the onset of a signal (stimulus) and the initiation of a response (e.g., the amount of time between the "go" signal for a swimming sprint race start and the beginning of the feet moving off the starting block).

TABLE 2.1   Two Categories of Motor Skill Performance Measures

Category	Examples of Measures	Performance Examples
1. Performance outcome measures	Time to complete a response, e.g., sec, min, hr	Amount of time to run a mile, or type a word
	Reaction time (RT), e.g., sec, msec	Time between starter's gun and beginning of movement
	Amount of error in performing criterion movement, e.g., AE, CE, VE	Number of cm away from the target in reproducing a criterion limb position
	Number or percentage of errors	Number of free throws missed
	Number of successful attempts	Number of times the beanbag hit the target
	Time on/off target	Number of seconds stylus in contact with target on pursuit rotor
	Time on/off balance	Number of seconds stood in stork stance
	Distance	Height of vertical jump
	Trials to completion	Number of trials it took until all responses correct
2. Performance production measures	Displacement	Distance limb traveled while performing action
	Velocity	Speed limb moved while performing action
	Acceleration	Acceleration/deceleration pattern while moving
	Joint angle	Angle of each joint of arm at impact in hitting ball
	Joint torque	Net joint torque of the knee joint at takeoff on a vertical jump
	Electromyography (EMG)	Time at which the biceps initially fired during a rapid flexion movement
	Electroencephalogram (EEG)	Brain cortex activation pattern while shooting an arrow in archery

include any movement related to the action, but only the time before movement begins.

The stimulus (or "go") signal is the indication to act. In laboratory or clinical settings, the signal can take one of a variety of forms, such as a light, a buzzer, a shock, a word on a screen, or a spoken word or sound. As such, the signal can relate to any sensory system, i.e., vision, hearing, or touch. The person can be required to perform any type of movement. For example, the person might be required to lift a finger off a telegraph key, depress a keyboard key, speak a word, kick a board, or walk a step. Finally, to assess optimal RT, some type of warning signal should be given prior to the stimulus signal.

Types of RT Situations

Figure 2.2 depicts three of the most common types of RT situations. For illustration purposes, this figure shows a light as the stimulus signal and lifting a finger from a telegraph key as the required movement. However, the three types of RT situations discussed here do not need to be limited to these characteristics.

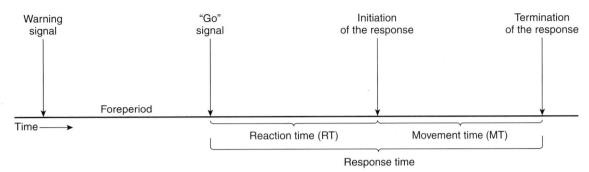

FIGURE 2.1   The events and time intervals related to the typical measurement of reaction time (RT) and movement time (MT).

When a situation involves only one signal and requires only one action in response, the RT situation is known as **simple RT.** In the example presented in figure 2.2 the person must lift a finger from the telegraph key when a light comes on. Another type of RT situation is **choice RT,** where there is more than one signal to which the person must respond, and each signal has a specified response. The example in figure 2.2 indicates that the person must respond to the red light by lifting the index finger from a telegraph key, to the blue light by lifting the middle finger, and to the green light by lifting the ring finger. The third type of RT situation is **discrimination RT,** where there is also more than one signal, but only one response. In the figure 2.2 example, the person is required to lift his or her finger from the telegraph key only when the red light comes on. If the blue or green light is illuminated, the person should make no response.

Although the examples of simple, choice, and discrimination RT situations just described refer to laboratory conditions, these different types of RT situations also exist in everyday life and in sport environments. For example, a sprinter in track is involved in a *simple RT situation* when he or she starts a race. He or she hears a verbal warning signal from the starter, then hears the gun sound, which is the signal to begin to run. *Choice RT situations* are more common in everyday activities, such as when driving a car you come to an intersection with a traffic signal, which has three possible signals, each of which requires a different action. If the light is red, you must depress the brake pedal

and come to a complete stop. If the light is yellow, you need to prepare to stop. And if the signal is green, you can continue to keep the accelerator pedal depressed to move through the intersection. Joggers experience *discrimination RT situations* when they find something in their path that indicates they need to step over it, such as a log or a curb. There are many different stimuli in the jogger's environment, but only those with specific, distinct features will specify to the jogger to engage in the action of stepping up and over an object. Thus the jogger engages in this specific action only when the environmental stimuli have these features.

RT Interval Components
Through the use of electromyography (EMG) to measure the beginning of muscle activity in an RT situation, a researcher can *fractionate* RT into two component parts. The EMG recording will indicate

---

simple RT   the reaction time when the situation involves only one signal (stimulus) that requires only one response.

choice RT   the reaction time when the situation involves more than one signal and each signal requires its own specified response.

discrimination RT   the reaction time when the situation involves more than one signal but only one response, which is to only one of the signals; the other signals require no response.

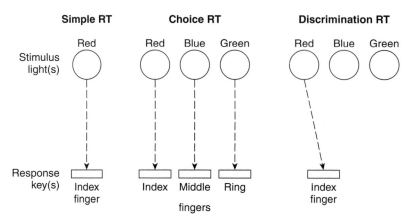

FIGURE 2.2   Three different types of reaction time (RT) test situations: simple RT, choice RT, and discrimination RT.

the time at which the muscle shows increased activity after the stimulus signal has occurred. However, there is a period of time between the onset of the stimulus signal and the beginning of the muscle activity. This "quiet" interval of time is the first component part of RT and is called the *premotor time.* The second component is the period of time from the increase in muscle activity until the actual beginning of observable limb movement. This RT component is called the *motor time.* You can see some examples of fractionated RTs at the end of this chapter in figure 2.8, which presents examples of EMG recordings. The RT interval is shown along with EMG recordings for three muscle groups. Although not indicated in the figure, the premotor time for each EMG recording is the interval of time prior to the beginning of muscle activity; the motor time is the remainder of the RT interval in which muscle activity is recorded.

By fractionating the RT interval into two parts, researchers interested in understanding the action preparation process are able to obtain more specific insights into what occurs as a person prepares to move. Most researchers agree that the premotor time is a measure of the receipt and transmission of information from the environment, through the nervous system, to the muscle itself. This time interval seems to be an indicator of *perceptual and cognitive decision-making activity* in which the person engages while preparing an action. The

motor time interval indicates that there is muscle activity before observable limb movement occurs. Researchers commonly agree that this activity indicates a time lag in the muscle that it needs in order to overcome the inertia of the limb after the muscle receives the command to contract.

The Use of RT in Research
Reaction time has a long history as a popular measure of human motor skill performance. Although RT can be used as a performance measure to assess how quickly a person can initiate a required action, researchers also use it as a basis for inferring other characteristics. The most common is to identify the environmental context information a person may use while preparing to produce a required action, which will be the topic of discussion in chapter 7. For example, if one performance situation yields a longer RT than another situation, the researcher can determine what may have led to the different RT lengths, which then can tell us something about influences on the amount of time it takes us to prepare an action.

Another use of RT is to assess the capabilities of a person to anticipate a required action and determine when to initiate it. In a sport situation, a basketball coach may want to know how long it takes a point guard to recognize that the defender's actions indicate the guard should pass the ball rather than shoot it. When used in this way, RT provides information about decision making. Thus, in addition to indicating how fast a person responds to a signal, RT also provides a window for examining how a person interacts with the performance environment while preparing to produce a required action.

Relating RT to Movement Time and Response Time

In any situation in which a person must perform an action in response to a signal, two additional performance measures can be assessed. These were shown in figure 2.1 as movement time (MT) and response time. **Movement time (MT)** begins when RT ends. It is the interval of time between the initiation and the completion of an action. **Response time** is the total time interval, involving both RT and MT.

An important characteristic of RT and MT is that they are relatively *independent* measures. This means that RT does not predict MT, or vice versa. The independence of RT and MT as performance measures indicates that if one person in a group of people has the fastest RT in a performance situation, that person may not have the fastest MT in the group. Thus, RT and MT measure different aspects of human performance. You will learn more about the independence of these two performance measures in chapter 3.

ERROR MEASURES

The amount of error a person makes as a result of performing a skill has had a prominent place in human performance research and in everyday living activities and sport. Error measures allow us to evaluate performance for skills for which *accuracy* is the action goal. Skills such as reaching to grasp a cup, throwing a dart at a target, walking along a prescribed path, and driving a car on a street require people to perform actions that demand spatial and/or temporal accuracy. To assess performance outcome for this type of skill, the amount of error a person makes in relation to the goal is a meaningful performance measure.

Error measures not only provide indicators of performance accuracy; certain types of error mea-

LAB LINKS

Lab 2 in the Online Learning Center Lab Manual for chapter 2 provides an opportunity for you to measure and compare RT and MT.

sures also tell us about possible causes of performance problems. This is especially true if performance is assessed for more than one trial. For a series of trials (typical in a sport skill instruction or a rehabilitation setting), the instructor or therapist can determine whether the observed movement inaccuracy is due to problems associated with *consistency* or to those associated with *bias*. These important measures provide the professional with a basis for selecting the appropriate intervention to help the person overcome the inaccuracy. *Consistency problems* indicate a lack in acquiring the basic movement pattern needed to perform the skill, whereas *bias problems* indicate that the person has acquired the movement pattern but is having difficulties adapting to the specific demands of the performance situation.

Assessing Error for One-Dimension Action Goals

When a person must move a limb a specified amount in one dimension, as when a patient attempts to achieve a certain knee extension, the resulting error will be a certain distance short of or past the goal. Similarly, if a pitcher in baseball is attempting to throw the ball at a certain rate of speed, the resulting error will be either too slow or too fast in relation to the goal. Measuring the amount of error in these situations simply involves

movement time (MT)   the interval of time between the initiation of a movement and the completion of the movement.

response time   the time interval involving both reaction time and movement time; that is, the time from the onset of a signal (stimulus) to the completion of a response.

A CLOSER LOOK

Examples of the Use of RT and MT to Assess Skill Performance Problems in Decision-Making Situations

Sport Skill Example

An offensive lineman in football must perform his assignment as quickly as possible after the center snaps the ball. If the lineman is consistently slow in carrying out his assignment, the problem could be that he is not giving enough attention to the ball snap, he is not sure about his assignment, or he moves too slowly when carrying out his assignment. The first two problems relate to RT (the time between the ball snap and the beginning of foot movement); the third relates to MT (the time between the beginning of foot movement and the completion of the assignment). By assessing both RT and MT in an actual situation, the coach could become more aware of the reason for the lineman's problem, and begin working on helping the lineman improve that specific part of the problem.

Car Driving Example

Suppose you are helping a student in a driving simulator to reduce the amount of time he or she requires to stop the car when an object suddenly appears in the street. Separating RT and MT would let you know if the slow stopping time is related to a decision-making or a movement speed problem. If RT (the time between the appearance of the object and the person's foot release from the accelerator) increases across various situations, but MT (the time between the foot release from the accelerator and foot contact with the brake pedal) is constant, you know that the problem is primarily related to attention or decision making. But if RT remains relatively constant but MT changes across various situations, you know the problem is movement related. In either case, you can more specifically help the person to improve his or her performance in these situations.

subtracting the achieved performance value (e.g., 15 cm, 5°, 20 sec) from the target or goal amount.

We can calculate at least three error measures to assess the general accuracy characteristics of performance over repeated performances, and to assess what may be causing the accuracy problems. To obtain a general indicator of how successfully the goal was achieved, we calculate **absolute error (AE).** AE is *the absolute difference between the actual performance on each trial and the goal.* For multiple-trial situations, summing these differences and dividing by the number of trials will give you the average absolute error for the trials. AE provides useful information about the *magnitude of error* a person has made on a trial or over a series of trials. This score gives you *a general index of accuracy* for the session for this person. But evaluating performance solely on the basis of AE hides important information about the source of the inaccurate performance. To obtain this information, we need two additional error measures.

One reason a person's performance may be inaccurate is that the person has a tendency to over-

shoot or to undershoot the goal, which is referred to as *performance bias.* To obtain this information, we must calculate **constant error (CE),** which is the signed (+/–) deviation from the goal. When calculated over a series of trials, CE provides a meaningful *index of the person's tendency to be directionally biased* when performing the skill. Calculating CE involves making the same calculations used to determine AE, except that the algebraic signs are used for each trial's performance.

Another reason for performance inaccuracy for a series of trials is *performance consistency* (or, conversely, variability), which is measured by calculating **variable error (VE).** To determine this consistency index, calculate the *standard deviation of the person's CE scores for the series of trials.*

Assessing Error for Two-Dimension Action Goals

When the outcome of performing a skill requires accuracy in the vertical and horizontal directions, the person assessing error must make modifications to the one-dimension assessment method. The gen-

A CLOSER LOOK

Calculating and Using Error Scores to Assess Accuracy, Bias, and Consistency

Suppose that you are a physical therapist working with Joe and Sam. You are working with them to maintain a consistent 50 cm stride length while walking. To determine the intervention approach each of them will need, you have both of them walk six strides on a runway. The following illustration shows their performance for each stride. The 50 cm distance targets for each stride are marked as vertical lines across the runway; the numbers represent the location of the foot placement on each stride by showing the direction (+ = too far; – = too short) and distance (cm) Joe and Sam missed the target stride length.

Note that both Joe and Sam have the *same AE,* but that

- Joe has a high negative CE but a low VE, which means that his 6 strides tend to be consistently short of the target stride length for his stride lengths
- Sam has a low positive CE but a high VE, which means that his 6 strides are inconsistently long and short of the target stride length

Discussion question: Based on the CE and VE differences, would the physical therapist have a more difficult rehabilitation problem ahead with Joe or Sam? Why?

| Sam | | +15 | −12 | | +10 | −12 | | +12 | | +5 |
| Joe | −15 | | −12 | −10 | | −12 | −12 | | −5 | |

Calculating the average AE, average CE, and VE:

	AE	AE	CE	CE
Stride No.	Joe	Sam	Joe	Sam
1	15	15	−15	15
2	12	12	−12	−12
3	10	10	−10	10
4	12	12	−12	−12
5	12	12	−12	12
6	5	5	−5	5
Total	66	66	−66	18
Avg	11	11	−11	3
VE (SD)			3.3	12.1

eral accuracy measure for the two-dimension situation is called *radial error (RE),* which is similar to AE in the one-dimension case. To calculate RE for one trial, calculate the hypotenuse of the right-angle triangle formed by the intersection of the X-axis (extended horizontally from the center of the target) and the Y-axis (extended vertically from the center of the location of the performance result). This calculation involves the following steps:

- Measure the length of the error in the horizontal direction (i.e., X-axis); square this value

absolute error (AE) the unsigned deviation from the target or criterion, representing amount of error. A measure of the magnitude of an error without regard to the direction of the deviation.

constant error (CE) the signed (+/–) deviation from the target or criterion; it represents amount and direction of error and serves as a measure of performance bias.

variable error (VE) an error score representing the variability (or conversely, the consistency) of performance.

- Measure the length of the error in the vertical direction (i.e., Y-axis); square this value

- Add the squared X-axis and Y-axis error values; take the square root of the total

An example of the calculation of RE is shown in figure 2.3. To determine the average RE for a series of trials, simply calculate the mean of the total RE for the series.

Performance bias and consistency are more difficult to assess for the two-dimension case than in one dimension, because the algebraic signs + and − have little meaning for the two-dimension case. Hancock, Butler, and Fischman (1995) have presented a detailed description of calculating measures of bias and consistency in the two-dimension situation. Rather than go into the details of this calculation, we will consider a general approach to the problem here. For a series of two-dimensional movements, a researcher can obtain a qualitative assessment of bias and consistency by looking at the actual grouping of the movement locations. If the grouping tends to be in one quadrant of the target, then a performance bias is evident, whereas responses scattered in all quadrants would indicate no apparent performance bias. Consistency in these two examples would be much better in the former than in the latter case. Again, as for the one-dimension situation, the practical benefit of assessing these characteristics is that the strategies used to improve performance would differ for the bias and the consistency cases.

Assessing Error for Continuous Skills
The error measures described in the preceding two sections are based on accuracy goals for discrete skills. Continuous motor skills also require accuracy. For example, when a person must walk along a specified pathway, performance assessment can include measuring how well the person stayed on the pathway. Or, if a person is in a car simulator and must steer the car along the road as projected on a screen, a measure of performance can be based on how well the person kept the car on the road. Error measures for these types of skills must be different from those used to assess discrete skill performance.

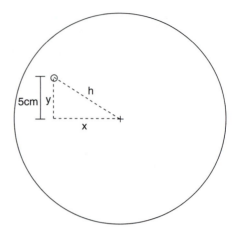

FIGURE 2.3   An example of measuring radial error (RE) to assess performance accuracy.   The performance situation involves a person throwing a dart at a circular target. The goal of the throw is to hit the center of the target (represented by the +). The throw hit the location indicated by the O. RE is the hypotenuse (h) of the right-angle triangle formed by the intersection of the X-axis and Y-axis. The following example of X-axis and Y-axis distances associated with this location demonstrates the calculation of RE for this throw.

$$
\begin{aligned}
\text{X-axis distance} &= 10\,\text{cm} \rightarrow 10^2 = 100 \\
\text{Y-axis distance} &= 5\,\text{cm} \rightarrow 5^2 = \underline{25} \\
\text{Sum} &= 125 \\
\text{RE} &= \sqrt{125} = 11.2\,\text{cm}
\end{aligned}
$$

A common error score for continuous skills is the **root-mean-squared error (RMSE),** which you can think of as AE for a continuous task. To understand how this error measure is determined and used, consider the following example, taken from performing a continuous skill known as *pursuit tracking*. To perform this skill, subjects move a joystick, steering wheel, or lever to make an object, such as a cursor, follow a specified pathway. The criterion pathway can be described kinematically as a displacement curve. Figure 2.4 provides an example. A displacement curve can represent the subject's tracking performance. To determine how accurately the subject tracked the criterion pathway, we would calculate an RMSE score.

Calculate RMSE by determining the amount of error between the displacement curve produced by the subject's tracking performance and the

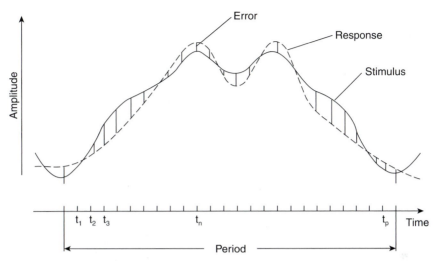

FIGURE 2.4   The difference between the subject's response and the stimulus at each specified time interval is used to calculate one root-mean-squared error (RMSE) score.   [From Franks, I. M. et al. (1982). The generation of movement patterns during the acquisition of a pursuit tracking task. *Human Movement Science,* 1:251–272. Copyright © 1982 Elsevier/North-Holland, Amsterdam, The Netherlands. Reprinted by permission.]

displacement curve of the criterion pathway (see figure 2.4). The actual calculation of RMSE is complex and requires a computer program that can sample and record the subject's position in relation to the criterion pathway at specified points of time, such as 100 times each second (100 Hz; note that 1 Hz = 1 time/sec). At each sampling point, the difference between the criterion pathway location and the subject's location is calculated. For the 100-Hz example, this yields 100 error scores each second. If the criterion pattern were 5 sec, there would be 500 error scores for the trial. The computer then derives one score, RMSE, from these by calculating an average error score for the total pathway.

KINEMATIC MEASURES

Kinematic measures, traditionally associated with biomechanics, have become important descriptors of performance in research on motor learning and control. The term **kinematics** refers to the description of motion without regard to force or mass. Three of the most common of such descriptors

refer to an object's changes in position, its speed, and its changes in speed. The terms used to refer to these kinematic characteristics are *displacement, velocity,* and *acceleration.*

Kinematic measures are performance production measures that are based on recording the movement of specific body segments while a person is performing a skill. A typical procedure is first to mark the joints associated with the body segments of interest in a distinctive way with tape, a marking pen, special light-reflecting balls, or

---

root-mean-squared error (RMSE)   an error measure used for continuous skills to indicate the amount of error between the performance curve produced and the criterion performance curve for a specific amount of time during which performance is sampled.

kinematics   the description of motion without regard to force or mass; it includes displacement, velocity, and acceleration.

light-emitting diodes (LEDs). The researcher then records the person's performance of the skill on videotape, or by using special LED-reading cameras. Computer software developed to calculate kinematic measures then analyzes the recordings. This approach is used in commercially available movement analysis systems.

Another way to obtain kinematic measures is to record the person's movement of an object, which was the case for the pursuit tracking task described earlier and depicted in figure 2.4. Here, a computer samples (i.e., detects at a specified rate per second) and records the movements of the tracking device. In this example, a horizontal lever on a tabletop was the movement device. A potentiometer attached to the axle of the lever provided movement-related information that the computer sampled. Similar samplings of movement can be taken from the movement of a joystick, a mouse, or a rollerball.

Displacement

The first kinematic measure of interest is **displacement,** which is *the spatial position of a limb or joint during the time period of the movement.* Displacement describes changes in spatial locations as a person carries out a movement. We calculate displacement by using a movement analysis system to identify where the movement device or marked joint is in space (in terms of its X-Y coordinate in two-dimensional analysis or its X-Y-Z coordinate in three-dimensional analysis) at a given time. The system then determines the location of that joint for the next sampled time. The analysis system samples these spatial positions at specific rates, which vary according to the analysis system used. For example, a common videotape sampling rate is 60 Hz. Faster sampling rates are possible, depending on the analysis system used. Thus, the spatial location of a movement device or limb can be plotted for each sampled time as a displacement curve.

Velocity

The second kinematic measure of interest is **velocity,** which is a time-based derivative of displacement. *Velocity,* which we typically call speed in everyday terms, refers to *the rate of change in an*

This participant in a research study has reflective markers attached to various joints, and body and head locations for kinematic movement analysis purposes.

object position with respect to time. That is, how rapidly did this change in position occur and in what direction was this change (faster or slower than its previous rate)? Movement analysis systems derive velocity from displacement by dividing it by time. That is, divide a change in spatial position (between time 1 and time 2) by the change in time (from time 1 to time 2). Velocity is always presented on a graph as a position-by-time curve (see figure 2.5, in which the velocity curve is based on the same movement as the displacement curve). We refer to velocity in terms of an amount of distance per an amount of time. The example in figure 2.5 shows velocity as the number of degrees per second. As the slope of this curve steepens, it represents increasing velocity, whereas negative velocity is represented by a slope that goes downward. Zero velocity is indicated by no change in positive or negative position of the curve.

Acceleration

The third kinematic measure is **acceleration,** which describes *change in velocity during movement.* We derive acceleration from velocity by dividing change in velocity by change in time. We also depict acceleration curves as a function of time, as you can see in the acceleration graph in figure 2.5, which is based on the displacement and velocity graphs also in that figure. The acceleration curve depicts the speeding up and slowing down of the movements as the subject moves. Rapid acceleration means that a velocity change occurred quickly.

Linear and Angular Motion

In kinematic descriptions of movement, the measures of displacement, velocity, and acceleration can refer to either linear or angular motion. The distinction between these types of motion is important to understand, and is a critical distinction in the analysis of movement. *Linear motion* refers to motion in a straight line and involves all the body or object moving the same distance over the same amount of time. *Angular motion,* which is sometimes called *rotary motion,* refers to motion that occurs about an axis of rotation and involves specific body segments as they rotate about joints, which are the axes of rotation for body segment movement. For example, if you want to describe the kinematics of walking, linear motion descriptions are appropriate for movement from one location to another, because the whole body is moving linearly. However, if you want to describe the foot movement characteristics during walking, angular motion descriptions are more appropriate, because the foot rotates about the ankle joint during walking.

A common way researchers describe angular motion is by measuring the motion of a limb segment as it rotates about a joint while a movement is occurring. Two examples are shown in figure 2.6. The top part of this figure shows an angle-angle diagram for a skilled runner. According to Enoka (2002), because we move by rotating body segments about each other, angle-angle diagrams pro-

vide an insightful means of examining movement by looking at the relationship between two joints during a movement. The angle-angle diagram usually plots the angle between two adjacent body segments against the angle of one body segment.

In figure 2.6, the angular displacement of the knee joint is compared to that of the thigh during the four discrete events of a running stride: takeoff, opposite footstrike, opposite foot takeoff, and opposite footstrike. Note that this angle-angle diagram produces a heart-shaped pattern, which is the classic knee-thigh relationship pattern during gait. The bottom part of the figure shows similar diagrams for three persons who have had amputation below the knee. What is noticeable here is that the amputees do not flex the knee joint at the beginning of the stance as the skilled runner does. These examples demonstrate that an important benefit of kinematic measures is that they allow us to describe the characteristics of critical components of a skill during movement.

KINETICS

The term **kinetics** refers to the consideration of force in the study of motion. Whereas *kinematics* refers to descriptors of motion without concern for the cause of that motion, *kinetics refers to*

---

displacement a kinematic measure describing changes in the spatial positions of a limb or joint during the time course of the movement.

velocity a kinematic measure describing the rate of change of an object's position with respect to time. It is derived by dividing displacement by time (e.g., m/sec, km/hr).

acceleration a kinematic measure that describes change in velocity during movement; we derive it from velocity by dividing change in velocity by change in time.

kinetics the study of the role of force as a cause of motion.

FIGURE 2.5   Recordings of displacement, velocity, and acceleration of the wrist joint during the performance of a dart throw. The X-axis in each graph is the percent of the total movement time of the arm movement for the dart throw. The vertical line in each graph indicates the release of the dart, which occurred at approximately 51% of the total movement time of the arm movement.   [Data from one participant in an experiment that was part of: Jeansonne, J. J. (2003). *The effect of environmental context on performance outcomes and movement coordination changes during learning of complex motor skill.* Ph.D. dissertation, Louisiana State University.]

FIGURE 2.6 Angle-angle diagrams showing knee-thigh relationships during running by a skilled runner (top) and three below-knee amputees (bottom). The abbreviations indicate ipsilateral (left) footstrike (IFS), ipsilateral takeoff (ITO), contralateral (right) footstrike (CFS), and contralateral takeoff (CTO), which are the four components of a running stride.

[From Enoka, R. M. et al. (1978). Below knee amputee running gait. *American Journal of Physical Medicine and Rehabilitation, 61*, 70–78. Copyright © 1978 Williams & Wilkins Company, Baltimore, Maryland. Reprinted by permission.]

force as a cause of motion. Susan Hall (2003), in her textbook on biomechanics, states that "a force can be thought of as a push or pull acting on a body" (p. 63). Human movements can involve both external and internal sources of force. For example, gravity and air resistance are external forces that influence running and walking; water resistance is an external force that influences swimming movements. Muscles provide the basis for internal forces by pushing and pulling on joints of the body.

One way to see the importance of the role of force in our understanding of human movement is to note that all three of *Newton's laws of motion* refer to the role of force. In his first law, force is presented as necessary to start, change, or stop motion. His second law indicates that force influences the rate of change in the momentum of an object. And his third law presents force as being involved in the action and reaction that occurs in the interaction between two objects.

An important force-related characteristic of human movement is that human motion involves rotation of body segments around their joint axes. The effect of a force on this rotation is called *joint torque,* or rotary force (see figure 2.7 for an example of how to graphically present joint torque). Because of the many different types of force, and their influence on human movement, researchers studying motor skill learning and control are increasingly including the measurement of forces as part of their research.

Researchers can measure certain forces directly using devices such as force plates, force transducers, and strain gauges. They use force plates to measure ground reaction forces, which are involved in the interaction between an object, such as a person, and the ground. Force plates are popular force measurement devices in laboratories and clinics in which locomotion research and rehabilitation take place. Researchers use force transducers and strain gauges to measure force that is muscle produced; these are popular in laboratory and clinical settings to determine the magnitude of force generated while a subject is performing limb movement tasks.

Newton's second law of motion allows us to measure force indirectly by taking into account the relationship of force to velocity or acceleration and to the mass of the object: force = mass × acceleration. Because of this, we can calculate force without needing to use mechanical and electronic force measurement instruments, if acceleration can be assessed from a kinematic analysis of the movement.

EMG MEASURES

Movement involves electrical activity in the muscles, which can be measured by **electromyography (EMG).** Researchers commonly accomplish this by either attaching surface electrodes to the skin over muscles, or inserting fine wire electrodes into a specific muscle. These electrodes detect muscle electrical activity, which then can be recorded by a computer or polygraph recorder. Figure 2.8 shows some EMG recordings of electrical activity in the ipsilateral biceps femoris (BFi) and contralateral biceps femoris (BFc) of the legs and the anterior deltoid (AD) of the shoulder girdle for a task that required the person to move his or her arm, on a signal, from the reaction-time key to a position directly in front of the shoulder. The EMG signals presented for these muscles show when electrical activity began in the muscles; we can identify this activity by the increase in the frequency and height of the traces for each muscle. The actual beginning of movement off the RT key is designated in the diagram by the vertical line at the end of the RT recording (line 5 of figure 2.8).

Researchers can use EMG information in a variety of ways. One that is most relevant to motor learning and control issues is the use of EMG recordings to indicate when a muscle begins and ends activation. Muscle activation begins when the EMG recording increases in frequency and height compared to when the muscle is not active. When EMG recordings include several muscles involved in the same movement, researchers can gain insight into the process of movement coordination by observing the sequence of muscle activation patterns. For example, in figure 2.8, the first muscle to show activation after the signal to move the arm was the

FIGURE 2.7 Results of an experiment by Sanders and Allen showing knee torques for one subject during contact with a surface after the subject drop-jumped from a platform and immediately initiated a vertical jump for maximum height. Each line on the graph represents performance for the trial noted in the key on the graph. [Reprinted from Sanders, R. H., & Allen, J. B. (1993). *Human Movement Science, 12*, pp. 299–326, with kind permission of Elsevier Science-NL, Sara Burgerharstraat 25, 1055 KV Amsterdam, The Netherlands.]

ipsilateral biceps femoris (Bfi), which is a leg muscle on the same side of the body as the arm that moved; next in sequence was the anterior deltoid (AD), which moves the arm for the type of movement in the experiment. This activation sequence tells the researcher that more than arm muscle activity is involved for the simple arm movement performed in the experiment. The researcher would interpret the sequence of muscle activity as indicating that the body prepares itself for an arm movement like this one by first activating leg muscles responsible for stabilizing body posture.

MEASURING COORDINATION

One of the more interesting phenomena of recent motor learning and control research is the investigation of complex skills. One reason for this is methodologically based. Prior to the advent of computer-based technology for movement analy-

sis, kinematic measurement of movement was an expensive, labor-intensive, and time-consuming process involving frame-by-frame analysis of slow-motion film. With the development of the computer-based movement analysis systems, there has been a dramatic increase in research involving complex skills.

A measurement issue that has developed in the study of complex skills concerns how best to assess coordination. As you will study in chapter 4, coordination involves the movement of limb segments in specific time- and space-based patterns. We can easily observe these patterns in angle-angle

electromyography (EMG) a measurement technique that records the electrical activity of a muscle or group of muscles. It indicates the muscle activity.

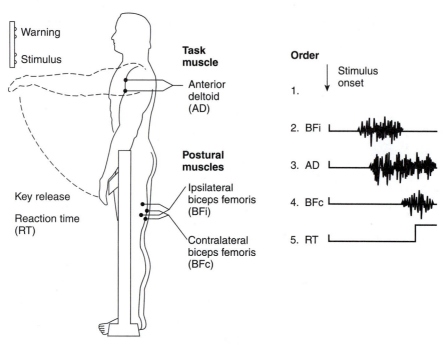

FIGURE 2.8   Using EMG recordings to measure a movement response.   The figure on the left shows the reaction-time apparatus and where each electrode was placed to record the EMG for each muscle group of interest. The figures on the right show the EMG recordings for each of the three muscle groups and the reaction-time interval for the response. [From Lee, Wynne. (1980). *Journal of Motor Behavior, 12*, 187. Reprinted by permission of the author.]

plots of the movements of limb segments, such as the ones depicted in figure 2.6. However, a measurement issue has arisen concerning angle-angle diagrams. Many researchers report only these qualitative kinematic descriptions and do not provide quantitative assessments of them. Some researchers question whether the qualitative pattern representation of limb segment relationships is sufficient for inferring coordination and suggest that quantitative assessment of these descriptions is needed as well.

A problem in resolving this issue is that there is little agreement among researchers about how to quantify coordination patterns such as the one in figure 2.6. Although several researchers have suggested techniques (see, e.g., Sparrow et al., 1987; Newell & van Emmerik, 1989; Vereijken et al., 1992), each has inherent problems, contributing to the current lack of general acceptance of any one

technique. Attempts to establish appropriate quantitative techniques continue (e.g., Sidaway, Heise, & Schoenfelder-Zohdi, 1995). Until researchers can resolve this issue, qualitative presentations of limb segment relationships will remain the norm for assessing coordination.

SUMMARY

An essential element in understanding motor learning is the measurement of motor performance. All concepts presented in this text are based on research in which researchers observed and measured motor performance. Measuring motor performance is essential for the assessment of motor deficiencies, as well as for the evaluation of performance by students or patients as they progress through practice and therapy regimes. In this chapter, we

A CLOSER LOOK

Quantifying Coordination Patterns

Motor control researchers have suggested several techniques for quantifying the angle-angle plots that are popular for describing coordination patterns, such as the classic heart-shaped pattern of the knee-hip joints relationship during gait. While the regularity of the pattern is easy to observe, this qualitative approach does not allow for statistical between-pattern comparisons to determine reliable differences or similarities. Following are two quantitative approaches to this problem.

• The most common method is to cross-correlate time-related position changes in the angle of one joint with changes in another joint, (e.g., Newell & van Emmerik, 1989; Vereijken et al., 1992). The resulting correlation coefficient is interpreted as a ratio expressing the extent to which the two joints follow similar patterns of movement. A high corre-

lation indicates strong coordination between the joints, whereas a low correlation shows little between-joint coordination.

• Sidaway, Heise, and Schoenfelder-Zohdi (1995) argue that a correlation approach is flawed because it assumes a linear relationship between the joints. In contrast, angle-angle plots of movement patterns are typically nonlinear. To accommodate both linear and nonlinear situations, they propose a normalized root-mean-squared error technique, which they call NoRMS. This method involves comparing a number of cycles of a continuous task, or a series of trials for a discrete task. From this series, the mean of the angle-angle plots is calculated. Then the root-mean-squared error (RMSE) is determined for each cycle or trial of the series, totaled, and then normalized with respect to the number of cycles or trials.

focused on different ways to measure motor performance, along with the ways we can use these measurements in motor learning research and applied settings.

The performance measurement issues and examples discussed in this chapter were these:

• Two categories of performance measures: performance outcome measures (which measure the result of the performance of a movement activity) and performance production measures (which measure movement-related characteristics that produce the performance outcome of a movement activity)

• Performance outcome measure examples: reaction time (RT), movement time (MT), and three measures of performance outcome error (AE, CE, and VE)

• Performance production measures examples: three kinematic measures (displacement, velocity, and acceleration), joint torque as a kinetic measure, and EMG

• Concerns about the qualitative and quantitative measurement of movement coordination

RELATED READINGS

Clarys, J. P., Cabri, J., De Witte, B., Toussaint, H., de Groot, G., Huying, P., & Hollander, P. (1988). Electromyography applied to sport ergonomics. *Ergonomics, 31,* 1605–1620.

Kim, J., Chung, S., Tennant, L. K., Singer, R. N., & Janelle, C. M. (2000). Minimizing error in measurement of error: A proposed method for calculation of error in a two-dimensional motor task. *Perceptual and Motor Skills, 90,* 253–261.

Mah, C. D., Hulliger, M., Lee, R. G., & Marchand, A. R. (1994). Quantitative analysis of human movement synergies: Constructive pattern analysis for gait. *Journal of Motor Behavior, 26,* 83–102.

Reeve, T. G., Fischman, M. G., Christina, R.W., & Cauraugh, J. H. (1994). Using one-dimensional task error measures to assess performance on two-dimensional tasks: Comment on "Attentional control, distractors, and motor performance." *Human Performance, 7,* 315–319.

Soderberg, G. L., & Knutson, L. M. (2000). A guide for use and interpretation of kinesiologic electromyographic data. *Physical Therapy, 80,* 485–498.

Sparrow, W. A. (1992). Measuring changes in coordination and control. In J. J. Summers (Ed.), *Approaches to the study of motor control and learning* (pp.147–162). Amsterdam: Elsevier.

STUDY QUESTIONS

1. (a) Describe the differences between performance outcome measures and performance production measures. (b) Give three examples for each of these measures of motor performance.

2. (a) Describe how simple RT, choice RT, and discrimination RT situations differ. (b) What does it mean to fractionate RT? (c) How does MT differ from RT?

3. What different information can be obtained about a person's performance by calculating AE, CE, and VE when performance accuracy is the movement goal?

4. How can performance error be determined for a continuous skill such as pursuit tracking?

5. Describe three kinematic measures of movement and explain what each measure tells us about the movement.

6. What is meant by the term *kinetics* as it is related to measuring human movement?

7. What information about a movement can be obtained by using EMG?

8. How can angle-angle diagrams be used to tell us something about the coordination characteristics of two limbs or two limb segments?

CHAPTER

Motor Abilities

*Concept: A variety of abilities underlie
motor skill learning and performance success*

After completing this chapter, you will be able to

- Define the term *ability* and distinguish it from the term *skill*

- Explain the difference between the general motor ability hypothesis and the specificity of motor abilities hypothesis

- Name and describe several motor ability categories, and explain how researchers have identified the various motor ability categories

- Describe how motor abilities relate to motor skill performance

Application

Some people perform many different physical activities very well. Why is this the case? Are they born with some special "motor ability" that enables them to be successful at all they do? Have they had an abundance of good training and practice in a wide variety of activities? Are they really good at everything, or only at certain activities?

Also, people differ in how quickly and successfully they learn motor skills. If you observe a physical activity class for beginners, you will see various degrees of success and failure during the first few days. For example, in a beginning golf class, when the students first start to hit the ball, some will spend an inordinate amount of time simply trying to make contact with the ball. But some will be at the other extreme, able to hit the ball rather well. The remainder of the class usually will be distributed somewhere along the continuum of success between these two extremes. We can ob-

serve parallel differences in other physical activity situations, such as dance classes, driving instruction classes, and physical therapy sessions.

Discussion

In chapters 1 and 2, you were introduced to motor skills and the measurement of motor skill performance. Now, you will be introduced to a type of personal characteristic known as *ability,* which influences the way people perform and learn motor skills.

ABILITY AND MOTOR ABILITY

One of the difficulties in studying the concept of ability as it relates to motor skill performance is that the term *ability* is used in so many different ways. For example, physical and occupational therapists refer to "functional ability"; a baseball coach might refer to a player's "running ability"; educators often refer to students' "cognitive ability" or "intellectual ability." The list of examples could go on, but these few examples illustrate the problem. As a result, it is important to specify the precise manner in which the term will be used.

For this discussion, the term *ability* will be used according to its meaning in the area of psychology that involves the study of *individual differences.* People who study individual differences are concerned with the identification and measurement of abilities that characterize and differentiate individuals. Individual-difference psychologists also investigate the relationship between abilities and the performance and learning of skills. In this context, the term **ability** means *a general trait or capacity of the individual that is a relatively enduring characteristic which serves as a determinant of a person's achievement potential for the performance of specific skills.* When the term **motor ability** is used in this context, it refers to *an ability that is specifically related to the performance of a motor skill.* It is important to note that some researchers and practitioners use terms such as "psychomotor ability" and "perceptual motor ability" to refer to what we will call motor ability.[1]

The identification of specific motor abilities is not an easy task. As a result, few researchers have ventured into this area of study. However, those who have undertaken this challenge have provided us with useful information that helps us have a better understanding of an important factor related to determining why people differ in achievement levels of motor skill performance.

Abilities as Individual-Difference Variables

The individual differences we observe in the levels of success that people achieve in the performance of a motor skill depends in large part on the degree to which the person has the motor abilities that are important for the performance of that skill. For ex-

ample, people with differing levels of the motor abilities important for playing tennis will have differing *achievement potentials* in tennis. This example indicates that various motor abilities underlie the performance of a complex motor skill such as tennis, and that people have different levels of these abilities. It also indicates that if two people have the same training experiences and amount of practice, but differ in their levels of the motor abilities important for playing tennis, the one with the higher levels of the appropriate abilities has the potential to perform at a higher level. Although researchers generally agree with this view, they debated for many years, especially in the 1950s and 1960s, how motor abilities relate to one another within the same person.

The controversy over general versus specific motor abilities. In the debate about the relationship of motor abilities, one viewpoint holds that motor abilities are *highly related* to each other. The opposite view is that they are *relatively independent* of one another. This debate is not commonly pursued in the current research literature. However, an understanding of the different points of view will facilitate your application of the concept of motor abilities to motor skill performance achievement.

The **general motor ability hypothesis** maintains that although many different motor abilities can be identified within an individual, they are highly related and can be characterized in terms of a singular, global motor ability. It holds that the level of that ability in an individual influences the ultimate success that person can expect in performing any motor skill. This viewpoint has been in existence for quite some time (e.g., Brace, 1927; McCloy, 1934). This hypothesis predicts that if a person is highly skilled in one motor skill, then he or she has the potential to be highly skilled in all motor skills. The reasoning behind this prediction is that there is *one* general motor ability. In fact, one proponent of this view developed a motor ability test battery that he proposed could be used to classify students into one of five homogeneous motor ability subgroups for purposes of teaching and engaging in physical activities (Barrow, 1957).

---

[1]Although the terms *motor ability, psychomotor ability,* and *perceptual-motor ability* can have specific meanings, they are sufficiently similar, for purposes of this book, to use the term *motor ability* to refer to all three terms.

But contrary to the expectations of proponents of the general motor ability hypothesis, very little research evidence supports this viewpoint. One suspects that the basis for the continued existence of this hypothesis is its intuitive appeal. Tests of general motor ability are convenient, appealing to those who seek an easy explanation for why certain people are successful or unsuccessful at performing motor skills. The fact that these tests are poor predictors of specific motor skill performance has not diminished the appeal of the general motor ability hypothesis.

The alternative perspective, for which there has been substantial support, is the **specificity of motor abilities hypothesis.** Franklin Henry is generally credited with deriving the specificity hypothesis to explain results from his research that the general motor ability hypothesis could not explain (e.g., Henry, 1961). This specificity view states that individuals have many motor abilities, and these abilities are relatively independent. This means, for example, that if a person exhibited a high degree of balancing ability, we could not predict how well that person would do on a test of reaction time.

Support for the specificity hypothesis has come from experiments that were reported primarily in the 1960s. These experiments were based on the common assumption that if motor abilities are specific and independent, then the relationship between any two abilities will be very low. Thus, in the simplest of cases, the relationship would be very low between any two abilities such as balance and reaction time, or between reaction time and speed of movement, or between static and dynamic balance.

The research evidence in the 1960s that provided most of the initial support for the specificity hypothesis, and became an impetus for further research, came from the laboratory of Franklin Henry at the University of California, Berkeley. This research was based on the premise that motor abilities are relatively independent. Henry and his colleagues reasoned that they could demonstrate this independence rather simply by investigating the relationship between reaction time and arm movement speed. Recall from the discussion in chapter 2 that reaction time is the amount of time

to see, hear, or feel a stimulus (i.e., a "go" signal) and then initiate the required movement; movement time is the amount of time from the initiation of the movement to its completion. The common result from many experiments from Henry's laboratory (e.g., Henry, 1961a, 1961b) was that reaction time and movement speed are uncorrelated, which means that each is an independent motor ability.

Balance and timing abilities. Although researchers now generally accept the specificity of motor abilities hypothesis, some have raised questions about the generality of certain specific motor abilities. That is, do certain motor abilities represent one ability, or are there several variations of these abilities, each of which is task specific and relatively independent of the other(s)? Two examples of these motor abilities are balance and timing.

Although static and dynamic *balance* are generally regarded as two types of balance, *balance* is often regarded as one motor ability. This means that static balance, which refers to the maintaining of equilibrium while in a stationary position, is considered to be a simpler variation of dynamic balance, which refers to the maintaining of equilibrium while in motion. This viewpoint is seen, for example, when rehabilitation protocols specify that a person should develop static postural balance

---

ability a general trait or capacity of an individual that is a determinant of a person's achievement potential for the performance of specific skills.

motor ability an ability that is specifically related to the performance of a motor skill.

general motor ability hypothesis a hypothesis that maintains that the many different motor abilities that exist in an individual are highly related and can be characterized in terms of a singular, global motor ability.

specificity of motor abilities hypothesis a hypothesis that maintains that the many motor abilities in an individual are relatively independent.

A CLOSER LOOK

The Relationship between Reaction Time (RT) and Movement Time (MT) as Support for the Specificity of Motor Abilities Hypothesis

Franklin Henry's research concerning the RT-MT relationship are now considered the classic experiments for establishing evidence against the traditional general motor ability hypothesis. These experiments typically involved participants responding to either an auditory or a visual signal by lifting their finger from a telegraph key and then moving their arm in a specified direction, or directions, to hit a target, such as a ball hanging on a string. Results of these experiments were notably consistent in producing low correlations[1] between RT and MT. The following is a summary of the results of several of these experiments, which Henry reported in a *Research Quarterly* article published in 1961. These results demonstrate the type of evidence on which Henry and others concluded that motor abilities are independent.

The first of these experiments investigated the RT-MT relationship for *gender* and the *complexity of the movement.* Among the various levels of movement complexity were a simple movement (Movement A,

which was a forward arm movement of 117 cm to a string target); a two-part movement (Movement B, which was an initial upward arm movement followed by a forward movement of 30 cm to a ball-grasp target); and a three-part movement (Movement C, which was an initial upward and lateral movement, followed by a lateral downward direction reversal to a target, and then a forward movement to a target).

In addition to gender and movement complexity effects on the RT-MT relationship, Henry also reported the following results:

Stimulus complexity effects: For simple, choice, and discrimination RT situations, the average RT-MT correlation was 0.02.

Maturation effects: For participants in five age groups (8, 12, 18, 24, and 30 yrs) for movements A and B described above, the average RT-MT correlation was 0.11.

Movement	A	B		C	
Gender	**Males**	**Males**	**Females**	**Males**	**Females**
RT	225 ms	195 ms	205 ms	204 ms	219 ms
MT[a]	195 ms	93 ms	130 ms	481 ms	522 ms
RT-MT Correlation	0.01	−0.32	0.10	0.18	0.29

[a]Note that the longer MT for Movement A than for Movement B occurred because A involved a much longer movement than B, even though B involved two parts.

[1]A correlation is a statistical technique to determine the relationship between two performance measures. The number that results from a correlation, referred to as a coefficient, will be within the range of −1.0 to +1.0. A 0 indicates no relationship between the measures; a 1.0 indicates a high relationship. The minus and plus indicate the direction of the relationship; the minus indicates that when the value of one measure increases, the other measure decreases, and the plus indicates that the values of both increase or decrease.

capabilities before engaging in activities requiring dynamic postural balance, such as walking. However, research evidence consistently indicates that static and dynamic balance are relatively independent motor abilities. For example, Rose et al. (2002) reported that 14 of 23 children with gait disorders related to cerebral palsy showed normal standing balance characteristics.

Research evidence also indicates that several relatively independent variations of static and dynamic balance exist. Drowatzky and Zuccato (1967) reported an excellent example of this research many years ago. In this experiment, participants performed six different balancing tasks that generally have been regarded as measures of either static or dynamic balancing ability. The results of

TABLE 3.1 Results from the Experiment by Drowatzky and Zuccato (1967) Showing the Correlations among Six Different Tests of Static and Dynamic Balance

Test	Static Balance Tests			Dynamic Balance Tests		
	1 Stork Stand[1]	**2** Diver's Stand[2]	**3** Bass Stick Stand[3]	**4** Sideward Leap[4]	**5** Bass Stepping Stone Test[5]	**6** Balance Beam Test[6]
1	—	0.14	−0.12	0.26	0.20	0.03
2		—	−0.12	−0.03	−0.07	−0.14
3			—	−0.04	0.22	−0.19
4				—	0.31	0.19
5					—	0.18
6						—

[1]*Stork stand*—Person stands for as long as possible on the foot of the dominant leg while placing the other foot on the inside of the supporting knee and the hands on the hips.

[2]*Diver's stand*—Person stands erect with both feet together, arms extended in front. When ready he or she rises onto the balls of the feet, closes his or her eyes, and maintains this position for as long as possible.

[3]*Bass stick test*—Person stands for as long as possible, up to 60 sec, with the ball of the foot of the dominant leg crosswise on a 1 in. wide × 1 in. high × 12 in. long stick; the other foot must be off the floor.

[4]*Sideward leap*—Person stands on the left foot, leaps sideward to the right to a mark on the floor (distance = person's leg length), leans forward to push small object off a mark (18 in. in front of landing mark), then holds balance for 5 sec.

[5]*Bass stepping stone test*—Person stands on the right foot on the starting mark, then leaps to a series of targets located in front of the person, alternating left and right feet. At each target, the person maintains balance for as long as possible, up to 5 sec.

[6]*Balance beam test*—On a balance beam (4 in. wide, 4.5 in. off the floor, 10 ft long) person walks, with hands on hips, heel to toe for 10 steps or until falls; if falls, gets back on beam, continues walking; stops walking at 10 steps or second fall.

Source: From Drowatzky, J. N. & Zuccato, F. C. (1967). Interrelationships between selected measures of static and dynamic balance. *Research Quarterly for Exercise and Sport, 38,* 509–510. Copyright © 1967 American Alliance for Health, Physical Education, Recreation, and Dance. Reprinted by permission.

the correlations among all the tests (table 3.1) showed that the highest correlation (.31) was between the sideward stand and the Bass stand. Most of the correlations ranged between 0.12 and 0.19. A more recent study by Tsiglis, Zachopoulou, and Mavridis (2001) supported the Drowatsky and Zucatto results for various types of dynamic balance. The highest correlation between two of three different types of dynamic balance tests was .22. The two other correlations between the tests were .05 and .13.

On the basis of results such as these, it would be difficult to conclude that only one test could be considered a valid measure of balancing ability. We need to subdivide the ability we generally call "balance" into various types of balance.

Timing, as a motor ability, concerns the external timing required to precisely time a bat swing with a pitched ball in baseball, and the internal timing required to perform a well-timed sequence of movements, such as those produced by a skilled dancer or pianist. Some researchers propose that people possess a general timing ability that underlies the performance of skills involving both external and internal timing (e.g., Ivry & Hazeltine, 1995). Others argue that timing is specific to the requirements of a skill, which means that there are various types of timing abilities. According to Zelaznik and his colleagues (e.g., Zelaznik, Spencer, & Doffin, 2000), research that supports a general timing ability have restricted the comparison of skills to those that have similar timing characteristics, such the

LAB LINKS

Lab 3 in the Online Learning Center Lab Manual
for chapter 3 provides an opportunity for you to
experience several different types of balance tests
and compare your results to the predictions of the
general motor ability and specificity of motor abilities hypotheses.

repetitive tapping of a finger at either a preferred
rate of speed (referred to as self-paced, or unpaced,
timing) or in time with a metronome (externally-
paced timing). When Zelaznik et al. (2000) compared externally-paced rates of repetitive finger
tapping and continuous circle drawing, which involve similar timing requirements for different
types of tasks, the correlations were generally low.
Thus, it seem reasonable to conclude that although
people are capable of precise timing when performing motor skills, timing ability is specific to the requirements of the skill being performed rather than
a general timing ability.

The "all-around athlete." If motor abilities are numerous and independent, then how can we explain
the so-called "all-around athlete," the person who
is very proficient at a variety of physical activities?
According to the specificity view, abilities fall
somewhere along a range containing low, average,
and high amounts within individuals. Because people differ, it seems reasonable to expect that some
people have a large number of abilities at an average level, and other people have a majority of abilities at either the high or the low end of the scale.

According to the specificity hypothesis, the person who excels in a large number of physical activities has high levels of a large number of abilities.
We would expect that a person would do very well
in those activities for which the underlying abilities required for successful performance matched
the abilities for which the person was at the high
end of the scale.

In actual fact, the true all-around athlete is a rare
individual. Typically, when a person shows high

performance levels in a variety of physical activities, a close inspection of those activities reveals
many foundational motor abilities in common. We
would expect a person exhibiting high levels for a
variety of abilities to do well in activities for which
those abilities were foundational to performance.
However, we would expect average performance if
this person engaged in activities for which those
abilities were less important, activities based on
other abilities, of which the person possessed only
average levels.

Identifying Motor Abilities

As a capacity, an ability is a relatively enduring attribute of an individual. Researchers who study individual differences assume that we can describe
the skills involved in complex motor activities in
terms of the abilities that underlie their performance. For example, the ability called spatial visualization is related to the performance of such
diverse tasks as aerial navigation, blueprint reading, and dentistry (Fleishman, 1972). An important
step in understanding how abilities and skill performance are related is identifying abilities and
matching them with the skills involved.

When researchers and practitioners identify specific motor abilities, they usually refer to the work
of Edwin Fleishman (see Fleishman & Quaintance,
1984, for a description of this work). His research,
which was carried out for four decades beginning
in the 1950s, continues to influence our understanding and study of motor abilities and how they
relate to motor skill performance. Perhaps the most
significant achievement of Fleishman's work was
the development of a taxonomy of motor abilities,
which he designed to identify the fewest possible
ability categories that could be applied to the greatest variety of motor skills.

A taxonomy of motor abilities. From the results of
extensive batteries of perceptual motor tests given to
many people, Fleishman developed a "taxonomy of
human perceptual motor abilities" (Fleishman,
1972; Fleishman & Quaintance, 1984). The goal of
the taxonomy was "to define the fewest independent

A CLOSER LOOK

A Value of Identifying Motor Abilities

Identifying and assessing motor abilities can allow a teacher, coach, or therapist to

- Identify the source of problems or difficulties in performing a skill. Often a person has difficulty learning a new skill because he or she lacks adequate experience involving the motor ability essential to performing that particular skill.

  Example: A child may be having difficulty catching a thrown ball because of a poorly developed ability to visually track a moving object.

- Develop appropriate physical activities to improve performance in a variety of skills involving the same motor ability.

  Example: Dynamic balance is a foundational ability to many different skills. As a result, movement experiences that provide people the opportunity to develop their dynamic balance ability in a variety of movement situations should benefit learning skills requiring dynamic balance.

---

ability categories which might be most useful and meaningful in describing performance in the widest variety of tasks" (Fleishman, 1967, p. 352). The taxonomy included two broad categories of human abilities in the perceptual motor and physical domains: *perceptual motor abilities* and *physical proficiency abilities.* Table 3.2 presents and defines the eleven perceptual motor ability categories Fleishman proposed. Note that table 3.2 also includes an example of one of the tests he used to assess each ability and an example of a motor skill whose performance would be associated with the ability category.

In addition to perceptual motor abilities, Fleishman also identified nine abilities that he designated as *physical proficiency abilities.* These abilities differ from the perceptual motor abilities in that they are more generally related to gross motor skill performance. Most people would consider these abilities physical fitness abilities. The physical proficiency abilities identified by Fleishman are as follows: (1) *static strength,* the maximum force that a person can exert against external objects; (2) *dynamic strength,* the muscular endurance used in exerting force repeatedly; (3) *explosive strength,* the ability to mobilize energy effectively for bursts of muscular effort; (4) *trunk strength,* the strength of the trunk muscles; (5) *extent flexibility,* the ability to flex or stretch the trunk and back muscles; (6) *dynamic flexibility,* the ability to make repeated,

rapid trunk-flexing movements; (7) *gross body coordination,* the ability to coordinate the action of several parts of the body while the body is in motion; (8) *gross body equilibrium,* the ability to maintain balance without visual cues; and (9) *stamina,* the capacity to sustain maximum effort requiring cardiovascular effort.

We should not consider Fleishman's lists to be exhaustive inventories of all the abilities related to motor skill performance, because Fleishman wanted to identify the smallest number of abilities that would describe the tasks performed in the test battery. Although he used hundreds of tasks to identify those abilities, the inclusion of additional types of tasks besides those Fleishman used could lead to the identification of other motor abilities. For example, Fleishman did not include the following abilities in his two lists:

- *Static balance*—The ability to maintain postural stability on a stable surface or when not engaging in locomotor activities (e.g., standing on the floor while reading a book)

- *Dynamic balance*—The ability to maintain postural stability on a moving surface or when engaging in locomotor activities (e.g., walking on a sidewalk)

- *Visual acuity*—The ability to see clearly and precisely (e.g., reading a street sign)

TABLE 3.2 Perceptual Motor Ability Categories Identified by Fleishman (1972) as a Result of Numerous Research Studies. The Ability Labels, Definitions, and Tests Are as Fleishman Presented Them in Two Reports on His Work (Fleishman, 1972, pp. 1019f; Fleishman & Quaintance, 1984, pp. 164f).

Ability Category	Definition	Ability Category Test and Related Motor Skill Example
Multilimb coordination	Ability to coordinate movements of a number of limbs simultaneously	*Complex coordinator task:* Person simultaneously controls two levers, one with each hand, and two pedals, one with each foot, in response to signals *Skill example:* Playing the piano or organ, where both hands and feet are involved
Control precision	Ability to make rapid and precise movement adjustments of control devices involving single arm-hand or leg movements; adjustments are made to visual stimuli	*Rotary pursuit task:* Person keeps a hand-held stylus in contact with a small disk embedded in a phonograph-like turntable as it rotates at 60 rpm *Skill example:* Operating a joy stick in a computer video game
Response orientation	Ability to make a rapid selection of controls to be moved or the direction to move them in	*Visual discrimination tasks, e.g., choice reaction time task:* Person responds as quickly as possible when one of several visual signals illuminates *Skill example:* Soccer player with the ball responding to defensive player's movements by dribbling past the player, passing, or making a shot at the goal
Reaction time	Ability to respond rapidly to a signal when it appears	*Visual or auditory simple reaction time task:* Person responds as quickly as possible to a visual (e.g., a light) or auditory (e.g., a buzzer) signal *Skill example:* Start of a sprint in swimming
Speed of arm movement	Ability to rapidly make a gross, discrete arm movement where accuracy is minimized	*Two-plate reciprocal tapping task:* Person moves a hand-held stylus back and forth between two metal plates, 25 cm apart, as rapidly as possible for 10 sec *Skill example:* Throwing a ball for speed rather than for accuracy
Rate control	Ability to time continuous anticipatory movement adjustments in response to speed and/or direction changes of a continuously moving target or object	*Pursuit tracking task:* Person moves a computer mouse to move a cursor on a computer monitor to maintain contact with a target cursor that changes in speed and direction *Skill example:* Driving a car on a highway
Manual dexterity	Ability to make skillful arm-hand movements to manipulate fairly large objects under speeded conditions	*Minnesota Manual Dexterity task:* Person picks up with one hand and turns over as quickly as possible a series of wooden pegs in holes *Skill example:* Dribbling and maintaining control of a basketball while running
Finger dexterity	Ability to make skillful, controlled manipulations of tiny objects involving primarily the fingers	*Purdue Pegboard task:* Person picks up and assembles small peg, washer, and collar units and inserts them into small holes *Skill example:* Buttoning a shirt
Arm-hand steadiness	Ability to make precise arm-hand positioning movements where strength and speed are minimized; includes maintaining arm-hand steadiness during arm movement or in a static arm position	*Track tracing task:* Person moves a hand-held stylus through a trough in a board without touching the sides of the trough; and *Hand-steadiness task:* Person holds a stylus in a small hole without touching the sides of the hole *Skill example:* Applying eye-liner
Wrist, finger speed	Ability to make rapid and repetitive movements with the hand and fingers, and/or rotary wrist movements when accuracy is not critical	*Tapping task:* Person holds a pencil and taps its point as many times as possible in a large circle for a specified amount of time *Skill example:* Handwriting for speed
Aiming	Ability to rapidly and accurately move the hand to a small target	*Manual aiming task:* Person holds a pencil and rapidly makes a dot in a series of very small circles *Skill example:* A drummer rapidly moving a stick from a snare drum to a small cymbal

A CLOSER LOOK

The Relationship between Perceptual Motor Abilities and Handwriting Speed

Slow handwriting speed can affect children's school performance by preventing them from completing hand-written work that must meet time constraints. To investigate factors that are associated with slow handwriting, Tseng and Chow (2000) administered three perceptual or motor abilities tests and a vigilance test to 7- to 11-year-old Chinese schoolchildren who were either slow or normal speed handwriters.

Handwriting speed: The amount of time required for the children to copy in pencil a previously studied text (speed = the number of Chinese characters written per minute)

The abilities tests assessed:
- arm movement speed and hand dexterity
- nonmotor visual perception (including discrimination, sequential memory, figure closure, etc.)
- visual-motor integration (which required the copying in sequence of a set of geometric forms)
- ability to focus and maintain attention over time

Results: The following abilities were predictors of slow handwriting:
- Arm speed and hand dexterity
- Focusing and maintaining attention
- Visual memory
- Visual-motor integration
- Visual sequential memory

Author's conclusion: These results suggest that "intervention for slow handwriting should focus on facilitating visual processing, including memory and visual-motor integration, rather than the fine motor training so often emphasized in occupational therapy programs" (p. 87).

- *Visual tracking*—The ability to visually follow a moving object (e.g., watching the flight of a ball that is thrown to you to catch)
- *Eye-hand or eye-foot coordination*—The ability to perform skills requiring vision and the precise use of the hands (e.g., correctly typing a sentence on a keyboard) or feet (e.g., kicking a penalty kick in soccer)

An important assumption of this view of human abilities is that all individuals possess these motor abilities. Another is that because it is possible to measure these motor abilities, it is also possible to determine a quantified measure of the level of each ability in a person. People differ in the amount of each ability they possess. Their motor abilities indicate limits that influence a person's potential for achievement in motor skill performance.

Relating Motor Abilities to Motor Skill Performance

An approach presented by Ackerman (1988) helps us see where motor abilities fit into the broader issue of motor skill performance. He described motor abilities as one of three categories of human abilities that affect motor skill performance. One category is general intelligence, or general ability. Included are cognitively oriented abilities and memory-related processes, such as acquiring, storing, retrieving, combining, and comparing memory-based information, as well as using it in new contexts. The second category is perceptual speed ability. This category includes abilities associated with a person's facility for solving problems of increasing complexity, and with the person's speed at processing information he or she must use to solve problems. Tests of such tasks as finding the *X*s in an array of letters and transcribing symbols on a list assess these abilities. Finally, *psychomotor ability* (i.e., motor ability) is the third category. Abilities in this category, which is the focus of our discussion, are related to speed and accuracy of movements that place little or no cognitive demand on the person. To fully understand individual differences, we must see performance of all types of skills in terms of these three foundational categories of abilities. However, for the purposes of the present discussion, we will limit our attention to motor abilities.

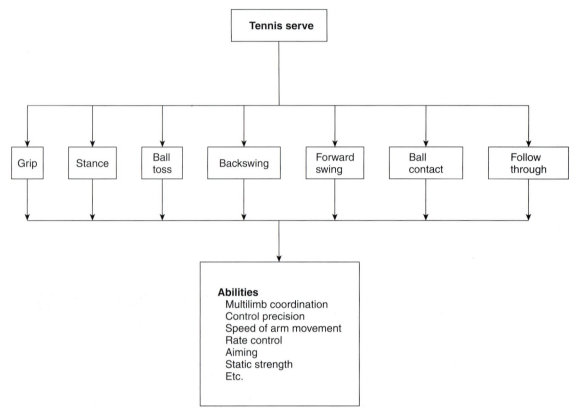

FIGURE 3.1   A task analysis for the tennis serve indicating the component parts of the serve and some examples of perceptual motor abilities underlying performance of the serve.

Figure 3.1 illustrates the view that motor abilities are underlying, foundational components of motor skill performance. This figure shows how we can analyze complex motor skills by a process known as *task analysis* in order to identify the abilities that underlie any motor skill. For example, to serve a tennis ball successfully, a player must perform certain components of that skill properly. Figure 3.1 identifies these components, which are the first level of analysis of the tennis serve, in the middle tier of the diagram. Identification of these components helps us identify more readily the underlying motor abilities that are involved in the successful performance of this task. The bottom tier of the diagram presents these abilities. Based on Fleishman's lists, they include such abilities as multilimb coordination, con-

trol precision, speed of arm movement, rate control, aiming, and static strength. You undoubtedly could add others. However, these few examples should serve to illustrate the foundational role perceptual motor and physical proficiency abilities play in the performance of motor skills.

SUMMARY

- The term *ability* refers to a general trait or capacity of the individual that is related to the performance of a variety of skills or tasks. A variety of motor abilities underlie the performance of a motor skill; people have different amounts, or quantities, of these abilities.

- Researchers have debated for many years how the various motor abilities relate to one another. The two hypotheses proposed to describe this relationship are the general motor ability hypothesis, which states that the abilities are highly related, and the specificity hypothesis, which argues that the abilities are relatively independent of one another. Research evidence has consistently supported the specificity hypothesis.

- There has been some debate among those who hold the specificity hypothesis concerning the generality of certain specific motor abilities, such as balance and timing. Research evidence has consistently shown that balance consists of static and dynamic balance as two relatively independent motor abilities, and that several relatively independent variations of each exist. Timing ability, which refers to both the precise external and internal timing involved in performing motor skills, appears to be specific to the requirements of the task being performed.

- An important approach to the identification of motor abilities was Fleishman's taxonomy of perceptual and physical proficiency abilities. The abilities identified in this taxonomy, along with others not included, play a foundational role in the performance of motor skills. Because it is possible to measure these abilities, we can assess a person's level of each ability. Research evidence shows that people differ in their amounts of each ability. These levels indicate limits that influence a person's potential for achievement in specific motor skills.

RELATED READINGS

Ackerman, P. L., & Cianciolo, A. T. (1999). Psychomotor abilities via touch-panel testing: Measurement innovations, construct, and criterion validity. *Human Performance, 12,* 231–273.

Franchignoni, F., Tesio, L., Martino, M. T., Ricupero, C. (1998). Reliability of four simple, quantitative tests of balance and mobility in healthy elderly females. *Aging—Clinical and Experimental Research, 10,* 26–31.

Proctor, R. W., & Dutta, A. (1995). *Skill acquisition and human performance.* Thousand Oaks, CA: Sage. [Read ch. 10: Individual Differences]

Robertson, S. D., Zelaznik, H. N., Lantero, D. A., Gadacz, K. E., Spencer, R. M., Doffin, J. G., & Schneidt, T. (1999). Correlations for timing consistency among tapping and drawing tasks: Evidence against a single timing process for motor control. *Journal of Experimental Psychology: Human Perception and Performance, 25,* 1316–1330.

Stelmach, G. E., & Nahom, A. (1992). Cognitive-motor abilities of the elderly driver. *Human Factors, 34,* 53–65.

Tseng, M. H., & Cermak, S. A. (1993). The influence of ergonomic factors and perceptual-motor abilities on handwriting performance. *American Journal of Occupational Therapy, 47,* 919–926.

STUDY QUESTIONS

1. (a) How do people who study individual differences define the term *abilities?* (b) Distinguish the meaning of *abilities* from the term *skill.*

2. (a) What is the difference between the general motor ability hypothesis and the specificity of motor abilities hypothesis? (b) Give an example of research evidence indicating which of these hypotheses is more valid.

3. How is balance an example of a motor ability that includes at least two types of relatively independent variations?

4. How can a specificity view of motor abilities explain how a person can be very successful at performing a lot of different motor skills?

5. (a) Name and describe five perceptual motor abilities identified by Fleishman. (b) What other motor abilities can you identify?

6. Describe how motor abilities relate to motor skill performance.

INTRODUCTION TO MOTOR CONTROL

Motor Control Theories

*Concept: Theories about how we control coordinated movement differ
in terms of the roles of central and environmental features of a control system*

After completing this chapter, you will be able to

- Discuss the relevance of motor control theory for the practitioner

- Define the term *coordination* as it relates to the performance of motor skills

- Describe the *degrees of freedom problem* as it relates to the study of human motor control

- Compare and contrast an open-loop control system and a closed-loop control system

- Describe a primary difference between a motor program–based theory of motor control and a dynamic pattern theory of motor control

- Define a generalized motor program and describe an invariant feature and a parameter proposed to characterize this program

- Define the following terms associated with a dynamic pattern theory of motor control: order and control parameters, self-organization, coordinative structures, and perception-action coupling

- Discuss how a motor program–based theory and a dynamic pattern theory each explain the basis for the relative-time characteristics of human walking and running

Application

To successfully perform the wide variety of motor skills we use in everyday life, we must coordinate various muscles and joints to function together. These muscle and joint combinations differ for many skills. Some skills, such as hitting a serve in tennis or getting out of a chair and into a wheelchair, require us to coordinate muscles and joints of the trunk and limbs. Other skills involve coordination of the arms, hands, and fingers; examples

are reaching to pick up a pencil, playing the guitar, and typing on a keyboard. For still other skills, where only one arm and hand are involved, we must coordinate only a few muscles and joints. We do this when we manipulate a computer joystick or a car's gearshift.

Motor skill performance has other important general characteristics in addition to body and limb coordination. For example, we perform some skills with relatively slow movements; think of how we position a bow before releasing an arrow, or pick up a cup to take a drink from it. Other skills, such as throwing a ball or jumping from a bench to the floor, require fast, ballistic movements. Some motor skills, such as writing a numeral or buttoning a shirt, have few component parts; other skills, such as performing a dance routine or playing the piano, are very complex.

Also, we can produce remarkably accurate and consistent movement patterns from one performance attempt to another. We are capable of performing well-learned skills with a remarkable degree of success in a variety of situations, even though we have never before been in similar situations. For example, a skilled tennis player will have to use a forehand stroke in many different situations in matches. The many different characteristics in any situation, such as the ball's flight pattern, speed, spin, bounce, and location on the court, as well as the opponent's position, the wind and sun conditions, and so on, provide little chance that any two situations can be exactly alike. Yet a skilled player can hit the ball successfully.

Discussion

Before we discuss some theories of how the nervous system controls coordinated movement, we will consider the importance of having an understanding of the basic components of motor control theory. Then, we will clarify a few terms, to provide a foundation for understanding those theories.

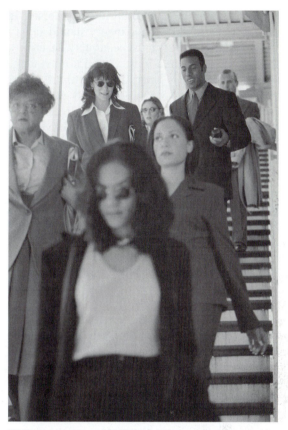

Walking down a crowded flight of stairs is a good example of an action that requires a person to adapt his or her pattern of head, body, and limb movements to the characteristics of the stairs and the other people on the stairs.

THEORY AND PROFESSIONAL PRACTICE

Students who are preparing for professions in which their primary responsibilities involve motor skill instruction often question the need to study motor control theory. This type of questioning often comes from those who believe their preparation needs to involve only "practical" information that will help them carry out their day-to-day responsibilities in the workplace. Unfortunately, this view is often the result of a lack of understanding

of the relevance of theory to professional practice. In this section, we will discuss what a theory is and the relevance of motor control theory for teachers, coaches, and therapists.

What Is a Theory?

If we base our understanding of the term *theory* on how it is commonly used in everyday language, we come away with the view that a theory has little relevance to reality. But this view is short-sighted and misleading. In science, a theory helps us understand phenomena and explains the reasons why these phenomena exist or behave as they do. Stephen Hawking (1996), the world-renowned theoretical physicist at Cambridge University in England, states that a good theory should satisfy "two requirements. It must accurately describe a large class of observations . . . and it must make definite predictions about the results of future observations" (p. 15). In Hawking's domain of physics, theories are developed to help us understand various aspects of the physical universe in which we live. They do this by providing us with explanations of observable physical events, such as identifying the variables that make a rolling ball eventually stop rolling. By identifying these variables, we can then predict how far a ball will roll given specific characteristics of these variables.

In the behavioral sciences, which include the study of human motor learning and control, theories focus on explaining human behavior. When the human behavior of interest is the performance and learning of motor skills, we look to theories to provide us with explanations about why people perform skills as they do, which means identifying the variables that account for the performance characteristics we observe. For example, we know from our observations of people performing skills that a person can perform the same skill in a variety of different situations. A skilled basketball player can shoot a one-hand jump shot from a variety of locations on the floor and in a variety of game-related situations. A good theory of motor control will explain why this capability is possible.

The Relevance of Motor Control Theory for the Practitioner

A benefit of a basic understanding of motor control theory is that it provides the practitioner with a base of support on which he or she can develop effective skill instruction and practice environments. Figure 4.1 illustrates the connection between theory and practice by indicating some of the many applications that will be enhanced when a practitioner has knowledge about the variables that influence motor skill performance. To use the example given at the end of the preceding section, if we know *why* people can adapt to a variety of situations when they perform a motor skill, we can use this knowledge to develop practice conditions

that we can confidently predict will facilitate this adaptation capability. Consider a different example. Suppose you need to help a person reacquire the capability to walk. Knowledge about the motor control mechanisms that underlie human locomotion and the environmental variables that affect it will allow you to develop more appropriate assessment and intervention strategies, because they will be based on variables that influence locomotion.

MOTOR CONTROL THEORY

In the earlier section titled "What is a theory?" you read that a good theory should describe and provide explanations for a large class of observable events. In light of this requirement, what should a good theory of motor control describe and explain? Researchers generally acknowledge that it should describe and explain how the nervous system produces coordinated movement such that we are able to successfully perform a variety of motor skills in a variety of environmental contexts. In many respects, the attempt to understand how we produce coordinated movement is similar to wanting to know how a watch, which also involves the precise coordination of many components, keeps time.

The following sections discuss two essential issues important to a theory of motor control: the meaning of the term *coordination* as it applies to motor skill performance, and the "degrees of freedom problem." Although researchers have proposed additional issues that a theory of motor control should address,[1] these two will provide a sufficient foundation on which to base your introduction to the two prominent motor control theories discussed in this chapter.

It is important to note that the theories described here address motor control from a predominantly *behavioral level of analysis*. This means that they focus on explaining observed behavior without attempting to specify neural-level features of the con-

---

[1]For broader and more in-depth discussions of issues that are relevant for a theory of motor control, see books devoted to motor control issues, e.g., Kelso (1995), Rosenbaum (1991), and Rothwell (1995).

FIGURE 4.1 Motor control theory provides a foundation on which practitioners can base many tasks and responsibilities.

trol process (for an example of a neural model of motor control, see Bullock & Grossberg, 1991). An important goal of behaviorally based motor control theories is to propose laws and principles that govern coordinated human motor behavior. A neural-level theory would be expected to describe neural mechanisms or neural mechanism interactions that explain how the nervous system is involved in these behavioral principles (e.g., see Willingham, 1998).

Coordination

The performance of a motor skill involves a person's organization of the activation of muscles in such a way that the goal of an action can be accom-

plished. It is this organizational feature that is at the heart of the definition of the term *coordination.* For the purposes of this textbook, we will use a definition based on one provided by Turvey (1990): **coordination** is the patterning of head, body, and limb movements relative to the patterning of environmental objects and events.

---

coordination   the patterning of body and limb motions relative to the patterning of environmental objects and events.

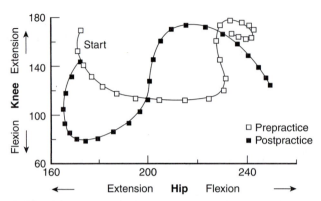

FIGURE 4.2 Angle-angle diagram from an experiment by Anderson and Sidaway showing coordination changes resulting from practice for the hip and knee relationship while performing a soccer kick. [Reprinted with permission from *Research Quarterly for Exercise and Sport,* Vol. 65, pp. 93–99, Copyright © 1994 American Association for Health, Physical Education, Recreation, and Dance, 1900 Association Drive, Reston, VA 20191.]

This definition contains two parts. Each is important to consider further. First, note that the definition specifies that coordination involves *patterns of head, body, and/or limb movements.* Although a common use of the term *coordination* relates it to a characteristic of skilled performance, it should not be limited to this use. When used in reference to a movement pattern associated with the performance of a skill, coordination refers to the organizational characteristics of the head, body, and limb movements involved in the performance, regardless of the skill level of the performer. This means that when we consider the assessment of movement characteristics of the performance of a skill, it is necessary to consider coordination as referring to the relationship among the head, body, and/or limbs *at a specific point in time* during the skill performance.

A common way to portray movement patterns is to represent graphically the relationship between the displacement patterns of limbs as they move while performing the skill. An example of this type of representation can be seen in figure 4.2, where the coordination of the knee-hip joint angles during a soccer kick is shown.

The second part of the definition states that the pattern of head, limb, and body motion is *relative to the pattern of environmental objects and events.* This is important because it establishes the need to

consider motor skill coordination in relation to the context in which the skill is performed. The characteristics of the environmental context constrain the head, body, and limbs to act in certain ways so that the goal of the action can be achieved.

For example, to walk along a pathway, people must adapt their head, body, and limb movement patterns to the characteristics of the pathway. If, for example, a person is walking on a sidewalk and encounters a tree branch lying across it, he or she must use a new pattern of movement in order to step over the branch. The characteristics of the tree branch will dictate the characteristics of the movement pattern. If it is small, the person may need to take only a large step, whereas if it is a large branch, he or she may have to climb over it.

The Degrees of Freedom Problem

Because coordination involves head, body, and limb movement patterns, an important question in the study of motor control is this: How does the nervous system control the many muscles and joints involved in producing a given pattern? To answer this question, we must consider an important problem that was first posed by Nicolai Bernstein, a noted Russian physiologist whose work, produced from the 1930s to the 1950s, did not become known to the Western world until 1967. His work

A CLOSER LOOK

Looking at the Degrees of Freedom Problem at the Level of Muscles and Joints

We know that there are 792 muscles in the human body that can act to make the one hundred joints behave in different ways. And each joint has mechanical characteristics that define its degrees of freedom for movement. On the basis of these features, Turvey (1990) put the coordination control problem into perspective this way. If all the joints were only hinge joints like the elbow, there would be one hundred mechanical degrees of freedom to be controlled at the joint level. But if two specific characteristics, such as position and velocity, needed to be defined for these joints to carry out a specific act, the degrees of freedom would increase to two hundred.

continues to influence research and theory related to motor control. Bernstein proposed that to perform a well-coordinated movement, the nervous system had to solve what he termed the "degrees of freedom problem."

The **degrees of freedom** of any system reflect the number of independent elements or components of the system. The **degrees of freedom problem** arises when a complex system needs to be organized to produce a specific result. The control problem is as follows: How can an effective yet efficient control system be designed so that a complex system, having many degrees of freedom, is constrained to act in a particular way?

Consider the following example of the degrees of freedom control problem in a mechanical system. A helicopter is designed so that it can fly up or down, to the left or the right, forward or backward, and so on, and at a variety of speeds. The helicopter designer must enable the pilot to control many different features so that the helicopter can do all these things. And the designer must help the pilot do so as simply as possible. If the pilot had to control one switch or lever for each component needed to make the helicopter fly a certain way, the pilot's job would be overwhelming. Therefore, the designer reduces the complexity of the task by providing control sticks and pedals that the pilot can control simultaneously with his or her hands and feet. Each stick or pedal controls several functions at once.

When the nervous system must control the human body so that it performs a complex motor skill, such as hitting a baseball, it faces a degrees of freedom control problem similar to that involving the helicopter. The determination of the actual number of degrees of freedom that must be controlled in coordinated human movement depends on which level of control we are considering. At a very basic level, we might consider motor units as the elements that must be controlled. At another level, we could consider muscles as the element of interest. Regardless of the control level considered, it becomes evident that for any motor skill, the control problem involved in enabling a person to perform that skill is an enormous one. However, as you will see in chapter 11, when a person practices a skill and progresses from being a beginner to being a skilled performer, the motor control system solves the degrees of freedom problem in ways that are evident from the changes we can observe in specific coordination characteristics.

---

degrees of freedom   the number of independent elements or components in a control system and the number of ways each component can act.

degrees of freedom problem   a control problem that occurs in the designing of a complex system that must produce a specific result; the design problem involves determining how to constrain the system's many degrees of freedom so that it can produce the specific result.

OPEN-LOOP AND CLOSED-LOOP CONTROL SYSTEMS

Most theories of motor control incorporate two basic systems of control. These two systems, called **open-loop** and **closed-loop control systems,** are based on mechanical engineering models of control. Rather than provide exact descriptions of the control processes in complex human movement, these two models are basic descriptions of different ways the central and peripheral nervous systems initiate and control action. These models serve as useful guides that illustrate some of the basic components involved in that process.

Figure 4.3 presents diagrams illustrating simple open-loop and closed-loop control systems. These are the typical diagrams you would see in any general presentation of these types of control systems. Notice that each of these systems has a *control center.* The control center is sometimes referred to as an *executive.* An important part of its role is to generate and issue movement instructions to the *effectors,* which, in the human, are the muscles and joints involved in producing the desired movement.

Both control systems also contain *movement instructions* that come from the control center and go to the effectors.

Differences between the Systems

These systems differ in two ways. First, a closed-loop control system involves **feedback,** whereas an open-loop system does not. In human movement, the feedback is *afferent* information sent by the various sensory receptors to the control center. The purpose of this feedback is to update the control center about the correctness of the movement while it is in progress.

In terms of the involvement of feedback in human movement control, figure 4.3 is somewhat misleading. The diagram indicates that the "effectors" that enable the head, body, and limbs to move are the only source of feedback. But in complex human movement, feedback can come also from several other sources, such as visual and auditory receptors.

The second important difference between open- and closed-loop control systems relates to the

FIGURE 4.3 Diagrams illustrating the open-loop and closed-loop control systems for movement control.

movement instructions issued by the control center. In the open-loop system, because feedback is not used in the control of the ongoing movement, the instructions contain all the information necessary for the effectors to carry out the planned movement. Although feedback is produced and available, it is not used to control the ongoing movement. This may be so because feedback is not needed, or because there is not enough time to use feedback to effectively control the movement after it is initiated. In the closed-loop system, the movement instructions are quite different. First, the control center issues an initial instruction to the effectors that is sufficient only to initiate the movement. The actual execution and completion of the movement depend on feedback information that reaches the control center. The feedback provides information about the status of the movement, which serves to enable the control center to do one of several things: allow the movement to continue as initially instructed, provide additional instructions to continue the movement in progress, or correct a movement error.

TWO THEORIES OF MOTOR CONTROL

We can classify theories of how the nervous system controls coordinated movement in terms of the relative importance given to movement

open-loop control system   a control system in which all the information needed to initiate and carry out an action as planned is contained in the initial instructions to the effectors.

closed-loop control system   a system of control in which during the course of an action, feedback is compared against a standard or reference to enable an action to be carried out as planned.

feedback   information from the sensory system that indicates the status of a movement to the central nervous system; in a closed-loop control system, feedback is used to make corrections to an ongoing movement.

A CLOSER LOOK

Mechanical and Human Motor Skill Examples of Open-Loop and Closed-Loop Control Systems

Open-Loop Control
Mechanical Example
- **Videocassette recorder.** It can operate as an open-loop control system by being programmed to tape television programs on specified dates and at specified times. The VCR will turn on and off at the specified times. (Note that it will turn off at the specified time even if the program being taped continues past that time.)

Human Motor Skill Example
- **Throwing a dart at a dartboard.** When the person initiates the throw, the arm movement and dart release occur as specified by movement instructions developed before the initiation of the arm movement.

Closed-Loop Control
Mechanical Example
- **Thermostat in a house.** It controls the air-conditioning and heating systems in a house. The desired room temperature is set on the thermostat. This setting becomes a reference against which actual room temperatures are compared. The room temperature serves as the feedback to the thermostat to indicate when to turn the air-conditioning or heating system on or off.

Human Motor Skill Example
- **Driving a car.** When a person drives a car on a street or highway, he or she must keep the car within a specified lane. To do this the driver uses visual and proprioceptive feedback to control the steering wheel to make the needed adjustments to keep the car from going outside the lane boundaries.

---

instructions specified by central components of the control system and by the environment. Theories that give prominence to instructions specified by the central nervous system in the control process have in common some form of memory representation, such as a motor program, that provides the basis for organizing, initiating, and carrying out intended actions. In contrast, other theories give more influence to movement instructions specified by the environment and to the dynamic interaction of this information with the body, limbs, and nervous system.

Motor Program–Based Theory

At the heart of central control–oriented theories is the **motor program,** a memory-based construct that controls coordinated movement. Various theoretical viewpoints attribute different degrees of control to the motor program. Undoubtedly, the view that best characterizes present-day thinking about the motor program comes from the work of Richard Schmidt (1988; Schmidt & Lee, 1999).

He proposed that a serious problem with previous views was that they limited the motor program to specific movements or sequences of movements. To overcome this limitation, Schmidt hypothesized the **generalized motor program** as a mechanism that could account for the adaptive and flexible qualities of human coordinated-movement behavior.

Schmidt's generalized motor program. Schmidt proposed that a generalized motor program controls a *class of actions,* rather than a specific movement or sequence. He defined a class of actions as a set of different actions having a common but unique set of features. For Schmidt, these features, which he called **invariant features,** are the "signature" of a generalized motor program, and form the basis of what is stored in memory. These movement-related features remain consistent from one performance of an action to another. In order for a person to produce a specific action to meet the demands of a performance situation, the person must

A CLOSER LOOK

The Evolution of the Motor Program Concept

- Early Greek philosophers such as *Plato* talked about a person's creation of an "image" of an act preceding the action itself.
- *William James* (1890) alluded to Plato when he stated that to perform an action, a person must first form a clear "image" of that action.
- *Karl Lashley* (1917) is regarded as the first person to use the actual term *motor program.* He initially viewed motor programs as "intention[s] to act," but later described them as "generalized schemata of action which determine the sequence of specific acts" (Lashley, 1951, p. 122). He proposed that these schemata were organized to provide central control of movement patterns.
- *Sir Frederick Bartlett* (1932) implied that a motor program exists when he used the term *schema* to describe internal representations and organizations of movements.
- *Miller, Galanter, and Pribram* (1960) proposed the notion of a "Plan," which was "essentially the same as a program for a computer" (p. 16), and was responsible for controlling the sequence of events of an action.

- *Franklin Henry* (Henry & Rogers, 1960) gave the motor program concept a needed conceptual and empirical boost. He hypothesized that the "neural pattern for a specific and well-coordinated motor act is controlled by a stored program that is used to direct the neuromotor details of its performance" (p. 449). Henry's concept of the motor program was also that of a computer program. He proposed that when initiated, the program controls the exact movement details, with essentially no modifications possible during the execution of the movement.
- *Stephen Keele* (1968) offered a view similar to Henry's by defining the motor program as "a set of muscle commands that are structured before a movement sequence begins, and that allow . . . the entire sequence to be carried out uninfluenced by peripheral feedback" (p. 387).
- *Richard Schmidt* (1975) proposed that the motor program is not specific muscle commands, but is an abstract memory-based representation of a class of actions, with each class defined by invariant features.

retrieve the appropriate program from memory and then add movement-specific **parameters.** These are movement-related features of the performances of an action that can be varied from one performance to another.

Rather than use a computer analogy, Schmidt proposed a phonograph record analogy to describe the characteristics of the generalized motor program. The invariant features of a record specify the rhythm and the dynamics (force) of the music. The parameters include the adjustable speed and volume controls. Even if a record is played faster than normal or louder than normal, the rhythmic and dynamic structure of the music remains intact.

Invariant features and parameters. Although many possible characteristics could be invariant features of the generalized motor program, three are most commonly proposed. These include the

motor program   a memory representation that stores information needed to perform an action.

generalized motor program   the general memory representation of a class of actions that share common invariant characteristics; it provides the basis for controlling a specific action within the class of actions.

invariant features   a unique set of characteristics that defines a generalized motor program and does not vary from one performance of the action to another.

parameters   features of the generalized motor program that can be varied from one performance of a skill to another; the features of a skill that must be added to the invariant features of a generalized motor program before a person can perform a skill to meet the specific demands of a situation.

a. Normal speed (10 sec)

30%   20%   40%   10%

b. Faster (5 sec)

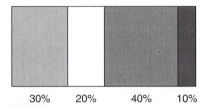

30%   20%   40%   10%

c. Slower (15 sec)

30%   20%   40%   10%

Time scale (sec) ⟶

0   1   2   3   4   5   6   7   8   9   10   11   12   13   14   15

FIGURE 4.4   An illustration of invariant relative time for a hypothetical four-component motor skill when it is performed normally at a 10-sec duration (a), speeded up to a 5-sec duration (b), and slowed down to a 15-sec duration (c).

relative time (which is analogous to rhythm) of the components of the skill; the relative force used in performing the skill; and the order, or sequence, of the components. The term *relative* in *relative time* and *relative force* indicates that what is invariant are the percentages, or proportions, of overall force and timing of the components of a skill.

Figure 4.4 presents an illustration of how to interpret the concept of invariant relative time. Suppose you move your arm as quickly as possible to hit four switches in sequence. Now, suppose that the four components of this task yield the following movement time proportions: component 1

takes up 30 percent of the total performance time; component 2, 20 percent; component 3, 40 percent; and component 4, 10 percent. If the performance of this skill under typical conditions has an overall duration of 10 sec [represented in part (a) of the figure], then regardless of how much you speed up or slow down this overall duration, the actual amount of time characteristic of each component changes proportionately. In figure 4.4, parts (b) and (c) represent this proportional component change for speeding up the skill [part (b)] and slowing it down [part (c)]. Thus, if you typically perform this skill in 10 sec, then the amount of time you spend

**Defining the Motor Program: A Memory Representation
versus a Plan of Action Prepared Just Prior to Moving**

A problem that has arisen over the years has led to difficulties in understanding what the motor program is and how it functions. This problem is that the term *motor program* has been used to describe different functional constructs. In some discussions, the motor program refers to the memory representation of a movement or action. The generalized motor program construct in Schmidt's schema theory is a good example. The theoretical arguments about the memory-representation type of motor program focus on which

characteristics of a movement or action are stored in memory as a part of the motor program. We use the term this way in the present chapter.

The other use of the term *motor program* refers to what is constructed or prepared just prior to movement initiation, but following an intention to act. This use of the term, sometimes referred to as *motor programming,* is the focus of chapter 7, although we do make some reference to this preparation aspect of motor program–based control in the present chapter.

---

performing each component is 3, 2, 4, and 1 sec respectively. If you performed the skill twice as fast, in 5 sec, then each component would change proportionately to be 1.5, 1, 2, and 0.5 sec respectively. If you slowed down your overall performance time to 15 sec, then each component would change to 4.5, 3, 6, and 1.5 sec respectively.

Although motor program theory proposes that the invariant features of a generalized motor program are rather fixed from one performance of a skill to another, it also holds that there are other features, called *parameters,* that can be varied. Examples include the *overall force,* the *overall duration,* and the *muscles* that must be used to perform the skill. Skilled performers can easily change these from one performance situation to another, readily adapting them to the specific requirements of each situation.

The following two examples illustrate the relationship between invariant features and parameters. One relates to figure 4.4, which, as just discussed, portrayed relative time as an invariant feature. This figure also illustrates the parameter of *overall duration.* The normal, faster, and slower speeds in the figure show that a person can change the overall amount of time taken to move without altering the relative time structure of the components of the movement. This type of situation occurs, for example, when a person walks faster or slower than his or her typical speed.

The second example concerns *muscles* as parameters. Research evidence shows that whether you sign your name with a pen held in your preferred hand, in the opposite hand, between your toes, or with your teeth, the two signatures have distinct invariant spatial as well as relative time and force features (see Wright, 1990 for an excellent review of this research). These results suggest that you can change the muscles involved in writing your signature without altering the invariant features represented in the generalized motor program. Interestingly, Rijntjes et al. (1999) provided neurological evidence for muscles as a movement parameter related to the signing of one's name by comparing brain regions activated by people signing their name with the finger of the preferred hand and with the big toe. Additional evidence and examples of muscles as parameters will be discussed in chapter 12, when we consider the topic of bilateral transfer.

Schmidt's schema theory. A formalized theory of how the generalized motor program operates to control coordinated movement is Schmidt's

---

relative time   the proportion of the total amount of time required by each of the various components of a skill during the performance of that skill.

schema theory (Schmidt, 1975, 1988). A **schema** is a rule or set of rules that serves to provide the basis for a decision. It is developed by abstracting important pieces of information from related experiences and combining them into a type of rule. For example, your concept of *dog* is the result of seeing many different types of dogs and developing a set of rules that will allow you to identify correctly as a "dog" an animal you have never seen before.

Schmidt used the schema concept to describe two control components involved in the learning and control of skills. Both are characterized as based on abstract rules. The first is the *generalized motor program,* which, as just described, is the control mechanism responsible for controlling the general characteristics of classes of actions, such as throwing, kicking, walking, and running. The second component is the *motor response schema,* which is responsible for providing the specific rules governing an action in a given situation. Thus, the motor response schema provides parameters to the generalized motor program.

The schema theory provides an explanation for how well a person can *adapt* to new situations or environmental contexts. People can successfully perform a skill requiring movements that have not been made in that same way before. For example, when you walk in a crowded mall or return a tennis serve, characteristics of the situation change in ways that you have not previously experienced. It is possible to perform the skill successfully in these situations because the person can use the rules from the motor response schema to generate appropriate parameter characteristics; the person adds these to the generalized motor program to perform the skill.

Schmidt's schema theory claims to *solve the degrees of freedom problem* in movement coordination through an executive control operation that organizes motor programs and schemas. An important emphasis in this approach is the abstract, or general, nature of what is stored in the control center. The generalized motor program and recall schema work together to provide the specific movement characteristics needed to initiate an action in a given situation. The action initiation is an

open-loop control process. However, once the action is initiated, feedback can influence its course if there is sufficient time to process the feedback and alter the action.

Testing the invariant relative-time feature. Researchers have attempted to provide empirical support for motor program–based control by investigating Schmidt's claim that a generalized motor program controls a class of actions defined by specific invariant features. Of the proposed invariant features, relative time has generated the most research interest. Support for the invariance of this feature has come from many experiments investigating several different skills, such as typing, gait, handwriting, prehension, and sequences of key presses, among others. (For reviews of this evidence, see Heuer, 1991; Schmidt, 1985, 1988.)

Researchers typically have investigated relative time invariance by observing changes in relative time across a range of values of an associated parameter, such as overall duration or speed. The most commonly cited research example in this regard is a study by Shapiro, Zernicke, Gregor, and Diestel (1981) in which people walked and ran at different speeds on a treadmill. The researchers were interested in the percentages of the total step-cycle time (i.e., relative time) that would characterize the four components, or phases, of the step cycle at each treadmill speed (i.e., the overall duration parameter). Their hypothesis was that if relative time is invariant for the generalized motor program involved in controlling walking and/or running gait patterns, then the percentages for a specific gait component should remain constant across the different speeds.

The results were consistent with the hypothesis of relative time invariance (see figure 4.5). As gait sped up or slowed down (at least up to 6 km/hr and beyond 8 km/hr), the percentage of time accounted for by each step-cycle component remained essentially the same for different speeds. The differences between the relative time characteristics of walking and running are especially notable in the pie charts in the (b) section of figure 4.5. The pie charts show the relative time percentages for the average

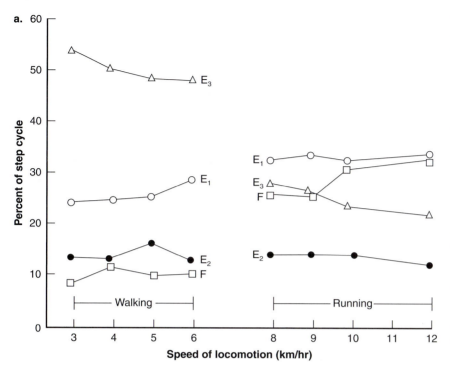

a.

Percent of step cycle / Speed of locomotion (km/hr)

Walking — Running

b. **Walking**

Running

FIGURE 4.5 **Results of the experiment by Shapiro et al.** (a) The relative time percentage of total step-cycle time for each of the four step-cycle phases (Phillipson step cycle) at different speeds of walking and running. F = Flexion phase (from toe-off to beginning of knee extension); E_1 = Extension phase 1 (from beginning of knee extension to heelstrike); E_2 = Extension phase 2 (from heelstrike to maximum knee-angle flexion); E_3 = Extension phase 3 (from maximum knee-angle flexion to toeoff). [From Shapiro, D. C., et al. (1981). Evidence for generalized motor programs using gait pattern analysis. *Journal of Motor Behavior, 13,* 33–47. Copyright © 1981 Heldref Publication, Inc. Washington, DC. Reprinted by permission.]

(b) The average (of the four speeds) relative time percentages of total step-cycle time for each of the four step-cycle phases for walking and running.

of the walking speeds and the running speeds for each of the four step-cycle phases. Because the relative time percentages differed between walking and running, the authors concluded that *different* motor programs control walking and running gaits. Within each gait pattern, the overall duration (i.e., speed) parameter could be increased or slowed down while the relative timing among the components of the step cycle was maintained.

Dynamic Pattern Theory

In sharp contrast to the motor program–based theory of motor control is an approach commonly

schema a rule or set of rules that serves to provide the basis for a decision; in Schmidt's schema theory, an abstract representation of rules governing movement.

FIGURE 4.6   (a) shows the hand and finger placement for performing the finger movement task used in the experiments by Kelso. (b) and (c) show fingertip movement position as a function of time, during which movement frequency increased. (b) shows fingertip positions for both index fingers as they moved from being out of phase to in–phase. (c) shows the relationship of the left index finger's peak extension to the right finger's peak extension as a different way to portray the phase transition shown in (b). [Reprinted from Kelso J.A.S., & Schöner, G. (1988). Self-organization of coordinative movement patterns. *Human Movement Science, 7,* 27–46, with kind permission of Elsevier Science-NL, Sara Burgerharstraat 25, 1055 KV Amsterdam, The Netherlands.]

referred to as **dynamic pattern theory** (and some-times referred to as *dynamical systems theory, co-ordination dynamics theory, ecological theory,* and *action theory.*) The basis for this theoretical viewpoint is a multidisciplinary perspective in-volving physics, biology, chemistry, and mathe-matics. Proponents of this theory see human movement control as a complex system that behaves in ways similar to those of any complex biological or physical system. As a complex sys-tem, human motor control is seen from the per-spective of *nonlinear dynamics;* this means that behavioral changes over time do not follow a con-tinuous, linear progression, but make sudden abrupt changes. For example, in the physical world, when the temperature of water is increased gradually, there is a specific temperature (100° C) at which the water boils, its behavior abruptly changes. This type of change represents a **nonlinear behavior.**

Those who study dynamic pattern theory are particularly interested in how a system changes over time from one stable state to another because of the influence of a particular variable. In addition, they are interested in identifying physical and mathematical laws that govern such behavior. Although this approach has been used to model many complex systems in the physical world (see Gleick, 1987), only since the 1980s has it captured the attention of scientists interested in understanding and explaining human movement control.

Nonlinear changes in movement behavior. A series of experiments by Kelso and his colleagues established for movement scientists that the systematic change in the level of a variable can cause a nonlinear behavioral change in human coordinated movement (e.g., Kelso, 1984; Kelso & Scholz, 1985). The top panel in figure 4.6 illustrates the type of task used in these experiments. Participants began moving their right and left index fingers at a specified rate of speed so that they were *out of phase* (sometimes referred to as *antiphase*). This means that the muscle groups controlling the right and left fingers were operating simultaneously but in opposite ways: when the right finger was flexed, the left finger was extended. Quantitatively, the fingers were 180° out of phase with each other throughout the movement cycle. The participants systematically increased the speed of their finger movements by keeping their finger speed consistent with that of a metronome controlled by the experimenters. The result was that at a critical speed the finger movements spontaneously shifted to an *in-phase* coordination state, where both were flexed or extended at the same time (i.e., 0 or 360° in phase with each other).

The shift to the in-phase coordination state occurred during the *transition* between the stable out-of-phase and in-phase states. As you can see in figure 4.6, the transition was a mixture of both out-of-phase and in-phase finger movements.[1] But at slower speeds, only out-of-phase movements occurred, whereas at faster speeds, only in-phase

movements occurred. Thus, a linear increase in movement speed led to a nonlinear change in the fundamental pattern of movement.

When viewed from the perspective of coordination patterns, these experiments established that distinct coordination patterns can spontaneously develop as a function of a change in a specific variable. In the case of the finger movement task used in the Kelso experiments, the out-of-phase and in-phase finger movement relationships are stable coordination patterns. The importance of these experiments is that they provided an initial step in the investigation of coordination changes that can occur without resorting to a mechanism such as a motor program to account for the change.

Another example of spontaneous coordination change that results from the systematic increase or decrease of a variable is the change from walking to running coordination patterns that occur at specific speeds. The experiment by Shapiro et al. (1981), which was discussed in this chapter, was an early demonstration of this spontaneous gait pattern change. Since that experiment, the walk-to-run and, conversely, the run-to-walk gait changes that occur

---

[1] Although the transition in the experiment described in figure 4.6 shows a mixture of in-phase and out-of-phase movements, not all transitions between two stable coordination states are mixtures of the two states. Transitions can take various forms (for detailed information about transition forms, see Kelso, 1995).

---

dynamic pattern theory   an approach to describing and explaining the control of coordinated movement that emphasizes the role of information in the environment and the dynamic properties of the body and limbs; it is also known as the dynamic systems theory.

nonlinear behavior   a behavior that changes in abrupt, nonlinear ways in response to systematic linear increases in the value of a specific variable (e.g., the change from smooth to turbulent water flow in a tube at a specific increase in water velocity; the change from a walking to a running gait at a specific increase in gait velocity).

A CLOSER LOOK

Two Views about the Source of Relative Time Invariance

Relative time invariance is a common component of both the generalized motor program and dynamic pattern views of motor control. However, one of the important differences between these views is the source of the invariance.

- The *generalized motor program view* emphasizes that relative time, as an invariant feature of the generalized motor program, is included in the movement commands sent to the musculature. Because of this, the resulting action is obliged to perform according to this time constraint. Relative time invariance across variations of a parameter is an indicator of a class of movements that are controlled by the same generalized motor program.
- The *dynamic pattern view* prefers to use the term "temporal pattern" rather than relative time invari-

ance. Although different with respect to some specific characteristics, temporal pattern is an analogous concept to relative time invariance. More important, the invariance seen in relative time for many actions is the result of the person interacting with characteristics of the task and/or environment, or the mechanical dynamics involved in the body and limb movements. Relative time invariance across variations of a control parameter is an indicator of coordination pattern stability.

---

as a function of speed have been demonstrated numerous times, and have become the basis for an increasing amount of research (e.g., Diedrich & Warren, 1995, 1998; Wagenaar & van Emmerik, 1994).

Stability and Attractors

At the heart of the dynamic pattern view is the concept of **stability.** In dynamic terms, stability refers to the behavioral steady state of a system. It is important to note that this use of this term is different from the concept of invariance. As used here, stability incorporates the notion of variability by noting that when a system is slightly perturbed, it will return spontaneously to a stable state.

By observing characteristics of a stable state, scientists can gain understanding of the variables that influence a system to behave as it does. For example, in the reciprocal rhythmic finger movements in the Kelso experiment just described, the researchers observed behavioral stability when the fingers were in out-of-phase and in-phase relationships with each other. These two stable states indicate two coordinated movement patterns. Between these states, as finger speed increased, a *phase transition* occurred during which instability characterized the behavioral patterns. The instability

continued until finger speed reached a point at which a new stable state spontaneously occurred.

The stable behavioral steady states of systems are known as **attractors** (or *attractor states*). In terms of human coordinated movement, attractors are *preferred behavioral states,* such as the in-phase and out-of-phase states for rhythmic finger movements described in the Kelso experiment. Attractors represent stable regions of operation around which behavior typically occurs when a system is allowed to operate in its preferred manner.

For example, when people locomote at a speed of 3 mi/hr (i.e., 4.8 km/hr), the arms and legs are "attracted to" a coordination relationship that produces a walking gait. This gait pattern represents the preferred behavioral state for engaging in a locomotion action. But when people locomote at a speed of 10 mi/hr (~16 km/hr), the walking gait is not the preferred locomotion state. At this speed, most people run, which, as you saw in figure 4.5, involves a coordination pattern that is different from a walking gait pattern.

Finally, attractor states are not only stable states characterized by minimal behavioral variability, but also optimally *energy-efficient* states. This means that when a person is moving at a preferred rate or using a preferred coordination pattern, that person uses less energy than he or she would if moving at a nonpreferred rate.

Order and Control Parameters

Proponents of the dynamic pattern view place a priority on developing formal nonlinear equations of motion that specify the stability and loss of stability of performance in addition to changes that result from learning and development. To develop these equations, scientists must identify the variables responsible for and associated with coordination. Primary among these variables are **order parameters** (sometimes the term *collective variables* is used). These are functionally specific and abstract variables that define the overall behavior of a system. The order parameters enable a coordinated pattern of movement that can be reproduced and distinguished from other patterns.

Because order parameters define a movement pattern, it is essential to identify specific types. The most prominent of the order parameters identified by researchers is *relative phase* for rhythmic movements. Relative phase refers to a quantified value that represents the movement relationship between two movement segments. For example, the bottom panel (c) of figure 4.6 illustrates that for the rhythmic finger movement task in the Kelso (1984) experiment, the relative phase for the in-phase movement relationship was 360° (which is the same as 0°); the relative phase for the out-of-phase movement relationship was 180°. These two relative phases were determined by establishing that the maximum adduction of a finger had a phase value of 360° (i.e., 0°), and the maximum abduction had a phase value of 180°. On the basis of a common starting point, the relative phase was then calculated as the difference between the phase values of the two fingers at any point during the movement. For the in-phase movement, both fingers had a common starting point of maximum adduction (i.e., 360°). The fingers then moved together to a maximum abduction position (180°), and then returned to the initial maximum adduction position. At any time during the fingers' movement, they had a relative phase of 360°, indicating that both fin-

gers are at the same abduction position. The opposite holds for the out-of-phase pattern. At any point, the one finger is abducting the same amount as the other is adducting, which means the two fingers have a relative phase of 180°. Another way to consider this relationship is from the perspective of the amount of simultaneous adduction and/or abduction movement. When moving in-phase with each other, both fingers abduct or adduct the same amount at the same time; when moving out of phase with each other, both fingers move the same amount simultaneously, but one is adducting while the other is abducting.

The **control parameter** represents the variable that when increased or decreased will influence the stability and character of the order parameter. For example, in the Kelso experiment, movement frequency (i.e., speed) was the control parameter. As

---

stability   a behavioral steady state of a system that represents a preferred behavioral state and incorporates the notion of invariance by noting that a stable system will spontaneously return to a stable state after it is slightly perturbed.

attractors   the stable behavioral steady states of systems. In terms of human coordinated movement, attractors characterize preferred behavioral states, such as the in-phase and out-of-phase states for rhythmic bimanual finger movements.

order parameters   functionally specific variables that define the overall behavior of a system; they enable a coordinated pattern of movement to be reproduced and distinguished from other patterns (e.g., relative phase); known also as collective variables.

control parameters   coordinated movement control variables (e.g., tempo, or speed, and force) that freely change according to the characteristics of an action situation. According to the dynamic pattern view of motor control when a control parameter is systematically varied (e.g., speed is increased from slow to fast), an order parameter may remain stable or change its stable state characteristic at a certain level of change of the control parameter.

the movement frequency was systematically increased by the metronome, the phase relationship between the two fingers underwent distinct changes. You can see in figure 4.6 in both panels (b) and (c) that the in-phase relationship was maintained through several frequencies, but then began to destabilize as frequency continued to increase. Notice in the figure that neither an in-phase nor an out-of-phase relationship was detectable during a period of increasing frequencies, which is known as a *phase transition*. However, as the frequency continued to increase, there was a critical frequency at which the new out-of-phase relationship emerged and became stable. From an experimental point of view, the control parameter is important to identify because it becomes the variable to manipulate in order to assess the stability of the order parameter, which in turn provides the basis for determining attractor states for patterns of limb movement.

From an applied perspective, the control parameter can be the basis for assessing the stability of a coordination pattern, and may provide insights into a person's coordination characteristics that might not otherwise be observed. This application can be especially useful in rehabilitation settings. For example, van Emmerik and Wagenaar (1996) demonstrated that Parkinson's disease patients had more difficulty than healthy age-matched control participants in adapting a specific coordination pattern while walking to gradually increasing speeds (i.e., the control parameter) on a treadmill. In this study, the relative phase (i.e., the order parameter) of interest was based on the relationship between the arm and leg swings while walking. The researchers concluded from their results that the assessment of the stability of the phase relationship for the arm and leg swings at various walking speeds provides a sensitive technique to diagnose and detect early stages of Parkinson's disease.

Self-organization. An important element of the dynamic pattern perspective is the concept of **self-organization.** This means that when certain conditions characterize a situation, a specific stable pattern of behavior emerges. Many examples of self-organization exist within the physical world that illustrate applications of this concept to the human movement domain. For example, there is no hurricane program in the universe, but hurricanes commonly occur. However, they occur only when certain wind and water temperature conditions exist. When these variables achieve certain characteristics, a hurricane will self-organize in an identifiable pattern that distinguishes it from a tropical depression, or any other weather system.

When applied to human movement coordination, the concept of self-organization means that when certain conditions characterize a situation, a specific pattern of limb movement emerges. Thus, rather than being specified by a motor program, the coordinated pattern of movement self-organizes within the framework of the characteristics of environmental conditions and limb dynamics. For example, in the bimanual finger-movement task performed in the Kelso experiments, the in-phase coordination pattern self-organized as a function of the movement speed (i.e., the control parameter). This same type of self-organization is seen for the walk-to-run, or run-to-walk, gait transitions that occur as gait speed increases or decreases.

Coordinative Structures

Another important aspect of the dynamic pattern view relates to the unit of behavior that is controlled. Proponents of the view assert that skilled action results when a person's nervous system constrains *functionally specific synergies of muscles and joints* to act cooperatively, so that the person can carry out an action according to the dictates of the situation. An individual may develop these functional synergies, called **coordinative structures,** through practice or experience, or they may exist naturally.

An example of a coordinative structure is the muscles and joints (the degrees of freedom to be controlled) involved in the action of reaching and grasping an object. The individual groups of muscles and joints that must act together to enable a person to successfully reach and grasp an object are "converted" through practice into a task-specific ensemble. The action occurs when a person has the intention to reach and grasp a cup and the environmental conditions specify that this action should occur. Then, in accordance with the characteristics of the limb and of the environmental constraints, the coordinative structure self-organizes to carry out the action.

Coordinative structures can be intrinsic or developed through practice. *Intrinsic coordinative structures* are involved in actions such as walking, running, and bimanual coordination. When we perform these actions, the muscles and joints of the limbs involved have a natural tendency to demonstrate interlimb coordination patterns that have characterized our performance of them since early in life. For example, when performing a skill involving bimanual coordination, which requires the simultaneous use of both arms and hands, both infants (e.g., Corbetta & Thelen, 1996) and adults (e.g., Kelso, Southard, & Goodman, 1979) typically demonstrate a similar natural tendency to move the arms and hands in synchrony, i.e., simultaneously both spatially and temporally. This means that when people first learn to perform a tennis serve, which requires each arm to simultaneously move in different ways, their initial tendency is to move their arms in the same way at the same time. In contrast, *coordinative structures developed through practice* become new combinations of muscles and joints that act together to produce a coordination pattern that will allow the achievement of an action goal. The tennis serve just described is a good example of the development of a new coordinative structure as a result of extensive practice.

For the learning of certain skills, the intrinsic coordinative structures can lead to initial performance difficulties, as in the case of learning a tennis serve. However, after overcoming these initial difficulties, the person's performance of the skill will benefit from the newly developed coordinative structure, because it will allow him or her to achieve an action goal even though some slight perturbation occurs during the action. For example, if a tennis player is serving, and during the serve a gust of wind makes the ball deviate from its intended path, the player can quickly and easily adjust the movements involved in his or her serving

action and achieve a successful serve. Similarly, if a person is jogging on a sidewalk and must step over a curb, the jogger can quickly and easily adjust movement characteristics of his or her gait pattern to avoid tripping while maintaining the jogging coordination pattern.

Perception and action coupling. Proponents of the dynamic pattern view emphasize the interaction of the performer and the physical environment in which the skill is performed. From a motor control perspective, this interaction involves perception and movement variables that must be taken into account in any attempt to explain the mechanisms involved in the control of open motor skills, which, as discussed in chapter 1, involve a person or object in motion. The dynamic pattern theory proposes that this interaction, which is referred to as **perception-action coupling,** is an essential element in accounting for skillful performance of open skills. The perception part of the interaction detects and uses critical invariant information in the environment (e.g., the amount of time until the object contacts the person, or vice versa); the action part involves the setting and regulating of movement control features that enable the person

---

self-organization   the emergence of a specific stable pattern of behavior due to certain conditions characterizing a situation rather than to a specific control mechanism organizing the behavior; e.g., in the physical world hurricanes self-organize when certain wind and water temperature conditions exist.

coordinative structures   functionally specific collectives of muscles and joints that are constrained by the nervous system to act cooperatively to produce an action.

perception-action coupling   the interaction between perceptual and movement variables that results in specific movement dynamics of an action in accordance with specific characteristics of the perceptual variable (e.g., the specific kinematic characteristics of a reach-and-grasp action associated with specific object characteristics).

A CLOSER LOOK

Evidence for Relative Time in Brain Activity and Coordinated Movement

In an excellent discussion comparing and contrasting the motor programming and dynamic pattern views of motor control, Kelso (1997) addressed various issues related to relative time, which is a key variable common to both views. One of the issues that motor control researchers have struggled with over the years is determining the relationship between brain activity and observable performance characteristics associated with movement. A possible breakthrough in this struggle appears possible through the use of functional brain imaging technology, which enables researchers to observe brain activity while a person engages in performing a motor skill.

Below are two key findings from research by Kelso and his colleagues in which they used this technology to investigate the issue of relative time. In these experiments, participants performed bimanual coordination skills to produce either in-phase or out-of-phase (antiphase) movement coordination patterns

to a signal that specified movement speed, which was systematically increased (see figure 4.6).

• At low speeds, relative time remained stable (i.e., invariant) across a range of speeds for both in- and out-of-phase coordination patterns.
• Spontaneous transitions from out-of-phase to in-phase coordination patterns occurred (i.e., a new coordination pattern self-organized) at a critical movement speed.

The results indicated that for relative time, the brain produced essentially the same pattern of activity as was observed at the movement level during the performance of a motor skill. Kelso stated that an important implication of these results for the motor control theory controversy is that the dynamic pattern view predicts these results, whereas the motor programming view does not.

---

to achieve the action goal (e.g., kinematic and kinetic components of movements).[2]

An example of a perceptual variable involved in this type of coupling process is known by the Greek letter *tau* (τ), which is related to the time-to-contact between an object and a person's eye. (We will discuss *tau* further in chapters 5 and 6.) Researchers have demonstrated that *tau* guides actions such as steering a car, catching a ball, hitting a ball, jumping from a platform, and performing the long jump. As a person gains experience, the perceptual variable couples with the dynamics of movement so that a distinct coordination pattern can be reproduced as needed.

Some additional examples of perception-action coupling include the coordination pattern people use to get on or over an obstacle, climb stairs, and go through a doorway. Researchers have found that

obstacles in a person's pathway, stairs, and door openings specify size-related information that a person perceives in terms of an invariant relationship between an object's size and her or his own leg length (in the case of obstacles and stairs) or body size (in the case of door openings). Thus the person will step or climb over the obstacle on the basis of this perceived relationship, choose one of various stair-climbing options, and walk through a doorway sideways or face-forward depending on this perceived relationship between the environmental feature and his or her own body size–related feature.

THE PRESENT STATE OF THE CONTROL THEORY ISSUE

The motor program–based theory and the dynamic pattern theory are the predominant behavioral theories currently addressing how the nervous system produces coordinated movement. Debate and research continue as scientists attempt to answer this

[2] For an excellent discussion of perception-action coupling and its application to sport skill performance, see Buekers, Montagne, & Laurent, 1999.

A CLOSER LOOK

Walk-to-Run Gait Changes: Interpretations According to Motor Program Theory and Dynamic Pattern Theory

People spontaneously change from a walk to a run gait pattern at a certain speed of locomotion. Although individuals vary in terms of the actual speed at which this change occurs, the shift appears to be common to all people. The motor program and dynamic pattern theories differ in their explanations of why this coordination change occurs.

- **Motor Program Theory** The relative time structure of a coordination pattern distinguishes one generalized motor program from another. Because walking and running gaits are characterized by different relative time structures, they are controlled by different generalized motor programs. The walk-to-run gait pattern change occurs at a certain speed because the person chooses to change from the program that controls walking to the program that controls running.

- **Dynamic Pattern Theory** Interlimb and body coordination patterns self-organize as a function of specific control parameter values and environmental conditions. For walking and running gait patterns, speed is a critical control parameter. The walk-to-run gait transition involves a competition between two attractors. At slow speeds, the primary attractor state is a walking coordination pattern. But as walking speed increases, there is a certain range of speeds at which this attractor state loses stability, which means that for this range of

speeds, the walking pattern undergoes some change as a running coordination pattern self-organizes and eventually becomes the stable attractor state for gait at a certain speed.

Interpreting the Shapiro et al. (1981) Experiment Results (Figure 4.5)

Motor program theory. Gait is controlled by one generalized motor program when walking gait is observed (3–6 km/hr) and by a different generalized motor program when the running gait is observed (8–12 km/hr).

Dynamic pattern theory. The walking and running gaits represent two attractor states that remain stable within the speed ranges of 3–6 km/hr and 10–12 km/hr. But for gait speeds of 7–9 km/hr, the order parameter becomes unstable during a transition period in which a new gait pattern (running) self-organizes and becomes stable for a certain range of speeds.

important theory question. A benefit of the debate between proponents of these theories is that critical issues have become clarified and future directions more evident. We now know, for example, that a theory of control cannot focus exclusively on the movement information that is specified by the central nervous system. Theorists also must take task and environmental characteristics into account. As Newell (1986) rightly stated, the optimal pattern of coordination is determined by the interaction among constraints specified by the person, the environment, and the task.

Opinions vary in terms of the resolution of the motor control theory debate. For example, some researchers foresee a compromise between the two

theories, which would lead to the development of a hybrid theory that incorporates the strengths of each theory (e.g., see Abernethy & Sparrow, 1992; Walter, 1998). Some research evidence that suggests the potential for some compromise was reported by Amazeen (2002). In a series of experiments, she demonstrated that the application of specific aspects of a dynamic pattern theory to the generalized motor program theory could account for performance characteristics associated with the acquisition of rhythmic bimanual coordination skills that the generalized motor program theory alone could not. However, she left open the possibility that her results could be interpreted as support for only the dynamic pattern theory.

A CLOSER LOOK

Implications of the Dynamic Pattern View for Physical Rehabilitation

In 1996, the journal *Human Movement Science* published a special issue in which the articles addressed the relevance of the dynamic pattern view of motor control to the field of physical rehabilitation. In the concluding article, van Wieringen highlighted the key implications from the articles. The following summarizes some of those implications.

- Movement problems observed in children with movement disorders may be related to perceptual difficulties. Because of perception-action coupling, deficiencies in detecting visual information can limit movement capabilities.
- Therapy treatments for movement problems should engage patients in the performance of actions that are as realistic as possible. Because many actions occur as a function of environmental context characteristics that afford (i.e., allow) such actions, realistic task environments facilitate the improvement of movement capabilities.
- Practitioners should assess movement problems and capabilities for functional tasks across a range of personal, environmental, or task characteristics that may, at a critical value, elicit change in a person's movement form. (See Scholz, 1990, for a detailed discussion about using this approach to

assess coordination problems for a child with cerebral palsy who locomotes using a "bunny-hop" or hopping pattern.)
- Coordination patterns observed in people with movement disorders may be optimal because of the constraints imposed on the motor control system by the pathological condition. For example, the typical gait pattern of a person with spastic cerebral palsy may be the result of weak muscles that do not allow a "normal" gait pattern, which would suggest that the observed cocontraction of muscles involved in the gait pattern is due to a compensation for the weak muscles rather than to the disease itself. In this case, rehabilitation should be directed toward muscle strengthening rather than decreasing the level of the muscle cocontraction.

Others argue that a hybrid theory is unlikely. For example, Abernethy and Sparrow (1992) speculated that a compromise theory would not emerge because the two theories represent two vastly different approaches to explaining the control of coordinated movement. They reasoned that because of this difference, the history of science would predict that one will eventually become the predominant theory. Kelso (1997) expressed a similar view, but was more specific in his projections. He argued that because many aspects of the motor program view can be subsumed within the dynamic pattern theory, especially those related to invariant features and control parameters, and because the dynamic pattern theory can explain and predict more of the behavioral features of coordinated movement, the dynamic pattern theory will eventually become the predominant theory. However, at

this point in time, that predominance has yet to be established.

SUMMARY

- Motor control theory, like any theory, provides an explanation for why observable phenomena or behavior exist or behave as they do. It also provides the practitioner with a base of support on which to develop effective motor skill instruction and practice environments.

- The term *coordination* refers to the patterning of head, body, and/or limb movements in relation to the patterning of environmental objects and events. When the term *coordination* is used in reference to the movement patterns associated with the performance of a skill, it refers to the relationship among head, body, and/or limbs at a specific point in time during the skill performance.

- For a person to learn to produce a well-coordinated movement that achieves an intended action goal, the motor control system must solve the degrees of freedom problem, which concerns constraining the many degrees of freedom that characterize the muscles, joints, etc. A theory of motor control should provide an explanation of how the motor control system solves this problem.

- Theories of motor control typically incorporate features of open-loop and closed-loop control systems. Both involve a control center, movement instructions, and effectors. The closed-loop system also includes feedback as part of the system. In an open-loop system, the control center sends the effectors all the movement instructions they need to perform a skill from beginning to end. In contrast, the control center in a closed-loop system sends movement instructions to the effectors that enable them to initiate the performance of a skill; feedback from the effectors and other sources provides the control center with the information needed to give the effectors the instructions to continue and end the movement.

- Motor control theories can be distinguished in terms of the relative importance given to the movement instructions specified by central components of the control system or by the environment. Theories that give prominence to instructions from the control center have in common some form of stored memory representation, such as a motor program, that provides the movement instructions to the effectors. In contrast, theories that give prominence to movement instructions specified by the environment emphasize the dynamic interaction of this information with the body, limbs, and nervous system.

- Motor program–based theories include a memory-based construct known as the motor program that serves as the basis for controlling coordinated movement. Schmidt's schema theory is the most popular representative of this type of theory. It proposes that a generalized motor program serves as the central mechanism for the control of motor skill performance. The generalized motor program is an abstract representation of a class of movements that is stored in memory and retrieved when an action involving that class of movements is to be performed. Stored in the generalized motor program are invariant features of the movement class, such as the order of movement events and the relative time and relative force of the movement components. When a specific action is to be performed, specific parameter values must be added to the generalized motor program; these include the overall duration and overall force of the movement as well as the muscles that will be used.

- The dynamic pattern theory takes issue with the importance motor program theories give to memory-based representations for the control of motor skills. The dynamic pattern theory proposes that factors such as environmental invariants and limb dynamics can account for much of the control ascribed to the motor program. The theory views coordinated movement as following rules associated with nonlinear dynamics. The theory incorporates dynamic features such as attractor states, which are preferred, stable patterns that define specific coordination patterns; order parameters, such as relative phase, that functionally define attractor states; and control parameters, such as speed or frequency, that influence the stability and instability of attractor states. Coordinated movement self-organizes as coordinative structures according to the characteristics of the interactions among the person, the environment, and the skill to be performed.

- At present, there are strong proponents of both the motor program and the dynamic pattern theories of motor control. Opinions vary in terms of how the current theory debate will be resolved.

RELATED READINGS

Barton, S. (1994). Chaos, self-organization, and psychology. *American Psychologist, 49,* 5–14.

Bongaardt, R., & Meijer, O. G. (2000). Bernstein's theory of movement behavior: Historical development and contemporary relevance. *Journal of Motor Behavior, 32,* 57–71.

Clark, J. E. (1995). On becoming skillful: Patterns and constraints. *Research Quarterly for Exercise and Sport, 66,* 173–183.

Feigenberg, I. M., & Meijer, O. G. (1999). The active search for information: From reflexes to the model of the future (1966). *Motor Control, 3,* 225–236.

Mussa-Ivaldi, F. A. (1999). Modular features of motor control and learning. *Current Opinion in Neurobiology, 9,* 713–717.

Swinnen, S. (1994). Motor control. *Encyclopedia of human behavior.* (Vol. 3, 229–243). New York: Academic Press.

Wallace, S. A. (1996). Dynamic pattern perspective of rhythmic movement: An introduction. In H. N. Zelaznik (Ed.), *Advances in motor learning and control* (pp. 155–194). Champaign, IL: Human Kinetics.

Worringham, C. J., Smiley-Owen, A. L., & Cross, C. L. (1997). Neural basis of motor learning in humans. In H. N. Zelaznik (Ed.), *Advances in motor learning and control* (pp. 67–86). Champaign, IL: Human Kinetics.

Zanone, P. G., & Kelso, J. A. S. (1991). Relative timing from the perspective of dynamic pattern theory: Stability and instability. In J. Fagard & P. Wolff (Eds.), *The development of timing control and temporal organization in coordinated action* (pp. 69–92). Amsterdam: Elsevier.

STUDY QUESTIONS

1. Define the term coordination and describe how a limb movement displacement graph can portray a coordinated movement pattern.

2. What is the *degrees of freedom problem* as it relates to the study of human motor control?

3. Describe the similarities and the differences between a closed-loop control system and an open-loop control system. For each system, describe a motor skill that could be characterized as having that type of control system.

4. Define a generalized motor program and describe two invariant features and two parameters proposed to characterize this program.

5. Describe an example of nonlinear changes in human coordinated movement.

6. Define and give an example of the following key terms used in the dynamic pattern theory of motor control: (a) stability; (b) attractors; (c) order parameters; (d) control parameters; (e) coordinative structures; (f) self-organization.

7. Discuss how relative-time characteristics of human walking and running gaits are explained by (a) motor program–based theory and (b) dynamic pattern theory.

CHAPTER

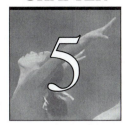

Performance Characteristics
of Complex Skills

*Concept: Specific characteristics of the performance
of various motor skills provide the basis for much of our
understanding of the processes involved in motor control*

After completing this chapter, you will be able to

- Describe Fitts' law and explain how it relates to the speed-accuracy trade-off phenomenon

- Define the term *prehension,* describe a prehension example, and discuss, from a motor control perspective, the relationship among the components of a prehension action

- Describe how handwriting provides a good example of the concept of motor equivalence

- Describe the difference between symmetric and asymmetric bimanual coordination, and discuss why asymmetric bimanual coordination is more difficult to maintain than symmetric

- Describe the rhythmic relationships associated with walking and running gait patterns, the role of maintaining head stability during locomotion, and the characteristics associated with gait transitions that occur at certain speeds of locomotion

Application

Appropriate instruction and practice intervention procedures are important to develop to help people acquire or rehabilitate skills effectively and efficiently. As you saw in chapter 4, a basic understanding of motor control theory and the processes involved in motor control form important parts of a foundation on which to base the development of these procedures. Consider the following two examples. If a person were having difficulty reaching, grasping, and drinking from a cup, how would the therapist determine the reason for this problem

and then develop an appropriate intervention strategy to help the person perform this type of skill? An important part of the answer to these questions comes from research concerned with the motor control involved in prehension. Or, suppose a beginning student in a tennis class is having problems learning to serve because he or she cannot coordinate the ball toss and racquet movement that must simultaneously occur to perform a successful serve. Motor control researchers have identified some distinct characteristics of bimanual coordination that provide teachers and coaches some insight into how to overcome the tennis serve problem.

Discussion

The motor control theories discussed in chapter 4 were derived from researchers' observations of people performing a variety of everyday and sport skills in many different situations. These observations have established that each type of skill involves distinct performance characteristics that are essential to consider in a theory of motor control, and to provide guidance for practitioners as they help people learn or rehabilitate skills. In the following sections, we will consider some of the more prominent types of motor skills researchers have investigated with these goals in mind.

SPEED-ACCURACY SKILLS

Many motor skills require a person to perform with both speed and accuracy. For example, kicking a penalty kick in soccer, pitching a fastball for a strike in baseball and softball, playing a song on a piano at a fast tempo, and speed typing all require fast and accurate movement to achieve successful performance. When both speed and accuracy are essential to the performance of a motor skill, we commonly observe a phenomenon known as the **speed-accuracy trade-off.** This means that when the person emphasizes speed, accuracy is reduced. And conversely, when he or she emphasizes accuracy, speed is reduced. For example, to accurately thread a needle with sewing thread, you will thread a needle with a large eye more quickly than one with a small eye. Also, you will typically type a sentence more slowly if you try not to make any errors than if you aren't concerned with the number of errors you make.

Fitts' Laws

The speed-accuracy trade-off is such a common characteristic in motor skill performance that a mathematical law describes it. Fitts' law, based on the work of Paul Fitts (1954), has become one of the most significant "laws" associated with human performance. In science, a *law* refers to a situation in which a result, or outcome, can be predicted when certain variables are involved. **Fitts' law** pre-

dicts the movement time for a situation requiring both speed and accuracy in which a person must move to a target as quickly and accurately as possible. The variables that predict the performance outcome are the *distance* to move and the *target size.* According to Fitts' law, if we know the spatial dimensions of these two variables, we can predict the movement time required to hit the target. In mathematical terms, Fitts' law describes this relationship as

$$MT = a + b \log_2(2D/W)$$

where

MT is movement time
a and b are constants
D is the distance moved
W is the target width, or size

That is, movement time will be equal to the $\log_2$ of two times the distance to move divided by the width of the target. As the target size becomes smaller or as the distance becomes longer, the movement speed will decrease in order to allow for an accurate movement. In other words, there is a speed-accuracy trade-off.

Fitts indicated that because of the lawful relationship between target size and movement distance, the equation $\log_2(2D/W)$ provides an **index of difficulty (ID)** for speed-accuracy skills. The index specifies that the higher the ID is, the more difficult the task will be. This is because more difficult tasks will require more movement time.

Figure 5.1a shows several examples of reciprocal tapping task dimensions that would characterize different IDs. Figure 5.1b shows approximate movement times for tasks with these, and other, IDs to illustrate the relationship between task difficulty (ID) and movement speed when people are instructed to move accurately, i.e., hit the target.

Fitts based his original calculation on a reciprocal tapping task in which participants made repetitive back-and-forth movements as fast as possible between two targets for a specified period of time. For this task, they were told to place an emphasis on accuracy. Since Fitts' initial work, other researchers have found that the lawful speed-accuracy relationship generalizes to a wide range of motor skill performance situations. For example, research evidence shows that when people perform manual aiming tasks, such as moving pegs from one location to insert them into a hole, throwing darts at a target, reaching or grasping containers of different sizes, and moving a cursor on a screen to a target, their actions demonstrate movement time characteristics predicted by Fitts' law.

If we apply Fitts' law to the sport skills described earlier in this section, the implications of this law for instruction and practice become more evident. For example, suppose a soccer player is asked to practice scoring a goal on a penalty kick by kicking the ball so that it travels as fast as possible to each of three different-sized areas in the goal. Fitts' law predicts that the highest speed will occur for the ball kicked to the largest area. Conversely, the slowest speed will characterize the ball kicked to the smallest area. Later in this book (Unit VI), we will discuss the practice conditions that will help a person achieve both speed and accuracy in these types of situations.

PREHENSION

Prehension is the general term used to describe actions involving the *reaching for and grasping of objects.* Research evidence has shown that at the movement level, prehension consists of three distinct components: *transport, grasp,* and *object manipulation.* The object manipulation component refers to the functional goal for the prehension action. In other words, an important part of understanding the control of prehension relates to what the person intends to do with the object after grasping it. The importance of this component is that it influences the kinematic and kinetic characteristics of the transport and grasp components. For example, if a person intends to pick up a cup to drink from it, the transport and grasp characteristics will differ from those associated with the person picking up the cup and moving it to a different location on a table (see Newell & Cesari, 1999, for a discussion of the motor control implications of this issue). In fact, it is because of the relationship of

LAB LINKS

Lab 5a in the Online Learning Center Lab Manual for chapter 5 provides an opportunity for you to perform reciprocal tapping tasks with characteristics that will allow you to experience how Fitts' law describes the speed-accuracy trade-off.

the object manipulation component to the other two components that *prehension must be considered an action that is different from the action of reaching and pointing to an object.*

The Relationship of Prehension Components
From a motor control perspective, prehension involves the arm transporting the hand to an object as the hand forms the grip characteristics that are needed to grasp the object. A motor control question of interest here concerns the relationship between the transport and grasp components. Although initial attempts to answer this question proposed that these components were relatively independent

speed-accuracy trade-off   a characteristic of motor skill performance in which the speed at which a skill is performed is influenced by movement accuracy demands; the trade-off is that increasing speed yields decreasing accuracy, and vice versa.

Fitts' law   a human performance law specifying the movement time for an aiming action when the distance to move and the target size are known; it is quantified as $MT = a + b \log_2(2 D/W)$, where a and b are constants and W = target width, and D = distance from the starting point to the target.

index of difficulty (ID)   according to Fitts' law, a quantitative measure of the difficulty of performing a skill involving both speed and accuracy requirements; it is calculated as the $\log_2(2 D/W)$, where W = target width, and D = distance from the starting point to the target.

prehension   the action of reaching for and grasping an object that may be stationary or moving.

FIGURE 5.1
(a). Examples of indexes of difficulty (ID) for reciprocal tapping tasks with different target size and/or distance characteristics. Task difficulty is indexed according to the ID such that the higher the ID is, the more difficult is the task. The ID is calculated according to the Fitts' law equation: $ID = \log_2 (2 \cdot Distance/ Width)$ [Note that W is measured from the near edge of each target.]

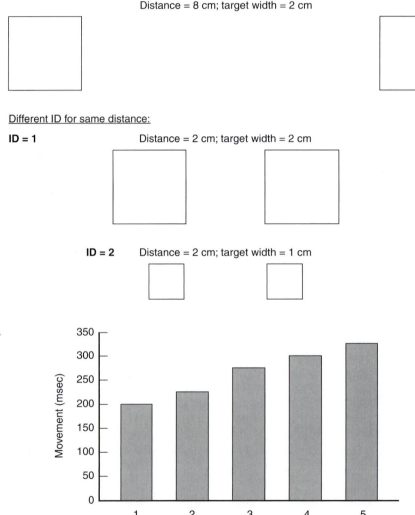

a. Same ID for different distances and target widths:

ID = 3   Distance = 4 cm; target width = 1 cm

Distance = 8 cm; target width = 2 cm

Different ID for same distance:

ID = 1   Distance = 2 cm; target width = 2 cm

ID = 2   Distance = 2 cm; target width = 1 cm

(b). Approximate movement times (in msec) for each tap of reciprocal tapping tasks of five different indexes of difficulty.

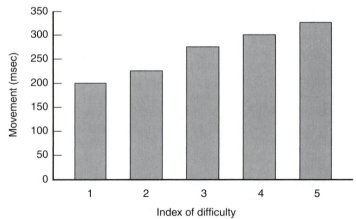

b. Movement (msec) vs Index of difficulty

The most compelling evidence demonstrating this relationship has come from movement analy-

(e.g., Jeannerod, 1981, 1984), more recent evidence has established that these two components interact synergistically (i.e., cooperatively) according to task demands. This means that the reach and the grasp are not two separate movement components, but function in an interdependent manner.

A CLOSER LOOK

The Controversy Related to Explaining Fitts' Law

Although researchers consistently provide evidence that demonstrates the wide range of skill performance situations to which Fitts' law applies, they have not agreed on a motor control explanation for the speed-accuracy trade-off. Below is a sampling of some of the prominent hypotheses that continue to have proponents. It is important to understand that these hypotheses relate to explanations for the speed-accuracy trade-off associated with rapid manual-aiming tasks, which were the types of tasks involved in the initial demonstration of the trade-off.

- **Intermittent feedback hypothesis.** Crossman and Goodeve (1983) proposed that open-loop control is involved in the initiation of a rapid manual aiming task. But as the arm moves toward the target, the person intermittently uses feedback to generate submovements, which are small corrections in the trajectory, until the target is contacted. Movement time (MT) increases for longer distances or narrower targets because the number of corrections increases. For a reciprocal aiming task, some of the MT increase occurs because the person spends more time in contact with each target to evaluate visual feedback and plan the movement to the next target.
- **Impulse-timing hypothesis.** Schmidt and colleagues (1979) proposed that many speed-accuracy tasks involve movements that are too fast to allow for the use of visual feedback to make corrections during the movement. In these situations, they hypothesize that a person programs commands in advance of movement initiation. These commands are forwarded to the muscles as "impulses," which are the forces produced during

a specific amount of time. The result is that the arm is forcefully driven toward the target and achieves accuracy based on the specified amount of force and time. Because amounts of force and time relate to movement variability, increases in movement velocity result in more variable movement. To correct an inaccurate outcome, the person would need to slow arm speed on the next attempt.
- **Multiple submovements hypothesis.** Meyer and colleagues (1988, 1990) adopted elements of both the intermittent-feedback and impulse-timing hypotheses. They proposed that before initiating movement, the person programs an initial impulse, which is then executed. If the movement is accurate, nothing further is required. But if feedback during the movement indicates that the movement will be inaccurate, the person prepares and executes submovements that adjust the initial velocity. This process continues until the person produces an accurate movement. The number of submovements made relates to movement time and the target distance and width (see also Yao & Fischman, 1999).

ses of the fingers and thumb as the hand moves toward the object. For example, Jakobson and Goodale (1991) showed that the object's size and distance from the hand influenced the timing of the distance between the fingers and thumb reaching its maximum during the reach, as well as the velocity profile of the transport component. Interestingly, they, along with others (e.g., Chieffi & Gentilucci, 1993), found that regardless of object size and distance, hand closure occurred at approximately two-thirds of the total movement time involved in the action. In addition, research evidence has shown that the kinematics of both the transport and grasp components are modified when the object is suddenly

and unexpectedly moved during the transport phase (e.g., Gentilucci, Chieffi, Scarpa, & Castiello, 1992), and when an obstacle needs to be avoided to get to the object (e.g., Saling, Alberts, Stelmach, & Bloedel, 1998). These kinematic changes have led to the conclusion that there is a strong *coupling* between the reach and grasp components of a prehension action. Thus, prehension serves as an additional example to those described in chapter 4 of how muscles and joints involved in a complex action operate as a *coordinative structure* to enable people to achieve an action goal in a variety of situations.

It is also important to note that the person's intended manipulation of the object and the visual

A CLOSER LOOK

The Use of Functional Objects Enhances Prehension Performance in Rehabilitation Settings

An experiment related to the rehabilitation of reaching performance for cerebrovascular accident (CVA) patients demonstrates the benefit of the use of functional objects during therapy. Wu, Trombly, Lin, and Tickle-Degnen (1998) engaged fourteen men and women CVA patients in the performance of two types of tasks, which required them to reach a distance of 20 cm to a food chopper and then grasp and push down its handle. The "enriched" task involved chop-

ping a mushroom, which the participants could see. The "impoverished" task involved chopping, but there was nothing in the chopper, and the chopper itself was covered so that its shape and content could not be seen. All participants performed ten trials of each task. Analysis of the hand movements indicated that the enriched task resulted in patients reaching for the chopper faster, more directly, and more smoothly than they did for the impoverished task.

 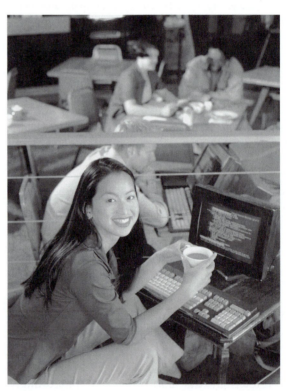

The same object manipulation goal for a prehension action can be achieved with different grasp characteristics.

information the person obtains about the distance to the object, its size, shape, weight, etc., preset the motor control system to initiate the reach and grasp movements. This presetting involves specifying "ballpark" estimates of the spatial and temporal characteristics that the transport and grasp components will need to reach and grasp the object. However, as the arm moves toward the object, visual feedback influences needed modifications to these component specifications (if there is sufficient

A CLOSER LOOK

Initial Difficulties in Controlling an Upper Extremity Prosthesis for Prehension

An experiment by Wallace et al. (1999) involved people without an amputation wearing simulated upper extremity artificial limbs as a way to gain insight into the motor control difficulties associated with initial attempts to use these devices to perform a prehension action. Because the simulators were mechanically similar to the actual prostheses worn by amputees, and the participants were required to perform a novel task, the researchers reasoned that the results would provide a reasonable estimate of initial performance by amputees.

The simulators included a figure-8 harness, cable, and split-hook prehensor (identical to a regular prosthesis). They were designed to mimic a prosthesis for a person with an amputation.

The prehension action involved reaching forward 290 mm, removing a vertically oriented dowel (150 mm long, 25 mm in diameter, 155 gm in weight) from a hole, and then putting it into a hole 88 mm from the start position as quickly as possible. The holes were 38 mm deep and 30 mm in diameter.

Performance trials consisted of 10 trials for each of the following: the participant's own right limb, the participant's own left limb, the right prosthetic limb, and the left prosthetic limb.

Results showed that performance with the prosthetic limb took approximately three times longer than with the person's own limb. And although there were no movement time differences between the right and left prosthetic limbs, the participants reported more difficulty controlling the right-limb device (possibly because it is controlled by the contralateral shoulder of their nondominant limb).

time). In addition, the grasp itself may undergo further modifications, especially to size and force, after contact with the object and as the intended manipulation is carried out.

Prehension and Fitts' Law

One final point that is important to note with regard to the motor control aspects of prehension is that it demonstrates speed-accuracy trade-off characteristics. In fact, researchers have established that Fitts' law consistently applies to prehension for both laboratory tasks and activities of daily living. For example, in an experiment by Bootsma, Marteniuk, MacKenzie, and Zaal (1994), movement distance and object width influenced movement time during prehension in accordance with the predictions of Fitts' law. In addition, these object characteristics influenced the movement kinematics of the action. The relevance of the kinematic evidence is that it provides a way to explain why movement time increases as object width decreases. The kinematics showed that as objects decrease in size, the amount of time involved in the deceleration phase of the movement increases, suggesting that the

increase in movement time associated with the smaller objects is due to the person reducing the speed of the limb as it approaches the object. This means that when a person reaches for a cup that has a small handle, not only will the transport and grasp kinematics differ from reaching for a cup with no handle, but the movement time will also be slower, because of the increased accuracy demands of grasping the small handle.

Implications for Practice

From an applied perspective, the motor control research evidence about prehension has important implications for the development of practice conditions to help people improve their prehension capabilities. Because of the cooperative relationship between the reach, grasp, and object manipulation components, it is essential that prehension practice or therapy strategies involve functional activities (e.g., Wu, Trombly, Lin, & Tickle-Degnen, 1998). In addition, because movement characteristics of reach and grasp components interact in various ways according to object characteristics, it is important that practice involve reaching, grasping,

A CLOSER LOOK

Prehension Situations Illustrate Motor Control Adaptability

An experiment by Steenbergen, Marteniuk, and Kalbfleisch (1995) provides a good illustration of how adaptable the motor control system is. We see this adaptability when people alter movements of a specific action to accommodate characteristics of the task situation. The authors asked the participants to reach and grasp with the right or left hand a Styrofoam cup that was either full or empty. Participants had to grasp the cup, located 30 cm in front of them, then place it on a round target 20 cm to the right or left. Movement analyses of the hand transport and grasp phases revealed interesting differences at the movement level depending on which hand a person used and whether the cup was full or empty. For ex-

ample, during the transport phase, hand velocity was distinctly faster and peak velocity was earlier when the cup was empty. The grasp aperture time also varied according to the cup characteristic. Maximum grasp aperture occurred earlier in the transport phase for the full cup, a situation demanding more movement precision. In terms of coordination of the joints involved in the action, participants froze the degrees of freedom of the shoulder, elbow, and wrist joints during the prehension movements for both full and empty cups. However, when the cup was full, participants increased stabilization during the movement by making a trunk postural adjustment that moved the shoulder forward.

and manipulating a variety of object characteristics and manipulation goals. Finally, because of the interdependent relationship of the components of prehension, it would not be beneficial to separate the reach, grasp, and object manipulation goal so that a person could practice each component separately.

HANDWRITING

Investigation of the control mechanisms responsible for handwriting is a prominent theme in the study of motor control. Researchers generally agree that different control mechanisms are involved in controlling *what people write* (letters, words, numbers, etc.) and *how they write it* (the writing strokes producing the letters, words, etc., on the writing surface).

When we consider the act of handwriting from an anatomical perspective, we see that there is a great deal of individual variation in terms of limb segment involvement. But when researchers obtain handwriting samples from one person, they offer strong evidence for what Bernstein (1967) referred to as **motor equivalence.** That is, a person can adapt to the specific demands of the writing context and adjust size, force, direction, and even muscle involvement to accommodate those demands.

The notable outcome is that there is a great degree of similarity in characteristics such as letter forms, writing slant, relative force for stroke production, and relative timing between strokes. People have little trouble varying characteristics such as movement time and writing size, among others.

The complexity of handwriting control makes it difficult to develop a simple control model describing the components of this process. A person can write his or her signature or a familiar phrase with the preferred hand, with the nonpreferred hand, with a foot, or by holding a pen in the mouth. This suggests that at least the spatial features of writing are represented in the memory system in an abstract form. Also, this motor equivalence capability suggests the involvement of coordinative structures in handwriting control.

Another interesting feature of the act of handwriting is that several control processes occur at the same time. To write a sentence, a person must use lexical, semantic, and motor control processes. Writing requires the person to retrieve words from memory. These words must have meanings that fit what the writer intends to convey. The written sentence requires specific grammatical construction. The words require a certain spelling, which involves the person's movement of the limb to produce spe-

A CLOSER LOOK

A Handwriting Demonstration of Motor Equivalence

Write Your Signature

1. with a pen in your preferred hand.
2. with a pen in your nonpreferred hand.
3. with a pen held in your mouth by your teeth.
4. with your preferred hand on the chalkboard.

Compare the Spatial Characteristics of the Four Handwriting Samples

1. Describe the similarities you see.
2. Describe the differences you see.

Undoubtedly, specific elements of your signature remained constant regardless of which muscle groups were involved in the writing action. Your ability to engage various muscle groups to write your signature demonstrates how the act of handwriting illustrates the concept of motor equivalence.

cific letters that are of an appropriate size and shape for what he or she is writing on. Further, the individual must hold the writing instrument with an appropriate amount of force to allow these letters to be formed. The capability of human beings to carry out these various cognitive and motor elements in relatively short amounts of time demonstrates both the complexity and the elegance of the control processes underlying the act of handwriting.

BIMANUAL COORDINATION SKILLS

In addition to unimanual coordination skills, people perform many motor skills that require the simultaneous performance of the two arms, i.e., **bimanual coordination.** Sometimes the two limbs do essentially the same thing (*symmetric bimanual coordination*); this occurs when someone rows a boat or when a person in a wheelchair rolls the wheels of the chair in order to go straight forward or backward. But more interesting from a motor control perspective are *asymmetric bimanual coordination* situations in which each limb must do something different. For example, a guitar player holds strings with one hand to determine chords, while plucking or striking strings with the other hand to produce sound. A skilled drummer can produce one rhythm with one hand while producing another with the other hand. The serve in tennis requires the player to toss the ball into the air with one arm while moving the racquet with a very different movement pattern with the other.

Bimanual Coordination Preferences

An important characteristic of the performance of skills that require either symmetric or asymmetric bimanual coordination is that the two limbs *prefer* to do the same thing at the same time. This preference helps the performance of symmetric bimanual skills, but can lead to problems for asymmetric skills. For example, why is it difficult to rub your stomach with one hand while at the same time tapping the top of your head with the other hand? The reason is that your two arms want to simultaneously do one of the actions, but not both.

The earliest research to demonstrate the motor control system's preference to coordinate the two arms to move together involved the simultaneous performance of discrete movements. In what is now seen as a classic series of experiments, Kelso, Southard, and Goodman (1979) had people perform rapid aiming movements to targets that had the same or different Fitts' index of difficulty (ID) values (see figure 5.2). Results showed a *temporal*

---

motor equivalence   the capability of the motor control system to enable a person to achieve an action goal in a variety of situations and conditions (e.g., writing your signature with either hand).

bimanual coordination   a motor skill that requires the simultaneous use of the two arms; the skill may require the two arms to move with the same or different spatial and/or temporal characteristics.

basis for the coordination of the two arms as they moved with similar movement times not only to targets with the same ID values, but also to targets that had different ID values (note that the movement times are not identical, but similar). In addition the results of this experiment demonstrated that the bimanual movements to targets with different ID values did not adhere to Fitts' law. The apparent strength of the preference for the two arms to temporally move together overcame the influence of the speed-accuracy trade-off characteristic for the same movement when it was performed by only one arm.

In the Kelso et al. bimanual coordination situation, the *more difficult task* influenced the performance of the arm doing the less difficult task. That is, the arm that was required to move a shorter distance (i.e., had the less difficult task) slowed down in comparison to when it moved the same distance alone. Similar results have been shown when *task complexity* differences characterized the bimanual coordination task. For example, the task used in an experiment by Swinnen, Schmidt, Nicholson, and Shapiro (1990) required participants to rapidly move their arms in different spatial-temporal patterns. The task involved moving one arm in a simple one-direction arm-flexion movement while at the same time moving the other in a two-part flexion and extension movement. Both arms were to complete their movements in a movement time of 800 ms. At the beginning of practice, participants generally produced with each arm the similar movement patterns, which typically resembled the more complex two-part movement required by one arm.

Motor Control of Bimanual Coordination
Researchers are not certain how the motor control system is involved in the control of bimanual coordination. At present, we know that there is a coupling of the arms, which forms a natural coordinative structure that prefers to operate in spatial-temporal symmetry. And an in-phase relationship between the arms (i.e., both arms flexing and extending at the same time) appears to be the predominant symmetrical relationship. In addition, we know that

LAB LINKS

Lab 5b in the Online Learning Center Lab Manual for chapter 5 provides an opportunity for you to perform symmetric and asymmetric bimanual coordination tasks that will allow you to experience the intrinsic coordination characteristic of symmetric bimanual coordination even though the achievement of the action goal of the skill requires asymmetric bimanual coordination.

with practice, a person can learn to uncouple (sometimes referred to as "dissociate") the two limbs and simultaneously move his or her arms asymmetrically. But, we do not yet understand the control mechanisms involved in this dissociation process. Some researchers report evidence that *proprioceptive feedback* is important in this process (e.g., Vershueren et al., 1999a), while others propose that *visual feedback* is the basis for performing the complex asymmetric bimanual coordination task (e.g., Mechsner, Kerzel, Knoblich, & Prinz, 2001). We will look at these two sources of feedback in chapter 6.

In terms of motor control theory perspectives on learning to uncouple the limbs, researchers have proposed distinctive views. Those who support the motor program theory argue for generalized motor program involvement, but there is disagreement about whether two new generalized motor programs develop so that each arm becomes controlled by a separate program, or one generalized motor program develops in which each arm can perform somewhat independently. From a dynamic pattern theory perspective, the control issue is rather straightforward. The initial tendency for the arms to be spatially and temporally coupled represents an attractor state in which a specific relative phase relationship is the order parameter. But, with practice, the stable relationship becomes unstable as the new relationship becomes more stable and a new attractor state emerges.

Implications for Practice
Teachers, coaches, and therapists who are aware of bimanual coordination tendencies will recognize

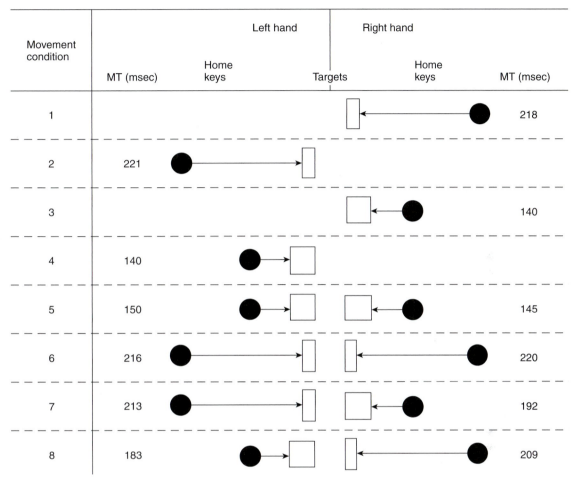

Movement condition		Left hand			Right hand	
	MT (msec)	Home keys		Targets	Home keys	MT (msec)
1						218
2	221					
3						140
4	140					
5	150					145
6	216					220
7	213					192
8	183					209

FIGURE 5.2 Movement time scores for one- and two-hand movements to targets of different distances and sizes reported in Kelso, Southard, and Goodman's second experiment. [Source: Kelso, J. A., Southard, D. L., & Goodman, D. (1979). On the coordination of two-handed movements. *Journal of Experimental Psychology: Human Perception and Performance, 5,* 229–238. Copyright © 1979 the American Psychological Association. Adapted with permission.]

the need to give special attention to people who are learning skills that require the arms to perform different spatial-temporal movement patterns. The required unlinking of bimanual movements can be a difficult process for people. But, as both experience and research evidence (e.g., Lee, Swinnen, & Verschueren, 1995; Swinnen et al., 1990; Walter & Swinnen, 1994) tell us, people can achieve success in performing these types of skills when they receive appropriate instruction, feedback, and practice. We will consider some of the strategies

practitioners can use to facilitate the learning of asymmetric bimanual coordination skills in Units V and VI.

GAIT

There is little argument that at the nervous system level, *central pattern generators* in the spinal cord are involved in the control of human gait. These mechanisms provide the basis for stereotypic locomotive patterns. We can trace evidence for this

A CLOSER LOOK

Applying the Dynamic Pattern View of Gait Control to Physical Therapy Interventions

We can see the involvement in locomotor control of dynamic interactions between the person and the environment in the effectiveness of a therapy strategy that helps reestablish normal rhythmic gait. Based on the dynamic pattern control perspective, Wagenaar and van Emmerik (1994) recommended that therapists use various methods to help patients attain spontaneous production of the appropriate rhythmic structures for specific gait patterns by systematically altering gait speeds.

Wagenaar and Beek (1992) showed an example of the effectiveness of this procedure. They used a metronome to present rhythms to hemiplegic patients. When the authors systematically increased the rhythmic beat from 60 to 96 steps a minute, these patients improved the phase relationships of their arms and legs; this in turn positively influenced trunk rotation.

---

spinal level of control to the work of the British Nobel laureate Charles Sherrington and his colleagues at the end of the nineteenth and beginning of the twentieth centuries (e.g., Sherrington, 1906).

Using a procedure known as decerebration, which involves severing the spinal cord from the brain, Sherrington observed that decerebrated cats performed locomotor rhythmic muscular activity similar to that performed by intact animals. Later, Brown (1911) went a step further by additionally severing a cat's sensory pathways to the spinal cord; still, the cat showed rhythmic leg contractions appropriate for walking. More recent research (e.g., Grillner, 1981, 1985) has confirmed and extended these earlier observations (see Field-Fote, 2000, for an excellent overview of the spinal cord's role in the control of locomotion).

The Rhythmic Structure of Locomotion

To understand how humans control the wide range of gait they are capable of, we must consider higher-level nervous system involvement, along with musculoskeletal dynamics and environmental interactions. The rhythmic structure of locomotor actions is an important characteristic that will serve to illustrate the roles of these various factors.

In the discussion in chapter 4 of the study by Shapiro et al. (1981), you saw that on the basis of an analysis of the four components of the Phillipson step cycle, walking and running each have a distinct rhythmic structure. In fact, this rhythmic characteristic is so common for walking and running gaits that mathematical models have been developed to describe their structures. Those who have developed these models view the leg movements in walking and running gaits as operating similar to a pendulum (see Wagenaar & van Emmerik, 1994, and Donker et al., 2001, for discussions about these models).

The rhythmic structure of gait patterns is not limited to leg movements. For example, when a person walks, distinct *rhythmic relationships exist between the movement of the arms and that of the legs,* and the specific character of this relationship relates to walking speed. Craik, Herman, and Finley (1976) first demonstrated this relationship by providing evidence that there are two arm-leg coordination patterns for walking: a 2:1 ratio (i.e., two arm swings to each leg stride) for very slow walking, and a 1:1 ratio for walking at speeds greater than 0.75 m/s (1.7 mi/hr, or 2.72 km/hr). Van Emmerik and Wagenaar (1996) reported that additional research has established that the transition from the 2:1 to the 1:1 arm-leg relationship occurs within the walking speed range of 0.2 to 1.2 m/s (0.5 to 2.7 mi/hr, or 0.3 to 4.32 km/hr). In addition to the arm-leg relationship, the pelvis and thorax also demonstrate a rhythmic relationship during walking. At lower speeds, they move in phase with each other, but out of phase at higher walking speeds.

What is the practical benefit of knowing about these various coordination characteristics of gait

A CLOSER LOOK

Avoiding Obstacles While Walking or Running

Research by James Cutting and his colleagues at Cornell University (e.g., Cutting, 1986; Vishton & Cutting, 1995) has shown that if a person is walking or running and wishes to maintain footspeed while avoiding an obstacle, three time periods are critical:

The Time Needed to

1. recognize that an object needs to be avoided;

2. adjust the footfall;

3. turn the foot to avoid the obstacle.

Of these three periods, the first is the most critical and takes up about 75 percent of the distance covered while the subject is approaching an object.

Implication for Clinical Rehabilitation and Sport
Because of the importance of early visual recognition of an object to be avoided, it is important to train people to actively visually search the environment in which they locomote. To avoid collision, a person must recognize objects sufficiently early to allow appropriate movement adjustments. Therefore, the therapist or coach who focuses training on only the movement-adjustment aspect of this task ignores the most critical component of object recognition.

patterns? Van Emmerik and Wagenaar (1996) presented an excellent argument, along with research evidence, to support their view that knowing about these characteristics and using them as assessment techniques allow us to identify coordination problems in the trunk and extremities, especially for people with Parkinson's disease. For example, when walking at preferred speeds, Parkinson's patients show pelvis and thorax phase relationships that are exactly opposite those described in the previous paragraph for healthy people.

Head Stability and Locomotion
When a person engages in locomotor activity, a goal of the motor control system is to *maintain head stability.* Researchers have demonstrated that head stability, as measured by the vertical orientation and minimal horizontal motion, is maintained during locomotor actions such as walking, walking in place, running in place, and hopping (for brief reviews of this research literature, see Cromwell, Newton, & Carlton, 2001, and Holt, Ratcliffe, & Jeng, 1999). Why is head stability so important to maintain during these types of actions? The answer relates to the role the head plays in these activities. When we consider that the head contains the complex of sensory and motor nervous system components essential for us to navigate through an

environment and maintain postural stability so that we don't fall, it becomes evident that head stability is important to maintain during locomotion. In addition, maintaining a stable head position during locomotion optimizes the use of vision in actions in which vision of an object while running is essential for achieving the action goal. For example, a baseball or tennis player must visually track the flight of the ball while running in order to catch or hit it. Finally, it is interesting in light of the importance of head stability during locomotion that researchers have found that children with cerebral palsy and adults with neurological impairment commonly adopt what could be considered "abnormal" postural and gait characteristics as strategies to enable them to maintain head stability while walking (e.g., Holt, Jeng, Ratcliffe, & Hamill, 1995; Holt, Ratcliffe, & Jeng, 1999).

Gait Transitions
Another important gait characteristic, which was briefly described in chapter 4, is the spontaneous change from a walking to a running gait (and vice versa) at certain speeds. Although these spontaneous gait transitions are common to all people, the speed at which transition occurs varies between individuals. Some people continue to walk at higher speeds than others, whereas some people continue

to run at lower speeds than others. In addition, the walk-to-run transition typically occurs at higher speeds than the run-to-walk transition. The issue of interest to researchers who study human locomotion is *why* this transition occurs. There is general agreement that the reason is not due to physical limitations. As a result, researchers have developed and tested several hypotheses. The most prevalent of these has been that the transition occurs to minimize metabolic energy consumption (i.e., VO_2). Although researchers have provided evidence that supports this hypothesis, others have reported results that fail to support it (see Hreljac, 1993). At present, no single cause for gait transitions has been determined. Interestingly, Turvey et al. (1999), after reporting results that did not support their hypothesis based on the role of kinetic energy, expressed doubts that a single cause can be identified because of the nature of complex biological systems. Kao (2001) found evidence that supported their conclusion by demonstrating that multiple factors that may be specific to individuals underlie gait transitions. However, until further research is carried out, the identification of the reason(s) why people spontaneously change gaits at certain speeds remains a puzzle for researchers to solve.

Finally, it is important to note that vision provides an additional component of gait control, as you will see in chapter 6. Vision provides information that directs a person's walking speed, body alignment, and navigation through the environment.

SUMMARY

Much of our understanding of the control processes underlying the performance of motor skills comes from research evidence that has identified specific performance characteristics associated with a variety of types of skills. This discussion highlighted several of these characteristics.

- *Speed-accuracy skills,* which require a person to produce movement that is both fast and accurate, typically demonstrate a speed-accuracy trade-off. That is, if the movement must be as accurate as possible, people move at a slower rate of speed than when accuracy is not important. Fitts' law provides a mathematical basis for predicting this trade-off on the basis of the task's movement distance and target size characteristics.

- Performance of *prehension skills,* which involve the reaching for and grasping of objects, demonstrates the synergistic coupling of movement components that allow a person to achieve an action goal in a variety of situations. The transport and grasp components function interdependently by adjusting certain movement kinematics to adapt to specific characteristics of the object to be grasped and the manipulation goal of the prehensive action. Different from manual aiming, pointing, and reaching, prehension movement kinematics vary during both the transport and the grasp phases as a function of what the performer intends to do with the object after it is grasped.

- *Handwriting* demonstrates an important motor control characteristic known as motor equivalence, which means that a person can achieve the same action goal in a variety of situations that require movement adaptations dictated by the environmental context or by task characteristics such as size, force, direction, and muscles involved. The movement adaptations result in remarkable similarities in handwriting characteristics such as letter forms and the relative time relationship between strokes, among others.

- *Bimanual coordination skills* require the simultaneous performance of the two arms. Some tasks require symmetric bimanual coordination (i.e., both arms perform in the same way at the same time); others require asymmetric bimanual coordination (i.e., each arm performs differently). An important motor control characteristic of these skills is the natural, or intrinsic, spatial and temporal coupling of the arms, which means that we have a preference to move the arms symmetrically. Personal experience and research evidence shows that people can learn to uncouple the arms to perform asymmetric bimanual coordination skills. At the present time, researchers have not determined the specific motor control mechanism that underlies the control of arms in this uncoupled, asymmetric state.

• The performance of *locomotion* actions, such as walking and running, is characterized by the rhythmic relationships that exist between step-cycle components, arm and leg movements, and the movement of the pelvis and thorax. Also, the maintenance of head stability is an important characteristic associated with locomotor activities. And a locomotion characteristic that has yet to be explained in terms of why it occurs is that spontaneous gait transitions (from walking to running, and running to walking) occur at certain gait speeds.

RELATED READINGS

Bennett, K. M. B., Adler, C. H., Stelmach, G. E., & Castiello, U. (1993). A kinematic study of the reach to grasp movement in a subject with hemi-Parkinson's disease. *Neuropsychologia, 31,* 709–716.

Bonnard, M., & Pailhous, J. (1993). Intentionality in human gait control: Modifying the frequency-to-amplitude relationship. *Journal of Experimental Psychology: Human Perception and Performance, 19,* 429–443.

Cutting, J. E., Vishton, P. M., & Braren, P. (1995). How to avoid collisions with stationary and with moving objects. *Psychological Review, 102,* 627–651.

Elliott, D. E., Helsen, W. F., & Chua, R. (2001). A century later: Woodworth's (1899) two-component model of goal-directed aiming. *Psychological Bulletin, 127,* 342–357.

Holt, K. G. (1996). "Constraint" versus "choice" in preferred movement patterns. *Behavioral and Brain Sciences, 19,* 76–77.

Kelso, J. A. S., Fuchs, A., Lancaster, R., Holroyd, T., Cheyne, D., & Weinberg, H. (1998). Dynamic cortical activity in the human brain reveals motor equivalence. *Nature, 392,* 814–818.

Li, L. (2000). Stability landscapes of walking and running near gait transition speed. *Journal of Applied Biomechanics, 16,* 428–435.

Semjen, A., Summers, J. J, & Cattaert, D. (1995). Hand coordination in bimanual circle drawing. *Journal of Experimental Psychology: Human Perception and Performance, 21,* 1139–1157.

STUDY QUESTIONS

1. How is Fitts' law related to the speed-accuracy trade-off phenomenon observed in many motor skills?

2. (a) Describe a prehension situation. (b) Indicate the components of this situation. (c) Describe the movement characteristics involved in each component, and how they might change in different prehension situations.

3. Discuss how the skill of handwriting can provide a good example of the meaning of the term *motor equivalence.*

4. Discuss why the performance of a skill requiring asymmetric bimanual coordination is difficult when it is first attempted.

5. (a) What are two examples of the rhythmic structures involved in walking and running? (b) Describe how gait lends itself to the use of an identified order parameter and control parameter to be the basis for assessment of coordination problems.

6. Discuss why it is important to maintain head stability during locomotion.

CHAPTER

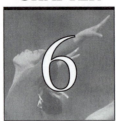

Proprioception and Vision

Concept: Proprioception and vision are important components of motor control

After completing this chapter, you will be able to

- Describe several methods used to investigate the role of proprioception in the control of movement

- Describe several movement characteristics for which proprioception plays an important motor control role

- Discuss the role vision plays in the motor control aiming movements

- Discuss how vision is involved in the motor control of prehension

- Discuss how vision is involved in the motor control of handwriting

- Discuss how vision is involved in the motor control of locomotion for several types of action goal

- Discuss how vision is involved in the motor control of catching a moving object

- Discuss how vision is involved in the motor control of striking a moving object

Application

When you reach for a glass of water to drink from it, both the proprioceptive and the visual sensory systems come into play as you carry out the action. Vision helps you locate the glass and grasp it with your hand and fingers. Proprioception helps you lift the glass, move it toward your mouth, and not have the glass slip out of your hand. Without the sensory information provided by these two key sensory systems, you would have considerably more difficulty carrying out relatively simple tasks like drinking from a glass. You accomplish other everyday skills, such as putting your door key into the keyhole, maneuvering around people as you walk in a hallway, and driving your car with ease, because of the information that proprioception and vision provide your motor control system. Similarly, sport activities also require and benefit from the roles played by the proprioceptive and visual sensory systems. For example, to catch a ball, you must see where the ball is, time its arrival to your hand, position your hand in space, and then close your fingers around the ball when it is in your hand.

Discussion

A key feature of any theory of motor control is the role played by sensory information in controlling action. Sensory receptors located in various parts of the human body provide this information. Two of the most important types of sensory information sources influencing the control of coordinated movement are proprioception and vision.

PROPRIOCEPTION AND MOTOR CONTROL

Proprioception refers to our sensation and perception of limb, trunk, and head position and movement.[1] Although it is often overlooked as one of our basic senses, proprioception is sensory information transmitted to the central nervous system about such movement characteristics as direction, location in space, velocity, and muscle activation. In closed-loop models of movement control, proprioceptive feedback plays a significant role, whereas in open-loop models, central commands control movement without involving proprioceptive feedback. Questions about whether we can control movements without proprioceptive feedback, and what role proprioceptive feedback plays in the control of coordinated movement, have intrigued movement scientists for many years (see Willingham, 1998, pp. 574f for a brief historical review).

Researchers have taken a variety of experimental approaches to determine the role of proprioception in controlling coordinated action. We discuss a few of these next to introduce you to the current thinking about this issue.

Investigating the Role of Proprioception

Proprioception is an important source of feedback. When action is under closed-loop control, proprioceptive information allows us to make movement corrections as we move. When an action is under open-loop control, as in a rapid, ballistic movement, proprioceptive feedback is available, but we cannot make movement corrections as we move because of time limitations.

Researchers have used several techniques to investigate the role of proprioception in the control of movement. We will consider four techniques in this discussion. Three of the techniques involve the observation of movement after **deafferentation** in some way. This means that the proprioceptive afferent pathways to the central nervous system are not available. The fourth involves the observation of movement while a tendon of a muscle involved in the control of a movement is vibrated, which distorts the proprioceptive feedback that is normally received from the muscle and tendon proprioceptors.

Surgical Deafferentation

One method used to investigate the role of proprioception in the control of movement involves the observation of movement of animals or humans following surgical deafferentation, which means that the afferent neural pathways associated with the movements of interest have been surgically severed or removed. Several studies have been reported in which a surgical deafferentation procedure was

---

[1]*Kinesthesis* is a term that is related to the term *proprioception*. There has been considerable debate about the distinction between them. Sometimes they are used to refer to specific types of sensory information; in other cases they are used synonymously. For the purposes of this book, the term *proprioception* is used to refer to sensory information about body and limb position and movement that is transmitted to the CNS from the proprioceptors.

---

proprioception   the perception of limb, body, and head movement characteristics; afferent neural pathways send to the central nervous system proprioceptive information about characteristics such as limb movement direction, location in space, and velocity.

deafferentation   a procedure that researchers use to make proprioceptive feedback unavailable (through surgically severing or removing afferent neural pathways involved in the movement); it also can result from injury or surgery to afferent neural pathways involved in proprioception

A CLOSER LOOK

Proprioceptors

The sensory receptors responsible for detecting body and limb position and movements, called proprioceptors, are located in the muscles, tendons, ligaments, and joints. In general, they function to provide the central nervous system (CNS) with information about body and limb position and changes in position. The various types of proprioceptors provide information concerning specific characteristics of body and limb position and movement. The following is a brief description of the proprioceptors and their function.

- **Muscle spindles.** Located in all skeletal muscles, lying in parallel with extrafusal muscle fibers and attached directly to the muscle sheath; consist of two types of sensory neurons: groups Ia (annulospiral endings) and II (flower-spray endings). Function to detect change in muscle fiber length, limb movement velocity and acceleration, and limb spatial position.
- **Golgi tendon organs (GTO).** Located at the junction of tendon and skeletal muscle; consist of Ib sensory neuron fibers (approximately one GTO for every ten muscle fibers). Function to detect force through the tendon due to lengthening

of skeletal muscle (work in synergy with muscle spindles); also involved in detecting spatial position.
- **Joint receptors.** Located in joint capsules and ligaments of all synovial joints; consist of four types of sensory neuron endings: Golgi-type endings (in ligaments), spray-type endings (in joint capsule), Pacinian corpuscle (near ligament attachments), and free nerve endings. Function to help detect joint spatial position, joint velocity, and joint direction; rather than provide information about the full range of joint position, they appear to act to detect the limits of a flexion or extension.

---

used with monkeys. Two sets of classic research studies in which this method of investigation was used will serve as examples of how researchers have used this technique to study proprioception.

Taub and Berman (1963, 1968) observed monkeys before and after surgical deafferentation as they performed well-developed motor skills, such as climbing, reaching, and grasping. Taub and Berman consistently found that the deafferented monkeys were still capable of performing the skills, although the degree of precision was notably less than it had been.

Taub and Berman looked at skills that were well developed. What would happen if experimenters used the same surgical deafferentation procedure with *newly learned skills?* Bizzi and his colleagues at Massachusetts Institute of Technology (e.g., Bizzi & Polit, 1979; Polit & Bizzi, 1978) took this approach in several experiments. They trained monkeys to point an arm at one of a series of lights when it came on. The monkeys could see the lights, but not their arms making the pointing movement. After they learned to point accurately to each light

when required, the monkeys were surgically deafferented so that no proprioceptive feedback information from the pointing arm was available during the movement. When the monkeys were again directed to point at each light as it came on, they were able to position their limbs accurately in the deafferented state. In fact, they could make accurate pointing movements from starting positions that were different from the starting positions used during training.

Surgically deafferenting human subjects for experimental purposes is not possible, for obvious reasons. However, some people are surgically deafferented because of certain trauma- or disease-related problems. For example, rheumatoid arthritis patients who have had finger *joint replacement* surgery have no joint receptors available. A good example of using this approach to the study of proprioception is an experiment done many years ago by Kelso, Holt, and Flatt (1980). Patients who had had their metacarpophalangeal joints removed and replaced with flexible silicone rubber implants performed finger-positioning movements. On each

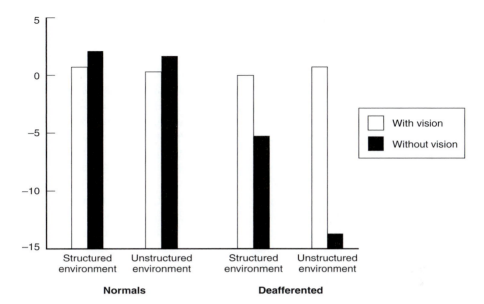

FIGURE 6.1   Results of the experiment by Blouin et al. showing the amount of error during the reproduction of an arm position for normal and deafferented subjects with vision of the environment available (structured) or not available (unstructured), and vision of the moving arm available or not.   [Source: Data from Blouin, J., et al. (1993). Reference systems for coding spatial information in normal subjects and a deafferented patient. *Experimental Brain Research, 93*, 324–331, Springer-Verlag, New York, NY.]

trial, participants moved their fingers to a criterion finger position or a criterion distance, returned their fingers to a new starting point, and then attempted to reproduce the criterion position or distance. Results indicated that the patients had little difficulty in accurately reproducing the criterion finger *position* from a starting point that was different from the original starting point. However, they did have problems reproducing the movement *distance* from these new starting points.

Deafferentation Due to Sensory Polyneuropathy

The observation of movement characteristics of people who have a *sensory polyneuropathy* involving a limb provides a non-surgical technique for investigating deafferented humans. For these people, the large myelinated fibers of the limb are lost, leading to a loss of all sensory information except pain and temperature. The efferent motor pathways are typically intact. A good example of this research strategy is an experiment by Blouin et al.

(1993). They compared a sensory polyneuropathy patient with normal participants on a pointing task involving an arm moving a pointer. On some trials, participants could see the apparatus environment, whereas on other trials, they performed without this visual information available. Results, shown in figure 6.1, were that with vision, the patient performed as accurately as the normal participants. However, without vision of either the environment or the arm while moving, the deafferented patient consistently undershot the target. Thus, without visual feedback, the deafferented patient was not able to reproduce movement accurately to a specific location in space.

Temporary Deafferentation

The third proprioceptive feedback removal technique, which is used with humans, is known as the *nerve block technique.* To investigate an arm movement, the researcher places a blood pressure cuff just above the participant's elbow and then inflates until the person no longer can feel anything with the fingers. In a phenomenon similar to what you experience when your arm is "asleep," the ischemic condition keeps afferent pathways from functioning. However, the efferent pathways remain unaffected. In several studies (e.g., Kelso & Holt, 1980; Laszlo, 1966, 1967), people could perform finger and arm spatial positioning in the absence of afferent sensory information from the muscles and joints of the fingers, hand, and forearm.

Tendon Vibration Technique

A procedure in which movement is observed while proprioceptive feedback is distorted rather than removed involves the high-speed vibration of a tendon connected to a muscle that is an agonist in the movement of interest. This vibration distorts muscle spindle firing patterns, which leads to a distortion of proprioceptive feedback. Examples of the use of this technique can be found in several experiments reported by Verschueren. For example, one experiment (Verschueren, Swinnen, Cordo, & Dounskaia, 1999a) applied vibration to the tendons of the biceps and/or anterior deltoids of the preferred arm of blindfolded participants as they simultaneously drew circles with each arm. The results (see figure 6.2) showed that the vibration influenced the spatial characteristics of the circles drawn by the vibrated arm, but not for the nonvibrated, nonpreferred arm. In addition, the vibration of the preferred arm influenced the relative phase relationship between the two arms during the circle drawing.

The Role of Proprioceptive Feedback

Research evidence shows that people *can* carry out certain limb movements in the absence of proprioceptive feedback. However, there appear to be several distinct limitations to this capability. Because of these limitations, it is possible to identify the various roles of proprioceptive feedback in the control of human movement. We will consider three that are especially notable.

First, proprioception influences *movement accuracy.* Several results from the experiments just discussed support this conclusion. In the Taub and Berman studies, the monkeys were clumsier while

climbing, grasping, and reaching than they had been before deafferentation. In fact, they had difficulty grasping food with their hands in this condition. In the Bizzi experiments, the researchers noted that when the animal's posture was altered, pointing accuracy diminished in the deafferented condition. And in the Kelso, Holt, and Flatt experiment, the human participants maintained only positioning accuracy following joint capsule replacement; distance movements were severely disrupted.

It is important to point out that movement accuracy effects have also been demonstrated when researchers block or distort a person's vision while performing a movement. Although this is an indirect method for investigating the role of proprioception (vision is the only sensory system that participants cannot use; all other sensory sources of information remain available), the movement accuracy results of experiments that have used this technique correspond with those described earlier that directly blocked or distorted proprioception. For example, Robertson and Elliot (1996) showed that distorting the vision of skilled gymnasts increased the number of steps they used to walk as fast as possible along a balance beam and increased their movement form errors. When their vision was completely blocked, only their movement form errors increased. When Danion, Boyadijan, and Marin (2000) blocked the vision of skilled gymnasts, they veered from a straight line as they walked. And Glover and Dixon (2001) showed that the lack of vision of an object while reaching for it, even though participants had seen it before initiating their movement, resulted in their limb trajectory being less accurate during the initial portion of its flight.

The influence of proprioception on movement accuracy appears to be due to the specific kinematic and kinetic feedback provided by the proprioceptors to the central nervous system (CNS). Feedback about limb displacement provides the basis for spatial position corrections, which enable the limb to achieve spatial accuracy by a continuous updating of limb position to the CNS, which in turn can send movement commands that will modify the position

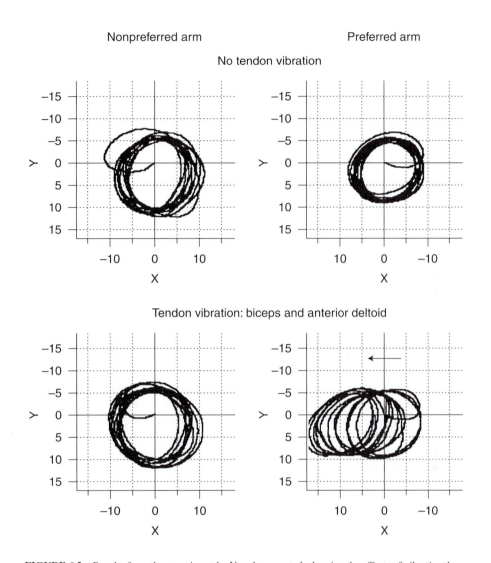

FIGURE 6.2   Results from the experiment by Verschueren et al. showing the effects of vibrating the tendons attached to the biceps and anterior deltoid of the preferred arm during bimanual circle drawing with no vision of the arms. The top row shows one participant's drawings during one trial when no tendon vibration was applied. The bottom row shows the drawings by the same participant during one trial with tendon vibration. [Adapted from Figure 1A–D, p. 185, of Verschueren, Swinnen, Cordo, & Dounskaia (1999). *Experimental Brain Research, 127*, 182–192. Copyright © 1999 Springer-Verlag, New York, NY.]

accordingly, provided that the movement occurs for a sufficient amount of time to allow movement corrections to occur. In addition, proprioceptors provide feedback about limb velocity and force, which influence movement distance accuracy.

Second, proprioceptive feedback influences the *timing of the onset of motor commands.* An experiment by Bard et al. (1992) provides a good example of evidence for this role. They compared movements of normal participants with a patient deafferented due to a sensory polyneuropathy. The participants were asked to simultaneously extend an index finger and raise the heel of the ipsilateral foot. When they performed this task in reaction to an auditory signal, both the normal and the deafferented participants performed similarly by initiating the finger extension first. We would expect this if a common central command were sent to each effector. Because of the difference in distance of efferent neural pathways to the finger and heel, finger movement would occur first. Conversely, when asked to do the task at their own pace, the normal participants raised the heel first; this suggests that they based timing of the finger movement onset on proprioceptive feedback about heel movement. In contrast, the deafferented patients performed as they had in the reactive situation, indicating that they used a central command rather than proprioceptive movements feedback as the basis for the timing of the onset of the heel and finger movements.

Finally, proprioception plays an important role in various aspects of the *coordination of body and limb segments*. Three coordination characteristics influenced by proprioceptive feedback will serve to demonstrate this role.

First, *postural control* requires proprioceptive feedback. Although a considerable amount of research evidence shows that postural control is a function of many interacting variables, such as vision, the musculoskeletal system, activity of the cerebellum and basal ganglia, cognitive processes, the tactile sensory system, and proprioception, problems with any of these will lead to postural dysfunction. Jeka and colleagues have demonstrated (e.g., Jeka, Ribiero, Oie, & Lackner, 1998) the importance of proprioception in postural control by showing that proprioception, together with tactile information, functions to provide essential information to the CNS to enable a person to control upright stance posture in body sway situations.

The second coordination characteristic involves the *spatial-temporal coupling between limbs and limb segments*. Results of the experiment by Verschueren et al. (1999a), which we considered earlier, show the importance of proprioceptive feedback for the spatial and temporal coupling between the arms when we perform bimanual coordination tasks. And in another study by this same researcher and colleagues (Verschueren et al. 1999b), they demonstrated that proprioception influences the coupling between two limb segments of the same limb, such as the upper arm and forearm. Also, Jackson et al. (2000), in a study that involved a woman whose left arm was temporarily deafferented because of a stroke, showed that she had limb-coupling problems during the performance of a task involving prehension.

The third coordination characteristic influenced by proprioceptive feedback is the *adapting to movement situations that require the use of non-preferred coordination patterns*. Bonnard and Pailhous (1999) demonstrated this effect when they asked an adult patient who was deafferented, due to sensory neuropathy 15 years earlier, to repetitively move a lever back and forth to maintain rhythmical movements for 100 sec. When the patient could choose the movement amplitude (i.e., distance) to maintain with the rhythm specified by a metronome (i.e., frequency), she maintained consistent movement amplitude and frequency (see figure 6.3), even when she could not see the results of her movements. But when asked to perform at the same frequency, but with the movement amplitude 95 percent larger (the experimenter-constrained condition), she maintained the frequency but not the amplitude, which drifted over time toward her preferred amplitude. In contrast, when non-deafferented adults performed the same task, they maintained the frequency and amplitude for both the preferred and the experimenter-constrained conditions.

VISION AND MOTOR CONTROL

There are two components of visual function. Each component receives information in a different segment of the field of vision, which is said to extend to 200 degrees horizontally and 160 degrees vertically. One component is *central vision,* sometimes referred to as foveal vision. Central vision detects information only in small areas, having a range of

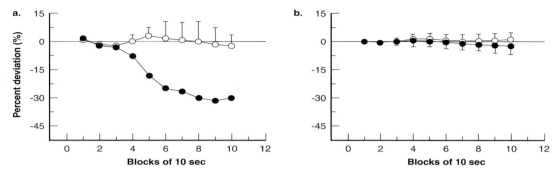

FIGURE 6.3 Results of the experiment by Bonnard and Pailhous showing the percentage of deviation from the initial amplitude for repetitive rhythmical arm movements for the preferred (open circles) and constrained (filled circles) initial movements, which the deafferented patient (graph A) and a normal control subject (graph B) attempted to maintain without seeing the results of their movements. Note that for the constrained but not for the preferred rhythm, the amplitude of the deafferented patient's movements began to deviate farther from the goal amplitude as the amount of time increased within a trial. [*Source:* Figure 2, panels c and d, p. 571 in Bonnard, M., & Pailhous, J. (1999). Contribution of proprioceptive feedback to preferred versus constrained space-time behavior in rhythmical movements. *Experimental Brain Research, 128,* 568–572.]

about 2 to 5 degrees. The detection of information in the visual field outside these limits occurs by means of *peripheral vision.*

Vision Predominates
Our Sensory-Perceptual Systems

Of all our sensory systems, we tend to use and trust vision the most. For example, when you first learned to type or play the piano, you undoubtedly felt that if you could not see your fingers hit each key, you could not perform accurately. Beginning dancers and stroke patients learning to walk have a similar problem. They often act as if they cannot perform the activity if they cannot watch their feet.

These anecdotal experiences illustrate our tendency to give vision a predominant role when we perform motor skills. Empirical research evidence also supports this phenomenon. The best example is a classic experiment by Lee and Aronson (1974) that is often referred to as the "moving room" experiment. Participants stood in a room in which the walls could move up or down, as well as forward or backward. However, the floor was stationary and did not move. The researchers observed the participants' postural responses to the movement of the walls. When the walls moved, children and adults made posture correction adjust-

ments that were in keeping with trying to maintain their standing balance when the walls and floor were moving. But because the floor did not move, their proprioceptors were not signaling that their bodies were losing stability. Only their visual systems detected any loss of balance.

The moving room experiment demonstrates the special priority we assign to vision in our daily activities. In that experiment, when the proprioceptors and vision provided conflicting information to the central nervous system, people gave attention to vision while ignoring the proprioceptors. The result was that they initiated unnecessary postural adjustments.

In the sections that follow, we will look at several types of motor skills to see the role that vision plays when people perform them. Some of these skills were included in chapter 5, where we considered performance characteristics that provided insight into how the motor control system operates to enable performance. Although vision was described as being involved in the control of these skills, the specific roles played by vision were not discussed. It will be helpful to make the connection between the discussion of these skills in the following sections with what you learned from chapter 5 about the control of these skills.

VISION AND MANUAL AIMING

A manual aiming task requires a person to move one or both arms over a prescribed distance to a target. In real-world settings, this action is required when a person puts a key in a keyhole, places a pen in a penholder, types on a keyboard, or plays the piano. Laboratory approximations of this type of action typically involve a person's holding a stylus on a starting point and then moving it to hit a target as accurately as possible. In some experiments the participants must hit the target while moving as quickly as possible, whereas in others they must move at specific speeds.

Vision's Role Depends on the Phases of the Aiming Movement

Vision is involved in different ways at different times during an aiming movement. Research evidence has shown that there are three distinct phases of performing a manual aiming movement (see figure 6.4). The role vision plays in the control of the movement is different in each phase.

The first phase is the *movement preparation phase,* which begins as soon as a person has made the decision to perform a manual aiming action. Here, the person uses vision to determine the specific movement characteristics required by the situation, such as the direction and distance the limb must travel and the target spatial orientation and size. These characteristics are the regulatory characteristics we discussed in chapter 1. The next two phases involve the actual movement of the limb. The second phase, the *initial flight phase,* includes the beginning of the limb movement in the general direction of the target. This phase is typically ballistic (which means it occurs very rapidly) and open-loop, i.e., without the influence of feedback. Vision plays a minor role in this phase, although it acquires early limb displacement and velocity information that is used later for error correction purposes. The third phase is the *termination phase,* which begins just before and ends when the target is hit. If the individual has sufficient time to use visual feedback and make movement modifications, vision plays a critical role in providing the information he or she needs to make these alterations so that the limb will hit the target.

The Coordination of Vision and Hand Movement in Manual Aiming

When a person makes an aiming movement with a hand, how do the eyes and hand work together to carry out this action? Researchers have addressed this question by using eye movement tracking equipment and 2-D or 3-D motion analysis equipment to analyze a person's eye and hand movements when he or she performs a manual aiming task. For eye movement analysis, the characteristic of interest is the *point of gaze,* which is the specific location in the environment on which central (i.e., foveal) vision is fixated at any particular moment. To assess the coordination of vision and hand movement, researchers calculate the relationship between the timing and/or location of the termination of the point of gaze with the timing and/or location of the hand movement. If the point of gaze and hand movement are temporally or spatially coupled during an aiming movement, the point of gaze should be at a specific location at a consistent proportion of the total movement time and/or distance of the hand movement.

A good example of research evidence that demonstrates the coupling between vision and hand movement is an experiment by Helsen, Elliott, Starkes, and Ricker (1998). Participants were seated at a table and were asked to move their index fingers 40 cm to the right from a starting location in front of them to a 1-cm by 2-cm target as fast as possible. Both point of gaze and hand movements tended to undershoot the target and then made one or more corrections to hit the target. The analysis of eye and finger movements showed that the participants typically initiated eye movements approximately 70 ms *before* they began to move their hands from the start location. The initial eye movement moved the point of gaze very close to the target after which they made a second eye movement to correct the undershooting of the first. The initial hand movement traveled about 95 percent of the total distance, after which one or two additional accelerations were made to home in on the target. The point of gaze typically arrived at the target 450 msec *before* the finger, which would allow for in-flight hand movement corrections based on visual feedback. The researchers found evidence for *tem-*

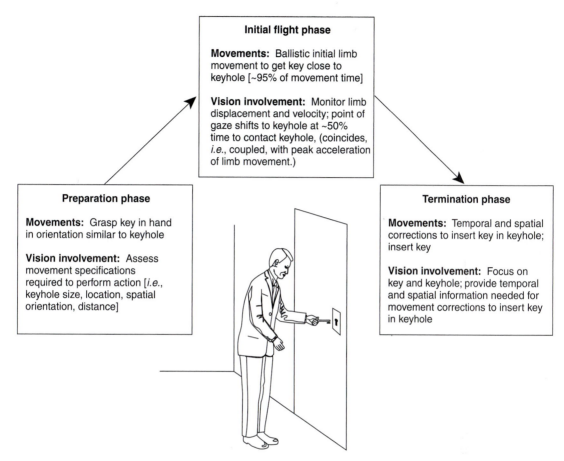

FIGURE 6.4 The three phases of manual aiming task in which vision plays an important role can be illustrated by the task of putting a key into a keyhole in a lock on a door.

poral coupling between the eye movements and hand movements because the completion of the initial eye movement coincided with the timing of the peak acceleration and velocity of the hand movement. Evidence for *spatial coupling* was shown by the point of gaze consistently terminating on the target when the hand movement was at 50 percent of the total movement distance.

More recently, the same researchers (Helsen, Elliott, Starkes, & Ricker, 2000) showed that the initiation of elbow and shoulder movements is also coupled in time with eye and finger movement initiation. The sequence of events was that the eyes

moved first, followed by the shoulder, then the elbow, and finally the finger. The initial eye movement traveled approximately 90 percent of the distance to the target, before moving to the target. On every trial for every participant, the point of gaze was on the target long before the hand arrived at the target. The results of these experiments, and others like it (e.g., Helsen, Starkes, & Buekers, 1997), support the importance of vision in the three phases of performing an aiming task described earlier. It is important to note that the actual limb movement part of the aiming task involves only the second and third of these phases, which has led

A CLOSER LOOK

The Eye and Hand Movements of Artists Painting and Drawing

An excellent website (http://www.physiol.ox.ac.uk/~rcm/pem/) presents an exhibit titled, "The Painter's Eye Movements," which is a nine-page exhibition of the eye and hand movements of skilled artists as they paint and draw from models. The site includes a brief description, with pictures, of eye-movement tracking equipment and how it is used with hand-movement equipment to provide information about eye and hand movements.

some researchers to refer to a two-phase model of limb control for visually directed movements. As the Helsen et al. experiments have nicely demonstrated, the initial flight phase is a ballistic movement prepared from visually detected information before the initiation of movement. This phase continues for as much as 90 percent of the distance to the target. Then, the termination phase begins in which visual feedback is used to correct the trajectory and speed of the arm movement so that the target will be hit.

The Amount of Time Needed to Make Vision-Based Movement Corrections

An important factor that influences the role of vision in an aiming movement is the amount of time available to use visual feedback to make movement corrections while the movement is in progress. Corrections can occur only when the person has sufficient time to detect and modify the movement. This means there is a minimum total movement time requirement in order for the performer to be able to use visual feedback to correct movement errors prior to the completion of the movement.

The important question here is, *what is the minimum amount of time required* for movement corrections to be carried out on the basis of visual feedback? Researchers have been attempting to answer this question since the end of the nineteenth century (e.g., Woodworth, 1899). The most vigorous effort to investigate this question occurred in the latter part of the twentieth century, beginning with an influential experiment by Keele and Posner in 1968. Unfortunately, all this research effort has not provided us with a precise answer to the question (see Carlton, 1992, for an excellent review of this research). Part of the problem is that different experimental procedures have resulted in a variety of time estimates for the processing of visual feedback.

The most common experimental procedure has been to have people perform manual aiming movements with different goal movement times. On some trials, the lights would go out just as the person began to move, whereas on other trials the lights remained on. The logic to this procedure was that if visual feedback were necessary, aiming accuracy would decrease with the lights out because the person could not see the target and therefore would not be able to use visual feedback. When participants did not know when the lights would be on or off, the amount of time to process visual feedback was estimated to be between 190 and 260 ms. However, later experiments used the same lights-on-or-off technique, but participants knew when they would perform under each condition (e.g., Zelaznik, Hawkins, & Kisselburgh, 1983; Elliott & Allard, 1985). This advance knowledge indicated that visual feedback could be used in less than 100 ms.

Other experimental procedures have led researchers to conclude that visual feedback can be processed in amounts of time that are faster or slower than those estimated by the lights-on-or-off procedure. These have included such procedures as distorting the visual information by having people wear prism glasses (e.g., Smith & Bowen, 1980, estimated the time to be about 150 msec); moving the target location after the person initiated a movement to a target (e.g., Brenner & Smeets, 1997, estimated the time to be about 110 msec); and preventing visual feedback for portions of the distance to the target (e.g., Spijkers & Lochner, 1994, estimated the time to be about 135 msec).

Although it is not possible to establish an exact minimum amount of time required to use visual feedback to enable movement corrections, it appears that an estimate of *100 to 160 msec* is reasonable for simple manual aiming tasks. How well this generalizes to other skills is not known at this time, although several researchers have investigated this question using tasks that require people to intercept a moving object, such as ball catching or hitting (e.g., Bootsma & van Wieringen, 1990). Although the time estimates are again related to the procedures used in the experiments, the 100 to 160 msec estimate would capture the time estimates reported in these experiments.

In terms of the three-phase model of a manual aiming movement described earlier, the minimum amount of time required to make visual feedback–based corrections establishes a time limit for situations to which this model can apply. If the limb movement is faster than the minimum amount of time, only the first two phases of the model describe the movement. In this situation the "initial flight phase" becomes the only flight phase; the movement must terminate at the end of this phase without the possibility of modifying movement errors. Thus, the entire movement would be under open-loop control, which means that the accuracy of the movement would depend on the quality of the preparation before the initiation of movement.

Is this issue about the minimum time required to use visual feedback of any consequence to the performance of skills other than the manual aiming tasks performed in laboratories? If we generalize the notion of manual aiming to skills involving the "aiming" of the arm to catch a ball, or to hit a ball, or the "aiming" of the foot to step on a stair step, then the minimum time issue becomes relevant to sports skills and activities of daily living. For example, whether or not a person will have time to adjust his or her initial hand movement to catch a ball will depend on the amount of time available to catch the ball. If the ball speed is too fast or the distance the ball travels is too short to allow any movement modification, success at catching the ball will depend on the initial hand position. Similarly, if a person is stair climbing at a pace that is too fast to allow foot-position adjustments while the foot is in flight, the risk of falling increases.

VISION AND PREHENSION

In chapter 5, we considered evidence showing that prehension and manual aiming are different actions. An important difference between them is the object manipulation goal of the prehension action. Although target characteristics influence the control of both manual aiming and prehension, contact with the target does not terminate a prehension action. What the person does with the object after it is contacted is an essential component of prehension. But because of the similarities between the two actions, vision is involved in the control of prehension in some ways that are similar to its role in the control of manual aiming.

As in manual aiming, vision provides information prior to the initiation of movement, such as the distance to the object and important regulatory characteristics of the object, such as its shape, texture, and the environmental context in which the object is located. The motor control system uses this information to initiate the transport phase of prehension, during which the hand and fingers begin to form the grasp characteristics required when the object is contacted and manipulated. Then, like manual aiming, vision provides information to the CNS while the limb is in flight so that the hand can make needed movement modifications as it approaches and grasps the object. As was the case for manual aiming, a person can make these in-flight arm and hand movement modifications only if there is sufficient time to do so.

Monocular versus Binocular Vision

One of the questions researchers have investigated concerning vision and prehension relates to *the use of monocular (i.e., one eye) compared to binocular (i.e., two eyes) vision* to reach and grasp an object. Research evidence (e.g., Goodale & Servos, 1996; Coull et al., 2000; Servos, 2000) has shown that the motor control system operates more effectively and efficiently when it receives visual information from *both* eyes. Although people can reach and pick up

A CLOSER LOOK

Time to Contact: The Optical Variable Tau

In situations in which a person moves toward an object to make contact with it, or the object moves toward the person, such as when a person is catching or hitting a thrown ball, vision plays an important role in specifying *when* to initiate the action and make contact with the object. The important visual information in these situations is the *time to contact,* which is the amount of time remaining until the object contacts the person (or vice versa) from a specific distance (see Bootsma & Peper, 1992). Time to contact is specified according to the relative rate of change of the size of the image of the object on the retina of the eye. As the person approaches the object, or vice versa, the object produces an increasingly larger retinal image. When this image attains a certain critical size, it triggers the action required by the situation.

In the early 1970s, David Lee (1974) provided evidence that time to contact is specified by an optical variable, which he termed *tau* (τ). He also showed that *tau* can be quantified mathematically by relating object size, the distance of the object from the person, and the angle subtended at the person by the object size and distance. In mathematical terms, *tau* is the inverse of the relative rate of change of the visual angle subtended by the moving object, given the speed of approach of the object is constant.

The motor control benefit of the *tau* variable is its predictive function, which allows action initiation and object contact to occur "automatically" at a specific time to contact regardless of the speed of the object or person. When driving a car, for example, the driver's initiation and amount of braking action to avoid collision with another car is not dependent on the driver's cognitive knowledge of the distance to and velocity of the other car. Rather, by specifying the time to contact at any distance and velocity, the rate of change of the size of the retinal image of the other car provides the information needed by the driver to determine the type of braking, or deceleration, required by the situation

---

objects when the use of only one eye is available, the accuracy and efficiency of the movement decrease as the distance to the object increases. Experiments (e.g., Coull et al., 2000) that have shown this influence of distance provide support for the view of the importance of binocular vision for *depth perception.*

The monocular vision problem appears to be due to a preparation-phase problem that results from an underestimation of the distance to objects and their size prior to the initiation of movement. Movement kinematic evidence for this problem is the lower peak velocities and smaller grip apertures (i.e., the distance between thumb and fingers in the grasp position) during the transport phase. Interestingly, when people are not permitted to use binocular vision, and must reach for and grasp an object using monocular vision, they will move their heads in a manner that enables them to obtain more accurate information about the size of an object and the distance to it (see Marotta, Kruyer, & Goodale, 1998).

Central and Peripheral Vision

Another question of interest concerning the motor control of prehension relates to the *roles of central and peripheral vision.* The current understanding of these roles is that each makes specific contributions to the prehension action. For example, research by Sivak and MacKenzie (1990) showed that peripheral vision provides the CNS with information about the environmental context and the moving limb. When they blocked the participants' use of peripheral vision, which meant they could use only central vision for reaching and grasping an object, the organization and control of the transport phase was affected, but not the grasp phase. Central vision provides information specific to the object itself, such as the size and shape of the object. When the researchers blocked the participants' use of central vision, which meant they could use only peripheral vision for reaching and grasping an object, problems occurred with both the transport and grasp phases.

A CLOSER LOOK

Visual Cues Can Aid Walking for People with Parkinson's Disease

One of the primary movement disorders common to people who have Parkinson's disease is slowness of gait (i.e., gait hypokinesia). Two questions have interested researchers and physical therapists concerning this gait problem. One, what movement characteristic accounts for the slowness? Two possibilities are cadence, which would mean that the difficulty relates to the rhythm, or beat, of the walking pace, and stride length, which would mean that the slowness is due to strides that are shorter than normal. The answer to this question is important for the second question: Is there a rehabilitation strategy that would help patients improve their control of walking gait speed?

To address these questions, Morris, Iansek, Matyas, and Summers (1994) compared walking gaits of Parkinson's patients with age-matched controls (60–85 years old) for instructions to walk along a 12-m walkway at "a comfortable pace" and at a "fast speed." *The results showed this:*

* *The Parkinson's patients walked more slowly than the control participants at both speeds, and had shorter stride lengths, but similar cadences.*

Then, the researchers provided visual cues to the Parkinson's patients by placing 50-cm by 5-cm laminated strips of cardboard on the walkway at intervals matching the mean stride lengths of the control participants for each speed. The patients were instructed to walk over each floor marker as they walked along the walkway. *The results showed this:*

* *The patients' velocity and stride lengths were similar to the controls for both speeds.*

The researchers concluded from their results that the regulation of stride length was the "key deficit" in gait slowness for patients with Parkinson's disease. And visual cues can be an effective rehabilitation strategy for helping these patients regulate gait speed.

In light of these results, it is interesting to note that several researchers (e.g., McIntosh, Brown, Rice, & Thaut, 1997) have provided evidence to show the effectiveness of rhythmic auditory stimulation, which involves embedding a tone at specific intervals in music to provide a stepping pace for Parkinson's patients. Walking speeds can be varied by using music of different tempos

---

The results of the Sivak and MacKenzie experiment match those reported in other research by showing the distinct roles played by central and peripheral vision in the control of aiming and prehension movements (see Jeannerod & Marteniuk, 1992, for a review of this research). Consider, for example, that when a person sits at a table with the intent to reach up and pick up a cup, central vision fixates on the cup during this prehension preparation phase to obtain information on size, shape, etc. Then, in the transport phase, as the person's hand begins to move toward the cup, the moving hand will be seen by peripheral vision. As the grasp phase begins, when the hand nears the cup, central vision again is used to provide the information needed to accurately grasp the cup.

These distinctive behavioral roles for central and peripheral vision, along with supporting neurophysiological evidence, have led some re-

searchers to propose that the visual system is actually two anatomical systems that operate in parallel (see Bridgeman, 1996, for a more detailed discussion of the two vision systems). Paillard (1980), for example, proposed that a *kinetic* visual channel was responsible for processing visual information in peripheral vision. This channel would process high-speed movement information and control limb movement direction. To process visual information in central vision and for slow-speed movements, Paillard proposed a *static* visual channel.[2] Other researchers have proposed similar two-channel visual systems but have given them different names. Some examples include the *perception* system, which would be responsible for

[2] For a review of research that has tested Paillard's two visual systems model, and two experiments that support and extend this model, see Proteau, Bolvin, Linossier, and Abahnini (2000)

FIGURE 6.5 Handwriting examples from the experiment by Smyth and Silvers showing errors related to writing without vision available (bottom line in (a); right side of arrows in others) as compared to writing with vision available. (a) shows errors as deviating from the horizontal; (b) shows errors as adding and deleting strokes; (c) shows adding and deleting of letters; (d) shows adding or deleting of repetitions of double letters; (e) shows reversing of letters. [Reprinted from Smyth, M.M., & Silvers, G. (1987). Functions of vision in the control of handwriting. *Acta Phychologica, 65,* 47–64. With kind permission of Elsevier Science-NL, Sara Burgerhartstraat 25, 1055 KV Amsterdam, The Netherlands.]

recognizing and describing what a person is seeing, and the *perception-action* system which would be responsible for perceptually guided movements (Goodale & Milner, 1992); another is the *focal* vision system, which is responsible for the detection of static objects by central vision, and the *ambient* vision system, which detects objects and movement around us, involving peripheral vision (Trevarthen, 1968). One important characteristic of the two systems relates to our conscious awareness of the information detected by each system. We are generally consciously aware of information detected by the visual system related to central vision, but not of that detected by the system related to peripheral vision.

VISION AND HANDWRITING

A substantial amount of research evidence indicates that vision plays an important role in the control of handwriting actions. A good example of this

role was provided by Smyth and Silvers (1987), who presented evidence showing that a person who is asked to write with his or her eyes closed adds extra strokes to some letters, omits strokes from some letters, and duplicates some letters. And if visual feedback is delayed while a person is writing, that person makes many errors, including repeating and adding letters.

On the basis of their own research and that of others, Smyth and Silvers proposed that vision performs two distinct functions in the control of handwriting. One function is to help the writer *control the overall spatial arrangement of words on a horizontal line.* We see an example of this function in figure 6.5, where handwriting samples taken from people writing without vision available show distinct deviations from a horizontal line. The second function for vision is to help the writer *produce accurate handwriting patterns,* such as the appropriate strokes and letters required for the written material. Again, evidence of this is seen in figure

A CLOSER LOOK

Gymnasts' Use of Vision on the Balance Beam

Shannon Robertson and her colleagues (e.g., Robertson, Collins, Elliott, & Starkes, 1994; Robertson & Elliott, 1996) have shown that skilled gymnasts use visual information as they perform their routines on a balance beam. In several studies, they involved gymnasts walking as fast as possible across a standard balance beam (5 m long x 10.5 cm wide). In the Robertson and Elliott (1996) experiment, nine female college varsity gymnasts performed the task with full vision, no vision, or distorted vision (goggles with a prism oriented vision to the left or right). Results for each condition were as follows:

	Amount of time to cross the beam	Number of times stepped off beam	Number of steps to cross beam	Number of form errors
Full Vision	3.0 sec.	0.2	7	10
No Vision	4.0 sec.	2.5	8	30
Distorted Vision	7.5 sec.	8.4	9	42

The increase in form errors when the gymnasts had no vision or distorted vision was due primarily to deviations from an upright posture. These deviations resulted from the gymnasts' postural adjustments to maintain their balance as they walked. When these results are considered in terms of our discussion of the role of vision in human motor control, they are consistent with experiments involving locomotor daily living activities by demonstrating the significant role vision plays in helping us maintain dynamic posture.

6.5. People who wrote without vision available added or omitted strokes, added extra letters, deleted letters, and reversed letters.

VISION AND LOCOMOTION

Although scientists in a variety of fields have studied locomotion, the study of the role of vision in the control of locomotion does not have a long history. However, we have learned from this research that vision plays important roles in the motor control of locomotion. To introduce you to these roles, we will consider the following three types of locomotion situations, each of which is defined by the locomotion action goal.

Maintaining Dynamic Postural Balance

In both daily activities and sports, we engage in locomotor activities in which an essential goal is to maintain postural balance. Although the situations may involve other action goals, the maintenance of postural balance is critical to achieve them. Consider,

for example, situations such as walking in an empty hallway on your way to class, or performing a balance-beam routine as a gymnast. In each of these situations, the people involved would find it difficult to achieve the primary action goals of the activity without maintaining dynamic postural balance.

How does vision enable people to maintain their balance in locomotion situations like these? For locomotion in general, research evidence indicates that *peripheral vision* plays a key role (e.g., Assaiante & Amblard, 1992). More specifically, peripheral vision detects visual cues in the environment by assessing **optical flow** patterns. Optical flow refers to the pattern of rays of light that strike the retina of the eye from all parts of the environment. The word "flow" is significant because it indicates

optical flow The patterns of rays of light that strike the retina of the eye that emanate from and are specific to objects and features in the environment.

the dynamic nature of this visually detected information. As we move in an environment, or when something in our environment moves, our visual system detects and interprets invariant patterns of light rays that are specific to and emanate from objects and features in that environment. As a result, vision's use of optical flow allows us to locomote through an environment and helps us to achieve action goals. (For an excellent review of research concerning optical flow and locomotion, and an experiment involving the use of optical flow and locomotion, and an experiment involving the use of optical flow, see Konczak, 1994.)

Contacting Objects

When an athlete performs a long jump, the athlete needs to make contact with the take-off board at maximum running speed. This run-up portion of the long jump can be thought of as similar to an aiming task; it requires the athlete to move a certain distance and then hit a target. The target is the take-off board, which is about 20 cm long (from front to back) and 1.2 m wide (from side to side). If any part of the athlete's foot extends beyond the back edge of the board (i.e., the edge nearer the landing pit), a foul is called and the jump does not count. On the other hand, if the tip of the foot strikes short of the board, the jump is that amount shorter because the jump distance is measured from the back edge of the board.

The motor control question related to the run-up is this: What does the athlete do during the run-up to hit the take-off board as accurately as possible? One possibility is that the athlete performs the same programmed step pattern during each run-up on each jump. This would mean that any error in hitting the take-off board would be due to an error in the programmed step pattern. However, research evidence has shown that this is *not* what the athlete does. Although each long jumper takes a number of steps during each run-up that is specific to him or her, the step lengths of the last few steps vary across run-ups. Most scholars now agree that the reason for this is that the athletes use visual information that specifies the amount of time it will take to contact the take-off board. The motor

control system uses this *time-to-contact* information, which is specified by the visual variable *tau* (τ), to make stride-length adjustments during the last few steps to correct for the distance error that has accumulated during the run-up. Without these adjustments, the athlete would either be short or long of the take-off board.

In what has become a classic experiment demonstrating this time-to-contact influence for a locomotor skill requiring object contact, Lee, Lishman, and Thomson (1982) filmed three highly skilled female long jumpers during their approaches to the take-off board. By analyzing stride-length changes as each athlete approached and contacted the take-off board for a series of six long jumps, the researchers observed several important gait pattern characteristics. We will examine these using the results from one of these athletes (an Olympic-level performer), presented in figure 6.6.

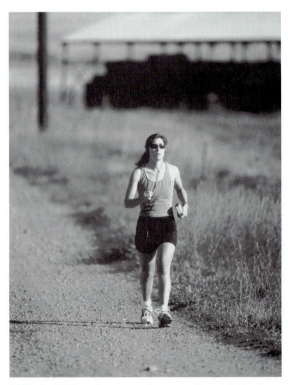

Vision is used in various ways when we walk on a dirt road.

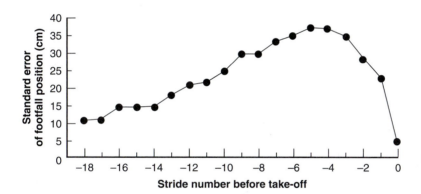

FIGURE 6.6   Redrawn from results of the experiment by Lee, Lishman, and Thomson showing the stride-length characteristics (top) and the standard errors for 6 long jumps by an Olympic-class female long jumper. [From Lee, D.N., Lishman, J.R., & Thomson, J.A. (1982). Regulation of gait in long jumping. *Journal of Experimental Psychology: Human Perception and Performance, 8,* 448–459. Copyright © 1982 The American Psychological Association. Adapted with permission.]

Initially, the athlete's stride length increased at a relatively constant rate for the first five to six strides; it then began to become similar for the next six strides. These strides were relatively consistent across the six jumps. Then, *on the final six strides*, something different occurred. The athlete made stride-length adjustments so that she could hit the board accurately. In fact, she made almost 50 percent of these adjustments on the last stride. The lower half of the figure shows why she had to make these adjustments. As the athlete ran down the track, small inconsistencies in each stride had a cumulative effect, so that when she was five strides from the board the error had risen to 37 cm. If she had not adjusted her stride lengths on the remaining strides, she would have missed hitting the take-off board by a long distance.

These stride-length characteristics led the authors to describe the long jump run-up as consisting of two phases: an *initial accelerative phase*, where an athlete produces stereotypic stride patterns, followed by a *zeroing-in phase,* where the athlete modifies stride patterns to eliminate accumulated error. They concluded that a long jumper bases the correction process during the second phase on visual information obtained *in advance of* these strides. This means that the visual system picks up time-to-contact information from the board and directs the locomotor control system to make appropriate stride-length modifications for the strides remaining until contact with the take-off board.

It is worth noting that the use of visual time-to-contact information to regulate gait does not depend on the expertise of the person. Although the participants in the Lee and authors long jump study were highly skilled, novice long jumpers also have demonstrated similar stride-length adjustments consistent with the influence of *tau* (Berg, Wade, & Greer, 1994).

In the second phase of the run-up, the percentage of the total stride-length corrections made on each stride can be used as a way to demonstrate the perception-action coupling involved in the long jump run-up. If *tau* is the visual variable that influences the long jumper's performance during this phase of the run-up, we would expect to see evidence of a coupling between the visually detected time-to-contact and movement corrections. This coupling would be best demonstrated by a linear relationship between the percentage of the total adjustment and the number of strides remaining to hit the take-off board. Montagne et al. (2000) presented evidence of this relationship in a study involving long jumpers of various levels of expertise. As you can see in figure 6.7, the percentage of the total amount of adjustment increased linearly for the final five strides from the take-off board. And, similar to what Lee et al. (1982) found for elite jumpers, approximately 40 percent of the total amount of adjustment occurred on the stride before the take-off board.

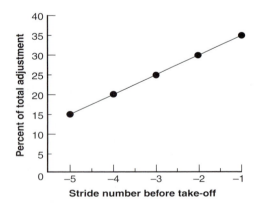

FIGURE 6.7   The percentage of the total amount of stride-length adjustments for the final five strides for the long-jumpers in the experiment by Montagne et al. [Modified Figure 3 from Montagne et al. (2000). A perception-action coupling type of control in long jumping. *Journal of Motor Behavior, 32,* 37–43.]

Researchers have found that other types of gait also involve adjustments during locomotion on the basis of visual time-to-contact information. Some examples are walking a given distance and stepping on the target with a specified foot (Laurent & Thomson, 1988); running and stepping on targets, as people do when crossing a creek on rocks (Warren, Young, & Lee, 1986); doing run-ups to the springboard and horse while performing the vault in women's gymnastics (Meeuwsen & Magill, 1987). In all of these activities, the persons adjust stride length on the basis of time-to-contact information as they near the targets.

Avoiding Contact with Objects

When you walk through a doorway, you want to avoid contact with the sides of the doorway. How do you successfully achieve the action goal of this locomotor activity? Research evidence indicates that vision provides the motor system with *body-scaled information* about the size of a specific body part in relation to the size of the doorway. A person decides how to orient his or her body to walk through an open doorway on the basis of visually perceived information related to the proportion of his or her shoulder width to the width of the door opening. More specifically, Warren and Whang (1987) reported that a doorway needs to be 1.3 times wider than the person's shoulder width for the person to determine that he or she can walk through it without having to turn his or her shoulders.

A different type of object avoidance situation occurs when we need to go safely over an obstacle in our pathway. People can employ a variety of avoidance strategies while walking or running to accomplish this goal. Patla and his colleagues have reported several studies in which they investigated the role vision plays in the strategy people select to go over an obstacle (e.g., Patla, Rietdyk, Martin, & Prentice, 1996). Here again, vision provides predictive information that specifies to the motor control system the type of step-pattern alteration that will be needed to step over the object. The primary information is specified by the height, width, and shape of the object. In addition, predictions about

A CLOSER LOOK

Vision Provides Body-Scaled Information When We Climb Stairs

Stair climbing is a common, everyday activity. But, how do we know that the stairs we need to climb are actually climbable? That is, how do we know that we can use a typical forward-stepping movement to climb a set of stairs? Vision operates in this situation in a way that is similar to how it enables us to determine if we can walk through a doorway without having to turn our shoulders to avoid contact with the sides of the doorway. The visual system detects and uses body-scaled information that involves

the *relationship between the stair/step height and the person's leg length.* Researchers (e.g., Warren, 1994) have shown that if the riser height is equal to or less than 88 percent of the person's leg length, the person will judge that stair step to be climbable by a normal, forward-stepping movement. If the proportion exceeds 88 percent, the person will use a different movement pattern to climb the stair steps, such as children often do when they sit on the step first, or lift a knee to put the lower leg on the step first.

---

how solid or fragile the object is are also important. For example, people will increase the height of their leading leg, which increases the amount of toe clearance, more for an obstacle perceived to be fragile than for an object perceived to be solid.

VISION AND JUMPING FROM HEIGHTS

Jumping from a platform to the floor is another skill for which experimental results have supported the view that the visual variable *tau* triggers specific preparatory movement–related activities so that a person can achieve an action goal. For example, in an experiment by Sidaway, McNitt-Gray, and Davis (1989), people jumped from three different heights: 0.72 m, 1.04 m, and 1.59 m. The researchers instructed the participants to land with both feet on a force plate on the floor, and to direct their visual attention toward this force plate throughout the jump.

A unique characteristic of this experiment is that the researchers measured the EMG activity of the rectus femoris so that they could assess the onset of activity in this agonist muscle in relation to the distance the person was from landing on the floor. The logic here was that if the visual variable *tau* acts as a triggering mechanism for initiating a certain action, there should be a specific relationship between *tau* and the onset of rectus femoris activ-

ity, regardless of the height of the jump. The results of this experiment support this prediction, which means that the visual variable *tau* mediated the control of the onset of the muscle activity required for jumping from different heights.

VISION AND CATCHING

In many ways, catching an object is like the prehension action discussed earlier. However, there are two important differences. First, catching involves a moving object; prehension typically involves a stationary object. Second, the grasp of the object in the catching action ends the action; prehension typically involves doing something with the grasped object. Although in some sport situations, such as baseball and softball, there are occasions in which a player must remove the ball from the glove after the catch and throw the ball, this situation is uniquely sport and situation specific and will not be included in this discussion of catching.

Three Phases of Catching an Object

To catch an object, the person must first move the arm and hand toward the oncoming object. Then, he or she must shape the hand to catch the object. Finally, the fingers must grasp the object.

Williams and McCririe (1988) provided research evidence demonstrating the phases of catching with their study of 11-year-old boys trying to

FIGURE 6.8   The arm, hand, and fingers movement characteristics involved in catching a ball in relation to the percentage of ball flight time. [Data from Williams & McCririe (1988). *Journal of Human Movement Studies, 14,* 241–247.]

catch a ball with one hand (figure 6.8). A movement analysis of the catching action showed the following sequence. There was no arm motion for the first 160 to 240 msec of the ball flight. Then, elbow flexion gradually began and continued slowly and uniformly for about 80 percent of the ball flight. At about the same time, the fingers began to extend. The hand began to withdraw from the oncoming ball until about one-half of the ball flight time had elapsed. Then the upper arm accelerated about the shoulder, which resulted in the hand's being transported to the spatial position required for intercepting the ball. Boys who caught the ball began final positioning action 80 msec earlier than boys who failed to catch it. By the time 75 percent of the ball flight was complete (113 msec prior to contact), each successful boy had his hand and fingers in a ready state for catching the ball.

These results indicate that vision provides advance information enabling the motor control system to *spatially and temporally set the arms, hands, and fingers before the ball arrives* so that the individual can catch the ball. It is especially noteworthy here that the person bases the grasping action on visual information obtained *before* the ball actually makes contact with the hand, rather than on feedback obtained after the ball has hit the hand. The extent of involvement of proprioception during pre–ball contact stages is not well understood. However, we know that proprioceptive and tactile feedback become involved after contact because the catcher needs to make adjustments to the grasp. Research evidence also shows that both central and peripheral vision operate when a person picks up information critical to catching an object.

Vision of the Object and Catching

Catching an object, such as a ball, is a complex action that has challenged researchers in their efforts to understand how the visual and motor control systems interact to enable people to successfully catch a moving object. The results of these research efforts have identified several factors that influence successful catching that relate specifically to the visual observation of the object.

One factor is the *amount of time of visual contact with the moving object.* Research evidence indicates that constant visual contact is needed during two critical periods of time in the object's flight: the initial part of the flight and the period of time just prior to contact with the hand(s). How much time is required during each of these time periods has not been established, and undoubtedly depends on the situation. Some researchers have reported evidence indicating that observation of the initial flight should continue until the ball reaches its zenith (Amazeen, Amazeen, Post, & Beek, 1999), although others have indicated that only the first 300 ms of flight are important (e.g., Whiting, Gill, & Stephenson, 1970). The important point here is that visual contact with the object is needed for an amount of time during its initial flight phase that is sufficient to obtain information to determine estimates of the direction and distance of the flight.

In terms of visual contact with the object during its final portion of flight, research evidence indicates that the time period between 200 and 300 ms before hand contact is critical for successful catching (Savelsbergh, Whiting, Pijpers, & van Santvoord, 1993), although the precise amount of

A CLOSER LOOK

The Use of Looming in Television and Movies: An Illustration of Our Use of *Tau*

In their review of the issues related to determining the visual information people use to time the approach of an oncoming object, Abernethy and Burgess-Limerick (1992) stated that if a *tau*-based method for picking up time to contact is viable, "observers must first and foremost be sensitive to information provided by optical expansion or 'looming'" (p. 366). They went on to describe several research studies supporting this prediction. Although these studies are important to establish scientific support for *tau*, we can find evidence of our sensitivity to looming from a common everyday experience.

Have you ever watched a television program or movie and experienced the illusion of an object flying out of the screen directly at you? Because television and movies are two-dimensional media, creators of visual effects implement the concept of looming to create the three-dimensional quality of an object moving from far away and then acting as if it were flying out of the screen directly at the viewer. This illusion is created by making the object appear small on the screen and then having it nonlinearly expand in size (i.e., slowly at first and then rapidly). This change in the rate of expansion creates the optical illusion that the object will fly out of the screen and hit you. Undoubtedly you have observed this looming illusion, and have actually responded to it by moving your head to avoid the object hitting you. What is especially interesting about this behavioral reaction is that it occurs even though you know it is not possible for the object to physically fly out of the screen and hit you. The important point here is that the object made no distance and velocity changes; only size changed. It is this size-based change, and its nonlinear rate of expansion, that is the basis for *tau* providing a means for people to time the approach of an oncoming object.

time may depend on the specific characteristics of the situation, especially the length of time the object is in flight and its velocity (see Bennett, Davids, & Craig, 1999). The need to see the ball during the final portion of its flight is to obtain specific time-to-contact information for the final spatial positioning of the hand and fingers, and the timing of the closing of the fingers during the grasp of the object.

What about visual contact with the object in flight between these two time periods? Research evidence, primarily from Elliott and his colleagues (e.g., Elliott, Zuberec, & Milgram, 1994), indicates that continuous visual contact with the ball during this period of time is *not* essential. The Elliott et al. (1994) study showed that people can catch a ball that has a flight time of 1 sec by *intermittently seeing brief "snapshots"* (approximately 20 msec) of the ball every 80 msec of its flight. Interestingly, these results are remarkably similar to those reported for people walking on a balance beam (Robertson et al., 1999) and across a horizontal ladder (Assaiante, Marchand, & Amblard, 1989).

Thus, people can use visual samples of ball flight characteristics to obtain the information they need to catch the ball. This capability to use intermittent visually detected information to catch an object helps us understand how an ice hockey goalie can catch a puck or a soccer goalkeeper can catch a ball even though he or she must visually track it through several pairs of legs on its way to the goal.

Another important motor control question concerning vision of the object and catching is this: *Does the motor control system use the visual variable* tau *to enable people to catch an object?* Although there is considerable debate about the answer to this question (see Abernethy & Burgess-Limerick, 1992, for a more complete discussion of this issue), a significant amount of research evidence indicates that *tau* is involved in solving the time-to-contact problem when catching an object (Abernethy & Burgess-Limerick, 1992; Bootsma & Peper, 1992). When an object moves directly toward a person, the angle created at the person's eyes by the top and bottom edges of the object increases in size in a nonlinear way as the

LAB LINKS

Lab 6 in the Online Learning Center Lab Manual
provides an opportunity for you to compare catching a ball when you can and when you cannot see
your hands.

object approaches the person. The nonlinearity
refers to the perceived slowness of this angle increase when the ball is farther away from the person and the rapid increase in size as it gets close to
the person. It is this rate of expansion of angular
size, which is often referred to as *looming,* that the
visual system uses to determine when collision of
the object with the person will occur. For the action of catching, this optical expansion establishes
when the appropriate movement characteristics for
the arm, hand, and finger will be in place to catch
the object. For objects that do not move directly toward the person but require the person to run to
catch them, *tau* also provides the visual basis for
timing the catch, although the mathematics for calculating *tau* are distinctly more complex.

Vision of the Hands and Catching

An important question related to catching is this:
*Must a person be able to see his or her hands
throughout the flight of a ball to successfully catch
the ball?* In one of the first experiments investigating this question, Smyth and Marriott (1982) attached a screen to the participants so they could see
the oncoming ball, but not their hands. When the
participants were able to see their hands, they averaged 17.5 catches out of 20 balls thrown. However,
when they could *not* see their hands, they were able
to catch an average of 9.2 balls out of 20. More important, when they could *not* see their hands, participants typically made a hand-positioning error:
they could not get their hands into the correct spatial position to intercept the ball. But when they
could see their hands, their typical errors involved
grasping: they initiated too early the finger flexion
they needed to grasp the ball.

Interesting as the Smyth and Marriott results
may be, research since their work has shown that
experience is an important factor influencing a person's catching success when he or she cannot see
his or her hands. We might expect this, as Davids
(1988) argued, because the effective use of peripheral vision is a function of age and experience. Because we use peripheral vision to see our hands as
we try to catch an oncoming object, it is logical to
expect that our need to see our hands to catch a ball
will depend on our age and experience.

Fischman and Schneider (1985) provided empirical evidence that supports the influence of experience. Using the same experimental procedures
as those of Smyth and Marriott, they included participants who had had at least five years' experience in varsity baseball or softball. The results of
this experiment (figure 6.9) showed that although
the number of catches decreased when the people
could not see their hands, the type of error did not
depend on whether or not the participants could see
their hands. However, for the inexperienced ball
catchers, more positioning errors than grasp errors
occurred when they could not see their hands.

Researchers now generally agree that both ball
catching experience and skill level influence the
need for a person to see his or her hands while
catchinga ball (see Bennett, Davids, & Craig,
1999).More-experienced and skilled catchers do
not need to see their hands; less-experienced and
low-skill catchers require vision of their hands. The
reason for this difference appears to relate to a person's capability to use proprioceptive feedback to
catch a moving object. The less-experienced, low-
skilled person needs visual feedback to assist in the
use of proprioceptive feedback to spatially position
his or her arms and hands, and to effectively grasp
the object. In terms of helping people improve their
catching skill, this relationship between experience
and the need for vision of the hands suggests that
beginners and less-skilled people should practice
catching primarily in situations where they can see
their hands throughout the ball flight, from the
point where the ball leaves the thrower's hand until
the ball is grasped.

A CLOSER LOOK

"Watch the Ball All the Way to Your Bat!"

A common instruction coaches give when teaching hitting in baseball is to tell players, "Watch the ball all the way to your bat." In light of this, it is interesting to note that research (e.g., Bahill and LaRitz, 1984) indicates that batters probably never see the bat hit the ball. If they do, it is because they have jumped in their visual focus from some point in the ball flight to the bat contact point. They do not visually track the ball continuously all the way to bat contact because this is virtually a physical impossibility. Batters commonly track the ball to a certain point and then visually jump to a point where they predict the ball will be at bat contact.

It is worth noting that more-skilled batters watch the ball for a longer amount of time than less-skilled players. Beginners tend to have the bat swing initiation movement influence their head position and "pull" their head out of position to see the ball/bat contact area.

From an instruction point of view, these characteristics suggest that *it is worthwhile* to instruct a person, "Watch the ball all the way to your bat." Even though the person can't really do that, this instruction directs the person's visual attention so that the person tracks the ball for as long as physically possible, and keeps his or her head in position to see the ball/bat contact area.

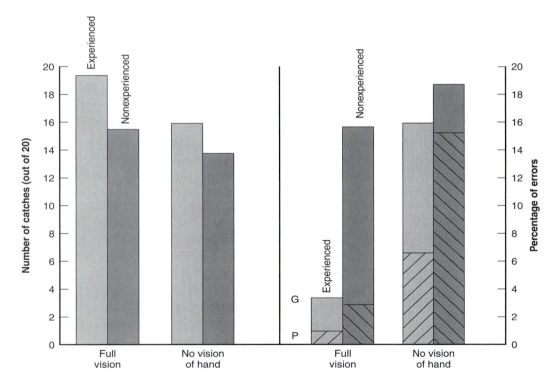

FIGURE 6.9 Results of the experiment by Fischman and Schneider showing the number of right-hand catches made (out of 20 chances) for experienced softball/baseball players and nonexperienced subjects, and the percentage of errors made (based on 360 attempts) by each group that were classified as positioning (P) or grasp (G) errors when subjects either could or could not see their hands. [*Source:* Data from Fischman, M.G., & Schneider, T. (1985). Skill level, vision, and proprioception in simple one-hand catching. *Journal of Motor Behavior, 17,* 219–229.]

A CLOSER LOOK

How Does a Person Catch a Ball That Requires Running to Catch It?

In many sports, players must run to catch a ball. A motor control question concerning this situation that has intrigued scientists for many years is this: *What control strategy does a person use to catch a ball that requires running some distance to catch it?* This question has generated interest because people seem to be able to learn to successfully perform this skill relatively easily, which is evident when we observe how quickly children learn this skill. The primary approach taken by scientists to answer this question has been to develop mathematical models that identify the critical favors involved in this skill and describe how the motor control system manages these factors.

The mathematical models identify two angles of two triangles as the critical factors involved in this catching situation (see McLeod, Reed, & Deines, 2001). These triangles and the angles are shown in figure 6.10.

FIGURE 6.10   An illustration depicting the critical angles that McLeod, Reed, and Dienes propose the motor control system must manage so that a fielder can run and catch a ball. The filled circles represent the locations of the ball during its flight; the open circles represent the locations of a fielder who must run to catch the ball. The figure shows a ball hit to the fielder's right. To make the figure represent a ball hit along the line directly in front or behind the fielder, the lines that converge to form angles α and β (which are to the left of the final ball and fielder location) would converge to form these angles along line C_2 in front of or behind the final ball and fielder location. [*Source:* Modified Figure 1, p. 1348 in McLeod, P., Reed, N., & Dienes, Z. (2001). Toward a unified fielder theory: What we do not yet know about how people run to catch a ball. *Journal of Experimental Psychology: Human Perception and Performance, 27,* 1347–1355.]

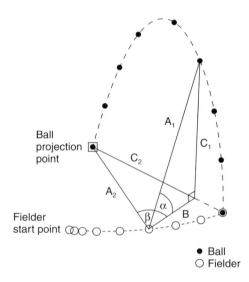

VISION AND STRIKING A MOVING OBJECT

Two experiments investigating the striking of a moving object illustrate how vision is involved in this action.

Vision and Baseball Batting

The most commonly cited experiment related to the role of vision in baseball batting was performed many years ago by Hubbard and Seng (1954). Using photographic techniques, they found that professional baseball players tracked the ball only to a point, at which time they made their swing. This point did not coincide with the point where the bat made contact with the ball. Each batter tended to synchronize the start of the step forward with the release of the ball from the pitcher's hand. And, perhaps most important, the durations of the batters' swings were remarkably consistent from swing to swing, indicating that it was the initiation of the swing that batters adjusted according to the speed of the oncoming pitch. Interestingly, these findings agree precisely with expectations from a *tau*-based strategy for hitting. That is, the initiation of the batting action occurred at a critical time to contact.

Some of the findings of Hubbard and Seng have been either verified or extended in research reported since their study. For example, thirty years later, Bahill and LaRitz (1984) used more sophisticated technology to closely monitor eye and head

A CLOSER LOOK (*continued*)

- *Triangle 1* involves the ball flight and the fielder's position. Within this triangle, the critical angle is the angle of elevation of the fielder's point of gaze above the horizontal (angle α). This angle is created by a line from the ball location in the air at any moment to the fielder's position on the ground at that moment, and a line from the fielder's position to the location on the ground directly under the ball.
- *Triangle 2* involves the ball flight, the ball projection point, and the fielder's position. Within this triangle, the critical angle (β) is the angle created by a line from the ball projection point to the fielder's position and a line from the fielder's position to the location on the ground directly under the ball.

Research based on this type of mathematical model has resulted in some general agreement with Chapman's (1968) original model for the catching situation in which the person must run straight forward or backward. However, there is no consensus among scientists for the situation in which the person must run to the side to catch the ball.

- *To catch a ball that requires running directly forward or backward,* angle α is the primary angle involved because the fielder's position would be along A_2 and its extension. Fielders time their arrival at the ball by running forward or backward at a speed that maintains α between 0° and 90°.
- *To catch a ball that requires running to the side,* both angles α and β are critical. As in the situation in which the fielder must run forward or backward, fielders time their arrival at the ball by running forward or backward at a speed that maintains α between 0° and 90°. However, researchers do not yet know why fielders choose the spatial path they follow to make the catch, which involves the control of β.

McLeod, Reed, and Dienes (2001) summed up the status of our current knowledge about the issue of how people run to catch a ball by saying: "We understand how α is controlled but not β" (p. 1355). Regardless of how this issue is resolved, the important point in terms of the discussion in this chapter is the critical involvement of the visual system. And vision appears to be involved in a way that requires little conscious control of the movements that must be executed to enable a person to achieve the action goal.

movements of a major league baseball player and several college baseball players. The study was done in a laboratory situation that simulated players' responses to a high-and-outside fastball thrown by a left-handed pitcher to a right-handed batter. The major league player visually tracked the ball longer than the college players did. The college players tracked the ball to a point about 9 ft in front of the plate, at which point their visual tracking began to fall behind the ball. The major league player kept up with the ball until it reached a point about 5.5 ft in front of the plate before falling behind in his tracking. Also, regardless of the pitch speed, the major league player followed the same visual tracking pattern and was very consistent in every stance he took to prepare for the pitch. His

head position changed less than one degree across all pitches. Interestingly, he made slight head movements while tracking the ball, but never moved his body.

Vision and Table Tennis Striking

In a study of five top table tennis players in the Netherlands, Bootsma and van Wieringen (1990) showed from movement analysis results that the players could not rely completely on consistent movement production. Players seemed to compensate for differences in the initiation times of their swings in order to hit the ball as fast and as accurately as possible. For example, when time to contact was shorter at swing initiation, players compensated by applying more force during the

General Vision Training Programs for Athletes: Do They Improve Sports Performance?

Bruce Abernethy and his colleagues at the University of Queensland in Australia have asserted for many years that although general vision training programs (e.g., Eyerobics) may help to improve certain basic vision functions, they do not improve sport-specific performance. Abernethy and Wood (2001) presented three lines of reasoning, all of which are supported by research evidence, as the basis for their position:

- Above-normal basic visual function (e.g., foveal and peripheral acuity, contrast sensitivity) does not favor elite athletes. A significant amount of research has shown that the visual advantage of elite athletes is sports-specific and perceptual in nature, i.e., the interpreting and use of visual information to specific sports activities. (We will discuss this aspect of vision and motor control in chapters 7 and 8).

- Although many commonly measured visual functions can improve with training and repetitive practice, many of the reported improvements occur for people with visual defects. And, the exercises used to train specific visual functions are commonly procedures that are the same as, or similar to, the tests used to evaluate the functions.

- Experimental evidence is lacking to validate the effectiveness of general vision training programs for improving sports performance. In fact, in the experiment reported in this article, two visual training programs (Sports Vision and Eyerobics) led to performance improvements that were no better than reading about and watching televised tennis matches during the four-week training time, which consisted of four 20-min sessions each week.

stroke. And evidence suggests that some of these players were making very fine adjustments to their swings while they were moving. Thus, whereas visual information may trigger the initiation of the swing and provide information about its essential characteristics, vision also provides information that the player can use to make compensatory adjustments to the initiated swing, although these are very slight in terms of time and space quantities.

SUMMARY

Proprioception and vision are two important sources of feedback involved in movement control.

- To investigate the role of proprioception in motor control, researchers have used several experimental techniques to remove or distort proprioceptive feedback. Results of experiments that have used these techniques have shown that proprioceptive feedback provides important information that influences motor control functions such as movement accuracy, the timing of the onset of motor commands, and various

aspects of the coordination of limb and body segments.

- Vision tends to dominate as a source of sensory information, which is well illustrated by a movement response to visual information in situations in which vision and proprioception provide conflicting information, as was demonstrated in the "moving room experiment."

- Research evidence has shown that vision plays several important roles in the motor control of complex daily activities and sports skills. We examined how these roles are involved in the performance of several types of motor activities and skills, namely, manual aiming actions; prehension actions; handwriting; locomotion actions, including those that involve maintaining dynamic postural balance, contacting objects, and avoiding contact with objects; jumping from heights; catching a ball; and hitting a baseball and a table tennis ball.

- As a result of our examination of several types of motor activities and skills, we determined that vision is critically involved in motor control functions, such as the preparation of movements required to initiate and carry out an action; the guidance and correction of limb-movement kinematics; the maintaining of postural balance; and the timing and spatial positioning involved in the contacting or intercepting of objects, and in avoiding contact with objects.

RELATED READINGS

Bingham, G. P., Bradley, A., Bailey, M., & Vinner, R. (2001) Accommodation, occlusion, and disparity matching are used to guide reaching: A comparison of actual versus virtual environments. *Journal of Experimental Psychology: Human Perception and Performance, 27,* 1314–1334

Bootsma, R. J. (1991). Predictive information and the control of action: What you see is what you get. *International Journal of Sport Psychology, 22,* 271–278.

Carnahan, H., Goodale, M. A., & Marteniuk, R. G. (1993). Grasping versus pointing and the differential use of visual feedback. *Human Movement Science, 12,* 219–234.

Dietz, V. (2002). Proprioception and locomotor disorders. *Nature Reviews Neuroscience, 3,* 781–790

Haggard, P. (1997). Coordinating actions. *Quarterly Journal of Experimental Psychology, 50A,* 707–725

Inhoff, A. W., & Gordon, A. M. (1997). Eye movements and eye-hand coordination during typing. *Current Directions in Psychological Science, 6,* 153–157.

Hibbard, P. B., & Bradshaw, M. F. (2003). Reaching for virtual objects: Binocular disparity and the control of prehension. *Experimental Brain Research, 148,* 196–201

Michaels, C. F., Zeinstra, E. B., & Oudejans, R. R. D. (2001). Information and action in punching a falling ball. *Quarterly Journal of Experimental Psychology, 50A,* 69–93.

Portier, S. J., & van Galen, G. P. (1992). Immediate vs. postponed visual feedback in practicing a handwriting task. *Human Movement Science, 11,* 563–592.

Starkes, J., Helsen, W., & Elliot, D. (2002). A ménage a trois: The eye, the hand and on-line processing. *Journal of Sports Sciences, 20,* 217–224

STUDY QUESTIONS

1. Describe four methods for investigating the role of proprioception in the control of movement. What do the results of the investigations using these methods tell us about the role of proprioception in controlling movement?

2. What two roles does vision play in controlling manual aiming movements? How is the duration of the movement a variable influencing these roles?

3. Discuss how vision is involved in controlling prehension. Use an example to illustrate.

4. Discuss how time to contact is involved in the control of locomotion when the goal is to contact a target. Include in this discussion the role vision plays in this situation.

5. Discuss how vision is involved when a person must (a) catch a thrown ball; (b) strike an oncoming ball.

CHAPTER

Action Preparation

Concept: Performing voluntary, coordinated movement
requires preparation of the motor control system

After completing this chapter, you will be able to

- Discuss why reaction time (RT) can be an index of preparation required to perform a motor skill

- Explain how Hick's law describes the relationship between the number of alternatives in a choice-RT situation and RT

- Describe various task and situation characteristics that influence action preparation

- Describe various performer characteristics that influence action preparation

- Discuss several motor control activities that occur during action preparation

Application

Many sport and daily activities demonstrate our need to prepare the motor control system to carry out an intended action. For example, many sporting events, such as running, swimming, and trap shooting, incorporate the importance of preparation into the rules of the activity, which require an audible signal warning the competitors to get ready.

Certain performance characteristics of activities also provide evidence of the need to prepare for the action. For example, when you decide to pick up a glass of water for a drink, there is a slight delay between your decision and the intended action. In another example, if you are driving a car along a street and another car unexpectedly pulls out in front of you, there is a measurable time delay be-

tween the moment you see this and the moment you begin to move your foot off the accelerator and onto the brake pedal. In each of these very different action scenarios, intended action is preceded by an interval of time in which the motor control system is prepared according to the demands and constraints of the situation.

Consider the preparation of action from a different perspective. Undoubtedly, at some time or other you have said, following a poor performance in an activity, I wasn't "ready". By saying this, you imply that if you had been "ready" you would have performed much better than you just have. Or, if you work with physical therapy patients, you undoubtedly have heard one tell the therapist, "Don't rush me. If I get out of this chair before I'm ready, I'll fall."

Discussion

In chapters 4 through 6, we focused on factors influencing the control of an ongoing action. Although there was occasional mention of the initiation of the action, we only touched on what is involved in the actual preparation of an intended action. In the present discussion, our interest is in what occurs between the intention to act and the initiation of the action itself. In the motor control literature, researchers sometimes use the term *movement preparation* to designate this activity. However, in keeping with the distinction we made in chapter 1 between actions and movements, we will use the term **action preparation** when referring to this process.

In this context, *preparation* does not refer to the long-term preparation that occurs during the days prior to an event, but to the specific preparation the motor control system makes *just prior to initiating an action.* We will address two preparation issues here. First, how do different skill, performance-context, and personal factors influence the preparation process? Second, exactly what is the motor control system preparing that makes preparation such a critical part of any performance? Before we discuss these issues, we will establish how we know that the motor control system needs to be prepared for action.

ACTION PREPARATION REQUIRES TIME

The principle that the motor control system needs preparation before it can initiate an action has its roots in research carried out in the middle of the nineteenth century by Donders (1868/1969), a Dutch physician. This principle is derived from an inference based on the effects of various factors on observed differences in the amount of time between the production of a signal telling a person to begin performing a skill and the instant experimenters actually observe the beginning of movement. As you studied in chapter 2, we call this interval of time *reaction time (RT)*. When considered in the context of action preparation, *RT is an index of preparation* required to produce an action.[1] By investigating factors that increase or decrease this time interval and the mental activities that occur during this interval, we can gain some understanding of the action preparation processes our motor control system engages in to enable us to perform a skill.

One of the things that RT tells us is that preparing to produce voluntary movement takes time. Planned movement does not occur instantaneously. Certain actions and circumstances require more preparation than others. In the following sections, we discuss a variety of factors that influence the amount and type of preparation needed.

TASK AND SITUATION CHARACTERISTICS INFLUENCING PREPARATION

One set of factors that influence action preparation includes characteristics of both the task itself and the situation in which it must be performed.

The Number of Response Choices

An important characteristic of task and performance situations that influences preparation time is the number of response alternatives the performer has to choose from. *As the number of alternatives increases, the amount of time required to prepare the appropriate movement increases.* The easiest way to demonstrate this relationship is by looking at the choice-RT situation you were introduced to in chapter 2. RT increases according to the number of stimulus or response choices. The fastest RTs occur in simple-RT situations, which have only one stimulus and one response. RT slows down when

---

[1]When RT is used as an index of action preparation, it is often used as described in chapter 4, to determine the amount of time required for "motor programming."

---

action preparation   the activity that occurs between the intention to perform and the initiation of an action; sometimes, the term *motor programming* is used to refer to this activity.

A Historical Look at the Use of Reaction Time to Study Action Preparation

The study of reaction time (RT) as an indicator of mental operations has a history that can be traced back to the middle of the nineteenth century. Scientists were becoming interested in determining the basic elements of thought. The investigation of RT provided a useful means of investigating this question because it represented the time interval between the detection of a stimulus and the initiation of a response to it. Dr. F.C. Donders, a Dutch physician, hypothesized that specific mental operations occur in a specific series of stages during the RT interval, and was certain that he could identify each stage. He initiated research that was published in 1868 (Donders, 1868/1969), and continues to influence researchers today. To test his hypothesis, he set up three different "methods" for performing reaction-time tasks.

- *Simple reaction-time task* (Donders called this the *a* method): The participant pressed a telegraph-type key as soon as possible when a light illuminated.
- *Choice reaction-time task* (Donders called this the *b* method): The participant pressed a telegraph-type key as soon as possible with the right hand when the right light illuminated and with the left hand when the left light illuminated.
- *Discrimination reaction-time task* (Donders called this the *c* method): The participant pressed a telegraph-type key as soon as possible when a light of specified color illuminated, but not when any other light illuminated (e.g., respond to the red light, but not to the green light).

Donders reasoned that the RTs for the three tasks would be different because of the different "mental operations" involved in identifying the stimulus and selecting the appropriate response for each task. He developed the following subtraction method to determine the speed of each of the two mental operation stages:

- RT for the *c* task – RT for the *a* task = Amount of time for the *stimulus discrimination* stage
- RT for the *c* task – RT for the *b* task = Amount of time for the *response selection* stage

The simple-RT task provided the baseline RT because it involved only stimulus identification and the selection of one response, whereas the choice– and discrimination–reaction time tasks required the discrimination of different stimuli and the selection of one response from more than one possible response.

Unfortunately, few researchers following Donders' lead with any degree of effort until after World War II, when in 1952 Hick reported his work concerning the systematic influence of the number of stimulus-response alternatives on RT (which is discussed in this chapter). Since that time, the study of reaction time as a means of understanding the action preparation process, which is now a part of the area of study referred to as *mental chronometry,* has generated a substantial amount of research (for a review of this research, see Meyer et al., 1988).

more than one stimulus and more than one response are possible, as in the choice-RT situation.

The relationship between the amount of RT increase and the number of response choices is so stable that a law, known as Hick's law, was developed that predicts a person's RT when his or her simple RT and the number of choices are known. **Hick's law** (Hick, 1952) states that RT will increase logarithmically as the number of stimulus-response choices increases. This means that when we calculate the logarithm of the number of choices in a choice-RT situation and plot the

resulting RT on a graph, RT increases linearly as the number of choices increases. The equation that describes this law is $RT = K \log_2 (N + 1)$, where K is a constant (which is simple RT in most cases) and N equals the number of possible choices. Figure 7.1 illustrates how we can predict the magnitude of this increase mathematically by applying Hick's equation.

The important component of Hick's law is the $\log_2$ function, because it designates that the RT increase is due to the information transmitted by the possible choices, rather than to the actual

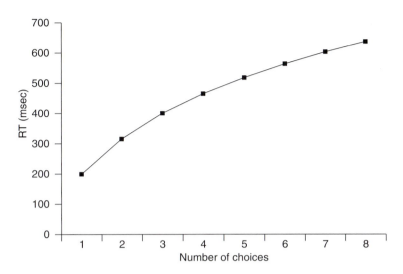

FIGURE 7.1 Predicted reaction times (RT), according to Hick's law, for one through eight choice-RT situations, based on a simple (i.e., one choice) RT of 200 msec.

number of choice alternatives. In information theory, log_2 *specifies a bit of information. A* bit, short for *bi*nary digi*t,* is a yes/no (i.e., 1/0) choice between two alternatives. In a 1-bit decision, there are two alternatives; there are four alternatives in a 2-bit decision; a 3-bit decision involves eight choices; and so on. The number of bits indicates the smallest number of "yes/no" decisions needed to solve the problem created by the number of choices involved. For example, if eight choices were possible in a situation, an individual would have to answer three yes/no questions to determine the correct choice. Thus, an eight-choice situation is a 3-bit decision situation. Accordingly, Hick's law not only correctly predicts that RT increases as the number of choice alternatives increases; it also predicts the specific size of increase to expect.

The Predictability of the Correct Response Choice

If a number of response alternatives exist in a performance situation and one alternative is more predictable than the others, response preparation time will be shorter than it would if all the alternatives were equally likely. Research evidence has consistently shown that *as the predictability of one of the possible choices increases, RT decreases.*

An experimental procedure, popularized in the early 1980s by Rosenbaum (1980, 1983), is commonly used to investigate this relationship. In this procedure, known as the *precuing technique,* researchers provide participants with differing amounts of advance information about which movement must be made in a choice situation. In Rosenbaum's experiments, participants had to move the appropriate finger as quickly as possible to hit the signaled target key. There were three response dimensions, all of which involved a two-choice situation: the *arm* to move (left or right); the *direction* to move (away from or toward the body);

Hick's law a law of human performance stating that RT will increase logarithmically as the number of stimulus-response choices increases.

and the *extent* of the movement (short or long). Prior to the signal to move, the participants could receive advance information (the precue) specifying the correct upcoming response for none, one, two, or all three of the dimensions. The results showed that as the number of precued dimensions increased, the RT decreased, with the fastest RT occurring when all three dimensions were precued. The benefit of the advance information was that participants would need to prepare only the remaining non-precued dimensions after the "go" signal.

The Influence of the Probability of Precue Correctness
An interesting twist to the precuing situation occurs when the advance information may or may not be correct. The critical factor influencing preparation time in this situation is the *probability* of the advance information's correctness. For example, in a two-choice situation, if the advance information has only a 50-50 chance of being correct, the performer will ignore it and respond as if no advance information has been given. This occurs because the probability of correctness of the advance information is no greater than the probability of correctness of the information the person already has. However, if the advance information has an 80 percent chance of being correct, the performer will *bias* his or her preparation toward making that response.

What happens when the signal requires the non-prepared movement? In other words, what is the

price of preparing the wrong movement before preparing the correct one? We can learn the answer from the results of experiments such as one by Larish and Stelmach (1982), which has become the model approach to study this issue. Participants received advance information about whether the right hand or the left hand should hit the target. But this information was correct only 20 percent, 50 percent, or 80 percent of the time. The results (shown in figure 7.2) illustrate the **cost-benefit trade-off** associated with this situation. When there was a 50-50 chance (50 percent correct condition) of the precue's being correct, participants responded as if the task were a two-choice RT task. However, in the 80-20 condition, participants obviously biased their responses to move in the direction of the precued target. When they were correct, there was a benefit; their RTs were *faster* than if they had not biased their responses. However, when they were wrong (the 20 percent case), there was a cost: their RT was *slower* than it was in the 50-50 condition.

Stimulus-Response Compatibility
Another task characteristic that influences the movement preparation time is the physical relationship between the stimulus and response choices. The study of what is termed **stimulus-response compatibility** has a long history that dates back to World War II (for a discussion of this history, see Proctor & Reeve, 1990). This extensive study has shown consistently that *RT will be faster as the*

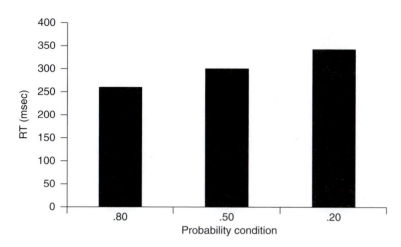

FIGURE 7.2 Results from the experiment by Larish and Stelmach showing the effects on RT of different probabilities of a precue's correctness. [Adapted from Larish, D., & Stelmach, G. E. (1982). Preprogramming, programming, and reprogramming of aimed hand movements as a function of age. *Journal of Motor Behavior, 14,* 322–340. Copyright © 1982 Heldref Publications, Inc., Washington, DC. Reprinted by permission.]

relationship between the stimulus events and their required response becomes more compatible. Conversely, RT will be slower as this relationship becomes less compatible.

The spatial relationship between the stimulus and response devices is the most common way of considering stimulus-response compatibility. For example, suppose a person has to push one of three keys in response to the illumination of one of three lights. If the lights and keys are arranged horizontally with the key to be pushed located under the light indicating that response, then the situation is more compatible than if the lights are vertical and the buttons are horizontal. A more compatible relationship would lead to faster RTs than a less compatible situation. Also, as compatibility decreases, the number of choice errors will increase.

A different type of stimulus-response compatibility situation occurs when the appearance of the stimulus suggests one type of response, but the situation requires a different response. The best example of this is the *Stroop effect,* which is a phenomenon that occurs when a person must verbally respond to the ink color of a word that names a color. When the word name and ink color of the word are the same, RT is faster than if the word is a different color than its name. For example, if BLUE is the word, people will say "blue" faster when the ink color is blue than when the word name is RED but the ink color is blue. In terms of stimulus-response compatibility, a compatible situation exists when the ink color of a word is the same as the color it names and the person must say the ink color; but an incompatible situation exists when the word is written in a color that is different from the one it names and the person must say the ink color.

To account for the effect of stimulus-response compatibility on RT, Zelaznik and Franz (1990) presented evidence showing that when stimulus-response compatibility is low, RT increases are due to response selection problems. On the other hand, when stimulus-response compatibility is high, response selection processing is minimal, so that any

cost-benefit trade-off   the cost (in terms of slower RT), and benefit (in terms of faster RT) that occur as a result of biasing the preparation of an action in favor of one of several possible actions (as opposed to preparing as if each possible action were equally probable).

stimulus-response compatibility   a characteristic of the spatial arrangement relationship between a stimulus and a response. This relationship includes the spatial arrangement of stimuli and the limb movements required to respond to them, and the physical characteristics or meaning of a stimulus and the type of response required. This relationship will influence the amount of preparation time in a reaction time task involving stimulus and response choices.

A CLOSER LOOK

Biasing Actions Is Common in Many Sport Contexts

In many sport activities, athletes often bias their action preparation to produce one particular action rather than some other possible one. For example, if a basketball player knows that the player he or she is defending goes to the right to make a shot only on rare occasions, the defensive player undoubtedly will bias his or her movement preparation by anticipating the need to defend moves to the left when the offensive player has the ball, rather than preparing to defend moves to the left or right with equal probability. In racquet sports, players who consistently hit to one side of the court will find their opponents anticipating the ball's being hit to that side by standing closer to that side or leaning somewhat in a way that will allow them to move more quickly to that side. Baseball players commonly bias their hitting decisions and actions according to a pitcher's tendency to throw a certain pitch in a specific situation.

In each of these examples, the players have found that they can gain an advantage by "playing the percentages" and biasing their preparation. The clear advantage is that if they are correct, they can initiate the appropriate action faster than they could otherwise. But they run the risk of being wrong. If they are, the appropriate action will take longer to initiate than it would if no biasing had occurred. And this extra preparation time can lead to an unsuccessful performance.

RT changes reflect motoric processes related to preparation of the selected response. Weeks and Proctor (1990) further developed this point by demonstrating that the specific response selection problem is due to translation problems involving the mapping of the stimulus locations to the response locations. Because this translation process requires time, RT increases.

Foreperiod Length Regularity
A part of the preparation process begins when a person detects a signal indicating that the signal to respond will occur shortly. The interval between this "warning" signal and the stimulus, or "go" signal, is known as the **foreperiod.** In simple-RT situations the regularity of the length of this interval influences RT. If the foreperiod is a constant length, i.e., the same amount of time for every trial, RT will be shorter than the amount of time that typically characterizes simple RT.

We can attribute the shorter RT associated with constant foreperiods to *anticipation* by the performer. Because it is a simple-RT situation, the person knows before the warning signal what response will be required. And because every trial has the same foreperiod length, he or she knows when the go signal will occur after the warning signal. As a

result, the person can prepare the required action in advance of the go signal, such that the actual initiation of it begins before the go signal.

The starts of sprint races in track or swimming illustrate the need to implement an understanding of the effect on RT of a constant foreperiod length. If the starter of these races maintains a constant amount of time between his or her signal for the athletes to get ready and the gun or sound to start running or swimming, the athletes can anticipate the go signal and gain an unfair advantage over other athletes who did not anticipate the signal as accurately. We would expect some variation in the actual initiations of movement because people vary in terms of their capability to time the precise amounts of time typically involved in the RT foreperiods of sprint starts.

Movement Complexity
Movement complexity is based on the number of parts to a movement. Research evidence demonstrating the effect of movement complexity on RT was reported primarily in the 1960s through the early 1980s, beginning with the now classic experiment by Henry and Rogers (1960). They demonstrated that for a ballistic task, which requires both fast RT and fast movement, RT increases as a function of the

Several situation and performer characteristics discussed in this chapter influence a swimmer's preparation to start a race.

number of component parts of the required action. Numerous other experiments have confirmed these findings since that time (e.g., Anson, 1982; Christina & Rose, 1985; Fischman, 1984). From a preparation-of-action perspective, these results indicate that the complexity of the action to be performed influences the amount of time a person requires to prepare the motor control system.

A question that arose from these experiments related to whether, in fact, the key factor is the number of component parts involved in the action. Because the amount of time to perform the action and the number of component parts of the action are confounded when actions of different complexity are compared, it is possible that the amount of time required may be the cause of the RT increase. To investigate which of these two factors influenced RT in the Henry and Rogers experiment, Christina and colleagues (e.g., Christina, Fischman, Lambert, & Moore, 1985; Fischman

LAB LINKS

Lab 7b in the Online Learning Center Lab Manual provides an opportunity for you to experience the influence of movement complexity on RT by participating in an experiment that is similar to the one by Henry and Rogers (1960).

1984) carried out a series of experiments that provided support for the Henry and Rogers conclusion that the number of component parts is the key in the RT increase.

Movement Accuracy
As the accuracy demands for a movement increase, the amount of preparation time required also increases. Researchers have nicely demonstrated this effect in comparisons of RTs for manual aiming tasks that differed according to the target sizes. For example, Sidaway, Sekiya, and Fairweather (1995) had people perform manual aiming tasks in which they had to hit two targets in sequence as quickly as possible. Two results showed the influence on preparation of the accuracy demands of the task. First, RT increased as target size decreased. Second, when the first target was a constant size, the dispersion of the location of hits on that target was related to the size of the second target. This result indicated that preparation demands increased as movement accuracy demands increased, due to the additional preparation required for a person to constrain his or her limb to move within spatial constraints imposed by the smaller target.

The Repetition of a Movement
A well-known characteristic of human performance is that when the performance situation requires a person to repeat the same response on the next attempt, that person's RT for the next trial will

foreperiod   in a reaction time paradigm, the time interval between a warning signal and the go signal, or stimulus.

The Classic Experiment of Henry and Rogers (1960)

Henry and Rogers (1960) hypothesized that if people prepare movements in advance, a complex movement should take longer to prepare than a simple one. In addition, the increased preparation time should be reflected in changes in reaction time (RT). To test this hypothesis, they compared three different rapid-movement situations that varied in the complexity of the movement. The least complex movement required participants to release a telegraph key as quickly as possible after a gong (movement A). The movement at the next level of complexity (movement B), required participants to release the key at the gong and move the arm forward 30 cm as rapidly as possible to grasp a tennis ball hanging from a string. The most complex movement (movement C) required participants to release the key at the gong, reach forward and strike the hanging tennis ball with the back of the hand, reverse direction and push a button, and then finally reverse direction again and grasp another tennis ball. Participants were to perform all of these movements as quickly as possible.

The results supported the hypothesis. The average RT for movement A was 165 msec; for movement B the average RT was 199 msec; and for movement C the average RT was 212 msec.

The researchers held that the cause of the increase in RT was the increase in the amount of movement-related information that had to be prepared. They proposed that the mechanism involved in this movement preparation was a motor program, similar to a computer program, that would control the details of the sequence of events required to perform the movement.

---

be faster than it was for the previous attempt. As the number of trials increases, the influence of the repetitions on RT lessens. Again, as in other performance situations, the decrease in preparation time is due to a reduction in the response-selection process (see Campbell & Proctor, 1993).

The Time Between Different Responses to Different Signals

There are some performance situations that require a person to respond to a signal with one action and then very quickly respond to another signal with a different action. For example, when a basketball player is confronted by a defensive player in a one-on-one situation, he or she might fake a move in one direction (the first signal) before moving in the opposite direction (the second signal). Each "signal" by the offensive player requires the defensive player to initiate a movement. In this situation, RT will be slower for the defensive player's second movement than for his or her first.

The RT delay for the second movement is due to the **psychological refractory period (PRP)**, which can be thought of as a delay period (the term *refractory* is synonymous with *delay*) during which a person cannot select the second movement until after he or she selects and initiates the first. As such, the PRP reflects a distinct limitation in the action preparation process.

Figure 7.3 illustrates the PRP using the basketball one-on-one situation described earlier. The player with the ball (Player A) fakes a move to the left but then quickly moves to the right. He or she gains extra time to carry out the move to the right because of the RT delay created by the PRP that results from Player B's initial reaction to the fake. The illustration shows that Player B's RT would be the same amount of time for Player A's move to the right if it had not been preceded by a fake move to the left. But the fake requires Player B to initiate a response to the fake before he or she can initiate a response to the move to the right.

PERFORMER CHARACTERISTICS INFLUENCING PREPARATION

In addition to task and situation characteristics, certain characteristics of the performer also influence the process of action preparation. We should think of these characteristics as situational, because they

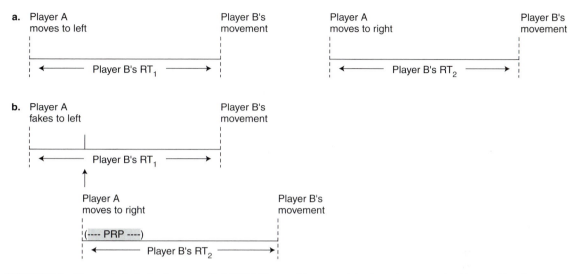

FIGURE 7.3 The psychological refractory period (PRP) illustrated in terms of the time advantage gained by an athlete for moving to the right when it follows a fake for moving to the left. (a) Player B's RT when Player A moves to the left (RT_1) or the right (RT_2), when neither is preceded by a fake in the opposite direction. (b) Player B's RT when Player A first fakes moving to the left but then moves to the right. In this situation, Player A gains extra time to carry out the move to the right because of the increased RT_2 for Player B, which results from the delay caused by the PRP.

refer to the state of the person at the time a skill must be performed. It is important to note here that these performer characteristics typically influence not only the time needed to prepare a voluntary movement but also the quality of its performance.

Alertness of the Performer

An important principle of human performance is that the degree of alertness of the performer influences the time he or she takes to prepare a required action, as well as the quality of the action itself. In two types of performance situations, the role of alertness is especially critical. One type is the RT task, where a person does not have to wait for any length of time beyond a few seconds, but must respond as quickly and as accurately as possible. The other type, involving the long-term maintenance of alertness, is the task for which fast and accurate responding is important, but the signals to which the person must respond occur infrequently and irregularly.

For RT tasks, a way to increase the likelihood that a person is optimally alert and prepared to re-

spond appropriately is to provide some type of *warning signal* that indicates he or she must respond within the next few seconds. Researchers demonstrated the benefit of this warning signal more than a century ago, in the early days of human performance research. For example, in a review of RT research, Teichner (1954) reported that there was sufficient evidence accumulated in the first half of the 1900s to conclude that RT is significantly faster when the signal to respond is preceded by a warning signal than when there is no warning signal.

An important point is that after the warning signal, there is an optimal length of time for the person to develop and maintain alertness while waiting for the go signal. If the go signal occurs too

---

psychological refractory period (PRP) a delay period during which a person seems to put planned action "on hold" while executing a previously initiated action.

FIGURE 7.4   An illustration of the warning signal to "go" signal time relationship necessary to ensure optimal readiness to respond in a reaction time situation. The actual amounts of time for these events depend on the task and situation in which they are performed.

soon after the warning signal, or if the person must wait too long, RT will be longer than if the go signal occurs sometime between these two points in time. These performance effects indicate that people require a minimum amount of time to develop optimal alertness and that we can maintain that level of alertness for a limited amount of time.

As you can see in figure 7.4, there is an optimal time range during which the go signal should occur following the warning signal. The exact amounts of time to insert in this figure will depend on the skill and situation. However, for simple-RT situations, a reasonable rule of thumb is this: *the optimal foreperiod length should range between 1 and 4 sec.*

Tasks that involve long-term maintenance of alertness are known as **vigilance** tasks. In vigilance situations, an individual must perform an appropriate action when he or she detects a signal to act. The problem is that *signals occur very infrequently and irregularly.* There are many vigilance situations in skill performance contexts. In sports, a situation involving vigilance occurs when a baseball outfielder must maintain alertness throughout an inning in the field despite having only one ball hit his or her way, out of the many pitches thrown. In industry, a worker who must detect and remove defective products from the assembly line will see many products move past him or her for long periods of time, but only a few will be defective. Similarly, driving a car along an uncrowded freeway is a vigilance task when a person drives for an extended time. Lifeguarding at a pool or beach can be a vigilance problem, because during a long shift on duty, situations requiring a response are very infrequent. Medical personnel often are required to work long hours and still be able to identify symptoms of health problems correctly and perform surgical techniques requiring precise motor control.

In each of these situations, RT increases as a function of the amount of time the person must maintain alertness to detect certain signals. Detection errors increase as well. Scientists first reported this phenomenon during World War II (see Mackworth, 1956). In experiments investigating the detection of signals simulating those observed on a radar screen, results showed that both the RT to a signal and the accuracy of detecting signals deteriorated markedly with each half hour during a two-hour work interval.

Eason, Beardshall, and Jaffee (1965) nicely demonstrated that alertness deterioration contributes to the performance decrements associated with long-term vigilance. They provided physiological evidence consistent with decreases in vigilance performance over one-hour sessions. Skin conductance in participants decreased, indicating increased calming and drowsiness over the session. In addition, participants' neck tension steadily increased, as their nervous systems attempted to compensate by increasing muscle activity in the neck.

Attention Focused on the Signal versus the Movement

Many motor skills, such as sprints in track and swimming, require a person to move as fast as possible when the signal to move occurs. In these situations, there are two important components, the RT and the movement time (MT). To prepare to initiate his or her movement, the person can focus on the signal itself (a *sensory set*) or on the movement

A CLOSER LOOK

Vigilance Problems Result from Closed-Head Injury

Closed-head injury involves brain damage and often results from an auto accident or a fall. Numerous cognitive and motor problems can accompany this type of injury, depending on the area of the brain that is damaged. Included in the problems associated with closed-head injury is difficulty sustaining attention over a period of time in vigilance tasks.

Loken et al. (1995) provided evidence for this difficulty by comparing patients with severe closed-head injuries to non-brain-injured people. All participants observed on a computer screen sets of two, four, or eight small blue circles (1.5 mm diameter). On some trials, one of the circles was solid blue (this occurred on only 60 percent of the 200 trials). When participants detected the solid blue circle, they were to hit a specified keyboard key. The set of trials lasted 20 min, with only 2 to 5 sec between trials.

The authors pointed out that the following results were most noteworthy because they added to previous knowledge of vigilance problems related to closed-head injury. *In contrast to the non-brain-injured participants,* the patients showed that their

1. **overall vigilance performance** was differentially affected by the complexity of the stimulus array on the computer screen (i.e., detection performance decreased as the set size of circles increased).
2. **detection time latency** (RT) increased as a function of the length of time engaged in performing the task (i.e., the amount of time taken to detect a solid blue circle increased linearly across the 200 trials).

required (a *motor set*). Research evidence, first provided by Franklin Henry (1961), indicates that which of the two components the performer consciously focuses attention on influences RT.

However, because Henry's results were based on the participants' opinions of what their sets were, Christina (1973) imposed on each participant either a sensory or a motor set to initiate a fast arm movement. The sensory-set group was told to focus attention on the sound of the go signal, a buzzer, but to move off the response key as fast as possible. The motor-set group was told to focus on moving as quickly as possible. Results showed that the sensory-set group had an RT 20 msec faster than that of the motor-set group. Interestingly, MT was not statistically different for the two groups. Thus, participants' focusing of attention on the signal and allowing the movement to happen naturally shortened the preparation time required and did not penalize movement speed, yielding a faster overall response time.

Jongsma, Elliott, and Lee (1987) replicated these laboratory results in a sport performance situation. They compared sensory and motor sets for a sprint start in track. To measure RT, the authors embedded a pressure-sensitive switch in the rear-foot starting block. They measured MT as the time from the release of this switch until a photoelectric light beam was broken 1.5 meters from the starting line. Results showed that for both novices and experienced sprinters, RT was faster for the sensory-set condition.

WHAT OCCURS DURING PREPARATION?

On the basis of the discussion so far, you can see that the process of preparing an action is complex. It includes perceptual, cognitive, and motor components. One way to demonstrate that the preparation process includes these components is to divide an EMG recording of the RT interval into components by using a technique known as *fractionating RT,* which was introduced in chapter 2.

vigilance   maintaining attention in a performance situation in which stimuli requiring a response occur infrequently.

A CLOSER LOOK

A Summary of Task and Performer Characteristics That Influence the Amount of Time Required to Prepare an Action

Characteristics That *Increase* Action Preparation Time

- An increase in the number of movement alternatives
- An increase in the unpredictability of the correct movement response alternative
- Following an expectation bias toward performing one of several movement alternatives, the required movement not being the one expected
- An increase in the degree of spatial incompatibility between environmental features and the movements required
- An increase in the irregularity of foreperiod lengths in an RT situation
- No previous experience (i.e., practice) performing the task in the required situation
- A decrease in performer alertness
- An attention focus on the movement rather than the "go" signal

Characteristics That *Decrease* Action Preparation Time

- A decrease in the number of movement alternatives
- An increase in the predictability of the correct movement response alternative
- Following an expectation bias toward performing one of several movement alternatives, the required movement being the one expected
- An increase in the degree of spatial compatibility between environmental features and the movements required
- An increase in the regularity of foreperiod lengths in an RT situation
- An increase in the amount of experience (i.e., practice) performing the task in the required situation
- An increase in performer alertness
- An attention focus on the "go" signal rather than the movement

Evidence from Fractionating RT

To fractionate RT, we divide into two distinct components the EMG recording taken from the agonist muscle involved in a movement (see figure 7.5). The first is the *premotor* component (sometimes referred to as electromechanical delay). Notice that the EMG signal does not change much from what it was prior to the onset of the signal. However, shortly after the onset of the signal, the EMG signal shows a rapid increase in electrical activity. This indicates that the motor neurons are firing and the muscle is preparing to contract, even though no observable movement has yet occurred. In this period of time, the *motor* component is the increased EMG activity preceding the observable movement.

The premotor and motor components of RT represent two distinct activities that occur prior to observable movement and reflect different types of movement preparation processes. The premotor component includes the perceptual or cognitive processing of the stimulus information and preparing the movement features of the required action. The motor component begins the actual motor output phase of a movement. During this time, the specific muscles involved in the action are firing and preparing to begin to produce observable movement.

By fractionating RT, we can gain insight into what occurs during the action preparation process. Researchers look at which of these RT components is influenced by the various factors we discussed earlier that influence RT. For example, Christina and Rose (1985) reported that the changes in RT due to increases in *response complexity* were reflected in increases in the premotor component. For a two-part arm movement, the premotor component increased an average of 19 msec over that for a one-part arm movement, whereas the motor component increased only 3 msec. Siegel (1986) found that RT increased linearly as *movement durations* increased from 150, through 300 and 600, to 1200 msec, the length of the premotor component also increased linearly. The motor component, on the other hand, remained the same length until the response duration became 1200 msec; then it showed

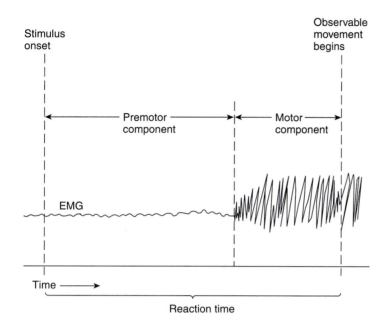

FIGURE 7.5 Schematization of fractionated reaction time indicating the relationship between the EMG signal activity and the premotor and motor components of the RT interval.

a slight increase. Sheridan (1984) showed that the premotor component was also responsible for RT increases due to increases in *movement velocity*. However, Carlton, Carlton, and Newell (1987) found changes in both the premotor and motor components by altering *force-related characteristics* of the response.

Postural Preparation

When a person must perform arm or leg movements, a part of the preparation process involves organizing supporting postural activity. EMG recordings of postural muscle activity provide evidence for this preparation.

Weeks and Wallace (1992) reported an example of research that demonstrates postural preparation for an arm movement. They asked people to perform an elbow-flexion aiming movement in the horizontal plane while standing in an erect posture. Participants learned to make this movement in three different velocities defined by criterion movement times. The authors made EMG recordings from various muscles of both legs and the responding arm. The results showed that a specific sequence of supporting postural events occurred; for each movement velocity, the muscles of the contralat-

eral and ipsilateral legs (biceps femoris and rectus femoris) activated *prior to* the onset of the arm agonist muscles (biceps brachii). And as the arm velocity increased, the onset of the anticipatory postural muscle activity occurred at an earlier time prior to arm agonist muscle activation. The authors found different onset orders for the various postural muscles.

Similar postural preparation effects were found in a study by Mercer and Sahrmann (1999) for leg movements. People of three age groups (8–12, 25–35, and 65–73 yrs) who had no neuromuscular impairments performed two types of stair-stepping movements: stepping onto a stair step with one foot (the "place task"); and stepping onto a stair step with one foot and then putting the other foot on the step (the "step task"). The experimenters analyzed EMG recordings from four muscles of the stance leg (tibialis anterior, gastrocnemius-soleus, hamstring, and gluteus maximus) and two muscles of the moving leg (rectus femoris and gluteus maximus). When the experimenters analyzed the EMG results in terms of the onset (i.e., activation) times for each muscle for all participants, they found that the tibialis anterior (TA) of the stance leg was the first muscle to activate. On average, it activated

Fractionated Visual Reaction Time Can Provide Insights into the Locus of Developmental Coordination Disorder

Children with developmental coordination disorder (DCD) have no evident physical or mental condition that would result in motor disabilities, yet they display motor performance levels below those of age-matched peers, and have significant difficulties with activities of daily living. In their attempts to better understand DCD, researchers have presented evidence that children with DCD have slower visual reaction time (RT) for a simple voluntary movement compared to normally coordinated children. Many of those researchers hypothesized that this slower RT is due to problems related to selecting the appropriate action or preparing the movements required for that action. Annette Raynor (1998) investigated this hypothesis by fractionating simple visual RT for six- and nine-year-old children with and without DCD. With the children in a sitting position, she asked them

to kick their right leg forward as fast as possible when a light in front of them illuminated. The results showed:

- Children with DCD had slower RTs than children who were not diagnosed with DCD.
- The fractionated RTs showed slower *premotor and motor* components for the DCD children.

The results of the fractionated RT not only supported the premotor locus hypothesis, but also presented new evidence that the motor component contributes to the coordination difficulties. Thus, the RT fractionation technique enabled the researcher to gain insights into DCD not previously seen. From this new base of understanding, researchers can plan investigations to identify the specific reasons for the movement planning and implementation delays.

215 ms *before* the initiation of movement by the opposite leg for the stepping task, and 307 ms *before* movement initiation for the place tasks. This initial activation of the TA in the stance leg ensured postural stability when the opposite leg stepped forward. Another important result of this experiment is the variety of muscle activation sequences demonstrated by each participant and across the participants for each task. Figure 7.6 shows the specific muscle activation sequences exhibited for the two tasks and the number of participants in each age group who displayed each sequence on at least 75 percent of the trials (which the experimenters referred to as representative of a "preferred" sequence). These results demonstrate that no specific sequence of muscle activation characterized all or any one of the participants for either task.

The sequences of muscle activation reported in these two experiments demonstrate that the preparation of postural stability is an important part of action preparation. And both experiments show that postural preparation involves organizing a *flexibly organized synergy* of postural muscles. This conclusion is important because movement scien-

tists traditionally have assumed that postural muscle preparation is rigidly temporally organized. The advantage of the flexibly organized synergy is that anticipatory postural activity can occur according to the person's equilibrium needs of various pre-movement postures.

Preparation of Limb Movement Characteristics
An essential part of the action preparation process is selecting and organizing the specific movement characteristics of the limbs to perform according to the dictates of task constraints and characteristics. Because an individual often can perform the same action using several different limbs or different segments of the same limb, he or she must specify and prepare the limb or limb segments to be involved in performing a given task.

One feature of limb movement a person must prepare is the *direction* or directions in which the limbs must move. For a very rapid movement, a person may prepare several different directions before initiating the movement. Another feature related to direction preparation is the *trajectory* the arm will follow during movement. For a task re-

FIGURE 7.6 Results of the experiment by Mercer and Sahrmann (1999) showing the number of children, young adults, and older adults who exhibited specific "preferred" sequences of muscle activation for the stance leg for the place and step tasks. Each sequence indicates the order of activation for the muscles listed (TA = tibialis anterior, GM = gluteus maximus, HS = hamstring, GS = gastrocnemius-soleus). *Source:* Figure 4, p. 1149 in Mercer, V. S., & Sahrmann, S. A. (1999). Postural synergies associated with a stepping task. *Physical Therapy, 79,* 1142–1152.

quiring a ballistic movement and spatial *accuracy,* an individual must prepare in advance, constraining the limb movement to meet the accuracy constraints of the task. In addition, as we discussed in chapter 6, a person catching a ball must prepare his or her hand and finger movements before the oncoming ball reaches him or her.

Preparation of Movements for Object Control
When the action to be performed involves manipulating an object, a part of the preparation process involves specifying certain movement features needed to control the object. Three examples illustrate some of those features that can be involved in this aspect of movement preparation.

One feature is the specification of pen pressure on the writing surface and grip force of the fingers on the writing instrument (Wann & Nimmo-Smith, 1991). Experienced writers adjust the amount of pen pressure on the writing surface according to certain characteristics of the surface to allow

energy-efficient, continuous, fluent motion. In contrast, children with handwriting problems often use excessive pen pressure and grip the pen barrel with excessive force.

Another movement feature prepared prior to manipulating an object is setting the amount of force required to lift or move the object. As an illustration of this type of preparation, think about situations in which you have looked at an object and, because of certain characteristics, judged it to be heavy. But when you began to lift it, you discovered it was light. Undoubtedly, you lifted the object much more quickly and higher in the air than you had intended. Why did you respond in this way? The reason is that because of certain observable characteristics of the object, such as a beverage can that looks unopened although it is actually empty, you anticipated that a certain amount of muscular force would be required to lift the object. This anticipated amount of force was used to prepare the musculature for the lifting action.

A CLOSER LOOK

Achieving a Standing Posture from Various Sitting Postures: An Example of How Functional Demands Affect Action Preparation

Changing from a sitting posture to a standing posture (referred to as a sit-to-stand action) is a common everyday activity that provides a good example of how the motor control system adapts to allow the same action to occur from a variety of initial postural positions. Shepherd and Gentile (1994) presented evidence of this adaptability by having healthy adults sit in different postures on a chair (an erect trunk, a fully flexed trunk, and a partially flexed trunk, i.e., flexed between the fully flexed and erect positions), and then stand. Analyses of the various joint movements involved in this action showed this:

• *In the erect and partially flexed sitting postures:* The knee began to extend before the hip joint began to extend.

• *In the fully flexed sitting posture:* the hip joint began to extend before the knee began to extend.

These different initiation patterns of joint movements illustrate how functional demands influence the order of muscle activation in preparing an action. Because different sitting postures will require different support, propulsion, and balance characteristics during the sit-to-stand action, the order of the initiation of movement of the knee or hip joints is a critical factor in enabling a person to carry out the intended action without losing balance.

Researchers have used this common everyday experience to provide evidence that the movement force characteristics are prepared in advance of the manipulation of objects. For example, Butler et al. (1993) showed that when men did not know the weight of a box that looked like it was filled with heavy objects, they performed with a jerking motion. Movement kinematics of these lifts showed that velocities at the shoulders and knees were much higher than the velocities when the men knew the actual weight of the box.

A third object control feature that individuals prepare is what Rosenbaum and Jorgenson (1992) referred to as *end-state comfort*. This means that when a person has several options for specifying how an object will be manipulated, as when he or she must pick up an object and place it in a specified location, the person will organize the limb movements so that a comfortable limb position will result at the completion of the action. For example, if a person must pick up an object and place it upside down on a tabletop, the person typically will pick up the object with a hand position that will yield the most comfortable position when the object is placed upside down.

Of the several hypotheses proposed to explain the end-state comfort effect, one that continues to gain support is the precision hypothesis (e.g., Rosenbaum, van Heutgen, & Caldwell, 1996; Short & Cauraugh, 1999). This hypothesized explanation proposes that precision in limb positioning will be greater, and the movement will be faster, when a person's limb is in a comfortable position. Thus, to ensure a faster and more accurate final limb and object position, a person prepares movement characteristics according to the comfort of the final rather than the starting position of the limb. Although this strategy may require some awkward hand and arm postures when picking up an object, it enables the person to more effectively and efficiently achieve the object manipulation goal.

Preparation of Sequences of Simple Movements
Playing the piano and typing on a keyboard are examples of skills that involve the sequencing of series of simple movements. Two types of research evidence indicate that short sequences of these movements are prepared in advance of the initial movement. One is the systematic increase in RT as movement complexity increases, which we dis-

A CLOSER LOOK

Correcting Handwriting Problems Due to Grip and Pen Force

The results of the experiment by Wann and Nimmo-Smith (1991) showed that when handwriting, children with handwriting problems often do so because they use excessive pen pressure and grip the pen barrel with excessive force. The have not acquired the necessary association between the "feel" of the pen against the surface and the appropriate pen pressure to apply. The researchers speculated that adults who made the appropriate force adjustments had acquired this capability through experience, which had led to their nonconsciously learning the amount of pressure required based on sensations in the fingers holding the pen.

Teachers and therapists who work with children struggling with this type of problem can encourage an increasing sensitivity in the children to appropriate pen pressure. One way to do this is by providing handwriting experiences with a variety of writing surfaces. A teacher or therapist should monitor each child's grip force, with the goal of keeping it at the minimum amount of force needed to produce a visible trace on the writing surface.

cussed earlier in this chapter. The other type of evidence is the kinematic characteristics of hand movements during the performance of typing and piano playing (e.g., Engel, Flanders, & Soechting, 1997; Soechting & Flanders, 1992). For example, in the Engel, Flanders, & Soechting study, skilled pianists played short excerpts from three pieces written for the piano. In one piece, the first four notes were the same for the right hand. However, the fourth note in one phrase is typically played by a different finger from the fourth note of the other phrase. For one phrase, the sequence of finger movements for the same first four notes was: thumb—index finger—middle finger—ring finger; but for the other phrase it was: thumb—index finger—middle finger—thumb. To hit the fourth note with the thumb the pianists moved the thumb under the fingers and repositioned the hand between the third and fourth notes. Because of the consistency of the kinematics of the third and fourth note movements for several trials of playing these phrases, the researchers concluded that movements for each phrase were prepared in advance. If the hand and finger repositioning had not been prepared in advance of playing the previous three notes, the kinematics of the hand and finger positioning would have been somewhat variable across the several trials.

Preparation of Spatial Coding

In performance situations requiring specified responses to certain stimuli, such as choice-RT situations, people take into account the spatial relationships of the stimulus and response locations in the movement preparation process. They translate these relationships into meaningful codes that they then use to produce the required responses. Research has shown that this spatial coding accounts for many stimulus-response compatibility effects (see Weeks & Proctor, 1990 for a discussion of these). The simplest spatial coding, which leads to the fastest preparation (i.e., RT), occurs when left and right stimulus locations are compatible with left and right response locations. Beyond that arrangement, it appears that up-to-right and down-to-left stimulus-to-response relationships lead to faster preparation times. The limb involved in performing the required response is not as critical as the spatial relationship of the stimulus location to the response location.

Rhythmicity Preparation

Many skills require that the component movements follow specific rhythmic patterns. We can see this characteristic in any of the various types of gait, performance of a dance sequence, shooting of a free throw in basketball, and so on. In some of these activities, the participant can take time before performing it to engage in some preperformance activities that are commonly referred to as rituals. Interestingly, rhythmic patterns also characterize preperformance rituals and appear to influence performance. Although this relationship has not

TABLE 7.1   Types of Behaviors Involved in Preperformance Rituals in Activities Investigated by Southard and Amos (1996)

Activity	Behaviors in Preperformance Rituals
Golf putt	1. Swinging the putter back and forth without contacting the ball 2. Pause; no movement for 1 sec or more 3. Moving the toes or either foot up and down 4. Swaying the body back and forth without swinging the putter 5. Lifting the putter vertically
Tennis serve	1. Bouncing the ball with the racquet or the hand not holding the racquet 2. Pause; no movement for 1 sec or more 3. Moving the racquet forward to a position in front of the body waist high 4. Moving the racquet back from the front of the body and then forward again 5. Moving the racquet to a ready position in order to initiate serving the ball
Basketball free throw	1. Bouncing the ball 2. Pause, no movement for 1 sec or more 3. Bending at the knees or waist 4. Moving the ball upward with the arms 5. Spinning the ball 6. Bringing the ball to an initial shooting position

Table based on text and table 1 (p. 290) in Southard, D., & Amos, B. (1996). Rhythmicity and preperformance ritual: Stabilizing a flexible system. *Research Quarterly for Exercise and Sport, 67,* 288–296.

been widely studied, the few research studies investigating it have consistently shown a positive correlation between the rhythm of the preperformance routine and the success of the performance itself (e.g., Southard & Miracle, 1993; Southard & Amos, 1996; Wrisberg & Pein, 1992). In terms of the preparation of action, the preperformance rituals would appear to stabilize the motor control system and orient it to engaging in a rhythmic activity.

The Southard and Amos (1996) study will serve as a good example of how these researchers have determined that such a relationship exists. They video recorded fifteen basketball free throws, golf putts, and tennis serves for experienced university men who had established rituals for each of these activities. Each video recording was analyzed to determine the preperformance behaviors each participant used on each trial. The types of behaviors for each activity are listed in table 7.1. It is important to note that although each of the behaviors was

observed, individual participants did not exhibit every behavior. The researchers also analyzed the total time to perform the ritual and the relative time for each behavior in the ritual, which was the percentage of time engaged in each behavior in the ritual. Results showed a moderately high .77 correlation between the relative time for the ritual behaviors and successful performance. This relationship suggests that the consistent relative timing of preperformance ritual behaviors may be an important part of the successful performance of closed motor skills that provide an opportunity for the performer to engage in preperformance rituals.

Mack (2001) provided additional evidence that the consistent performance of the components of a preperformance routine is more important than the total amount of time taken to perform the routine. Although he did not assess the relative time of the components of a routine, he compared the influence of altering a normal routine in terms of its duration and component activities. He found essentially no influence on the free-throw shooting performance of university basketball players when they had to double the amount of time they normally took for their pre-shot routine, but a decrease in performance when they had to include some new activities in their normal routine.

SUMMARY

To perform a motor skill, a person must prepare the motor control system.

- The preparation process requires time, which can be measured by reaction (RT); the amount of time required depends on a variety of task, situation, and personal characteristics.

- *Task and situation characteristics* that influence the amount of time required to prepare an action include

    ‣ the number of movement response alternatives in the situation from which the performer must choose only one

    ‣ the predictability of the correct movement response alternative when there are several from which to choose

    ‣ the degree of stimulus-response compatibility

    ‣ the regularity of the length of the RT foreperiod

    ‣ movement complexity

    ‣ movement accuracy demands

    ‣ the amount of movement response repetition involved in a situation

    ‣ the amount of time available between different movement responses

- *Personal characteristics* that influence the amount of time required to prepare an action include

    ‣ the degree of the performer's alertness

    ‣ attention focus on the signal to move or on the movement required at the signal

- The premotor and motor components of the RT interval, which can be identified by fractionating the interval on the basis of EMG recordings from the agonist muscles, can provide insight into the extent to which various preparation activities involve perceptual, cognitive, or motor processes.

- Motor control activities that occur during action preparation include

    ‣ postural organization

    ‣ limb performance characteristics

    ‣ object control characteristics

    ‣ sequences of simple movements

    ‣ spatial coding

    ‣ movement rythmicity

RELATED READINGS

Carson, R., Chua, G. R., Goodman, D., & Byblow, W. D., (1995). The preparation of aiming movements. *Brain and Cognition, 28,* 133–154.

Klapp, S. T. (1996). Reaction time analysis of central motor control. In H. N. Zelaznik (Ed.); *Advances in motor learning and control* (pp.13–35). Champaign, IL: Human Kinetics.

Mohagheghi, A. A., & Anson, J. G. (2002). Amplitude and target diameter in motor programming of discrete, rapid aimed movements: Fitts and Peterson (1964) and Klapp (1975) revisited. *Acta Psychologica, 109,* 113–136

Stelmach, G. E., Teasdale, N., & Phillips, J. (1992). Response initiation delays in Parkinson's disease patients. *Human Movement Science, 11,* 37–45.

Weeks, D. J., Proctor, R. W., & Beyak, B. (1995). Stimulus-response compatibility for vertically oriented stimuli and horizontally oriented responses: Evidence for spatial coding. *Quarterly Journal of Experimental Psychology, 48A,* 367–383.

Wing, A. M., & Ledeman, S. J. (1998). Anticipating load torques produced by voluntary movements. *Journal of Experimental Psychology: Human Perception and Performance, 24,* 1571–1581

Wright, D. L., Black, C., Park, J. H., & Shea, C. H. (2001). Planning and executing simple movements: Contributions of relative-time and overall-duration specification. *Journal of Motor Behavior, 33,* 273–285

STUDY QUESTIONS

1. Discuss how we can use reaction time (RT) as an index of the preparation required to perform a motor skill.

2. Discuss how Hick's law is relevant to helping us understand the characteristics of factors that influence motor control preparation.

3. What is the cost-benefit trade-off involved in biasing the preparation of an action in the expectation of making one of several possible responses? Give a motor skill performance example illustrating this tradeoff.

4. Describe two performer characteristics that can influence action preparation. Discuss how these characteristics can influence preparation.

5. Select a motor skill and describe two motor control features of that skill that a person prepares prior to the initiation of performance of the skill.

UNIT

III

ATTENTION
AND MEMORY

CHAPTER

8

Attention as a Limited
Capacity Resource

*Concept: Preparation for and performance of motor skills
are influenced by our limited capacity
to select and attend to information*

After completing this chapter, you will be able to

- Define the term *attention* as it relates to the performance of motor skills

- Discuss the concept of *attention capacity,* and identify the similarities and differences between fixed and flexible central-resource theories of attention capacity

- Describe *Kahneman's model of attention* in relationship to a motor skill situation

- Discuss *dual-task techniques* that researchers use to assess the attention demands of performing a motor skill

- Explain the different types of *attentional focus* a person can employ when performing a motor skill

- Define *visual search* and describe how it relates to attention capacity limits and to the performance of a motor skill

- Describe two different types of techniques that researchers have used to help understand visual search in a motor skill performance situation

- Discuss how skilled performers engage in visual search in the performance of different types of motor skills

Application

When you are driving your car on an open highway that has little traffic, it is relatively easy for you to carry on a conversation with a passenger in the car or on a cell phone at the same time. But what happens when the highway you are driving on becomes congested with other traffic? Isn't it difficult to carry on a conversation with your passenger or on your phone while driving under these conditions?

Consider some other examples in which doing more than one activity at a time may or may not be a problem. A skilled typist can easily carry on a conversation with someone while continuing to type—

but a beginner cannot. A child learning to dribble a ball has difficulty dribbling and running at the same time, whereas a skilled basketball player does these two activities and more at the same time. A physical therapy patient tells the therapist not to talk to her while she is trying to walk down a set of stairs.

These examples raise an important human performance and learning question: Why is it easy to do more than one thing at the same time in one situation, but difficult to do these same things simultaneously in another situation? The answer to this question comes from the study of *attention* as it relates to the performance of multiple activities at the same time.

Another aspect of attention occurs when you need to visually select and attend to specific features of the environmental context before actually carrying out an action. For example, when you reach for a cup to drink the coffee in it, you visually note where the cup is and how full it is before you reach to pick it up. When you put your door key into the keyhole, you first look to see exactly where it is. When you need to maneuver around people and objects as you walk along a corridor, you look to see where they are, what direction they are moving in, and how fast they are going. To drive your car, you also must visually select information from the environment so that you can get safely to your destination.

In sport activities, visual attention to environmental context information is also essential. For example, visually selecting and attending to ball- and server-based cues allows the player to prepare to hit a return shot in tennis or racquetball. Skills such as determining where to direct a pass in soccer or hockey, or deciding which type of move to put on a defender in basketball or football, are all dependent on a player's successful attention to the appropriate visual cues prior to initiating action.

Discussion

When the term is used in the context of human performance, **attention** refers to engagement in the perceptual, cognitive, and motor activities associated with performing skills. These activities may be performed consciously or nonconsciously. For example, detecting information in the environment is an attention-demanding activity. We observe and attend to the environment in which we move to detect features that help us determine what skill to perform and how to perform it. Although this observation and detection activity demands our attention, it does not always require that we are consciously aware of what we observe and detect that directs our actions.

Since the earliest days of investigating human behavior, scholars have had a keen interest in the study of attention. For example, as early as 1859, Sir William Hamilton conducted studies in Britain dealing with attention. Around the same time, William Wundt, generally acknowledged as the "father of experimental psychology," investigated the concept of attention at the University of Leipzig in Germany. In America, William James provided one of the earliest definitions of attention in 1890, describing it as the "focalization, concentration, of consciousness."

Unfortunately, this late-nineteenth- and early-twentieth-century emphasis on attention soon waned, as those under the influence of behaviorism deemed the study of attention no longer relevant to the understanding of human behavior. A renaissance in attention research occurred, however, when the practical requirements of World War II included the need to understand human performance in a variety of military skills. Researchers were interested in several attention-related areas, such as the performance of more than one skill at the same time; the selection of and attention to relevant information from the performance environment; the performance of tasks where people had to make rapid decisions when there were several response choices; and the performance of tasks where people had to maintain attention over long periods of time. The discussion in this chapter will

---

attention   in human performance, the conscious or nonconscious engagement in perceptual, cognitive, and/or motor activities before, during, and after performing skills; the human information-processing systems includes limitations to the number of these activities that can be performed simultaneously.

address two of these issues: the simultaneous performance of multiple activities, and the selection of and attention to relevant information from the environment.

ATTENTION AND MULTIPLE TASK PERFORMANCE

Scientists have known for many years that we have attention limits that influence performance when we do more than one activity at the same time. In fact, in the late nineteenth century, a French physiologist named Jacques Loeb (1890) showed that the maximum amount of pressure that a person can exert on a hand dynamometer actually decreases when the person is engaged in mental work. Other researchers in that era also pointed out this multiple-task performance limitation (e.g., Solomons & Stein, 1896). Unfortunately, it was not until the 1950s that researchers began to try to provide a theoretical basis for this type of behavioral evidence.

Attention Theories

The most prominent among the first theories addressing attention limitations[1] was the *filter theory* of attention, sometimes referred to as the *bottleneck theory*. This theory, which evolved into many variations, proposed that a person has difficulty doing several things at one time. The reason for this limitation is that the human information-

[1]For an excellent review and discussion of the history and evolution of attention theories, see Neumann (1996).

processing system performs each of its functions in serial order, and some of these functions can process only one piece of information at a time. This means that somewhere along the stages of information processing, the system has a *bottleneck*, where it filters out information not selected for further processing (see figure 8.1). Variations of this theory were based on the processing stage in which the bottleneck occurred. Some contended it existed very early, at the stage of detection of environmental information (e.g., Welford, 1952, 1967; Broadbent, 1958), whereas others argued that it occurred later, after information was perceived or after it had been processed cognitively (e.g., Norman, 1968).

This type of theoretical viewpoint remained popular for many years, until it became evident that the filter theories of attention did not adequately explain all performance situations. The most influential alternative proposed that attention limits were the result of the *limited availability of resources* needed to carry out the information-processing functions. Just as you have limited economic resources to pay for your activities, we all have limited attention resources to do all the activities that we may attempt at one time.

Theories emphasizing attentional resource limits propose that we can perform several tasks simultaneously, as long as the resource capacity limits of the system are not exceeded. However, if these limits are exceeded, we experience difficulty performing one or more of these tasks. Theorists who adhere to this viewpoint differ in their views of *where* the resource limit exists. Some propose that there is one central resource pool from which

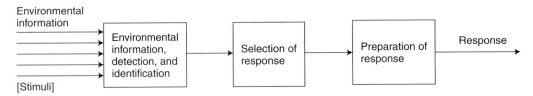

FIGURE 8.1   A generic information-processing model on which filter theories of attention were based. The figure illustrates the several stages of information processing and the serial order in which information is processed. Filter theories varied in terms of the stage at which the filter occurred. Prior to the filter, the system could process several stimuli at the same time. In the model illustrated in this figure, the filter is located in the detection and identification stage.

all attention resources are allocated, whereas others propose multiple sources for resources.

Finally, more recent attention theories have moved away from the concept of a central capacity limit to one that emphasizes the selection and integration of information and activities associated with the various functional aspects of human performance, such as those depicted in figure 8.1. The primary focus of these theories has been in the area of visual selective attention, which will be discussed later in this chapter.

Central-Resource Capacity Theories

According to some attention theories, there is a central reserve of resources for which all activities compete. Following the analogy of your economic resources, these **central-resource theories** compare human attention capacity to a single source from which all activities must be funded. To illustrate this view, consider the available attention resources as existing within one large circle, like the one depicted in figure 8.2. Next, consider as smaller circles the specific tasks that require these resources, such as driving a car (task A) and talking with a friend (task B). Each circle by itself fits inside the larger circle. But for a person to successfully perform both tasks simultaneously, both small circles must fit into the large circle. Problems arise when we try to fit into the large circle more small circles than will fit.

A good example of a central resource theory is one proposed by Nobel laureate Daniel Kahneman (1973). Although this theory was originally presented many years ago, it continues to influence our present views about attention. And although some researchers have pointed out shortcomings in Kahneman's theory in terms of accounting for all aspects of attention and human performance (e.g., Neumann, 1996), it continues to serve as a useful guide to direct our understanding of some basic characteristics of attention-related limits on the simultaneous performance of multiple activities. In his model (see figure 8.3), the *capacity limits of the central pool of resources are flexible.* This means that the amount of available attention can vary depending on certain conditions related to the indi-

FIGURE 8.2 Diagram showing that two tasks (A and B) can be performed simultaneously (e.g., driving a car while talking with a passenger) if the attention demanded by the tasks does not exceed the available attention capacity. Note that the amount of available capacity and the amount of attention demanded by each task to be performed may increase or decrease, a change that would be represented in this diagram by changing the sizes of the appropriate circles.

vidual, the tasks being performed, and the situation. According to the illustration in figure 8.2, this flexible central-capacity theory states that the size of the large circle can change according to certain personal, task, and situation characteristics.

Kahneman views the *available* attention that a person can give to an activity or activities as a general *pool of effort,* which involves the mental resources necessary to carry out activities. The person can subdivide this one pool so that he or she can allocate attention to several activities at the same time. Allocation of resources is determined by characteristics of the activities and the allocation policy of the individual, which in turn is influenced by situations internal and external to the individual.

Figure 8.3 depicts the various conditions that influence how a person will allocate the available resources. First, notice that the central pool of available resources (available capacity) is

---

central-resource theories   attention-capacity theories that propose one central source of attention resources for which all activities requiring attention compete.

A CLOSER LOOK

An Attention-Capacity Explanation of the Arousal-Performance Relationship

A widely held view of the relationship between arousal and performance is that it takes the form of an inverted U. This means that when we graph this relationship, placing on the vertical axis the performance level ranging from poor to high, and placing on the horizontal axis the arousal level ranging from very low to very high, the plot of the relationship resembles an inverted U. This type of relationship indicates that arousal levels that are either too low or too high will result in poor performance. However, between these extremes is a range of arousal levels that should yield high performance levels.

If, as Kahneman's model indicates, arousal levels influence available attention capacity in a similar way, then it would follow that we can attribute the arousal level-performance relationship to available attention capacity. This means that arousal levels that are too low or too high lead to poor performance, because the person does not have the attentional resources needed to perform the activity. When the arousal level is optimal, sufficient attention resources are available and the person can achieve a high level of performance.

FIGURE 8.3 Kahneman's model of attention. [From Kahneman, D. (1973). *Attention and effort,* © 1973, p.10. Reprinted by permission of Prentice Hall, Inc., Englewood Cliffs, NJ]

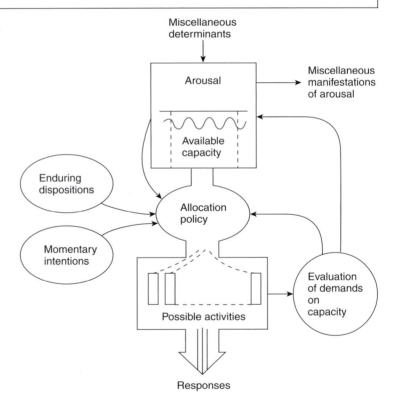

represented as a box at the top of the model. The wavy line indicates that the amount of attention available, the capacity limit, is flexible. Attention capacity will increase or decrease according to the *arousal level* of the person. **Arousal** is the general state of excitability of a person, reflected in the activation levels of the person's emotional, mental, and physiological systems. If the person's arousal level is too low or too high, he or she has a smaller available attention capacity than he or she would if the arousal level were in an optimal range. This means that for a person to have available the maximum attention resources, the person must be at an optimal arousal level.

Second, another critical factor determining whether there are sufficient attentional resources is the *attention demands, or requirements, of the tasks to be performed.* This factor is represented in Kahneman's model in figure 8.3 as the *evaluation of demands on capacity.* Because tasks differ in the amount of attention they demand, the person must evaluate these demands to determine if he or she can do them all simultaneously, or if he or she will not be able to perform some of them.

Finally, *three rules influence how people allocate attentional resources.* One is that we allocate attention to ensure that we can complete one activity. Another is that we allocate attentional resources according to our *enduring dispositions.* These are the basic rules of "involuntary" attention, which concern those things that seem to naturally attract our attention (i.e., distract us). We typically will "involuntarily" direct our attention to (or be distracted by) at least *two types of characteristics of events* in our environment, even though we may be attending to something else at the time.

One is that the event is *novel* for the situation in which it occurs. These events can be visual or auditory. In terms of novel visual events, think about why fans at a basketball game who sit behind the basket like to stand and wave objects in the air while a player is attempting to shoot free throws. Or, consider why you become distracted while driving your car when a ball rolls onto the street in front of you. That we spontaneously and involuntary allocate our visual attention to novel events such as these is well supported by research evidence (see Cole, Gellatly, & Blurton, 2001, and Pashler & Harris, 2001, for excellent reviews of this evidence).

Unexpected noise also presents a novel event that spontaneously and involuntarily attracts our attention. For example, how many times have you directed your attention away from the person teaching your class to one of your classmates when he or she sneezes very loudly or drops a book on the floor? Consider a different type of example. Why is a professional golfer who is preparing to putt distracted by a spectator talking, when a basketball player who is preparing to shoot a free throw is not distracted by thousands of spectators yelling and screaming? The most likely reason is that the golfer does not expect to hear someone talking while preparing to putt, but for the basketball player, the noise is a common part of the game. As a result, the noise is novel in one situation but not in the other.

The second characteristic of events that will involuntarily direct our attention is the *meaningfulness* of the event to us personally. A classic example of this characteristic is known as the *cocktail party phenomenon,* which was first described in the 1950s (Cherry, 1953). Undoubtedly, you have experienced this phenomenon yourself. Suppose you are at a party in a room filled with people. You are attending to your conversation with another person. Suddenly you hear someone near you mention your name in a conversation that person is having with other people. What do you do? You probably redirect your attention away from your own conversation to the person who said your name. Why did you do this? The reason relates to the meaningfulness of your name to you. Even though you were attending to your own conversation, this meaningful event caused you to spontaneously shift your attention. In sports, it is not uncommon to hear athletes say that while they are performing, the only person they hear saying something to them is the coach. Why? In this competitive situation, the person's coach is very meaningful to the athlete.

The third rule in Kahneman's model concerning our allocation of attention relates to a person's *momentary intentions.* That is, a person allocates attention in a situation according to his or her specific intentions. Sometimes, these intentions are self-directed, which means the person has personally decided to direct attention to a certain

---

arousal   the general state of excitability of a person, involving physiological, emotional, and mental systems.

This bicycle rider, who can drink water, steer the bike, pedal the bike, maintain balance, see ahead to determine where to go and how to avoid road hazards, etc., demonstrates the simultaneous performance of multiple activities.

aspect of the situation. At other times, momentary intentions result from instructions given to the person about how or where to direct his or her attentional resources. For example, if a physical therapist tells a patient to "pay close attention to where you place your foot on the stair step," the patient has the "momentary intention" to allocate his or her attention according to the therapist's instruction.

Multiple-Resource Theories
Multiple-resource theories provide an alternative to theories proposing a central resource pool of attention resources. Multiple-resource theories contend that we have several attention mechanisms, each having limited resources. Each resource pool is specific to a component of performing skills. Using a government analogy, the resources are available in various government agencies, and competition for the resources occurs only among those activities related to the specific agencies. The most prevalent of the multiple-resource theories were proposed by Navon and Gopher (1979), Allport (1980), and Wickens (1980, 1992).

Wickens proposed what has become the most popular of these theories. He stated that resources for processing information are available from three different sources. These are the *input and output modalities* (e.g., vision, limbs, and speech system), the *stages of information processing* (e.g., perception, memory encoding, response output), and the *codes of processing information* (e.g., verbal codes, spatial codes). Our success in performing two or more tasks simultaneously depends on whether those tasks demand our attention from a common resource or from different resources. When two tasks must be performed simultaneously and share a common resource, they will be performed less well than when the two tasks compete for different resources.

For example, the multiple-resource view would explain variations in the situation involving driving a car while talking with a passenger in the following way. When there is little traffic, driving does not demand many resources from any of the three different sources. But when traffic gets heavy, resource demand increases from these two sources: input-output modalities and stages of information processing. These are the same two sources involved in providing attention resources for carrying on a conversation with a friend. As a result, to maintain safe driving, the person must reduce the resource demand of the conversation activity.

An advantage of multiple-resource theories is their focus on the types of demands placed on various information—processing and response outcome structures, rather than on a nonspecific resource capacity. The resource—specific attention view provides a practical guide to help us determine when task demands may be too great to be performed simultaneously. For example, if one task requires a hand response and one requires a vocal response, a person should have little difficulty performing them

A CLOSER LOOK

Attention and Cell Phone Use While Driving

A common concern throughout the world is the use of cell phones by people who are driving motor vehicles. Many countries, and some cities in the United States, have passed laws that prohibit cell phone use while driving. In some instances, the laws prohibit the use of both hand-held and hands-free cell phones, while in other cases, laws allow hands-free cell phone use. The following information, taken from an article by Strayer and Johnston (2001), provides some basis for concern.

- A study by the United States Department of Transportation indicated that as many as half of the motor vehicle accidents in the U.S. can be related to driver inattention and other human error.
- A survey of cell phone owners reported that approximately 85 percent use their phones while driving, 27 percent of whom use them on half of their trips (Goodman et al., 1999; a summary of their report is available online at www.nhtsa.dot.gov)
- A study of cell phone records of 699 people who had been involved in motor-vehicle accidents reported that 24 percent were using their cell phones within the 10-min period before the accident (Redelmeier & Tibshirani, 1997).

Although research evidence supports a relationship between cell phone use and motor vehicle accidents, the issue of cell phone use as the cause of accidents remains unsolved. However, researchers who have investigated this issue, in either car simulators or simulated driving situations in laboratories, report evidence that indicates an attention-related basis for driving accidents. In their article, Strayer and Johnson reported a series of experiments in which participants engaged in a simulated driving task in a laboratory. The results indicated these things:

- Participants missed two times more simulated traffic signals when they were engaged in cell phone conversations; and, when they responded correctly to the signals (i.e., red lights), their reaction time (RT) was significantly slower than when they were not using the cell phone.
- No significant differences were found between hand-held and hands-free cell phone use for the number of missed traffic signals and RT (a result that is problematic for a multiple-resource theory of attention).
- The generation of phone conversations influenced the number of missed traffic signals and RT more than did listening to the radio or to a section of a book on audiotape.

simultaneously, because they do not demand attention from the same resource structure. Conversely, people have difficulty performing two different hand responses simultaneously because they both demand resources from the same structure.

PROCEDURES FOR ASSESSING ATTENTION DEMANDS

A common experimental procedure used to investigate attention-limit issues is the **dual-task procedure.** The general purpose of experiments using this technique is to determine the attention demands and characteristics of the simultaneous performance of two different tasks. Experimenters' general approach has been to determine the atten-

tion demands of one of the two tasks by noting the degree of interference caused on that task while it

multiple-resource theories   theories of attention proposing that there are several attention resource mechanisms, each of which is related to a specific information-processing activity, and is limited in how much information it can process simultaneously.

dual-task procedure   an experimental procedure used in the study of attention to determine the amount of attention required to perform an action, or a part of an action; the procedure involves assessing the degree of interference caused by one task when a person is simultaneously performing another task.

A CLOSER LOOK

Dual-Task Techniques Used to Assess Attention Demands of Motor Skill Performance

Researchers typically have used one of two dual-task techniques in their investigations of the attention demands associated with the preparation and performance of motor skills. Each technique relates to a specific attention-demand issue.

Continuous Secondary-Task Technique

Purpose. To determine if attention capacity is required *throughout* the performance of a motor skill.

Procedure. A person performs the primary and secondary tasks separately and simultaneously. When the person performs both tasks simultaneously, he or she is instructed to concentrate on the performance of the primary task while continuously performing the secondary task.

Rationale. If the primary task demands full attention capacity, performance will be poorer on a secondary task while performing it together with the primary task than when performing only the secondary task. If attention capacity can be shared by both tasks, simultaneous performance should be similar to that of each task alone.

Example. As a person walks from one end of a hallway to the other, he or she must listen to words spoken through earphones; when the person hears each word, he or she must repeat the word that was spoken just prior to that word (i.e., the secondary task is a short-term memory task that involves interference during the retention interval).

Secondary-Task Probe Technique

Purpose. To determine the attention demands required by the *preparation* of a skill, by the performance of *specific components* of a skill, or at *specific times* during the performance of a skill.

Procedure. A person performs the primary and secondary tasks separately and simultaneously. The secondary task (a discrete task) is performed at predetermined times before or during primary-task performance (i.e., the secondary task "probes" the primary task).

Rationale. If a probed site of the primary task demands full attention capacity, performance will be poorer on a secondary task while performing it together with the primary task than when performing only the secondary task. If attention capacity can be shared by both tasks at the probed site, simultaneous performance should be similar to that of each task alone.

Example. As a person reaches for and grasps a cup of water to drink from it, he or she must listen through earphones for a "beep" sound at any time just before or during the performance of the activity. As soon as the person hears the "beep" he or she says "bop" into a microphone (i.e., the secondary task is a simple auditory-reaction time task that requires a vocal response).

---

is performed simultaneously with another task, called the *secondary task.*

The *primary task* in the dual-task procedure is typically the task of interest, whose performance experimenters are observing in order to assess its attention demands. Depending on the purpose of the experiment, the performer may or may not need to maintain consistent primary-task performance, whether performing that task alone or simultaneously with the secondary task.

If instructions in the experiment require the participant to pay attention to the primary task so that it is performed as well alone as with the secondary task, then secondary-task performance is the basis researchers use to make inferences about the atten-

tion demands of the primary task. On the other hand, if the experiment does not direct the person to attend primarily to either task, performance on both tasks is compared to performance when each task is performed alone.

FOCUSING ATTENTION

In addition to having to distribute attention among several activities, people also direct attention to specific features of the environment and to action preparation activities. This attention-directing process is known as **attentional focus.** As opposed to attentional demands, which concern the distribution of attentional resources to various tasks that

A CLOSER LOOK

Dual-Task Interference During Gait in People with Parkinson's Disease

A study by O'Shea, Morris, and Iansek (2002) provides a good example of the use of the dual-task procedure to study attention demands of activities, and an opportunity to consider the relationship between movement disorders and attention demands as it relates to multiple task performance.

Participants: 15 people (mean age = 68.3 yrs) with Parkinson's disease (PD) and 15 comparison people (mean age = 67.7 yrs) without PD. The people with PD were in a self-determined "on" phase of their medication cycle.

Walking tasks: **1.** Walk 14 m at a self-selected speed (single task: free walking)

2. Walk while transferring as many coins as possible from one pocket to another on their opposite side (motor secondary task: manual object manipulation)

3. Walk while counting backward aloud by threes from a three-digit number (cognitive secondary task: subtraction)

Standing tasks: Perform the coin transfer task and the digit subtraction task while standing.

Results:

Walking tasks change from walking only to walking while performing a secondary task:

	Walking Speed		Stride Length	
	PD Group	No–PD Group	PD Group	No–PD group
With Coin Task:	−18.5%	−7.4%	−15.4%	−7.4%
With Subtraction Task:	−18.7%	−6.9%	−18.7%	−6.9%

Secondary tasks change from performing it while standing to performing it while walking:

	PD Group	No–PD Group
Coin task (coins/min rate)	−17.4%	0.0%
Subtraction task (responses/min rate)	−4.7%	+13.1%

Conclusions: People with PD showed

- a greater amount of deterioration in their walking gait characteristics when they had to simultaneously perform a manual object-manipulation task and cognitive task involving subtraction than comparably aged people who did not have PD.
- a slower rate of performing a manual object-manipulation task and a cognitive task involving subtraction when they had to perform these tasks while walking than when they performed them while standing.

need to be performed simultaneously, attentional focus concerns the marshalling of available resources in order to direct them to specific information sources.

We can consider attentional focus in terms of both width and direction of focus. *Width* indicates that our attention can have a *broad or narrow* focus on environmental information and mental activities. *Direction* indicates that our attention focus can

> **attentional focus**   the directing of attention to specific characteristics in a performance environment, or to action-preparation activities.

A CLOSER LOOK

An Attention-Related Strategy for Preparing to Perform a Closed Skill

Based on a review of research related to attention and performance, Singer and colleagues (Singer et al., 1991) presented a three-component strategy that should be employed by people as they prepare to perform a closed skill. People can use this strategy when performing a variety of sport skills (e.g., shooting a free throw in basketball, serving in tennis or badminton, shooting in archery and gun sports, hitting a golf ball) and everyday skills (e.g., getting out of bed, getting out of a chair, walking along a designated pathway, buttoning a jacket).

Those who use this strategy engage in three activities just prior to performing a skill:

1. **Relaxation** involves using breathing control and muscle relaxation to reduce tensions, to enhance attention focus and develop an optimal arousal level.
2. **Visualization** involves mentally seeing and feeling the desired performance before actually performing it.
3. **Focus** involves concentrating on a positive aspect of task performance that is vital to performing effectively.

be *external or internal:* attention may be focused on cues in the environment or on internal thoughts, plans, or problem-solving activities. Nideffer (1993) has shown that the broad and narrow focus widths and the external and internal focus directions interact to establish four types of attention-focus situations that relate to performance.

Individuals in performance situations require specific types of attention focus to achieve successful performance. For example, a person needs a broad/external focus to walk successfully through a crowded hallway, but a narrow/external focus to catch a ball. Sometimes, situations require us to shift the type of attention focus and the object of that attention. We do this by engaging in what is referred to as *attention switching.* It is an advantage to switch attention focus rapidly among environmental and situational pieces of information when we must use a variety of sources of information for rapid decision making. For example, a football quarterback may look to decide if the primary receiver is open; if not, he must find an alternate receiver. In the meantime, the quarterback must make decisions related to whether or not he is about to be tackled or kept from delivering a pass. Each of these activities requires attention and must be carried out in the course of a few seconds. To do

this, the player must rapidly switch attention between external and internal sources of information.

However, certain kinds of attention switching can be a disadvantage in the performance of some activities. For example, a person performing a skill that requires a rapid, accurate series of movements, such as typing, piano playing, or dancing, will be more successful if he or she focuses attention on a primary source of information for extended periods of time. Problems can arise if the person's attention is switched too frequently between appropriate and inappropriate sources of information. For example, if a pianist is constantly switching visual attention from the written music to the hands and keys, he or she will have difficulty maintaining the precise timing structure required by the piece being played.

Focusing Attention on Movements versus Movement Effects

If, as we just discussed, it is best for people to narrow their attention focus while performing certain skills, a relevant question concerns the specific location of the attention focus. Although Nideffer presented the options of internal and external to represent the location, there is an alternative way to use these terms when referring to the performance of a specific skill. Is it preferable to focus attention on one's own movements (internal focus) or on the effects of one's own movements (external focus)? This question has intrigued scientists for many years, which we can see if we look at the classic and influential work of William James (1890). He raised this same question more than a century ago, and offered as an answer that the directing of attention to the "remote effects" (i.e., outcome of a movement, or movement effects) would lead to better performance than attention to the "close effects" (i.e., the movements). He presented an example of a reaching/aiming movement to illustrate his point: "Keep your eye at the place aimed at, and your hand will fetch [the target]; think of your hand, and you will likely miss your aim" (p. 520).

More recently, the German scholar Wolfgang Prinz (1997) formalized this view by proposing the *action effect hypothesis,* which stated that actions are best planned and controlled by their intended effects. This means that attention focused on the intended outcome of the performance of a skill will be more effective than attention focused on one's own movements. An interesting application of this hypothesis was reported in an article in *The New Yorker* magazine (Acocella, 2003) about the great ballerina Suzanne Farrell. Although retired from performing, she teaches ballet to experienced students and professional dancers. In her teaching, she emphasizes that the dancers concentrate on the effect they want to create with movements rather than on the movements themselves. When researchers have investigated the action effect hypothesis, they have reported strong support with evidence based on a variety of laboratory and sports skills (e.g., Wulf, McNevin, & Shea, 2001; Wulf & Prinz, 2001). Although much of this research has investigated attention focus as it relates to learning motor skills, the results have been remarkably consistent in showing that when performers direct their attention focus to the movement effects, they perform the skill at a higher level than when their attention focus is on their own movements. We will consider this attention-focus

issue further in chapter 13, when we discuss verbal instructions and their effects on skill learning.

ATTENTION AND AUTOMATICITY

Automaticity is an important concept in our understanding of attention and motor skill performance. The term **automaticity** is commonly used to indicate that a person performs a skill or engages in an information-processing activity without demands on attention capacity. We briefly considered the attention capacity demands of a skill in the discussion of the evaluation of the task demands component of Kahneman's model of attention. Information-processing activities include the visual search of the environment that occurs as a person assesses the environmental context regulatory characteristics associated with performing a skill; the use of *tau* when moving toward an object to make or avoid contact with it, or when an object is moving toward a person who needs to catch or strike it; the storing of information in memory and the retrieval of information from memory; the selection of an action to perform and the movement characteristics that must be applied to carry out the action; and the actual production of an action. From an attention point of view, the question of interest with regard to these activities concerns the attention capacity demand of each activity.

Logan (1985, 1988, 1998), who has produced some of the most important research and thinking about the concept of automaticity and motor skill performance, views automaticity as an acquired skill that should be viewed as a continuum of varying degrees of automaticity. This means that rather than considering the attention capacity demand of an information—processing activity in terms of "yes, it demands capacity," or "no, it

---

automaticity　the term used to indicate that a person performs a skill, or engages in certain information-processing activities, without requiring attention resources.

doesn't demand capacity," the continuum view considers automaticity as related to demanding varying amounts of attention capacity. Logan proposes that, as with skill, people acquire automaticity with practice. As a result, the degree of automaticity for a skill or information-processing activity may be only partially automatic when the attention demand of the activity is assessed.

An important skill learning question that comes out of this view is this: *How automated do complex skills become?* Some skills such as performing a dance or gymnastics routine or playing a piano piece are highly complex. Do these become automated throughout the piece so that little, if any, attention is needed? The more likely response to this question is that the performer develops automated "chunks" of the entire piece. These chunks are parts of the piece that have been put together into groups and performed with little attention required within the chunks. Attention appears to be demanded, however, at the beginning or initiation of each chunk.

Anecdotal evidence for this view comes from discussions with skilled individuals. During performances, individuals indicate that they perform many parts of a routine without thinking about these parts. However, these performers indicate that there are also places in the routine to which they must direct conscious attention. Those places seem to be identified by distinct characteristics. The dancer may attend to the place where the tempo changes or a partner must be contacted or lifted; the pianist may attend to tempo changes. The gymnast may direct attention to parts of the routine that would make the routine dangerous if missed. All of these individuals indicate that they give attention to parts of the routine with which they have had difficulty.

VISUAL SELECTIVE ATTENTION

The consideration of **visual selective attention** extends the discussion not only of attention, but also of the role vision plays in the control of motor skills which you studied in chapter 6. Visual selective attention concerns the role of vision in motor skill performance in directing visual attention to environmental information (sometimes referred to as "cues") that influences the preparation and/or the performance of an action. Because the use of vision in this way is primarily an attention issue, it is included here rather than in chapter 6.

Researchers have disputed since the end of the nineteenth century about whether visual selective attention is active or passive (sometimes phrased as "top-down or bottom-up," or "goal directed or stimulus driven"). In terms of the information-processing model in figure 8.1, the basis for this dispute concerns how we select information from the environmental context to process in the first stage. Do we visually select relevant environmental cues according to our action intentions and goals, or do we visually attend to environmental cues because of their distinctiveness or meaningfulness in the situation? In their review of the visual attention research literature, Egeth and Yantis (1997) concluded that these two types of visual attention control "almost invariably interact" (p. 270). This means that in most performance situations, our intentions and goals as well as certain characteristics in the environment influence our visual attention. In other words, although we may actively seek environmental cues based on our action intentions and goals, we may also attend to certain cues because of their distinct characteristics. You will see evidence of this active-passive visual attention throughout this discussion.

The term **visual search** is used to describe the process of directing visual attention to locate relevant environmental cues. During the preparation process for performing many skills, people carry out visual search to select from the environment those cues that are relevant for the performance of a skill in a specific situation. In the following sections, we discuss the actual process of selecting appropriate information from the environment, and give examples from various sport and everyday skills to illustrate how visual search is an important component of the performance of both open and closed motor skills.

PROCEDURES FOR INVESTIGATING VISUAL SEARCH IN MOTOR SKILLS

Before considering the visual search process itself, we will examine how researchers have investigated visual selective attention as it relates to performing motor skills. Three experimental procedures have become popular for determining the visual search strategies used in skill performance situations. Two involve video simulation of a skill performance situation. The third involves monitoring of the person's eye movements as he or she performs a skill.

Video Simulation Techniques

In one popular technique for investigating visual search, researchers videotape real skill performance situations and then use the video to simulate the real situation. In the testing situation, the participant observes the video (or sometimes a film or a series of slides), and then is asked to perform specific actions as if he or she were actually in that situation. For example, a tennis player may be asked to act as if he or she is actually receiving the serve of the tennis player in the video. For the action component, the participant may be required to designate as quickly as possible the ball's landing position on the court of the serve.

Researchers have used two different procedures in the video simulation technique. Each determines one of two characteristics of the visual search process. The temporal occlusion procedure assesses the amount of time the person takes to select the information he or she needs in order to respond. The event occlusion procedure determines which characteristics of the observed performance the person uses to make a correct response.

Temporal Occlusion Procedure

This procedure allows an investigation of the amount of time a person requires for visual search. The experimenter determines the time periods of interest as they relate to the skill performed and then has the film or video stop at these predetermined time points during the action. The observer is then required to make a response as quickly as possible. An excellent example of the use of this procedure is in an experiment by Abernethy and Russell (1987), in which badminton players watched film sequences of a player making different shots. When the film stopped, participants marked their predictions of the landing positions of the shuttle. The film stopped at different times prior to, during, and after shuttle contact. By noting the relationship between the accuracy of a participant's predicted shuttle landing location and the moment he or she made the decision, the researchers could determine when in the time course of the observed action the participant had visually selected the information needed to make a decision.

Event Occlusion Procedure

To identify the specific information a person uses to make the required response, researchers use the *event occlusion procedure*. Parts of each frame of film or video are masked so that the observer cannot see selected parts of the action. Figure 8.4 presents an example of this procedure, taken from the second part of the Abernethy and Russell (1987) study. In their experiment, participants predicted the landing location of the shuttle when they could not see the arm and racquet, racquet, head, or legs of the person hitting the shuttle. The logic of this approach is that if the person performs worse without being able to see a specific feature of the opponent's action, then that feature includes the visual information the person uses to determine the location of the shot.

---

visual selective attention   the process of engaging vision in directing attention to specific environmental information (i.e., cues) that influence the preparation and/or performance of an action. It is selective because the specific cues attended to must be chosen from among other possible cues in the performance environment. The selective attention process may be active or passive.

visual search   the process of directing visual attention to locate relevant information in the environment that will enable a person to determine how to prepare and perform a skill in a specific situation.

FIGURE 8.4   Examples of what subjects saw in the Abernethy and Russell experiment when they watched a film of a badminton serve where various parts of the serving action were masked and could not be seen.   [*Source:* Abernethy, B. & Russell, D.G. (1987). Expert-novice differences in an applied selective attention task. *Journal of Sport Psychology, 9,* 326–345.]

Eye Movement Recording Technique

Another experimental procedure researchers use to investigate visual attention in motor skills is *eye movement recording.* This procedure requires the use of specialized equipment that tracks the movement of the eyes and records where the eyes are "looking" at a particular time. A researcher can record the displacement of *foveal vision* for a specific time interval, as well as the place and the length of time the person fixates his or her gaze while tracking. One way researchers use this technique is to have the participant observe a film sim-ulation of a performance situation and then make a response. The movement of the eye is then plotted on the film scene to determine the spatial location of the participant's eye movements (displacement), along with his or her gaze fixation characteristics related to observing the serving action. A more difficult way to use this procedure is to record eye movements while a person is actually performing a skill in the performance setting. Later in this discussion, we will discuss several examples of experiments that have used the eye movement recording technique.

Eye Movements and Visual Attention

Although eye movement recordings track the displacement characteristics of central vision while people observe a scene, an important question arises concerning how well this procedure assesses visual attention. The rationale for the use of the procedure is that what a person is looking at should give researchers insight into what information in the environment the person is attending to. But there is an important research question here: Is this a valid assumption? Can we validly relate eye movements to visual attention?

Two characteristics of the use of eye movement recordings provide an answer. First, research evidence (see Henderson, 1996, and Zelinsky et al., 1997, for reviews of this evidence) has shown consistently that it is possible to give attention to a feature in the environment without moving the eyes to focus on that feature. This would mean that peripheral vision was the source of picking up the relevant information. However, it is *not* possible to make an eye movement without a corresponding shift in attention. Second, because eye movement recordings are limited to the assessment of central vision, they do not assess peripheral vision. Research evidence has shown that peripheral vision is involved in visual attention in motor skill performance (see Bard, Fleury, & Goulet, 1994 for a brief review of this research). As a result of these two factors, eye movement recordings cannot provide a complete picture of the environmental features to which the person is directing visual attention. Therefore, eye movement recordings typically provide an *underestimation* of what a person is visually attending to. However, even with these limitations, the recording of eye movements is a useful technique to provide good estimates of those features in the environment that a person directs visual attention to as he or she prepares and performs a motor skill.

HOW WE SELECT VISUAL CUES

Theories concerning how we select certain cues in the environment address the selection of cues for nonmoving as well as moving objects. Both situations are important for the performance of motor skills. For example, visual search for regulatory characteristics of stationary objects is critical for successful prehension actions. Without detection of these characteristics a person would not have the information needed to prepare and initiate movement to reach for and grasp a cup, or any stationary object.

Visual Search and Intended Actions

The visual search for regulatory information in the performance environment is an active search that a person engages in according to the action he or she intends to perform. This means that the performer looks for specific cues that will enable him or her to achieve a specific action goal. For example, if a person intends to pick up a cup to drink from it, he or she will visually search for features of the cup and in the environment that will indicate the most appropriate movement characteristics to implement. This search could include looking to see how full the cup is, what type of liquid is in it, the location of the cup in terms of distance from the person, and whether or not there may be obstacles between the person and the cup. By actively looking for these regulatory features, the person can prepare the movement characteristics to reach for, pick up, and drink from the cup. This view of a visual search process fits well with the research evidence you saw in chapter 6 that showed the influence of various object and environment features on prehension movement kinematics.

Research evidence also supports the view that we actively visually search the performance environment according to action intentions. For example, Bekkering and Neggers (2002) demonstrated that the focus of initial eye movements differed when participants in their experiment were told to point or to grasp an object. For example, the intention to grasp an object directed participants' visual search to the spatial orientation of an object, whereas the intention to point to the object did not. These results led the authors to conclude that a specific action intention enhances the visual detection of those regulatory conditions that are relevant to the intended action.

A CLOSER LOOK

Visual Search and Attention Allocation Rules

If the key to successful selection of environmental information when performing motor skills is the distinctiveness of the relevant features, an important question is this:

What Makes Certain Features More Distinctive than Others?

Insight into answering this question comes from the attention allocation rules in Kahneman's theory of attention (1973), which we discussed earlier in this chapter:

- **Unexpected features attract our attention.** You can see this in your own daily experience. While concentrating on your professor during a lecture, haven't you been distracted when a classmate has dropped some books on the floor? Undoubtedly, you switched your visual attention from the profes-

sor to search for the source of the noise. When the environment includes features that typically are not there, the distinctiveness of those features increases. The result is that people have a tendency to direct visual attention to them.

- **We allocate attention to the most meaningful features.** In the performance environment, the most meaningful cues "pop out" and become very evident to the performer. Meaningfulness is a product of experience and instruction. As a person experiences performing in certain environments, critical cues for successful performance are invariant and increase in their meaningfulness, often without the person's conscious awareness. Instruction also plays a part in the way certain features of cues become more meaningful than others.

The Feature Integration Theory of Visual Selective Attention

Although researchers have proposed several theories to account for the characteristics of how we select certain cues in the environment and ignore others (see Neumann, 1996, for a review of these theories), one of the more popular theories is the *feature integration theory* proposed by Treisman in the 1980s (e.g., Treisman & Gelade 1980; Treisman 1988). This view indicates that during visual search, we initially group stimuli together according to their unique features, such as color or shape. This grouping occurs automatically. These groups of features form "maps" related to the various values of various features. For example, a color map would identify the various colors in the observed scene, whereas a shape map would indicate which shapes are observed. These maps become the basis for further search processes when the task demands that the person identify specific cues. For further processing, we must use attention, and must direct it to selecting specific features of interest.

The selection of features of interest occurs when a person focuses the *attentional spotlight* on the master map of all features. People can direct atten-

tion over a wide or a narrow area, and it appears that the spotlight can be split to cover different map areas. If the person's task is to search for a target having a certain distinct feature, then the target will "pop out" as a result of this search process, because the feature is distinct among the groupings of features. Thus, the more distinctive the feature is that identifies the target of the visual search, the more quickly the person can identify and locate the target. If the distinctive feature is a part of several cues, the search slows as the person assesses each cue in terms of how its characteristics match those of the target.

For movement situations, McLeod, Driver, Dienes, and Crisp (1991) proposed a *movement filter* in the visual system that would allow visual attention to be directed at just the moving items in the person's environment. They suggested that this movement filter mechanism can be related to Treisman's feature integration theory's emphasis on the importance of grouping in visual search by operating as a subsystem to a group's common movement characteristics. In light of this view it is interesting to note that Abernethy (1993) described research evidence to demonstrate that in sports involving

A CLOSER LOOK

Two Examples of Severe Time Constraints on Visual Search

There are some situations in sport in which researchers can determine the actual amount of time a person has to engage in visual search and to prepare an action. Two of these are returning a serve in tennis and hitting a baseball. In each of these situations, it is clearly to the player's advantage to detect the information needed as early as possible in order to prepare and initiate the appropriate action.

Preparing to Return a Tennis Serve A serve traveling at 90 to 100 mi/hr (145 to 161 km/hr) allows the receiver only 0.5 to 0.6 sec to hit the ball. This means that the person must search as soon as possible for the cues that will provide information about the direction, speed, landing point, and bounce characteristics of the ball so that he or she can select, organize, and execute an appropriate return stroke.	**Preparing to Hit a Baseball** When a pitcher throws a ball at a speed of 90 mph, it will arrive at home plate in approximately 0.45 sec. Suppose that it takes 0.1 sec for the batter to get his or her bat to the desired point of ball contact. This means that the batter has less than 0.35 sec after the ball leaves the pitcher's hand to make a decision and to initiate the swing. If the pitcher releases the ball 10 to 15 ft in front of the rubber, the batter has less than 0.3 sec of decision and swing initiation time.

fast ball action, such as racquet sports, skilled players visually search the playing environment for the "minimal essential information" necessary to determine an action to perform. This information has been shown to be the invariant perceptual features of a situation. We described one of these invariant features in chapter 6 when we discussed the importance of the use of time-to-contact information to catch a ball, contact or avoid an object while walking or running, and strike a moving ball.

Abernethy adds to this example of minimal essential information the detection of the coordination kinematics of an opponent's action, which involves the grouping of displacement characteristics of the joints involved in a coordinated movement pattern. As a person becomes more skillful, his or her visual attention becomes increasingly more attuned to detecting the important kinematic features, which provides the skilled player an advantage over the less-skilled player in anticipating the opponent's action in a situation. In effect then, this minimal essential information "pops out" for the skilled player, and directs the player's visual attention as he or she prepares an appropriate action to respond to his or her opponent's action.

VISUAL SEARCH AND ACTION PREPARATION

Visual search picks up critical cues that influence three parts of the action control process: *action selection, constraining of the selected action* (i.e., determining the specific movement features for performing the action), and *timing of action initiation.* By influencing these processes, the visual system enables a person to prepare and initiate an action that conforms to the specific requirements of the performance situation.

Research investigating visual search in performance situations has produced evidence about what is involved in these important preparation processes. The following research examples illustrate how researchers have investigated a variety of sports and everyday skills, and provide a sense of what we currently know about the characteristics of visual search processes related to the performance of open and closed motor skills.

Visual Search in Returning a Badminton Serve
The experiments by Abernethy and Russell (1987) described earlier in this chapter provide the best example of research investigations of visual search by

FIGURE 8.5 Illustration show-ing where tennis expert tennis players in the Goulet, Bard, and Fleury experiment were looking during the three phases of a tennis serve. [*Source:* Based on discussion in Goulet, C., et al. (1989). Expertise differences in preparing to return a tennis serve: A visual information processing approach. *Journal of Sport and Exercise Psychology, 11,* 382–398.]

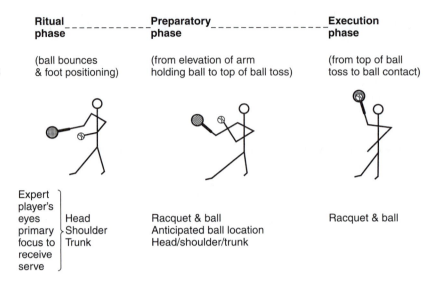

Ritual phase

(ball bounces & foot positioning)

Preparatory phase

(from elevation of arm holding ball to top of ball toss)

Execution phase

(from top of ball toss to ball contact)

Expert player's eyes primary focus to receive serve } Head Shoulder Trunk

Racquet & ball
Anticipated ball location
Head/shoulder/trunk

Racquet & ball

expert badminton players. They found that the time between the initiation of the badminton server's backswing and the shuttle's hitting the floor in the receiver's court is approximately 400 msec (0.4 sec). Within that time period, there appears to be a critical time window for visually picking up critical cues predicting where the shuttle will land. This window, which lasts from about 83 msec before until 83 msec after racquet-shuttle contact, provides information about racquet movement and shuttle flight that seems to resolve uncertainty about where the served shuttle will land. Experts use the 83-msec period prior to racquet-shuttle contact more effec-tively than novices. As a result, experts have more time to prepare their returns. The racquet and the arm are the primary sources to visually search for the anticipatory cues needed to prepare the return.

Visual Search in Returning a Tennis Serve

Results from two experiments by Goulet, Bard, and Fleury (1989) demonstrate how critical visual search strategies are to preparing to return tennis serves. Expert and novice tennis players watched a film showing a person serving and were asked to identify the type of serve as quickly as possible. The authors recorded the participants' eye move-ments as they watched the film. Three phases of the serve were of particular interest: the "ritual phase"

(the 3.5 sec preceding the initiation of the serve); the "preparatory phase" (the time between the ele-vation of the arm for the ball toss and the ball's reaching the top of the toss); and the "execution phase" (from the ball toss to racquet-ball contact).

As illustrated in figure 8.5, during the ritual phase, the expert players focused mainly on the head and the shoulder/trunk complex, where gen-eral body position cues could be found. During the preparatory phase, they directed visual search pri-marily around the racquet and ball, where it re-mained until ball contact. An interesting note was that the experts also looked at the server's feet and knees during the preparatory phase. The important difference between experts and novices was that the visual search patterns of the expert players al-lowed them to correctly identify the serve sooner than novices could.

In an effort to investigate the visual search char-acteristics of expert players in a more realistic setting, Singer et al. (1998) assessed the eye move-ment behaviors of five nationally ranked university male and female tennis players as they returned ten serves on a tennis court. Interestingly, all five play-ers did not use the same visual search strategies. During the phases of the serve that Goulet et al. (1989) called the ritual and preparatory phases, the two highest-ranked players fixated primarily on the arm-racquet-shoulder region of the server, whereas two fixated on the racquet and expected ball toss area. All the players included head fixations during these phases. The players demonstrated more individual variation during the ball toss phase of the serve. Two players visually tracked the ball from the server's hand to the highest point of the toss, one player made a visual jump from the server's hand to the highest point of the toss, one player fixated only on the predicted highest point of the toss, and one player did not fixate on the ball toss but only on the racquet. Differences again were found for the visual search strategies used by the players after the server hit the ball. The two highest-ranked players visually tracked the ball to its landing location, two players did not track the ball after contact but visually jumped to the predicted landing location, and one player used a combination of these two strategies to return serves.

When compared to the Goulet et al. (1989) results, the Singer et al. (1998) study shows that expert players exhibit more individual variation in their visual search strategies than Goulet and his colleagues reported. With this qualification in mind, it is important to note that the description of visual search characteristics of expert tennis players presented in figure 8.5 can be viewed as a general description of these characteristics; individual players may not match them completely.

Visual Search in Baseball Batting

An example of research describing characteristics of the visual search processes involved in baseball batting is a study by Shank and Haywood (1987). They recorded eye movements for college and novice players as they watched a videotape of a right-handed pitcher as if they were right-handed batters. Twenty randomly presented fastballs and curves from both the windup and stretch positions were observed. For each pitch, the players' task was to indicate verbally if the pitch was a fastball or a curve. The expert players correctly identified almost every pitch, whereas the novices were correct only about 60 percent of the time. Participants in both groups did not begin to track the ball until about 150 msec after the ball had left the

pitcher's hand. During the windup, experts fixated on the release point, whereas novices tended to shift fixations from the release point to the pitcher's head.

More recently, Kato and Fukuda (2002) investigated the eye movements of nine expert baseball batters as they viewed the pitcher's motion during different types of pitches. The distribution of eye movement fixations indicated that the batters looked primarily at the pitcher's elbow, shoulder, and head, with the primary focus on the elbow. In results similar to those of Shank and Haywood, the batters' visual attention involved the release point. But a difference from the Shank and Haywood results was the batters' direction of their foveal vision on the elbow as a type of "pivot" point from which they could include and evaluate the release point, as well as the entire arm motion and initial ball trajectory, in their peripheral vision.

Visual Search in Soccer Actions

To determine whether to shoot, pass, or dribble in soccer, the player must use visual search that is different from that involved in the situations described above. The soccer situation involves many players in the visual scene that must be searched for relevant cues. An experiment by Helsen and Pauwels (1990) provides a good demonstration of visual search patterns used by experienced and inexperienced male players to determine these actions. Participants acted as ball handlers as they viewed slides of typical attacking situations. For each, the person indicated as quickly as possible whether he would shoot at the goal, dribble around the goalkeeper or opponent, or pass to a teammate. The experts took less time to make the decision. Eye movement recordings showed that the experts gained this time advantage because they fixated on fewer features of the scene and spent less time at each fixation.

Another visual search situation in soccer involves anticipating where a pass will go. Williams, Davids, Burwitz, and Williams (1994) showed that experienced players and inexperienced players look at different environmental features to make this determination. Results based on subjects' eye-movement characteristics while watching an actual soccer game showed that the experienced players fixated more on the positions and movements of other players, in addition to the ball and the ball handler. In contrast, inexperienced players typically fixated only on the ball and the ball handler.

Finally, Williams and Davids (1998) reported a comprehensive investigation of visual selective attention and search strategies of experienced and less experienced soccer players in three-on-three and one-on-one situations. The experiments demonstrate the benefit of using eye-movement recordings, the spatial-occlusion procedure, and individual verbal reports to provide a more complete picture of visual selective attention in complex and fast-paced skill performance situations. Among the many results in this study, two are especially noteworthy for our discussion. One is that in the one-on-one situations, the experienced players visually fixated longer on the opponent's hip region more than the less experienced players, which indicated their knowledge of the relevant information to be acquired from the specific environmental feature. The other is that in the three-on-three situations, the experienced players used peripheral vision to select relevant information more than the less experienced players. Evidence for the use of peripheral vision came from the results of the spatial occlusion procedure, in which the masking of areas of the video scene surrounding the ball and the player with the ball had a more negative effect on the performance of the experienced players.

Visual Search When Shooting a Basketball

When a basketball player shoots a jump shot, when does the player visually search for and detect the relevant information needed to determine when and how to make the shot? To address this question, researchers in The Netherlands used the temporal occlusion procedure to investigate expert basketball players shooting a jump shot (Oudejans, van de Langenberg, & Hunter, 2002). The researchers established a simulated game situation in which the players watched a scene on a video project in front of them. The players performed jump shots at a

basket on the basis of the actions of the defensive players in the video. The players saw all, none, or only parts of the video. The results indicated that the players' shooting performance was less successful when they could not observe the scene just before they released the ball. The researchers concluded that to successfully shoot a jump shot, players determine their final shooting movement characteristics by visually searching for and using information detected until they release the ball.

Each of the sports skills discussed so far is an open skill. Visual search is clearly an important part of the preparation and performance of these skills. But visual search is important for closed skills as well. The basketball free throw provides a good example of a closed skill in which the quality of the visual search prior to shooting the ball plays a critical role in the success of the shot. Vickers (1996) reported an experiment that nicely demonstrates this effect. She recorded the eye movements of elite Canadian women basketball players as they prepared to shoot, and then shot, free throws. Two results are especially noteworthy. First, the "experts" (they had made an average of 75 percent of their free throws during the just-completed season) looked directly at the backboard or hoop for a longer period of time just prior to shooting the ball than did the "near experts" (they had made an average of 42 percent of their free throws during the just-completed season). This was especially the case for the final eye movement fixation just prior to the release of the ball. Second, as can be seen in figure 8.6, the amount of time devoted to the final fixation prior to releasing the ball was related to the shooting success of the players Vickers classified as experts. They fixated on the backboard or hoop for just over 1.4 sec for shots they made, but almost 0.2 sec less for shots they missed. It is interesting to note that the final fixation duration for the near experts was just the opposite, with a longer fixation time on shots they missed than on shots they made. Vickers interpreted this finding as evidence that the near experts did not fixate long enough just prior to the release of the ball for the shots they made or missed to allow them to attain the shooting percentage of the expert.

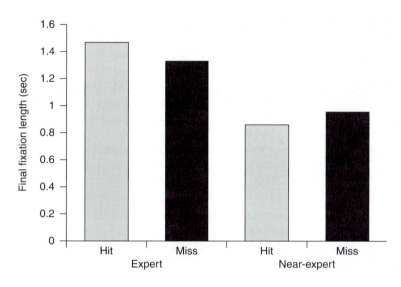

FIGURE 8.6 Results from Vickers (1996) showing expert and near-expert basketball players' mean duration of their final eye movement fixations just prior to releasing the ball during basketball free throws during shots they hit and missed. These final fixations were on the backboard or hoop. [Modified figure 6 (p. 348) in Vickers, J. (1996). Visual control when aiming at a far target. *Psychology: Human Perception and Performance, 22,* 342–354. Copyright © 1996 the American Psychological Association. Adapted with permission.]

Visual Search When Putting a Golf Ball

Another closed skill that involves visual search as a part of the preparation for performing the skill is putting a golf ball. In another experiment by Vickers (1992), she reported eye movement data for lower-handicap golfers (0 to 8 handicaps) and higher-handicap golfers (10 to 16 handicaps). In golf, the lower-handicap golfers are more skilled than those with higher handicaps. Vickers reported that during a series of putts, several differences were found between these two groups during the preparation phase of each putt, which she defined as the interval of time just after the golfer completed positioning the ball and just before the initiation of the backswing of the putter. First, the low-handicap golfers had a shorter preparation phase (approximately 3.7 sec) than the high-handicap golfers (approximately 4.8 sec). Second, the low-handicap golfers directed more eye movement fixations to the ball during this phase than the high-handicap golfers, who directed more fixations to the putter. Third, there was a relationship between the eye movement fixation during the preparation phase and the success of a putt. Fixations on the club led to more missed putts, whereas fixations on the ball led to more successful putts.

Vickers also described an interesting point that is relevant to our discussion on visual attention. She noted that golfers generally are not con- sciously aware of eye movements during putting. Golfers tend to associate visual attention with head position, which means they consider a change in visual attention to be related to a change in head movement. However, their head movement to shift visual attention from one location to another is generally initiated by eye movement.

Visual Search While Driving a Car

Driving a car is a nonsport performance situation in which vision provides information to select and constrain action. In a study that was done many years ago, but continues to be preferred as a demonstration of this role for vision, Mourant and Rockwell (1972) had novice and experienced drivers drive a 2.1-mi neighborhood route and a 4.3-mi freeway route. The novices were students in a driver education class. The results of the eye movement recordings showed that novice drivers concentrated their eye fixations in a small area more immediately in front of the car. More experienced drivers visually searched a wider area that was further from the front of the car. This broader scanning range increases the probability for the detection of important cues in the environment. On the freeway, the novices made pursuit eye movements, whereas the experienced drivers made specific eye fixations that jumped from location to location. That is, the experienced drivers knew

A CLOSER LOOK

The Influence of Distractors on Prehension: Implications for Rehabilitation Treatment Protocols

In our daily activities, we often need to pick up an object from a table or desk that is cluttered with objects other than the one we want. To what extent do these other objects influence the way in which we visually search for the desired object and perform the prehension action to pick it up? The answer to this question is valuable not only because it would add to our knowledge about visual selective attention, but also because it has implications that are especially relevant for physical and occupational therapists for prehension rehabilitation. Kritikos, Bennett, Dunai, and Castiello (2000) provide some answers to this question in a review of previous research and two of their own experiments. They report that compared to situations in which there are no distractor objects (i.e., objects other than the target object), the presence of distractor objects

- increases reaction time and movement, which indicates that the person requires more time for decision making to select the target object and move to it
- alters movement kinematic characteristics of the reach and grasp in ways that relate to the number, size, shape, color (especially in relation to the target object) and location of the distractor objects

An important implication of these results for rehabilitation contexts is this:

- Experiences with prehension actions should not be limited to situations in which the target object is by itself, but should also include the target object in the presence of different numbers of other objects that vary in terms of their size, shape, color, location, etc.

---

which cues were important and specifically searched for those cues. The experienced drivers looked into the rear- and side-view mirrors more frequently than the novices, whereas the novices looked at the speedometer more than the experienced drivers did.

More recently, Chapman and Underwood (1998) extended these findings. They monitored eye movements of novice and experienced drivers as they watched various driving-related scenes that included at least one dangerous situation. In these situations, both types of drivers narrowed their visual search and increased the durations of their eye movement fixations. But the more experienced drivers tended to fixate for shorter amounts of time on specific parts of the scene than the novice drivers. This result indicates that more experienced drivers require less time to detect and process the information obtained from a fixation, which gives them an advantage in determining the appropriate driving action to take in the situation. In addition, the experienced drivers tended to be less variable in where they fixated their eye move-

ments while watching the driving scenes, which, in agreement with the findings of Mourant and Rockwell (1972), indicates their greater knowledge of which environmental cues to look at to obtain the most relevant information.

Visual Search During Prehension While Walking
When a person must walk to a table to pick up an object, such as a pen or book, visual search plays an important role in setting into motion the appropriate action coordination. An experiment by Cockrell, Carnahan, and McFayden (1995) demonstrated this role for visual search. Participants were required to walk 3.75 m to a table and pick up an aluminum can or a pencil as they walked by. Results showed that before they began any prehensive action, their eyes moved to fixate on the target. Head movement also preceded the initiation of reaching movements. Thus, the eyes' searching of the environment to determine the location and characteristics of the object started a chain of events to allow the participants to grasp the object successfully.

A CLOSER LOOK

A Visual Search Training Program to Teach Anticipation Skills in Squash

Abernethy, Wood, and Parks (1999) engaged university male and female students in a four-week training program designed to teach them to improve their anticipation skills in squash by improving their visual search strategies. None of the students had competitive experience in any racquet sport. The training program consisted of the following:

• A 20-min session of supervised perceptual training exercises related to squash on four days of each week. These exercises involved
  — formal instruction on the biomechanics of the forehand and backhand drives, which emphasized the proximal-to-distal development of stroke kinematics
  — formal instruction on locating the most important anticipatory cues for racquet sports and a brief summary of expert-novice differences in the use of these cues
  — practice in focusing on appropriate information sources in video sequences
  — practice in verbally predicting stroke direction and force from spatially occluded video displays, with feedback given about prediction accuracy

  — practice on making anticipatory predictions from temporally occluded video displays, with feedback given about prediction accuracy
  — practice in which a simulated movement rather than verbal response to the video was required
• A 20-min session of supervised practice of squash on one day of each week. This practice session involved
  — hitting forehand drives while moving or stationary (balls were projected from a ball machine)

The results of a posttest given after the completion of this training program showed that the participants

• improved their anticipatory prediction accuracy for ball direction and location
• consistently made their predictions before ball contact in a temporal occlusion test
• performed the tests better than other participants who had experienced a more general training program, or who had only physically practiced squash during the training sessions

Visual Search While Locomoting Through a Cluttered Environment

Walking and running through a cluttered environment can occur in everyday situations—we walk around furniture in the house or walk through a crowded mall—and in sport situations: a player runs with a football or dribbles a basketball during a game. People's ability to maneuver through environments like these indicates that they have detected relevant cues and used them in advance to avoid collisions. Visual search is an important part of this process.

According to research by Cutting, Vishton, and Braren (1995), the most important cues involved in avoiding collision in these situations come from the relative location or motion of objects around the object the person needs to avoid. When visually fixating on the object he or she needs to avoid,

the person uses relative-displacement and/or velocity information about both the object to be avoided and other objects in front of or behind the object. It is important to note that this decision making is done automatically by the visual system and provides the basis for appropriate action by the motor control system. The key practical point here is that the person needs to visually fixate on the object or objects that he or she wishes to avoid.

TRAINING VISUAL SEARCH STRATEGIES

Each of the motor skill performance examples discussed in the preceding section had in common the characteristic that people with more experience in an activity visually searched their environment and located essential information more effectively and efficiently than people with little experience. Therefore, we know that as people become more experienced and skilled in an activity, they acquire better visual search skills. How do people acquire this capability? In many cases, experience alone is the key factor in the acquisition of effective visual search strategies. These strategies are often acquired without specific training and without the person's conscious awareness of the strategies they use. But is it possible to facilitate the acquisition of effective search strategies by teaching novices to use strategies that experts use? A positive answer to this question would provide teachers, coaches, and physical rehabilitation therapists with guidance about how to more effectively design practice and intervention strategies.

Researchers have demonstrated the benefits of providing novices with instructions concerning what to look for and attend to, along with giving them a sufficient amount of practice implementing these instructions. A result of this type of intervention strategy is an increase in the probability that important environmental cues will "pop out" when the person is in the performance situation (see Czerwinski, Lightfoot, & Shiffrin, 1992). However, Abernethy, Wood, and Parks (1999) emphasized that it is essential for this type of training to be specific to an activity. They pointed out that research evidence has demonstrated the lack of benefit derived from generalized visual training programs, such as those often promoted by sports optometrists (e.g., Wood & Abernethy, 1997). The problem with a generalized training approach to the improvement of visual attention is that it ignores the general finding that experts recognize specific patterns in their activity more readily than do novices (a point that will be discussed in chapter 11).

Several examples of effective visual search training programs have been reported in the research literature (e.g., Abernethy, Wood, & Parks, 1999; Farrow, et al., 1998; Haskins, 1965; Singer et al., 1994). Each of these programs has been sport specific, and has shown that video-based simulations can serve as the basis for effective self-paced training of athletes outside of their organized prac-

tice time. However, as Abernethy, Wood, and Parks (1999) point out, the studies that have reported the effectiveness of these programs have not tested their efficacy in actual performance situations or in competition environments. Although these programs show promise to benefit athletes' performance, it remains for researchers to establish that this type of visual search training will transfer to the sports performance environment. In addition, whether similar training programs could be effective in physical rehabilitation contexts to facilitate the performance of skills requiring visual search also remains to be determined.

SUMMARY

We have considered the concept of attention as it relates to human motor skill performance in two ways: the simultaneous performance of multiple activities, and the visual selection of action-relevant information from the environment. In the discussion of attention and the simultaneous performance of multiple activities, we discussed the following:

- People have a *limited attention capacity* for performing the perceptual, cognitive, and motor activities associated with the performance of motor skills, which often limits the ability to perform more than one activity at the same time.

- *Kahneman's attention theory* is an example of a centrally located, flexible limited capacity view of attention. His theory proposes that our attention capacity is a pool of resources that has a limited amount of resources to be allocated to activities to be performed. The amount of capacity can increase or decrease according to the general arousal level of the performer. The allocation of resources is influenced by several factors related to the person and the activities.

- *Multiple-resource theories* provide an alternative view of a limited capacity view of attention. These theories propose that several different resource pools exist from which attention can be allocated. The resources are specific to a component of performing a skill. Wickens' model states that these components include input and output modalities, stages of information processing, and codes of processing information.

- The most common experimental procedure used to investigate the attention demands of motor skill performance is called the *dual-task procedure.*

- *Attentional focus,* which refers to where a person directs his or her attention in a performance situation, can be considered in terms of its width (i.e., broad or narrow) and direction (i.e., internal or external), or in terms of whether attention is focused on the movements or the movement effect.

- *Automaticity* is an important attention-related concept that relates primarily to skilled performance in which the performer can implement knowledge and procedures with little or no demand on attention capacity.

In the discussion of attention and the visual selection of action-relevant information from the environment, we dicussed the following:

- *Visual selective attention* to action-relevant information in the performance environment is an important part of preparing to perform a motor skill.

- The performer usually engages in an active *visual search* of the performance environment according to the information needs to prepare and perform an intended action, although sometimes the environmental information attended to provides the basis for selecting an appropriate action.

- Researchers have typically used three different types of experimental procedures to investigate the visual search strategies associated with the performance of motor skills:
  - ▸ temporal occlusion of video or film
  - ▸ spatial, or event, occlusion of video or film
  - ▸ eye-movement recordings

- The *feature integration theory* of visual selective attention, one of the more popular explanations of how people visually select and attend to certain cues in the performance environment and ignore others, proposes that during visual search for static objects, we automatically group stimuli together according to their unique features and develop maps for each feature. The selection of features for attention occurs when a person focuses the attentional spotlight on the master map of all features, which allows a distinctive feature of interest to "pop out." For movement situations, a movement filter allows visual attention to be directed to just the movement items in the person's environment. Skilled performers visually search the performance environment to select the minimal essential information needed to perform an action.

- We looked at research related to the visual search involved in the performance of several different sport skills (badminton return of serve, tennis return of serve, baseball batting, various soccer skills, shooting a basketball, and putting a golf ball), and everyday skills (driving a car, prehension, and locomotion through a cluttered environment). Each skill provided evidence that effective visual search strategies are distinctly specific to the requirements of the action and to the skill level of the performer.

- Activity-specific training programs facilitate the use of effective visual search strategies more successfully than general-vision training programs.

RELATED READINGS

Abernethy, B., & Burgess-Limerick, R. (1992). Visual information for the timing of skilled movements: A review. In J. J. Summers (Ed.), *Approaches to the study of motor control and learning* (pp. 343–384). Amsterdam: Elsevier.

Bourdin, C., Teasdale, N., & Nougier, V. (1998). Attentional demands and the organization of reaching movements in rock climbing. *Research Quarterly for Exercise and Sport, 69,* 406–410.

Briem, V., & Hedman, L. R. (1995). Behavioural effects of mobile telephone use during simulated driving. *Ergonomics, 38,* 2536–2562.

Maltz M., & Shinar, D. (199). Eye movements of younger and older drivers. *Human Factors, 41,* 15–25.

Moreno, F. J., Ona, A., & Martinez, M. (2002). Computerized simulation as a means of improving anticipation strategies and training in the use of the return in tennis. *Journal of Human Movement Studies, 42,* 31–41.

Nougier, V., & Rossi, B. (1999). The development of expertise in the orienting of attention. *International Journal of Sport Psychology, 30,* 246–260.

Osborne, K., Rudrud, E., & Zezoney, F. (1990). Improved curveball hitting through the enhancement of visual cues. *Journal of Applied Behavior Analysis, 23,* 371–377.

Spikman, J. M., Timmerman, M. E., van Zomeren, A. H., & Deelman, B. G. (1999). Recovery versus retest effects in attention after closed head injury. *Journal of Clinical Experimental Neuropsychology, 21,* 585–605.

Tenenbaum, G., Levy-Kolker, N., Sade, S., Liebermann, D. G., & Lidor, R. (1996). Anticipation and confidence of decisions related to skilled performance. *International Journal of Sport Psychology, 27,* 293–307.

van Gemmert, A. W. A., Teulings, H. L., & Stelmach, G. E. (1998). The influence of mental and motor load on handwriting movements in Parkinsonian patients. *Acta Psychologica, 100,* 161–175.

Whitall, J. (1996). On the interaction of concurrent verbal and manual tasks: Which initial task conditions produce interference? *Research Quarterly for Expertise and Sport, 67,* 349–354

STUDY QUESTIONS

1. Discuss the similarities and differences between fixed and flexible central-resource theories of attention capacity.

2. Describe a motor skill situation in which two or more actions must be performed simultaneously, and then discuss how Kahneman's model of attention could be applied to the situation to explain conditions in which all the actions could be performed simultaneously and when they could not be.

3. Discuss two different dual-task techniques that researchers use to assess the attention demands of performing a motor skill. Give an example of each.

4. (a) Describe the width and direction of attention focus options a person has when performing a motor skill. (b) For each type, describe a motor skill situation in which that focus option would be preferred.

5. Discuss whether a person should focus attention on his or her own movements or on the movement effects. Give an example.

6. What is the meaning of the term *automaticity* as it relates to attention and the performance of motor skills? Give an example.

7. What is the meaning of the term *visual search* when it applies to the performance of a motor skill? Give an example.

8. (a) Describe two different types of video simulation techniques and the eye-movement recording technique that can be used to help us understand visual search in a motor skill performance situation. (b) What are the benefits and limitations of each of these three techniques?

9. Discuss how skilled performers engage in visual search in the performance of four different types of motor skills.

CHAPTER

9

Memory Components, Forgetting, and Strategies

***Concept: Memory storage and retrieval
influence motor skill learning and performance***

After completing this chapter, you will be able to

- Compare and contrast *working memory* and *long-term memory* in terms of duration and capacity of information, and processing activities in each

- Distinguish *procedural, episodic,* and *semantic* memory as components of long-term memory

- Define *declarative* and *procedural* knowledge

- Give examples of *explicit* and *implicit* memory tests and describe how each relates to assessing, remembering, and forgetting

- Discuss several causes of forgetting for working memory and long-term memory

- Discuss effective strategies to help remember a movement or sequence of movements that must be performed

- Define the *encoding specificity principle* as it relates to practice and test contexts associated with the performance of motor skills

Application

Have you ever had the experience of calling an information operator to ask for a telephone number and then finding out that you didn't have a pen? Hurriedly, you dialed the number as quickly as possible after the operator gave it to you. Why did you do this? "Obviously," you say, "because I would have forgotten it if I hadn't dialed right away." Do you need to do this with your home telephone number? You can quite readily recall your home number at almost any time, without any assistance.

Consider a few other memory situations. When you are at a party and you are introduced to someone, you often find it very difficult to recall that person's name, even a very short time later. Compare that to remembering a teacher's name from your elementary school. You can probably name most of your teachers with little difficulty. Consider also a situation when you were shown how to serve a tennis ball for the first time. When you tried it, you found that you had some difficulty remembering all the things that you were supposed to do to perform a successful serve. That situation differs quite drastically from how well you can hop onto a bicycle, even after you have not been on one for many years, and ride it down the street.

Discussion

Memory plays an important role in virtually all our daily activities. Whether in conversation with a friend, working mathematical problems, or playing tennis, we are confronted by situations that require the use of memory to produce action.

What is memory? We often think of memory as being synonymous with the words *retention* or *remembering*. As such, most people consider that the word *memory* indicates a capacity to remember. Endel Tulving (1985), a leading contemporary memory researcher and theorist, has stated that *memory* is the "capacity that permits organisms to benefit from their past experiences" (p. 385).

In the discussion that follows, we will consider various issues and questions concerning human memory as it applies to the learning and performance of motor skills. First, we will discuss the different storage systems included in memory. We will then build on this foundation by considering the issue of the causes of forgetting, and finally address how these causes can be overcome by the use of strategies that can help develop a more durable and accessible memory for the skills being learned.

MEMORY STRUCTURE

Views about the structure of memory have gone through many different phases throughout the history of the study of memory, which can be traced back to the early Greek philosophers. However, one characteristic of memory structure that is now commonly accepted is that a part of memory is oriented toward events that have just occurred, while a part is related to events in the past. This is not a new idea. In fact, in 1890, William James wrote of an "elementary" or "primary" memory that makes us aware of the "just past." He distinguished this from a "secondary memory" that is for "properly recollected objects." To primary memory, James allocated items that are lost and never brought back

into consciousness, whereas to secondary memory, he allocated ideas or data that are never lost. Although they may be "absent from consciousness," they are capable of being recalled.

The debate about the structure of memory has centered around how this distinction between memory for immediate things and memory for things in a more distant past fits into a structural arrangement. At present, the bulk of the evidence supports the view that there are two components of memory.[1] The evidence for this comes from two different but complementary research approaches to the study of human memory. One of these is taken from the study of cognitive psychology, where inferences about the structure and function of memory are based on observing the behavior of individuals in memory situations. The other approach is that of the neuropsychologist or neurophysiologist, who is interested in explaining the structure of memory in terms of what is occurring in the nervous system during behavioral changes related to memory. Research evidence from both of these approaches provides convincing evidence that the memory system comprises at least two components that are definable by their distinct functions. Also, it is important to note that after reviewing and evaluating the relevant research literature, Healy and McNamara (1996) concluded that although some elaboration of various aspects of the component model of memory is needed, the model remains a useful means of understanding human memory.

A Two-Component Memory Model

Several different models of human memory have been developed to represent its component structure. One of the most enduring and influential was presented by Atkinson and Shiffrin in 1968. Using a computer analogy, they conjectured that memory structure should be thought of as similar to computer hardware. They considered that the software that allows the computer to function constitutes the "con-

---

[1] Although some models and discussions of memory include "sensory memory" as a third component, its role in motor skill learning and performance has not been well established. As a result, it is not included in this discussion.

trol processes," which involve memory processes such as storage and retrieval of information, and are under the control of the person. The structural components, they concluded, comprise a sensory register, short-term store, and long-term store.

Since the time of Atkinson and Shiffrin's presentation of theory of memory structures, the primary theoretical problem has been to determine the exact nature of these structures. While debate continues about memory structure, there is general agreement that this structure of memory should include different memory storage components in addition to serving a functional role for what the person does with the information in each component.

One approach that accommodates these characteristics was proposed by Baddeley (1986, 1995). According to this view, memory is seen as comprising two functional components, *working memory* and *long-term memory.* Each memory component is defined in terms of its functions. Although a number of different functions have been proposed, we will focus primarily on three: putting information in memory (referred to as storage processes), getting information out of memory (referred to as retrieval processes), and specific functions in each component.

WORKING MEMORY

The **working memory** should be thought of as a system that incorporates characteristics and functions traditionally associated with sensory, perceptual, attentional, and short-term memory processes. Working memory operates in all situations requiring the temporary use and storage of information and the execution of memory and response production processes (see Baddeley, 1995). As such, working memory includes memory functions traditionally ascribed to *short-term memory,* as well as other functions typically associated with the attention-related processes we discussed in chapter 8 (Engle, 2002).[2]

Working Memory Functions
Working memory must be thought of both as a place where information is stored for a short time and as a functionally active structure. This functional characteristic of working memory enables people to respond according to the demands of a "right now" situation. To do this, *working memory plays a critical role in decision making, problem solving, movement production and evaluation, and long-term memory function.* With regard to influencing long-term memory function, working memory provides essential processing activity needed for the adequate transfer of information into long-term memory. Finally, it is important to note that an important working memory function is to serve as an *interactive workspace* where various memory processing activities can occur, such as integrating the information in working memory with information that has been retrieved from the more permanent, long-term memory.

Because working memory involves both storing and processing information, it is important to consider each function separately. In terms of storing information, two characteristics of working memory are essential to understand: the length of time information will remain in working memory, which is called *duration,* and the amount of information that will reside in working memory at any one time, which is called *capacity.*

Duration
Our understanding of the duration of information in working memory comes from research that investigated short-term memory. In terms of the history of science, this research is relatively recent. Peterson and Peterson (1959) were the earliest to report research related to the remembering of words

working memory   a functional component of the structure of memory that operates to temporarily store and use recently presented information; it also serves as a temporary work space to integrate recently presented information with information retrieved from long-term memory to carry out problem-solving, decision-making, and action-preparation activities.

---

[2] For a brief review of evidence that identifies neural mechanisms associated with working memory, see Smith (2000).

A CLOSER LOOK

Experimental Procedures to Assess the Duration of Movement Information in Working Memory

The Adams and Dijkstra (1966) experiment set the standard for the procedural protocol researchers have used to investigate the question concerning the duration of movement information in working memory. Because the researchers were interested in movement information, their procedures were designed to require participants to use only proprioceptive information to perform the task.

- **Apparatus.** An arm-positioning apparatus consisted of an almost friction-free handle that could be moved left or right along a metal trackway. This apparatus sat on a table facing the participant in the experiment.

- **Task.** To begin a trial, a blindfolded participant moved the handle of the apparatus along the trackway to a location specified by a physical block (the criterion arm position to be remembered). After returning the handle to the starting point and waiting for a certain amount of time (the retention interval), the participant performed a recall test by moving the handle to his or her estimate of the arm position just experienced (the physical block had been removed). The experimenter recorded the location and the participant returned the handle to begin a new trial, which involved moving to a new position along the trackway.

- **Determining duration.** To determine the length of time movement location information stayed in working memory, the researchers compared various durations of the retention interval. They determined the accuracy of the participants' recall movements for each retention interval length. Duration of the memory for the arm position was assumed to be related to the degree of accuracy of

the recall movement. As you can see in figure 9.1 below, arm-positioning recall accuracy decreased (i.e., error increased) very sharply for retention intervals up to 20 sec, and continued to decrease for longer interval lengths.

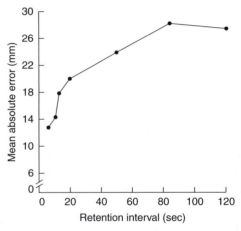

FIGURE 9.1   Results from the experiment by Adams and Dijkstra showing the mean absolute error for the recall of an arm-positioning task following different lengths of retention intervals.   [From Adams, J.A., & Dijkstra, S. (1966). Short-term memory for motor responses. *Journal of Experimental Psychology, 71,* 314–318. Copyright © 1966 by the American Psychological Association. Reprinted with permission.]

presented one time each. They showed that we tend to lose information (i.e., forget) from working memory after about only 20 to 30 sec. The first experiment published relating working memory storage duration to motor skills was by Adams and Dijkstra in 1966. Results of their experiment indicated that arm positions in space that are experienced one time each are lost from working memory at a rate comparable to that of words.

The results of many other studies that followed the Adams and Dijkstra investigation generally supported the conclusion that the duration of move-

ment information in working memory is about 20 to 30 sec. Information that is not processed further or rehearsed is lost.

Capacity

We are concerned with not only *how long* information will remain in short-term storage, but also *how much* information we can accommodate. The issue of capacity in working memory was originally presented by George Miller in 1956, in an article that has become a classic in the memory literature.

A CLOSER LOOK

Pitching in Baseball: A Demonstration of the Interactive Work Space Function of Working Memory

The situation. You are a baseball catcher or coach who needs to decide which pitch the pitcher should throw next. To make this decision, you must consider information about both the present situation and past experiences. In terms of the present situation you need to consider *who the batter is, the score, who and where the runners on base are, the number of outs, the locations of defensive players in the infield and outfield, the ball and strike count,* and so on. In terms of past experiences you need to consider *the batter's batting history in similar situations, the opposing team's tendencies in this situation-especially if they have runners on base, the pitcher's history of pitching in similar situations,* and so on.

Working memory involvement. The working memory serves as a temporary workspace to enable you to integrate the information about the present situation and past experiences so that you can select the best pitch for right now. After receiving your pitch choice, the pitcher will involve the working memory to retrieve from long-term memory the invariant characteristics of the type of pitch required, and then use the temporary workspace to apply specific movement-related features to the pitch, such as speed and location. After the pitch is delivered, the information in working memory is deleted to provide space for new information to allow the pitcher to respond to what the batter does, or to throw the next pitch you select.

Miller provided evidence to indicate that we have the capacity to hold about *seven items (plus or minus two items),* such as words or digits, in short-term storage. To increase the "size" of an item in memory involves a control process termed *organization,* which we will consider later in this discussion. The newly created larger item, or "chunk" as Miller called it, enables people to recall far more than five to nine individual items at a time. However, with no practice or rehearsal of newly presented information, the capacity limit of working memory is five to nine individual items.

Although few researchers have investigated the capacity limits of working memory for motor skills, the available evidence agrees with the 7 ± 2 range proposed by Miller. For example, in one of the first investigations of this issue, Wilberg and Salmela (1973) reported that an eight-movement sequence of arm-positioning movements was the upper limit of working memory capacity for movements. More recently, Ille and Cadopi (1999) asked twelve- and thirteen-year-old female gymnasts to reproduce a sequence of discrete gymnastics movements after watching the sequence one time on a videotape. The gymnasts' recall performance demonstrated a six-movement capacity limit for the more-skilled gymnasts and a five-movement limit for the less-

skilled gymnasts. The results for these young gymnasts are in line with those reported by Starkes, Deakin, Lindley, and Crisp (1987) for young skilled ballet dancers, who showed evidence that an eight-movement sequence was their capacity limit.

To account for research evidence that has shown that highly skilled individuals (i.e., experts) seem to have a working memory capacity that is greater than that of the general population, Ericsson and Kintsch (1995) proposed a memory mechanism they called *long-term working memory.* In addition to having a larger working memory storage capacity, experts also show evidence that performing certain secondary tasks does not interfere with their performance of the activity at which they are skilled. Experts in an activity use long-term working memory when they must have access to a large amount of relevant knowledge at their disposal to use while performing the activity. In addition, the experts use long-term working memory to integrate new information with previously acquired knowledge. It is important to note that as is commonly characteristic of expertise (which we will discuss more fully in chapter 11), long-term working memory is skill specific, which means that it develops as expertise in a skill rather than being a common component of working memory.

Processing Activities

Information that is active in working memory is processed (or manipulated) in such a way that it can be used to accomplish the goal of the problem at hand. The goal may be to remember what you have just been told or shown to do so that you can do the task. Or you may need to use this information to solve a specific movement problem. And in both cases, you would like to remember what you did in each performance situation so that you can use your experience as a reference to help you in some future performance situation. In each case, you will involve working memory processing activities to enable you to achieve different goals.

Consider some examples of motor skill performance situations in which these different information uses could occur. Suppose your golf instructor has just given you a specific instruction to concentrate on your hand position as you swing a golf club. You must not only remember this instruction as you swing, but also retrieve from long-term memory the correct hand position and evaluate your present hand swing compared with the ideal. Of course, how successfully you make this comparison on your own depends on your stage of learning. But carrying out this verbal instruction invokes the working memory.

Suppose you have just watched a dancer perform a sequence of dance movements and you must now perform that sequence, which is a common occurrence in instruction and dance audition situations. Working memory processing activity would be involved because you must keep in memory the visually presented sequence of movements and translate that visual information into motor performance. Involved in this translation process would be retrieving from long-term memory the movement information required to carry out the sequence.

Consider also the following example. You are a patient in an occupational therapy session and are given a complex puzzle to put together. You study the pieces and try to determine how the specific pieces fit together. You continually try to match pieces as in the completed puzzle. And you try to determine an appropriate movement strategy that would allow you to put the pieces together quickly and with little error. Working memory would be actively involved in this problem-solving situation because you carried out several activities requiring several different perception, remembering, and performance characteristics that must be done virtually simultaneously.

LONG-TERM MEMORY

The second component of the structure of memory is **long-term memory**, which is a more permanent storage repository of information. It is what we typically think of when the term *memory* is mentioned. William James (1890) considered long-term memory as "memory proper." This is the component of memory that contains information about specific past events as well as our general knowledge about the world.

In terms of the *duration* of information in long-term memory, it is generally accepted that the information resides in a relatively permanent state in long-term memory. (Note, however, a discussion of this by Loftus, 1980; Loftus & Loftus, 1980.) Usually, "forgotten" information that is stored in long-term memory is there, but the person is having difficulty locating it. Thus, measuring forgetting and remembering in long-term memory situations can be a tricky problem and one that often cannot be satisfactorily addressed by traditional recall and recognition tests. We will come back to this important point later in this chapter.

With regard to the *capacity* of long-term memory, it is generally agreed that there is a relatively unlimited capacity for information in long-term memory (e.g., Chase & Ericsson, 1982). In fact, we know neither how much information a person can store in memory nor how to measure the capacity of long-term memory. An unlimited capacity leads to unique problems, however. For example, organization of information in memory becomes much more critical in an unlimited capacity system than in one of a limited capacity. Thus, there is a need to understand how people organize the information stored in long-term memory. This and other related issues unique to long-term memory will be discussed throughout this chapter.

A CLOSER LOOK

An Alternative View of Long-Term Memory Capacity: "When the Brain's Mailbox Is Full"

An article titled "When the Brain's Mailbox Is Full" appeared in *The New York Times On The Web** on July 27, 1999. The article described an experiment by Dr. H. Lee Swanson, from the University of California at Riverside, that takes issue with the commonly held view that long-term memory has a limitless capacity. Swanson's study, which was reported in the July 1999 issue of the research journal *Developmental Psychology,* found evidence he interpreted as indicating that "As we get older, we run out of places to store information. We have a limited amount of space in our memory system." The decrease in memory capacity, he said, begins around age forty-five for most people, although "not all 'mailboxes' are the same size and people organize them differently. We have different abilities in what we store and some of us are more efficient in what we can store." From an aging perspective, Swanson's view would indicate that when older people have memory lapses, it may not be due to a failure on the brain's part to adequately process in-

formation, but "may signal that a mailbox of memory is full."

Because Swanson's study is unique in finding evidence for such a memory capacity limitation, other scholars were quoted in the article as being skeptical about the reliability of the evidence. Dr. Timothy Salthouse, a highly regarded cognitive psychologist at Georgia Tech who investigates age-related memory and human performance, commented that one problem researchers face in the investigation of this issue is, "We don't know how to measure storage capacity." Dr. Robert L. Kahn, a retired psychology professor who coauthored the book *Successful Aging,* which was based on the study of aging by the MacArthur Foundation, rejected Swanson's ". . .mechanistic notion that treats the brain as a bunch of shelves and pigeonholes which run out of space." Instead, he preferred the concept of "the lifelong elasticity of the human brain" and thought that training and mnemonic devices can sharpen memory skills.

*http://www.nytimes.com

In terms of information duration and capacity characteristics, it becomes obvious that long-term memory is distinct from working memory. Another distinct characteristic of long-term memory is the type of information that is stored there. In the following sections, three types of information stored in long-term memory will be discussed.

Procedural, Episodic, and Semantic Memory

In a commonly referred-to model of long-term memory, Tulving (1985) proposed that there are at least three "systems" in long-term memory: *procedural, episodic,* and *semantic* memories. Each of these systems differs in terms of how information is acquired, what information is included, how information is represented, how knowledge is expressed, and the kind of conscious awareness that characterizes the operations of the system. We will briefly consider each of these systems and how they function and differ.

Procedural memory may have the most direct relevance to our discussion of long-term memory because it relates specifically to storing information about motor skills. Procedural memory is best described as the memory system that enables us to know "how to do" something, as opposed to enabling us to know "what to do." This distinction is readily seen in situations where you can perform a skill very well (i.e., "how to do it"), but you are not able to verbally describe very well what you did (i.e., "what to do").

The procedural memory system enables us to respond adaptively to our environment by carrying out learned procedures so that we can achieve

---

long-term memory   a component of the structure of memory that serves as a relatively permanent storage repository for information.

specific action goals. For the performance of motor skills, procedural memory is critical, because motor skill is evaluated on the basis of producing an appropriate action, rather than simply verbalizing what to do. According to Tulving, an important characteristic of procedural memory is that procedural knowledge can be acquired only through "overt behavioral responses," which, for motor skills, means physical practice.

Semantic memory is, according to Tulving, characterized by "representing states of the world that are not perceptually present" (p. 387) to us right now. This means that we store in this memory system our general knowledge about the world that has developed from our many experiences. This includes specific factual knowledge, such as when Columbus discovered America or the name of the tallest building in America, as well as conceptual knowledge, such as our concepts of "dog" and "love." How information is represented in semantic memory is currently the source of much debate. The debate ranges from suggestions that all experiences are represented in some fashion in memory to suggestions that individual experiences are not represented in semantic memory, but rather, only abstractions, such as prototypes or schemas, are represented.

Episodic memory consists of knowledge about personally experienced events, along with their temporal associations, in subjective time. It is this memory system that enables us to "mentally 'travel back' in time" (Tulving, 1985, p. 387). An example here would be your memory of an important life event. You are very likely to recall this event in terms of both time and space. For example, if you were asked, "Do you remember the first time you drove a car by yourself?" you would retrieve that information from episodic memory. Episodic memory is usually expressed in terms of remembering some experience, or episode. For performing motor skills, episodic memory can be the source for information that prepares you for an upcoming performance or helps you determine what you are now doing wrong that at one time you did correctly.

Hitting a backhand groundstroke during a rally in tennis requires the player to know what to do in the situation and how to execute the stroke.

Distinguishing between Knowing "What To Do" and Doing It

An important part of relating the three memory systems of long-term memory with motor control is the distinction between knowing "what to do" and being able to successfully perform the action. Some learning theorists have argued that the information in the episodic and semantic memory systems should be considered **declarative knowledge** (e.g., Anderson, 1987). This knowledge is specified as what we are able to describe (i.e., declare) if we are asked to do so. Thus, declarative knowledge is specific to knowing "what to do" in a situation. This type of knowledge is distinct from *procedural knowledge,* which typically cannot be verbalized. As described earlier, **procedural knowledge** enables the person to know "how to do" a skill. This distinction is a useful one and will be referred to in various parts of this chapter.

One of the only experiments that has directly distinguished these two types of knowledge in a motor skill context was reported by McPherson and Thomas (1989). They classified nine- to twelve-year-old boys as "expert" or "novice" tennis players based on length of playing experience and tournament play. Novices had never played in tournaments and had only three to six months playing experience. The "experts," on the other hand, had at least two years of experience and had played in junior tournaments. These boys were clearly in an elite group for their age. The players were interviewed after each point (something that the researchers had previously established did not disrupt the quality of performance). Players were asked to state what they had attempted to do on the previous point. When this information was later compared with what they had actually done (which was analyzed from a videotape recording), some interesting results were obtained. First, in terms of having an effective strategy or action goal, the experts knew what to do nearly all the time, whereas the novices generally never knew what to do. Second, although the experts were quite capable of demonstrating that they knew what action goal to establish in a specific situation, they were not always able to accomplish it in their performance of the action. This suggests that the appropriate goal was established but there were problems in attaching the appropriate parameter values to the selected motor program. This evidence, then, supports the importance of distinguishing "what to do" from "how to do it" when discussing learning and control processes underlying complex motor skills.

REMEMBERING AND FORGETTING

In this section of our discussion, we will consider some evidence to indicate that a variety of reasons exist to explain forgetting. But before getting into this discussion, there are some terms that need to be identified and defined. **Encoding** is the transformation of information to be remembered into a form that can be stored in memory. *Storage* of information is the process of placing information in long-term memory. *Rehearsal* is a process that enables the individual to transfer information from the working memory to long-term memory. **Retrieval** involves the search through long-term memory for information that must be accessed in order to perform the task at hand.

ASSESSING REMEMBERING AND FORGETTING

Researchers generally determine what or how much has been remembered or forgotten by using one or both of two categories of memory tests.

Explicit Memory Tests
When we ask people to remember something, we are asking them to consciously call something to mind. Tests of memory that do this same type of thing are known as *explicit* memory tests. These tests assess what a person can *consciously remember*. Two types of explicit memory tests that have been popular in memory research are known as recall tests and recognition tests.

A **recall test** requires a person to produce a required response with few, if any, available cues or aids. This test asks the person to "recall" information that has been presented. In the verbal domain, these tests typically take the form of essay or fill-in-the-blank tests. For example, a recall test could ask, "Name the bones of the hand." In motor skills, a recall test requires the person to perform an action on command, such as "Perform the skill I just demonstrated to you" or "Show me how you tie your shoe."

---

declarative knowledge   knowledge about "what to do" in a situation; this knowledge typically is verbalizable.

procedural knowledge   knowledge that enables a person to know "how to do" a skill; this knowledge typically is difficult to verbalize, or is not verbalizable.

encoding   a memory process involving the transformation of information to be remembered into a form that can be stored in memory.

retrieval   a memory process involving the search through long-term memory for information needed to perform the task at hand.

recall test   an explicit memory test that requires a person to produce a required response with few, if any, available cues or aids.

A **recognition test,** on the other hand, provides some cues or information on which to base a response. In this type of test, a person's task is to recognize the correct response by distinguishing it from several alternatives. In the verbal domain, multiple-choice or matching tests are examples of recognition tests. For example, you could be asked, "Which of these is a bone of the hand?" You are then given four alternative answers from which to choose, where only one is correct. To answer the question, you need only to recognize which is the correct alternative, or which are the incorrect alternatives, to answer the question. For motor skills, recognition tests can involve having a person produce several different movements and then asking which of these is the one just demonstrated or most appropriate for a specific situation.

In terms of learning and performing motor skills, we are often confronted with both recall and recognition "tests," sometimes in the same situation. For example, if a person must climb a ladder, he or she must recall what to do and how it should be done in order to safely and effectively climb the rungs to the desired height. And a recognition test situation exists in a sport context when a football quarterback must visually inspect the defensive players to determine if their alignment is as it should be if he is to use the offensive play that has been called. Both recall and recognition tests are relevant to a baseball batter when deciding whether or not to swing at a pitch. He or she engages in a recognition test when determining if the ball is in the strike zone or not. Then, to produce the appropriate swing, the batter must recall what to do to carry out this action and then be able to recognize if the swing that has been initiated is appropriate for hitting the pitch where it is thrown.

An important benefit of recall and recognition tests is that each provides different information about what has been remembered or forgotten. It is possible for a person to fail to produce a correct response on a recall test, but be able to produce that response when it is one among several alternatives in a recognition test. A value of the recognition test, then, is that it enables the researcher to determine if information is actually stored in memory, even though retrieval cues or aids are needed by the person in order to gain access to that information.

Implicit Memory Tests

Many times people have information stored in memory, but it is stored in such a way that they have difficulty accessing that information so that they can respond correctly on explicit memory tests. For example, suppose you were asked to describe the grammatical rules of a sentence you had just said. Although you may not have been able to identify these rules, you confirmed your knowledge of them by the sentence you articulated. As a result, you demonstrated that you had knowledge about grammar rules stored in memory, but in a form that could not be brought to conscious level so you could verbalize the rules.

In the domain of motor skills, we can assess implicit memory by asking a person to verbally describe how to perform a skill and then asking him or her to perform it. As is often the case, especially with highly skilled people, the person can successfully perform a skill but cannot verbally describe what he or she did. For example, if you were asked to verbally describe how you tie your shoes, you might not be able to do it, or you might experience some difficulty doing it. Does this mean you don't know how to tie your shoes, or that you have forgotten how to tie your shoes? No; in terms of our earlier distinction between procedural and declarative knowledge, it means that you do not have access to, or immediate access to, your declarative knowledge about tying shoes. How would you provide evidence that you know how to tie your shoes? You would physically demonstrate tying your shoes, which would indicate that you had the procedural knowledge necessary to perform this skill.

On the other hand, it is possible to know what to do (i.e., have declarative knowledge), but not be able to actually do what you know you should do (i.e., have poor procedural knowledge). This phenomenon was demonstrated very nicely in the experiment by McPherson and Thomas (1989) that was discussed earlier. They gave young male basketball players an explicit paper-and-pencil test and asked them to indicate what they would do in a given bas-

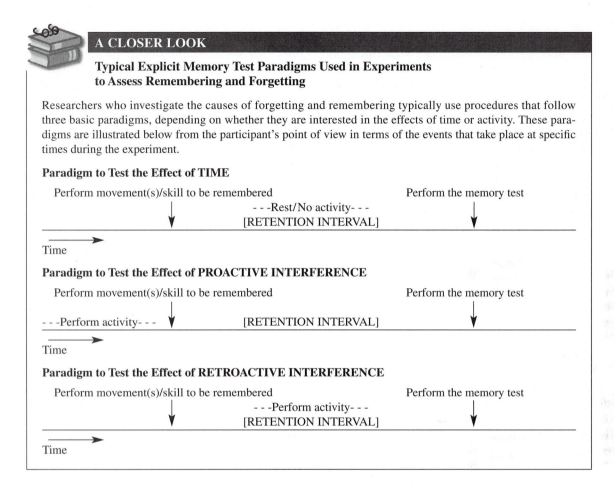

A CLOSER LOOK

Typical Explicit Memory Test Paradigms Used in Experiments to Assess Remembering and Forgetting

Researchers who investigate the causes of forgetting and remembering typically use procedures that follow three basic paradigms, depending on whether they are interested in the effects of time or activity. These paradigms are illustrated below from the participant's point of view in terms of the events that take place at specific times during the experiment.

Paradigm to Test the Effect of TIME

Perform movement(s)/skill to be remembered   Perform the memory test

- - -Rest/No activity- - -
[RETENTION INTERVAL]

Time →

Paradigm to Test the Effect of PROACTIVE INTERFERENCE

Perform movement(s)/skill to be remembered   Perform the memory test

- - -Perform activity- - -   [RETENTION INTERVAL]

Time →

Paradigm to Test the Effect of RETROACTIVE INTERFERENCE

Perform movement(s)/skill to be remembered   Perform the memory test

- - -Perform activity- - -
[RETENTION INTERVAL]

Time →

---

ketball game situation. This information indicated declarative knowledge about what to do. An implicit test was also administered by observing what the players actually did in a situation to determine if they had the procedural knowledge necessary to do what they indicated should be done. The results showed that many of the players knew what to do in each situation, but couldn't actually do it in a game.

THE CAUSES OF FORGETTING

Trace Decay

When forgetting occurs with the passing of time, the cause is generally termed *trace decay* in the memory literature. It should be noted that the term "trace" is not commonly used in contemporary memory research literature. However, it can be

thought of as synonymous with what is referred to in this discussion as the memory representation of an action.

An important point about trace decay is that it can be effectively tested as a cause of forgetting only in working memory. A major problem with testing it for long-term memory is the practical impossibility of maintaining a no-interference situation. For example, if you try to recall how to hit a slice serve in tennis after several years of not having performed it, you will have some initial

---

recognition test   an explicit memory test that requires a person to select a correct response from several alternative responses.

difficulty remembering how to do it. Although time is a factor, you undoubtedly experienced the potentially interfering influences of the many cognitive and motor activities you have performed since you last performed this type of serve. Hence, we observe the interaction of interference and time in the long-term memory situation. As a result, we know very little about the influence of time on forgetting information stored in long-term memory.

Although time undoubtedly influences forgetting of information stored in long-term memory, it is more likely that forgetting involves the misplacing of information rather than its decay or deterioration. One reason for this is the relative permanence characteristic for information stored in long-term memory. Thus, forgetting typically refers to a retrieval problem rather than to information no longer in memory.

Proactive Interference

Activity that occurs *prior to* the presentation of information that is to be remembered and negatively affects the remembering of that information is known as **proactive interference.** Relatively convincing research evidence suggests that proactive interference is a reason for forgetting movement information held in *working memory.* One of the best examples of this was provided in an experiment by Stelmach (1969). Participants moved to either zero, two, or four locations on an arm-positioning task *before* moving to the location to be recalled. Following a retention interval of 5, 15, or 50 sec, they moved in reverse order to their estimates of each of the locations they had moved to. Thus, the first location recalled was the criterion location. Results showed proactive interference effects as four prior movements and a retention interval of at least 15 sec yielded the largest amount of recall performance error, compared to the other time and activity conditions.

Several attempts have been made to explain why proactive interference affects remembering movement information. One plausible suggestion is that when the proactive interference takes the form of other movements, especially those that are similar to the criterion activity, *confusion* occurs. The individual is unable to make the criterion movement precisely because of the influence of the prior activities on the distinctiveness of the criterion movement.

Proactive interference seems to occur primarily when there is similarity between what is to be remembered and the interfering activity. This similarity seems to relate to "attribute" similarity. That is, if the information to be remembered and the interfering activity relate to the same movement attribute or characteristic, then proactive interference will build up as the number of similar movements preceding the movements to be remembered increases.

For movement information in *long-term memory,* the role of proactive interfering activities is virtually unknown. It appears that we can quite readily overcome proactive interference effects by actively rehearsing the information. This means that when we actively practice an action, we strengthen its representation in memory and thus notice few, if any, effects of proactive interference.

Retroactive Interference

If an interfering activity occurs after we perform a movement we need to remember (i.e., *during* the retention interval) and results in poorer retention performance than if no activity had occurred, the forgetting is said to be due to **retroactive interference.** In *working memory,* it seems that rather than just any activity causing interference to the extent that retention performance is negatively affected, the degree of similarity between the interfering activity and the movement that must be remembered is an important factor. For example, participants in experiments by Smyth and Pendleton (1990) were shown a sequence of four movements, such as a forward bend of the head, both arms raised to shoulder level in front of the body, a bend of the knees, and left leg raised to the side. Following a retention interval, they had to perform these movements, either in sequence (serial recall) or in any order (free recall).

The influence of five different retention interval time and activity conditions on recall performance can be seen in figure 9.2. As you can see, these results showed that only when the retention interval involved subjects in recalling movements that were

A CLOSER LOOK

Proactive Interference Influence on Gymnastic Judging

A series of studies by Diane Ste.-Marie and her colleagues provide interesting evidence that gymnastic judges' evaluations of a gymnast's performance may be influenced by their having watched the gymnasts during pre-competition warm-up sessions. In each study, the following procedures were used:

Participants: Female gymnastics judges certified by Gymnastics Canada

Study phase: The judges watched videotapes of individual gymnastic elements performed by several gymnasts. The elements were edited parts of actual routines the gymnasts performed. The judges' evaluated the performance of each as perfect or with a form error.

Test phase: The judges watched and evaluated the same gymnasts performing elements that were:

1. the same way as in the study phase (SAME);
2. a different way from in the study phase, i.e., with an error if perfect in study phase, or vice versa (DIFFERENT);
3. a new element, which was not in the study phase (NEW)

Results of each study:
- *Ste.-Marie and Lee (1991)* showed the following order of judgment accuracy percentages for the three test-phase conditions:

Highest: SAME; 2nd highest: NEW; Lowest: DIFFERENT

This order of test accuracy demonstrates that observing and evaluating the performance of previously seen elements biased the judges evaluations when the elements were performed differently from the previous observation. This bias is seen in the results that show lower judgment accuracy for elements the judges had seen previously, but performed differently, than for elements they had not seen previously. Interestingly, the bias occurred even though the judges were not consciously aware that they had seen the elements they evaluated in the same/different test conditions performed in the study phase.

- *Ste.-Marie and Valiquette (1996)* showed the same order of accuracy as the Ste.-Marie and Lee study when the test phase occurred immediately, one day, or one week after the study phases. These results indicate that the bias effects of previous observations persisted for at least one week.
- *Ste.-Marie, Valiquette, and Taylor (2001)* showed the same order of test accuracy as the previous two studies when the study phase involved judging the performance of each element, naming the element performed, or naming the apparatus involved. These results indicate that the test accuracy results in the previous studies were due to watching the gymnasts perform during the study phase and not to the judges' being involved in evaluating the performance of each element.

These studies provide excellent demonstrations of the influence of proactive interference on human memory, especially when the previous experiences involve characteristics that are similar to those involved in the test situation.

---

similar to those they had to remember did recall performance significantly suffer from activity in the retention interval.

Another characteristic of retroactive interference effects in working memory is one that we discussed for proactive interference. That is, activity during the retention interval causes interference that increases recall performance error only when there is a certain amount of activity. As long as the amount of information stays within this limit, remembering is not affected. However, when that limit is exceeded, forgetting occurs, which results in recall performance error increase (see, e.g., Roy & Davenport, 1972).

> **proactive interference**   a cause of forgetting because of activity that occurs prior to the presentation of information to be remembered.
>
> **retroactive interference**   a cause of forgetting because of activity occurring during the retention interval.

FIGURE 9.2 Free recall results of the experiment by Smyth and Pendleton showing the retroactive interference effects of performance similar movements to those that had to be remembered. [From Smyth, M. M., & Pendleton, L. R. (1990). Space and movement in working memory. *Quarterly Journal of Experimental Psychology, 42A,* 291–304. Reprinted by permission of the Experimental Psychology Society.]

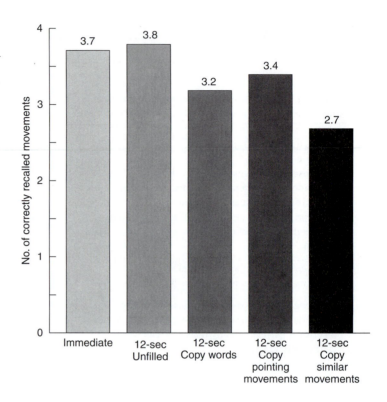

Thus, the available research evidence indicates that retroactive interference for remembering just-presented movements occurs in specific circumstances. These appear to be when the activity during the retention interval is similar to the movements that must be remembered, and when this activity and the movements to be remembered exceed working memory or attention-capacity limits.

Retroactive Interference and Long-Term Memory

It appears that retention interval length and/or activity does not have the same forgetting effects for all types of motor skills stored in *long-term memory*. Research evidence indicates that *certain types of motor skills are remembered better over long periods than are other types*. Your own experiences may provide some support for this. You probably had very little trouble remembering how to ride a bicycle, even after not having been on one for several years. However, you probably did experience

some difficulty in putting together the pieces of a puzzle that you had assembled quickly around the same time you learned to ride a bicycle.

The characteristic of skills that distinguishes these two situations relates to one of the classification systems discussed in chapter 1. That is, *continuous motor skills* are typically more resistant to long-term forgetting than are discrete skills, especially when the skill involves producing a series of discrete movements in what is sometimes referred to as a serial discrete skill.

Several reasons have been suggested to explain why this retention difference occurs. One is the difference in the *size of the verbal component* of the two types of skills. Serial discrete skills have a large verbal component, whereas this is small for continuous skills. This characteristic is significant because the verbal component of skills seems to deteriorate over time more readily than motor components. Another reason is that continuous skills are *practiced more* than are discrete skills. This is evident if you consider what a "trial" is for these

A CLOSER LOOK

Implications for Motor Skill Instruction of the Effects on Working Memory of Proactive and Retroactive Interference

- After you give instructions that describe or demonstrate what to do in a skill or how to do a skill, keep the amount of time before people physically practice the skill as short and free of activity (verbal and motor) as possible.

- Do not describe or demonstrate examples of "what *not* to do" before you give instructions that describe or demonstrate what to do in a skill or how to do a skill, and before people have an initial opportunity to physically practice the skill.

- If you describe or demonstrate examples of "what *not* to do" either before or after you give instruction about what to do in a skill or how to do a skill, do it after people have practiced the skill several times and limit the examples to one or two.

- If people ask questions after you give instructions about what to do in a skill or how to do a skill, repeat the instructions (i.e., verbally or demonstrate) after answering the question just before the people physically practice the skill.

two types of skills. One trial for a discrete skill, is usually one performance of the skill, whereas one trial for a continuous skill is several repetitions of the skill over a much longer period of time. Thus, fifty trials of a continuous skill yield many more practice repetitions of the skill than do fifty trials of a discrete skill.

MOVEMENT CHARACTERISTICS RELATED TO MEMORY PERFORMANCE

Location and Distance Characteristics

Actions have many characteristics that we can store in memory. For example, we could store the spatial position of various points of a movement, such as the beginning and the end point of a golf swing. We could also store the distance of a movement, its velocity, its force, and/or the direction of a movement. Two of these, *location* and *distance,* have been extensively examined with regard to how easily they can be stored in and retrieved from memory.

Investigation of the issue was very popular in the 1970s and focused primarily on working memory. Of particular interest were the short-term storage characteristics of spatial positioning movements of the arm. The initial research studies found that movement end-point location is remembered better than movement distance (e.g., Diewert, 1975; Hagman, 1978; Laabs, 1973). However, an

important finding showed that when movement end-point location information is a relatively reliable recall cue, people will use a location-type strategy to recall the movement (Diewert & Roy 1978). However, when location information is totally unreliable and only distance information will aid recall, people will use some nonkinesthetic strategy, such as counting, to help remember the distance of the criterion movement.

Another characteristic of remembering location information is that an arm-movement end location is more easily remembered when it is within the person's own body space (e.g., Chieffi, Allport, & Woodfin, 1999; Larish & Stelmach 1982). For limb-positioning movements, people typically associate the end location of a movement with a body part and use that as a cue to aid their recall performance. Other research, which will be considered later, suggests that people will also spontaneously associate the end location of limb positions with well-known objects, such as a clock face, to aid recall.

What does all this mean for teaching motor skills? One implication is that if limb positions are important for successful performance of the skill, the instructor can emphasize these positions in ways that will facilitate learning the skill. For example, if you are teaching a beginner a golf swing, the important phases of the swing that he or she should concentrate on are critical location points in

FIGURE 9.3   Results from the experiment by Laugier and Cadopi showing the influence of movement meaningfulness on remembering a four-element dance sequence. Scores reflect form and quality measures of novice dancers' one-time performance of the sequence after fifteen viewings of a skilled dancer performing the sequence. [Modified figure 2, p. 98, in Laugier, C., & Cadopi, M. (1996). Representational guidance of dance performance in adult novices: Effect of concrete vs. abstract movement. *International Journal of Sport Psychology, 27,* 91–108. Adapted with permission of the International Society of Sport Psychology.]

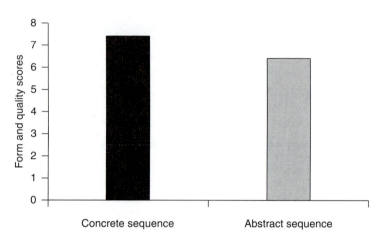

the swing. The keys could be the beginning point of the backswing or the location point of the top of the backswing. Or if a therapist is working with a patient who needs to work on flexing or extending his or her knee, emphasizing the position of the lower leg can help the patient remember where the last movement was or to establish a goal for future flexion attempts. If a dancer is having difficulty remembering where her arm should be during a particular sequence, a body-part cue about the location of the arm can help her remember the position more effectively.

The Meaningfulness of the Movement
Another characteristic that influences remembering movements is the *meaningfulness* of the movement. A movement or sequence of movements can be considered meaningful to an individual if that person can readily relate the movement to something he or she knows. For example, a movement that forms the shape of a triangle is considered more meaningful than one that makes an unfamiliar, abstract pattern. Or, if a movement is similar to one the person can do, then the new movement being learned takes on increased meaningfulness to the person.

The results of an experiment by Laugier and Cadopi (1996) illustrate the influence movement meaningfulness has on remembering movements.

Adult novice dancers watched a video of a skilled dancer perform a four-element sequence of dance movements, each of which involved two to four body, head, and/or limb movements. One sequence, which the researchers labeled as a "concrete" sequence, was a sequence commonly performed in dance. Another sequence, labeled as an "abstract" sequence, involved elements that did not belong to any particular style of dance. After fifteen viewings of the dancer performing the sequences, the participants performed the sequence one time. Analysis of the participants' performance indicated that the observation of the concrete sequence led to better form and quality than the observation of the abstract sequence (see figure 9.3). Interviews of the participants indicated that the concrete sequence had a higher degree of meaningfulness to them, which helped them remember the sequence when they performed it.

STRATEGIES THAT ENHANCE MEMORY PERFORMANCE

There are several different strategies people can use to help them remember important movement characteristics of a skill, which in turn facilitate learning the skill. Note that some of these strategies take advantage of the movement characteristics we just discussed that are more easily remembered than others. We will consider three general strategies that research evidence has shown to influence how well a movement is remembered.

Increasing a Movement's Meaningfulness

When people first practice a new skill, it is very likely that the skill will require that they coordinate their body and limbs in a new way. This characteristic makes it also likely that the new coordination pattern of movements will be more abstract than it is concrete. That is, the skill typically has little inherent "meaningfulness" to the learner in terms spatial and temporal characteristics of the limb coordination needed to perform the skill. As you saw earlier in this discussion, movements that are higher in their meaningfulness will be remembered better than those low in meaningfulness. The instructor can take advantage of this characteristic by presenting to the learner a strategy that will increase the meaningfulness of the movements required to perform the skill. Two strategies are especially effective: visual imagery and verbal labels.

The use of *visual imagery* as a memory strategy involves developing in your mind a picture of what a movement is like. As an instructor, is best to use an image of something that is very familiar to the learner. For example, rather than provide the complex instructions for how to coordinate the arm movements to perform a sidestroke in swimming, the instructor can provide the learners with a useful image to use while practicing the stroke. The image is of themselves picking an apple from a tree with one hand, bringing the apple down, and putting the apple in a basket.

Another effective strategy that increases the meaningfulness of a movement to attach a meaningful *verbal label* to the movement. One of the earliest demonstrations of the beneficial influence of attaching verbal labels to movements was by John Shea (1977), who had participants move a lever to a stop on a semicircular arm-positioning apparatus. When they arrived at the criterion location, those in one group were provided with a number that corresponded to the clockface location of the criterion location; another group received an irrelevant verbal label such as a nonsensical three-letter syllable;

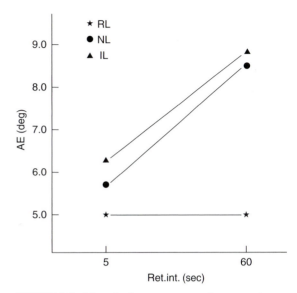

FIGURE 9.4 Mean absolute error computed across positions for the 5-sec and 60-sec retention intervals (ret. int.) for Experiment 1 by Shea. (RL = relevant label, NL = no label, IL = irrelevant label.) [From Shea, J.B. (1997). Effects of labeling on motor short-term memory. *Journal of Experimental Psychology: Human Learning and Memory, 3,* 92–99. Copyright © 1977 by the American Psychological Association. Reprinted with permission.]

another group received no verbal label about the criterion location. Results, as seen in figure 9.4, indicated that the group given a clockface label showed no increase in error over a 60-sec unfilled retention interval, whereas the other two groups showed a large increase in recall error. In a related experiment, Winther and Thomas (1981) showed that when useful verbal labels are attached to positioning movements, retention performance of young children (age seven) can become equivalent to that of adults.

There are at least four reasons why the use of visual imagery and verbal labels aid the learning of complex motor skills. First, they reduce the complexity of the verbal instructions that would be needed to describe all the movements involved in performing the skill, and their relationships to each other. Second, they help change an abstract, complex array of movements to a more concrete, meaningful set of movements. Third, they direct the performer's attention focus to the outcome of the movements rather than to the movements themselves, which, as we discussed in chapter 8, enhances the performance of skills. And fourth, they speed up the movement planning process by facilitating the retrieval of the appropriate memory representation of the action (Johnson, 1998).

The Intention to Remember

In all the memory experiments considered so far, participants have always known in advance that the movements they were presented or had to practice would be later subject to a recall test. But, suppose they were not given this information in advance? Suppose they were told that the goal of the experiment was to see how well they could move their arms to a specified location. If an unexpected recall test was given later, how well would they recall the movements made earlier?

The two situations just described are known in the memory research literature as *intentional* and *incidental* memory situations, respectively. In addition to investigating the influence of intention to remember as an effective remembering strategy, the comparison of these two situations provides insight into the encoding of movement information processes. That is, do we store only information to which we give conscious attention, as in the case of the intentional memory situation, or do we store more information, as would be shown by good memory performance, in the incidental memory situation?

This question has received little research interest in the study of memory for movements. However, the research that has been done indicates that, in general, intention to remember leads to better remembering than no intention to remember. (See Crocker & Dickinson, 1984 for a review of this research.) Yet retention test performance in the incidental situation is typically better than if no previous experience with the test movements had occurred. In fact, some reports show incidental memory test performance to be as good as it was for the intentional situation.

The investigation of intentional and incidental memory strategies is an important one to increase our understanding of memory processes related to encoding and storing information. Research indicates that we encode and store much more information than we are consciously aware of.

One implication that the intentional and incidental memory research provides for instructional situations is that memory performance and skill learning can be enhanced by telling students when they begin to practice a skill that they will be tested on the skill later. The effect of this advance knowledge about a test is that students will undoubtedly increase the amount of effort given in practice, a characteristic that you will repeatedly see in this text as beneficial for memory and learning. Also, when there are specific characteristics of a skill performance situation that must be remembered for a later test, a better test performance will result from telling people what these characteristics are.

Subjective Organization

A strategy frequently used by learners of large amounts of information is grouping or organizing the information into units. This strategy, which is known as *subjective organization,* involves the organizing of information that must be remembered in a way that is meaningful to the individual. Other terms that researchers have used to describe this strategy are chunking, clustering, and grouping, among others. An example of implementing this strategy is commonly seen when people need to learn a long monologue for a play, or a list of terms for a test. They often will organize the monologue or list by dividing it into shorter, more manageable chunks to begin memorizing the information. You would likely use a similar strategy if you had to play from memory a long piece of music on an instrument, or had to learn a dance or gymnastics routine. In each of these situations, continued practice typically leads to increasing the size of the chunks.

Although the role of subjective organization in motor skill learning has not been the subject of a large amount of research, there is evidence indicating that when given the opportunity to subjectively organize a sequence of movements, some people will spontaneously create an organized structure. And this subjectively determined organizational structure imposed on the sequence benefits recall performance (e.g., Magill & Lee, 1987). In addition, it is interesting to note that memory performance deficits often seen following a stroke (i.e., cerebrovascular accident) have been found to be due in part to a lack of ability to implement effective organizational strategies (e.g., Lange, Waked, Kirshblum, & DeLuca, 2000). Similarly, people with Parkinson's disease have been shown to have problems with implementing a subjective organization strategy without external guidance (Berger et al., 1999).

One way to apply the benefit of subjective organization to motor skill learning situations is to consider the way a novice approaches the learning of a complex skill. He or she tends to consider complex motor skills as comprising many parts. As the beginner develops his or her ability to execute the skill, the number of components of the skill seems to decrease. This does not mean the structure of the skill itself has changed. Rather, the learner's view of the skill has changed. A good example is a dance or gymnastic floor exercise routine, where each of the routines is made up of many individual parts. To the beginner, a dance routine is thought of step by step and movement by movement. Beginning gymnasts think of a floor exercise as so many individual stunts. As they practice, their approach to the skills changes. They begin to organize the routines into units or groups of movements. Three or four component parts are now considered as one. The result will be performing the entire routine with the requisite timing, rhythm, and coordination. With that result, moreover, will be the added effect of developing a more efficient means of storing the complex routine in memory.

Skilled performers organize information to such an extent that it appears they have an increased working memory capacity; this led Ericsson and Kintsch (1995) to propose the long-term working memory described earlier in this discussion. A good example of this type of subjective organization can be seen in the experiment with "novice" and "expert" eleven-year-old dancers by Starkes et al. (1987) that was mentioned earlier in the discussion of working memory capacity. When these dancers were presented sequences of eight elements that were organized as in a ballet routine, the expert dancers recalled the routine almost perfectly, whereas the novices recalled about half of the sequence correctly. However, when the same number of elements was presented in an unstructured sequence, there was no difference between the skilled and novice dancers in terms of the number of elements they correctly recalled. This result indicates that the organizational structure of the sequence of dance movements was an important factor in the experts' recall performance. In an interesting anecdote, the researchers reported observing an adult principal national-level ballet dancer being able to perform a sequence of ninety-six steps after having seen the sequence demonstrated one time. Thus, organization was apparently a strategy used to reduce the working memory load of this sequence and to increase the memorability of the sequence.

Similar organization effects were reported by Millslagle (2002) for experienced basketball players. Both male and female players were shown slides of structured and unstructured plays that could occur in game situations. On a recognition test given after the players viewed the slides, they more accurately remembered having seen slides that included the structured plays. Interestingly, when results were compared for the players who were guards, forwards, and centers, the guards' recognition accuracy was higher than it was for the forwards and centers. Because guards have more experience determining and implementing plays than the other two positions, the results of this experiment further emphasize the influence of expertise on the organizational structure of the information we store in memory.

PRACTICE-TEST CONTEXT EFFECTS

An important influence on the retention of motor skills is the relationship between the context of practice and the context at the time of the test. The context of a movement relates to both the environmental conditions in which the movement is performed and characteristics related to the person performing the movement. For example, if a memory experiment is performed in a laboratory, the

A CLOSER LOOK

Active and Passive Limb Movements: Evidence for the Application of the Encoding Specificity Principle to Motor Skills

An excellent example of research evidence supporting the application of the encoding specificity principle to the remembering of movements is an experiment done many years ago by Lee and Hirota (1980).

- **Apparatus.** An arm-positioning apparatus on a table facing the participant.

- **Task and experimental conditions.** On some trials, blindfolded participants actively moved the handle of the apparatus along the trackway to a criterion arm position that was specified by a physical block. On other trials, they were passively moved by the experimenter to a criterion arm position. For the recall test on each trial, participants were told to actively move to the arm position just experienced or were passively moved by the experimenter until the participant told the experimenter to stop. This procedure continued until all participants had actively and passively experienced the presentation of each criterion arm position and had performed recall tests in either the same way they had experienced the presentation of the criterion position or the opposite way.

- **Encoding specificity principle predictions.**
  - ▸ Active movements to the criterion arm movements should be recalled better when the

movements are actively recalled than passively recalled.
  - ▸ Passive movements to the criterion arm movements should be recalled better when the movements are passively recalled than when they are actively recalled.

- **Results.** As you can see in figure 9.5 below, the results supported the encoding specificity principle. When the movement during the recall test was performed in the same way as it was during the presentation of the criterion arm position (i.e., active–active, passive–passive), recall performance was more accurate than when the recall test was performed differently from the way it was during the presentation of the criterion arm position (i.e., active–passive, passive–active).
  - ▸ Note that there was no advantage to active over passive movements. The difference in recall accuracy related to the relationship between the presentation and recall conditions.

FIGURE 9.5 Results of the experiment by Lee and Hirota showing absolute error for recalling arm-position movements presented as either active or passive and recalled in either the same or opposite conditions. [From data in Lee, T.D., & Hirota, T.T. (1980). Encoding specificity principle in motor short-term memory. *Journal of Motor Behavior, 12*, 63–67.]

LAB LINKS

Lab 9 in the Online Learning Center Lab Manual provides an opportunity for you to experience practice and test conditions that demonstrate the effects of the encoding specificity principle on remembering movements.

environmental context includes such things as the room in which the experiment is done, the experimenter, the time of day, the noise the participant can hear, the lighting, and so on. Personal context involves such things as the mood of the individual, the limb used to make the movement, the sitting or standing position of the subject, and the sensory feedback sources that are available to the subject. As you will see in this section, differences in these conditions during the time the movement to be remembered or learned is presented or practiced and during the time the movement must be recalled can influence the success of the recall performance.

The Encoding Specificity Principle

An important point to consider regarding the influence of movement context on remembering or learning a motor skill is the relationship between the practice and test contexts. In some situations, especially for closed skills, the test goal is essentially the same as the practice goal. That is, to shoot a free throw, you must stand in essentially the same place and shoot the ball through a hoop that is the same distance from you as it was when you practiced it. In such closed-skill situations, what is known as the **encoding specificity principle** applies.

The encoding specificity principle was introduced by Tulving and Thomson (1973). According to this principle, the more the test context resembles the practice context, the better the retention performance will be. Evidence that this principle applies to motor skills has come primarily from laboratory-based experiments (e.g., Lee & Hirota, 1980; Magill & Lee, 1987). However, as you will see in the discussion in chapter 12 concerning the transfer of learning, ample evidence exists to have

confidence in generalizing this principle to the learning and performance of motor skills.

The encoding specificity principle is based on research findings that indicate that the memory representation for an action has stored with it important sensory and motor feedback information that is specific to the context conditions in which the action was practiced. Thus, the more the test conditions match the practice conditions, the more accurate the test performance will be expected to be.

The practical implications of the encoding specificity principle seem especially relevant to learning closed skills. In a closed skill, the test context is typically stable and predictable. Because of this, practice conditions can be established that will closely mimic the test conditions. In these cases, then, the more similar the practice setting is to the test setting, the higher the probability or successful performance during the test. Consider, for example, practice for shooting free throws in a basketball game. Free throws are always one, two, or one-and-one situations. According to the encoding specificity principle, it is essential that players have practice experiences in which these gamelike conditions prevail. This does not say that this is the only way that free throws can be practiced. However, if game performance is the test of interest, it is essential that gamelike practice be provided.

Consider also a physical therapy example where a knee joint replacement patient is working on knee joint flexion and extension. Based on the encoding specificity principle, because test conditions involve active limb movement, practice conditions should emphasize active rather than passive limb movement. Similar practice-test relationships can be established for a variety of skill practice situations.

---

encoding specificity principle   a memory principle that indicates the close relationship between encoding and retrieval memory processes; it states that memory test performance is directly related to the amount of similarity between the practice and the test contexts, i.e., the more similarity, the better the test performance will be.

SUMMARY

- Memory is best viewed as consisting of two functional components: working memory and long-term memory.

- Working memory serves two functions: a short-term storage system for information just presented or retrieved from long-term memory, and a temporary workspace for manipulating information just received and just retrieved from long-term memory in order to solve a specific problem, make a decision, or prepare an action required in a specific situation.

- Working memory has a limited capacity for information storage and the information remains for only a brief amount of time.

- Long-term memory stores different types of information on a more permanent basis. It appears to have no limits in terms of how much information can be stored or the length of time the information will remain there.

- Forgetting is a term used to describe the loss of memory or the inability to retrieve information from memory. Forgetting is usually measured by determining the amount of information that a person can recall or recognize following a retention interval.

- Both time and activity influence forgetting in both working memory and long-term memory. The causes of forgetting associated with these factors are referred to as trace decay, which means the memory representation deteriorates over time, and interference, which can occur before (proactive interference) or after (retroactive interference) the presentation of the movement to be remembered.

- Movement-related characteristics that influence the remembering of a movement are the movement distance, movement end-location, and the meaningfulness of the movement.

- Strategies that increase how well movements are remembered include the use of visual imagery and verbal labels; the subjective organization of a complex sequence of movements into meaningful units; and the intention to remember.

- The relationship between the practice and test context characteristics influences the remembering of movements according to the encoding specificity principle, which states that increasing the similarity between these context characteristics increases performance on a memory test.

RELATED READINGS

Awh, E., Jonides, J., Smith, E. E., Buxton, R. B., Frank, L. R., Love, T., Wong, E. C., & Gmeindl, L. (1999). Rehearsal in spatial working memory: Evidence from neuroimaging. *Psychological Science, 10,* 433–437.

Christina, R. W., & Bjork, R. A. (1991). Optimizing long-term retention and transfer. In D. Druckman & R. A. Bjork (Eds), *In the mind's eye: Enhancing human performance* (pp. 23–56). Washington, DC: National Academy Press.

Kimberg, D. Y., D'Esposito, M., & Farah, M. J. (1998). Cognitive functions in the prefrontal cortex: Working memory and executive control. *Current Directions in Psychological Science, 6,* 185–192.

Kimbrough, S. K., Wright, D. L., & Shea, C. H. (2001). Reducing the saliency of intentional stimuli results in greater contextual-dependent performance. *Memory, 9,* 133–143.

McIsaac, H. K., & Eich, E. (2002). Vantage point in episodic memory. *Psychonomic Bulletin & Review, 9,* 146–150.

Roediger, H. L. (1990). Implicit memory: Retention without remembering. *American Psychologist, 45,* 1043–1056.

Shadmehr, R., BrashersKrug, T. (1997). Functional stages in the formation of human long-term motor memory. *Journal of Neuroscience, 17,* 409–419

STUDY QUESTIONS

1. Discuss how working memory and long-term memory differ in terms of the duration and capacity of information in each.

2. Describe the meaning of the terms *declarative* and *procedural* knowledge. Give a motor skill example of each.

3. Discuss the primary causes of forgetting in working memory and in long-term memory.

4. Discuss two effective strategies a person can use to help him or her remember a movement or sequence of movements that he or she must perform. Give an example of the use of each strategy in a motor skill performance situation.

5. What is the *encoding specificity principle,* and how does it relate to the performance of motor skills?

UNIT

IV

INTRODUCTION TO MOTOR SKILL LEARNING

Defining and Assessing Learning

Concept: People who assess learning must make inferences from observing performance during practice and tests

After completing this chapter, you will be able to

- Define and distinguish between the terms *performance* and *learning*

- Identify four general performance characteristics typically observable as motor skill learning occurs

- Describe several different methods to assess motor skill learning

- Discuss two reasons performance during the practice of a motor skill may misrepresent the amount of learning that occurred during practice

Application

Any professional involved in motor skills instruction typically has to provide some type of assessment to determine whether or not the student or patient has learned what the professional has taught. The following two situations, common in physical education and rehabilitation settings, provide examples of the importance of assessing learning.

Suppose you are a physical educator teaching a tennis unit. If you are teaching your students to serve, how do you determine if they are actually learning what you are teaching them? What will you look for to assess their progress in learning to serve? How can you be certain that what you are observing is the result of learning and not just luck?

Or suppose you are a physical therapist helping a stroke patient to re-learn how to walk without support. What evidence will tell you that this patient is learning to do what you have taught him or her to do? What characteristics of the patient's per-

formance will make you confident that the patient is learning this skill and will be able to walk without assistance at home as well as in the clinic?

Discussion

In any discussion about the assessment of learning, we need to keep two important terms distinct: *performance* and *learning*. This distinction helps us establish an appropriate definition for the term *learning;* it also helps us consider appropriate conditions under which we should observe performance so that we can make valid inferences about learning.

PERFORMANCE DISTINGUISHED FROM LEARNING

Simply put, **performance** is *observable behavior.* If you observe a person walking down a corridor,

A CLOSER LOOK

The Terms "Performance" and "Learning"

Performance	Learning
• Observable behavior	• Inferred from performance
• Temporary	• Relatively permanent
• May not be due to practice	• Due to practice
• May be influenced by performance variables	• *Not* influenced by performance variables

you are observing him or her perform the skill of walking. Similarly, if you observe a person hitting a baseball, you are observing a performance of the skill of hitting a ball. When used in this way, the term *performance* refers to the execution of a skill at a specific time and in a specific situation. *Learning,* on the other hand, cannot be observed directly, but can only be inferred from characteristics of a person's performance.

Before considering a more formal definition for learning, think about how often we make inferences about people's internal states based on what we observe them doing. For example, when someone smiles (an observable behavior), we infer that he or she is happy. When someone cries, we infer that he or she is sad, or perhaps very happy. When a person yawns, we assume that the person is tired. In each of these situations, certain characteristics about the individual's behavior are the basis for our making a particular inference about some internal state we cannot observe directly. However, because we must base our inference on observed behavior, it is possible for us to make an incorrect inference. For example, if a student sitting beside you in class yawns during the lecture, you might infer from that behavior that the person is tired because of lack of sleep the night before. However, it may be that he or she is bored.

Learning Defined
We will use the following general definition for the term **learning:** *a change in the capability of a person to perform a skill that must be inferred from a relatively permanent improvement in performance as a result of practice or experience.* It is impor-

tant to note from this definition that the person has increased his or her *capability, or potential,* to perform that skill. Whether or not the person actually performs the skill in a way that is consistent with this potential will depend on the presence of what are known as *performance variables.* These include factors that can affect a person's performance but not the degree of learning the person has achieved. Some examples include the alertness of the person, the anxiety created by the situation, the uniqueness of the setting, fatigue, and so on. As a result, it is critical that methods used to assess learning take factors such as these into account to allow accurate inferences about learning.

GENERAL PERFORMANCE CHARACTERISTICS OF SKILL LEARNING

We generally observe four performance characteristics as skill learning takes place.

Improvement
First, *performance of the skill shows improvement over a period of time.* This means that the person performs at a higher level of skill at some later time

---

performance   the behavioral act of executing a skill at a specific time and in a specific situation.

learning   change in the capability of a person to perform a skill; it must be inferred from a relatively permanent improvement in performance as a result of practice or experience.

than at some previous time. It is important to note here that learning is not necessarily limited to improvement in performance. There are cases in which practice results in bad habits, which in turn result in the observed performance's failure to show improvement. In fact, performance actually may become worse as practice continues. But because this text is concerned with skill acquisition, we will focus on learning as it involves improvement in performance.

Consistency

Second, as learning progresses, *performance becomes increasingly more consistent.* This means that from one performance attempt to another, a person's performance characteristics should become more similar. Early in learning, performance is typically quite variable from one attempt to another. Eventually, however, it becomes more consistent.

A related term here is *stability,* which was introduced in chapter 4. As performance consistency of a skill increases, certain behavioral characteristics of performance become more stable. This means that the acquired new behavior is not easily disrupted by minor changes in personal or environmental characteristics.

Persistence

The third general performance characteristic we observe during learning is this: *the improved performance capability is marked by an increasing amount of persistence.* This means that as the person progresses in learning the skill, the improved performance capability lasts over increasing periods of time. A person who has learned a skill should be able to demonstrate the improved level of performance today, tomorrow, next week, and so on. However, because of some forgetting or other factors, the person may not achieve the same performance level on each of these occasions as he or she did at the end of the practice time devoted to the skill. The persistence characteristic relates to the emphasis in our definition of learning on a *relatively permanent improvement in performance.*

Adaptability

Finally, an important general characteristic of performance associated with skill learning is that *the improved performance is adaptable to a variety of performance context characteristics.* We never really perform a skill for which everything in the performance context is exactly the same each time. Something is different every time we perform a skill. The difference may be our own emotional state, the characteristics of the skill itself, an environmental difference such as a change in weather conditions, the place where we perform the skill, and so on. Thus, successful skill performance requires adaptability to changes in personal, task, and/or environmental characteristics. The degree of adaptability required depends on the skill and the performance situation. As a person progresses in learning a skill, his or her capability to perform the skill successfully in these changed circumstances also increases. Later in this book, we will explore some instruction and practice condition characteristics that can influence how well a person adapts to these various situations.

ASSESSING LEARNING BY OBSERVING PRACTICE PERFORMANCE

One way we can assess learning is to record levels of a performance measure during the period of time a person practices a skill. A common way to do this is to illustrate performance graphically in the form of a **performance curve.** This is a plot of the level achieved on the performance measure for each time period, which may be time in seconds or minutes, a trial, a series of trials, a day, etc. For any performance curve, the levels of the performance measure are always on the Y-axis (vertical axis), and the time over which the performance is measured is on the X-axis (horizontal axis).

Performance Curves for Outcome Measures

We can graphically describe performance by developing a performance curve for an outcome measure of performance. An example is shown in figure 10.1, which depicts one person's practice of a complex pursuit tracking task. The task required the per-

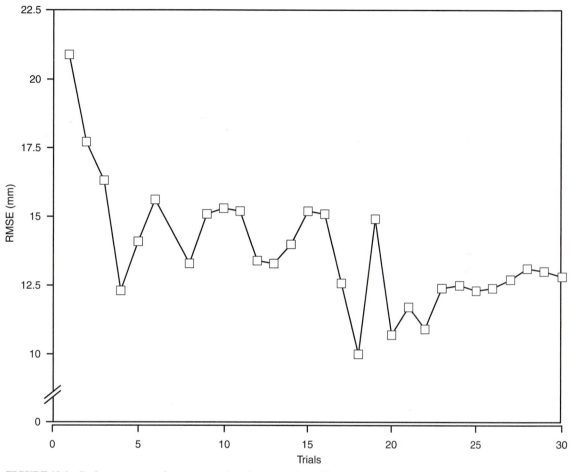

FIGURE 10.1 Performance curve for one person learning a pursuit tracking task. The performance measure is the root-mean-squared error (RMSE) for each trial. Notice that because the performance measure is error, lower values represent better performance than higher values.

son to track, or follow the movement of, a cursor on a computer monitor by moving the mouse on a tabletop. The goal was to track the cursor as closely as possible in both time and space. Each trial lasted about 15 sec. The outcome measure of performance was the root-mean-squared error (RMSE), which was described in chapter 2.

Notice that in this graph we can readily observe two of the four behavioral characteristics associated with learning. First, *improvement* is evident by the general direction of the curve. From the first to the last trial, the curve follows a general downward trend (note that because the performance measure

is error, improvement involves decreasing error). Second, we can also see *increased performance consistency* in this graph. The indicator of this

performance curve   line graph describing performance in which the level of achievement of a performance measure is plotted for a specific sequence of time (e.g., sec, min, days) or trials; the units of the performance measure are on the Y-axis (vertical axis) and the time units or trials are on the X-axis (horizontal axis).

A CLOSER LOOK

Examples of Motor Skill Performance Adaptability Demands

Closed Skills

- *Hitting a sand wedge in golf*
  - from wet sand, dry sand, etc.
  - from various locations in the sand trap
  - to various pin locations on the green
  - when shot has various implications for score

- *Shooting free throws in basketball*
  - one- and two-shot free throws at various times of the game
  - one-and-one shot situations at various times of the game
  - with various crowd conditions (e.g., quiet, loud, visible behind the basket)
  - various types of backboards

- *Walking*
  - on various types of surfaces
  - in various settings (e.g., home, mall, sidewalk)
  - while carrying various types of objects
  - alone or while carrying on a conversation with a friend

Open Skills

- *Hitting a baseball/softball*
  - various types, speeds, and locations of pitches
  - various ball-and-strike counts
  - various people-on-base situations with various numbers of outs
  - left-handed and right-handed pitchers

- *Catching a ball*
  - balls that are different shapes, weights, sizes, etc.
  - various speeds and directions
  - in the air, on the ground
  - with one or two hands

- *Driving a car*
  - various sizes of cars
  - various street and highway conditions
  - with or without passengers
  - various weather conditions

performance characteristic is performance on adjacent trials. According to figure 10.1, this person showed a high degree of inconsistency early in practice but became slightly more consistent from one trial to the next toward the end of practice. The expectation would be that the person would increase this consistency with additional practice trials.

When a person is acquiring a new skill, the performance curve for an outcome measure typically will follow one of *four general trends* from the beginning to the end of the practice period for a skill. This period of time may be represented as a certain number of trials, hours, days, etc. The trends are represented by the four different shapes of curves

in figure 10.2. Curve (a) is a *linear curve,* or a straight line. This indicates proportional performance increases over time; that is, each unit of increase on the horizontal axis (e.g., one trial) results in a proportional increase on the vertical axis (e.g., one second). Curve (b) is a *negatively accelerated curve,* which indicates that a large amount of improvement occurred early in practice, with smaller amounts of improvement later. This curve represents the classic power function curve of skill learning, which we will discuss in some detail in chapter 11 as a characteristic of the power law of practice. Curve (c) is the inverse of curve (b) and is called a *positively accelerated curve.* This curve

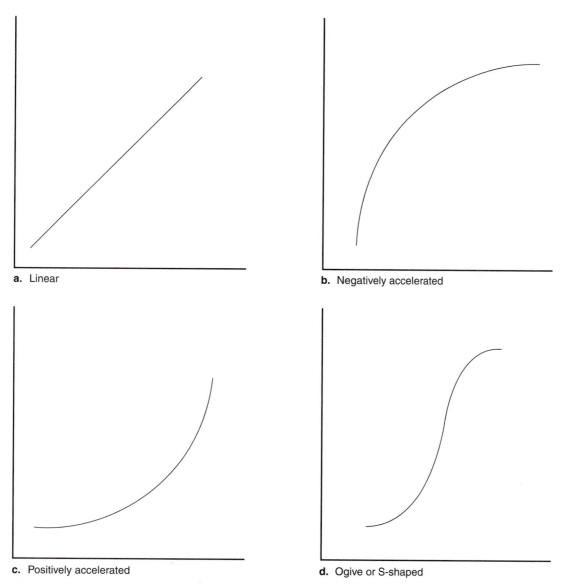

a. Linear

b. Negatively accelerated

c. Positively accelerated

d. Ogive or S-shaped

FIGURE 10.2   Four general types of performance curves.   Each curve is based on higher performance scores (which would be on the *y*- or vertical axis) represents better performance than lower scores.

indicates slight performance gain early in practice, but a substantial increase later in practice. Curve (d) is a combination of all three curves, and is called an *ogive* or *S-shaped curve.*

It is important to note that in contrast to figure 10.2, each curve shows better performance as the curve slopes upward. There are, however, instances in which the slope of the curve in a downward direction indicates performance improvement. This occurs when the performance measure is one for which a decrease in the performance level means better performance. Measures involving error (as in figure 10.1) or time (such as speed and reaction time) follow this characteristic as performance is

FIGURE 10.3   Results of an experiment by Marteniuk and Romanow showing changes in performance accuracy (displacement) on a tracking task at different practice trial blocks for one participant. The graph at the top shows the criterion pathway for the tracking task. [From Marteniuk, R. G., & Romanow, S. K. E. (1983). Human movement organization and learning as revealed by variability of movement, use of kinematic information, and fourier analysis. In R. A. Magill (Ed.), *Memory and control of action.* Copyright © 1983 Elsevier/North-Holland, Amsterdam, The Netherlands. Reprinted by permission.]

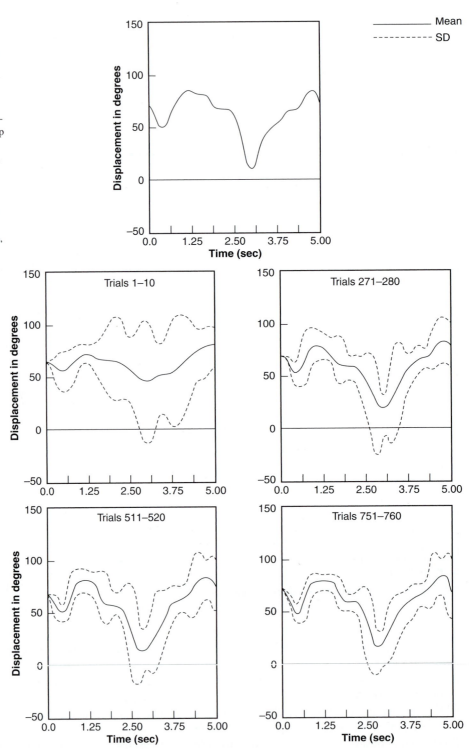

improving when the amount of error or time decreases. In such cases, the directions of the performance curves would be opposite to those just described, although the shapes of the curves would be the same.

The four curves presented in figure 10.2 are hypothetically smoothed to illustrate general patterns of performance curves. Typically, performance curves developed for individuals are not smooth but erratic, like the one in figure 10.1. However, there are various statistical procedures that can be used for curve smoothing when the reporting of research results warrants it. Finally, various individual, instructional, and motor skill characteristics can influence the type of curve that will characterize a person's performance as he or she learns a skill. You will learn about several of these characteristics in various chapters of this textbook.

Performance Curves for Kinematic Measures

When we use performance production measures, such as kinematics, we cannot always develop performance curves like the one in figure 10.1. This is the case because a kinematic measure typically does not lend itself to being represented by one number value for each trial. Kinematic measures involve performance over time *within* a trial. It is important to include this time component in the graphic representation of a kinematic measure.

To assess improvement and consistency in performance for a series of practice trials, researchers commonly show one performance curve graph for each trial. To show improvement and consistency changes, they depict a representative sample of trials from different stages of practice.

We can see an example of this approach to kinematic measures in figure 10.3. The task required participants to move a lever on a tabletop to produce the criterion movement displacement pattern shown at the top of this figure. Each participant observed the criterion pattern on a computer monitor before attempting to produce it by moving the lever. The four graphs located below the criterion pattern show one person's performance for 800 trials. The graphs show the practice trials in blocks of ten trials each. To demonstrate performance

changes during practice, figure 10.3 shows four of the blocks of trials, each representing a different segment of the 800-trial session. Each graph shows two performance characteristics: the person's average (mean) pattern drawn for the block of ten trials (the solid line); and the variability (sd, or standard deviation) of the patterns drawn for the same block of trials (dashed lines).

To determine *improvement in performance,* compare the early to the later practice trials by examining how the shape of the person's produced pattern corresponds to the shape of the criterion pattern. As the person practiced more, the produced pattern became more like the criterion pattern. In fact, in trials 751 through 760, the participant was making a pattern almost identical to the criterion pattern.

To assess *changes in consistency,* compare how far the standard deviation lines are from the mean pattern for each block of trials. For trials 1 through 10, notice how far the standard deviation lines are from the mean. This shows a large amount of trial-to-trial variability. However, for trials 751 through 760, these lines are much closer to the mean, indicating that the person more consistently produced the same pattern on each trial of that block of trials.

ASSESSING LEARNING BY RETENTION TESTS

Another means of inferring learning from performance examines *the persistence characteristic of improved performance* due to practicing a skill. A common means of assessing this characteristic is to administer a retention test. You have been experiencing this approach to assessing learning since you began school. Teachers regularly give tests that cover units of instruction. They use these **retention tests** to determine how much you know, or have retained from your study. The teacher

---

retention test   test of a practiced skill that a learner performs following an interval of time after practice has ceased.

makes an inference concerning how much you have learned about a particular unit of study on the basis of your test performance.

The typical way to administer a retention test in a motor skill situation is to have people perform the skill they have been practicing after a period of time during which they have not actually practiced the skill. The purpose is to determine the degree of permanence or persistence of the performance level achieved during practice; having a period of time with no practice allows this type of assessment. The actual length of time between the end of practice and the test is arbitrary. But the amount of time should be sufficiently long to allow the influence of any performance variables to dissipate to determine what was learned during practice. The critical assessment is the difference between the person's performance level on the first practice day and that on the test. If there is a significant improvement between these two periods of time, then you can be confident that learning has occurred.

ASSESSING LEARNING BY TRANSFER TESTS

The third means of inferring learning examines the *adaptability aspect of performance changes* related to learning. This assessment method involves using **transfer tests,** which are tests involving some novel situation, so that people must adapt the skill they have been practicing to the characteristics of this new situation. Two types of novel situations are especially interesting. One is a new context in which the people must perform the skill; the other is a novel variation of the skill itself.

Novel Context Characteristics

Test administrators can use various kinds of context changes in transfer tests. One characteristic they can change is the *availability of augmented feedback,* which is the performance information a person receives from some external source. For example, in many practice situations, the person receives augmented feedback in the form of verbal information about what he or she is doing correctly or incorrectly. If you were assessing learning to

discover how well the person could rely on his or her own resources to perform the skill, then your requirement that the person perform without augmented feedback availability would be a useful context change for the transfer test. It is important to note that some researchers refer to a test that involves this type of context change as a retention rather than a transfer test, because the practiced skill is performed during the test.

Another context characteristic a test administrator can change is the *physical environment* in which a person performs. This is especially effective for a learning situation in which the goal is to enable a person to perform in locations other than those in which he or she has practiced. For example, if you are working in a clinic with a patient with a gait problem, you want that patient to be able to adapt to the environmental demands of his or her everyday world. Although performing well in the clinic is important, it is less important than performing well in the world in which the patient must function on a daily basis. Because of this need, the transfer test in which the physical environment resembles one in the everyday world is a valuable assessment instrument.

The third aspect of context that can be changed for a transfer test is the *personal characteristics* of the test taker as they relate to skill performance. Here, the focus is on how well a person can perform the skill while adapting to characteristics of himself or herself that were not present during practice. For example, suppose you know that the person will have to perform the skill in a stressful situation. A test requiring the person to perform the skill while emotionally stressed would provide a useful assessment of his or her capability to adapt to this situation.

Novel Skill Variations

Another aspect of adaptability related to skill learning is a person's capability to successfully perform a novel variation of a skill he or she has learned. This capability is common in our everyday experience. For example, no one has walked at all speeds at which it is possible to walk. Yet, we can speed up or slow down our walking gait with little diffi-

ASSESSING LEARNING FROM COORDINATION DYNAMICS

Another method of assessing learning involves the observation of the stabilities and transitions of the dynamics of movement coordination related to performing a skill. Proponents of this approach, which is gaining in popularity in learning research, assume that when a person begins to learn a new skill, he or she is not really learning something new, but is evolving a new spatial and temporal coordination pattern from an old one. When viewed from this perspective, learning involves the transition from the initial pattern (i.e., the intrinsic dynamics), represented by a preferred coordination mode the person uses when first attempting the new skill, to the establishment of the new coordination mode (see Zanone & Kelso, 1994, for a more detailed discussion). *Stability and consistency* of the coordination pattern are important criteria for determining which coordination state (initial, transition, or new) characterizes the person's performance.

For example, a person who is learning handwriting experiences an initial state represented by the coordination characteristics of the upper arm, forearm, and hand while engaged in handwriting at the beginning of practice. These characteristics make up the preferred spatial and temporal structure the person and the task itself impose on the limb, so the limb can produce movement approximating what is required. This initial stable state must be changed to a new stable state in which the person can produce fluent handwriting. Learning is the process that occurs during the transition between these two states, and during the development of the consistency and stability of the new state.

An example of this approach to assessing skill learning is an experiment by Lee, Swinnen, and Verschueren (1995). The task (see figure 10.4)

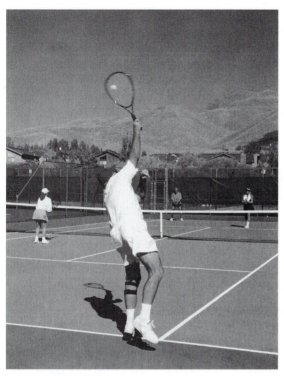

One way to assess how well a person learns a serve in tennis is to use a transfer test, such as performing the serve in a tennis match.

culty. Similarly, we have not grasped and drunk from every type of cup or glass that exists in the world. Yet when we are confronted with some new cup, we adapt our movements quite well to the cup characteristics and successfully drink from it. These examples illustrate the importance to people of producing novel variations of skills. One of the ways to assess how well a person can do this is to use a transfer test that incorporates this movement adaptation characteristic.

Note that one of the ways we get people to produce a novel skill variation is to alter the performance context in some way so that they must adapt their movements to it. In this way, the transfer test designed to assess capability to produce novel skill variations resembles a transfer test designed to assess capability to adapt to novel performance context features. The difference is the learning assessment focus.

---

transfer test   test in which a person performs a skill that is different from the skill he or she practiced, or performs the practiced skill in a context or situation different from the practice context or situation.

FIGURE 10.4   The task and results from the experiment by Lee, Swinnen, and Verschueren. The top panel shows the task, in which participants moved two levers to draw ellipses on the computer monitor (the dotted lines on each graph represent the goal ellipse pattern). The series of graphs shows the results as the left-arm × right-arm displacements of one person for the pretest and posttest (and some intermediate) trials for each of three practice days. [From Lee, T. D. et al. (1995). Relative phase alterations during bimanual skill acquisition. *Journal of Motor Behavior, 27,* 263–274. Reprinted with permission of the Helen Dwight Reid Educational Foundation. Published by Heldref Publications, 1319 Eighteenth Street NW, Washington, DC 20036–1802. Copyright © 1995].

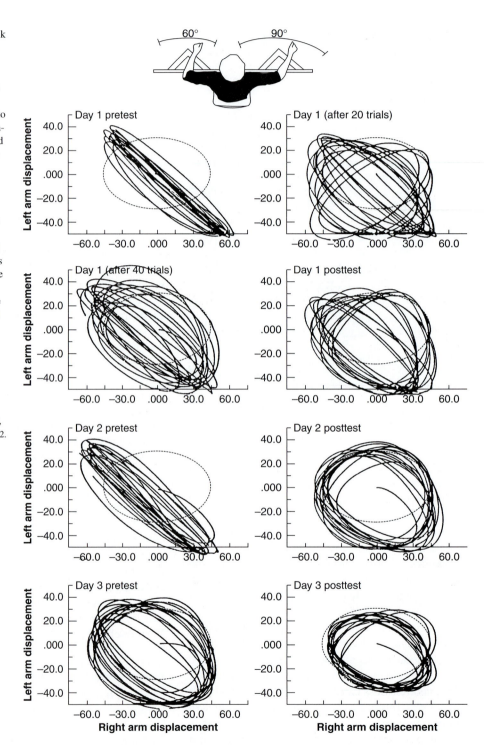

required participants to learn a new asymmetric bi-manual coordination pattern. (We briefly considered in chapter 4 the motor control difficulties associated with these types of tasks.) To perform the task, they simultaneously moved two levers toward and away from the body at the same rate (15 times in 15 sec). Their goal was to produce ellipses on the computer monitor. To accomplish this, they had to coordinate the movement of their arms so that the right arm on each cycle was always 90 degrees out-of-phase with the left arm. The initial coordination pattern for the two arms for one participant is shown in figure 10.4 as the arm-to-arm displacement relationship performed on the pretest. The diagonal lines seen in the day 1 (pretest) graph were the result of the person moving the arms in-phase, in a motion resembling that of windshield wipers. The consistency of this coordination pattern is indicated by the amount of overlap of the fifteen diagonal lines produced during the pretest. Notice the person's tendency to produce that same diagonal pattern on the pretest trial on day 2, after having performed sixty practice trials of the ellipse pattern on day 1.

By the end of day 3, this person had learned to produce the ellipse pattern. Evidence for this is the consistent production of fifteen ellipses in both the pretest and the posttest trials on day 3. However, notice the instability of the performance in the many trials between the old and the new stable patterns (exhibited on the day 1 pretest and the day 3 posttest). This instability occurs during the transition between two stable states and characterizes the process of learning a new skill.

PRACTICE PERFORMANCE MAY MISREPRESENT LEARNING

It may be misleading to base an inference about learning solely on observed performance during practice. There are at least two reasons for this. One is that the practice situation may involve a performance variable, which was described earlier in this discussion as having the potential to artificially inflate or depress performance. The second reason is that practice performance may be misleading if it involves performance plateaus.

LAB LINKS

Lab 10 in the Online Learning Center Lab Manual provides an opportunity for you to experience the influence of a performance variable during practice as you learn a new motor skill.

Practice Performance May Overestimate or Underestimate Learning

In this textbook, you will see examples of variables whose presence during practice influences performance in such a way that performance overestimates or underestimates learning. One way to overcome these problems is to use retention or transfer tests to assess learning. If a person's practice performance does represent learning, then that person's performance on a retention test should demonstrate the persistence characteristic and not deviate too much from his or her performance at the end of practice. Similarly, transfer test performance should demonstrate the person's increased capability to adapt to novel conditions.

Performance Plateaus

Over the course of learning a skill, it is not uncommon for a person to experience a period of time during which improvement seems to have stopped. But for some reason, at some later time, improvement starts to occur again. This period of time during which there appears to be no further performance improvement is known as a **performance plateau.**

Examples of performance plateaus are difficult to find in the motor learning research literature because most of this research presents performance curves that represent the average for a group of participants. To find evidence of a performance plateau, individual participant's results are needed. An experiment

---

performance plateau while learning a skill, a period of time in which the learner experiences no improvement after having experienced consistent improvement; typically, the learner then experiences further improvement with continued practice.

FIGURE 10.5 Results from the experiment by Franks and Wilberg showing the results from one participant performing the complex tracking task for ten days, with 105 trials per day. Notice the performance plateau for three days (days 5, 6, and 7) where performance leveled off before the subject showed improvement again. [From Franks, I. M., & Wilberg, R. B. (1982). The generation of movement patterns during the acquisition of a pursuit tracking task. *Human Movement Science, 1,* 251–272. Copyright © 1982 Elsevier/North-Holland, Amsterdam, The Netherlands. Reprinted by permission.]

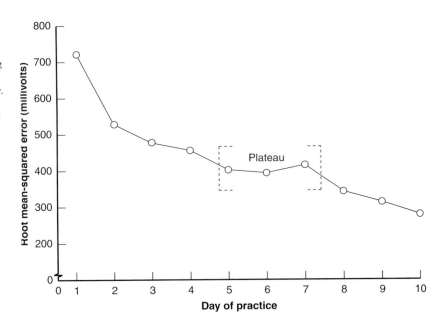

reported by Franks and Wilberg (1982) is an example of this latter case, and it provides a good illustration of a performance plateau (figure 10.5). This graph shows one individual's performance on a complex tracking task for ten days, with 105 trials each day. Notice that this person showed consistent improvement for the first four days. Then, on days 5 through 7, performance improvement stopped. However, this was a temporary characteristic; performance began to improve again on day 8 and the improvement continued for the next two days. The steady-state performance on days 5 through 7 is a good example of a performance plateau.

The concept of a performance plateau has a historical place in motor learning research. The first evidence of a plateau during skill learning is attributed to the work of Bryan and Harter (1897), who published their observations of new telegraphers learning Morse code. The authors noted steady improvement in the telegraphers' letters-per-minute speed for the first twenty weeks. But then a performance plateau occurred that lasted six weeks; this was followed by further performance improvement for the final twelve weeks. Since this early demonstration, researchers have been debating about whether a plateau is a real learning phenomenon or

merely a temporary performance artifact (see Adams 1987 for the most recent review of plateau research). At present, most agree that *plateaus are performance rather than learning characteristics.* This means that plateaus may appear during the course of practice, but it appears that learning continues during these times.

There are several *reasons performance plateaus* occur. One is that the plateau represents a period of transition between two phases of acquiring certain aspects of a skill. During this transition, the person is developing a new strategy that the task requires to increase the level of performance already achieved. Consequently, no performance improvement occurs until the new strategy is successfully implemented. Other possible explanations for a performance plateau may be that it represents a period of poor motivation, a time of fatigue, or a lack of attention directed to an important aspect of a skill. Finally, it is possible the plateau may be due not to these performance characteristics but to limitations imposed by the performance measure. This is the case when the performance measure involves what are known as *ceiling* or *floor effects.* These effects occur when the performance measure will not permit the score to go above or below a certain point.

A CLOSER LOOK

An Example of Practice Performance That Misrepresents Learning

An experiment by Winstein et al. (1996) is a good example of how practice performance may not represent the influence of a variable on the learning of a motor skill.

- **Purpose of the experiment:** Which of three different augmented feedback conditions would be best as an aid to help people learn a partial-weight bearing task? This task is a skill often taught by physical therapists. (Augmented feedback refers to performance-based information a person receives from a source external to himself or herself.)

- **The task:** The participants' goal was to learn to support 30 percent of their body weight while stepping on a floor scale with a preferred leg while on crutches. The target amount of weight was marked on the scale for each person. Participants in one group could see the scale needle move as they were stepping on the scale (concurrent augmented feedback). These participants were able to correctly adjust their weight on each trial. Two other groups received augmented feedback after performing the task (terminal augmented feedback). Participants in these groups could not see the scale needle during each trial, but saw a red line on the scale after completing one trial or a five-trial set (the five-trial group saw five red lines, each marked with the corresponding trial number of the set).

- **Practice trials and retention test:** All three groups performed eighty practice trials on one day. Two days later, they performed a retention test that consisted of twenty trials without any feedback about the amount of weight they applied to the scale.

- **Results:** *During the practice trials* the concurrent feedback group performed with very little error. The two terminal feedback groups performed with significantly more error than the concurrent group. However, *on the retention test* the concurrent group performed significantly worse than at the end of the practice trials, and worse than both of the terminal groups. The terminal feedback groups performed with about the same amount of error as they produced at the end of the practice trials.

- **Conclusion:** It is important to notice that if the retention test had not been given, the conclusion about the best augmented feedback condition for learning this task would have favored the concurrent condition. However, this conclusion would be based on performance when the various types of augmented feedback were available to the participants. The more valid way to determine which feedback condition is best for learning is when no augmented feedback is available, because it reflects the therapy goal of enabling people to perform the partial-weight bearing task in daily living conditions, which is with no augmented feedback. When the participants were tested under this condition on the retention test, the conclusion was that the *concurrent feedback was the worst learning condition.* Thus, performance during practice misrepresented the influence of the augmented feedback conditions on learning.

SUMMARY

- To effectively study concepts and issues related to the learning of motor skills, it is important to distinguish the terms *performance,* which is an observable behavior, and *learning,* which is inferred from the observation of performance.

- People typically demonstrate four general performance characteristics as they learn a motor skill:

performance *improvement* over a period of time, an increase in trial-to-trial performance *consistency,* a *persistence* of an improved performance capability, and the capability to *adapt* to a variety of performance context characteristics.

- The assessment of one or more of the four general performance characteristics forms the basis for four methods commonly used to assess motor skill learning:

1. *Performance curves* of performance outcome and kinematics provide a way to observe performance improvement and consistency over a period of time.

2. *Retention tests* assess persistence of an improved performance capability by requiring the performance of the practiced skill after a period of time during which the skill was not practiced.

3. *Transfer tests* assess the acquired capability to adapt to performance situations and contexts that were not experienced during practice.

4. Graphical representations of *movement coordination patterns* during practice and tests provide a means of assessing the consistency and stability of coordination characteristics associated with performing a motor skill.

• The assessment of learning on the basis of practice performance only can sometimes lead to incorrect inferences about learning, because

1. Certain *performance variables* can artificially inflate or depress practice performance so that the observed performance during practice over- or underestimates the amount a person has learned during practice. Retention and transfer tests provide ways to determine the extent to which performance during practice represents learning.

2. *Performance plateaus,* which appear on performance cues as periods of time during which performance does not improve, give the appearance that learning has stopped even though it has not. Providing additional practice trials can establish a means of determining if learning continued during a performance plateau.

RELATED READINGS

Christina, R. W. (1997). Concerns and issues in studying and assessing motor learning. *Measurement in Physical Education and Exercise Science, 1,* 19–38.

Langley, D. J. (1997). Exploring student skill learning. A case for investigating subjective experience. *Quest, 49,* 142–160.

Lee, T. D., & Swinnen, S. P. (1993). Three legacies of Bryan and Harter: Automaticity, variability, and change in skilled performance. In J. L. Starkes & F. Allard (Eds.), *Cognitive issues in motor expertise* (pp. 295–315). Amsterdam: Elsevier.

Slifkin, A. B., & Newell, K. M. (1998). Is variability in human performance a reflection of system noise? *Current Directions in Psychological Science, 7,* 170–177.

STUDY QUESTIONS

1. Explain how the terms *performance* and *learning* differ, and why we must *infer* learning from performance situations.

2. What four performance characteristics are generally present if learning of a skill has occurred?

3. What is an advantage of using transfer tests in making a valid assessment of learning? Give an example of a real-world situation that illustrates this advantage.

4. What is a performance plateau? What seems to be the most likely reason a performance plateau occurs in motor skill learning?

5. Describe a motor skill learning situation in which it may be possible to under- or overestimate the amount of learning during practice. Indicate how you would demonstrate this misrepresentation.

CHAPTER

The Stages of Learning

Concept: Distinct performance and performer characteristics
change during skill learning

After completing this chapter, you will be able to

- Describe characteristics of learners as they progress through the stages of learning as proposed by Fitts and Posner and by Gentile

- Describe several performer- and performance-related changes that occur as a person progresses through the stages of learning a motor skill

- Discuss several characteristics that distinguish an expert motor skill performer from a nonexpert

- Discuss two types of research evidence that help predict a person's future performance achievement

- Relate Ackerman's model of individual differences to the stages of learning a motor skill

Application

Have you ever noticed that people who are skilled at performing an activity often have difficulty teaching that activity to a beginner? This difficulty is due in part to the expert's failure to understand how the beginner approaches performing the skill each time he or she tries it. To facilitate successful skill acquisition, the teacher, coach, or therapist must consider the point of view of the student or patient and ensure that instructions, feedback, and practice conditions are in harmony with the person's needs.

Think for a moment about a skill you are proficient in. Remember how you approached performing that skill when you first tried it as a beginner. For example, suppose you were learning the tennis serve. Undoubtedly you thought about a lot of things, such as how you held the racquet, how high you were tossing the ball, whether you were transferring your weight properly at contact, and so on. Now, recall what you thought about after you had had lots of practice and had become reasonably proficient at serving. You probably did not continue to think about all the specific elements each time you served.

In the rehabilitation clinic, imagine that you are a physical therapist working with a stroke patient and helping him or her regain locomotion function. Like the tennis pro, you are a skilled performer (here, of locomotion skills); the patient is like a beginner. Although there may be some differences between the sport and the rehab situations because the patient was skilled prior to the stroke, in both cases you must approach skill acquisition from the perspective of the beginner.

Now, think about another aspect of the relationship between skilled performers and beginning learners. Have you ever observed someone who has just begun to learn a motor skill and thought about how well that person would perform the skill after he or she had had a lot of practice and experience? Predicting a person's future achievement is something we commonly talk about with friends and colleagues as we watch beginners perform a skill. A part of the reason for this may be a rather natural inclination for people to want to predict the future, which is something we see and hear regularly in the news. However, there are valid professional reasons for making these kinds of predictions. For example, a teacher who wants to subdivide a large physical education class into smaller, more homogeneous groups may make the decision about how to select the groups on the basis of how each student performs a skill on a pretest or during the first class in which the skill is taught. The teacher may place students who exhibit high initial performance levels into one group, those who exhibit poor initial performance levels into another group, and so on.

Predictions about future performance achievement also occur in other contexts. In sports, young athletes will be invited to participate in "development" leagues or camps if they show potential to become national- or international-level players. In industry and the military, people are placed into specific types of jobs on the basis of their performance on a variety of types of tests or experiences. And in physical rehabilitation, therapists often determine the therapy intervention strategies to use with a patient on the basis of the patient's initial performance on a skill for which therapy is required.

Discussion

An important characteristic of learning motor skills is that all people seem to go through distinct stages as they acquire skills. Several models have been proposed to identify and describe these stages. We discuss two of the more influential of these next. It is important to note that each of these models presents performer and performance characteristics associated with each stage of learning that we will refer to throughout the chapters that follow.

Learning to compete in wheelchair racing involves distinct stages of learning while progressing from being a beginner to being a highly skilled performer.

THE FITTS AND POSNER THREE-STAGE MODEL

Fitts and Michael Posner presented the acknowledged classic learning stages model in 1967. Their model continues to be referred to by researchers today. They proposed that learning a motor skill involves three stages. During the *first stage,* called the **cognitive stage** of learning, the beginner[1] focuses on cognitively oriented problems. For example, beginners typically try to answer questions such as these: What is my objective? How far should I move this arm? What is the best way to hold this implement? Where should this arm be when my right leg is here? Additionally, the learner must engage in cognitive activity as he or she listens to instructions and receives feedback from the instructor.

Performance during this first stage is marked by a large number of errors, and the errors tend to be large ones. Performance during this stage also is highly variable, showing a lack of consistency from one attempt to the next. And although beginners may be aware that they are doing something wrong, they generally do not know what they need to do to improve.

The *second stage* of learning in the Fitts and Posner model is called the **associative stage** of learning. The cognitive activity that characterized the cognitive stage changes at this stage, because the person has learned to associate certain environmental cues with the movements required to achieve the goal of the skill. The person makes fewer and less gross errors since he or she has acquired the basic fundamentals or mechanics of the skill, although they need to be improved. Because this type of improvement still is required, Fitts and Posner referred to this stage as a *refining* stage, in which the person focuses on performing the skill successfully and being more consistent from one attempt to the next. During this refining process, performance variability begins to decrease. Also during this associative stage, people acquire the capability to detect and identify some of their own performance errors.

After much practice and experience, which can take many years, some people move into the **autonomous stage** of learning, which is the *final*

LAB LINKS

Lab 11a in the Online Learning Center Lab Manual for chapter 11 provides an opportunity for you to learn a new motor skill and experience a progression through some learning stages.

stage of learning. Here the skill has become almost *automatic,* or habitual. People in this stage do not consciously think about what they are doing while performing the skill, because they can perform it without conscious thought. They often can do another task at the same time; for example, they can carry on a conversation while typing. Performance variability during this stage is very small: skilled people perform the skill consistently well from one attempt to the next. Additionally, these skilled performers can detect their own errors, and make the proper adjustments to correct them. Fitts and Posner pointed out the likelihood that not every person learning a skill will reach this autonomous stage. The quality of instruction and practice as well as the amount of practice are important factors determining achievement of this final stage.

It is important to think of the three stages of the Fitts and Posner model as parts of a continuum of practice time, as figure 11.1 depicts. Learners do not make abrupt shifts from one stage to the next. There is a gradual transition or change of the learner's characteristics from stage to stage. Because of this, it is often difficult to detect which

---

cognitive stage　the first stage of learning in the Fitts and Posner model; the beginning or initial stage on the learning stages continuum.

associative stage　the second stage of learning in the Fitts and Posner model; an intermediate stage on the learning stages continuum.

autonomous stage　the third stage of learning in the Fitts and Posner model; the final stage on the learning stages continuum, also called the *automatic stage.*

---

[1] The term "beginner" is used here and throughout the following chapters to refer to a person who is beginning to learn, or relearn, a skill.

FIGURE 11.1   The stages of learning from the Fitts and Posner model placed on a time continuum.

stage an individual is in at a particular moment. However, as we will consider in more detail later in this discussion, the beginner and the skilled performer have distinct characteristics that we can observe and need to understand.

GENTILE'S TWO-STAGE MODEL

Another model that motor learning researchers commonly refer to was proposed by Gentile (1972, 1987, 2000). In contrast to Fitts and Posner, she viewed motor skill learning as progressing through two stages, and presented these stages from the perspective of the goal of the learner in each stage.

In the *initial stage,* the term Gentile used for the first stage, the beginner has two important goals to achieve. One is to acquire a *movement coordination pattern* that will allow some degree of success at achieving the action goal of the skill. This means that the beginner must develop movement characteristics that match the regulatory conditions of the environmental context in which the skill is performed. Recall from the discussion of Gentile's taxonomy of motor skills in chapter 1 of this text that the term *regulatory conditions* refers to those characteristics of the environmental context that determine the movement characteristics required to achieve an action goal. For example, if a person is beginning to rehabilitate his or her prehension skills, he or she must focus on developing the arm and hand movement characteristics that match the physical characteristics associated with the object to be grasped. If, in the prehension example, the person must reach and grasp a cup that is on a table, the regulatory conditions include the size and shape of the cup, location of the cup, and so on.

The second goal of the beginner is to learn to *discriminate between regulatory and nonregulatory conditions* in the environmental context in

which he or she performs the skill. Different from regulatory conditions, the **nonregulatory conditions** are those characteristics of the performance environment that do *not* influence the movement characteristics required to achieve an action goal. To continue with the example of reaching and grasping a cup, the color of the cup or the shape of the table the cup is on are nonrelevant pieces of information for reaching for and grasping the cup, and therefore do not influence the movements used to perform the skill.

To achieve these two important goals, the beginner explores a variety of movement possibilities. Through trial and error, he or she experiences movement characteristics that match and do not match requirements of the regulatory conditions. As a result, these experiences are successful as well as unsuccessful. In addition, because the learner has numerous problems to solve to determine how to achieve the action goal, he or she engages in a large amount of cognitive problem-solving activity. When the learner reaches the end of this stage, he or she has developed a movement coordination pattern that allows some action goal achievement, but this achievement is neither consistent nor efficient. However, as Gentile (2000) described it, "Although the learner now has a general concept of an effective approach, he or she is not skilled. The action-goal is not achieved consistently and the movement lacks efficiency" (p. 149).

In the second stage, which Gentile called the *later stages,* the learner needs to acquire three general characteristics. First, the person must develop the capability of *adapting* the movement pattern he or she has acquired in the first stage to the specific demands of any performance situation requiring that skill. Second, the person must increase his or her *consistency* in achieving the goal of the skill. Third, the person must learn to perform the skill with an *economy of effort.*

A CLOSER LOOK

Implications of Gentile's Learning Stages Model for Instruction and Rehabilitation Environments

During the Initial Stage

• Have the learner focus on achieving the action goal, which will allow the development of the basic movement coordination pattern of the skill.

• Establish practice situations that provide opportunities to discriminate regulatory from nonregulatory characteristics.

During the Later Stage

Closed skills. In practice situations, include characteristics as similar as possible to those the learner will experience in his or her everyday world, or in the environment in which he or she will perform the skill.

Examples:
• walking on similar surfaces in similar environments

• writing with the same type of implement on the same type of surface
• shooting basketball free throws as they would occur in a game
• shooting arrows under match conditions

Open skills. In practice, systematically vary the controllable regulatory conditions of actual performance situations, while allowing naturally varying characteristics to occur as they normally would.

Examples:
• walking from one end of a hallway to the other while various numbers of people are walking in different directions and at various speeds (systematically vary the hallway size and numbers of people; allow the people to walk at any speed or in any direction they wish)

A unique feature of the second stage in Gentile's model is that the *learner's goals depend on the type of skill.* More specifically, the open skill and closed skill classifications specify these goals. *Closed skills require* **fixation** of the basic movement coordination pattern acquired during the first stage of learning. This means that the learner must refine this pattern so that he or she can consistently achieve the action goal. The learner works toward developing the capability to perform the movement pattern with little, if any, conscious effort (i.e., automatically) and a minimum of physical energy. Thus, practice of a closed skill during this stage must give the learner the opportunity to "fixate" the required movement coordination pattern in such a way that he or she is capable of performing it consistently.

On the other hand, *open skills require* **diversification** of the basic movement pattern acquired during the first stage of learning. An important characteristic of open skills, which differ from

closed skills in this way, is the requirement for the performer to quickly adapt to the continuously changing spatial and temporal regulatory

---

nonregulatory conditions characteristics of the performance environment that do *not* influence the movement characteristics required to achieve an action goal.

fixation the learner's goal in the second stage of learning in Gentile's model for learning closed skills in which learners refine movement patterns so that they can produce them correctly, consistently, and efficiently from trial to trial.

diversification the learner's goal in the second stage of learning in Gentile's model for learning open skills in which learners acquire the capability to modify the movement pattern according to environmental context characteristics.

A CLOSER LOOK

The Initial Stage of Learning to Bowl

A study by Langley (1995) provides a good illustration of the performer and performance characteristics described for the initial stage of learning in both the Fitts and Posner and the Gentile learning stages models. Langley assessed student thought processes during a beginning bowling class that met for ten weeks. He had each student complete a questionnaire at the end of each class, he took extensive observational and interpretive notes, and he interviewed the students at the beginning, middle, and end of the ten-week session.

The results of this study indicated that student thoughts focused primarily on errors in task performance. In the first week, the primary errors of concern related to lack of control of the ball, which related to inconsistency of throws and aiming problems. In the middle week, students began to describe the movement characteristics and outcomes of their throws as keys to what they needed to focus on to improve. By the end of the course, students indicated problems with consistency and accuracy of the hook ball. Consistent with expectations of learning stages models, these beginning bowlers showed evidence of an initial lack of an appropriate movement pattern to achieve the action goal, inconsistent performance, a lack of knowledge about specific components of the skill (e.g., aiming), and the development of error detection capabilities.

---

conditions of the skill. These conditions change within a performance trial as well as between trials. This means that the learner must become attuned to the regulatory conditions and acquire the capability to modify movements to meet their constantly changing demands on the performer. As a result, rather than learning to automatically produce a specific set of movements, the learner must acquire the capability to monitor the environmental conditions and modify the movements accordingly. Thus, practice of an open skill during this stage must provide the learner with experiences that will require these types of movement modifications.

One aspect of the second stage of learning in Gentile's model that requires further consideration concerns the features of the acquired movement pattern that the performer must change to meet performance situation demands. Although Gentile's model indicates that fixation of the pattern is the goal of the second stage for closed skills, the performer may need to make movement modifications. But closed skill pattern modifications differ from those required for open skills. You saw some examples of these differences in the discussion of the adaptability component of our definition of learning in chapter 10. You can relate these differences to the distinction between invariant features and parameters of a coordination pattern, which were discussed in chapter 4.

For *closed skills,* pattern modifications typically involve movement parameter changes rather than changes of the invariant features of the pattern itself. For example, in bowling, on the second ball of a frame the bowler is confronted with a different pattern of pins than he or she experienced with the first ball. But rather than change the movement coordination pattern in order to bowl the ball, the bowler modifies characteristics such as location of ball release or ball speed. In golf, a ball in different types of grass or sand may require the golfer to modify his or her stance or the trajectory of the downswing, but not the invariant features of the swing itself. Similarly, situations requiring prehension may require various widths of grasp apertures or amounts of grasp force, but the basic invariant features of the reach-and-grasp action will remain consistent. However, for *open skills,* the performer may be required to change either the invariant features or the parameters of the movement pattern. For example, if the action goal for a tennis player is to return a serve, he or she may prepare to hit a forehand groundstroke but have to change to a backhand when the serve is hit. Or if the action goal of a pedestrian is to cross a street at an intersection, he or she may begin to walk but have to change to a run partway across, because the traffic signal has changed.

Finally, it is important to note that the types of movement changes required by closed and open skills involve different action planning and preparation demands for the performer. Closed skills allow the learner to plan and prepare either without any or with a minimum of time constraints. However, time constraints severely limit the amount of time the performer has to plan and prepare the performance of an open skill. This difference indicates that during practice of open skills, the performer must acquire the capability to quickly attend to the environmental regulatory conditions as well as to anticipate changes before they actually occur.

PERFORMER AND PERFORMANCE CHANGES ACROSS THE STAGES OF LEARNING

Stages-of-learning models indicate that in each learning stage, both the person and the skill performance show distinct characteristics. In this section, we will look at a few of these characteristics. This overview has two benefits: first, it provides a closer look at the skill learning process, and second, it helps explain why instruction or training strategies need to be developed for people in different learning stages.

Changes in Rate of Improvement

As a person progresses along the skill learning continuum from the beginner stage to the highly skilled stage, the *rate* at which the performance improves changes. Although, as figure 10.2 showed, there are four different types of performance curves representing different rates of improvement during skill learning, the *negatively accelerated pattern is more typical of motor skill learning* than the others. This means that early in practice, a learner usually experiences a large amount of improvement relatively quickly. But as practice continues, the amount of improvement decreases.

This change in the rate of improvement during skill learning has a long and consistent history in motor learning. In fact, in 1926 Snoddy mathemat-

LAB LINKS

Lab 11b in the Online Learning Center Lab Manual for chapter 11 provides an opportunity for you to compare characteristics of novices and experts performing the same skill.

ically formalized a law known as the **power law of practice.** According to this law, early practice is characterized by large amounts of improvement. However, after this seemingly rapid improvement, further practice yields improvement rates that are much smaller. Exactly how long the change in rates takes to occur depends on the skill.

Crossman (1959) reported what is today considered a classic experiment demonstrating the power law of practice. He examined the amount of time it took cigar makers to produce one cigar as a function of how many cigars each worker had made since beginning to work at the factory. Some workers had made 10,000 cigars, whereas others had made over 10 million. The skill itself was a relatively simple one that could be done very quickly. The first notable finding was the relationship between performance improvement and the amount of experience. Workers still showed some performance improvement after seven years of experience, during which time they had made over 10 million cigars (see figure 11.2). In addition to this remarkable result, he found evidence of the power law of practice for these workers. As you can see in figure 11.2, the majority of all the improvement occurred during the first two years. After that, performance improvement increments were notably smaller.

The difference in rate of improvement between early and later practice is due partly to the amount

power law of practice   mathematical law describing the change in rate of performance improvement during skill learning; large amounts of improvement occur during early practice, but smaller improvement rates characterize further practice.

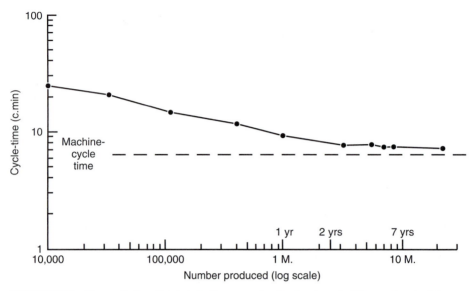

FIGURE 11.2   The results from the study by Crossman showing the amount of time workers took to make a cigar as a function of the number of cigars made across seven years of experience. Note that both axes are log scales.   [From Crossman, E. R. F. W. (1959). A theory of the acquisition of speed skill. *Ergonomics, 2,* 153–166. Copyright © 1959 Taylor and Francis, London.]

of improvement possible at a given time. Initially, there is room for a large amount of improvement. The errors people make during early practice trials are large and lead to many unsuccessful attempts at performing the skill. Because many of these errors are easy to correct, the learner can experience a large amount of improvement quickly. However, as practice continues, the amount of improvement possible decreases. The errors people make later in practice are much smaller. As a result, their correction of these errors yields less improvement than they experienced earlier in practice. And certainly from the learner's perspective, attaining notable improvement seems to take longer than it did before.

Changes in Movement Coordination
In the discussion in chapter 4, you saw that to perform a complex motor skill (i.e., one that involves several limbs or limb segments), the motor control system must solve the *degrees of freedom problem.* Recall that when we relate this problem to the muscles and joints, it concerns the need to constrain the many degrees of freedom of movement associated with the muscles and joints involved in performing

the skill. For the beginning learner, solving this problem is a critical part of the learning process. In fact, solving this problem underlies the achievement of an important goal for the learner in Gentile's initial stage of learning, which is to acquire a movement coordination pattern that would allow some success at achieving the action goal.

Bernstein, whom we noted in chapter 4 first identified this problem, described a strategy beginners typically use to gain initial control of the many degrees of freedom associated with performing a complex motor skill (Bernstein, 1967; Whiting, 1984). This strategy, which researchers now refer to as **freezing the degrees of freedom,** involves holding some joints rigid (i.e., "freezing" them) while performing the skill. For example, suppose a beginner must perform a skill such as a racquetball forehand shot, which involves the coordination of the wrist, elbow, and shoulder joints of one arm. This means that for the arm movement component of this skill, the person needs to control three degrees of freedom. The common strategy the beginner uses to achieve this control so that he or she can hit the ball is to keep the wrist and elbow joints "locked" (i.e., "frozen"). This strategy makes the arm and hand move as if they were a stick, with the arm and hand segments acting as one segment. But as the person practices the skill, a freeing of the degrees of freedom emerges as the "frozen" joints begin to become "unfrozen" and operate in a way that allows the arm and hand segments to function as a multisegment unit. This new unit eventually demonstrates characteristics of a *functional synergy,* which means that the individual arm and hand segments work together in a cooperative way to enable optimal performance of the skill. It is interesting to note that Southard and Higgins (1987) reported evidence demonstrating this kind of strategy and coordination development for the arm movement component of the racquetball forehand shot. They showed that a primary benefit of the development of the functional synergy of the arm segments was an increase in racquet velocity at ball impact.

Researchers have demonstrated similar coordination development characteristics for several other skills. For example, Anderson and Sidaway (1994) showed that when beginning soccer players initially tried to kick a ball properly, they limited the movements of their hip and knee joints. The problem with this strategy is that it limits the velocity that can be generated by the hip joint, because the player cannot use the knee joint effectively. With practice, however, players' kicking velocity increased, as their hip and knee joints acquired greater freedom of movement and increased functional synergy. Figure 4.2, which was presented in chapter 4 as an example of a graphic representation of coordination patterns, portrayed the pre- and post-practice knee-and-hip relationship results from this study.

In a final example, note that these coordination changes are not limited to sports skills or to people acquiring new skills. Stroke patients going through physical therapy to help them move from sitting to standing and then to sitting again show coordination development characteristics similar to those of people acquiring a new skill (Ada, O'Dwyer, & Neilson, 1993). In this experiment, recovering stroke patients progressed from being able to sit-stand-sit without assistance one time to being able to perform this sequence three times in a row in 10 sec. As the patients progressed, the coordination between the hip and the knee joints showed marked improvement changes which demonstrated the development of the functional synergy required for these joints to allow unaided standing.

Changes in Altering an Old or Preferred Coordination Pattern

Because we have learned to perform a variety of motor skills throughout our lives, we have developed preferred ways of moving. In fact, each of us has developed a rather large repertoire of movement patterns that we prefer to use. When confronted with learning a new skill, we often determine that it resembles a skill we already know how to perform. As a result, we typically begin practicing the new skill using movement characteristics similar to those of the skill we already know. For example, it is common for an experienced baseball player to use a swing resembling baseball batting when he or she first practices hitting a golf ball.

When a person is learning a new skill that requires altering an established coordination pattern, an interesting transition from old to new pattern occurs. The experiment by Lee, Swinnen, and Verschueren (1995) that we discussed in chapter 10 provides a good example of this change. Recall that participants had to learn to bimanually move two levers simultaneously in a 90-degree out-of-phase arm movement relationship in order to draw ellipses on the computer monitor. In chapter 10, figure 10.4 showed that when they first were confronted with this task, the participants' preferred way of coordinating their arms was to move both arms at the same time, producing diagonal patterns. The influence of this preferred movement

---

freezing the degrees of freedom   common initial strategy of beginning learners to control the many degrees of freedom associated with the coordination demands of a motor skill; the person holds some joints rigid (i.e., "freezes" them) while performing the skill.

A CLOSER LOOK

Controlling Degrees of Freedom as a Training Strategy in Occupational Therapy

A case study of a thirty-four-year-old hemiplegic woman who had suffered a stroke demonstrates how a therapist can use an understanding of the degrees-of-freedom problem to develop an occupational therapy strategy (Flinn, 1995). To increase impaired left-arm strength and function during the first two months of outpatient therapy, the therapist engaged the patient in *using the impaired arm* to perform several functional tasks for which the degrees of freedom were restricted.

- Initially, the therapist decreased the number of joints involved by restricting the movement of certain joints and decreasing the amount of movement required of the limb against gravity.
  Example: The patient used the impaired arm to apply her wheelchair brakes, dust tables, and provide postural stability as she brushed her teeth using her nonimpaired arm.
- During the next two months, as the patient's use of her left arm improved, the therapist increased the degrees of freedom by requiring the use of more joints to perform tasks.

Example: In the initial therapy period, the patient simply pushed silverware from the counter into the drawer; now she grasped each object from the counter, lifted it, and placed it in the drawer.

- Finally (a couple of months later), the therapist again increased the degrees of freedom demands by focusing treatment specifically on the everyday multiple degrees-of-freedom tasks the patient would have to perform at her regular workplace.

---

pattern remained for more than sixty practice trials. Participants did not produce the new coordination pattern consistently until they had performed 180 practice trials. Instability characterized the coordination patterns they produced on trials between these two demonstrations of stable patterns.

The Lee et al. experiment demonstrates several things. First, it shows that people approach skill learning situations with distinct movement pattern biases that they may need to overcome to achieve the goal of the skill to be learned. Second, it is possible for people to overcome these biases, but often this takes a lot of practice (the actual amount varies among people). Finally, as illustrated in figure 10.4, an observable pattern of stability-instability-stability characterizes the transition between production of the preferred movement pattern and production of the goal pattern. The initially preferred and the newly acquired goal movement patterns are distinguished by unique but stable kinematic characteristics over repeated performances. However, during the transition period between these stable patterns, the limb kinematics are very irregular or unstable.

People who provide skill instruction should note that this transition period can be a difficult and frustrating time for the learner. The instructor or therapist who is aware of this can be influential in helping the person work through this transition stage. One helpful strategy is providing extra motivational encouragements to keep the person effectively engaged in practice.

Changes in Muscles Used to Perform the Skill
If practicing a skill results in coordination changes, we should expect a related change in the muscles a person uses while performing the skill. EMG patterns produced while people practiced skills have shown that early in practice a person uses his or her muscles inappropriately. Two characteristics are particularly noteworthy. First, more muscles than are needed commonly are involved. Second, the timing of the activation of the involved muscle groups is incorrect. As a person continues to practice, the number of muscles involved decreases so that eventually a minimal number of muscles needed to produce the action are activated, and the

A CLOSER LOOK

Muscle Activation Changes during Dart-Throwing Practice

An experiment by Jaegers et al. (1989) illustrates how the sequence and timing of muscle activation reorganizes as a person practices a skill. Individuals who were inexperienced in dart throwing made forty-five throws at a target on each of three successive days. Several arm and shoulder muscles were monitored by EMG.

The *three muscles primarily involved in stabilizing the arm and upper body* were the anterior deltoid, latissimus dorsi, and clavicular pectoralis.

- *On the first day of practice:* The three muscles erratically initiated activation both before and after the dart release.
- *At the end of the last day of practice:* The three muscles initiated activation according to a specific sequence.
  - ▸ The clavicular pectoralis and anterior deltoid became active approximately 40 to 80 msec prior to dart release; they turned off at dart release.
  - ▸ The latissimus dorsi became active just before dart release and remained active for 40 msec after dart release. Then, the anterior deltoid again initiated activation.

The primary muscle involved in producing the forearm-extension–based throwing action was the lateral triceps.

- *During the initial practice trials:* The lateral triceps initiated activation erratically, both before and after dart release.
- *At the end of the last day of practice:* The lateral triceps consistently initiated activation approximately 60 msec prior to dart release and remained active until just after dart release.

---

timing of when the involved muscles are activated becomes appropriate.

Researchers have provided evidence showing these types of change during practice for a variety of physical activities. For example, muscle activation changes have been demonstrated for sport skills such as the single-knee circle mount on the horizontal bar in gymnastics (Kamon & Gormley, 1968), ball throwing to a target (Vorro, Wilson, & Dainis, 1978), dart throwing (Jaegers et al., 1989), and the lunge in fencing (Williams & Walmsley, 2000). Also, researchers have shown muscle activation differences resulting from practice in laboratory tasks, such as complex, rapid arm movement and manual aiming tasks (Schneider et al., 1989), as well as simple, rapid elbow flexion tasks (Gabriel & Boucher, 1998), and arm-extension tasks (Moore & Marteniuk, 1986).

The change in muscle use that occurs while a person learns a skill reflects a *reorganization of the motor control system* as that skill is acquired. As Bernstein (1967) first proposed, this reorganization results from the need for the motor control system

to solve the degrees-of-freedom problem it confronts when the person first attempts the skill. By structuring muscle activation appropriately, the motor control system can take advantage of physical properties of the environment, such as gravity or other basic physical laws. By doing this, the motor control system reduces the amount of work it has to do and establishes a base for successful skill performance.

Changes in Energy Cost

Because the performer and performance changes we have described in the preceding sections occur as a result of practicing a skill, we can reasonably expect that the learner would become a more economical (i.e., efficient) user of energy. This change, then, would be consistent with a proposal in Gentile's stages of learning model that the development of an economy of effort is an important goal of the later stages. Economy of movement refers to minimizing the energy cost of performing a skill. Beginners expend a large amount of energy (have a high energy cost), whereas skilled performers perform more efficiently, with minimum expenditure of energy.[2]

Several energy sources have been associated with performing skills. One is the *physiological energy* involved in skilled performance; researchers identify this by measuring the amount of oxygen a person uses while performing a skill. They also determine physiological energy use by measuring the caloric cost of performing the skill. People also expend *mechanical energy* while performing; scientists determine this by dividing the work rate by the metabolic rate of the individual. As we learn a skill, changes in the amount of energy we use occur for each of these sources. The result is that we perform with greater efficiency; in other words, our energy cost decreases as our movements become more economical.

Scientists have been accumulating research evidence only recently to support the prediction that energy cost decreases as a result of practicing a skill. For example, *oxygen use* decreased for people learning to perform on a complex slalom ski simulator in practice sessions over a period of several days (Durand et al., 1994; Almasbakk, Whiting, & Helgerud, 2001). Sparrow (Sparrow & Irizarry-Lopez, 1987; Sparrow & Newell, 1994) demonstrated that oxygen use, heart rate, and *caloric costs* decrease with practice of a motor skill for persons learning to walk on his or her hands and feet (creeping) on a treadmill moving at a constant speed. And Heise (1995; Heise & Cornwell, 1997) showed *mechanical efficiency* to increase as a function of practice for people learning to perform a ball-throwing task.

In addition to demonstrating a reduction in energy cost, learners also experience a decrease in their rate of perceived exertion (RPE). RPE, which is a measurable subjective perception, refers to the amount of effort (i.e., exertion, or energy) a person feels that he or she is expending while performing a skill. A nice demonstration of changes in both energy use economy and RPE was reported in an experiment by Sparrow, Hughes, Russell, and Le Rossingnol (1999). Novice rowers performed on a rowing ergometer for one practice session each day for six days. The results showed that when the rowers performed at their preferred stroke rates, metabolic energy expenditure economy increased, while heart rate, oxygen consumption, and RPE significantly decreased during the six days of practice.

Changes in Achieving the Kinematic Goals of the Skill

As you read in chapter 2, kinematic characteristics define the spatial and temporal features of the movements involved in performing a skill. Skilled performance has certain displacement, velocity, and acceleration limb-movement goals. As a person practices a skill, he or she not only becomes more successful in achieving these goals, but also acquires these kinematic goals at different times during practice, although in the same sequence. *Displacement* is the first kinematic goal persons achieve, indicating that spatial characteristics of a skill are the first ones people successfully acquire. The next goal people achieve is *velocity;* this is followed by *acceleration.* The instructional significance of this progression of kinematics is that it suggests the importance of focusing on spatial features of a skill first, and then progressing to the more temporal features.

Marteniuk and Romanow (1983) provided the best demonstration of this systematic progression of kinematic goal acquisition in an experiment that was briefly introduced in chapter 10. Participants practiced moving a horizontal lever back and forth to produce a complex displacement pattern (which was shown in figure 10.3). During 800 trials of practice, they became increasingly more accurate and consistent at producing the criterion pattern. An evaluation of the kinematic performance measures showed that the participants first achieved accuracy and consistency with the displacement characteristics. Then they acquired the velocity and finally the acceleration characteristics as practice progressed.

---

[2]Note that many prefer the term *economy* to *efficiency;* see Sparrow and Newell (1998).

Changes in Visual Selective Attention

Because vision plays a key role in the learning and control of skills, it is interesting to note how the use of vision changes as a function of practicing a skill. Because we discussed most of these changes at length in chapter 6, we will mention them only briefly here. Beginners typically look at too many things, which often leads them to direct their visual attention to inappropriate environmental cues. As a person practices a skill, he or she directs visual attention toward sources of information that are more appropriate for guiding his or her performance. In other words, the person gains an increased capability to direct his or her vision to the regulatory features in the environment that will provide the most useful information for performing the skill. Also, people get better at appropriately directing their visual attention earlier during the time course of performing a skill. This timing aspect of directing visual attention is important because it increases the time available in which the person can select and produce an action required by the situation.

A good example of research evidence that demonstrates the change in visual selective attention across the stages of learning is an experiment by Savelsbergh, Williams, van der Kamp, and Ward (2002). They recorded the eye-movement characteristics of novice and expert soccer goalkeepers in a simulated penalty kick situation. The goalkeepers observed life-size video clips of professional players taking penalty kicks that were directed to six areas of the goal. The goalkeepers moved a joystick to intercept the ball; if they positioned it in the correct location at the moment the ball crossed the goal line, a save was recorded. As expected, the expert goalkeepers performed better than the novices, especially in terms of making more saves, better predictions of ball height and direction. In addition, the experts initiated their joystick response closer to the time of foot-ball contact, and made fewer joystick position corrections. The visual search characteristics were identified in terms of time periods before and after foot-ball contact by the kicker. Overall, the experts made fewer eye-movement fixations of longer duration to fewer areas of the scene involving the kicker. These results indicated that the experts reduced the amount of visual information they needed to attend to, and they extracted more information from the most relevant parts of the scene. As the kicker began the approach to the ball and eventually made ball contact, the experts progressively moved their fixations from the kicker's head to the nonkicking foot, the kicking foot, and the ball. They made very few fixations on other areas of the kicker's body. In contrast, the novices spent more time fixating on the kicker's trunk, arms, and hip areas and less time on the head, nonkicking foot, and ball. Interestingly, at foot-ball contact, the expert goalkeepers fixated on the ball more than two times longer than the novices.

Changes in Conscious Attention When Performing a Skill

According to the Fitts and Posner learning stages model, early in practice the learner consciously thinks about almost every part of performing the skill. But as the person practices the skill and becomes more proficient, the amount of conscious attention he or she directs to performing the skill itself diminishes to the point at which he or she performs it almost automatically.

We see an everyday example of this change in the process of learning to shift gears in a standard shift car. If you have learned to drive a standard shift car, you undoubtedly remember how you approached shifting gears when you first learned to do so. Each part of the maneuver required your conscious attention. You thought about each part of the entire sequence of movements: when to lift off the accelerator, when to push in the clutch, how to coordinate your leg movements to carry out these clutch and accelerator actions, when and where to move the gear shift, when to let out the clutch, and finally, when to depress the accelerator again. But what happened as you became a more experienced driver? Eventually, you performed all these movements without conscious attention. In fact, you undoubtedly found that you were able to do something else at the same time, such as carry on a

A CLOSER LOOK

Driving Experience and Attention Demands of Driving a Standard Shift Car

Shinar, Meir, and Ben-Shoham (1998) used a dual-task procedure to determine the influence of years of driving experience on the attention demands for driving a standard shift car. They asked forty licensed drivers (ages eighteen to sixty-six years) to drive their own manual or automatic transmission cars along a 5-km route through downtown Tel Aviv. The route involved streets with multiple lanes, many intersections, many traffic signs, heavy traffic, and many pedestrians and pedestrian crossings. The secondary task involved the drivers observing traffic signs and verbally reporting each sign that indicated "Slow—Children on the Road" and "No Stopping."

The results showed that the experienced drivers (median = eight years of experience) of either the manual or automatic transmission cars detected similar percentages of the two signs. However, the novice drivers (median = one and one-quarter years of experience) of manual transmission cars detected lower percentages of the signs than those who drove automatic transmission cars. Thus, driving experience led to a reduction in the attention demanded by the action of gear shifting to such an extent that driving a manual transmission car in heavy traffic became similar to the attention demanded when driving an automatic transmission car.

conversation or sing along with the radio. You would have had great difficulty doing any of these things while shifting when you were first learning to drive. Evidence that this type of attention-demand change occurs with experience was provided by Shinar, Meir, and Ben-Shoham (1998) in a study that compared experienced and novice licensed car drivers in Isreal. Results showed that while shifting gears, the novice drivers tended to miss traffic signs that the experienced drivers did not miss.

Changes in Error Detection and Correction Capability

Another performance characteristic that improves during practice is the capability to identify and correct one's own movement errors. An individual can use this capability either during or after the performance of the skill, depending on the time constraints involved. If the movements are slow enough, a person can correct or modify an ongoing movement while the action is occurring. For example, if a person grasps a cup and brings it to the mouth to drink from it, he or she can make some adjustments along the way that will allow him or her to accomplish each phase of this action successfully. However, for rapid movements, such as initiating and carrying out a swing at a baseball, a person often cannot make the correction in time during the execution of the swing, because the ball

has moved past a hittable location by the time the person makes the correction. For both types of skills, performers can use errors they detect during their performance to guide future attempts.

An excellent example of research evidence that demonstrates the change in error detection and correction capability is a study involving gymnasts at different stages of learning (Robertson, Collins, Elliott, & Starkes, 1994). Novice and skilled gymnasts walked across a balanced beam as quickly as possible with either full or no vision of the beam as they walked. Results showed that with no vision, both groups made significantly more form errors (unintentional deviations from a relaxed upright standing position) than with vision, but the novices made many more than the skilled gymnasts (see figure 11.3). In addition, with no vision available, the skilled gymnasts maintained the amount of time they took to transverse the beam with full vision, while the novices took almost two times longer. The skilled gymnasts maintained their movement time in the no-vision condition by taking more steps and making more form errors. The authors concluded that the results indicate that "part of becoming skilled involves developing the ability to rapidly and efficiently correct movement errors" (p. 338). It is important to add to this comment that these corrections indicate the capability to detect the errors. And, as we discussed in chap-

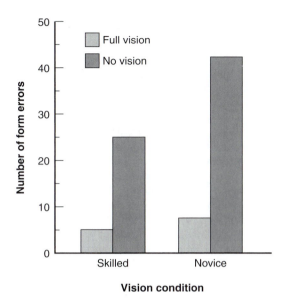

FIGURE 11.3 The results of the experiment by Robertson et al. showing the number of form errors made by novice and skilled gymnasts as they walked across a balance beam with full vision or no vision as they walked. [Source: Modified Figure 4, p. 337 in Robertson, S., Collins, J., Elliott, D., & Starkes, J. (1994). The influence of skill and intermittent vision on dynamic balance. *Journal of Motor Behavior, 26*, 333–339.]

ter 6, vision is an essential source for detecting and correcting these movements errors while traversing the beam.

A PERFORMER CHARACTERISTIC THAT DOES NOT CHANGE ACROSS THE STAGES OF LEARNING

Researchers who have investigated the use of sensory feedback across the stages of learning have consistently shown that *learning is specific to the sources of sensory feedback available during practice.* This means that if we use visual feedback during practice in the first stage of learning, we continue to need to use it in the same way as we become more skillful in later stages. Proteau and Marteniuk (1993) presented a good example of research evidence of this feedback dependency. They allowed participants to see their movements as they practiced to learn to perform a 90 cm aiming movement in 550 ms. Then, after 200 or 2,000 practice

trials, the visual feedback was removed. We would expect that if the participants had learned to rely on sensory feedback sources other than vision as they practiced, increasing the amount of practice with vision would decrease the need for vision to perform the skill. However, the results showed just the opposite effects. Participants who had visual feedback removed after 2,000 trials performed less accurately than those who had it removed after 200 trials. Rather than decreasing their dependency on visual feedback, the participants increased dependency. Similar results were reported for participants learning the same type of manual aiming task with visual feedback but then having it removed after 100, 1,300, and 2,100 trials (Khan, Franks, & Goodman, 1998). Other types of motor skills have also shown this effect, such as walking across a balance beam (which you saw in the preceding section), walking a specific distance on a narrow line on the floor (Proteau, Tremblay, & DeJaeger, 1998), a serial arm-movement skill (Ivens & Marteniuk, 1997), and a weightlifting skill (Tremblay & Proteau, 1998).

Why does dependency increase for sensory feedback sources available during practice as a person advances through the stages of learning? Proteau and his colleagues hypothesize that the dependency develops because the sensory feedback becomes part of an integrated sensory component of the memory representation of the skill. As a result, if the person must perform without the same sensory feedback available, retrieval of the representation from memory is less than optimal, because the sensory information available in the performance context is not compatible with the sensory information stored in the memory representation of the skill. As a result, performance is less accurate than it would have been with all the stored sensory information available in the performance context.

EXPERTISE

If a person practices a skill long enough and has the right kind of instruction, he or she eventually may become skilled enough to be an *expert*. On the

A CLOSER LOOK

Mirrors in Dance Studios and Weight Training Rooms: Are They Necessary?

If you walk into most dance studios and weight training rooms, you will see full-length mirrors on at least one wall, if not more. The most common reason given for their presence is that they provide an added source of visual feedback that will help the dancers and lifters improve their technique. But according to the evidence discussed in this chapter about practicing with this type of visual feedback when the performance context does not include mirrors, the mirrors may hinder learning more than they help it. According to several studies by Proteau and others, the longer people practice in the presence of this type of visual feedback, the more dependent on that feedback they become. This means that when an individual must perform without the mirror, that person will not perform as well as if he or she had practiced without the mirror all along.

Tremblay and Proteau (1998) provided evidence that this view applies to powerlifters learning to "perfect" their form for the squat lift. When the lifters

who practiced with a mirror for 100 trials were asked to perform the lift without the mirror, they increased the amount of error of their knee joint angle by 50 percent. Rather than the mirror helping them perfect their form, it led to poorer form when the mirror wasn't available.

Although we don't have research evidence based on dancers, we have evidence that some professional dance teachers do not use mirrors during classes and rehearsals. Two examples were described in the magazine *The New Yorker* (January 6, 2003) in an article by Joan Acocella. After the author observed a dance class taught by the great ballerina Suzanne Farrell, she stated, "Again and again, she tells dancers to stop looking in the studio mirror" (p. 53). The other example involves George Ballanchine, the originator of the New York City Ballet Company, considered by many to have been one of the world's best choreographers. Ballanchine forbade his dancers to look in the mirror. He told them, "I'm the mirror" (p. 53).

---

learning stages continuum we presented earlier in this discussion (figure 11.1), the expert is a person who is located at the extreme right end. This person is in an elite group of people who are exceptional and outstanding performers. Although motor skill expertise is a relatively new area of study in motor learning research, we know that experts have distinct characteristics. Most of our knowledge about experts in the motor skills domain relates to athletes, dancers, and musicians. Although they are in seemingly diverse fields, experts in these skill performance areas have some similar characteristics. Some of these will be examined next.

Amount and Type of Practice Leading to Expertise

In an extensive study of experts from a diverse number of fields, Ericsson, Krampe, and Tesch-Romer (1993) reported that expertise in all fields is the result of *intense practice for a minimum of ten years.* Critical to achieving expertise is not only the length of time in which the person practices in-

tensely, but also the type of practice. According to Ericsson and his colleagues, the specific type of intense practice a person needs to achieve expertise in any field is *deliberate practice.* During this type of practice, the person receives optimal instruction, as well as engaging in intense, worklike practice for hours each day. As the person develops toward expertise, he or she begins to need personalized training, or supervision of the practice regime.

A characteristic of expertise that emerges from the length and intensity of practice required to achieve expertise in a field is this: *expertise is domain specific* (see Ericsson & Smith, 1991). This means that characteristics of experts are specific to the field in which they have attained this level of success. There is little transfer of the capabilities in the field of expertise to another field in which the person has no experience.

Experts' Knowledge Structure

A notable characteristic common to expert skill performers is that they know more about an activ-

A CLOSER LOOK

A Summary of Performer and Performance Changes across the Stages of Learning

• *Rate of improvement*	The amount of improvement decreases *(power law of practice)*
• *Movement coordination*	Coordination patterns change from a "freezing" of limb segments to the segments working together as a functional synergy
• *Altering an old or preferred coordination pattern*	Coordination patterns change from the old pattern to a transitional state of no evident pattern, and then to a new pattern
• *Muscles involved*	The number of muscles involved decreases and the timing pattern of muscle group activation becomes appropriate for the action situation
• *Energy cost/movement efficiency*	The amount of energy used decreases; movement efficiency increases
• *Achievement of kinematic goals*	A spatial-to-temporal goals sequence evolves
• *Visual selective attention*	Attention increasingly becomes directed to more appropriate sources of information
• *Conscious attention*	Amount of conscious attention to movement characteristics reduces
• *Error detection and correction*	Capability increases to detect and correct one's own performance errors

ity than nonexperts do. More important, this expert knowledge is structured quite differently as well. Research investigating experts in a number of diverse skills, such as chess, computer programming, bridge, and basketball, has shown that the expert has developed his or her knowledge about the activity into more organized concepts and is better able to interrelate the concepts. The expert's knowledge structure also is characterized by more decision rules, which he or she uses in deciding how to perform in specific situations. Additionally, because of the way the knowledge is structured, the expert can remember more information from one observation or presentation.

The benefit of these knowledge structure characteristics is that they enable the expert to solve problems and make decisions faster and more accurately than a nonexpert can, and to adapt to novel environments more easily. For example, an expert basketball player bringing the ball down the floor can look at one or two players on the other team and know which type of defense the team is using; he or she then can make decisions about whether to pass, dribble, or shoot. The beginner would need

to take more time to make these same decisions because he or she would need to look at more players to obtain the same information.

Experts' Use of Vision

When experts perform an activity, they use vision in more advantageous ways than nonexperts do. We discussed many of these characteristics in chapters 6 and 8. For example, experts search their environment faster, give more attention to this search, and select more meaningful information in less time. Also, experts do not need as much environmental information for decision making, primarily because they "see" more when they look somewhere. Undoubtedly due in part to their superior visual search and decision-making capabilities, experts can use visual information better than nonexperts to anticipate the actions of others. And experts recognize patterns in the environment sooner than nonexperts do. Experts achieve these vision characteristics after many years of experience performing a skill; studies have shown the characteristics to be a function more of experience than of better visual acuity or eyesight.

A CLOSER LOOK

Experts Compared to Novices: Vision

Bruce Abernethy, one of the world's leading researchers on the issue of expertise as it relates to the use of vision in the performance of motor skills, summarized some primary research findings in an article published in 1999 in the *Journal of Applied Sport Psychology*. The following are some of his key points about the comparison between experts and novices in their use of vision in performance situations in which there is a very brief window of time to detect and use visual information, such as hitting a pitched baseball or returning a racquetball serve.

No Differences

- General vision measures (e.g., visual acuity) and nerve function measures (e.g., nerve conduction velocity) show no differences. *Experts' superior performance relates more to the superior use of visual information.*
- Visual search patterns may or may not differ. *Experts exhibit superior use of visual information even when search patterns are similar.*

Differences

- Experts are faster and more accurate in recognizing patterns in their own skill domain. *"Patterns" refer to coordination patterns related to an action and to patterns involving several people.*
- Experts detect and use important action-directing cues faster. *The result is better anticipation and faster implementation of a required action.*

PREDICTING FUTURE ACHIEVEMENT

The focus of this discussion is on predicting a person's *potential* for future achievement on the basis of his or her performance as a beginner in the early stage of learning a person's actual future achievement. Whether or not an individual actually achieves his or her potential will depend on many factors, such as motivation, training, opportunities, etc. Thus, those who make predictions must limit their judgment to the assessment of a person's potential for success, given the appropriate opportunities to develop that potential.

RELATING INITIAL AND LATER ACHIEVEMENT

Researchers have used three different approaches to address the question of how well early learning stage performance predicts later stage achievement. Two involve determining the degree of relationship between early and later stage performance by employing correlational statistics. The third considers the role played by motor abilities at each learning stage.

Correlating Initial and Later Performance

One way to determine the relationship between initial and later performance achievement is to correlate performance scores of a person as he or she progresses across the stages of learning. The simplest method is to correlate early performance scores with later performance scores. In most cases, this correlation will be low, indicating a low relationship between initial and later achievement.

Although it was published many years ago, an experiment by Ella Trussell (1965) continues to be a classic example of research evidence with this typical result. College women practiced juggling three tennis balls for twenty-seven practice sessions (three sessions per week for nine weeks). Each session included seventy-five tosses. The author defined juggling performance as the number of errors or dropped balls. As expected, the women's performance improved with practice. As the top panel of figure 11.4 shows, error scores dropped from fifty errors per seventy-five tosses in the first practice period to twenty errors per seventy-five tosses in the final session. More important, however, is the bottom graph of this figure, which shows the extent to which scores for each practice period predicted final scores (practice

FIGURE 11.4 The top graph shows the performance curve from the experiment by Trussell for a juggling task. The errors are indicated for the practice periods. The bottom graph indicates the accuracy of prediction of final performance in the juggling task as a function of the amount of practice used for prediction. [From Trussell, E. (1965). Prediction of success in a motor skill on the basis of early learning achievement. *Research Quarterly,* 36, 342–347. 1965 American Alliance for Health, Physical Education, Recreation, and Dance. Reprinted by permission.]

periods 24 through 27). Note that the statistic denoting the prediction value is R^2, which is on the vertical axis of the graph. This statistic was derived by squaring the correlation between the participants' scores for a practice period and the average of the final four practice periods. Interpret the R^2 as indicating the degree of commonality, that is, similarity, between the initial and final sets of performance scores. In this experiment, the first five practice period scores correctly predicted the scores of the final periods only 50 to 60 percent of the time. These odds are about the same as those involved in flipping a coin. But this prediction

capability increased with more practice periods. Note, for example, that performance during practice period 15 predicted final performance with about 85 percent accuracy.

Intertrial Correlations

A more complex correlation procedure involves correlating all the practice trials with each other. This approach provides information about the relationship between the performance scores of any two trials. The common finding from this analysis has been that *trials that are close to each other in time are more highly correlated than trials that are farther from each other.* This between-trials relationship follows what has been called a **superdiagonal form.** This term describes the way the trial-to-trial correlations appear on a correlation matrix that compares all trials against each other, with the same trials located on both the vertical and the horizontal axes of the matrix. The correlation of a trial with the trial that succeeds it, such as that of trial 2 with trial 3, is found just above the diagonal of the matrix, where a trial would be correlated with itself. On the basis of the use of the prefix "super" to mean "above," a superdiagonal form occurs when the highest correlations in the matrix are along the diagonal that is just above the main diagonal of the matrix.

superdiagonal form a term describing the way the trial-to-trial correlations appear in a correlation matrix where all trials are correlated with each other; trials that are closer to each other have scores more highly correlated; the correlation decreases as trials become farther apart.

TABLE 11.1   The Intertrial Correlation Matrix from Performance on a Rhythmic Arm Movement Task Reported by Thomas and Halliwell (The correlations are based on the spatial error scores from the task.)

Trial	1	2	3	4	5	6	7	8	9	10	11	12	13	14	15
1	—	27	−.05	.33	.23	.08	.27	.15	.00	−.04	−.09	.11	−.05	.13	−.12
2		—	.63	.71	.57	.57	.64	.54	.57	.38	.54	.29	.15	.67	.25
3			—	.60	.46	.18	.56	.50	.45	.53	.48	.12	.09	.37	.24
4				—	.73	.45	.61	.62	.45	.29	.51	.15	.17	.49	.12
5					—	.37	.67	.57	.59	.32	.52	.22	.28	.52	.21
6						—	.53	.54	.50	.39	.68	.52	.41	.61	.35
7							—	.71	.67	.70	.65	.51	.57	.80	.50
8								—	.67	.67	.65	.52	.43	.59	.48
9									—	.47	.73	.54	.61	.78	.41
10										—	.56	.59	.63	.62	.64
11											—	.49	.57	.72	.62
12												—	.63	.58	.47
13													—	.71	.63
14														—	.53
15															—

Source: Thomas, J. R., & Halliwell, W. (1976). Individual differences in motor skill acquisition. *Journal of Motor Behavior, 8,* 89–100. Copyright © 1976 Heldref Publications, Inc., Washington, DC. Reprinted by permission.

An excellent example of this approach is in one of the few motor skill studies to apply this approach. In an experiment by Thomas and Halliwell (1976), participants learned three motor skills: the rotary pursuit task, the stabilometer task, and a rhythmic arm movement task. The correlation matrix in table 11.1 presents the results of participants' initial fifteen trials of practice on the rhythmic arm movement task. This task involved learning to move a lever held at the side of the body to a visual target in time with a metronome. Both spatial and temporal error constituted the performance score. As you can see in the table, the highest between-trial correlations are typically along the diagonal located just *above* the main diagonal of the correlation matrix. As you can see by looking to your right to compare a particular trial to other trials, the correlation between trials farther away is generally lower. For example, the correlation between trials 4 and 5 is 0.73, whereas the correlation between trials 4 and 12 drops to 0.15.

Thus, these results provide additional evidence that performance early in practice is a poor predictor of performance later in practice.

The Relationship between Motor Abilities and the Stages of Learning

The third approach to investigating the relationship between performance achievement early and later in learning is to compare the motor abilities that account for performance achievement at each stage. Although controversy exists concerning whether the abilities associated with performance remain constant or change during skill learning, the prevailing view is that abilities required to perform a skill can change as the person becomes more proficient at performing the skill. This means that the abilities related to performing the skill in the early stage of learning may not be the same as those related to performance in later stages. When considered in terms of how poorly we can predict performance between early and later stages of

A CLOSER LOOK

Individual Differences in Skill Learning from a Dynamic Pattern Perspective

According to a dynamic pattern view of skill learning (e.g., Zanone and Kelso, 1994), a person initiates practice to learn a new skill by using a coordination pattern that is familiar to him or her yet is similar in some way to the pattern that the person must learn. The pattern the person uses on the initial practice trial spontaneously results from his or her attempt to achieve the action goal of the new skill.

Because of previous skill performance experiences and certain physiological and biomechanical constraints, the person has developed distinct coordination-pattern preferences *(attractor states)*. These preferences represent stable patterns that the person can repeat with little variation and that involve optimal efficiency of energy use. Examples include preferred walking and running gaits and speeds, as well as rhythmic bimanual limb movements that are both in-phase (with simultaneous activation of homologous muscles) and antiphase (with alternate activation of homologous muscles).

Learning a new skill involves a transition from the preferred, stable coordination pattern to the new pattern. If the coordination dynamics of the new skill are similar to those characterizing the preferred pattern, competition between attractor states will lead to slower learning of the new skill than if the patterns were dissimilar. Thus, the practitioner must consider the individual's coordination-pattern tendencies at the time he or she begins practice for learning a new skill. These tendencies constitute an individual difference factor that influences the rate of skill learning.

---

learning, this view provides a basis for accounting for this poor prediction.

Ackerman (1988, 1992) provided insight into these changes when he proposed a model broadly describing the relationship between the types of abilities that are primarily responsible for performance in each of the three stages of learning of the Fitts and Posner model, which we discussed earlier in this chapter. Figure 11.5 presents a graphic representation of this relationship. In the cognitive stage of learning, in which the learner must acquire knowledge about task goal, rules, and strategies, general cognitive and broad-content abilities predominate to account for performance. General cognitive abilities include reasoning, problem solving, and verbal abilities, among others; broad-content abilities include spatial orientation, attention control, etc. As the person progresses to the associative stage, perceptual speed ability becomes more predominant in accounting for performance. This includes the facility to solve problems quickly, especially problems related to visual search and memory use. Finally, in the autonomous phase, the demand on perceptual and motor abilities increases

so that they become the abilities that are most highly correlated with performance.

Ackerman (1992) cites several examples of experiments that provide support for his model. In addition, he associates the relationship between the types of abilities that account for performance and

FIGURE 11.5 Ackerman's hierarchical model of the relationship between types of abilities and the Fitts and Posner stages of learning. [Adapted from Ackerman, P.L. (1992). Predicting individual differences in complex skill acquisition: Dynamics of ability determinants. *Journal of Applied Psychology, 77,* 598–614. Copyright © 1992 the American Psychological Association. Adapted with permission.]

A CLOSER LOOK

Teaching and Rehabilitation Implications of the Influence of Changes in Motor Abilities from Early to Later Practice

- A person eventually may perform better than his or her initial performance indicates. This means that you should not "give up" on a person because of such undependable evidence as early performance alone.
- Awareness of the coordination characteristics of a person's initial practice attempts can help a teacher or therapist determine the ease or difficulty the person will have learning the new skill. A change in the coordination pattern itself is more difficult to achieve than are changes in parameter components of the pattern.

- Skill analyses are important in helping the teacher or therapist distinguish between individual ability factors that will contribute to more or less successful skill performance during early and later practice trials.
- Screening tests to assess potential for future performance success should emphasize assessing in novices the specific abilities that are related to successful performance by people who are skillful performers.

the three learning stages. He indicates that the simple relationship between abilities and learning stages shown in figure 11.5 may relate *only* to skills in which motor performance requirements of the task are critical for task performance and the information-processing requirements do not change in various contexts in which the skill is performed. Although Ackerman does not use motor skill classification terminology, his description of these types of tasks would be most closely related to those classified in chapter 1 as closed motor skills in which regulatory conditions do not change from trial to trial. In contrast, for skills where information-processing demands change from one situation to another, the three types of abilities do not change in their relationship to performance at each stage of learning. Ackerman presented evidence based on the learning of an air traffic controller task as an example of this type of skill.

The Ackerman model must be viewed as a general description of three broad categories of human abilities and their relationship to skill performance at various stages of learning. Unfortunately, we do not know enough about the task-specificity aspect of the model to relate it to specific sport skills or skills of daily living. We must wait for additional research to provide this information. However, because the progression presented in the model depicted in figure 11.5 is in general agreement with

other views (e.g., Fleishman & Mumford, 1989) about the change of the abilities-performance relationship during skill acquisition, we can view this model as a key component of the explanation for poor early to later learning stage performance prediction for most complex motor skills.

The key point is that it is very difficult to predict future achievement in learning a motor skill when we base the prediction on early performance only. Abilities that account for a person's level of performance change in importance as the person moves from the early stage of learning to later stages. Those abilities that are important in accounting for a person's performance score early in practice are typically not as important later in practice. However, prediction of future performance improves if the teacher, coach, or therapist is aware of both the specific abilities that are essential to performance in the different stages of learning, and also the corresponding abilities within the learner.

SUMMARY

- When people begin to practice a new motor skill, and continue to practice the skill, they typically progress through distinct, although continuous, stages of learning. We discussed two models that describe these stages.

- The *Fitts and Posner model* proposes that the learner progresses through three stages:
  - *Cognitive stage*—The beginner engages in much cognitive activity such as problem solving, directing attention to the movements, etc.
  - *Associative stage*—In this intermediate stage the learner reduces the amount of cognitive activity involved in performing the skill and works to refine the skill to increase performance success and consistency.
  - *Autonomous stage*—The learner performs skillfully, almost automatically, with little conscious attention directed to the movements.
- *Gentile's model* proposes that the learner progresses through two stages:
  - *Initial stage*—The goals of the beginner are to develop a movement coordination pattern that will allow some degree of successful performance, and to learn to discriminate regulatory and nonregulatory conditions.
  - *Later stages*—The learner's goals are to acquire the capability of adapting the movement pattern acquired in the initial stage to specific demands of any performance situation; to increase performance success consistency; and to perform the skill with an economy of effort. Movement goals are skill specific in this stage, as closed skills require a *fixation* of the movement pattern; open skills require a *diversification* of the movement pattern.
- Several distinct performer and performance changes occur as the learner progresses through the learning stages. We discussed the following changes (a summary of each change is presented in A Closer Look on p. 223):
  - *Rate of improvement*
  - *Movement coordination*
  - *Altering an old or preferred coordination pattern*
  - *Muscles used to perform the skill*
  - *Energy cost/movement efficiency*
  - *Achievement of the kinematic goals of the skill*
  - *Visual selective attention*
  - *Conscious attention*
  - *Error detection and correction capability*

- A performer characteristic that *does not change* across the stages of learning is the reliance on sensory information that was available during the early practice stage.
- *Expertise* refers to a high level of skill performance that characterizes a person at the extreme opposite end of the learning continuum from the beginner.
  - Expertise is typically the result of *deliberate practice* for a minimum of ten years.
  - Experts have a *knowledge structure* that is organized into more concepts related to performing the activity and they are better able to interrelate the concepts. However, the knowledge structure is activity specific.
  - Experts who perform in activities that involve severe time constraints for decision making and anticipation visually search the performance environment in a way that allows them to select more meaningful information in a short amount of time.
- Investigations into the relationship between initial and later learning stages performance have generally used three different approaches:
  - *Correlations of early and later practice performance scores*—Results typically show very low relationship between initial practice performance and later performance.
  - *Intertrial correlations*—Results typically show a superdiagonal form of correlations in which correlations are highest for trials closest to each other, but become lower as trials farther from each other are compared.
  - *Comparisons of the influence of various motor abilities on performance at different stages of learning*—Results typically show that motor abilities associated with good performance early in practice become less associated later in practice as other motor abilities become associated with good performance.

RELATED READINGS

Benguigui, N., & Ripoll, H. (1998). Effects of tennis practice on the coincidence timing accuracy of adults and children. *Research Quarterly for Exercise and Sport, 69,* 217–223.

Broderick, M. P., & Newell, K. M. (1999). Coordination patterns in ball bouncing as a function of skill. *Journal of Motor Behavior, 31,* 165–188.

Davids, K., Lees, A., & Burwitz, L. (2000). Understanding and measuring coordination and control in kicking skills in soccer: Implications for talent identification and skill acquisition. *Journal of Sports Sciences, 18,* 703–714.

Durand-Bush, N., & Salmela, J. (2001). The development of talent in sport. In R. N. Singer, H. A. Hausenblaus, & C. M. Janelle (Eds.), *Handbook of sport psychology* (2nd ed., pp. 269–289). New York: John Wiley & Sons.

Henry, R. A., & Hulin, C. L. (1987). Stability of skilled performance across time: Some generalizations and limitations on utilities. *Journal of Applied Psychology, 72,* 457–462.

Levine, E. L., Spector, P. E., Menon, S., Narayanan, L., & Cannon-Bowers, J. (1996). Validity generalization for cognitive, psychomotor, and perceptual tests for craft jobs in the utility industry. *Human Performance, 9,* 1–22.

Sparrow, W. A., & Newell, K. A. (1998). Metabolic energy expenditure and the regulation of movement economy. *Psychonomic Bulletin & Review, 5,* 173–196.

Steenbergen, B., Marteniuk, R. G., & Kalbfleisch, L. E. (1995). Achieving coordination in prehension: Joint freezing and postural contributions. *Journal of Motor Behavior, 27,* 333–348.

STUDY QUESTIONS

1. Describe some characteristics of learners as they progress through the three stages of learning proposed by Fitts and Posner.

2. How does Gentile's learning stages model differ from the Fitts and Posner model? How does her model relate specifically to learning open and closed skills?

3. Describe four performer or performance changes that research has shown to occur as a person progresses through the stages of learning a motor skill.

4. Describe a performer characteristic that does *not* change across the stages of learning. Describe an example.

5. Describe what an expert is and how a person can become an expert motor skill performer. What are some characteristics that distinguish an expert from a nonexpert?

6. How accurately can you predict a person's future performance achievement on the basis of his or her performance in the practice sessions in which he or she begins to learn the skill? Discuss two types of research evidence that support your answer.

7. Discuss how Ackerman's model relates human abilities to stages of learning a motor skill.

Chapter

Transfer of Learning

Concept: Transfer of learning
from one performance situation to another
is an integral part of skill learning and performance

After completing this chapter, you will be able to

- Define *transfer of learning* as it applies to the learning of motor skills

- Discuss why transfer of learning is an important concept for motor learning

- Discuss two reasons proposed to explain why transfer occurs

- Define *negative transfer* and relate it to motor skill learning situations

- Discuss the difference between *symmetric* and *asymmetric* bilateral transfer

- Discuss hypotheses that attempt to explain why bilateral transfer occurs

Application

Why do we practice a skill? One reason is to increase our capability of performing the skill in a situation requiring it. We want to be able to accomplish specific action goals when we need to, whether we perform everyday skills, work skills, or sport skills. For example, if you were a physical therapist who was working with the gait problems of a stroke patient, you would want that person to be able to walk in environments outside the clinic. The patient should be able to walk at home, in the workplace, at the grocery store, in the mall, etc. Similarly, if you were a baseball coach, you would want your pitcher to pitch well in games as well as in practice. Each of these examples involves the concept of transfer of learning, because of the need

to transfer learned capabilities in one environment or situation to a different environment or situation. In fact, one of the goals of practicing a skill is developing the capability to transfer performance of the skill from the practice environment to some other environment in which the individual must perform the skill so that he or she can achieve the same action goal.

Discussion

Transfer of learning is one of the most universally applied principles of learning in education and rehabilitation. In educational systems, this principle is an important part of curriculum and instruction development, because it provides the basis for arranging the sequence in which the students will learn skills. In the rehabilitation clinic, this principle forms the basis for the systematic development of protocols that therapists implement with patients. Because of the widespread importance of transfer of learning, you need to have an understanding of this learning phenomenon as part of your conceptual foundation for studying motor learning.

In chapter 10, we used the concept of transfer of learning when we discussed transfer tests as a method of assessing learning. Those tests are based on the transfer of learning principle. That discussion provided you with a good basis for the present discussion, which will provide you with an understanding of the transfer of learning principle itself.

WHAT IS TRANSFER OF LEARNING?

Learning researchers generally define **transfer of learning** as the influence of previous experiences on performing a skill in a new context, or on learning a new skill. This influence may be positive, negative, or neutral (zero). **Positive transfer** occurs when previous experience facilitates performance of a skill in a new context or the learning of a new skill. Each of the examples presented at the beginning of this chapter involved positive transfer. **Negative transfer** occurs when previous experience hinders or interferes with performance of a skill in a new context or the learning of a new skill. For example, a person who has learned the forehand in tennis before learning the forehand in badminton often experiences some initial negative transfer for learning the mechanics of the stroke. The badminton forehand is a wrist snap, whereas the tennis forehand requires a relatively firm wrist. The third type of transfer of learning effect is *zero transfer,* which occurs when previous experience has no influence on performance of a skill in a new context or learning of a new skill. Obviously, there is no transfer from learning to swim to learning to drive a car. Nor can we assume that experience with some motor skills will always have an influence on learning new motor skills.

WHY IS TRANSFER OF LEARNING IMPORTANT?

We pointed out earlier that the principle of transfer of learning is an important part of educational curriculum development and instructional methodology, as well as the development and implementation of systematic approaches to rehabilitation protocols. Thus, from a practical point of view, the transfer principle is very significant. But the transfer principle also has theoretical significance, because it helps us understand processes underlying the learning and control of motor skills.

Sequencing Skills to Be Learned

The sequencing of mathematics skills provides a very useful practical example of the transfer principle as it relates to curriculum development in schools. The curriculum from grades K through 12 is based on a simple-to-complex sequence. Teachers present numeral identification, numeral writing, numeral value identification, addition, subtraction, multiplication, and division in this specific sequence, because each concept is based on the concepts that preceded it. A person presented with a division problem needs to know how to add, subtract, and multiply in order to solve the problem. We do not teach algebra before basic arithmetic. We do not teach trigonometry before geometry.

We can make the same point about skills taught in a physical education program, a sports program, or a rehabilitation clinic. Those who develop a curriculum or a protocol should incorporate the transfer of learning principle when they sequence skills. Learners should acquire basic or foundational skills *before* more complex skills that require mastery of these basic skills. In other words, there should be a logical progression of skill experiences. An instructor should decide when to introduce a skill by determining how the learning of that skill will benefit the learning of other skills. If the instructor does not use this approach, time is wasted while people "go back" to learn prerequisite basic skills.

Gentile's taxonomy of motor skills (discussed in chapter 1) provides a good example of how the transfer principle can be implemented in any skill training situation. That taxonomy presents sixteen categories of skills, systematically sequenced from less to more complex according to specific skill characteristics (see table 1.1). One use for this taxonomy is as a guide to help the therapist select functionally appropriate activities for a rehabilitation patient after making a clinical evaluation of the patient's motor function problems. Gentile based this taxonomy on the principle of positive transfer. She organized the sequence of activities by listing first the activities that a person must perform before performing more complex or difficult ones. The therapist can select appropriate functional activities for a rehabilitation regime by starting with activities related to the taxonomy category in which the therapist identified the skill performance deficit. Then the therapist can increase activity complexity by progressing through the taxonomy from that point, as described in chapter 1.

Instructional Methods

The second important practical application of the transfer of learning principle to motor skill instruction is in the area of instructional methods. For example, a swimming instructor might use dry land drills when teaching students the basic swimming strokes, before letting them try the strokes in the water. The instructor assumes that there will be positive transfer from the dry land drills to the performance of the strokes in water.

There are numerous other examples of incorporating the transfer principle in instructional settings. It is common, for example, to practice a part of a skill before practicing the entire skill (we will discuss this practice method in chapter 17). Sometimes an instructor simplifies an activity for a person before requiring the person to perform the skill in its actual context; for example, the coach has a person hit a baseball from a batting tee before hitting a moving ball. If the skill being acquired involves an element of danger, the instructor often allows the person to perform the skill with some type of aid so that the danger is removed. For example, a therapist may initially provide physical

guidance for a patient who is learning to get out of bed and into a wheelchair, so that the patient will not fall when first practicing this skill.

Assessing the Effectiveness of Practice Conditions

For any instructor, coach, or therapist who wants to determine the effectiveness of a practice routine or instructional method, the rule of thumb should be that *transfer test performance will provide the best assessment.* As you saw in our discussion in chapter 10 concerning the assessment of motor skill learning, a person's performance during practice can over- or underestimate what the person is actually learning. This same principle applies to the assessment of practice routines or instructional methods. We can know their effectiveness only by determining their impact on performance in the situation for which the practice or instruction was designed to prepare the student, athlete, or patient. For coaches of sports teams, the transfer test is usually the competition the athlete or team was preparing for. For instructor and therapists, the transfer test is not so easily determined. The instructor or therapist must identify the situations or environments in which the student or patient will need to perform. For the physical education instructor, the test may be performance on a skills test or in a tournament; for a dance instructor the test may be performance in a

---

transfer of learning   the influence of having previously practiced or performed a skill or skills on the learning of a new skill.

positive transfer   the beneficial effect of previous experience on the learning or performance of a new skill, or on the performance of a skill in a new context.

negative transfer   the negative effect of prior experience on the performance of a skill, so that a person performs the skill less well than he or she would have without prior experience.

A CLOSER LOOK

Assessing Positive Transfer of Learning

Researchers commonly use a simple experimental design to determine if positive transfer has occurred from either (1) experience with one skill to learning another skill or (2) performing a skill in one situation to performing it in another context. The design is as follows:

Experimental group	(1) Practice skill A	Perform skill B
	(2) Perform a skill in context A	Perform the same skill in context B
Control group	No practice	Perform skill B
		Perform the same skill in context B

The performance score of interest to the researcher is for skill B (1), or context B (2). If positive transfer is evident, then the performance of the experimental group should be better than that of the control group. Thus, prior experience is better than no prior experience for the skill or practice situation of interest.

To quantify the amount of positive transfer, researchers commonly calculate the *percentage of transfer,* which is the percentage of difference between the experimental and control groups' performance scores on skill B or in context B:

$$\text{Percentage of transfer} = \frac{\text{Experimental group} - \text{Control group}}{\text{Experimental group} + \text{Control group}} \times 100$$

It is important to be aware that a positive percentage will result for all performance measures except those for which a lower value indicates better performance (e.g., error, speed).

---

recital or concert; and for the physical or occupational therapist, the test may be performance of daily living activities at home or work activities in the workplace.

As support for the importance of the transfer test to assess practice conditions and instructional methods, one of the predominant theoretical viewpoints of why transfer of learning occurs emphasizes the importance of the transfer basis for this assessment. The *transfer-appropriate processing theory of transfer,* which will be presented later in this discussion, asserts that *the effectiveness of any practice condition should be determined only on the basis of how the practiced skill is performed in a "test" context.* This means that if we are deciding whether one instructional or practice strategy is superior to another to facilitate skill learning, we should not reach a conclusion until we have observed the person performing the practiced skill in its appropriate test performance situation.

WHY DOES POSITIVE TRANSFER OF LEARNING OCCUR?

The theoretical significance of the concept of transfer of learning becomes evident as we attempt to determine why transfer occurs. For example, if we know why transfer occurs, we have a better understanding of what a person learns about a skill that enables the person to adapt to the performance requirements of a new situation or to learn a new skill.

Although researchers have proposed several reasons over the years to explain why transfer of learning occurs, we will discuss only two of the more prominent hypotheses here. Both consider the *similarities* between the two situations to be critical for explaining transfer. However, they differ in their explanations of which similarities account for transfer. One hypothesis proposes that transfer of learning occurs because the components of the skills and/or the context in which skills are performed are similar. The other proposes that

If a person's goal for learning to ride a bicycle is to deliver newspapers, then the greatest amount of transfer between practice and test will occur when the practice experience includes opportunities for throwing a newspaper while riding a bicycle.

transfer occurs primarily because of similarities between the amounts and types of learning processes required (see figure 12.1).

Similarity of Skill and Context Components

The more traditional view of why positive transfer occurs contends that transfer is due to the similarity between the components of two skills or of two performance situations. In this view, the more similar the component parts of two skills or two performance contexts are, the greater will be the amount of positive transfer between them.

An important question concerning the similarity of skill components is this: What constitutes a "component part"? There are two answers to this question. One is any observable movement part of a skill, such as an overarm movement or a ball striking movement. However, it is important to note that the similarity of movement parts can also be considered in terms of their kinematic characteristics. Although we would expect positive transfer between two skills when compared at either level of similarity, different amounts of positive transfer would be expected when the similarities were compared at these two levels. For example, both baseball pitching and football passing include overarm throwing movements that are somewhat similar when compared in terms of observable movement, but become decidedly less similar when compared on the basis of their kinematics. The kinematic difference between these skills was nicely demonstrated in a study of high school and college baseball pitchers and football quarterbacks (Fleisig et al., 1996). The second answer is that a component part can relate to task-specific coordination dynamics, such as those we discussed in chapter 4. For example, from a dynamic pattern view of motor control, coordination tendencies and phase relationships that are common between tasks should promote positive transfer (e.g., Kelso & Zanone, 2002; Wenderoth, Bock, & Krohn, 2002).

This similarity of components view has its roots in some of the earliest motor learning research by E. L. Thorndike at Columbia University in the early part of the 1900s. To account for transfer effects, Thorndike (1914) proposed the **identical elements theory.** In this theory, "elements" are general characteristics of a skill or performance context—such as the purpose of the skill or the attitude of the person performing the skill—or specific characteristics of the skill, such as components of the skill being performed. Additionally,

---

identical elements theory   an explanation of positive transfer proposing that transfer is due to the degree of similarity between the component parts or characteristics of two skills or two performance contexts.

A CLOSER LOOK

Transfer from Virtual Reality Experience to a Real Environment

Virtual reality refers to three-dimensional computer-generated environments that can be explored and experienced in real time. Although there appear to be many potential applications of the use of virtual reality as a training strategy for motor skills, this potential remains to be determined. However, an interesting experiment by Wilson, Foreman, and Tlauka (1997) in England offers a look into one use of virtual reality in motor skills training contexts.

The focus of this study was on the training of people to be familiar with the spatial layout of a building, especially in terms of locating specific objects on three floors. Participants were in three groups: the real group, which experienced training in the real environment by being guided through the building floors; the computer group, which experienced being guided through a three-dimensional virtual reality version of the floors; and the control group, which did not experience training. Following training, par-

ticipants performed several tests to assess their spatial knowledge of the location of the objects pointed out during training. The results showed that the real and computer training groups performed better on the tests than the control group, and were not different from each other for two of the three floors. Interestingly, further investigation showed that the simulation of the floor for which the real group performed better was not as detailed as for the other two floors.

In addition to providing support for the identical elements theory of transfer, this study also suggests potential applications for motor skills training. For example, in rehabilitation contexts, virtual reality training could provide a preparatory experience for patients who need to experience locomoting in a variety of environmental contexts. Similar applications can be made for sports skills training where participation in new contexts will have an impact on the athletes' performance.

Thorndike considered identical elements to include mental processes that shared the same brain cell activity as the physical action.

According to a similarity of *skill components* comparison, we would expect the amount of transfer between the tennis serve and the volleyball serve to be greater than that between the tennis serve and the racquetball serve. And a comparison on the basis of the similarity of *context components,* we would expect a higher degree of transfer to occur when practice conditions included transfer test context characteristics than when they do not. In a clinical situation, for example, physical therapy protocols that include walking in the patient's everyday will yield more positive transfer than those that involve experiences only in the clinic.

Similarity of Processing Requirements

The second hypothesis explaining why positive transfer occurs proposes that it results from the *similarity of the cognitive processes* required by

the two skills or two performance situations. This hypothesis finds its clearest expression in the view that explains transfer effects in terms of transfer-appropriate processing (see Lee, 1988). This view maintains that although similarity in skill and context components explains some transfer effects, it cannot explain all transfer effects. A key point of the **transfer-appropriate processing theory** is the similarity between the learning or performance cognitive processes required by the two performance situations. In this view, two components of positive transfer are critical: the cognitive processing activity a person must do to be successful in performing the transfer task, and the similarity between that activity and the activity required during the training experience.

Some examples of transfer-appropriate processing include when the transfer task requires a person to engage in problem-solving activity, rapid decision making, application of rules, attention control, and the simultaneous performance of two or more tasks. For positive transfer to occur between the training and transfer tasks, the training

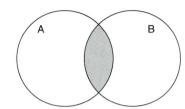

FIGURE 12.1   The two circles (A and B) in this figure can represent two skills or two performance contexts. For either theory proposed to explain why transfer of learning occurs, consider the amount of overlap between the two circles (the shaded area) as representing the degree of similarity between the two skills or performance contexts. More transfer should occur between the two skills or contexts in the set of circles on the left than in the one on the right.

task also must involve these same types of activities. What is especially important to note here is that the training and transfer tasks do not need to have similar movement components. The critical characteristic is the similarity between the cognitive processing demands of the training task and those of the transfer task.

Merit in Both Hypotheses

Although much remains unknown about the cause of transfer of learning, evidence points to the value of both hypotheses in accounting for transfer effect. As indicated by figure 12.1, we can expect the amount of positive transfer to be related to the amount of similarity between skills and performance contexts. It appears that the similarity-of-processing view is actually an extension of the components view that comes into play when skill components and context similarities are minimal, but cognitive processing activities are similar. However, as Schmidt and Young (1987) concluded in their extensive review of transfer in motor skills, we do not know very much about what accounts for the transfer phenomenon. Unfortunately, research investigating this question has been minimal during recent years, despite the fact that much more research is needed if we are to answer the question of *why* transfer occurs.

NEGATIVE TRANSFER

Although negative transfer effects appear to be rare and temporary in motor skill learning, people involved in motor skill instruction and rehabilitation need to be aware of conditions that may contribute to negative transfer. Because negative transfer effects can occur, it is important to know how to avoid such effects and to deal with them when they occur.

Negative Transfer Situations

Simply stated, negative transfer effects occur when an old stimulus requires a new but similar response. This means that the *environmental context characteristics of two performance situations are similar, but the movement characteristics are different.* Two situations that are especially susceptible to negative transfer effects involve a *change in the spatial locations of a movement* and a *change in the timing structure of the movement.*

An example of the *spatial location change* occurs when you must drive a car different from your own. If both cars are five-speed stick shifts, what happens when reverse is in a different location from the one you are accustomed to in your own car? Typically, you find yourself trying to shift to the location of reverse for your own car. This happens especially when you are not paying close attention to shifting. This example demonstrates that when

---

transfer-appropriate processing theory   an explanation of positive transfer proposing that transfer is due to the similarity in the cognitive processing characteristics required by the two skills or two performance situations.

A CLOSER LOOK

**Relating Transfer of Learning to Practice Conditions:
The Specificity of Practice Principle**

One of the oldest principles of motor learning is the "specificity of practice principle." Simply stated, this principle tells us that *to achieve optimal performance in a test, a person should experience practice conditions that match test conditions as closely as possible.* The specificity principle is a natural outgrowth of the various explanations about why positive transfer occurs. In fact, according to figure 12.1, the greatest amount of positive transfer would occur when practice and test conditions are the same. Although it is not always possible to create practice situations that will exactly match test situations, consider the following examples of some general practice and test features that can be matched as closely as possible.

Sensory/Perceptual Characteristics
Visual conditions. If the test requires performance without visual feedback about either the outcome of the performance or the limb or limbs performing the skill, practice should include performance situations without the visual feedback, e.g.,

- *practicing typing skills or piano playing*—Include practice opportunities without vision of the hands and keyboard
- *practicing basketball dribbling*—Include practice opportunities without vision of hands and ball
- *practicing "form/technique" with a mirror (e.g., gymnastics, dancing, weightlifting)*—Include practice opportunities without a mirror

Performance Context Characteristics
Environmental context. Include practice opportunities in the same environmental context as will exist for the test, e.g.,

- *rehabilitating locomotion*—Include practice opportunities in the person's home, workplace, shopping mall, etc.

- *rehabilitating occupational skills*—Include practice opportunities in the same setting the person experiences in daily living (or a simulation of it)
- *preparing for a night football game*—Include practice opportunities at night under the lights

Personal characteristics. Include practice opportunities that simulate the types of physical, mental, and emotional conditions the person may experience in the test, e.g.,

- *fatigue*—Practice shooting basketball free throws at the end of practice when fatigued
- *decision making*—Develop drills for soccer practice that will require a player with the ball to decide if he or she should pass to a teammate, shoot at the goal, or continue to keep control of the ball
- *anxiety*—Simulate conditions in practice that will require the person to control his or her anxiety levels while performing the skill

---

we learn a specific spatially oriented movement to accomplish an action goal, we require attention and time to learn a similar movement that is in a new direction or end-location, because of the negative transfer effect of the previous learning experience.

The second situation that leads to negative transfer effects involves a *change in the timing structure* of a sequence of movements from a previously learned sequence. Two different types of timing structure conditions are involved here. One is the *rhythmic pattern, or relative time structure,* learned

for a sequence of movements. When people learn a specific relative time structure for a sequence of movements, such as when they learn a piece of music, a dance sequence, etc., and then are asked to perform the sequence and ignore the rhythmic structure they learned, they typically produce the learned rhythmic structure for a number of trials (e.g., Summers, 1975). The second timing structure condition involves what appear to be *intrinsic bimanual coordination timing relationships.* An example of this situation can be seen in the results of

A CLOSER LOOK

An Example of Bilateral Transfer for Mirror Writing

Mark Latash (1999) reported a study in which students in his undergraduate class at Penn State University were required to learn a new skill as part of their class experience. The new skill was mirror writing, which involved handwriting a sentence on a piece of paper while looking in a mirror so that it would read correctly in the mirror, not on the paper. During a pretest the students wrote the sentence, "I can write while looking in the mirror," five times with one hand and then the other hand. For each trial, they timed how long it took to write the sentence and counted the errors they made. The students then prac-

ticed writing the sentence fifteen times a day, five days a week, for three weeks using the dominant hand only. At the end of the practice period, they did a posttest that required them to perform the task as in the pretest. By comparing the writing performance of the nondominant hand during the pre- and posttests, the students could determine if bilateral transfer resulted from the 225 practice trials with the dominant hand. The results showed that on the posttest for the nondominant hand, they wrote the sentence 40 percent faster than on the pretest, and their errors decreased by 43 percent.

the experiment by Lee, Swinnen, and Verschueren (1995) that was described in chapter 10. Participants were asked to produce a bimanual coordination pattern that is difficult to perform and varied markedly from their natural coordination pattern tendency, which was to move the arms in temporal synchrony. Recall that after achieving a small amount of progress in performing the new pattern by the end of the first day of practice (refer to figure 10.4), the participants reverted back to producing their natural symmetrical bimanual pattern. Thus the intrinsic coordination tendency to move the arms in temporal and spatial symmetry interfered with the participants' learning of a new asymmetrical movement pattern for the arms.

We often see either of the conditions that induce negative transfer effects when a person tries to "unlearn" a way of performing a skill and learn a new way to perform it. This type of situation occurs in many skill learning contexts. For example, athletes who go from high school to college commonly have to learn to perform a skill in a way that is different from how they performed it in high school. Even though the way they performed it in high school was successful, the college coach knows that to achieve success at the college level, the athlete needs to learn to perform the skill differently. In the rehab clinic,

physical and occupational therapists often interact with patients who have learned to perform a skill in a certain way because of a disability. However, the therapist knows that continued performance in this manner will lead to additional physical problems, which means the patient must acquire a different manner of performing the skill. In these types of situations, people typically show a decrement in performance when they begin practicing the skill in a new way. But with continued practice, performance begins to improve and eventually exceeds the level achieved previously.

Negative Transfer Effects Are Temporary
In each of the negative transfer situations described in this discussion, a common characteristic has been that the negative effects do not continue through all stages of learning. This is because negative transfer effects are temporary in nature and typically influence skill learning only in the early learning stage. However, it is important for the practitioner to be aware of this characteristic, because the negative transfer effects a person experiences early in practice may discourage a person's interest in pursuing the learning of the new skill or a new way to perform a well-learned skill. In addition, it is important that the practitioner be

aware of the aspects of a skill that will be most affected by negative transfer effects, and give particular instructional attention to these aspects to help the person overcome these effects.

Why Do Negative Transfer Effects Occur?

There are at least two likely reasons why negative transfer occurs. The first relates to the *memory representation* developed as a result of learning a skill. As a result of much practice performing a skill in one specific way, a specific perception-action coupling has developed between the perceptual characteristics of the task and the motor system. This coupling becomes a part of the memory representation for the action. When a person sees familiar perceptual characteristics in a performance environment, the motor system organizes itself in a preferred way to respond to those characteristics. Although this perception-action coupling allows for fast and accurate performing, it can become problematic when the familiar perceptual situation requires a movement that is different from what was learned. As you have seen in several discussions in this book, to change from the preferred state (i.e., the learned movement for the perceptual event) to a new state is difficult and takes practice.

Another possibility is that negative transfer results from *cognitive confusion.* In the car shift example, the requirements for shifting into reverse in the new car undoubtedly lead to some confusion in the driver about what to do. Undoubtedly you have had a similar experience when you have had to type on keyboards that differ in the locations of certain keys, such as the backspace or delete key. When you first begin typing on the new keyboard, you have difficulty striking the keys that are in different locations. What is notable here is that the problem is not with your limb control; you know how to strike keys in a sequence. Rather, the problem is related to the confusion created by the unfamiliar locations of the keys.

Fortunately, negative transfer effects can be overcome with practice. You probably have experi-

LAB LINKS

Lab 12 in the Online Learning Center Lab Manual provides an opportunity for you to experience the bilateral transfer phenomenon.

enced this for either gear shifting or typing, or for both. Just how much practice is required depends on the person and the task itself.

BILATERAL TRANSFER

When transfer of learning relates to learning of the same task but with the contralateral limb, it is known as **bilateral transfer,** although it is sometimes referred to as *cross-transfer* or *cross-education.* This well-documented phenomenon demonstrates our ability to learn a particular skill more easily with one hand or foot after we already have learned the skill with the contralateral hand or foot.

Experimental Evidence of Bilateral Transfer

Experiments designed to determine whether bilateral transfer does indeed occur have followed similar experimental designs. The most typical design has been the following:

	Pretest	Practice Trials	Posttest
Preferred limb	X	X	X
Nonpreferred limb	X		X

This design allows the experimenter to determine if bilateral transfer to the nonpracticed limb occurred because of practice with the other limb. In the sample experimental design, note that the practice limb is the preferred limb. However, this does not need to be the case; the preferred limb/nonpreferred limb arrangement could be reversed. In either case, the researcher compares pretest-to-posttest improvements for each limb.

A CLOSER LOOK

Using Bilateral Transfer in Occupational Therapy Treatment Strategies

Occupational therapists use various treatment strategies to help clients with impairments to one arm. One approach is to use a compensation strategy that will teach the client to compensate for the loss of the use of one arm either by using the nonimpaired arm in new ways, or modifying an environment to allow more opportunity to use the nonimpaired arm. However, another approach is to help the person improve the use of the impaired arm. When this type of therapy approach is used, the bilateral transfer phenomenon can provide a basis for the development of a specific therapy strategy, Nagel and Rice (2001) carried out the following experiment to determine if they could demonstrate bilateral transfer for a meaningful and purposeful activity that involved a fine motor skill.

- *Participants:* Graduate and undergraduate students who were right-hand dominant and without any neurological or orthopedic problems that would affect their task performance.
- *Task:* Participants performed a small maze-type game that required them to use one hand to move a metal ball through a maze. They moved the ball by holding a stem added to the maze with the thumb

and index finger and moving it to control the ball movement.

- *Experimental conditions and procedures:* A training group practiced the task with the left hand three times a day for seven days (i.e., 21 trials). A control group did not practice the task. Both groups performed a pretest and posttest with the right and left hands.
- *Results:* Bilateral transfer effects between the trained and untrained arms for the training group were found for movement time (the amount of time needed to complete the maze task on a trial) and the number of force oscillations (an index of movement efficiency). No statistically significant between-arm differences were found for the control group.

Although the participants in this experiment did not have unilateral limb impairments, the authors concluded that the results have implications for occupational therapy treatments. They suggested that occupational training with the unimpaired limb could be used as initial training, especially during the first few days after surgery or accident.

Although the practiced limb should show the greatest improvement, a significant amount of improvement should occur for the nonpracticed limb, indicating that bilateral transfer has occurred.

Investigation of the bilateral transfer phenomenon was popular from the 1930s through the 1950s. In fact, the bulk of the evidence demonstrating bilateral transfer in motor skills can be found in the psychology journals of that period. One of the more prominent investigators of the bilateral transfer phenomenon during the early part of that era was T. W. Cook. Between 1933 and 1936, Cook published a series of five articles relating to various concerns of bilateral transfer, which they called cross-education. Cook terminated this work by asserting that the evidence was sufficiently conclu-

sive to support the notion that bilateral transfer does indeed occur for motor skills.

Given such a foundation of evidence, very few experiments published since those by Cook have investigated only the question of the occurrence of the bilateral transfer phenomenon (e.g., Latash, 1999; Nagel & Rice, 2001; Rice, 1998). The bulk of the research literature since the 1930s has addressed several issues related to bilateral transfer. Among these are the direction of the greater amount of transfer, and the reason bilateral transfer occurs, both of which will be discussed next.

---

bilateral transfer transfer of learning that occurs between two limbs.

Symmetry versus Asymmetry of Bilateral Transfer

One of the more intriguing questions about the bilateral transfer effect concerns the direction of the transfer. The question is this: Does a greater amount of bilateral transfer occur when a person learns a skill using one limb before learning it with the contralateral limb **(asymmetric transfer)**, or is the amount of transfer similar when either limb is used first **(symmetric transfer)**?

Reasons for investigating this question are theoretical as well as practical. From a theoretical perspective, knowing whether bilateral transfer is symmetric or asymmetric would provide insight, for example, into the role of the two cerebral hemispheres in controlling movement. That is, do the two hemispheres play similar or different roles in movement control?

A more practical reason for investigating this question is that its answer can help professionals design practice to facilitate optimal skill performance with either limb. If asymmetric transfer predominated, the therapist, instructor, or coach would decide to have a person always train with one limb before training with the other; however, if symmetric transfer predominated, it would not make any difference which limb the person trained with first.

The generally accepted conclusion about the direction of bilateral transfer is that it is *asymmetric.* But there is some controversy about whether this asymmetry favors transfer from preferred to nonpreferred limb, or vice versa. The traditional view has been that there is a greater amount of transfer when a person practices initially with the preferred limb.

Although some controversy continues about this question, there is sufficient evidence to recommend that for most skill training and rehabilitation situations, the greater amount of transfer occurs *from the preferred to the nonpreferred limb.* This approach not only is consistent with the bulk of the research literature concerned with bilateral transfer, but also is supported by other factors that need to be taken into account, such as motivation. Initial

preferred-limb practice has a greater likelihood of yielding the types of success that will encourage the person to continue pursuing the goal of becoming proficient at performing the skill with either limb.

Why Does Bilateral Transfer Occur?

As we saw for explanations proposed to account for positive and negative transfer effects, cognitive and motor control explanations have been offered to answer the question of why bilateral transfer occurs. The *cognitive explanation* states that the basis for the positive transfer from a practiced to a non-practiced limb is the important cognitive information related to what to do to achieve the goal of the skill. This information is relevant to performing the skill regardless of the limb involved, and is critical information acquired during the initial stage of skill learning. As a result of practice with one limb, the relevant cognitive information is acquired, which makes it available when the skill is performed with the other limb.

The cognitive explanation of bilateral transfer can be related to the "identical elements" theory Thorndike proposed, which we discussed earlier. This explanation gives strong consideration to those elements of a skill related to the performer's knowing "what to do." For example, we can consider the performance of a skill with one limb and then the other to be essentially two distinct skills. Throwing a ball at a target using the right arm is a different task from throwing a ball with the left arm. However, elements of these skills are common to both, regardless of the hand the thrower is using. Examples would be the arm-leg opposition principle, the need to keep the eyes focused on the target, and the need to follow through. Each of these elements represents what to do to successfully throw the ball at a target and does not specifically relate to either arm.

Proponents of this view predict that if a person achieves proficiency at a skill using the right arm, the person does not need to relearn the common cognitive "what to do" elements when he or she be-

A CLOSER LOOK

Implementing Bilateral Transfer Training

For the person involved in motor skill instruction or rehabilitation, an important question concerns how to take advantage of the bilateral transfer phenomenon and implement it into the instructional or rehabilitation setting.

Recommended Guidelines
- Initiate practice with the preferred limb.
- In early practice sessions, concentrate on developing a reasonable degree of proficiency with one limb *before* beginning practice with the other limb.

- After initiating practice with the second limb, alternate practice for both limbs on the basis of set blocks of trials or amounts of time for practice with each limb.
- Use verbal encouragement to motivate the person to continue to practice with the nonpreferred limb.

---

gins practicing with the left arm. The person should begin with the left arm at a higher level of proficiency than he or she would have had if he or she had never practiced with the right arm.

The *motor control explanation* for bilateral transfer incorporates the generalized motor program and the transfer of motor output characteristics through the nervous system. There are two ways to establish this explanation. In the first, theorists look at the generalized motor program, which was described in chapter 4. Recall that the muscles required to produce an action are not an invariant characteristic of the generalized motor program. Rather, muscles are a *parameter* that a person must add to achieve the goal of the action.

Because a generalized motor program develops from practice, we would expect that following sufficient practice with one limb, a person would acquire the invariant characteristics of the action so that performing the action with the contralateral limb at some later time would simply be a matter of applying the muscle-specific parameter to those invariant characteristics. As a result, he or she could initially perform the action with the contralateral limb at a higher level. However, because of other factors, such as problems with perception, biomechanics, and specificity of training, we would not expect initial performance with the nonpracticed contralateral limb to be as good as performance with the practiced limb. But we would expect this initial performance to be better than it

would be if there were no practice at all with the other limb.

The second argument proponents of a motor control explanation offer is based on evidence showing that at least some bilateral transfer of skill is mediated in the brain by interhemispheric transfer of the motor components of the task (Hicks, Gualtieri, & Schroeder, 1983). Researchers have demonstrated this mediation by measuring the EMG activity in all four limbs when one limb performs a movement. When EMG activity occurs, it tells researchers that the central nervous system has forwarded commands to those muscles. In fact, research conducted as long ago as 1942 showed that the greatest amount of EMG activity occurs for the contralateral limbs (i.e., the two arms), a lesser amount occurs for the ipsilateral limbs (i.e., arm and leg on the same side), and the least amount occurs for the diagonal limbs (Davis, 1942).

Which of the two explanations of bilateral transfer is correct? Research evidence indicates that

---

asymmetric transfer bilateral transfer in which there is a greater amount of transfer from one limb than from the other limb.

symmetric transfer bilateral transfer in which the amount of transfer is similar from one limb to another, no matter which limb is used first.

both cognitive and motor factors are involved in bilateral transfer. There is no doubt that cognitive components related to "what to do" account for much of the transfer that results from practicing a skill with one limb. This is quite consistent with what we have discussed thus far in this book. For example, both the Fitts and Posner and the Gentile models of the stages of skill learning described in chapter 11 propose that determining "what to do" is a critical part of what a learner acquires in the first stage of learning. There is likewise no doubt that bilateral transfer involves a motor control basis as well. This is consistent with our discussion in chapter 4 of the control of coordinated action. It is also consistent with research evidence that there is some motor outflow to other limbs when one limb performs a skill.

SUMMARY

Transfer of learning concerns the influence of previous experiences on the performance of a skill in a new context or on learning a new skill.

- The influence of the previous experience may facilitate, hinder, or have no effect on the performance of a skill in a new context or on the learning of the new skill.
- The importance of the transfer of learning concept can be seen in its integral role in curriculum development in education, treatment protocol development in rehabilitation programs, and practice conditions in sports contexts.
- The transfer of learning concept is basic to the process of making inferences about the influence on motor skill learning of practice conditions and instructional methods.
- These are two of the hypotheses proposed to account for why positive transfer occurs:
  1. Positive transfer is a function of the similarity of the components of the skills performed and of the environmental contexts in which the skills are performed.
  2. Positive transfer is a function of the similarity of the cognitive processing activities involved in the two situations.
- Negative transfer effects, which are typically temporary and overcome with practice, occur primarily when a new movement is required for a familiar environmental context.
- Two hypotheses proposed to account for why negative transfer effects occur are the following:
  1. The difficulty inherent in altering a preferred perception-action coupling that has been developed for moving in a specific environmental context.
  2. The initial cognitive confusion that results when a person is not certain about how to move in a familiar environmental context.
- Bilateral transfer is a phenomenon in which improvement in the performance of a nonpracticed limb results from practice with the contralateral limb.
- Bilateral transfer is typically asymmetric, with the preferred-to-nonpreferred transfer direction yielding greater transfer than vice versa.
- Two hypotheses have been proposed to account for why bilateral transfer occurs:
  1. A cognitive hypothesis proposes that a person applies the knowledge acquired with practice of one limb about what to do to perform the skill to the initial performance of the skill with the contralateral limb.
  2. A motor control hypothesis proposes that the generalized motor program invariant characteristics acquired with the practice of one limb are applied as a parameter characteristic to the performance of the skill with the contralateral limb.

RELATED READINGS

Christina, R. W., & Bjork, R. A. (1991). Optimizing long-term retention and transfer. In D. Druckman & R. A. Bjork (Eds.), *In the mind's eye: Enhancing human performance* (pp. 23–56). Washington, DC: National Academy Press.

Ferguson, M. C., & Rice, M. S. (2001). The effect of contextual relevance on motor skill transfer. *American Journal of Occupational Therapy, 55,* 558–565.

Heikkilä, V. M. (2000). Relationship of laboratory and on-road tests for driving school students and experienced drivers. *Perceptual and Motor Skills, 90,* 227–235

Hesketh, B. (1997). Dilemmas in training for transfer and retention. *Applied Psychology: An International Review, 46,* 317–386.

Robertson, S., & Elliott, D. (1996). Specificity of learning and dynamic balance. *Research Quarterly for Exercise and Sport, 67,* 69–75.

Shields, R. K., Leo, K. C., Messaros, A. J., & Somers, V. K. (1999). Effects of repetitive handgrip training on endurance, specificity, and cross-education. *Physical Therapy, 79,* 467–475.

Tremblay, L., & Proteau, L. (1998). Specificity of practice: The case of powerlifting. *Research Quarterly for Exercise and Sport, 69,* 284–289.

Walter, C. B., & Swinnen, S. P., (1994). The formation and dissolution of "bad habits" during the acquisition of coordination skills. In S. P. Swinnen, H. Heuer, J. Massion, & P. Casear, (Eds.), *Interlimb coordination: Neural, dynamical, and cognitive constraints* (pp. 491–513). San Diego, CA: Academic Press

Winstein, C. J. (1991). Designing practice for motor learning: Clinical implications. In M. J. Lister (Ed.), *Contemporary management of motor control problems* (pp. 65–76). Fredericksburg, VA: Bookcrafters.

STUDY QUESTIONS

1. Define the term *transfer of learning.* Describe the three types of transfer of learning that can occur based on the type of influence of previous experiences.

2. What are two reasons proposed to explain why transfer occurs? For each of these, give a motor skill example.

3. What situation characteristics predict negative transfer? Give two motor skill performance examples of these characteristics and indicate why negative transfer would occur.

4. What is bilateral transfer? What is the issue underlying the question of whether bilateral transfer is symmetric or asymmetric?

5. Discuss two hypotheses that attempt to explain why bilateral transfer occurs.

6. Describe how you would organize practice for a skill in which the use of *either* arm or *either* leg to perform the skill would be beneficial.

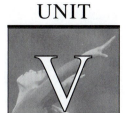

INSTRUCTION AND AUGMENTED FEEDBACK

Demonstration and Verbal Instructions

*Concept: Effective methods of providing instructions
for helping a person to learn motor skills
depend on the skills and the instructional goals*

After completing this chapter, you will be able to

- Describe what an observer perceives from a skilled demonstration of a motor skill, and procedures researchers have used to arrive at this conclusion

- Discuss the influence of beginners observing other beginners as they practice a skill

- Identify the main features of the two predominant theories about how observing a demonstration helps a person learn a motor skill

- Give examples of how instructions can influence where a person directs his or her attention when performing a motor skill

- Define *verbal cues* and give examples of how they can be used in skill learning or relearning situations

Application

If you wanted to instruct someone about how to perform a skill, how would you do it? Probably, you would verbally describe what to do, demonstrate the skill, or use some combination of both approaches. But do you know enough about the effectiveness of these different means of communication to know which one to prefer or when to use each one or both?

Demonstrating skills is undoubtedly the most common means of communicating how to perform them. We find demonstrations in a wide range of skill acquisition situations. For example, a physical education teacher may demonstrate to a large class how to putt in golf. An aerobics teacher may demonstrate to a class how to perform a particular sequence of skills. A baseball coach may show a player the correct form for bunting a ball. In a rehabilitation context, an occupational therapist may demonstrate to a patient how to button a shirt, or a physical therapist may demonstrate to a wheelchair patient how to get from a bed into the chair.

The instructor demonstrates a skill because he or she believes that in this way the learner receives the most amount of information in the least amount of time. But, we should know when demonstration is effective, and when it may be less effective than some other means of communicating how to perform a skill.

Similarly, the instructor should know when verbal instructions are an effective means of communicating how to perform a skill. And if verbal instructions are given, what characterizes the most effective instructions?

Discussion

It is ironic that although demonstration is a very common method of providing information about how to perform a skill, there is not as much research related to it as we might expect. However, in recent years researchers have shown an increased interest in the role of demonstration in motor skill learning.

There seem to be at least two reasons for the increased interest in demonstration and skill learning. One reason is the phenomenal growth of interest in the role of vision in skill learning. Because demonstrating how to do a skill typically involves visual observation on the part of the learner, researchers have been able to use the study of demonstration and skill learning to assess how the visual system is involved in skill acquisition and performance. Another reason for the current interest is that we know so little about how to effectively implement this very common instructional strategy. As a result, researchers have been making an increased effort to improve our understanding of the role of demonstration in skill instruction and learning.

DEMONSTRATION

The terms **modeling** and **observational learning** often are used interchangeably with the term *demonstration*. Because *demonstration* is more specific to the context of instruction about how to perform a skill, we will use this term in this text.

In the most recent comprehensive review of research investigating the role of demonstration in motor skill acquisition, McCullagh and Weiss (2001) discussed evidence that indicates demonstration is more effective under certain circumstances than under others. This conclusion suggests that an instructor should use demonstration only after determining that the instructional situation indeed warrants the use of demonstration, rather than

some other form of providing information about skill performance. In the following sections, we consider some of the concerns that professionals need to take into account before making this instructional decision.

What the Observer Perceives from a Demonstration

The decision about the situations in which demonstration would be preferred should be based on our knowledge of what a person actually "sees" when a skill is demonstrated. Note the use of the word "sees" rather than "looks at." As we pointed out in chapter 6, what we see and what we look at can be very different. What we "see" is what we *perceive* from what we look at. This distinction is particularly relevant to the discussion of demonstration, because what a person perceives from a skill demonstration is not necessarily something that he or she specifically looks at or looks for. It is also important to keep in mind that what we perceive may be at a conscious or nonconscious level of awareness. For example, when people are asked later to describe verbally what they saw in a demonstration that helped them perform a skill, they do not always give a very accurate accounting.

Research evidence has shown consistently that the observer perceives from the demonstration information about the coordination pattern of the skill (e.g., Scully & Newell, 1985; Schoenfelder-Zohdi, 1992; Whiting, 1988). More specifically, *the observer perceives and uses invariant features of the coordinated movement pattern* to develop his or her own movement pattern to perform the skill.

Two types of research evidence support this view. One involves the investigation of the visual perception of motion; the other is the investigation of the influence of demonstration on learning a

---

modeling   the use of demonstration as a means of conveying information about how to perform a skill.

observational learning   learning a skill by observing a person perform the skill; also known as *modeling*.

A CLOSER LOOK

Perceiving a Throwing Action from Observing a Point-Light Display

An experiment by Williams (1988) provides an example of use of the point-light technique. Eighty adults (ages eighteen to twenty-five years) and eighty children (ages fourteen to fifteen years) observed a video point-light display of a side view of the arm of a seated person throwing a small plastic ball at a target (see figure 13.1). The video showed only dots of light at the shoulder, elbow, and wrist joints of the

person throwing the ball. The author showed participants the video three times and then asked them what they had seen. Results showed that 66 percent of the children and 65 percent of the adults responded that they had seen a throwing motion. An additional 25 percent of the adults and 23 percent of the children made this response after seeing the video one additional time.

a.

b.

c.

FIGURE 13.1   An example of use of the point-light technique in motor learning research. (a) shows the model demonstrating the throwing of a small ball at a target. (b) shows a static image of the point-light display of the model's arm with lights at the shoulder, elbow, and wrist joints. (c) shows four still frames of the video shown to subjects. From left to right, these depict the arm at the start of the throw, at maximal flexion, at release of the small ball, and at completion of the throw.   [Reproduced with permission of author and publisher from Williams, J. G. (1989). Visual demonstration and movement production: Effects of timing variations in a model's action. *Perceptual and Motor Skills, 68,* 891–896. © Perceptual and Motor Skills 1989.]

complex skill. Taken together, these two types of research indicate that the visual system automatically detects in a movement pattern invariant information for determining how to produce the observed action. In some manner, which scientists do not fully understand and continue to debate, the person translates the perceived information into movement commands to produce the action.

The Visual Perception of Motion

Research investigating the perception of human motion attempts to answer questions about how people recognize movement patterns they see in their world. An important principle developed from this research is that people rarely use specific characteristics of the individual components of a pattern to make judgments about the pattern. Rather, they use relative information about the relationships among the various components.

Using a procedure known as the **point-light technique,** researchers have identified the relative information involved in the visual perception of human movement. This procedure involves placing lights or bright spots on the joints of a person who is then filmed or videotaped performing an action or skill. Then the researcher plays the film or video so that the person who watches the film or video sees only bright dots in motion. The first reported use of this procedure (Johansson, 1973) showed that people could accurately label different gait patterns, such as walking and running, by observing the moving dot patterns. Later, Cutting and Kozlowski (1977) showed that from observing moving dot patterns, people actually could identify their friends. Using a computer simulation, Hoenkamp (1978) showed that the movement characteristic people use to identify different gait patterns is not any one kinematic variable, but the *ratio of the time duration between the forward and return swings of the lower leg.*

This groundbreaking research on the perception of human movement provided two important conclusions that help our understanding of observational learning. First, people can recognize different gait patterns accurately and quickly without seeing the entire body or all the limbs move. Second, the most critical information people perceive in order to distinguish one type of gait pattern from another is not any one characteristic of the gait, such as velocity of the limbs. Instead, people use the invariant relative time relationship between two components of gait. From these conclusions we can hypothesize that the invariant relationships in coordinated movement constitute the critical information involved in observational learning.

Investigating What the Observer Perceives from a Skilled Demonstration

The second type of research providing evidence about what an observer uses from a skill demonstration provides more direct evidence that people perceive invariant relationships. An example is an experiment by Schoenfelder-Zohdi (1992) in which subjects practiced the slalom ski simulator task shown in figure 13.2. This simulator consisted of two rigid, convex, parallel tracks on which a movable platform stood. A participant stood on the platform with both feet and was required to move the platform to the right and then to the left as far as possible (55 cm to either side) with rhythmic slalom ski–like movements. The platform was connected on either side to each end of the apparatus by strong, springlike rubber bands, which ensured that the platform always returned to the center (normal) position. Thus, the participant had to learn to control the platform movement by using smooth ski–like movements, just as he or she would if actually skiing. Participants practiced this skill for several days after they had either observed a skilled model perform the task or received verbal information about the goal of the task. A movement analysis of limb movements showed that participants who had observed

---

point-light technique a research procedure used to determine the relative information people use to perceive and identify coordinated human actions; it involves placing LEDs or light-reflecting material on certain joints of a person, then filming or videotaping the person performing an action; when an observer views the film or video, he or she sees only joints in action.

FIGURE 13.2   A person performing on the slalom ski simulator. Note that the person has attached LED markers for movement analysis purposes.

the skilled demonstration developed coordinated movement patterns earlier in practice than did those who had not observed the demonstration. Figure 13.3 shows one example of these results.

The Influence of Skill Characteristics

Research investigating the influence on learning of demonstration has produced equivocal findings about the effectiveness of skill demonstration. Some researchers have found that demonstration leads to better skill learning than other forms of instruction; others have found that it does not. But as Magill and Schoenfelder-Zohdi (1996) pointed out, a closer inspection of that research leads to the conclusion that the influence of demonstration on skill acquisition depends on characteristics of the skill being learned. The most important characteristic leading to the beneficial effect of demonstration is that the skill being learned requires the *acquisition of a new pattern of coordination.*

We see this clearly when we organize into two categories the results of research investigating the

effect of demonstration on skill learning. In one category are those experiments in which participants learned more quickly after demonstration than after other forms of instruction. In experiments in this category, participants typically learned skills requiring them to acquire new patterns of limb coordination. In the other category are experiments in which participants usually learned skills no better after observing demonstrations than after receiving other forms of instruction. In these experiments, the participants practiced skills that required them to acquire new parameter characteristics for well-learned patterns of limb coordination.

Observing Skilled Demonstrations

A common guiding principle for demonstrating a skill is that the demonstrator should perform the skill correctly. Why would more accurate demonstration lead to better learning? Two reasons are evident from the research literature. The first reason follows our discussion of perception of inform-

FIGURE 13.3 Angle-angle diagrams of the left knee and left hip for two people practicing on the slalom ski simulator. Both graphs show the relationship of these joints after one day of practice. The top graph is from the person who watched a skilled model demonstrate; the lower graph is from the person who did not watch a demonstration. [From Schoenfelder-Zohdi, B. G. (1992). *Investigating the informational nature of a modeled visual demonstration,* Ph. D. dissertation, Louisiana State University. Reprinted by permission.]

ation in the preceding section. If the observer perceives and uses information related to invariant movement patterns, it is logical to expect the quality of performance resulting from observing a demonstration to be related to the quality of the demonstration. Another reason is that in addition to picking up coordination information, an observer also perceives information about the strategy used by the model to solve the movement problem. Typically, the observer then tries to imitate that strategy on his or her initial attempts at performing the skill.

A CLOSER LOOK

Beginners Learn by Observing Other Beginners: Learning the Tennis Volley

An experiment by Hebert and Landin (1994) nicely illustrates how instructors can facilitate skill acquisition for beginners by having them observe other beginners.

Participants: Female university students who had no previous formal training or regular participation in tennis

Task: tennis forehand volley with the non-dominant hand

Practice procedures: All participants first saw a brief instructional videotape that emphasized the basic elements of the volley

• *Learning model group:* Participants practiced the volley for 50 trials; the instructor provided verbal feedback after each trial. Each student in this group had a student, who was not in this group, observe and listen to a videotape of her practice trials.

• *Observer groups:* After observing the learning models, participants were divided into two groups and began their own 50 trials of practice.

___ *Observer group with verbal feedback:* Participants in this group received verbal feedback from the instructor after each practice trial.

___ *Observer group without verbal feedback:* Participants in this group did not receive verbal feedback from the instructor after each practice trial.

• *Control group:* Participants in this group practiced 50 trials of the volley without having observed the learning model participants or receiving verbal feedback from the instructor.

Results: On a posttest of the volley given after the practice trials, both observer groups performed better than the control group.

Conclusion: Having beginning tennis players observe other beginners practice a skill before they begin to practice will facilitate their learning of the skill.

Novices Observing Other Novices Practice

Although the theoretical predictions and the empirical evidence indicate that it is preferable for beginners to observe skilled demonstrators, evidence indicates that beginners can derive learning benefits even from observing unskilled demonstrators, especially if both the observers and the models are beginners. What this means is that the models are "demonstrators" only in that the observers are watching them practice.

One proposed benefit of this use of demonstration is that it discourages imitation of a skilled model's performance of the skill, and encourages the observer to engage in more active problem solving. We can trace evidence for the benefit of this approach to the 1930s (e.g., Twitmeyer, 1931), although widespread interest in this approach did not develop until Adams (1986) published some experiments. Since then, others have pursued the investigation of the use and benefit of observing an unskilled model (e.g., McCullagh & Meyer, 1997; Pollock & Lee, 1992; Weir & Leavitt, 1990). Results of this research have consistently shown that

beginners who observe other beginners practicing a skill will perform at a higher level when they begin to perform than the beginners they observed.

One way to effectively implement this use of demonstration is by pairing students, athletes, or patients in situations where one of the pair performs the skill while the other observes. After a certain number of trials or amount of time, the pair switches roles. On the basis of what we know from the research literature, learning of the skill can be facilitated for both the performer and the observer by having the teacher, coach, therapist, or some other knowledgeable person provide verbal feedback to the performer. Another effective strategy is to provide the observer of the pair with a checklist of key aspects of the skill. The observer should look for each aspect, check it on the list, and then provide some feedback to the performer. Under these conditions, the observer actively engages in problem-solving activity that is beneficial for learning. The learner observes what the unskilled model does, what the "expert" tells him or her is wrong with the attempt, what the model does to

LAB LINKS

Lab 13 in the Online Learning Center Lab Manual provides an opportunity for you to experience how a beginning learner observing another beginner practice can facilitate the learning of the observer when he or she begins to practice the skill.

correct errors, and how successful he or she is on the succeeding attempts.

The Timing and Frequency of Demonstrating a Skill

One of the reasons for demonstrating a skill is to communicate how to perform the skill. For the beginner, demonstration provides an effective means of communicating the general movement pattern of the action or skill. As we discussed in chapter 11, Gentile considered this to be the goal of the first stage of learning. When applied to the use of demonstration, Gentile's view suggests two things. The first is that it is beneficial to demonstrate a skill *before the person begins practicing it*. The second is that the instructor should *continue demonstrating during practice as frequently as necessary.*

Earlier, we pointed out that a skilled demonstration communicates the invariant characteristics of a movement pattern. If this is the case, then we would expect that the more frequently a beginner observes a skilled demonstration, the more opportunity the beginner will have to acquire the movement pattern. At least two research studies support this latter point. One, by Carroll and Bandura (1990), involves the learning of complex movement patterns of a computer joystick; the other, by Hand and Sidaway (1993), involves the learning of a golf skill. Both experiments provided evidence that more frequent observations of the model yielded better skill learning.

An experiment by Weeks and Anderson (2000), which investigated the issue of the timing of demonstrations, provides some additional insight into both the timing and frequency questions. The demonstrated skill involved a skilled volleyball player hitting an overhand serve. Participants, who had no previous experience hitting this serve, observed a video of 10 demonstrations and performed

30 serves. The all-prepractice group watched all 10 before performing the 30 serves; the interspersed group observed one demonstration and then performed three serves, in series throughout the practice period, and the combination group viewed 5 demonstrations before performing 15 serves, then viewed 5 demonstrations before performing the final 15 serves. All participants performed in two retention tests, which were 5 min and 48 hr respectively after the practice session. The results (figure 13.4) showed the benefit of the combination and all-prepractice conditions, as both led to better form and accuracy scores than the interspersed condition. In terms of the timing and frequency of demonstrations, these results indicate that several demonstrations should precede practice. Although it would be interesting to see how these demonstration schedules would have influenced learning had they been implemented in several days of practice, the results for one practice sessions reveal the importance of prepractice demonstrations.

Auditory Modeling

Our discussion so far has focused on visual demonstration. However, there are skills for which visual demonstration is less effective for learning than other forms of demonstration. An example is a skill for which the goal is to move in a certain criterion movement time or rhythm. For these types of skill, an auditory form of demonstration seems to work best.

A good research example of the effectiveness of auditory modeling when the goal is a specific movement time is an experiment by Doody, Bird, and Ross (1985). The task required people to perform a complex sequential movement with one hand in a criterion movement time of 2.1 sec. Visual and auditory demonstration groups observed a videotape of a skilled model before each practice trial. The visual demonstration group saw only the video portion of the tape and heard no sound. The auditory demonstration group heard only the audio portion of the modeled performance and did not see the task performed by the model. Results indicated that the group that heard the audio portion of the performance did better than the visual demonstration–only group.

FIGURE 13.4 The results of the experiment by Weeks and Anderson showing form and accuracy scores for practice trials and retention tests for an overhand volleyball serve for three groups that observed 10 skilled demonstrations in different amounts and at different times before and during practice. The form scores represent the mean of 10 aspects of form, each rated on a scale of 0 to 5, with 0 indicating a complete absence of the aspect, and 5 indicating the aspect was performed as recommended. [Source: Figures 1 (p. 266) and 2 (p. 267) in Weeks, D. L., & Anderson, L. P. (2002). The interaction of observational learning with overt practice: Effects on motor learning. *Acta Psychologica, 104,* 259–271.]

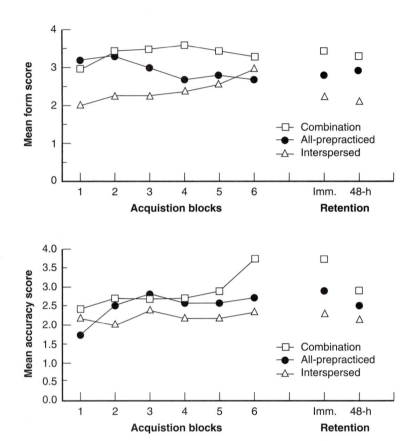

Two research examples of the benefit of auditory modeling to aid the learning of a rhythmic sequence involve a laboratory task and a sequence of dance steps. In an experiment by Wuyts and Buekers (1995), people who had no prior dance or music experience learned a sequence of thirty-two choreographed steps. For acquiring the rhythmic timing of this sequence, participants who heard only the timing structure learned it as well as those who both saw and heard the sequence performed by a model. The second example is an experiment by Lai, Shea, Bruechert, and Little (2002) in which they found that auditory modeling enhanced the learning of a sequence of five time intervals when two keyboard keys were alternately depressed. Before each practice trial, participants heard a sequence of tones that represented the timing sequence they were to learn.

How the Observing of Demonstrations Influences Learning

In terms of learning theory, an important question is this: Why does observing demonstrations benefit motor skill learning? Two different views propose answers to this question.

Cognitive mediation theory. The predominant view is based on the work of Bandura (1986) concerning modeling and social learning. This view, called the **cognitive mediation theory,** proposes that when a person observes a model, he or she translates the observed movement information into a symbolic memory code that forms the basis of a stored representation in memory. The reason the person transforms movement information into a cognitive memory representation is so that the brain can then rehearse and organize the information. The memory representation then serves as a guide for performing the skill and as a standard for error detection and correction. To perform the skill, the person first must access the memory representation and then must translate it back into the appropriate motor control code to produce the body and limb movements. Thus, cognitive processing serves as a mediator between the perception of the movement information and the performance of the skill by establishing a cognitive memory representation between the perception and the action.

According to Bandura, four subprocesses govern observational learning. The first is the *attention process,* which involves what the person observes and the information he or she extracts from the model's actions. Because of the importance of the attention process for learning, directing full attention to the demonstration rather than the mere observation of it is important for optimal learning. The second is the *retention process,* in which the person transforms and restructures what he or she observes into symbolic codes that the person stores in memory. Certain cognitive activities, such as rehearsal, labeling, and organization are involved in the retention process and benefit the development of this representation. The *behavior reproduction process* is the third subprocess; during it, the person translates the memory representation of the modeled action and turns it into physical action. Successful accomplishment of this process requires that the individual possess the physical capability to perform the modeled action. Finally, the *motivation process* involves the incentive or motivation to perform the modeled action. This process, then, focuses on all those factors that influence a person's motivation to perform. Unless this process is completed, the person will not perform the action.

Several research studies have provided support for the cognitive mediation theory by demonstrating evidence that is in line with predictions of the theory. For example, Ste.-Marie (2000) provided support for the prediction that *attention* is an important process in observational learning. In a series of four experiments, participants who had to divide their attention between performing a cognitive secondary task (counting backwards by threes)

and observing a model did not learn the skill as well as those who did not perform a secondary task. In an experiment discussed in chapter 9, Smyth and Pendleton (1990) showed that the prevention of the *rehearsal* process hindered learning a skill. In their experiment, some participants engaged in movement activity during the interval of time between the demonstration of a sequence of movements and their attempts to reproduce those movements. These participants recalled fewer movements than those who did not engage in activity during this time interval. And Blandin and Proteau (2000) provided evidence that observational learning involves the development of effective *error detection and correction,* which the cognitive mediation theory describes as an important function of the memory representation that develops during observational learning. In two experiments, participants' estimations of their performance error, and their use of that estimation on the next practice trials, were similar for an observational learning situation and one in which participants did not observe a model.

Dynamic view of modeling. The second view is based on the direct perception view of vision proposed many years ago by J. J. Gibson (1966, 1979). Scully and Newell (1985) adapted Gibson's view to the visual observation of a skilled demonstration and proposed the **dynamic view of modeling** as an alternative to Bandura's theory. The dynamic view questions the need for a symbolic coding step

---

cognitive mediation theory   a theory for explaining the benefit of a demonstration proposing that when a person observes a skilled model, the person translates the observed movement information into a cognitive code that the person stores in memory and uses when the observer performs the skill.

dynamic view of modeling   a theoretical view explaining the benefit of observing a skilled model demonstrate a skill; it proposes that the visual system is capable of automatically processing the observed movement in a way that constrains the motor control system to act accordingly, so that the person does not need to engage in cognitive mediation.

(the memory representation step) between the observation of the modeled action and the physical performance of that action. Instead, it maintains, the visual system is capable of automatically processing visual information in such a way that it constrains the motor control system to act according to what the vision detects. The visual system "picks up" from the model salient information that effectively constrains the body and limbs to act in specific ways. The person does not need to transform the information received via the visual system into a cognitive code and store it in memory. This is the case because the visual information directly provides the basis for coordination and control of the various body parts required to produce the action. Thus, the critical need for the observer in the early stage of learning is to observe demonstrations that enable him or her to perceive the important invariant coordination relationships between body parts. Additional observations of the model will benefit the learner by helping the person learn to parameterize the action.

In addition to the type of research evidence provided in the experiment by Schoenfelder-Zohdi (1992), which we considered earlier, evidence based on the use of the point-light display as the model has supported the prediction that the observer of a skilled demonstration perceives invariant coordination characteristics. An experiment by Horn, Williams, and Scott (2002) is a good example of this type of evidence. Female novice soccer players viewed a video of a skilled performer, a point-light display of a skilled performer, or no model. The skill involved chipping a soccer ball a distance of 5 m over a barrier (.35 m height) onto a target area located 2.5 m from the barrier. The point-light display, which was made from the video of the model performing the skill, showed 18 light-reflecting markers attached to the models major joints. The video and point-light display were shown life-size to the participants on a screen at three different times during the practice session. The results showed that during practice and on a retention test, target accuracy was similar for the video and point-light display groups, with both groups more accurate than the no-model group.

And the kinematic characteristics were similar for participants in the video and point-light display groups. As a result, the evidence provides support for the dynamic view's contention that the observer detects and uses coordination information based on the movement of limb segments, which is the only information the point-light display provided.

Which view is correct? Unfortunately, there is no conclusive evidence in the research literature that shows one of these two views of the modeling effect to be the more valid one. As you saw in the discussions of each view, both have research support for some specific assertions. As a result, until we have research evidence that one view cannot explain, we must consider with view as a possible explanation of why modeling benefits skill acquisition. The cognitive mediation theory has been the more prominent of the two, receiving more attention in motor skills research. However, the dynamic view is growing in popularity.

VERBAL INSTRUCTIONS AND CUES

Verbal instructions rank with demonstration as a commonly used means of communicating to people how to perform motor skills. Evidence supports the value of verbal instructions for facilitating skill acquisition. Several factors are particularly important for developing effective verbal instruction.

Verbal Instructions and Attention

An important performer characteristic we discussed in chapter 8 that relates to giving verbal instructions is that the person has a limited capacity to attend to information. Because of this limitation, the instructor must take into account the quantity of instructions. It is easy to overwhelm the person with instructions about what to do to perform a skill. We can reasonably expect that a beginner will have difficulty paying attention to more than one or two instructions about what to do. Because the beginner will need to divide attention between remembering the instructions and actually performing the skill, a minimal amount of verbal information can exceed the person's attention-

A CLOSER LOOK

Implementing Demonstration in Skill Instruction Settings

- Keep in mind that demonstrating a skill will have its greatest benefit when the skill being learned requires the acquisition of a *new pattern of coordination*. Examples include learning to serve in tennis, learning a new dance step, and learning to get into a wheelchair from a bed.
- Be aware that if the skill being learned involves learning a new control parameter characteristic for a previously learned pattern of coordination, demonstration will probably be no more beneficial than verbal instructions. Examples include learning to throw a ball at different speeds, learning to kick a ball from different distances, and learning to grasp and lift different sizes of cups.
- Demonstrate the skill several times before the observer attempts to perform it, and then as frequently as necessary after that during practice.
- To reduce a potential attention-capacity overload, do not give a continuous verbal commentary while demonstrating the skill. If it is important to direct

- the observers' attention to key aspects of the skill, use short, concise attention-directing verbal cues as needed.
- Be certain the observer can see the critical features of the skill you are demonstrating. It may be helpful to verbally direct the observer's attention to these features just before the demonstration.
- If you cannot demonstrate a skill very well, use some other way to provide a skilled demonstration, such as a film or videotape, or another person who can demonstrate the skill.
- In some situations, allow beginners to observe other beginners practice a skill. This can be an effective use of demonstration, and works well when there is limited space and/or equipment for every person in a group to perform the skill at the same time.
- Use auditory demonstrations of timing and rhythm goals. This is an effective way to communicate how to achieve these types of action goals.

---

capacity limits. In addition to concerns about attention capacity, the instructor should include other important attention-related considerations when giving verbal instructions. Several of these are discussed in the following sections.

Verbal Instructions to Focus Attention on Movement Outcomes

An important function of instructions is to direct learners' attention to focus on the features of the skill or environmental context that will enhance their performance of the skill. A key point with regard to the content of these instructions relates to our discussion of attention and consciousness in chapter 8. Recall that attention can be either conscious or nonconscious, with the person either aware or not aware of what is being attended to. When we relate this point to attention focus during the performance of a motor skill, we need to consider the research evidence we briefly discussed in chapter 8, which showed that a key part of skill learning is *where* a person directs his or her con-

scious attention when performing a skill. That research evidence was based on investigations of the **action effect hypothesis** (Prinz, 1997), which proposes that actions are best planned and controlled by their intended effects. The theory basis for this hypothesis relates to how we code sensory and motor information in memory. Prinz contends that we represent both in memory in a common code, which argues against the separation of perception and action as unique and distinct events. Without going further into the theory issues involved, the common coding view predicts that actions will be more effective when they are planned in terms of

action effect hypothesis the proposition that actions are best planned and controlled by their intended effects. When related to attention focus, this hypothesis proposes that the learning and performance of skills are optimized when the performer's attention is directed to the intended outcome of the action rather than on the movements themselves.

their intended outcomes rather than in terms of the movement patterns required by the skill. To test the action effect hypothesis in motor skill learning situations, researchers have designed experiments in which instructions that direct participants' attention to their own movements are compared to those that direct attention to the movement outcome (see Wulf & Prinz, 2001, for a review of this research).

The following research examples illustrate two types of experiments that have tested and supported the action effect hypothesis. And they demonstrate *two different ways to give verbal instructions to direct attention to movement outcomes.* The first involves instructions presented in a way that establishes a *discovery learning* situation. This means that the instructions focus the learner's attention on the action goal of the skill. Then, as the learner practices the skill, he or she "discovers" how to move to achieve that goal. The second example involves the *use of imagery* in instructions, which directs the learner's attention to move according to the image, which is the intended movement outcome of the skill.

In a study reported by Wulf and Weigelt (1997) participants practiced the slalom-ski simulator task (described earlier in this chapter and pictured in figure 13.2). Everyone was told that the goal of the task was to continuously move the platform for 90 sec as far as possible to the left and right at a rate of one complete cycle every 2 sec. Participants in one group were also told to try to exert force on the platform after it passed the center of the ski simulator, based on a movement characteristic of people who demonstrated high performance levels on the ski simulator. Another group was not given this additional instruction, which means the only instructions they received concerned the action goal (i.e., the desired effect of their movements). Because they were told only about the action goal, this group experienced a discovery learning situation.

As figure 13.5 shows, the additional movement attention-directing instructions led to poorer performance during practice trials and on a transfer test in which participants performed under stress (they were told they were being observed and evaluated by a skiing expert). Interestingly, in a follow-

up experiment, which was based on the assumption that more experience with the task would allow participants to direct more attention to the specific information in the instructions, the attention-directing instructions were given after three days of practice. But, once again, rather than aid learning, the instructions had a negative effect.

An experiment in which instructions used *imagery* to direct attention to the movement outcome was reported by Wulf, Lauterbach, and Toole (1999). Participants, who were university students with no previous experience playing golf, practiced hitting golf pitch shots into a circular target from a distance of 15 m. Everyone was given the same demonstration and instructions about the stance and how to grip the club. But one group was told to focus their attention on the swinging motion of the arms during each swing. These participants also received specific instructions about the various movements involved in the swing, and practiced several swings without holding a club before they practiced hitting a ball. A second group was told to focus their attention on the club head's pathway during the back- and down-swing (i.e., the "action effect"). They received specific instructions that emphasizes the pendulum-like motion of the club. The results showed that the participants who directed their attention to the club movement consistently produced higher target accuracy scores during practice trials and on a 24-hr retention test.

The instructions that involved imagery to direct participants' attention to the outcome of their movements told them to consider the club to be a pendulum and to focus their attention on the pendulum-like motion. Recall from the discussion in chapter 9 that the use of imagery is an effective strategy to help remember how to perform a skill. Now, we see that a reason for this is that the use of imagery focuses attention to movement outcomes rather than to the movements themselves.

Verbal Instructions to Focus Attention on Invariant Environmental Context Regulatory Conditions

Another issue associated with directing attention and the content of instructions relates to telling peo-

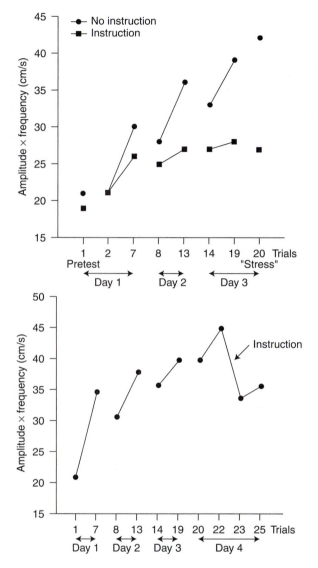

FIGURE 13.5 The top graph shows the results of the first experiment by Wulf and Weigelt which compared a group that received instructions about a movement component of the slalom ski simulator task and a group that did not receive the instructions. The bottom graph shows the results of their second experiment in which one group received the movement component instructions on the fourth day of practice. [Reprinted with permission from *Research Quarterly for Exercise and Sport,* Vol. 1, No. 4, 262–367. Copyright © 1997 by the American Alliance for Health, Physical Education, Recreation and Dance, 1900 Association Drive, Reston, VA 20191.]

ple what in the environment to look for that will help them perform a skill. The importance of this issue relates to a critical goal of the initial stage of learning, accordingly to Gentile's learning stages model. As we discussed in chapter 11, this goal is to learn the regulatory conditions that direct the movements required to achieve the action goal of the skill.

Sometimes we ask people to tell us what they were looking for or looking at when they performed a skill, so that we can help them correct their visual attention focus. However, research investigating the need for conscious awareness of environmental cues when learning skills reveals that these types of techniques do not have to be included in the student-teacher or patient-therapist interaction. This research shows that we learn to select relevant cues from the environment without being consciously aware of what those cues are.

A good example of research demonstrating that people attend to and use invariant environmental

FIGURE 13.6   The results of the experiment by Magill, Schoenfelder-Zohdi, and Hall (1990) showing the superior performance on the repeated segment A compared to the random segments B and C for a complex tracking task. [Source: R. A. Magill, et al., "Further Evidence for Implicit Learning in a Complex Tracking Task" paper presented at the annual meeting of the Psychonomics Society, November, 1990, New Orleans, LA.]

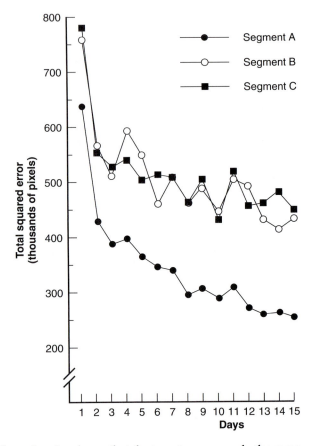

context features without conscious awareness of them is an experiment reported by Magill (1998). Participants watched a target cursor move in a complex waveform pattern across a computer monitor screen for 60 sec. The participants' task involved pursuit tracking of the target cursor: they were to manipulate a lever on a tabletop to make their own cursor stay as close as possible to the target cursor. The unique feature of the target cursor movement was that it moved randomly for the second and third 20-sec segments on every trial, but it made the same movements on every trial during the first 20-sec segment. The participants practiced this pursuit-tracking task for approximately twenty-four trials on each of fifteen days. The results, shown in figure 13.6, indicated that as they practiced, they performed better on the first segment than on the other two segments. But what is more important is that when interviewed, none of the participants indicated

that they knew that the target cursor made the same pattern during the first segment on every trial. Thus the participants attended to and used the regularity of the cursor movement during the first segment, even though they were not consciously aware of that characteristic. This lack of conscious awareness of the invariant movement pattern of the target cursor indicates that the participants *implicitly* learned the regulatory environmental context features that directed their movements as they tracked the target cursor.

Although the research just described indicates that people can learn to use relevant environmental context features without being instructed to look for them, there is a common assumption that we can facilitate skill learning by giving instructions that would make people aware of these features. For example, a tennis teacher may tell a student that a certain racquet-head angle at ball contact

A CLOSER LOOK

Training Anticipatory Skills in Tennis with an Implicit Instructional Strategy

An objective of tennis instruction is to enhance players' capabilities to anticipate as early as possible the direction of a ball hit by an opponent. This objective was at the heart of an experiment by Farrow and Abernethy (2002) in which they compared two training techniques designed to increase junior tennis players' anticipation skills for returning serves. Both techniques were based on the hypothesis that the sources of information used by the skilled players to anticipate serve direction could be used to train less skilled players. All participants experienced the following sequence of tests and training: *Pretest—Training (4 wks, 3 days/wk)—Posttest—Retention Test (32 days later)*

Tests and Training

Participants watched videotapes of skilled players' serves, which were from the receiver's view. During the tests, their task was to indicate as quickly as possible whether the serve direction was to their forehand or backhand. On some trials they verbally indicated the direction, while on others they moved with their racquets in the direction. Tapes were edited and programmed to stop at one of five time periods before and after racquet-ball contact (i.e., temporal occlusion): T1—900 ms before ball contact (start of ball toss); T2—600 ms before ball contact (ball toss almost at zenith); T3—300 ms before ball contact (racquet at top of backswing); T4—at ball contact; T5—after follow-through. Each training session consisted of watching temporally occluded videotapes of various professional tennis players hitting serves and then physically practicing the return of 50 serves.

Training Techniques

Explicit instruction: Participants received specific instruction about the relationship between information sources in the server's action and the direction of a serve. These sources were highlighted in instructional videos, verbal and written information, and verbal feedback provided during the physical practice trials.

Implicit instruction: participants received no specific instruction about the relationship between information sources in the server's action and the direction of a serve. They were told that their task was to estimate the speed of each serve seen on the videotape.

Results

Explicit rule information: Before and after the four-week training period, participants were asked to write down all the rules, coaching tips, and strategies they thought were important for returning serves. After training, the explicit training group wrote an average of 2.5 rules, while the implicit training group wrote an average of .5 rules.

Serve direction prediction accuracy: Overall, both training groups improved from the pretest to the posttest. But 7 of the 8 participants in the implicit training group improved prediction accuracy *at ball contact,* compared to 3 of 8 in the explicit group.

Conclusion

Although the prediction accuracy differences between the two training conditions were relatively minor, their similarity is important. That the implicit training led to test performance that was similar to that of explicit training indicates that the anticipatory information required to predict serve direction can be learned without being consciously aware of the specific sources for the information. However, it is important to note two important characteristics of the implicit training condition:

1. The participants directed attention to the server and the serve on each videotape, because they had to estimate the speed of the serve.

2. The training period involved a large number of trials of observing a variety of servers and serves that were temporally occluded at various times before and after each serve.

during a serve indicates a specific type of serve, which the student should try to look for to predict that type of serve. However, what is not so commonly known is that this type of instruction could actually hinder rather than facilitate learning, especially when the specific features looked for occur infrequently in a series of trials.

Green and Flowers (1991) reported an experiment that serves as a good example of the research evidence demonstrating this negative effect.

Participants played a computer game in which they manipulated a joystick to move a paddle horizontally across the bottom of the monitor to try to catch a "ball," which was a dot of light, that moved for 2.5 sec from the top to the bottom of the screen. The ball moved according to one of eight pathways. On 75 percent of the trials, the ball made deviations from the normal pathway that predicted the specific final position of the ball. Thus, participants' detection of these pathway-deviations characteristics could help them increase their catching accuracy. One group of participants received explicit instructions about these characteristics and their probability of occurring; the other group did not. Participants practiced for five days for a total of 800 trials. The results showed that both groups improved. However, the explicit-instructions group made more errors than the group that had had no instruction. The authors concluded that the instructed participants directed so much of their attentional resources to trying to remember the rule and looking for its occurrence that their performance was disrupted, because they did not have sufficient attention to devote to the catching task itself.

Verbal Instructions Influence Goal Achievement Strategies

Another factor that we need to consider is that verbal instructions direct the person's attention to certain performance goals of the skill. A good example of this is the way verbal instructions can bias the strategy a person uses to learn skills that must be performed both quickly and accurately. An experiment by Blais (1991) illustrates this type of strategy bias. The task was a serial pursuit tracking task in which participants controlled a device like a steering wheel to align a pointer in one of four positions on a screen in front of them. When a target position was illuminated, a participant had to move the pointer to that small area as quickly and as accurately as possible. When the person had achieved that goal, another target area was illuminated. This process was repeated many times. Three groups of participants received verbal in-structions that emphasized being accurate, being fast, or being both accurate and fast.

The instruction emphasis was especially evident during the first of the five days of practice. On this day, the "speed instruction" group recorded the fastest movement times, whereas the "accuracy group" produced the most accurate performance. An interesting result was that the group told to emphasize both speed and accuracy adopted a strategy that led to fast movement times—but at the expense of performance accuracy. And although the "accuracy instruction" group performed the most accurately, its participants did so in a manner that eventually gave them the fastest average overall response time, which included reaction time, movement time, and movement-correction time for errors. Thus, for this task, where both speed and accuracy were equally important for overall performance, instructions emphasizing accuracy led to the best achievement of the two-component goal.

Verbal Cues

One of the potential problems associated with verbal instructions is that they can contain too little or too much information and not provide the learner with what he or she needs to know to achieve the goal of the skill. To overcome this problem, instructors can use verbal cues to direct people to know what to do to perform skills (Landin, 1994). **Verbal cues** are short, concise phrases that serve to (1) direct the performer's attention to regulatory conditions in the environmental context, or (2) prompt key movement components of skills. For example, the cue "Look at the ball" directs visual attention, whereas the cue "Bend your knee" prompts an essential movement component. Research has shown these short, simple statements to be very effective as verbal instructions to facilitate learning new skills, as well as performing well-learned skills.

Teachers, coaches, or therapists can implement verbal cues in several different ways in skill learning settings. One way is to *give verbal cues along with a demonstration* to supplement the visual information (e.g., McCullagh, Stiehl, & Weiss, 1990;

A CLOSER LOOK

Considerations for Experts When Giving Verbal Instructions to Novices

We generally assume that beginners should be taught by people who are highly skilled in the activity to be learned. However, highly skilled performers (i.e., experts) can have problems when they give verbal instructions to beginners. We might expect certain types of problems because of some of the differences between experts and novices that we considered in chapter 11. Two differences that are especially relevant are these:

- *Their knowledge structures about the skill.* Compared to those of novices, experts' knowledge structures tend to be more conceptual and organized, with more interrelationship among the concepts. Novices, on the other hand, tend to have knowledge structures that involve more concrete and specific pieces of information, with few concepts and interrelationships among them.
- *The attention demands required to perform the skill.* Novices need to direct conscious attention

to more, and different, aspects of the performance of a skill than experts.

An experiment by Hinds, Patterson, and Pfeffer (2001) provides some evidence and insight about the problems experts can have providing instructions to novices. In this experiment, experts in the domain of electronics instructed novices about how to build an electronic circuit, which involved connecting wires in specific ways to make the electronic components for several different devices, such as a radio, motion detector, etc. Results showed that the experts provided instruction that was too conceptual and included too few concrete details to guide the novices. Interestingly, the experts' self-reported assessment of their teaching skill did not correlate well with the type of instructions they provided.

Zetou, Tzetzis, Vernadakis, & Rioumourtzoglou, 2002). When used this way, verbal cues aid in directing attention, and can guide rehearsal of the skill a person is learning. One caution about this use of verbal cues is that they may interrupt attention to the relative time patterns of skills and actually hinder skill learning (see Wiese-Bjornstal & Weiss, 1992).

Another way to use verbal cues is to *give cues to help learners focus on critical parts of skills.* For example, in an experiment by Masser (1993), first-grade classes were taught to do headstands. In one class, before students made each attempt to swing their legs up into the headstands, the instructor said, "Shoulders over your knuckles," to emphasize the body position critical to performing this skill. The cued students maintained their acquired skill three months after practice, whereas the students who had not received this verbal cue performed the headstand poorly three months later. A similar result occurred in an experiment using verbal cues to emphasize critical parts of the forward roll.

Performers also can *use verbal cues while performing* to cue themselves to attend to or perform key aspects of skills. Cutton and Landin (1994) provided a research example demonstrating the effectiveness of this technique for nonskilled individuals. Instructors taught university students in a beginning tennis class five verbal cues to say out loud each time they were required to hit a ball. These were as follows: "ready," to prompt preparation for the oncoming ball; "ball," to focus attention on the ball itself; "turn," to prompt proper body position to hit the ball, which included turning the hips and shoulders to be perpendicular with the net and pointing the racquet toward the back fence; "hit," to focus attention on contacting the ball; and

---

verbal cues short, concise phrases that direct a performer's attention to important environmental regulatory characteristics, or that prompt the person to perform key movement pattern components of skills.

A CLOSER LOOK

Guidelines for Using Verbal Cues for Skill Instruction and Rehabilitation

- Cues should be short statements of one, two, or three words.
- Cues should relate logically to the aspects of the skill to be prompted by the cues.
- Cues can prompt a sequence of several movements.
- Cues should be limited in number. Cue only the most critical elements of performing the skill.

- Cues can be especially helpful for directing shifts of attention.
- Cues are effective for prompting a distinct rhythmic structure for a sequence of movements.
- Cues must be carefully timed so that they serve as prompts and do not interfere with performance.
- Cues should initially be spoken by the performer.

"head down," to prompt the stationary position of the head after ball contact. The students who used verbal cues learned tennis groundstrokes better than those who did not, including a group that received verbal feedback during practice.

Verbal cues have also been used to *improve the performance of skilled athletes*. For example, Landin and Hebert (1999) had university female varsity tennis players use self-cueing to help them improve their volleying skills. Players learned to say the word "split," to cue them to hop to a balanced two-foot stop that would allow them to move in any direction. Then, they said, "turn," to cue them to turn their shoulders and hips to the ball. Finally, they said, "hit," to direct their attention to tracking the ball to the point of contact on the racquet and to cue themselves to keep the head still and hit the ball solidly. After practicing this cueing strategy for five weeks, the players showed marked improvements in both performance and technique.

Verbal cues can be used for two different purposes. Sometimes the cue *directs attention* to a specific environmental event or to specific sources of regulatory information (in our example, "ready," "ball," and "hit" are such cues). In other cases, the cue *prompts action,* for either a specific movement ("head down") or a sequence of movements ("turn"). The key to the effectiveness of verbal cues is that as the person practices and continues to use the cues, an association develops between the cue and the act it prompts. The benefit is that the person does not need to give attention to a large number of verbal instructions and can focus attention on the important perceptual and movement components of the skill.

SUMMARY

In this chapter, we discussed demonstration and verbal instructions and cues as effective means of communicating information about how to perform motor skills.

Demonstration
- A benefit of observing a skilled demonstration is that the observer detects the invariant characteristics of the movement pattern involved in the performance of the skill.
- Demonstration tends to be a more effective means of instruction when the skill being learned requires a new coordination of movement than when it involves a new parameter of a well-learned coordination pattern.
- Observation by a beginner of another beginner practicing a skill can lead to skill learning benefits.
- Skills should be demonstrated several times before a beginner practices a skill, with additional demonstrations during practice as needed.
- Auditory forms of demonstration are effective for the learning of motor skills that has a specific overall movement time goal and skills that require a specific rhythmic sequence or beat.
- Two prominent theoretical views that propose explanations for the benefit of demonstration on skill learning are
  ‣ The *cognitive mediation theory,* which proposes that observation of a demonstration leads to the development of a memory representation of the observed skill that the performer must access prior to performing the skill.

▸ The *dynamic view* which proposes that people do not need cognitive mediation because the visual system can constrain the motor control system to act according to what has been observed.

Verbal Instructions and Cues

- Several attention-related factors are important to consider when using verbal instructions to communicate how to perform a motor skill:
  ▸ Instructions should take into account learners' attention-capacity limitations.
  ▸ According to the movement effect hypothesis, instructions should direct the learner's focus of attention on movement outcomes rather than to the movements themselves.
  ▸ Novice learners can learn invariant environmental context regulatory conditions without conscious awareness of them (i.e., implicit learning), although attention focus on the environmental context is important.
  ▸ Instructions influence the novice learner to direct attention to certain performance goals, which influences the strategies the learner uses to begin practicing a skill.
- Verbal cues are short concise phrases that serve to
  ▸ Direct the performer's attention to regulatory conditions in the environmental context.
  ▸ Prompt key movement components of skills.
- Verbal cues can be given by an instructor or the performer to
  ▸ Direct an observer's attention during a demonstration of a skill.
  ▸ Direct a performer's attention to critical parts of skills.
- Verbal cues can help beginners learn a new skill, or skilled performers improve performance.

RELATED READINGS

Almeida, Q. J., Wishart, L. R., & Lee, T. D. (2002). Bimanual coordination deficits with Parkinson's disease: The influence of movement speed and external cueing. *Movement Disorders, 17,* 30–37.

Black, C. B., & Wright, D. L. (2002). Can observational practice facilitate error recognition and movement production? *Research Quarterly for Exercise and Sport, 71,* 331–339.

Deakin, J. M., & Proteau, L. (2002). The role of scheduling in learning through observation. *Journal of Motor Behavior, 32,* 268–276.

Laugier, C., & Cadopi, M. (1996). Representational guidance of dance performance in adult novices: Effect of concrete vs. abstract movements. *International Journal of Sport Psychology, 27,* 91–108.

McNevin, N. H., Wulf, G., Carlson, C. (200). Effects of attentional focus, self-control, and dyad training on motor learning: Implications for physical rehabilitation. *Physical Therapy, 80,* 373–385.

Starek, J., & McCullagh, P. (1999). The effect of self-modeling on the performance of beginning swimmers. *The Sport Psychologist, 13,* 269–287.

Sweeting, T., & Rink, J. E. (1999). Effects of direct instruction and environmentally designed instruction on the process and product characteristics of a fundamental skill. *Journal of Teaching Physical Education, 18,* 216–233.

Wulf, G., Shea, C., & Park, J. H. (2001). Attention and motor performance: Preferences for and advantages of an external focus. *Research Quarterly for Exercise & Sport, 72,* 335–344.

STUDY QUESTIONS

1. What are two types of research evidence that show that observing a skilled demonstration of a motor skill influences the acquisition of the coordination characteristics of the skill?

2. Describe how observing an unskilled person learning a skill could help a beginner learn that skill.

3. What are the main features of the two predominant theories about how observing a demonstration helps a person to learn that skill? How do these theories differ?

4. Describe two issues of concern that relate to instructions influencing *where* a person directs his or her attention when performing a motor skill.

5. Describe two purposes for using verbal cues. Give an example for each.

CHAPTER

Augmented Feedback

*Concept: Augmented feedback provides information
that can facilitate skill learning*

After completing this chapter, you will be able to

- Distinguish between task-intrinsic feedback and augmented feedback as they relate to performing a motor skill

- Define *KR* and *KP* and give examples of each

- Describe skill learning conditions in which augmented feedback would or would not influence learning

- Compare and contrast quantitative and qualitative augmented feedback

- Describe situations in which various types of augmented feedback, such as videotape replay, movement kinematics, and biofeedback would be effective for facilitating skill learning

- Identify situations in which concurrent augmented feedback would be beneficial or detrimental to skill learning

- Describe two time intervals associated with the giving of terminal augmented feedback during practice and how their lengths and the activity during each influence skill learning

- Describe various ways to reduce the frequency of giving augmented feedback as ways to facilitate skill learning

Application

Think about a time when you were beginning to learn a new physical activity. How much success did you experience on your first few attempts? Most likely, you were not very successful. As you practiced, you probably had many questions that you needed someone to answer to help you better understand what you were doing wrong and what you needed to do to improve. Although you may have been able to answer many of your questions on your own as you continued to try different

things while you practiced, you found that getting an answer from the instructor saved you time and energy.

This situation is an example of what commonly occurs in the early stage of learning a skill. It is equally typical for a person learning a new sport skill and a person relearning a skill following an injury or illness. The significance of this example is that it points out that an important role played by the teacher, coach, or therapist is to give augmented feedback to the learner to facilitate the skill acquisition process.

Consider the following situations. Suppose that you are teaching a golf swing to a class, or working in a clinic with a patient learning to walk with an artificial limb. In each situation, the people practicing these skills can make lots of mistakes and will benefit from receiving augmented feedback. When they make mistakes, which they do in abundance when they are beginners, how do you know which mistakes to tell them to correct on subsequent attempts? If you had a video camera available, would you videotape them and then let them watch their own performances? Or would it be even more beneficial to take the videotapes and have them analyzed so that you could show them what their movements looked like kinematically? There are many ways to provide augmented feedback. But before you as the instructor, coach, or therapist use any one of these, you should know how to implement that method most effectively and when to use it to facilitate learning.

Discussion

When people perform a motor skill, they can have available to them *two general types of performance-related information (i.e., feedback)* that will "tell" them something about the outcome of the performance or about what caused that outcome. One is **task-intrinsic feedback,** which is the sensory-perceptual information that is a natural part of performing a skill. Each of the sensory systems can provide this type of feedback. We discussed two of these in chapter 6: proprioception and vision. For example, if a person throws a dart at a target on the wall, he or she receives *visual* task-intrinsic feedback from seeing the flight of the dart and where it lands on the target. In addition, the person receives *proprioceptive* task-intrinsic feedback movement of his or her body posture along with arm and hand movement as the person prepares to throw the dart and as the dart is thrown. Other sensory systems can also provide task-intrinsic feedback, as does the *auditory* system when the person hears the dart hit, or not hit, the target.

The second general type of performance-related information is *in addition to* task-intrinsic feedback. Although various terms have been used to

identify this type of feedback, the term that will be used in this book is **augmented feedback.**[1] This adjective "augmented" refers to adding to or enhancing something, which in this case involves *adding to or enhancing task-intrinsic feedback.* It *enhances* the task-intrinsic feedback when augmented feedback provides information the person's sensory system can readily detect on its own. For example, a teacher or coach might tell a golfer where his or her hands were positioned at the top of the swing, even though the person could feel for himself or herself where they were. In a clinical environment, a therapist might show an amputee patient EMG traces on a computer monitor to enhance the patient's own proprioceptive feedback to help the patient activate appropriate muscles when learning to operate a prosthetic device.

In other situations, augmented feedback *adds* information that the person cannot detect using his or her sensory system. For example, the golf teacher or coach might tell the golfer where the ball went because the golfer was concentrating so much on keeping his or her head down during the swing that he or she did not see it after it was hit. Likewise, a therapist might tell a clinical patient how much his or her body swayed because vestibular problems prevent the patient from being able to detect this information. In each of these situations, augmented feedback provides performance information that otherwise would not be available to the person.

---

[1] Some researchers and motor learning textbooks use the term *task-extrinsic feedback* to refer to augmented feedback.

---

task-intrinsic feedback   the sensory feedback that is naturally available while performing a skill.

augmented feedback   a generic term used to describe information about performing a skill that is added to sensory feedback and comes from a source external to the person performing the skill; it is sometimes referred to as extrinsic or external feedback.

THE FEEDBACK FAMILY

Note that the term *feedback* is common to both categories of performance-related information described in the preceding paragraphs. As a result, it is important to consider the term "feedback" as a generic term that describes information people receive about their performance of a motor skill during or after the performance. To help conceptualize the relationship between the two general types of performance-related feedback, consider these two types of feedback as related members of the same family. Figure 14.1 graphically describes the feedback family relationships for task-intrinsic feedback and augmented feedback, as well as for the related specific types of each.

TYPES OF AUGMENTED FEEDBACK

In Figure 14.1, note that there are *two categories of types of augmented feedback:* knowledge of results and knowledge of performance. Each category can involve a variety of ways of presenting augmented feedback; this will be the topic of discussion later in this chapter.

Knowledge of Results (KR)

The category of augmented feedback known as **knowledge of results** (commonly referred to as **KR**) consists of *externally presented information about the outcome of performing a skill or about achieving the goal of the performance.* In some situations, KR describes something about the perfor-

mance outcome (i.e., result). For example, if a teacher tells a student in an archery class, "The shot was in the blue at 9 o'clock," the teacher is providing performance outcome information. Similarly, if a therapist shows a patient a computer-generated graph indicating that this leg extension was 3 degrees more than the last one, the therapist is giving KR to the patient about the outcome of his or her leg extension movement.

Sometimes, KR does not describe the performance outcome, but simply tells the performer whether he or she has achieved the goal of the performance. This is the case when some external device gives a "yes" or "no" signal indicating whether or not the performance goal was achieved. For example, to augment proprioceptive and visual feedback for a patient working on achieving a goal leg extension, the therapist could set a buzzer to be activated when the patient achieved the goal number of degrees of movement. Although the buzzer would provide no information about how close to the goal or how far from it the movement was if it had not been achieved, the patient would know that he or she had not achieved the goal unless the buzzer sounded. See table 14.1 for some additional examples.

It is important to point out that KR refers to a type of augmented feedback. Although a person can obtain knowledge about the results of an action from his or her own sensory system, such as seeing whether the basketball missed the basket or went in, this type of performance-related information is task-intrinsic. It does not refer to the specific type

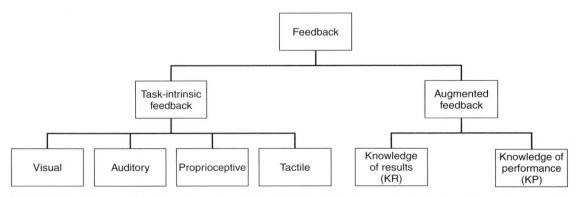

FIGURE 14.1   Illustration of the different types of feedback in the feedback family that are related to learning and performing motor skills.

TABLE 14.1   Examples of Augmented Feedback

• **A golf instructor tells a student:**	**KR** ➔ "Your shot went into the right rough."
	KP ➔ "You did not take your backswing back far enough before you began your downswing."
• **A physical therapist tells a patient:**	**KR** ➔ "You walked 10 feet more today than you did yesterday."
	KP ➔ "You should bend your knees more as you walk."
• **A student driver in a simulator**	**KR** ➔ sees the number of errors he or she made after completing a session.
	KP ➔ sees a light flash each time he or she makes an error while driving in a session.
• **A sprinter in track**	**KR** ➔ sees a posting on the scoreboard of the amount of time to run the race.
	KP ➔ sees a videotape replay of his or her race.
• **A gymnast**	**KR** ➔ sees the judges' scores after completing a routine.
	KP ➔ looks at a computer monitor to see a stick figure representation of his or her body, limb, and head displacement when he or she performed the routine.
• **A knee rehabilitation patient**	**KR** ➔ reads a display on an exercise machine that indicates the number of degrees of leg extension he or she had on that leg extension exercise repetition.
	KP ➔ hears a buzzer when a target muscle is active during a leg extension exercise.

---

of performance-related information the term KR refers to in this text. The importance of this distinction is that it allows us to distinguish the specific influences of task-intrinsic and augmented feedback on skill learning.

Knowledge of Performance (KP)

The second category of augmented feedback is **knowledge of performance** (known as **KP**). This is information about the *movement characteristics that led to the performance outcome.* The important point here is that KP differs from KR in terms of which aspect of performance the information refers to. For example, in the archery situation described above, the teacher would provide KP by telling the student that he or she pulled the bow to the left at the release of the arrow. Here, the teacher augments the task-intrinsic feedback by telling the student what he or she did that caused the arrow to hit the target where it did.

In addition to giving KP verbally, there are various nonverbal means of providing KP. For example, videotape replay is a popular method of showing a person what he or she did while performing a skill. Videotape replay allows the person to see what he or she actually did that led to the outcome of that performance. Another means of providing KP that is increasing in popularity as computer software becomes more accessible is showing the person computer-generated kinematic characteristics of the just-completed performance. In clinical environments, therapists also use biofeedback devices to give KP. For example, a therapist can attach a buzzer to an EMG recording device so that the person hears the buzzer sound when he or she activates

---

knowledge of results (KR)   category of augmented feedback that gives information about the outcome of performing a skill or about achieving the goal of the performance.

knowledge of performance (KP)   category of augmented feedback that gives information about the movement characteristics that led to a performance outcome.

A CLOSER LOOK

Augmented Feedback as Motivation

An instructor can use augmented feedback to influence a person's perception of his or her own ability in a skill. This is an effective way to influence the person's motivation to continue pursuing a task goal or performing a skill. The verbal statement "You're doing a lot better" can indicate to a person that he or she is being successful at an activity. Evidence supporting the motivational effectiveness of this type of verbal feedback comes from research relating to self-efficacy and performance of skills.

For example, Solmon and Boone (1993) showed that in a physical education class environment, students with high ability perceptions demonstrated longer persistence at performing a skill and had higher performance expectations than those with low ability perceptions. In her review of the self-efficacy literature as it relates to skill performance, Feltz (1992) concluded that the success or failure of past performance is a key mediator of a person's self-perceptions regarding ability.

The logical implication of these findings is that an instructor, coach, or therapist can present augmented feedback in a way that influences a person's feelings of success or failure which, in turn, influence a person to continue or to stop his or her involvement in participating in a physical activity.

---

the appropriate muscle during the performance of an action. In each of these situations, sensory feedback is augmented in a way that informs the person about the movement characteristics associated with the outcome of an action.

THE ROLES OF AUGMENTED FEEDBACK IN SKILL ACQUISITION

Augmented feedback plays two roles in the skill learning process. One is to *facilitate achievement of the action goal of the skill.* Because augmented feedback provides information about the success of the skill in progress or just completed, the learner can determine whether what he or she is doing is appropriate for performing the skill correctly. Thus, the augmented feedback can help the person achieve the skill goal more quickly or more easily than he or she could without this external information.

The second role played by augmented feedback is to *motivate the learner to continue striving toward a goal.* In this role, the person uses augmented feedback to compare his or her own performance to a performance goal. The person then must decide to continue trying to achieve that goal, to change goals, or to stop performing the activity. This motivational role of augmented feedback is not the focus of our discussion here. Others, however, have discussed it in the motor learning literature (e.g., Little & McCullagh, 1989). Scholars interested in the pedagogical aspects of physical education teaching (e.g., Solmon & Lee, 1996; Silverman, Woods, & Subramaniam, 1998) increasingly are studying the effects of augmented feedback on people's motivation to engage in, or continue to engage in, physical activities. In addition, augmented feedback functions as an important factor in influencing students' peceptions of ability (e.g., Fredenberg, Lee, & Solmon, 2001). And exercise psychologists have shown that augmented feedback is influential in motivating people to adhere to exercise and rehabilitation programs (e.g., Annesi, 1998; Dishman, 1993).

HOW ESSENTIAL IS AUGMENTED FEEDBACK FOR SKILL ACQUISITION?

When a researcher or practitioner considers the use of augmented feedback to facilitate skill acquisition, an important theoretical and practical question arises: Is augmented feedback *necessary* for a person to learn motor skills? The answer to this question has theoretical implications for the understanding of the nature of skill learning itself. The need, or lack of need, for augmented feedback to acquire motor skills tells us much about what characterizes the human learning system and how it functions to acquire new skills. From a practical perspective, determining the necessity for augmented feedback for skill learning can serve to guide the development and implementation of effective instructional strategies. As you will see, the answer to this question is not a simple yes or no. Instead, there are *four different answers.* Which one is appropriate depends on certain characteristics of the skill being learned and of the person learning the skill.

Augmented Feedback Can Be Essential for Skill Acquisition

In some skill learning situations, people, for various reasons, cannot use the task-intrinsic feedback to determine what they need to do to improve performance. As a result, augmented feedback is essential for learning. There are at least three types of situations in which a person may *not* be able to use important task-intrinsic feedback effectively.

First, some skill situations do not make critical sensory feedback available to the person. For example, when a performer cannot see a target that he or she must hit, the performer does not have important visual feedback available. In this case, augmented feedback adds critical information that is not available from the task performance environment itself.

Second, in some situations the person, because of injury, disease, etc., does not have available the sensory pathways needed to detect critical task-intrinsic feedback for the skill he or she is learning. For these people, augmented feedback serves as a substitute for this missing information.

Third, in some situations the appropriate task-intrinsic feedback provides the necessary information and the person's sensory system is capable of detecting it, but the person cannot use the feedback. For example, a person learning to move a limb a certain distance or to throw a ball at a certain rate of speed may not be able to determine the distance moved or the rate of speed of the throw because of lack of experience. In these situations, augmented feedback helps to make the available task-intrinsic feedback more meaningful to the performer.

Research evidence supports the need for augmented feedback in these learning situations. For example, in many of the earliest experiments the performance environment did not provide the learner with critical sensory feedback because the participants were blindfolded and thus could not see their movements or the performance environments. These experiments consistently showed augmented feedback, typically in the form of KR, to be essential for learning when, for example, the blindfolded persons had to learn to draw a line of a certain length (Trowbridge & Cason, 1932) or move a lever to a criterion position (e.g., Bilodeau, Bilodeau, & Schumsky, 1959). When the participants did not receive KR in these situations, they did not learn the skills.

Augmented Feedback May Not Be Needed for Skill Acquisition

Some motor skills *inherently provide sufficient task-intrinsic feedback,* so augmented feedback is redundant. For these types of skills, learners can use their own sensory feedback systems to determine the appropriateness of their movements and to make adjustments on future attempts. An experiment by Magill, Chamberlin, and Hall (1991) provides a laboratory example of this type of situation. Participants learned a coincidence-anticipation skill in which they simulated striking a moving object, which was a series of LEDs sequentially lighting along a 281-cm-long trackway. As they faced the trackway, they had to use a handheld bat to knock down a small wooden barrier directly under a target LED coincident with the lighting of the target. KR was the number of msec that they contacted the barrier before or after the target lighted. Four experiments showed that participants learned this task regardless of the number of trials on which they received KR during practice. In fact, receiving KR during practice did not lead to better learning than practice without KR.

A motor skill that does not require a person to have augmented feedback to learn it has an important characteristic: *a detectable external referent* in the environment that the person can use to determine the appropriateness of an action. For the

A CLOSER LOOK

Teacher Feedback Relationships in Physical Education Classes

Silverman, Woods, and Subramaniam (1999) examined the relationship between teacher feedback and several different practice and performance characteristics for eight classes of middle school physical education. Although each teacher taught one activity, the eight classes involved a variety of activities: volleyball, soccer, badminton, basketball, and ultimate. The teachers were videotaped for two classes in a row in which motor skill was the focus of instruction. The researchers observed the videotapes and recorded characteristics of several different teacher behavior categories, including teacher feedback. Among the various results

of the analysis of the data from this study was the finding that *the amount of teacher feedback given to students was significantly correlated with the amount of appropriate practice in which students engaged,* regardless of skill level. These results indicate that even though research has shown that teacher feedback and skill achievement are not highly correlated, teacher feedback has a positive impact on the students' participation in class by influencing them to engage in activity that is appropriate for helping them learn the skills that are the focus of the class instruction.

anticipation timing task in the Magill et al. experiment, the target and other LEDs were the external referents. The learner could see when the bat made contact with the barrier in comparison to when the target lighted; this enabled him or her to see the relationship between his or her own movements and the goal of those movements. It is important to note here that the learner may *not* be consciously aware of this relationship. The sensory system and the motor control system operate in these situations in a way that does not demand the person's awareness of the environmental characteristics (see Magill, 1998). Thus, the enhancement of these characteristics by providing augmented feedback does not increase or speed up learning of the skill.

Practice condition characteristics also influence the need for augmented feedback. One of these characteristics is the existence of an observational learning situation, which we discussed in chapter 13. Two different types of observational learning situations can be influential. In one, the learner observes a skilled model perform the skill. For example, in an experiment by Magill and Schoenfelder-Zohdi (1996), people who observed a skilled demonstration learned a rhythmic gymnastics rope skill as well as did those who received verbal KP

after each trial. In the other situation, the learner observes other beginners practice. For example, Hebert and Landin (1994) showed that beginning tennis players who watched other beginners practice learned the tennis forehand volley as well as or better than beginning players who received verbal KP. In both of these situations, beginners were able to practice and improve without augmented feedback.

There is an interesting parallel between skill learning situations in which learners do not need augmented feedback and results of studies investigating the use of teacher feedback in physical education class settings. These studies consistently have shown low correlations for the relationship between teacher feedback and student achievement (e.g., Lee, Keh, & Magill, 1993; Silverman, Tyson, & Krampitz, 1991). This finding suggests that the amount and quality of teacher feedback is influential for improving the skills of beginners in sport skills class settings, but we should not see it as the most important variable. Other variables, such as observational learning, appear to be capable of precluding the need for augmented feedback. Our understanding of the extent of this influence awaits further research.

Augmented Feedback Can Enhance Skill Acquisition

There are some types of motor skills that people can learn without augmented feedback, but they will *learn them more quickly or perform them at a higher level* if they receive augmented feedback during practice. For these skills, augmented feedback is neither essential nor redundant. Instead, it *enhances* the learning of these skills beyond what could be achieved without augmented feedback.

Skills in this category include those for which improvement does occur through task-intrinsic feedback alone, but because of certain skill or learner characteristics, performance improvement reaches only a certain level. One type of skill that fits this description consists of relatively simple skills for which achievement of the performance goal is initially easy to attain. An example is a movement goal of moving as quickly as possible. Initially, a person can assess if a particular attempt was faster than a previous one. However, usually because of the learner's lack of experience, which results in his or her decreased capability to discriminate small movement-speed differences, improvement seems to stop at a certain level of performance. To improve beyond this level of performance, the person requires augmented feedback. Research evidence shows that there is a point during practice at which people who receive KR about movement time for this type of skill continue to improve performance, whereas those who do not receive it level off in their performance.

Another type of skill for which augmented feedback enhances learning is any complex skill that requires a person to acquire an appropriate multi-limb pattern of coordination. For such skills, learners can attain a certain degree of success simply by making repeated attempts to achieve the performance goal. But this goal achievement process can be speeded up with the addition of KP. More specifically, the KP that works best is information about critical components of the coordination pattern.

The best research example of this type of skill is an experiment by Wallace and Hagler (1979).

Participants learned a one-hand basketball set shot with the nondominant hand, from a distance of 3.03 m from the basket, and 45 degrees to the left side of the basket. After each shot, one group received verbal KP about errors in their stance and limb movements during the shot. Another group received only verbal encouragement after each shot. Both groups could see the outcome of each shot. Figure 14.2 depicts the results. Note that KP provided an initial boost in performance for the first fifteen trials. Then, the verbal encouragement group caught up. However, similarity in performance between the two groups lasted only about ten trials; after this point, the verbal encouragement group showed no further improvement, whereas the group receiving KP continued to improve.

Augmented Feedback Can Hinder Skill Learning

An effect of augmented feedback on skill learning that many might not expect is that it can hinder the learning process and, in some cases, actually make learning worse than it would have been otherwise. This effect is especially evident when a beginning learner becomes dependent on augmented feedback that will not be available in a test situation. Typically, the performance improvement the learner experienced during practice deteriorates in the test situation. In fact, in some situations, not only does performance deteriorate when augmented feedback is withdrawn, but the test performance is no better than if augmented feedback had not been given at all.

The characteristic of tasks that is the most likely to lead to a dependency on augmented feedback is task-intrinsic feedback that is minimal or difficult to interpret. When performing these types of tasks, people typically substitute augmented feedback for task-intrinsic feedback, because it gives them an easy-to-use guide for performing correctly.

Several types of situations can lead a person to become dependent on augmented feedback. We will discuss three later in this chapter. One concern is the presentation of erroneous augmented feedback. Another situation involves the presentation

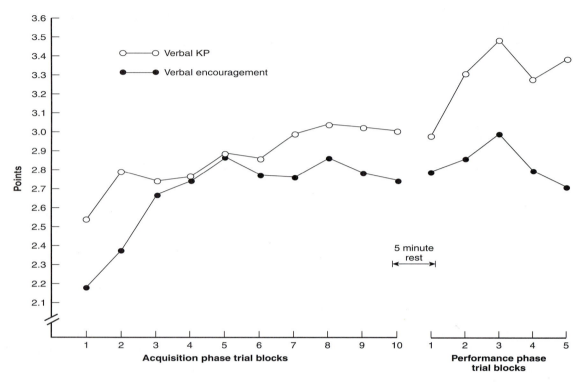

FIGURE 14.2   Results of the experiment by Wallace and Hagler showing the benefit of verbal KP for learning a basketball shooting skill.   [Reprinted with permission from *Research Quarterly for Exercise and Sport, Vol. 50, No. 2,* 265–271. Copyright © 1979 by the American Alliance for Health, Physical Education, Recreation and Dance, 1900 Association Drive, Reston, VA 20191.]

of concurrent augmented feedback, which refers to giving augmented feedback while a person performs a skill. The third occurs when augmented feedback is given too frequently during practice

THE CONTENT OF AUGMENTED FEEDBACK

In this section, we will focus on important issues concerning the content of augmented feedback, and then examine several types of augmented feedback that practitioners can use.

AUGMENTED FEEDBACK CONTENT ISSUES

We will consider five issues related to the content of augmented feedback. Each of these concerns

some of the kinds of information augmented feedback may contain.

Information about Errors versus Correct Aspects of Performance

An often debated issue about augmented feedback content is whether the information the instructor conveys to the learner should refer to the mistakes he or she has made or those aspects of the performance that are correct. Research evidence consistently has shown that *error information is more effective for facilitating skill improvement.* This evidence supports an important hypothesis, that focusing on what is done correctly while learning a skill, especially in the early stage of learning, is not sufficient by itself to produce optimal learning. Rather, the experience the person has in correcting errors by operating on error-based augmented feed-

A CLOSER LOOK

KP about Certain Features of a Skill Helps Correct Other Features

Participants in an experiment by den Brinker, Stabler, Whiting, and van Wieringen (1986) learned to perform on the slalom ski simulator. Their three-part goal was to move the platform from left to right as far as possible at a specific high frequency, and with a motion that was as fluid as possible. On the basis of these performance goals, each of three groups received a different type of information as KP after each trial. Researchers told participants in one group the *distance* they had moved the platform; they told another group's participants how close they were to performing at the criterion platform movement *frequency;* and they told participants in the third group

how fluid their movements were (i.e., *fluency*). All three groups practiced for four days, performing six 1.5-min trials each day, with a test trial before and after each day's practice trials. Early in practice, the type of KP an individual received influenced only the performance measure specifically related to that feature of performing the skill. However, on the last two days of practice, KP about *distance* caused people to improve all three performance features. Thus, giving KP about one performance feature led to improvement not only of that one, but also of the two other performance features.

back is especially important for skill acquisition (Lintern & Roscoe, 1980).

Another way of looking at this issue is to consider the different roles augmented feedback plays. Error information directs a person to change certain performance characteristics; this in turn facilitates skill acquisition. On the other hand, information indicating that the person performed certain characteristics correctly tells the person that he or she is on track in learning the skill and encourages the person to keep trying. When we consider augmented feedback from this perspective, we see that whether this feedback should be about errors or about correct aspects of performance depends on the goal of the information. Error-related information works better to facilitate skill acquisition, whereas information about correct performance serves better to motivate the person to continue.

KR versus KP

Two relevant questions concerning the comparison of the use of KR and KP in skill learning situations are these: Do practitioners use one of these forms of augmented feedback more than the other? Do they influence skill learning in similar or different ways?

Most of the evidence addressing the first question comes from the study of physical education

teachers in actual class situations. The best example is a study by Fishman and Tobey (1978). Although their study was conducted many years ago, it is representative of more recent studies, and it involves the most extensive sampling of teachers and classes of any study that has investigated this question. Fishman and Tobey observed teachers in eighty-one classes teaching a variety of physical activities. The results showed that the teachers overwhelmingly gave KP (94 percent of the time) more than KR. The majority of the KP statements (53 percent) were appraisals of students' performance, and 41 percent of the statements involved instructions on how to improve performance on the next trial. It is also worth noting that teachers gave praise or criticism 5 percent of the time.

An answer to the second question, concerning the relative effectiveness of KR and KP, is more difficult to provide because of the lack of sufficient and conclusive evidence from research investigating this question. The following examples of experiments provide some insight into a reasonable answer.

Two of the experiments indicate that KP is better than KR to facilitate motor skill learning. Kernodle and Carlton (1992) compared KR with videotape replays and verbally presented technique statements as KP in an experiment in which participants practiced throwing a soft, spongy ball as far as possible with the nondominant arm. KR was presented as the distance of the throw for each practice trial. The results showed that KP led to better throwing technique and distance than KR. Zubiaur, Oña, and Delgado (1999) reported a similar conclusion in a study in which university students with no previous volleyball experience practiced the overhead serve in volleyball. KP was specific information about the most important error to correct as it related to action either before hitting or in hitting the ball. KR referred to the outcome of the hit in terms of the ball's spatial precision, rotation, and flight. The results indicated that KP was more influential for learning the serve.

However, a study by Silverman, Woods, and Subramaniam (1999) provided evidence for the benefit of both KR and KP in terms of how each related to how often students in physical education classes would engage in successful and unsuccessful practice trials during a class. They observed eight middle school teachers teaching two classes each in various sport-related activities. The results indicated that teacher feedback as KR and as KP showed relatively high correlations with the frequency of students engaging in successful practice trials (0.64 and 0.67, respectively).

These studies indicate that *both KR and KP can be valuable* in skill learning sessions. With this in mind, consider the following hypotheses about conditions in which each of these forms of augmented feedback would be beneficial. KR will be beneficial for skill learning for at least four reasons: (1) Learners often use KR to confirm their own assessments of the task-intrinsic feedback, even though it may be redundant with task-intrinsic feedback. (2) Learners may need KR because they cannot determine the outcome of performing a skill on the basis of the available task-intrinsic feedback. (3) Learners often use KR to motivate themselves to continue practicing the skill. (4) Practitioners may want to provide only KR in order to establish a discovery learning practice environment in which learners are encouraged to engage in trial and error as the primary means of learning to perform a skill.

When giving verbal KP, it is important to provide information that is meaningful to the person to whom it is given.

On the other hand, KP can be especially beneficial when (1) skills must be performed according to specified movement characteristics, such as gymnastics stunts or springboard dives; (2) specific movement components of skills that require complex coordination must be improved or corrected; (3) the goal of the action is a kinematic, kinetic, or specific muscle activity; (4) KR is redundant with the task-intrinsic feedback.

Qualitative versus Quantitative Information
Augmented feedback can be qualitative, quantitative, or both. If the augmented feedback involves a numerical value related to the magnitude of some performance characteristic, it is called **quantitative augmented feedback.** In contrast, **qualitative augmented feedback** is information referring to the quality of the performance characteristic without regard for the numerical values associated with it.

For verbal augmented feedback, it is easy to distinguish these types of information in performance situations. For example, a therapist helping a patient to increase gait speed could give that patient qualitative information about the latest attempt in statements such as these: "That was faster than the last time"; "That was much better"; or "You need to bend your knee more." A physical education teacher or coach teaching a student a tennis serve could tell the student that a particular serve was "good," or "long," or could say something like this: "You made contact with the ball too far in front of you." On the other hand, the therapist could give the patient quantitative verbal augmented feedback using these words: "That time you walked 3 sec faster than the last time," or, "You need to bend your knee 5 more degrees." The coach could give quantitative feedback to the tennis student like this: "The serve was 6 cm too long," or "You made contact with the ball 10 cm too far in front of you."

Therapists and instructors also can give quantitative and qualitative information in nonverbal forms of augmented feedback. For example, the therapist could give qualitative information to the patient we have described by letting him or her hear a tone when the walking speed exceeded that of the previous attempt, or when the knee flexion achieved a target amount. The teacher or coach could give the tennis student qualitative information in the form of a computer display that used a moving stick figure to show the kinematic characteristics of his or her serving motion. Those teaching motor skills often give nonverbally presented quantitative information in combination with qualitative forms. For example, the therapist could show a patient a computer-based graphic representation of his or her leg movement while walking along, displaying numerical values of the walking speeds associated with each attempt, or the degree of knee flexion observed on each attempt. We could describe similar examples for the tennis student.

How do these two types of augmented feedback information influence skill learning? Although the traditional view is that quantitative augmented feedback is preferred, results from an experiment by Magill and Wood (1986) suggest a different conclusion. Each participant practiced moving his or her arm through a series of wooden barriers to produce a specific six-segment movement pattern. Each segment had its own criterion movement time, which participants had to learn. Following each practice trial, participants received either qualitative KR for each segment (i.e., "too fast," "too slow," or "correct") or quantitative KR for each segment (i.e., the number of msec too fast or too slow). Performance for the first sixty trials

showed no difference between the two types of KR. However, during the final sixty trials and on the twenty no-KR retention trials, quantitative KR resulted in better performance than qualitative.

These results suggest that people in the early stage of learning give attention primarily to the qualitative information, even when they have quantitative information available. The advantage of this attention focus is that the qualitative information provides an easier way to make a first approximation of the required movement. Put another way, this information allows learners to perform an action that is "in the ballpark" of what they need to do, which, as we discussed in chapter 11, is an important goal for the first stage of learning. After they achieve this "ballpark" capability, quantitative information becomes more valuable to them, because it enables them to refine characteristics of performing the skill that lead to more consistent and efficient achievement of the action goal.

Augmented Feedback Based on Error Size

A question that has distinct practical appeal is this: How large an error should a performer make before the instructor or therapist gives augmented feedback? To many, it seems reasonable to provide feedback only when errors are large enough to warrant attention. This approach suggests that in many skill learning situations, practitioners develop **performance bandwidths** that establish performance

---

quantitative augmented feedback   augmented feedback that includes a numerical value related to the magnitude of a performance characteristic (e.g., the speed of a pitched baseball).

qualitative augmented feedback   augmented feedback that is descriptive in nature (e.g., using such terms as *good, long*), and indicates the quality of performance.

performance bandwidth   in the context of providing augmented feedback, a range of acceptable performance error; augmented feedback is given only when the amount of error is greater than this range.

A CLOSER LOOK

Quantitative versus Qualitative Augmented Feedback and the Performance Bandwidth Technique

Cauraugh, Chen, and Radlo (1993) had subjects practice a timing task in which they had to press a sequence of three keys in 500 msec. Participants in one group received quantitative KR about their movement times (MT) when MT was *outside* a 10 percent performance bandwidth. A second group, in the reverse of that condition, received quantitative KR only when MT was *inside* the 10 percent performance bandwidth. Two additional groups had participants "yoked" to individual participants in the outside and inside bandwidth conditions. Members of these two groups received KR on the same trials their "yoked" counterparts did. This procedure provided a way to have two conditions with the same frequency of augmented feedback, while allowing a comparison between bandwidth and no-bandwidth conditions.

In terms of KR frequency, those in the outside bandwidth condition received quantitative KR on 25 percent of the sixty practice trials; those in the inside condition received KR on 65 percent of the trials. The interesting feature of this difference is that the remaining trials for both groups were implicitly qualitative KR trials, because when they received no KR, the participants knew that their performance was "good" or "not good." The retention test performance results showed that the two bandwidth conditions did not differ, but both yielded better learning than the no-bandwidth conditions. These results show that establishing performance bandwidths as the basis for providing quantitative KR yields an interplay between quantitative and qualitative KR that facilitates skill learning.

---

error tolerance limits specifying when they will or will not give augmented feedback. When a person's performance is acceptable, i.e., within the tolerance limits of the bandwidth, the practitioner does not give feedback. But if the performance is not acceptable, i.e., the amount or type of error is outside the bandwidth, the practitioner gives feedback to the person who performed the skill.

Research supports the effectiveness of the performance bandwidth approach. For example, in the first reported experiment investigating this procedure, Sherwood (1988) had subjects practice a rapid elbow-flexion task with a movement-time goal of 200 msec. Participants in one group received KR about their movement-time error after every trial, regardless of the amount of error (i.e., 0 percent bandwidth). Participants in two other groups received KR only when their error exceeded bandwidths of 5 percent and 10 percent of the goal movement time. The results of a no-KR retention test showed that the 10 percent bandwidth condition resulted in the least amount of movement time variability (i.e., variable error), whereas the 0 percent condition resulted in the most variable error.

Other researchers have replicated these results (e.g., Lee, White, & Carnahan, 1990; Cauraugh, Chen, & Radlo, 1993).

An important question related to implementing the performance bandwidth technique in skill learning situations concerns its relationship with the learner's stage of learning. It might seem reasonable, for example, to reduce the size of the error bandwidth as the learner advances from an early to a later stage of learning. However, at least two experiments have demonstrated that this type of reduction is not necessary. Goodwin and Meeuwsen (1995) compared a 0 percent and a 10 percent bandwidth for all practice trials with expanding (0-5-10-15-20 percent) and shrinking (20-15-10-5-0 percent) bandwidths for learning a golf putting task. Their results, which can be seen in figure 14.3, indicated that changing the bandwidth size during practice did not provide any additional learning benefit. In fact, both the expanding and constant 10 percent bandwidth conditions produced similar performance on a 48-hour retention test, and were superior to the contracting and 0 percent bandwidth conditions. Others have reported

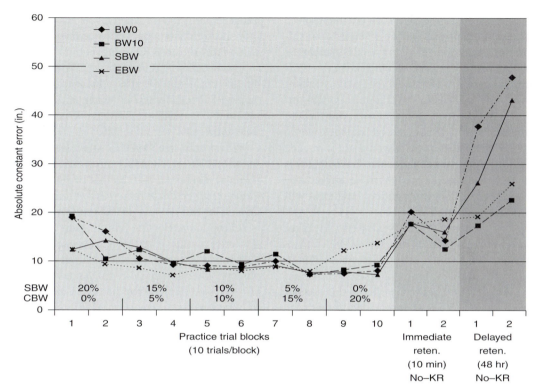

FIGURE 14.3 The results of the experiment by Goodwin and Meeuwsen, which compared four different performance-based bandwidth (BW) conditions for KR during the practice of a golf putting task. The BW0 is a 0 percent bandwidth, BW10 is a 10 percent bandwidth, SBW is a shrinking bandwidth, and EBW is an expanding bandwidth. Practice trial blocks show the mean of ten trials for each. The actual bandwidth for the SBW and EBW conditions are shown for each set of twenty trials. [Adapted from data in Goodwin, J. E., & Meeuwsen, H. J. (1995). Using bandwidth knowledge for results to alter relative frequencies during motor skill acquisition. *Research Quarterly for Exercise and Sport, 66,* 99–104.]

similar evidence that the changing of bandwidth sizes does not improve learning beyond the level achieved with a constant bandwidth during practice (e.g., Lai & Shea, 1999a).

Another practical issue concerning the use of the bandwidth technique relates to the instructions learners receive about the bandwidth procedure. This issue is relevant because when the learners receive no augmented feedback about their performance, the implicit message is that it was "correct." There is an instruction-related question here: Is it important that the learner explicitly be told this information, or will the learner implicitly learn this information during practice? Butler, Reeve, and Fischman (1996) in-

vestigated this question by telling one group of participants that when they received no KR after a trial, their performance was "essentially correct." A second group was not told this information. The task required a two-segment arm movement to a target in a criterion movement time. The results showed that the bandwidth technique led to better learning when the participants knew in advance that not receiving KR meant they were essentially correct.

Erroneous Augmented Feedback

One of the ways augmented feedback hinders learning is by providing people with erroneous information. While this statement may seem unnecessary because it makes such common sense, the statement gains importance when it is considered in the context of practicing a skill that can be learned *without* augmented feedback. In this skill learning situation, augmented feedback is redundant with the information available from task-intrinsic feedback. As a result, most people would expect that to provide augmented feedback would be a waste of time because it would not influence the learner. But research evidence shows that this is not the case, because even when augmented feedback is redundant information, beginners will use it rather than ignore it.

The first evidence of this type of effect was reported by Buekers, Magill, and Hall (1992). Participants practiced an anticipation timing task similar to the one used by Magill, Chamberlin, and Hall (1991), which was described earlier in this chapter as a task for which KR is not needed to learn the task. In the Buekers et al. experiment, three of four groups received KR after every trial. The KR was displayed on a computer monitor and indicated to the participants the direction and amount of their timing error. For one of these groups, KR was always correct. But for another group, KR was always erroneous by indicating that performance on a trial was 100 msec later than it actually was. The third KR group received correct KR for the first fifty trials, but then received the erroneous KR for the last twenty-five trials. A fourth group did not receive KR during practice.

The results (figure 14.4) showed two important findings. First, the correct-KR and the no-KR groups did not differ during the practice or the retention trials. Second, the erroneous KR information led participants to learn to perform according to the KR rather than according to the task-intrinsic feedback. This latter result suggested that the participants used KR, even though it was erroneous information. Even more impressive was that the erroneous KR influenced the group that had received correct KR for fifty trials and then was switched to the erroneous KR. After the switch, this group began to perform similarly to the group that had received the incorrect KR for all the practice trials. In addition, the erroneous information not only in-fluenced performance when it was available; it also influenced retention performance one day and one week later on no-KR. A subsequent experiment (McNevin, Magill, & Buekers, 1994) demonstrated that the erroneous KR also influenced performance on a no-KR transfer test in which participants were required to respond to a faster or slower speed than they practiced.

Why would erroneous KR affect learning a skill for which KR is redundant information? The most likely reason appears to be that beginners *rely on augmented feedback to help them deal with their uncertainty about what the task-intrinsic feedback is telling them.* For the anticipation timing task, the uncertainty may exist because the visual task-intrinsic feedback is difficult to consciously observe, interpret, and use. Evidence for an uncertainty-based explanation has been demonstrated in experiments by Buekers, Magill, and Sneyers (1994), and Buekers and Magill (1995).

The important message for practitioners here is that people who are in the early stage of skill learning will use augmented feedback when it is available, whether it is correct or not. Because of their uncertainty about how to use or interpret task-intrinsic feedback, beginners rely on augmented feedback as a critical source of information on which to base how they will move corrections on future trials. As a result, instructors need to be certain that they provide correct augmented feedback.

From a learning theory perspective, this reliance on augmented feedback by learners in the early stage of learning suggests that cognitive information can override the perception-action link, which suggests that the perceptual motor control system does not "automatically" use task-intrinsic feedback appropriately. The perceptual component of this system appears to require some calibration. If augmented feedback is available, the learner uses this information to carry out this calibration process. However, if augmented feedback is not available, and if the task is one where augmented information is not necessary for learning the skill, then this calibration process appears to occur by means of trial-and-error experience occurring during practice.

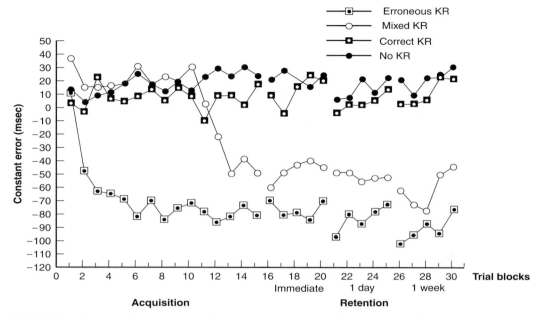

FIGURE 14.4   Results of the experiment by Buekers et al., showing the effects of erroneous KR compared to no KR and correct KR for learning an anticipation timing skill. Note that participants in the mixed-KR group received correct KR for their first fifty trials and then received erroneous KR for their last twenty-five practice trials. [From Buekers, M. J., Magill, R. A., & Hall, K. G. (1992). The effect of erroneous knowledge of results on skill acquisition when augmented information is redundant. *Quarterly Journal of Experimental Psychology. 44 (A),* 105–117. Reprinted by permission of The Experimental Psychology Society.]

TYPES OF KNOWLEDGE OF PERFORMANCE

Most of the research on which we base our knowledge of augmented feedback and skill learning comes from laboratory experiments in which researchers gave KR to participants. Although most of the conclusions from that research also apply to KP, it is useful to look at some of the research that has investigated different types of KP.

Verbal KP

One of the reasons practitioners give verbal KP more than verbal KR is that KP gives people more information to help them improve the movement aspects of skill performance. One of the problems that arises with the use of verbal KP is determining the appropriate content: what to tell the person practicing the skill. This problem occurs because skills are typically complex and KP usually relates to a specific feature of skill performance. The chal-

lenge for the instructor or therapist, then, is selecting the appropriate features of the performance on which to base KP.

To solve this problem, the first thing a teacher, coach, or therapist must do is perform a *skill analysis* of the skill being practiced. This means identifying the various component parts of the skill. Then, he or she should prioritize each part in terms of how critical it is for performing the skill correctly. Prioritize by listing the most critical part first, then the second most critical, and so on. To determine which part is most critical, decide which part of the skill absolutely must be done properly for the entire skill to be performed correctly. For example, in the relatively simple task of throwing a dart at a target, the most critical component is looking at the target. This part of the skill is the most critical because even if the beginning learner did all other parts of the skill correctly (which would be unlikely), there is a very low chance that he or she would perform the skill correctly without

---

A CLOSER LOOK

An Example of Basing Verbal KP on a Skill Analysis

In an experiment by Weeks and Kordus (1998), twelve-year-old boys who had no previous experience in soccer practiced a soccer throw-in. The participants' goal was to perform throw-ins as accurately as possible to a target on the floor. The distance to the target was 75 percent of each participant's maximum throwing distance. They received verbal KP on one of eight aspects of technique, which the researchers referred to as "form." Which aspect of form each participant received was based on the primary form problem identified for a throw-in. The researchers constructed a list of eight "form cues" on the basis of a skill analysis of the throw-in, and used this list to give verbal KP. The eight form cues were these:

1. The feet, hips, knees, and shoulders should be aimed at the target, feet shoulder width apart.
2. The back should be arched at the beginning of the throw.
3. The grip should look like a "W" with the thumbs together on the back of the ball.
4. The ball should start behind the head at the beginning of the throw.
5. The arms should go over the head during the throw and finish by being aimed at the target.
6. There should be no spin on the ball during its flight.
7. The ball should be released in front of the head.
8. Feet should remain on the ground.

---

looking at the target. In this case, then, looking at the target would be first on the skill analysis priority list, and would be the first part of the skill assessed in determining what to give KP about.

After determining which aspect of the skill about which to give KP, the practitioner needs to decide the content of the statement to make to the learner. There are *two types of verbal KP statements.* A **descriptive KP** statement simply describes the error the performer has made. The other type, **prescriptive KP,** not only identifies the error, but also tells the person what to do to correct it. For example, if you tell a person, "You moved your right foot too soon," you describe only the problem. However, if you say, "You need to move your right foot at the same time you move your right arm," you also give prescriptive information about what the person needs to do to correct the problem.

Which type of KP better facilitates learning? The answer is that it varies with the stage of learning of the person practicing the skill. For example, the statement, "You moved your right foot too soon," would help a beginner only if he or she knew the actual time at which the right foot was supposed to move. Thus, descriptive KP statements are useful to help people improve performance

only after they have learned what they need to do to make a correction. This suggests that *prescriptive KP statements are more helpful for beginners. For the more advanced performer, a descriptive KP statement often will suffice.*

Videotape as Augmented Feedback

The increasing availability and use of videotape as augmented feedback argues for the need for practitioners to know more about how to use it effectively. It is common to find articles in professional journals that offer guidelines and suggestions for the use of videotape replays as feedback (e.g., Franks & Maile, 1991; Jambor & Weekes, 1995; Trinity & Annesi, 1996). However, very little empirical research exists that establishes the effectiveness of videotape replays as an aid for skill acquisition. In fact, the most recent extensive review of the research literature related to the use of videotape as a source of augmented feedback in skill learning situations was published many years ago (Rothstein & Arnold, 1976).

Despite the age of that review, current research and practice related to the use of videotape as augmented feedback tends to follow or is based on its general conclusions. One of these was that the crit-

LAB LINKS

Lab 14a in the Online Learning Center Lab Manual provides an opportunity for you to develop a priority list of KP statements that you might give as feedback to people learning or relearning a motor skill.

ical factor for determining the effectiveness of videotape as an instructional aid was the *skill level of the learner rather than the type of activity.* For beginners to benefit from videotape replay, they required the assistance of an instructor to point out critical information. Advanced performers did not appear to need instructor aid as frequently, although discussions with skilled athletes suggests they receive greater benefit from observing replays when some form of attention-directing instructions are presented, such as verbal cues and checklists.

A good example of an experiment that demonstrated the benefit of having an instructor point out what the observer of the videotape replay should look for was reported by Kernodle and Carlton (1992). Participants practiced throwing a soft, spongy ball as far as possible with the nondominant arm. One group of participants received specific technique-related cues about what to look for on the videotape replays of each trial. Participants in a second group received this same information plus a verbal prescriptive KP statement that told them how to correct the technique problem. A third group watched only the video and received no cues or verbal KP. And a fourth group received verbal KR about the distance of each throw. The results showed that the participants in the two groups who received the specific technique cues to look for while watching the videotape replays learned to throw the ball farther and with better technique than the other two groups.

Research evidence also establishes that videotape replays *transmit certain types of performance-related information to the learner more effectively than other types.* One of the best examples of an experiment that supports this conclusion was one

conducted many years ago by Selder and Del Rolan (1979). They compared videotape replays and verbal augmented feedback (in the form of KP) in a study in which twelve-to-thirteen-year-old girls were learning to perform a balance beam routine. All the girls used a checklist to critically analyze their own performance after each trial. The verbal augmented feedback group used verbal KP to complete the checklist; the videotape feedback group completed the checklist after viewing videotape replays of each trial. At the end of six weeks of practice, the videotape group scored significantly higher on the routine than the verbal feedback group. More important, when each factor of the total routine score was evaluated, the videotape group scored significantly higher on only four of the eight factors: precision, execution, amplitude, and orientation and direction. The two groups did not differ on the other four: rhythm, elegance, coordination, and lightness of jumping and tumbling. These results suggest that videotape replay facilitates the learning of those performance features that the performer can readily observe and determine how to correct on the basis of the videotape replay. However, for performance features that are no more readily discernible, videotape replay is no more effective than verbal KP.

An alternative use of videotape replays is referred to as *self-modeling,* which combines modeling as a form of instruction with modeling as also a form of augmented feedback. An example of this use is seen in an interesting study by Starek and McCullagh (1999). Adult beginning swimmers

descriptive KP   a verbal knowledge of performance (KP) statement that describes only the error a person has made during the performance of a skill.

prescriptive KP   a verbal knowledge of performance (KP) statement that describes errors made during the performance of a skill and states (i.e., prescribes) what needs to be done to correct them.

A CLOSER LOOK

Skilled Athletes Progress Through Distinct Stages As They Learn to Use Videotape Replays

A study by Hebert, Landin, and Menickelli (1998) investigated the use of videotape replays as a part of the practice sessions for skilled female tennis players who needed to improve their attacking shots. Although the players who watched the videotape replays improved more than the players who did not, the athletes required a period of time to learn to use the replays effectively. According to the researchers' field notes and recordings of the athletes while they watched the videotapes, this period of time involved a progression through four stages in their use of the replays:

1. Players familiarized themselves with observing themselves on videotape. They made general

comments about how they personally looked on videotape as well as about their playing techniques.

2. Players began to recognize specific technical errors in their attack shots.

3. Players became more analytical as they made direct connections between their technique and the outcome of that technique.

4. Players began to use their observations of replays to indicate corrections they should make to their technique errors. They indicated awareness of the key aspects of their performance that related to successfully hitting the attack shot.

watched three-minute videotape replays of their swimming performance during the lesson of the previous day. The replay showed four swimming behaviors they had performed correctly, and four they had trouble performing. Then, some of the students saw only their own successfully performed skills from the previous day, whereas other students saw a skilled swimmer successfully perform these skills. The results showed that swimmers who saw their own videotaped performance performed better than those who saw the same skills performed by someone else.

Movement Kinematics as Augmented Feedback

With the widespread availability of computer software capable of providing sophisticated kinematic analysis of movement, it has become increasingly common to find sport skill instruction and physical rehabilitation situations in which students and patients can view graphically presented kinematic representations of their performances as a form of feedback. Unfortunately, as was the case with the use of videotape replays, there is little research evidence that provides definitive answers to questions concerning the effectiveness of this means of providing augmented feedback. However, the few studies that have been reported provide some insight into the use of this form of augmented feedback.

One of the first studies to investigate the use of movement kinematics did not involve a computer, and was carried out many years ago. This study is important because it illustrates the historical interest in this type of feedback, it involved a real-world training situation, and it exemplifies the positive effect that kinematic information can have on skill learning. Lindahl (1945) investigated the methods used to train industrial machine operator trainees to precisely and quickly cut thin disks of tungsten with a machine that required fast, accurate, and rhythmic coordination of the hands and feet. The traditional approach to training for this job was a trial-and-error method. To assess an alternative method, Lindahl created a mechanism that would make a paper tracing of the machine operator's foot movement pattern during the cutting of each disk. During training, the trainers showed the trainees charts illustrating the correct foot action (see the top portion of figure 14.5), and periodically showed them tracings of their own foot action. The results (see the bottom portion of figure 14.5) indicated that this training method based on movement kinematic information as augmented feedback enabled the trainees to achieve production performance levels in eleven weeks, compared to the five months required by trainees who used the traditional trial-and-error method. In addition, the trainees reduced their percentage of broken cutting wheels to almost zero in twelve weeks, a level not achieved by those trained with the traditional method in less than nine months.

A comprehensive series of experiments reported by Swinnen and his colleagues serve as good examples of laboratory research that has investigated the use of movement kinematics as augmented feedback (Swinnen et al., 1990; Swinnen, Walter, Lee, & Serrien, 1993). Participants in these experiments practiced a bimanual coordination task that required them to move two levers at the same time, but with each lever requiring a different spatial-temporal movement pattern. Kinematic information was presented as augmented feedback in the form of the angular displacement characteristics for each arm superimposed over the criterion displacements. In several experiments, the kinematic augmented feedback was compared with various other forms of augmented feedback. The results consistently demonstrated the effectiveness of the use of the displacement information.

An experiment by Wood, Gallagher, Martino, and Ross (1992) provides a good example of the use of graphically displayed movement kinematics for learning a golf shot with a five iron. A commercially marketed golf computer monitored the velocity, displacement, and trajectory path of each swing as the head of the club passed over light sensors on the platform from which the ball was hit. This information was then displayed on a monitor. One group of participants saw a template of an optimum pattern along with the kinematics; a second group did not see this template. A third group received the same kinematic information verbally in the form of numbers. A fourth group received no augmented feedback. On a retention test given one week later without augmented feedback, the group that had observed the graphic presentation of the swing kinematics along with the optimum pattern template performed best.

Finally, teachers, coaches, and therapists who use graphic displays of movement kinematics as augmented feedback, should take the stage of learning into account. Beginners benefit from kinematic information only when they can interpret and

FIGURE 14.5 The upper panel illustrates the foot action required by the machine operator to produce an acceptable disk cut in the experiment by Lindahl. The graph at the bottom indicates the production performance achieved by the trainees using graphic information during twelve weeks of training. The dashed lines indicate the levels of performance achieved by other workers after two, five, and nine months of experience. [From Lindahl, L. G. (1945) Movement analysis as an industrial training method. *Journal of Applied Psychology, 29,* 420–436, American Psychological Association.]

use it to improve their own performance. Thus, it is useful to show a template of the kinematic goal to beginners. More skilled performers can take advantage of more complex kinematic information.

Biofeedback as Augmented Feedback

The term **biofeedback** refers to an augmented form of task-intrinsic feedback related to the activity of

> **biofeedback** a type of augmented feedback that provides information about physiological processes through the use of instrumentation (e.g., EMG feedback).

A CLOSER LOOK

A Case Study of the Use of Biofeedback for Balance Training for Stroke Patients

A form of biofeedback that has been used for balance training in physical therapy contexts is the visual presentation on a computer monitor of a person's center of gravity. A case study reported by Simmons and associates (1998) is an interesting example of the effectiveness of this type of biofeedback in a clinical setting. The patient was a seventy-four-year-old post-stroke, hemiparetic male with whom therapists were working to help him regain balance control while standing. Following a pretest, the patient engaged in three balance training therapy sessions a week for four weeks. During each therapy session the patient stood on two force plates while looking at a computer monitor placed at eye level. On the monitor, he could see a small white dot superimposed on a white cross, which indicated an appropriate center of gravity while standing. During each therapy session, a clear plastic template marked with a circular pattern of

eight alphabetic letters was placed on the monitor. A verbal command to the patient indicated that he should initiate a weight shift that would cause the white dot to move from the center and hit the target letter and then return the dot back to the center cross. The patient did this for six 1-min intervals with a 45-sec rest between intervals. A posttest followed at the end of the four-week training period, and a retention test was given two weeks later. One of the tests simulated a sudden loss of balance, which involved a quick (400-msec) 5.7-cm forward and backward movement of the force plates on which the patient was standing. The patient's performance on this motor control test during the two-week retention test showed a 60 percent improvement for response strength of the affected leg, and a marked shift in balance onto the affected leg in the patient's attempts to regain balance.

physiological processes, such as heart rate, blood pressure, muscle activity, etc. Several forms of biofeedback have been used in motor skill learning situations. The most common is *electromyographic (EMG) biofeedback,* which provides information about muscle activity. Most of the research concerning the use of EMG as biofeedback has been undertaken in physical rehabilitation settings, and has shown positive results as an effective therapy intervention. The following examples illustrate different types of intervention purposes for the use of this form of augmented feedback.

Brucker and Bulaeva (1996) used EMG biofeedback with long-term cervical spinal cord-injured people to determine if it would help them increase their voluntary EMG responses from the triceps during elbow extension. Results of a post-treatment test indicated that participants who experienced only one 45-min treatment session significantly increased their triceps EMG activity; and those who experienced additional treatment sessions demonstrated even further increases.

The purpose of a study by Intiso and colleagues (1994) was to determine the effectiveness of EMG

biofeedback to help poststroke patients overcome foot drop of the paretic limb during the swing phase of walking. Some patients received EMG biofeedback during their physical therapy, whereas others did not. A unique characteristic of this study was the use of gait analysis to assess foot drop during the gait cycle. Results of this analysis demonstrated that the EMG biofeedback intervention led to better recovery than physical therapy without the biofeedback.

Another type of biofeedback was demonstrated by Chollet, Micallef, and Rabischong (1988). The researchers developed swimming paddles that would provide information to enable highly skilled swimmers to maintain their optimal velocity and number of arm cycles in a training session. The swimming paddles contained force sensors and sound generators that transmitted an audible signal to transmitters in a swimmer's cap. The sensors were set at a desired water-propulsion-force threshold; when the swimmer reached this threshold, the paddles produced a sound audible to the swimmer. The results showed that this device helped swimmers maintain their stroke count and swimming speed when they otherwise would have found it de-

A CLOSER LOOK

Guidelines for Giving Augmented Feedback to Facilitate Skill Learning

- **The person must be capable of using the information.** More specific or sophisticated augmented feedback is not necessarily better. Beginners need information to help them make a "ballpark" approximation of the required movements; they need more specific information as skill learning progresses.
- **A combination of error-based augmented feedback and information based on what was done correctly is most helpful,** to take advantage of the roles of augmented feedback for facilitating skill improvement and for motivating a person to continue practicing the skill.
- **Verbal KP should be based on the most critical error** made during a practice attempt; the practitioner should identify this error on the basis of a skill analysis and a prioritized list of components of the skill.

- **Prescriptive KP is better for novices,** whereas descriptive KP is more appropriate for more skilled people.
- **Videotape replays can be effective with beginners** if instructors or therapists provide direction to help them detect and correct errors as they watch the tape.
- **Computer-generated displays of the kinematics of a skill performance will be more effective for more advanced performers** than for novices to help facilitate skill improvement.
- **Biofeedback needs to give people information they can use to alter movements.** In addition, it must be presented in such a way that people do not become dependent on it.

creasing through the course of a long-distance practice session.

Finally, a rather unique type of biofeedback in motor skill learning contexts has been applied in the training of competitive rifle shooters (Daniels & Landers, 1981). Heartbeat biofeedback was presented audibly to help these athletes learn to squeeze the rifle trigger between heartbeats, which is a characteristic of elite shooters.

In general, research evidence has supported the effectiveness of biofeedback as a means of facilitating motor skill learning. However, debate continues concerning the specific situations in which the use of biofeedback is an effective and preferred form of augmented feedback (Moreland & Thomson, 1994; Moreland, Thompson, & Fusco, 1998).

TIMING ISSUES RELATED TO AUGMENTED FEEDBACK

Finally, three important questions arise about the timing of giving augmented feedback. To continue with the example in which you are teaching a person to play golf, one question is this: Should you give augmented feedback while the person swings, after he or she has hit the ball, or both times? If you give

feedback after the person hits the ball, the second question arises: How soon after the person's hitting of the ball should you give augmented feedback? The third question concerns whether you should give augmented feedback every time the person hits the ball, or only a few times during the practice session?

CONCURRENT AND TERMINAL AUGMENTED FEEDBACK

The first augmented feedback timing issue we will consider here is whether it is better to give augmented feedback while a person is performing a skill, in what is known as **concurrent augmented feedback,** or at the end of a practice attempt, in what we call **terminal augmented feedback.**

concurrent augmented feedback   augmented feedback that is provided while a person is performing a skill or making a movement.

terminal augmented feedback   augmented feedback that is provided after a person has completed the performance of a skill or a movement.

An important training question is whether concurrent or terminal presentation of augmented feedback is better for facilitating skill acquisition. Unfortunately, a search through the motor learning research literature suggests that there is no unequivocal answer to this question. However, a guideline emerges from that literature that can help us answer the question. Terminal augmented feedback can be effective in almost any skill learning situation, although the teacher or therapist must consider the nature of its effect in light of our discussion earlier in this chapter of the four different effects augmented feedback can have on skill learning. Concurrent augmented feedback, as you will see in the following sections of this discussion, seems to be most effective when the task-intrinsic feedback is difficult to use to determine how to perform the skill or improve performance. Because most of the discussion thus far in this chapter has involved terminal augmented feedback, the focus of this section will be on concurrent augmented feedback.

Effects of Concurrent Augmented Feedback on Learning

Research evidence has shown two general types of effects for the use of concurrent augmented feedback in skill learning situations. The more common is *a negative learning effect*. Although performance improves very well during practice when the feedback is available, it declines on retention or transfer trials during which the augmented feedback is removed. In these situations, the concurrent augmented feedback influences learners to direct their attention away from the critical task-intrinsic feedback and toward the augmented feedback. The result is that they substitute the information derived from augmented feedback for the important information they should acquire from task-intrinsic feedback. The result is that the augmented feedback becomes an integral part of what is learned, and therefore necessary for future performance.

Two experiments, one involving a continuous skill and the other involving a discrete skill, provide examples of research that has demonstrated this negative learning effect. Verschueren, Swinnen, Dom, and DeWeerdt (1997) had elderly healthy adults and Parkinson's patients practice the continuous bimanual coordination task described in chapters 10 and 11 (see figure 10.4). The task required that they learn to move two levers simultaneously for 20 sec in such a way that they would draw ellipses on the computer monitor. During the practice trials, participants saw on the monitor the drawings produced as they moved their arms. The results showed that participants in both groups made considerable improvement during practice when the concurrent

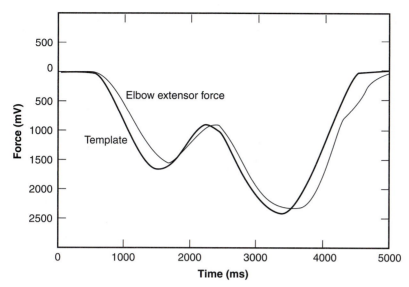

FIGURE 14.6 An example from the Vander Linden et al. experiment of what a participant saw during and/or after a trial on which they attempted to produce a 5-sec elbow-extension force trace that replicated as closely as possible the template trace. [Reprinted from Vander Linden, D. W. et al. (1993). "The effect of frequency of kinetic feedback on learning an isometric force production task in nondisabled subjects," *Physical Therapy, 73,* 79–87 with permission of the American Physical Therapy Association.]

visual augmented feedback was available. But their performance dropped dramatically on retention test trials without the augmented feedback.

The negative learning effect has also been demonstrated for the learning of a discrete task. Vander Linden, Cauraugh, and Greene (1993) compared concurrent and terminal augmented feedback for learning a 5-sec isometric elbow-extension force production task, which is illustrated in figure 14.6. Participants received augmented feedback by seeing the force produced during the performance of the task on each trial. One group received this feedback concurrently. Two other groups received this feedback after they completed performing the task. One of these two groups saw this information after every trial; the other saw it after every other trial. During the practice trials, the concurrent augmented feedback group performed the task better than the two terminal groups. However, forty-eight hours later on a retention test with no augmented feedback, the concurrent group's performance declined to a level that was the poorest of the three groups.

The second general effect is that concurrent augmented feedback *enhances skill learning.* A variety of situations have produced this effect. Some of these are the training of flight skills for airplane pilots (e.g., Lintern, 1991), the rehabilitation of

motor skills in physical therapy (e.g., Intiso et al., 1994), the activation of specific muscles or muscle groups (e.g., Brucker & Bulaeva, 1996), and the learning of certain types of bimanual coordination laboratory tasks (e.g., Swinnen et al., 1993). In these experiments, concurrent augmented feedback enhanced relevant features of the task-intrinsic feedback that were difficult to discern without the enhancement. Because most of these experiments are described elsewhere in this book, there is no need to describe them here.

Predicting Learning Effects of Concurrent Augmented Feedback

Two related hypotheses have been proposed to help us better understand how to predict when concurrent augmented feedback will have a positive or negative effect on learning. First, Annett (1959, 1969, 1970) stated that augmented feedback should be considered in terms of its information value, which he related to the "informativeness" of the task-intrinsic feedback and the augmented feedback. *When the information value of task-intrinsic feedback is low, but the information value of the augmented feedback is high, concurrent augmented feedback will most likely lead to a dependency on the augmented feedback.*

Lintern and his colleagues (Lintern, 1991; Lintern, Roscoe, & Sivier, 1990) added another dimension to Annett's hypothesis by proposing that practicing with augmented feedback will benefit learning to the extent that the feedback sensitizes the learner to properties or relationships in the task that specify how the system being learned can be controlled. This means that *for concurrent augmented feedback to be effective, it must facilitate the learning of the critical characteristics or relationships in the task as specified by the task-intrinsic feedback.* Negative learning effects will result when the augmented feedback distracts attention away from these features. But positive learning effects will result when the augmented feedback directs attention to these features.

Consider how these two hypotheses apply to the experiments described earlier as examples of the negative and positive learning effects of concurrent augmented feedback. In the Verschueren et al. and Vander Linden et al. experiments, which yielded negative effects, task-intrinsic feedback was difficult to interpret for both tasks. The limb movement relationship required by the bimanual coordination task and the amount of isometric force required by the elbow-extension task involved the need to discern proprioceptive feedback in ways that are unusual to most people. Thus the information value of the task-intrinsic feedback was low, which made it difficult to use to perform the skill. As a result, the concurrent augmented feedback became a very appealing source of information to help perform the skill. Although this information enabled the learners to improve their performance quite rapidly when it was present, it led to a dependence that distracted them from learning the proprioceptive task-intrinsic feedback critical to successful performance of the tasks. However, in the situations in the experiments in which concurrent augmented feedback facilitated learning, the concurrent augmented feedback directed the learners' attention to important features of the tasks that would be almost impossible to attend to otherwise because there is nothing inherent in the tasks themselves that tells a person how to perform a skill correctly.

THE KR-DELAY AND POST-KR INTERVALS

The second timing issue related to augmented feedback concerns when the feedback is given terminally. Two intervals of time are created between two trials: the **KR-delay interval** and the **post-KR interval.**[1] These intervals are depicted graphically in figure 14.7. To understand the relationship between these intervals and skill learning, we must understand the influence of two variables: *time,* i.e., the length of the interval, and *activity,* i.e., the cognitive and/or motor activity during the interval.

The Length of the KR-Delay Interval

It is not uncommon to see statements in textbooks indicating that a learner should receive augmented feedback as soon as possible after performing a skill, because delaying it beyond a certain amount of time would lead to poorer learning. A significant problem with this viewpoint is that it has little research evidence to support it. Such a view comes from research based predominantly on animal learning (see Adams, 1987). Research has established that human learners see augmented feedback as more than a reward: augmented feedback has informational value that humans use to solve problems associated with learning a skill. Whereas animal learning studies have shown that delaying reward leads to decreased learning, human skill learning studies have shown that delaying augmented feedback does not have this negative effect.

Although delaying the presentation of augmented feedback does not appear to affect skill learning, there does seem to be a *minimum amount of time* that must pass before it is given. Swinnen, Schmidt, Nicholson, and Shapiro (1990) demonstrated this in experiments in which participants learned to move a lever to achieve a specific

---

[1] Note that the terminology used to describe these two intervals follows the traditional labels used in the majority of the research literature, even though we have been using the term KR in a more specific way than these interval labels imply. It is important to see these intervals as relevant to *all* forms of augmented feedback.

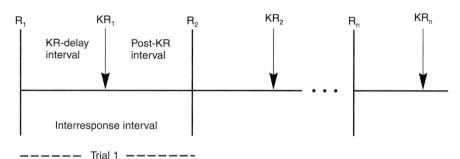

FIGURE 14.7 Intervals of time related to KR during the acquisition of a skill.

movement-time goal, or coincident in time with the appearance of a target light. They received KR at three different times: immediately upon completing the required movement (i.e., "instantaneously"), or 3.2, or 8 sec after completing it. The results showed that giving KR instantaneously upon completing a movement had a negative effect on learning.

Why would receiving augmented feedback immediately after completing a movement not be good for learning a skill? One possibility is that when learners receive augmented feedback too soon after the completion of a movement, they are not able to engage in their own analysis of task-intrinsic feedback, which is essential for them to develop error-detection capabilities. When augmented feedback is delayed by just a few seconds, these capabilities can develop more effectively.

Activity During the KR-Delay Interval
Researchers investigating the effects of activity during the KR-delay interval have found *three types of outcomes*. The most common effect of activity during the KR-delay interval on skill learning is that it has *no influence on learning*. Experiments have demonstrated this result since the 1960s (e.g., Bilodeau, 1969; Boulter, 1964; Marteniuk, 1986).

The second type of effect is much less common. There is some evidence, although it is sparse, that activity during the KR-delay interval *hinders learning*. Two specific types of activities have shown this negative effect. A study by Marteniuk (1986) tested the hypothesis that if KR-delay inter-

val activity were to interfere with learning, it would have to interfere with the same learning processes required by the primary task being learned. The results of two experiments showed that when the participants had to learn either a motor or a cognitive skill during the KR-delay interval, these activities interfered with learning of the primary skill.

The other type of KR-delay interval activity that research has shown to hinder skill learning involved estimating the movement-time error of another person's movement, which the second person performed during the interval. In an experiment by Swinnen (1990), people learned to move a lever a specified distance, involving two reversals of direction, in a criterion movement time. Participants who engaged in the error estimation activity during the KR-delay interval showed worse performance on a retention test than those who did nothing or who performed a nonlearning task during the interval.

Third, certain activities during the KR-delay interval actually can *benefit learning*. One type of activity that has consistently demonstrated this effect requires the person to evaluate his or her own performance. We will refer to this activity as the

---

KR-delay interval   the interval of time between the completion of a movement and the presentation of augmented feedback.

post-KR interval   the interval of time between the presentation of augmented feedback and the beginning of the next trial.

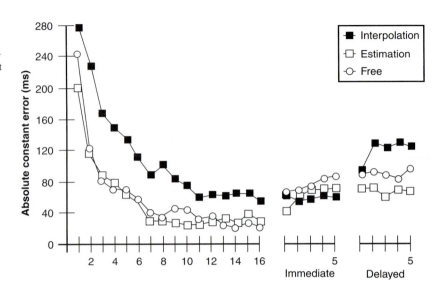

FIGURE 14.8   Results from the experiment by Swinnen showing the influence of estimating the experimenter's movement error (interpolation group) and the influence of estimating the participant's own error (estimation group) during the KR-delay interval, compared with no activity during the interval (free group). [From Swinnen, S. P. (1990). Interpolated activities during the knowledge of results delay and post-knowledge of results interval: Effects on performance and learning. *Journal of Experimental Psychology: Learning, Memory, and Cognition, 16,* 692–705. Copyright © 1990 by the American Psychological Association. Reprinted with permission.]

subjective performance evaluation strategy. Research has established the effectiveness of two approaches to the use of this strategy. One requires the estimation of the outcome of the performance, the other requires the evaluation of the movement-related characteristics of the performance of the skill. Swinnen (1990), in the experiment described above, compared the strategies of the participant estimating his or her own performance outcome error with estimating performance outcome error of another person's movement. Figure 14.8 shows that the subjective performance estimation strategy led to a learning benefit, but the strategy of estimating another person's performance hindered learning.

The second type of beneficial subjective performance estimation involves the estimation of specific characteristics of some of the movement-related components of an action. In an experiment by Liu and Wrisberg (1997) participants practiced throwing a ball at a target as accurately as possible with the nonpreferred arm and without vision of the target. Participants received KR by seeing where on the target the ball had landed on each trial. During the KR-delay interval, some of the participants rated on 5-point scales the appropriateness of the force, angle of ball release, and ball trajectory of the throw, and then estimated the

throw's point value on the target. The results indicated that these participants performed more accurately on a retention than those who had not used the estimation strategy.

We find an interesting parallel to the subjective performance estimation strategy in what researchers call the *trials-delay procedure.* Here, experiment participants receive KR for a trial after they complete performance on a later trial. Anderson, Magill, and Sekiya (1994) reported one of the most recent experiments providing evidence for the effectiveness of this effect. Participants practiced making a blindfolded aiming movement. One group received KR about distance error after every trial (delay–0). A second group received KR two trials later (delay–2), which meant that they were told their error for trial 1 after completing trial 3. Results (figure 14.9) were that while the delay condition hindered performance during practice, it led to better performance on a twenty-four-hour retention test.

What do these different effects of activity reveal about learning processes that occur during the KR-delay interval? Our conclusion is that during this time interval the learner is actively engaged in learning processes involving activities such as developing an understanding of the task-instrinsic feedback and establishing essential error detection capabilities.

LAB LINKS

Lab 14b in the Online Learning Center Lab Manual provides an opportunity for you to experience the effects on motor skill learning of estimating your own error during the KR-delay interval during practice.

For instructional purposes, the most significant implication of the various types of effects of activity during the KR-delay interval is that people who are practicing a skill can use a beneficial strategy after they complete the performance of a skill and before a teacher, coach, or therapist gives them augmented feedback. Before they receive augmented feedback, they could verbally describe what they think they did wrong that led to a less than desired performance outcome.

The Length of the Post-KR Interval

The significance of the post-KR interval is that it is during this period of time that the learner develops a plan of action for the next trial. This planning occurs during this interval because the learner now has available both task-intrinsic feedback and augmented feedback.

If the learner processes critical skill learning information during the post-KR interval, we would expect there to be a minimum length for this interval. Although there is not an abundance of research that has investigated this issue, there is empirical evidence that has shown that indeed, this interval can be too short (e.g., Weinberg, Guy, & Tupper, 1964; Rogers, 1974; Gallagher & Thomas, 1980). For optimal learning, a minimum amount of time is needed for the learner to engage in the learning processes required. Conversely, there is no evidence indicating an optimal length for the post-KR interval. Research consistently has shown no apparent upper limit for the length of this interval.

Activity During the Post-KR Interval

The effect of engaging in activity is similar for the post-KR interval to that for the KR-delay interval. Depending on the type of activity, activity can have no effect on learning, interfere with learning, or benefit learning.

The most common finding has been that activity during the post-KR interval *has no effect on skill*

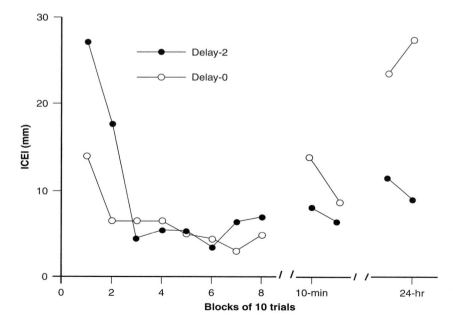

FIGURE 14.9 Results of the Anderson et al. experiment showing the beneficial effects of delaying a trial's KR for two trials (delay-2) compared to presenting KR after each trial (delay-0) for learning a manual aiming task. (Reprinted with permission from *Research Quarterly for Exercise and Sport, Vol. 65, No. 3,* 286–290. Copyright © 1994 by the American Association for Health, Physical Education, Recreation, and Dance, 1900 Association Drive, Reston, VA 20191.)

A CLOSER LOOK

Practical Implications of the Effects of KR-Delay and Post-KR Intervals

- A brief time interval should occur between a person's completion of a movement and the teacher's or therapist's giving of augmented feedback.
- Although an instructor's delaying of augmented feedback for a considerable length of time does not negatively affect learning of the skill, it undoubtedly influences the motivation of the person to continue to try to achieve the activity goal.
- A useful technique to facilitate skill learning is to have the person overtly focus attention on what he

or she did wrong on a practice attempt by having the person respond, before being told what he or she did wrong, to this question: "What do you think you did wrong that time?"
- There is little need to be concerned about the length of the activity engaged in during the post-KR interval in terms of its influence on the degree of skill learning. However, the teacher or therapist should take motivational considerations into account on an individual basis.

learning. The best example is in an experiment by Lee and Magill (1983) in which participants practiced making an arm movement in 1050 msec. During each post-KR interval, one group attempted the same movement in 1350 msec, one group engaged in a cognitive activity involving number guessing, and a third group did no activity. At the end of the practice trials, the two activity groups showed poorer performance than the no-activity group. However, this was a temporary performance effect rather than a learning effect: on a no-KR retention test, the three groups did not differ.

Several researchers have reported results indicating that activity during the post-KR interval *hinders learning.* Of these, only those by Benedetti and McCullagh (1987) and Swinnen (1990, experiment 3) included appropriate tests for learning. In both of these experiments, the interfering activity was a cognitive activity. Participants in the experiment by Benedetti and McCullagh engaged in a mathematics problem-solving task, whereas those in the experiment by Swinnen guessed the movement-time error of a lever movement the experimenter made during the post-KR interval.

Only one experiment (Magill, 1988) has demonstrated that *beneficial learning effects* can result from activity in the post-KR interval. Participants learned a two-component arm movement in which each component had its own criterion movement time. During the post-KR interval, one group had to learn two additional two-component move-

ments, one group had to learn a mirror-tracing task, and a third group did not engage in activity. Results showed that although there were no group differences on a no-KR retention test, the two groups engaged in activity during the post-KR interval performed better than the no-activity group on a transfer test in which participants learned a new two-component movement.

What do these different effects of activity tell us about learning processes that occur during the post-KR interval? They support the view we discussed earlier that learners engage in important planning activities during this time period. They use this planning time to take into account the discrepancy between the task-intrinsic and the augmented feedback, to determine how to execute the next attempt at performing the skill. Much of this planning seems to require cognitive activity; we see this in the experiments showing that engaging in cognitive problem-solving activity during this interval hinders learning.

FREQUENCY OF PRESENTING AUGMENTED FEEDBACK

For many years, the view was that augmented feedback should be given during or after every practice trial (i.e., 100 percent frequency), because no learning occurred on trials without augmented feedback. However, beginning with the influential review and evaluation of the KR literature by

Salmoni, Schmidt, and Walter (1984) and continuing to the present time, this traditional view has been revised as researchers have provided evidence that is contrary to predictions of that viewpoint.

The Reduced Frequency Benefit

Sufficient research evidence has now accumulated for us to say confidently that the optimal frequency for giving augmented feedback is *not* 100 percent. The best example of the initial evidence to support this conclusion was from an experiment by Winstein and Schmidt (1990). They had participants practice producing the complex movement pattern shown in the top panel of figure 14.10 by moving a lever on a tabletop to manipulate a cursor on a computer monitor. During the two days of practice, participants received KR after either 100 percent or 50 percent of the trials. For the 50 percent condition, the experimenters used a *fading technique* in which they systematically reduced the KR frequency; they provided KR after each of the first twenty-two trials of each day, then had participants perform eight trials with no KR, then systematically reduced the frequency from eight to two trials for the remaining eight-trial blocks each day. The results of this experiment are presented in the bottom panel of figure 14.10. In a no-KR retention test given one day later, the faded 50 percent frequency condition led to better retention performance than the 100 percent condition produced. In fact, people who had received KR after every practice trial showed retention test performance at a level resembling that of their first day of practice.

The Winstein and Schmidt (1990) study has generated a great deal of research since it was published. The research has focused on two predominant themes: providing additional empirical support for the reduced frequency benefit, and determining whether or not an optimal frequency exists to enhance skill learning. Two interesting conclusions have resulted from these research efforts. First, although a reduced frequency of augmented feedback can benefit motor skill learning, it may *not* benefit the learning of all motor skills. Second, an optimal relative frequency appears to be specific to the skill being learned.

LAB LINKS

Lab 14c in the Online Learning Center Lab Manual provides an opportunity for you to compare the effects on motor skill learning of different frequencies of receiving KR during practice

Theoretical Implications of the Frequency Effect

The challenge for those interested in developing motor learning theory is to establish why giving augmented feedback less than 100 percent of the time during practice is better for skill learning. One possible reason is that when people receive augmented feedback after every trial, they eventually experience an attention-capacity "overload." After several trials, the cumulative effect is that there is more information available than the person can handle.

A more likely possibility is that giving augmented feedback on every trial leads to engaging the learner in a fundamentally different type of learning processing than he or she would experience if it were not given on every trial. Schmidt and his colleagues (e.g., Salmoni, Schmidt, & Walter, 1984; Winstein & Schmidt, 1990) proposed this view, which they called the **guidance hypothesis.** According to this hypothesis, if the learner receives augmented feedback on every trial (i.e., at 100 percent frequency), then it will effectively "guide" the learner to perform the movement correctly. However, there is a negative aspect to this guidance process. By using augmented feedback as the guidance source, the learner develops a dependency on the availability of augmented feedback so that when he or she must

guidance hypothesis a hypothesis indicating that the role of augmented feedback in learning is to guide performance to be correct during practice; however, if it is provided too frequently, it can cause the learner to develop a dependency on its availability and therefore to perform poorly when it is not available.

FIGURE 14.10 The top panel shows the goal movement pattern in the Winstein and Schmidt experiment. A sample of one participant's attempt to produce this pattern is superimposed. The RMS error score is shown as the subject saw it. Note that the goal pattern lasted for 0.8 sec while the participant produced a 1.0-sec pattern. The bottom panel shows the results of this experiment for the 100 percent KR frequency and 50 percent KR frequency groups, where the 50 percent group had KR frequency "faded" from 100 percent to 0 percent. [From Winstein, C. J., & Schmidt, R. A. (1990). Reduced frequency of knowledge of results enhances motor skill learning. *Journal of Experimental Psychology: Learning, Memory and Cognition, 16,* 677–691. Copyright © 1990 American Psychological Association. Reprinted by permission.]

perform the skill without it, performance will be poorer than if augmented feedback were provided. In effect, augmented feedback becomes a crutch for the learner that is essential for performing the skill.

The hypothesis further proposes that receiving augmented feedback less frequently during practice encourages the learner to engage in more beneficial learning strategies during practice. For example, active problem-solving activities increase during trials with no augmented feedback. The learner does not become dependent on the availability of augmented feedback, and therefore can perform the skill well, even in its absence.

TECHNIQUES THAT REDUCE AUGMENTED FEEDBACK FREQUENCY

Now that we have established that it is generally more effective to provide augmented feedback less frequently than on every practice trial, a question that remains concerns how to implement ways that

A CLOSER LOOK

Practical Implications of the Reduced Frequency Effect

The conclusion that augmented feedback does not need to be given after every practice trial

- reduces the demand on the instructor, coach, or therapist to provide augmented feedback all the time. This should be especially comforting for those who work with groups, because research evidence shows that they typically do not provide augmented feedback with 100 percent frequency. In fact, in group practice situations, the teacher, coach, or therapist provides augmented feedback about one or two times per minute, with the same student rarely receiving more than a few feedback statements throughout a class session or practice

period (e.g., see Eghan, 1988; Fishman & Tobey, 1978; Silverman, Tyson, & Krampitz, 1991).
- is based on the use of augmented feedback to provide error correction information. However, it is important not to ignore the role of augmented feedback as a source of motivation when considering the frequency question. Although learners do not need externally presented error correction information after every trial, they may benefit from feedback statements that are motivation oriented on some intervening trials.

reduce frequency. The fading technique, described in the previous section, is one useful approach to reducing frequency. But there are several other techniques that are effective as well.

Performance-Based Bandwidths

When the decision to give augmented feedback is determined by performance-based bandwidth criteria, which we discussed earlier in this chapter, the frequency of giving augmented feedback will be less than on every trial. Recall from that discussion that this bandwidth technique for giving augmented feedback involves providing it only when performance is *not* within a preestablished tolerance limit (i.e., bandwidth). If we relate the bandwidth technique to the augmented feedback frequency issue, we can see how the bandwidth technique influences the frequency of presenting augmented feedback.

Lee, White, and Carnahan (1990) were the first to investigate this relationship. In their experiment they paired individual participants so that one of each pair received KR only on the trials on which the other of the pair received KR in 5 percent and 10 percent bandwidth conditions. The reason for the pairing of participants (a procedure known as "yoking") was to control for the possibility that the performance-based bandwidth benefit for learning was due to a reduced KR frequency. Thus, KR fre-

quency was the same for each pair of participants, but the KR frequency for the participant in the bandwidth condition depended on the 5 and 10 percent criteria. Results showed that the bandwidth-based KR conditions led to better retention performance. The researchers concluded that although the performance-based bandwidth technique reduces augmented feedback frequency, there are additional reasons why the technique enhances learning.

Two additional experiments will serve as examples of research that help us better understand the relationship between the performance-based bandwidth technique and augmented feedback frequency. In the experiment by Goodwin and Meeuwsen (1995) which was described earlier in this chapter, 0 percent and 10 percent error bandwidth conditions were compared with those that were systematically expanded (0-5-10-15-20 percent) and contracted (20-15-10-5-0 percent) while practicing putting a golf ball a criterion distance. The two conditions that resulted in the best retention test performance showed interesting KR frequencies. The frequencies for the 10 percent bandwidth condition reduced from 62 percent during the first twenty trials, to between 47 percent and 50 percent on the remaining trials. For the expanding bandwidth condition, KR frequencies began at 99 percent for the first twenty trials when the bandwidth was 0 percent, but then eventually reduced to 19 percent by the end of the practice trials, as the bandwidths increased in size. These results indicate that it is the reduction of KR frequency during practice that is important to improved learning. More recently, Lai and Shea (1999a) reported similar findings for the learning of a complex spatial-temporal movement pattern.

The results of these experiments raise interesting questions concerning why the bandwidth technique facilitates skill learning. We know part of the reason is that the technique reduces augmented feedback presentation frequency. Lee, White, and Carnahan (1990) proposed that the benefit resulting from the bandwidth technique is due to combining the presentation of augmented feedback with what the motor control system is capable of doing. Early in practice, the system is not capable of correcting errors with the precision required within a narrow bandwidth, as when errors must be corrected within a 5 percent or 10 percent tolerance limit. However, later in practice the system has acquired this capability.

From an instructional perspective, the bandwidth technique provides a useful means of *individualizing the systematic reduction of the frequency of augmented feedback* in practice situations. The bandwidth technique gives the practitioner a specific guideline for when to provide augmented feedback that encourages the learner to engage in important learning strategies. And because the bandwidth is related to individual performance, the learner can engage in these strategies at his or her own rate.

Self-Selected Frequency

Another technique that bases the frequency of augmented feedback on the individual who is learning the skill involves the learner receiving augmented feedback only when he or she asks for it. The learning benefits derived from this approach appear to result from the learner participating more actively in determining characteristics of the practice conditions by self-regulating the presentation of augmented feedback. An experiment by Janelle, Kim, and Singer (1995) provided initial evidence that

this strategy can enhance the learning of motor skills. College students practiced an underhand golf ball toss to a target on the ground. The students received KP about ball force, ball loft, and arm swing during practice. Compared to groups that received KP according to experimenter-determined frequencies (all of which received it less frequently than on every trial), the participants who controlled KP frequency themselves, performed more accurately on the retention test.

Janelle substantiated and extended these results in a later study in which videotape replay was a source of augmented feedback in addition to verbal KP (Janelle, Barba, Frehlich, Tennant, & Cauraugh, 1997). Participants in the self-regulated group controlled the augmented feedback schedule by requesting KP at will during 200 practice trials. An important characteristic of this experiment was that individual participants in another group were paired (i.e., yoked) to participants in the self-regulated condition to receive KP on the same trials, but without requesting it. The importance of this yoked condition was to control for the possibility that the effect of self-regulation of augmented feedback is due only to reduced frequency. Results showed that participants in the self-regulated condition learned the throwing accuracy task with more accuracy and better throwing technique than participants in the other KP and yoked conditions.

In terms of augmented feedback frequency, it is interesting to note that participants in the self-controlled condition requested KP on only 7 percent of the practice trials in the Janelle et al. (1995) experiment, and on only 11 percent in the Janelle et al. (1997) experiment. These low frequencies indicate that there is some relationship between the self-controlled procedure and the reduced relative frequency of augmented feedback. However, because people in the self-controlled conditions in both experiments performed better on retention tests than those in the frequency-yoked conditions, the benefit of the self-controlled situation is more than a simple frequency effect.

Why do beginners ask for feedback from an instructor? An experiment by Chiviakowsky and Wulf (2002) asked this question to participants in an experiment involving the learning of a sequential timing task. Each participant was asked on a questionnaire, "When/why did you ask for feedback?" Two-thirds of the participants answered that it was after what they considered to be a good trial. None indicated they asked for feedback after what they thought was a bad trial. These results indicate the importance of augmented feedback as a source of information to confirm a learner's subjective evaluation of his or her performance. The use of augmented feedback in this way allows beginners to engage in their own problem-solving strategies as they learn the skill and to test the validity of their own assessment of their progress in achieving the action goal.

Summary and Averaged Augmented Feedback
Another way to reduce the frequency of augmented feedback presentations is to give a listing of performance-related information after a certain number of practice trials. This technique, which is known as *summary augmented feedback,* reduces the presentation frequency of augmented feedback while providing the same amount of information as if it were given after every trial.

The summary technique could be advantageous in several types of skill learning situations. For example, suppose that a therapy patient must do a series of ten leg extensions in relatively rapid succession. To give augmented feedback after every extension may not be possible, if time limits restrict access to performance information after each attempt. A summary of all ten attempts could help overcome this limitation. Or, suppose that a person is practicing a shooting skill for which he or she cannot see the target because of the distance involved. Efficiency of practice could be increased if that person did not receive augmented feedback after each shot, but received information about each shot after every ten shots.

The first study to generate a great deal of interest in the summary technique was a laboratory-based experiment by Schmidt, Young, Swinnen, and Shapiro (1989). The task involved moving a lever along a trackway to achieve a goal movement time. During the practice trials, participants re-

ceived KR after every trial or in summary form after five, ten, or fifteen trials. The results of this experiment (see figure 14.11) showed very little difference between the conditions during practice and on a retention test given ten minutes after practice. But on a retention test two days later, the group that had received KR after every trial performed the worst, whereas the group that had received summary KR after every fifteen trials performed the best.

In an experiment involving the learning of target shooting with rifles, Boyce (1991) provided one group with KP after every shot, and another group with KP about every shot after each fifth shot. The results showed no difference in eventual shooting performance by these groups. Although the summary method did not yield better performance than the method giving KP after every shot, its effectiveness as an instructional technique was established, because it was just as effective for improving performance as the other method.

The decade of the 1990s saw several studies published that provided evidence supporting the benefit of the summary technique for motor skill learning (e.g., Schmidt, Lange, & Young, 1990; Wright, Snowden, & Willoughby, 1990; Guay, Salmoni, & Lajoie, 1999). However, a very practical question remains to be answered: What is the optimal number of performance attempts, or practice trials, to include in a summary augmented feedback statement? Although there have been several attempts to determine if a specific number of trials is optimal, the results have been equivocal. Two answers appear reasonable at the present time on the basis of results of research that has investigated this question. First, Sidaway, Moore, and Schoenfelder-Zohdi (1991) concluded that the positive effects of the summary technique are not due to the number of trials summarized, and stated that their results argue against the notion of an "optimal summary length." Instead, they argued that the summary effect is related either to the reduced frequency of presenting augmented feedback, or to the trials delay involved in presenting augmented feedback using the summary technique (note that the summary technique has characteristics similar to the trials-delay procedure,

FIGURE 14.11 Results of the experiment by Schmidt et al., showing the effects of learning a timing movement with different summary KR conditions. (Sum 1 = KR after every trial; Sum 5 = KR for five trials presented every five trials, etc.) [From Schmidt, R. A., et al., (1989). Summary knowledge of results for skill acquisition: support for the guidance hypothesis. *Journal of Experimental Psychology: Learning, Memory and Cognition. 15,* 352–359. Copyright © 1989 American Psychological Association. Reprinted by permission.]

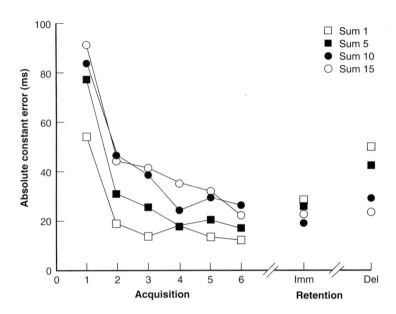

which we discussed earlier in this chapter). An alternative answer to the question is one we have seen related to many of the issues discussed in this book. The "optimal" summary length may be specific to the skill being learned. Guadagnoli, Dornier, and Tandy (1996) provided evidence for this possibility by showing that longer summaries are better for the learning of simple skills, whereas shorter summaries lead to better learning of more complex skills.

One of the possible strategies people may use when presented with a listing of augmented feedback is to *estimate an average for the series of trials* that the summary includes. The research literature provides some evidence that this may occur. In experiments in which the learner receives the average score for all the trials in a series, the results have shown that this procedure leads to better learning than presenting augmented feedback after every trial (Young & Schmidt, 1992), and no better or worse than after every trial or after every third trial (Wulf & Schmidt, 1996). But when compared to the summary technique, no differences are found in terms of their influence on skill learning (Guay, Salmoni, & Lajoie, 1999; Weeks & Sherwood, 1994; Yao, Fischman, & Wang, 1994).

Finally, why are these two feedback presentation methods effective? Their effectiveness is undoubtedly due to the same factors that lead to the benefit of reducing augmented feedback frequency, as explained by the guidance hypothesis. During practice trials on which they receive no augmented feedback, people engage in beneficial learning activities that are not characteristic of people who receive augmented feedback after every trial.

SUMMARY

- Augmented feedback is performance-related feedback that is provided by an external source; it adds to or enhances *task-instrinsic feedback,* which is performance-related feedback directly available to the sensory system during the performance of a skill.
- Two types of augmented feedback are distinguished on the basis of the aspect of a skill performance to which the information refers:
  ‣ *Knowledge of results (KR)* refers to the performance of a skill.

 ▸ *Knowledge of performance (KP)* refers to the movement-related characteristics associated with the outcome of the performance of a skill

- Augmented feedback plays two roles in the skill learning process:
  ▸ To facilitate achievement of the action goal of the skill.
  ▸ To motivate the learner to continue to strive toward the achievement of a goal.
- The need for augmented feedback for skill learning can be described in four different ways:
  ▸ It can be essential for skill learning.
  ▸ It may not be essential for skill learning.
  ▸ It can enhance skill learning beyond what is possible without it.
  ▸ It can hinder skill learning.
- Augmented feedback content issues include the following:
  ▸ Should the information conveyed to the learner refer to the errors made or to those aspects of the performance that were correct?
  ▸ Should the augmented feedback be KR or KP?
  ▸ Should the augmented feedback be quantitative or qualitative?
  ▸ Should the augmented feedback be based on the size of the error(s) and/or number of errors?
  ▸ What is the effect of erroneous augmented feedback on skill learning?
- KP can be presented to the learner in several different forms:
  ▸ Verbal KP, which can provide either descriptive or prescriptive information.
  ▸ Videotape replays of skill performances.
  ▸ Movement kinematics associated with a performance of a skill.
  ▸ Biofeedback.
- In addition to giving augmented feedback after a person has completed a trial, or after the performance of a skill (i.e., *terminal augmented feedback*), it can be presented during the performance (i.e., *concurrent augmented feedback*).
- Concurrent augmented feedback can have negative and positive effects on skill learning.
- Two intervals of time associated with terminal augmented feedback are the KR-delay inter-

val and the post-KR interval. Both require a minimum length of time, although a maximum length has not been determined. Engaging in activity during these intervals can hinder, benefit, or have no effect on skill learning.
- Research evidence indicates that the optimal frequency for giving augmented feedback is less than on every practice trial. The guidance hypothesis represents the most commonly held view for explaining the learning benefit of a reduced frequency.
- Several techniques will reduce augmented feedback frequency:
  ▸ Performance-based bandwidths.
  ▸ Performer-selected frequency.
  ▸ Summary and averaged augmented feedback.

RELATED READINGS

Carnahan, H., Vandervoort, A. A., & Swanson, L. R. (1996). The influence of summary knowledge of results and aging on motor learning. *Research Quarterly for Exercise and Sport, 67,* 280–287.

Chen, D. D., Hendrick, J. L., & Lidor, R. (2002). Enhancing self-controlled learning environments: The use of self-regulated feedback information. *Journal of Human Movements Studies, 43,* 69–86

Downing, J. H., & Lander, J. E. (2002, Nov./Dec.). Performance errors in weight training and their correction. *Journal of Physical Education, Recreation, and Dance, 73,* 44–52

Guadagnoli, M., Holcomb, W., & Davis, M. (2002). The efficacy of video feedback for learning the golf swing. *Journal of Sports Sciences, 20,* 615–622

Lee, A. M., Keh, N. C., & Magill, R. A. (1993). Instructional effects of teacher feedback in physical education. *Journal of Teaching in Physical Education, 12,* 228–243.

Magill, R. A. (2001). Augmented feedback and skill acquisition. In R. N. Singer, H. A. Hausenblaus, & C. Janelle (Eds.), *Handbook on research in sport psychology* (2nd ed.) pp. 86–114. New York: Wiley.

Schmidt, R. A., & Wulf, G. (1997). Continuous concurrent feedback degrades skill learning: Implications for training and simulation. *Human Factors, 39,* 509–525.

Swinnen, S. P. (1996). Information feedback for motor skill learning: A review. In H. N. Zelaznik (Ed.), *Advances in motor learning and control* (pp. 37–66). Champaign, IL: Human Kinetics.

Swinnen, S. P. (1998). Age-related deficits in motor learning and differences in feedback processing during the production of a bimanual coordination pattern. *Cognitive Neuropsychology, 15,* 439–466.

Wrisberg, C. A., Dale, G. A., Liu, Z., & Reed, A. (1995). The effects of augmented information on motor learning: A multidimensional assessment. *Research Quarterly for Exercise and Sport, 66,* 9–16.

STUDY QUESTIONS

1. Describe the two general types of performance-related feedback a person can receive during or after performing a motor skill. In your description, indicate the characteristic that differentiates the two.

2. What are the two types of information referred to by the terms KR and KP? Give two examples of each.

3. Describe skill learning conditions where augmented feedback would (a) be necessary for learning, (b) not be necessary for learning, and (c) not be necessary for learning but would enhance learning.

4. How do quantitative and qualitative augmented feedback differ, and how do they influence the learning of motor skills?

5. Describe a situation in which you would use videotape replay as a form of augmented feedback to (a) help a beginner learn a new skill, (b) help a skilled person correct a performance problem.

6. (a) What do we currently know about the use and benefit of kinematic information as augmented feedback to help someone learn a motor skill? (b) Describe a situation in which you would use this type of information and explain why you would use it.

7. (a) Discuss the different types of learning effects that biofeedback has been shown to have on skill learning. (b) Describe a skill learning situation in which you would use some form of biofeedback. Indicate how you would use it, and why you would expect it to enhance the learning of the skill.

8. What is the difference between concurrent and terminal augmented feedback? Give two examples of each.

9. (a) What are two types of activity during the KR-delay interval that have been shown to benefit skill learning? (b) Why does this benefit occur?

10. (a) What seems to be the most appropriate conclusion to draw regarding the frequency with which an instructor should give augmented feedback during learning? (b) How does the guidance hypothesis relate to the issue of augmented feedback frequency?

11. Describe a skill learning situation in which (a) giving summary augmented feedback would be a beneficial technique, (b) using the self-selected frequency strategy would be beneficial.

UNIT

VI

PRACTICE CONDITIONS

CHAPTER

Practice Variability

*Concept: Variability of practice experiences
is important for learning motor skills*

After completing this chapter, you will be able to

- Explain the meaning of the term *practice variability* and its relation to predictions of theories of motor skill learning

- Discuss ways to implement practice variability in skill learning or relearning contexts

- Describe how the *contextual interference effect* relates to organizing variable practice

- Discuss the relevance of contextual interference as a basis for scheduling practice for novice learners and skilled performers

- Identify reasons that contextual interference benefits motor skill learning

Application

A primary reason a person practices a skill is to increase his or her capability of performing it in future situations that will require the skill. For example, some people will need to perform sport skills successfully in skills tests, games, and matches. Dancers need to perform in recitals, performances, and competitions. And rehab patients practice skills so that they can perform them as needed in their everyday environment. Because of this future performance requirement, teachers, coaches, and therapists must design and establish practice conditions that will lead to the greatest probability of successful performance in the situations that will require the skills.

One practice characteristic that increases the chances for future performance success is the variability of the learner's experiences while he or she

practices. This includes variations of the characteristics of the context in which the learner performs the skill, as well as variations of the skill he or she is practicing. The teacher, coach, or therapist must address several important questions to determine how to optimize the types and amount of variation to include in practice experiences. First, what aspects of performing the skill should he or she vary? Second, how much variety of experiences is optimal? Third, how should the variety of experiences be organized in the practice sessions? We consider these questions in the discussion that follows.

Discussion

A consistent characteristic of theories of motor skill learning is their emphasis on the learning benefits derived from practice variability. In these theories, **practice variability** refers to the variety of movement and context characteristics the learner experiences while practicing a skill. For example, in Schmidt's (1975) schema theory, a key prediction is that successful future performance of a skill depends on the amount of variability the learner experiences during practice. Similarly, Gentile's learning stages model (1972, 2000) emphasized the learner's need during practice to experience variations of regulatory and nonregulatory context characteristics. And dynamic pattern views of skill learning stress the learner's need to explore the perceptual motor workspace and to discover optimal solutions to the degrees-of-freedom problem posed by the skill (e.g., McDonald, Oliver, & Newell, 1995; Vereijken & Whiting, 1990).

THE FUTURE PERFORMANCE BENEFIT OF PRACTICE VARIABILITY

The primary benefit a learner derives from practice experiences that promote movement and context variability is an increased capability to perform the skill in a future test situation. This means that the person has acquired an increased capability to perform the practiced skill, as well as to adapt to novel conditions that might characterize the test situation. When viewed from the perspective of transfer of learning, the inclusion of movement and context variability in practice can be seen as a means of enhancing the probability of positive transfer from the practice to the test contexts.

One way to establish that practice variability benefits future performance is to compare the effects on retention or transfer test performance of practice situations involving one variation of a skill (i.e., *constant practice*) with those involving several variations of the skill (i.e., *variable practice*). This type of comparison has been the standard research strategy for testing Schmidt's (1975) schema theory hypothesis that greater amounts of variable practice lead to better learning than lesser amounts. Although an abundance of published research studies have investigated this hypothesis (see van Rossum, 1990, for a review of this research), two

examples will illustrate these studies, which have generally supported Schmidt's hypothesis.

In two experiments reported by Shea and Kohl (1990, 1991), the participants' goal was to learn to use 175N of force to press a handle. A constant practice group practiced this skill for 289 trials, while a variable practice group practiced producing four different amounts of force (125N, 150N, 200N, and 225N). Notice that none of the variations practiced by the variable practice group was the 175N goal. When both groups performed a retention/transfer test for the 175N goal (the test was a retention test for the constant group but a transfer test for the variable group), the variable group performed more accurately than the constant group.

An experiment involving a sports skill also showed that variable practice yielded better learning than constant practice (Shoenfelt, Snyder, Maue, McDowell, & Woolard, 2002). In this study, participants practiced shooting basketball free throws. The constant practice group, which practiced only from the free-throw line, improved during the three weeks of practice, but two weeks later on a retention test, returned to their pretest level of performance. On the other hand, three variable practice groups, only one of which included shooting from the free-throw line, improved during practice and performed on the retention test at a higher level than they had on the pretest.

An interesting irony concerning the benefit of an increased amount of practice variability is that it is usually associated with an *increased amount of performance error during practice*. However, this relationship is consistent with research evidence that shows more performance error can be better than less error for skill learning, when it occurs in the initial learning stage. A good example of this evidence is an experiment by Edwards and Lee (1985). Each participant had to learn to move

---

practice variability   the variety of movement and context characteristics a person experiences while practicing a skill.

A CLOSER LOOK

Constant and Variable Practice for Learning to Shoot Free Throws in Basketball

The experiment by Shoenfelt, Snyder, Maue, McDowell, & Woolard (2002) involved university students who were not skilled basketball players practicing basketball free throws.

Practice and Test Schedules

Pretest	40 free throws (20 sets of 2 shots)
Practice	40 free throws per day (20 sets of 2 shots) M, T, W, Th, each week for 3 weeks
Weekly tests	Each Monday's session of 40 free throws was a weekly progress test
Retention test	40 free throws (20 sets of 2 shots) two weeks after the last practice session

Practice Variability Conditions

Constant practice (C)	Free-throw shooting from the free-throw line only
Variable practice – Front & Back (VFB)	Free-throw shots from 2 ft in front of and 2 ft behind the free-throw line (randomly assigned in each practice session)
Variable practice – Combination (VC)	Combination of C and VFB conditions
Variable practice – Random (VR)	Free-throw shots from the "elbow" to the left and to the right of the key, and from the top of the key (randomly assigned in each practice session)

Results

FIGURE 15.1 Results from the experiment by Shoenfelt et al. showing the pre- to post-test percentage of improvement for the four practice variability groups (C = Constant practice; VFB = Variable Front and Back practice; VC = Variable Combination practice; VR = Variable Random practice). [*Source:* Data from Schoenfelt, E. L., Snyder, L. A., Maue, A. E., McDowell, C. P., & Woolard, C. D. (2002). Comparison of constant and variable practice conditions on free-throw shooting. *Perceptual and Motor Skills, 94,* 1113–1123.]

his or her arm through a specified pattern in 1200 msec. Participants in the prompted group were told that if they moved according to a "ready and 1, 2, 3, 4, 5" count on a tape, they would complete the movement in the criterion time. Each person practiced until he or she could do three trials in a row correctly at 1200 msec. Those in the trial-and-error group were told the goal movement time and received knowledge of results (KR) about their timing error after each trial. The results indicated that the two groups performed similarly on the retention test, but the trial-and-error group performed the 1800-msec novel transfer task more accurately.

What is particularly interesting about these results is how much the two groups differed in the amount of error each produced during practice. The prompted group performed with very little error during practice, whereas the trial-and-error group experienced much error, especially during the first fifteen trials. Yet experiencing less error during practice was no more beneficial for retention test performance, and it was detrimental for transfer to a novel variation of the practiced movement.

IMPLEMENTING PRACTICE VARIABILITY

The first step in determining how to provide an appropriate amount of practice variability is to assess the characteristics of the future situations in which the learner will perform a skill. Of particular relevance here are the *characteristics of the physical context* in which he or she will perform the skill and the *skill characteristics* that the performance situation will require. If you again view this situation as a transfer of learning situation, then you will see the value of using the test conditions to determine what the practice environment should be like. As we discussed in chapter 12 and illustrated in figure 12.1, effective transfer is a function of the similarities between skill, context, and cognitive processing characteristics of the practice and test situations. A high degree of similarity between these characteristics in the two situations enhances transfer between the practice and the test.

Varying Practice Contexts

It is important to keep in mind that when people perform skills, they do so in contexts that have identifiable characteristics. As we discussed in chapter 1, Gentile (2000) pointed out that some features of the performance context are critical for determining the movement characteristics of an action (which she called regulatory conditions), whereas other features (nonregulatory conditions) have no influence.

Consider some examples of *regulatory conditions* that influence a person's walking behavior.

LAB LINKS

Lab 15 in the Online Learning Center Lab Manual provides an opportunity for you to experience and compare the effects of constant and variable practice on learning a motor skill.

Certain movement characteristics will be different when you walk on a concrete sidewalk from when you walk on ice or on sand. Also, you walk differently on a busy sidewalk that is cluttered with other people than on a sidewalk empty of people. When regulatory conditions like these may vary from one performance context to another, it is important that practice conditions include a variety of similar conditions.

Nonregulatory conditions also play a role in influencing transfer between practice and test. For walking, some nonregulatory conditions would include the physical environment around the walking pathway, such as buildings, trees, and open space. Although these features do not influence the pattern of movement directly, they nonetheless can influence the degree of success a person may achieve in carrying out the action in a unique context. Again, when nonregulatory conditions will vary from one performance context to another, practice conditions should provide opportunities to experience these characteristics.

Varying the regulatory conditions when practicing snowboarding increases the person's capability to snowboard in conditions not previously experienced.

TABLE 15.1   Examples of Varying Practice Conditions for Two Types of Closed Skills

---

Intertrial Variability of Regulatory Conditions	**No Intertrial Variability of Regulatory Conditions**
Golf shot using a 7-iron The goal is to successfully make shots with the 7-iron during a golf match.	**Basketball free throw** The goal is to shoot free throws successfully in basketball games.
Regulatory conditions that remain constant in a match • 7-iron characteristics • golf ball characteristics	**Regulatory conditions that remain constant in games** • basket height • basket distance from free-throw line • basketball characteristics
Regulatory conditions that can vary in a match • goal for the shot • distance of required shot · • location of ball	**Nonregulatory conditions that can vary in games** • number of free throws to be taken • importance to game of making the free throws • crowd noise • length of the game
Nonregulatory conditions that can vary in a match • number of hole being played • number of strokes ahead or behind • cloudy or sunny skies • importance of a particular shot	*Practice conditions* should include as many *nonregulatory* conditions as possible to be similar to those that could be experienced in a game.
Practice conditions should simulate as many *regulatory* and *nonregulatory* conditions as possible to be similar to those that could be experienced in a match.	

Varying Practice Conditions for Closed Skills

The first step in making the decision about what to vary during the practice of a closed skill is to determine whether or not the skill involves intertrial variability for the regulatory conditions in the test situation. *For closed skills that do not involve intertrial variability of regulatory conditions,* nonregulatory conditions may be novel. For the practice of these types of skills, regulatory conditions should remain constant, but nonregulatory conditions should vary according to expectations for the test situation. *For closed skills that involve intertrial variability,* both regulatory and nonregulatory conditions are likely to be novel in the test situation, which means that both should be varied in practice. Examples of practice condition characteristics for each of these types of closed skills are presented in table 15.1.

Varying Practice Conditions for Open Skills

Each performance of an open skill is unique, because in each performance of the skill, certain char-

acteristics are new to the performer. That is, to perform the skill the person must produce certain movements that he or she has not made before in exactly the same manner this situation requires. The performer needs to modify previously produced movements in order to achieve the goal of the skill. For example, if you are preparing to return a serve in tennis, it is likely that certain characteristics of the ball action will be unique to this particular serve. Thus, in addition to variations of nonregulatory conditions, practice of open skills also needs to include a variety of experiences with regulatory conditions that change from one attempt to another.

ORGANIZING VARIABLE PRACTICE

Having established that practice variability benefits skill learning, we next must consider how the teacher, coach, or therapist should organize the variable experiences within a practice session or unit of instruction. The following example illus-

		Class day					
		1	2	3	4	5	6
Blocked practice	30 min	All overhand	All overhand	All underhand	All underhand	All sidearm	All sidearm
Random practice	5 min 5 min 5 min 5 min 5 min 5 min	Underhand Overhand Underhand Sidearm Underhand Overhand	Overhand Sidearm Sidearm Underhand Overhand Overhand	Sidearm Overhand Sidearm Underhand Underhand Sidearm	Overhand Sidearm Sidearm Underhand Overhand Overhand	Underhand Overhand Underhand Sidearm Underhand Overhand	Sidearm Overhand Sidearm Underhand Underhand Sidearm
Serial practice	5 min 5 min 5 min 5 min 5 min 5 min	Overhand Underhand Sidearm Overhand Underhand Sidearm	Overhand Underhand Sidearm Overhand Underhand Sidearm	Overhand Underhand Sidearm Overhand Underhand Sidearm	Overhand Underhand Sidearm Overhand Underhand Sidearm	Overhand Underhand Sidearm Overhand Underhand Sidearm	Overhand Underhand Sidearm Overhand Underhand Sidearm

FIGURE 15.2   A six-day unit plan demonstrating three different practice structures (blocked, random, and serial) for teaching three different throwing patterns (overhand, underhand, and sidearm). All classes are 30 min long and all but the blocked practice schedule are divided into 5-min segments. Each practice condition provides an equal amount of practice for each throwing pattern.

trates how this practice organization question is involved as the motor skills professional develops practice conditions.

Suppose you are an elementary school physical education teacher organizing a teaching unit on throwing for your classes. You have determined that you will devote six class periods to this unit. You want the students to experience three variations of the throwing pattern: the overhand, underhand, and sidearm throws. How should you arrange these three different throws for practice during the six class periods? Figure 15.2 shows three possible arrangements. One is to practice each throw in blocks of two days each (blocked practice). Another possibility is to practice each throw in a random arrangement with 5-min blocks devoted to each particular pattern (random practice). Thus, each day students would experience six 5-min blocks, with no specified order of occurrence for the three patterns; the only stipulation would be that they practice all three an equal amount over the course of the unit. The third arrangement, serial practice, also involves a 5-min block for each pattern. However, in this approach students practice each pattern for two sets of five minutes every day in the same order.

This organization question is not unique to physical education. It applies to any situation in

which learners must practice and learn several variations of a skill. Consider a few examples. In a therapy situation, a patient may need to practice grasping objects of different sizes, weights, and shapes. A patient who has had a knee joint replacement may need to practice walking on different types of surfaces. In a dance setting, a dancer may need to practice tempo variations in a routine or other variations of particular components of a routine. Each of these situations involves the same organization problem: How should the schedule of practice for these variations be organized within the practice time available?

The Contextual Interference Approach to Organizing Variable Practice

One way to solve the variable practice schedule problem is to apply the learning phenomenon known as the *contextual interference effect*. William Battig (1979), who first demonstrated this effect, introduced the term **contextual interference** to refer to

---

contextual interference   the interference that results from performing variations of a skill within the context of practice.

Amount of contextual interference

Practice schedules

FIGURE 15.3   The amount of contextual interference that is possible in a practice situation is portrayed as a continuum ranging from high to low. Also presented are sample variable practice schedules in terms of how each relates to the amount of contextual interference created by the schedule.

the *interference* that results from performing various tasks or skills within the *context* of practice. Different amounts of contextual interference can result from the organization of the practice schedule. The practice schedule organization options described earlier can be viewed as located along a continuum of contextual interference (see figure 15.3). A *high amount of contextual interference* occurs at one extreme, when the practice schedule involves a random arrangement of trials so that all the task variations are performed in each practice session. In this schedule, the task variation practiced on each trial would be randomly determined. At the opposite extreme, a *low amount of contextual interference* results from a schedule that organizes the practice of each task variation in its own block, or unit, of time. Other schedules, such as the serial schedule described earlier, fall along the continuum between these two extremes.

The **contextual interference effect** occurs when a high amount of contextual interference results in better learning (i.e., retention and transfer performance) of the task variations than a low amount. What is especially noteworthy about this effect is that prior to Battig's initial demonstration of it, researchers traditionally viewed interference as something that hinders learning. According to that view, a low amount of contextual interference during practice should lead to better learning than a high amount. However, Battig's research showed an important exception to the traditional view of interference. It is important to note in this regard that a negative influence of interference is often

found for high contextual interference schedules during practice. But this interference turns out to be a learning benefit, because the high contextual interference practice schedules result in better performance on retention and transfer tests than low contextual interference practice schedules.

The first evidence of the contextual interference effect for motor skill learning was reported by Shea and Morgan (1979). Participants practiced three variations of movement patterns in which the goal was to move one arm through a series of small wooden barriers as rapidly as possible. One group followed a blocked practice schedule (i.e., low contextual interference) in which each movement pattern was practiced in its own unit of trials. A second group practiced the three patterns according to a random practice schedule (i.e., high contextual interference) in which the practice of each pattern was randomly distributed throughout the practice trials. Results showed that the random practice schedule led to poorer performance during practice, but better performance on retention and transfer tests. Thus, random practice resulted in better learning of the three pattern variations and allowed for better performance for a new pattern. Since the Shea and Morgan experiment, numerous other studies have been reported (see Brady, 1998; Magill & Hall, 1990). The evidence from this research establishes that the contextual interference effect is generalizable to learning motor skills.

One of the striking negative effects of low contextual interference practice is that it inhibits performance of the practiced skills in novel perfor-

A CLOSER LOOK

A Professional Golfer's Use of Random Practice

Amy Alcott, a professional golfer on the LPGA tour, described in *Golf Magazine* (December, 1991) a drill she uses to help her make a swing of the correct length and strength for the distance. She practices pitch shots that are 20, 40, 60, and 80 yards from flags marking each distance. Before she hits a ball, her teacher, Walter Keller, calls out the yardage for the

shot. She looks at the flag, sets up, and swings. Then, her teacher calls out another yardage for the next shot. She says that "One after another, he'd call out yardages—60, 20, 40, 80, 40, 60." Alcott states that she finds this type of practice "invaluable," and repeats it from time to time throughout the season.

mance contexts. Contextual interference experiments commonly show this. Although blocked practice sometimes leads to blocked retention test performance that is similar to performance following random practice, a large decrement in retention performance is typical when researchers test the skills under random conditions (e.g., Shea, Kohl, & Indermill, 1990). On the other hand, high contextual interference practice does not show the same transfer problem. Thus, low contextual interference practice appears to develop a practice context dependency that decreases a person's capability to adapt to novel test contexts.

The Contextual Interference Effect
Outside the Laboratory

Battig's original demonstration of the contextual interference effect was based on the learning of cognitive skills, such as word lists. Much of the research involving motor skills has been based on the learning of laboratory tasks, such as the barrier-knockdown task used by Shea and Morgan (1979). Because it is important to establish that learning phenomena demonstrated in the laboratory also exist in real-world settings, we will look at some of the research that provides evidence that the contextual interference effect applies to learning situations outside the laboratory.

One of the first experiments that presented this type of evidence was reported by Goode and Magill (1986). College women with no prior badminton experience practiced the short, long, and drive serves from the right service court. They practiced these serves three days a week for three weeks with

36 trials in each practice session, for a total of 324 trials (108 trials per serve) during the practice period. The low contextual interference condition was a modification of the blocked condition used in previous studies; in this study, the blocked practice group practiced one serve each day of each week. The group on a random practice schedule practiced each serve randomly in every practice session. In this condition, the experimenter told each participant which serve she should perform next.

As you can see in figure 15.4, the results demonstrated the contextual interference effect. The group that practiced with the random schedule outperformed the blocked practice group on the retention and transfer tests. What is especially remarkable is that on the transfer test, which involved serving from the left service court, the random group showed no deterioration in performance. On the other hand, students in the group that had practiced in a blocked schedule were not able to adapt well to this new performance context. In fact, learners in this group performed in the new context about as well as they had when they had begun practicing the serves from the right court three weeks earlier.

contextual interference effect the learning benefit resulting from performing multiple skills in a high contextual interference practice schedule (e.g., random practice), rather than performing the skills in a low contextual interference schedule (e.g., blocked practice).

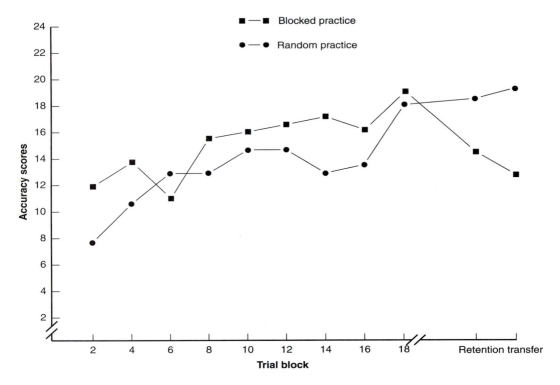

FIGURE 15.4   Results from the experiment by Goode and Magill showing the effects of blocked and random schedules of practice for three types of badminton serves on acquisition, one-day retention, and transfer. [Reprinted with permission from *Research Quarterly for Exercise and Sport, Vol. 57, No. 4,* 308–314. Copyright © 1986 by the American Alliance for Health, Physical Education, Recreation, and Dance, 1900 Association Drive, Reston, VA, 20191.]

The Goode and Magill study showed the benefit of high contextual interference for *beginners* learning an actual sport skill (the badminton serve). However, although their experiment used a sport skill, the authors carried it out in controlled experimental conditions. Those who seek even more real-world validity should note that Wrisberg and Liu (1991) attained the same results as Goode and Magill, but in an actual class setting. In that study, students learned the serves in a unit of instruction in an actual physical education class.

Another experiment worth noting demonstrates that the contextual interference effect for real-world skills exists not only for beginners, but also for *skilled individuals.* Hall, Domingues, and Cavazos (1994) had skilled baseball players practice hitting different types of pitches to improve their batting performance. The players engaged in forty-five extra pitches of batting practice three days a week for five weeks. Batters hit fastballs, curves, or change-ups according to a blocked or random schedule. In the blocked schedule, players practiced hitting one of these pitches on each day, whereas in the random schedule, they hit all three types of pitch, randomly presented, each day. The results showed that on a test involving a random sequence of pitches, like one that would occur in a game, players who had experienced the random practice schedule performed better than those who had practiced according to the blocked schedule.

In addition to these few examples, several other studies have found evidence that demonstrates the contextual interference effect for the learning of real-world skills. These include basketball shooting skills, tennis ground strokes, volleyball serves, rifle shooting, and computer game skills (see

Brady, 1998, for discussions of the various studies involving these skills). When considered together with the research based on laboratory tasks, research involving real-world skills establishes the contextual interference effect as an important motor learning phenomenon.

What Are the Limits of the Contextual Interference Effect?

Although researchers have provided a large amount of evidence supporting the contextual interference effect, they also have shown that it does not apply to all motor skill learning situations. As a result, it is important to determine those characteristics that limit the generalization of the effect. Both task and learner characteristics have been the focus of speculations and investigations of this issue.

Task characteristics were proposed as the primary limiting factor for the contextual interference effect in the first comprehensive review of the research literature (Magill & Hall, 1990). They hypothesized that the contextual interference effect would more likely be found for task variations controlled by different generalized motor programs (discussed in chapter 4) than by the same program. For example, when a person practices learning several skill variations characterized by different relative time patterns, a high contextual interference practice schedule should lead to better learning than a low contextual interference schedule. However, when the skill variations are characterized by the same relative time patterns, but different overall speeds, there should be no advantage to a high over a low contextual interference practice schedule. Thus, when removed from the context of the generalized motor program, the Magill and Hall hypothesis proposed that for the learning of skill variations, the contextual interference effect should be found when the characteristics of the variations are more dissimilar than similar.

In his assessment of the research that has investigated this hypothesis, Brady (1998) concluded that research involving laboratory tasks tends to support the hypothesis (e.g., Wood & Ging, 1991; Wulf & Lee, 1993). But when research involves applied settings, higher amounts of contextual in-

terference tend to enhance the learning of skill variations that are more similar than different. For example, compared to a low contextual interference practice schedule, moderate and high contextual interference practice schedules produced better learning of one-hand basketball set shots from different distances and angles (Landin & Hebert, 1997), but not better learning of three different volleyball skills (French, Rink, & Werner, 1990).

Two reasons may account for this discrepancy between the laboratory and applied settings. First, the learning of sport skills requires more practice than has been included in those studies that have not found the effect. Because sport skills tend to be more complex and difficult than the typical laboratory skills used in contextual interference research, much more practice would be required to learn the sport skills. The second reason is that the learning of sport skills may require a progression of low to high amounts of contextual interference rather than only a high amount. Unfortunately, these two possibilities remain speculative until we have research evidence that supports or does not support them.

Researchers have also proposed that several *learner characteristics* may limit the effect of contextual interference on skill learning. Of the characteristics suggested, age and skill level appear to be the most likely limiting factors. When participants in studies have been children, the highest amounts of contextual interference typically do not enhance learning. In fact, Brady's (1998) review points out that for children, practice schedules that produce lower amounts of contextual interference tend to produce better learning. In terms of skill level, Hebert, Landin, and Solmon (1996) found that low-skilled students in university tennis classes performed forehand and backhand strokes better on a retention test following blocked practice, whereas high-skilled students performed no differently following blocked or alternating-trials practice schedules.

In summary, we know that certain factors limit the extent of the generalization of the contextual interference effect in motor skill learning situations. Unfortunately, we do not have a definitive account of the specific characteristics that establish those

A CLOSER LOOK

An Application of the Contextual Interference Effect to the Physical Therapy of Stroke Patients

A study by Hanlon (1996) demonstrated the benefit of a random practice schedule for the physical therapy of unilateral stroke patients who needed to rehabilitate the use of their hemiparetic (i.e., paralyzed) arm to perform functional movement sequences.

Participants: 24 adult patients with chronic hemiparesis due to a unilateral cerebrovascular accident (CVA), which is commonly called a stroke.

Movement sequence practiced: Participants used their hemiparetic arm to perform a 5-step sequence designed to approximate steps needed to (1) open a cupboard door, (2) grasp a coffee cup by the handle, (3) lift the cup off its shelf, (4) place the cup on the counter, and (5) release the grasp.

Practice conditions:
- *Random practice schedule* — 10 trials in one session per day until participants achieved the performance criterion of 3 consecutive correct trials. Between each trial of the movement sequence, participants performed 3 other tasks with the hemiparetic arm: (1) pointing, (2) touching specified objects, (3) touching specified spots on a horizontal surface.
- *Blocked practice schedule* — 10 trials in one session per day until participants achieved the performance criterion of 3 consecutive correct trials.

- *No practice control condition* — No practice trials

Retention tests: All participants performed the 5-step movement sequence for five trials 2 and 7 days after the end of the practice sessions.

Results:
Practice trials:
- No statistically significant difference between the random and blocked practice groups for the mean number of trials required to achieve the performance criterion.

Retention tests:
- The *random practice group* performed significantly more successful trials on both retention tests than the blocked practice group and the no-practice control group.
- Interestingly, the blocked practice group did not differ from the no-practice control group on the number of correctly performed trials on the first retention test, but performed significantly better on the second retention test.

---

limits. Although there is general agreement that both task- and learner-related characteristics influence the degree to which contextual interference influences the learning of motor skill variations, we must wait for much more research evidence to allow us to confidently identify the specific characteristics.

Implications for the Practitioner

Given the inconclusive nature of our present knowledge about the specific factors that limit the generalization of the effect of contextual interference on skill learning, what should the practitioner do? To answer this, refer to figure 15.3. It is important to keep in mind that our present knowledge is different for the top and bottom portions of the continuum in this figure. In terms of the top half, we know that moderate and high amounts of contextual interference generally produce better learning of skill variations than low amounts. However, the bottom half of the figure remains unresolved in terms of the amount of contextual interference specific practice schedules produce when they are used for the learning of specific skill variations. As a result, view the continuum in figure 15.3 as representing a generic relationship between the various practice schedules and the amount of contextual interference each produces.

For the practitioner, when several variations of a skill must be learned, the best course of action would

A CLOSER LOOK

The Effectiveness of a Moderate Contextual Interference Practice Schedule

It may be preferable to learn some motor skill variations by practicing according to a schedule that involves a moderate rather than a high amount of contextual interference. A study by Landin and Hebert (1997) provides a good example of this type of practice situation.

Participants were university undergraduate students who had very little experience playing basketball. They practiced the one-hand set shot from six positions on the basketball court that varied in angle and distance from the basket. The *low contextual interference* group practiced according to a blocked schedule by shooting six consecutive shots from each position on each of three practice days. The *moderate contextual interference* group followed a blocked-serial schedule by shooting three shots from each position in sequence and then repeating the sequence. The *high contextual interference* group followed a serial schedule by taking one shot from each position in sequence and then repeating the sequence six times.

On the day after the end of practice, each group performed three transfer tests: a twelve-trial blocked schedule for three of the practice positions; a twelve-trial serial schedule for the same three positions; and a ten-trial free-throw test (the free-throw line was one of the six practiced positions). All three groups improved their shooting performance during practice, but they did not differ from each other at the end of practice. However, the blocked-serial practice schedule group performed better than the other two groups on all three tests. In addition, low amounts of contextual interference during practice led to poor adaptation to change. The blocked practice group maintained their end-of-practice performance level for the blocked and free-throw tests, but their performance on the serial test decreased to the level of their first day of practice.

---

be to select a practice schedule that should produce a moderate to high amount of contextual interference (according to figure 15.3). But he or she should be prepared to modify the schedule after practice begins in order to accommodate individuals who do not respond well to the practice schedule. For example, some individuals may require a practice schedule that produces a lower amount of contextual interference, such as a blocked schedule, until they acquire the basic movement patterns of the skill variations. However, it is important that the practitioner base any practice schedule modification on performance difficulties evident from retention or transfer tests rather than on those from practice sessions.

ACCOUNTING FOR THE CONTEXTUAL INTERFERENCE EFFECT

An important question that remains unanswered is this: Why does the contextual interference effect occur? Two hypotheses predominate the several accounts for this effect. One is the *elaboration hy-*

pothesis; the other is known as the *action plan reconstruction hypothesis.* Although we will not debate these two hypotheses at length, we will consider each briefly.

The Elaboration Hypothesis

In their experiment that first showed the contextual interference effect for learning motor skills, Shea and Morgan (1979) proposed that the effect is related to the elaboration of the memory representation of the skill variations that a learner is practicing.[1] During random practice, a person engages in more strategies, as well as more different strategies, than an individual who practices according to a blocked schedule. Also, because in a random practice schedule the person retains in working memory all the skill variations he or she is practicing, the person can compare and contrast the variations so that each becomes distinct from the other.

---

[1] Shea and Zimny (1983) developed a more formal version of the elaboration hypotheses.

A CLOSER LOOK

The Relationship of Practice Variability to Practice Specificity and Contextual Interference

Practice Variability and Practice Specificity: In chapter 12, one of the A Closer Look boxes related transfer of learning to the specificity of practice hypothesis, which indicates that optimal test performance is a function of the degree of similarity (i.e., specificity) of practice and test characteristics.

- The practice specificity hypothesis seems to be at odds with the practice variability hypothesis by emphasizing the importance of practice characteristics variety rather than specificity. However, research evidence indicates that each hypothesis relates to different practice and test characteristics:

  ▸ *Practice specificity hypothesis:* Relates primarily to the following characteristics associated with practice and test situations: (a) the sensory-perceptual information available, (b) the environmental context in which the skill is performed, (c) the cognitive processing requirements, and (d) the physical, mental, and emotional state of the performer (e.g., Coull, Tremblay, & Elliott, 2001; Lee, 1998; Proteau, Tremblay, & DeJaeger, 1998; Wright & Shea, 1994).

  ▸ *Practice variability hypothesis:* Relates primarily to movement characteristics of the skill performed in practice and test situations; performance context characteristics can be involved, especially when the context requires the performance of several variations of a skill (e.g., Schmidt, 1975; Schmidt & Lee, 1999).

Practice Variability and Contextual Interference:

- The *practice variability hypothesis,* which Schmidt (1975) proposed in his schema theory, specifically relates to parameter variations of a generalized motor program (GMP). It predicts that practicing several variations of an action leads to better performance of a novel variation of that action than practicing one variation. The hypothesis does not include predictions about the organization, i.e., schedule, of practice for the several variations.

- *Contextual interference* relates to the practice organization of several variations of a skill. Although there has been some question concerning the contextual interference influence on the learning of several parameter variations of an action associated with a GMP (Magill & Hall, 1990; Hall & Magill, 1995), several researchers have reported evidence that demonstrates this influence (e.g., Sekiya & Magill, 2000; Shea, Kohl, & Indermill, 1990).

- On the basis of the research results for both the variability of practice hypothesis and the contextual interference effect, we can make the following practice variability predictions:

  ▸ Practicing several variations of a skill will result in better learning than practicing one variation;

  ▸ Practicing several variations of a skill according to schedules that involve higher amounts of contextual interference (e.g., random and serial schedules) will result in better learning than practicing them according to schedules that involve low amounts of contextual interference (e.g., blocked schedules).

The result of engaging in these cognitive activities during practice is that the learner develops a memory representation for the skills that he or she then can access more readily during a test.

The Action Plan Reconstruction Hypothesis

An alternative hypothesis, by Lee and Magill (1985), stated that high amounts of contextual interference benefit learning because the interference requires a person to reconstruct an action plan on the next practice trial for a particular skill varia-

tion. This is necessary because the person has partially or completely forgotten the action plan he or she developed on the previous practice trial for that skill variation, because of the interference of the intervening practice trials of the other skill variations. In contrast, the person following a blocked practice schedule can use the same action plan he or she used on the previous trial, or a slightly modified one.

Consider the following illustration of how these different practice schedules would require different types of action plan activity. If you must add a long set of numbers and then you are immediately asked to do the same problem again, you probably will not re-add the numbers, but will remember and repeat only the answer. In contrast, if you are required to add several additional lists of numbers and then are given the first list again, you probably will have forgotten the solution to that problem, and therefore will have to add the same numbers again. The intervening problem-solving activity requires you to re-solve a problem you have solved already.

Lee and Magill hypothesized that the high contextual interference practice condition is like the addition situation in which there are several other problems to solve before you see the first problem again. When a learner practices a motor skill, the interference created by the practice trials between two trials of the same skill variation causes the person to forget much of the action plan he or she developed for the first trial. As a result, the learner must reconstruct and modify that plan to attempt the skill on the next trial. On the other hand, the blocked practice schedule is like the addition problem in which the next trial follows immediately, and it is easy to remember the solution and therefore be successful on the next trial.

In the motor learning context, high contextual interference conditions require learners to engage more actively in problem-solving activity during practice. Although this activity typically leads learners to perform more poorly during practice than they would with a low contextual interference schedule, this short-term performance deficit becomes a long-term benefit, because it leads to better retention and transfer test performance.

Research Supports Both Hypotheses

Much research is needed to determine which of the two hypotheses best accounts for the contextual interference effect. In his review of the research literature, Brady (1998) discussed several studies that provide support for each hypothesis. This means that it may be that more than one explanation accounts for the contextual interference effect.

Regardless of which hypothesis, or combination of hypothesis, accounts for the contextual interfer-

ence effect, two important learner-related characteristics have been demonstrated to be associated with the effect. One is that *higher levels of contextual interference involve greater attention demands during practice* than lower levels, which is predicted by both the elaboration and reconstruction hypotheses. Li and Wright (2000) provided research evidence of the greater attention demands for random compared to blocked practice by requiring participants to perform a secondary choice reaction-time task between practice trials and just before initiating their movements for a practice trial. These results help explain earlier results that showed higher physiological activation associated with higher levels of contextual interference (e.g., Husak, Cohen, & Schandler, 1991). The second characteristic, which was identified by Simon and Bjork (2001), is that *people who practice according to a blocked schedule tend to overestimate how well they are learning during practice.* The experimenters asked participants to make predictions about their own learning at various times during their practice sessions and before performing a retention test. Participants who engaged in a blocked practice schedule expected to perform better on the retention test than those who followed a random practice schedule.

SUMMARY

Variations of movement and context experiences are important ingredients for practice conditions that increase a person's capability to perform the practiced skill successfully and to adapt to conditions he or she has not experienced previously.

- Research evidence shows that *variable practice* leads to superior retention and transfer test performance when compared to *constant practice.*
- To determine the characteristics of a test context that should be varied in practice, identify the regulatory and nonregulatory conditions of the test context. Which of these conditions should be varied in practice depends on whether the skill is a closed or open skill.

- An important practice condition concern is how to organize the variety of experiences for a practice session unit of instruction, or therapy protocol. The *contextual interference effect* provides a basis for scheduling these experiences during practice.
- The contextual interference effect occurs when practice schedules that include higher amounts of contextual interference (e.g., random practice schedules) lead to better learning than those that include low amounts (e.g., blocked practice schedules).
- Research evidence indicates that the contextual interference effect applies to beginners as well as to skilled performers, and to laboratory skills and a wide range of sports and everyday skills; however, the effect is not applicable to the learning of all motor skills or to all learning situations. Researchers have not identified the specific factors that limit the generalization of the contextual interference effect.
- Two hypotheses predominate as explanations for why the contextual interference effect occurs: the *elaboration hypothesis* and the *action plan reconstruction hypothesis*.

RELATED READINGS

Albaret, J. M., & Thon, B. (1998). Differential effects of task complexity on contextual interference in a drawing task. *Acta Psychologica, 100,* 9–24.

Green, D. P., Whitehead, J., & Sugden, D. A. (1995). Practice variability and transfer of a racket skill. *Perceptual and Motor Skills, 81,* 1275–1281.

Hall, K. G. (1998, November/December). Using randomized drills to facilitate motor skill learning. *Strategies,* pp. 27–28, 35.

Immink, M. A., & Wright, D. A. (2001). Motor programming during practice conditions high and low in contextual interference. *Journal of Experimental Psychology: Human Performance and Perception, 27,* 423–437.

Lee, T. D., Swanson, L. R., & Hall, A. L. (1991). What is repeated in a repetition? Effects of practice conditions on motor skill acquisition. *Physical Therapy, 71,* 150–156.

Lee, T. D., Wishart, L. R., Cunningham, S., & Carnahan, H. (1997). Modeled timing information during random practice eliminates the contextual interference effect. *Research Quarterly for Exercise and Sport, 68,* 100–105.

Sherwood, D. E. (1996). The benefits of random variable practice for spatial accuracy and error detection in a rapid aiming task. *Research Quarterly for Exercise and Sport, 67,* 35–43.

Shewokis, P. A., Del Rey, P., & Simpson, K. J. (1998). A test of retroactive inhibition as an explanation of contextual interference. *Research Quarterly for Exercise and Sport, 69,* 70–74.

Wright, D. L., Li, Y., & Coady, W. (1997). Cognitive processes related to contextual interference and observation learning: A replication of Blandin, Proteau, and Alain (1994). *Research Quarterly for Exercise and Sport, 68,* 106–109.

STUDY QUESTIONS

1. What is meant by the term *practice variability* and why is it important for skill learning?

2. Give an example of how you would implement practice variability for (a) a closed skill without intertrial variability; (b) a closed skill with intertrial variability; (c) an open skill.

3. (a) How is contextual interference related to the issue of organizing practice for learning several related motor skills and variations of a motor skill? (b) Describe four practice schedules and locate each on a contextual interference continuum.

4. Describe an example that illustrates how you would implement an appropriate amount of contextual interference into the practice schedule for (a) a novice learning a skill; (b) a skilled person.

5. What are two reasons researchers have proposed for the benefits of contextual interference for motor skill learning?

CHAPTER

16

The Amount and Distribution of Practice

*Concept: The amount of practice and the spacing
or distribution of that practice can affect both
practice performance and the learning of motor skills*

After completing this chapter, you will be able to

- Define *overlearning* in terms of how it relates to the decision about the amount of practice time needed to learn motor skills

- Describe how an overlearning practice strategy influences the learning of procedural skills and dynamic balance skills

- Discuss the relationship between overlearning and other practice condition variables

- Describe how the concept of practice distribution is related to the intertrial interval and to the length and distribution of practice sessions

- Discuss evidence supporting the benefit for distributed practice for the distribution of practice sessions

- Compare and contrast massed and distributed intertrial interval schedules for discrete and continuous motor skills

- Describe how to implement knowledge of massed and distributed practice in various situations

Application

Teachers, coaches, and therapists must make important decisions about the amount of practice people should engage in, as well as how much time to devote to various activities within and across practice sessions within the total amount of practice time available. In terms of the amount of practice needed to learn a skill, the conventional wisdom seems to be that the more practice a person has, the better his or her performance will be in some future situation. Consider some examples. It seems likely that a dance teacher would encourage a dancer who was a bit tentative in certain parts of a routine to spend as much time as possible going over the routine repeatedly in practice. A golf instructor would probably try to help a person be more successful when putting by encouraging the person to spend as much time as possible on the practice putting green. And a therapist would typically encourage a rehabilitation patient to practice the skill he or she was relearning as often as possible. Our experiences in situations like these lead us to accept the "more practice is better" approach. But ironically, although this approach seems logical, research evidence indicates that it is not always the best alternative.

After having determined the amount of practice time people need to learn a motor skill, the professional needs to determine how much time to devote to various activities within and across practice sessions. He or she must determine the amount of time to devote to each activity in a session, the amount of rest between activities within a session, the length of each session, and the amount of time between sessions.

If you are a physical education teacher organizing a volleyball unit, you need to determine how much time you should devote in each class period to working on the various skills, drills, and other activities that you plan to include. If you have determined the total amount of practice time you want to devote to a given activity in the unit, and you know how many class periods you will have in the unit, you will know how much time you need to spend in each class period on that activity.

Similarly, if you are a physical or occupational therapist, you need to determine how much time a patient will spend on each activity within a session, how much rest time you should allow between activities in a session, when the next session should be, and so on. You also may need to instruct the patient concerning how to arrange his or her time schedule to do prescribed activities at home.

Discussion

The amount of practice a person devotes to a skill is critical for learning motor skills. This is especially the case when the person has the attaining of expertise as a goal. As we discussed in chapter 11, the impressive work by Ericsson has shown that expertise in any field is the result of intense practice for a minimum of ten years (Ericsson et al., 1993). Clearly, for achieving expertise, more practice is better than less. However, the amount of practice required to attain expertise is not our focus here. Instead, we will focus on the amount of practice a person needs to ensure achieving a specific learning goal associated with a specific period of practice.

There are many situations in which it is important to determine the amount of practice people should experience to achieve specific skill learning goals. Although limitations may exist in many of these situations in terms of the amount of time available for practice, the need to determine the amount of practice required remains. For example, a physical education teacher needs to determine the number of classes within a unit to devote to a specific activity. In sports settings, the amount of practice time available is restricted by a season's schedule or by rules established by professional associations. And, in rehabilitation contexts, the amount of time available for therapy is typically restricted by health care provider agencies.

As we address the issue of optimal amounts of practice, we will limit our discussion to these types of situations, and establish some guidelines for the effective and efficient use of available practice time. As suggested by the examples we just considered, this limited focus is particularly relevant to those involved in settings that involve strict practice time limitations on teachers, coaches, and therapists.

OVERLEARNING AND LEARNING MOTOR SKILLS

Researchers historically have investigated the relationship between the amount of practice and the achievement of specific performance goals within the topic of *overlearning*. **Overlearning** is the continuation of practice beyond the amount needed to achieve a certain performance criterion. A teacher, coach, or therapist implements an overlearning strategy by establishing a performance criterion, determining the amount of practice time the learner need to attain that criterion, and then requiring some percentage of that practice time as extra practice.

When we view it from a theoretical perspective, the idea of assigning extra practice has merit. Those who hold a motor program-based view of motor learning would say that extra practice helps strengthen the generalized motor program and response schema for the skill a person is learning, so that the person can call it into action more readily when necessary. From a dynamic patterns perspective, extra practice is a means by which a learner increases the stability of the coordination and control characteristics in the performance of the skill.

Driskell, Willis, and Copper (1992) presented a review and analysis of fifteen research studies that investigated several hypotheses related to over-learning. The first notable point about this review is that the issue of overlearning has not generated a great deal of research over the years. The fifteen studies covered research articles published from 1929 to 1982. However, these studies involved almost 4,000 subjects, which gives us a good basis for discerning the influence of overlearning on skill acquisition and how various factors influence over-learning. The results of this review indicated that for motor skill learning, overlearning has a positive influence on retention performance. And when 50 to 200 percent amounts of extra practice were analyzed, the higher percentages resulted in relatively proportionate higher retention test performance.

Although the Driskell et al. (1992) review provides a comprehensive overview of overlearning as it relates to skill acquisition, it does not evaluate effects related to specific types of motor skills. Because motor learning research has shown that certain types of skills relate to some distinct characteristics with regards to overlearning, we will consider three examples in the following sections.

The Overlearning Strategy for Learning Procedural Skills

Procedural skills constitute one type of motor skill particularly well suited to deriving benefits from an overlearning practice strategy. A procedural skill is an interesting combination of cognitive and motor components. It typically requires a person to perform a series of movements that individually are relatively easy to execute. However, to accomplish the total task, the performer must know which movements to make, and in what order. These types of skills are especially common in occupational, industrial, and military settings. For example, people are performing procedural skills when

their jobs require them to sort mail into appropriate bins, put together the components of a circuit board for a computer, or type from a written text.

A common problem with procedural skills is that people tend to forget what to do to carry out the entire procedure. This is particularly characteristic of procedural skills that they do not perform routinely every day. For example, several years ago, the U.S. Army was interested in improving the performance of soldiers assembling and disassembling machine guns. This skill is especially interesting to study because soldiers typically learn it in a short training period, but do not perform it again until some time after training; it is not a routine part of their daily duties. The problem was that when they performed a later test on this skill, the soldiers typically showed a large decrement in performance, compared to how they had performed at the end of training. To overcome this problem, researchers for the U.S. Army Research Institute (Schendel & Hagman, 1982) proposed that an overlearning training strategy (which they referred to as *over-training*) would be effective for decreasing the amount the soldiers forgot about the procedure.

The researchers compared two forms of over-training with a no-overtraining situation. An "immediate" overtraining condition required soldiers to perform 100 percent more trials than were necessary to achieve a performance criterion of one correct assembly/disassembly trial. The second overtraining condition also involved an additional 100 percent more practice trials, but these trials were administered as "refresher" training midway through the 8-week retention interval used for all subjects. Results showed that both of these over-training groups performed better than the no-overtraining control group on the retention test, which required the soldiers to practice until they were again able to assemble and disassemble the

---

overlearning   practice that continues beyond the amount needed to achieve a certain performance criterion.

gun correctly on a trial. However, the two over-training groups did not differ from each other in the number of trials it took to retrain to the criterion performance of one correct trial.

Based on the results of this experiment, the authors recommended the immediate overtraining procedure, because it was more cost- and time-effective. Because the trainees were already in the training session, it would take less time and money to have them engage in additional practice there than to bring them back several weeks later for a refresher training session.

The Overlearning Strategy for Learning Dynamic Balance Skills

In an experiment that involved learning a skill that has less of a cognitive component than the gun disassembly/assembly skill, Melnick (1971) investigated the use of overlearning for a dynamic balance skill. Although carried out many years ago, this experiment continues to be the only one reported in the research literature that involves the overlearning of dynamic balance skills. In addition to addressing the question of whether practice beyond what the learner needed to achieve a performance criterion was beneficial, Melnick asked whether there was an optimal amount of extra practice. In this experiment, people practiced balancing on a stabilometer until they were able to achieve a performance criterion of 28 out of 50 sec. After achieving this criterion, each group was required to perform further trials in one of the following amounts: 0 percent (none), 50 percent, 100 percent, or 200 percent of the initial number of trials of practice. Then, all participants performed a retention test twice, one week and then one month after practice.

The results showed that extra practice was beneficial. All the groups that engaged in practice beyond what they needed to achieve the performance criterion performed better on the retention tests. More interesting, however, was the result that there appeared to be *a point of diminishing returns* for the amount of retention performance benefit in relation to the amount of extra practice. The group that had 50 percent additional practice did as well

on the retention tests as the groups that had 100 percent and 200 percent extra practice. So, although additional practice was beneficial, increasing the amount of additional practice beyond a certain amount was not proportionally more beneficial to retention performance.

The Overlearning Strategy in a Physical Education Class

Researchers also have demonstrated the presence of this phenomenon of "diminishing returns" from increases in the amount of practice for learning skills in physical education classes. A good example of this is an experiment by Goldberger and Gerney (1990). In a unit of instruction, fifth-grade boys and girls practiced several football skills. The goal of this unit was to help students improve their performance of these skills. To simplify matters, we will look only at the two-step football punt. One group practiced these skills according to a teacher-rotated format, in which the teacher divided the class into five subgroups and assigned each to one of five stations where they practiced the skills for 5 min. At the end of every 5 min, students rotated to a new station. Another group of students practiced according to a learner-rotated format: they received index cards describing what they needed to do at each station and then were told to use their 25 min efficiently to practice each skill. Everyone practiced like this for two class periods on two days. The next week, the students performed the skills in a test.

The results showed that the two groups differed in terms of the number of practice trials for this skill, but not in test performance. The teacher-rotated format group actually practiced the skill an average of 7 more trials than the learner-rotated format group. Students in the learner-rotated format group performed from 0 to 67 trials, whereas students in the teacher-rotated group performed from 0 to 87 trials. But there was no difference between the groups in the amount of improvement in their punting performance scores. The additional practice time induced by the teacher-rotated format did not yield an additional skill improvement benefit. Thus, given the time constraints of the unit of instruction, the learner-rotated format was superior, because it provided more efficient use of that time.

THE OVERLEARNING STRATEGY CAN LEAD TO POOR TEST PERFORMANCE

Although the overlearning strategy typically benefits skill learning, some evidence shows that learning deficits may result from providing *too many* extra practice trials. Shea and Kohl (1990) reported an example of this effect in an experiment in which participants learned to push a handle with a specified amount of force (175N). One group practiced this skill for 85 trials. Another group also practiced this skill for 85 trials, but in addition practiced the same skill at four other force goals (125N, 150N, 200N, and 225N) for 51 trials each, for a total of 289 practice trials. A third group practiced the skill with the 175N goal force for 289 trials. One day later, all participants engaged in a retention test in which they performed the skill with the goal force of 175N for 10 trials.

The results showed that the group that practiced the 175N goal force for 289 trials had the poorest performance on the initial 5 trials of the retention test. In contrast, the group that practiced the variable goals performed best. Results for the group that practiced only 85 trials of the 175N goal fell between those of the two other groups. The differences between these groups were most distinct on the first retention trial. However, on the final 5 trials of the retention test, all three groups performed similarly. These results were replicated in another experiment by the same authors (Shea & Kohl, 1991).

Similarly, Travlos (1999) reported that increasing the amount of practice beyond a certain number of trials resulted in poorer transfer test performance. In this experiment, participants attempted to learn the distance of a horizontal line by touching a digitizing tablet with a stylus at locations they estimated to be the beginning and end of the line. Although they could not see their movements, the participants received knowledge of results (KR) about their estimate in terms of the distance it deviated from the 8-in. criterion. Five groups experienced different amounts of practice: 42, 77, 102, 127, and 152 trials. At the end of practice, they performed a transfer test for five trials. This test required them to estimate the horizontal length of a 10-in. line. The results, which you can see in figure 16.1, showed that at the end of practice, all groups performed similarly. However, performance on the transfer test was very much influenced by the amount of practice. Those who practiced the task for 77 and 102 trials performed the transfer test with less error than the other practice groups. Interestingly, 42 practice trials were two few, but 127 and 152 trials were too many; additional practice beyond 102 trials led to decrement in transfer test performance rather than an enhancement of it.

The significance of the results reported in these three experiments is that they run counter to what most people would expect. The addition of more practice beyond a certain amount did not improve retention and transfer test performance.

Why would more practice lead to poorer retention and transfer test performance than less practice? One reason could be that because the skills practiced in these experiments were so simple, boredom became a problem after a certain amount of practice. As a result, the learners reduced the amount of attention the task required to improve performance. Or, as Lee, Swinnen, and Serrien (1994) described it, the learners ceased to engage in the amount of *cognitive effort* required to improve task performance. A second explanation relates to both the motor program–based and the dynamic pattern theories concerning the importance of *practice variability,* which you studied in chapter 15. According to these theories, continued practice of the same movement results in a decreasing capability to remember the movement as well as to transfer to a movement variation, whereas the practice of variations of the movement results in enhancing the capability to remember and transfer to a related movement. It is interesting to note in this regard that in the Shea and Kohl experiments, practice of criterion task variations resulted in better retention performance than the same amount of

FIGURE 16.1   The results of the experiment by Travlos. Shown here is the amount of absolute error at the end of practice (black bars) and for the transfer test (grey bars) for five amounts of practice. [*Source:* Travlos, A. K. (1999). More practice does not necessarily enhance transfer of learning: Evidence and interpretations. *Perceptual and Motor Skills, 89,* 1161–1175.]

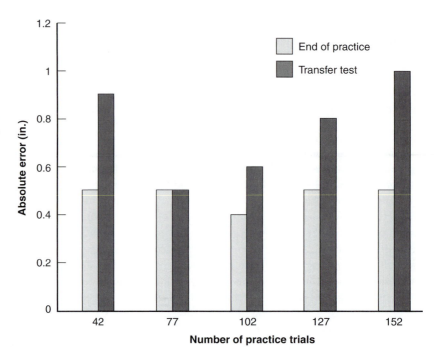

practice of the criterion task only. If these results were extended to performance on a transfer test, we would expect similar results.

OVERLEARNING AND OTHER PRACTICE VARIABLES

It can be useful for a learner to continue to practice a skill even though he or she can perform it correctly; such practice increases the permanence of the person's capability to perform the skill at some future time. However, the research investigating the overlearning strategy has shown rather conclusively that *the amount of practice is not the critical variable influencing motor skill acquisition.* In keeping with the commonly heard expression, "Practice does not make perfect; perfect practice makes perfect," the amount of practice invariably interacts with some other variable to yield optimal skill learning. You have seen this interaction with a number of practice-related variables, such as the type and frequency of augmented feedback and the variability of practice. From this perspective, the amount of practice is beneficial to a point. To es-

tablish an optimal learning environment, the instructor and/or learner also must take other practice condition characteristics into account. This does not mean that the amount of practice is unimportant. It does mean that the amount of practice cannot be considered in isolation, but in terms of its interaction with other practice condition variables.

THE DISTRIBUTION OF PRACTICE

Practice distribution (sometimes referred to as the spacing of practice) has been a popular topic for research in motor learning for many years. The most popular era for this study extended from the 1930s through the 1950s, when practice distribution was seen as a way to test learning theories popular at that time. However, researchers have continued to investigate practice distribution issues because of its relevance to applied settings in a variety of contexts.

One of the issues that was the focus of much of the early research concerned the amount of rest people need between practice trials to ensure an optimal learning environment. At issue was the question of

A CLOSER LOOK

Implementing the Overlearning Strategy

- The overlearning practice strategy works best when the teacher, coach, or therapist knows how much practice (i.e., number of trials or amount of time) a learner needs to achieve a certain performance level.
- Overlearning practice is effective for skills that a learner will practice during a specified period only, but will not perform for some time after that. The task in the Schendel and Hagman (1982) experiment of disassembling and assembling the machine gun is a good example. Although the soldiers did not need to perform this task every day, they needed to know how to do so in case a situation arose in which they were required to follow those procedures. The most effective practice procedure required the soldiers to engage in 100 per-

cent more practice trials than the number they required *to perform the skill correctly one time.*
- The instructor should *not* base the amount of extra practice on the notion that "more is better." There can be a point of diminishing returns, and it is even possible that the additional practice can lead to negative test performance. Although the instructor needs to determine the actual amount of extra practice that is best for each situation, a good place to start is to require 100 percent additional practice beyond the amount the learner requires to achieve the specified performance criterion.
- Practice requiring the performance of variations of skill characteristics can be an effective means of establishing an overlearning practice situation.

---

whether *massed or distributed* practice trials provided for better learning of motor skills. Some researchers argued that distributed practice was better; others maintained that it did not make much difference which spacing strategy an instructor followed.

Although this early controversy focused on between-trial rest intervals, the study of practice distribution also concerns the amount of practice during each session of practice and the amount of rest between sessions. In this second practice distribution issue, the question of concern is whether it is better to have fewer but longer sessions, or more but shorter sessions.

DEFINING MASSED AND DISTRIBUTED PRACTICE

Researchers use the terms **massed practice** and **distributed practice** in a general way to distinguish practice distribution schedules rather than assign specific amounts of time, which would allow for more objective definitions for these terms. The best way to understand these terms is to know that a massed practice schedule involves longer active practice, or work time, and shorter rest periods than a distributed schedule. Although rather vague, these

definitions are necessary because of the types of situations to which they apply.

When applied to the *length and distribution of practice sessions,* a *massed schedule* will have fewer practice sessions than a distributed schedule, with each massed practice session requiring more and/or longer practice. A *distributed schedule,* on the other hand, will distribute the same amount of practice time across more sessions, so that each session is shorter than each session in the massed schedule; the distributed practice sessions must be extended over a longer period to achieve the same total amount of practice.

When these terms apply to the *rest intervals between trials,* a *massed schedule* will have either no rest or a very short rest interval between trials. A *distributed schedule* will have much longer rest

> **massed practice**   a practice schedule in which the amount of rest between practice sessions or trials is very short.
>
> **distributed practice**   a practice schedule in which the amount of rest between practice sessions or trials is relatively long.

intervals than a massed schedule. Some researchers have specified that the length of the rest interval for a massed schedule is shorter than the amount of time required to perform the skill, but is as long or longer as the skill performance time for a distributed schedule. Although this conditional approach provides a more objective definition, it does not always describe these schedules as researchers have implemented them, especially for many discrete skills that may require less than one second to perform.

THE LENGTH AND DISTRIBUTION OF PRACTICE SESSIONS

For most instruction and rehabilitation situations, the primary practice distribution concern is how to use an allotted amount of time within and between practice sessions. Similar to our discussion earlier in this chapter, an important consideration here is that many instruction and rehabilitation situations have specified limits for the amount of time available. For most clinical applications, a patient may receive treatment for only a limited number of sessions because of health care management restrictions. Also, in teaching and coaching situations, there is often little flexibility in the number of days available for classes or practice sessions. For example, if a teacher has only ten days for a unit of instruction, then the practice schedule must fit that limit. Similarly, if a dancer must perform in a concert that is one month away, then the rehearsal schedule must adjust accordingly. Thus, outside limitations may determine how many days a person should devote to practice. However, the instructor, coach, or therapist still decides the number of practice sessions and the length of each one.

The Benefit of More and Shorter Sessions

Although there is not an abundance of research addressing the optimal number and length of practice sessions, the available evidence points to *the benefit of distributed practice.* The general result of experiments comparing a few long practice sessions with more frequent and shorter sessions is that practicing skills during shorter sessions leads to better learning.

The classic example of research supporting this general conclusion is a study published many years ago by Baddely and Longman (1978). They were attempting to determine the best way to schedule training sessions for postal workers on a mail-sorting machine, which required operating a typewriterlike keyboard. The training time limitations were a total of 60 hours and 5 days each week. The researchers distributed this practice time in four different ways. Two groups practiced for 1 hour in each session. One of these groups practiced for only one session each day, which resulted in a total training time of 12 weeks, whereas the second group had two sessions each day, thereby reducing the number of weeks in training to 6. Two other groups practiced for 2 hours in each session. One of these groups had only one session each day, whereas the other had two sessions per day. These latter two groups therefore had 6 weeks and 3 weeks of training, respectively. As this situation demonstrates, there are a variety of ways to distribute 60 hours of practice. The most distributed schedule required workers to train for 12 weeks, whereas the most massed schedule allowed them to complete their training in only 3 weeks. The difference lay in how long each session was and how many sessions occurred each day.

Table 16.1 describes two performance measures used to determine the effectiveness of the different practice schedules. One was the amount of time the trainees needed to learn the keyboard. The shortest time was 34.9 hours, whereas the longest was 49.7 hours; these figures represent the most distributed and the most massed schedules, respectively. Thus, for learning the keyboard, keeping practice sessions short and having only one session a day led to faster learning.

The second performance measure, which assessed motor performance, was typing speed. The trainees' goal was to type eighty keystrokes per minute. Only those in the most distributed schedule group attained this goal in the allotted training time of 60 hours (they did it in 55 hours). All of the other groups required additional practice time. It is interesting that those in the most massed schedule group, which practiced two 2-hour sessions each

TABLE 16.1 Results of the Baddeley and Longman Experiment with Practice Distribution Schedules for Training Postal Workers

Practice Schedule	Number of Hours to Learn Keyboard	Number of Hours to Type 80 Keystrokes/Minute
1 hr/session–1 session/day (12 weeks training)	34.9	55
1 hr/session–2 sessions/day (6 weeks training)	43	75
2 hrs/session–1 session/day (6 weeks training)	43	67
2 hrs/session–2 session/day (3 weeks training)	49.7	80+

Source: Data from Baddeley, A. D., & Longman, D. J. A. (1978). The influence of length and frequency training session on the rate of learning to type. *Ergonomics, 21,* 627–635.

day, never achieved this goal. After 80 hours of practice they were still doing only a little better than seventy keystrokes per minute.

Retention tests were given 1, 3, and 9 months after the workers had finished training. After 9 months, the most massed group performed worse on the typing speed test than the other groups, which performed about equally. Finally, the researchers obtained a very revealing result from the trainees' own ratings of the training schedules. Although most workers preferred their own schedule, those in the most massed group preferred theirs the most, whereas members of the most distributed liked theirs the least. Interestingly, these preferences were exactly opposite to the performance test results.

The results of this experiment indicate that fitting 60 hours of training into 3 weeks, where there had to be two 2-hour practice sessions each day, was a poor practice schedule. Although those in the most distributed schedule generally attained performance goals in the shortest time, they did not perform any better than two of the other groups on the retention tests. Given all the results, the authors concluded that the 1-hour training sessions were more desirable than the 2-hour sessions, and that one session per day was only slightly more effective than two sessions per day. However, having two 2-hour sessions each day was not a good training regime.

More recent studies have shown similar learning benefits for distributed practice for a variety of motor skills, as the following three examples demonstrate. Annett and Piech (1985) found that two 5-trial training sessions separated by one day led to better learning of a computer target-shooting game than one ten-trial session. One trial involved shooting at ten singly presented moving targets. The authors assessed learning by a performance test given one day after the end of the training session. The distributed group not only had more "hits" on the test but also had less error in the shooting attempts.

Bouzid and Crawshaw (1987) reported similar results for the learning of word processing skills. Typists who practiced twelve skills during two sessions of 35 and 25 min each, separated by a 10-min break, required less time to learn the skills and had fewer errors on a test than typists who practiced the skills during one 60-min session.

Finally, Shea et al. (2000) showed that distributing practice sessions across days resulted in better learning than massing all the sessions within one day for a continuous dynamic balance task and a discrete key-press timing task. The results for the continuous balance task are shown in figure 16.2. Note that for the first session of trials (each trial involved 90 sec of continuous balancing), both the one-day practice (massed) and the two-day practice (distributed) groups performed similarly. However, during the second practice session the groups began to perform differently. By the end of this session, the distributed group, for whom this session was the next day, had significantly less balancing error. Importantly, this difference continued during the retention test, which each group performed one day after the end of the practice sessions.

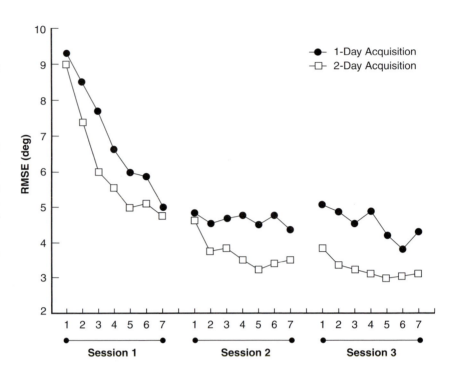

FIGURE 16.2. Results of the experiment by Shea et al. in which one group participated in two practice session's on one day (circles) and another participated in one session on each of two days (squares). The graph shows the amount of balancing error (RMSE, which was calculated as the amount of deviation, in degrees, from horizontal) for each 90-sec trial on a dynamic balance task. [*Source:* Figure 3, p. 745 in Shea, Lai, Black, & Park. (2000). Spacing practice sessions across days benefit the learning of motor skills. *Human Movement Science, 19,* 737–760.]

Explanations for the Distributed Practice Benefit

There are at least three possible reasons why the distribution of practice sessions across more days leads to better learning than massing the sessions within fewer days. One is that *fatigue* negatively influences learning for massed practice schedules. Although none of the experiments discussed in this section assessed participants' levels of fatigue, it is possible to suspect that fatigue influenced learning because of the task performance requirements. For example, in the Shea et al. (2000) experiment, participants performed a continuous dynamic balance task for 90 sec on each trial. The massed practice schedule required them to perform 14 trials on the same day with only 20-min break between trials 7 and 8. On the other hand, participants in the distributed practice schedule performed the second set of seven trials on the following day. If we were to assume that fatigue led to the learning differences between these two practice schedules, then one way to test this assumption would be to apply the

important principle concerning the assessment of learning, which we discussed in chapter 10. That is, we should base the assessment of the effect of a practice variable on retention or transfer test performance during which that variable should not influence performance. If fatigue influenced learning during the massed practice trials in the Shea et al. experiment, performance on the retention trials should be similar to performance during the second practice session. As you can see in figure 16.2, the performance differences for the second practice session carried over to the retention trials 24 hours later, which supports the possibility that the fatigue developed during practice influenced learning.

Second, the massing of practice within a day or a few days may diminish the amount of *cognitive effort* used on each trial as practice continues beyond a certain critical amount. We considered this explanation earlier in this chapter when we discussed reasons why more practice beyond a certain amount could lead to diminished learning. The massing of practice trials may institute a practice condition in

A CLOSER LOOK

Implications from Research on Massed versus Distributed Practice for Scheduling Practice or Rehabilitation Sessions

- **Practice sessions can be too long.** When in doubt about how long a session should be, opt for a shorter rather than a longer amount of time. If learners need more time, add more sessions.
- **More frequent practice sessions are preferable** to fewer sessions.
- **Time saved in terms of the number of days of practice can be a false savings,** because massing sessions too close together can lead to poorer long-term results.
- **The length and number of sessions desired by students, trainees, or patients may not represent the best schedule** for learning the skill. In the Baddeley and Longman study, if the postal trainees had been given their choice, they would have chosen the schedule that allowed them to complete their training in the fewest days, but that was the poorest schedule for learning the skill.

- **Make practice trials relatively short for skills that last a reasonably long time and require repetitive movements.** For beginners learning skills such as swimming, bicycling, typing, piano playing, and dancing: shorter practice trials that are repeated more frequently lead to better learning than longer trials that are infrequently repeated. For more advanced learners, the common dictum, "Keep trying it until you get it right," should be used only if the continuous attempts are relatively short in length and interspersed with ample amounts of rest (or other activity).
- **Make rest intervals relatively short for skills that involve relatively brief amounts of time.** For beginners learning skills such as hitting a golf ball, serving a tennis ball, shooting a basketball, throwing darts, prehensive actions: short rest intervals between trials lead to better learning than longer rest intervals between trials.

---

which performance of the skill on each trial becomes so repetitious that it becomes monotonous or boring. As a result, the learner begins to decrease the amount of cognitive effort involved in each trial, which in turn diminishes the level of learning.

The third explanation relates to *memory consolidation,* which is a long-term memory storage process. The memory consolidation hypothesis proposes that to store in memory the relevant information we need to learn a skill, certain neurobiochemical processes must occur. These processes, which transform a relatively unstable memory representation into a relatively permanent one, require a certain amount of time without additional practice of the same skill. The distribution of practice across several days provides a better opportunity for the memory consolidation process to take place than does the massing of practice within a day or a few days (see Brashers-Krug, Shadmehr, & Bizzi, 1996; Shadmehr & Brashers-Krug, 1997).

THE INTERTRIAL INTERVAL AND PRACTICE DISTRIBUTION

By far the greatest amount of research on the distribution of practice has investigated the length of the intertrial interval. One of the problems confronted when trying to understand this research relates to the definition problem described earlier in this chapter.

To elaborate on the general definitions presented earlier, we shall define *massed practice* as practice in which the amount of rest between trials is either very short or nonexistent, so that practice is relatively continuous. *Distributed practice* is practice in which the amount of rest between trials or groups of trials is relatively long. Although the terms "very short" and "relatively long" in these definitions are somewhat ambiguous, they allow us to generalize as much as possible from the research literature on massed versus distributed practice to motor skill learning situations.

Relating Practice Distribution and Contextual Interference to Skill Learning Contexts

The concept of contextual interference can be incorporated into practice distribution by organizing practice sessions to include principles related to both. The following are some examples that relate to three different skill learning contexts.

- **Physical education class.** If several drills or other kinds of activity are planned for the day's lesson, use a station-organization approach by assigning each skill or activity to a location in the gym or on the field so that there are several stations. Divide the class into groups and assign each to a station. Let the groups stay in their stations for about 12–15 minutes and then rotate to the next station. Continue this rotation approach for the entire period. If the class period is sufficiently long, allow for two or more rotations.
- **Sports-related practice.** Practices for team and individual sports typically include several activities. Rather than spend an extended amount of time on any one activity, divide in half the amount of time planned for each activity, and do each activity as two sets during practice. The two sets can be randomly or serially scheduled during the practice session.
- **Physical rehabilitation session.** Similar to sports-related practice sessions, rehab sessions typically involve several activities. If the planned activities allow, apply the approach described for sports-related practice by dividing in half the total amount of time planned for each activity, and do each activity as two randomly or serially scheduled sets during the session.

A History of Controversy

Although a great deal of research literature exists concerning the distribution of practice as it relates to the length of the intertrial interval, it is filled with controversy about which schedule leads to better learning. The controversy is evident in reviews of this literature as well as motor learning textbooks; both provide a variety of answers to the practice distribution question.

Two problems underlie the controversy surrounding this issue. The first relates to the issue of practice performance versus learning effects. Many of the experiments on massed versus distributed practice did not include retention or transfer trials. The second problem is that researchers generally have failed to consider that the two practice distribution schedules may have different learning effects on different types of skills.

Two reviews of the distributed practice research literature have helped resolve these problems and the controversy about which practice schedule is better for learning motor skills (Donovan & Radosevich, 1999; Lee & Genovese, 1988). Both reviews involved a statistical analysis, known as meta-analysis, to evaluate the research literature. Their conclusion was that the *type of task* was an important variable in determining practice distribution effects for schedules related to the length of intertrial rest intervals. More specifically, Lee and Genovese (1988, 1989) provided evidence that the type of practice distribution schedule that results in better learning depends on whether the skill is continuous or discrete. We will look at each of these types of skills next.

Continuous skills. Continuous skills have been the most common type of motor skills used to investigate the effects of massed versus distributed practice between trials. And the most popular task has been the rotary pursuit task, in which a person must keep a handheld stylus in contact with a small disk on a rotating turntable for as long as possible. A trial is usually a specified length of time, such as 20 or 30 sec. What makes this type of task useful for investigating the issue of massed versus distributed practice is that it is quite easy to specify

LAB LINKS

Lab 16 in the Online Learning Center Lab Manual provides an opportunity for you to experience a comparison of the effects of massed and distributed practice on the learning of a discrete motor skill.

massed and distributed intertrial interval lengths. Massed practice schedules typically have few, if any, seconds of rest between trials, whereas the intervals in distributed schedules are as long as or longer than the trials themselves. Because of this, researchers can establish intertrial interval lengths that are readily identifiable as distinctly massed or distributed. The Lee and Genovese (1988) review found that the consistent result has been that *distributed schedules lead to better learning* than massed schedules for learning continuous motor skills.

Discrete skills. When researchers use discrete skills to investigate the issue of intertrial massed versus distributed practice, a problem arises that is directly related to the definition problem we discussed earlier. If a massed schedule allows no rest between trials, whereas a distributed schedule involves a rest interval that is the same length as the practice trial, then the two contrasted intertrial intervals will be essentially the same length, because a discrete response is typically very short. For example, if people are practicing a rapid-aiming task that has a duration of approximately 150 msec, the distributed practice condition could, by definition, have a 150-msec intertrial interval. But if the massed condition had no rest between trials, only 150 msec would separate the two practice schedules. Thus, the operational definition of the terms "massed" and "distributed" becomes especially important in experiments using discrete tasks. Probably one reason this has not troubled researchers is that discrete tasks seldom have been used for comparing massed to distributed practice. In fact, in their comprehensive review, Lee and Genovese

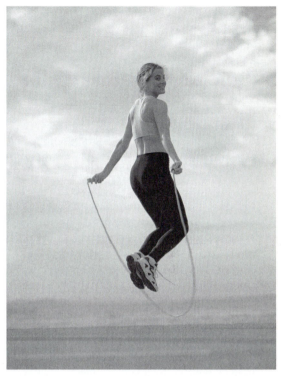

To enhance the learning of continuous motor skills, such as jumping rope, practice sessions should follow distributed schedules.

(1988) found only one study in the research literature that used a discrete task (Carron, 1969). The results of that study, and one subsequently reported by Lee and Genovese (1989), provided evidence that *massed practice schedules result in better learning* for discrete motor skills.

SUMMARY

Issues concerning the *amount of practice* needed to achieve specific skill performance goals historically have been discussed and investigated within the topic of *overlearning.*

• Overlearning is the continuation of practice beyond the amount needed to achieve a certain performance criterion.

- Research investigation of overlearning as a practice strategy has shown that the view that "more is better" is not always appropriate for the learning of motor skills, especially in terms of the benefits derived in relation to the amount of practice experienced; that is, there appears to be a *point of diminishing returns* for amount of practice.
- Research has shown evidence for a point of diminishing returns when an overlearning practice strategy is used to learn certain procedural skills, dynamic balance skills, and sports skills.
- Research has shown that learning deficits can result when too much overlearning is involved in learning of motor skills that are simple and easy to learn; this effect is probably due to a decrease in the amount of cognitive effort applied after a certain amount of practice.

Issues related to the *distribution of available practice time* involve massed and distributed practice schedules. The terms *massed* and *distributed* are generally defined in relation to each other according to the practice schedule characteristics of each.

- One type of practice distribution schedule involves the *length and frequency of practice sessions;* this type typically concerns a massed schedule of longer sessions within a day or a few days compared to a distributed schedule of shorter sessions across more days than the massed schedule.
- Research evidence shows that practice sessions can be too long and too infrequent to lead to optimal learning. Typically, better learning results when people practice skills in larger numbers of shorter practice sessions than when they do so in sessions that are long and fewer in number.
- We discussed three hypotheses proposed to explain why distributed practice sessions lead to better learning than massed sessions: a fatigue hypothesis, a cognitive effort hypothesis, and a memory consolidation hypothesis.
- The second type of practice distribution schedule involves the *length of the intertrial interval,* which is the rest period between practice trials.

- Research evidence shows that the optimum length for the intertrial interval depends on whether the skill is continuous or discrete. For continuous skills, distributed practice schedules are typically better for learning, but massed practice schedules are preferable for discrete skills.

RELATED READINGS

Ammons, R. B. (1988). Distribution of practice in motor skill acquisition: A few questions and comments. *Research Quarterly for Exercise and Sport, 59,* 288–290.

Croce, R. V., & Jacobson, W. H. (1986). The application of two-point touch cane technique to theories of motor control and learning: Implications for orientation and mobility training. *Journal of Visual Impairment and Blindness, 80,* 790–793.

Kwakkel, G., & Wagenaar, R. C. (2002). Effect of duration of upper- and lower-extremity rehabilitation sessions and walking speed on recovery of interlimb coordination in hemiplegic gait. *Physical Therapy, 82,* 432–448

Mackay, S., Morgan, P., Datta, V., Chang, A., & Darzi, A. (2002). Practice distribution in procedural skills training—A randomized controlled trial. *Surgical Endoscopy and Other Interventional Techniques, 16,* 957–961

Rhodenizer, L., Bowers, C. A., & Bergondy, M. (1998). Team practice schedules: What do we know? *Perceptual and Motor Skills, 87,* 31–34.

Schmidt, R. A., & Bjork, R. A. (1992). New conceptualizations of practice: Common principles in three paradigms suggest new concepts for training. *Psychological Science, 3,* 207–217.

STUDY QUESTIONS

1. What is meant by the term *overlearning* as it relates to learning motor skills?

2. (a) Define the term "procedural skill" as it is commonly used in the motor learning literature. (b) What was the recommendation from the results of the Schendel and Hagman study for using an overlearning strategy to help people learn a procedural skill? Indicate why they made this recommendation.

3. Discuss the evidence that would support the view that "more is better" may not be the best approach to implementing an overlearning strategy to help people learn a motor skill.

4. Describe how the concept of practice distribution is related to the intertrial interval and to the length and distribution of practice sessions. Describe a motor skill learning situation for each.

5. Discuss the Baddeley and Longman study with postal worker trainees in terms of how the study demonstrates the benefit of distributed over massed practice sessions for learning a motor skill.

6. (a) How do massed and distributed intertrial interval schedules differentially influence the learning of discrete and continuous motor skills? (b) Why do you think there is a difference in how massed and distributed intertrial interval schedules influence the learning of discrete and continuous skills?

7. Describe how you would implement your knowledge about massed and distributed practice in *one* of the following situations: a physical education or dance class; a practice session for a sport; a physical or occupational therapy session.

CHAPTER

Whole and Part Practice

Concept:Base decisions about practicing skills as wholes or in parts on the complexity and organization characteristics of the skills

After completing this chapter, you will be able to

- Define the terms *complexity* and *organization* as they relate to the relationships among the parts or components of a complex motor skill

- Describe ways to apply the part practice methods of *fractionization* and *segmentation* to the practice of motor skills

- Describe several ways to apply *simplification* methods to the practice of motor skills

Application

An important decision you must make when you teach any motor skill concerns whether it is better to have the learner practice the skill in its entirety or by parts. Consider the following sport skill instruction situation as an example. Suppose you are teaching a beginning tennis class. You are preparing to teach the serve. Most tennis instruction books break down the serve into six or seven parts: the grip, stance, backswing, ball toss, forward swing, ball contact, and follow-through. You must decide whether to have the students practice all of these parts together as a whole or to have them practice each component or group of components separately.

The question of whether to use whole or part practice also confronts professionals in a rehabilitation setting. For example, when a patient needs to learn the task of getting out of bed and getting into a wheelchair, this decision comes into play. Although this task has distinct and identifiable parts,

the therapist must determine whether to have the patient practice each part separately or always practice the whole sequence.

Discussion

The issue of whether to use whole or part practice has been a topic of discussion in the motor learning literature since the early 1900s. Unfortunately, that early research often led to more confusion than understanding. One of the reasons was that researchers tended to investigate the issue in terms of whether one or the other type of practice is better for learning specific skills, without concern for observing skill-related characteristics that could help them make useful generalizations about which practice scheme would be preferable for certain skills. For example, the question of whole versus part practice was investigated by Barton (1921) for learning a maze task; Brown (1928) for learning a piano score; Knapp and Dixon (1952) for learning to juggle; and Wickstrom (1958) for learning gymnastic skills. Although this research provided useful information about teaching these specific skills, it did little to establish a guiding principle for decisions about whether to use whole or part practice.

SKILL COMPLEXITY AND ORGANIZATION

A breakthrough in understanding the issue of whole versus part practice occurred in the early 1960s, when James Naylor and George Briggs (1963) hypothesized that the organization and complexity characteristics of a skill could provide the basis for a decision to use either whole or part practice. This hypothesis made it possible for instructors to predict for any skill which method of practice would be preferable.

Naylor and Briggs defined **complexity** in a way that is consistent with the term's use in this text. They stated that *complexity* refers to the number of parts or components in a skill, as well as the attention demands of the task. This means that a highly complex skill would have many components and demand much attention, especially from a beginner. Performing a dance routine, serving a tennis ball, and getting out of bed and into a wheelchair are examples of highly complex skills. Low-complexity skills have few component parts and demand relatively limited attention. For example, the skills of shooting an arrow and picking up a cup are low in complexity. It is important to keep the term *complexity* distinct from *difficulty*. As you saw in the discussion of Fitts' law in chapter 5, a low-complexity skill can be difficult to perform.

The **organization** of a skill refers to the relationships among the component parts of a skill. A skill has a *high level of organization* when its component parts are spatially and temporally interdependent. This means that the successive parts of a highly organized skill are like a chain of events in which the spatial-temporal performance characteristics of any one part are dependent on the spatial-temporal performance characteristics of the part performed just before it. Because of this char-

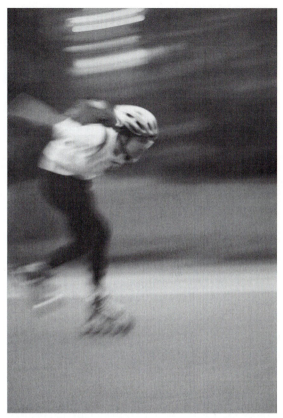

An important part of teaching the skill of rollerblading is the decision to have the students practice it as a whole skill or to use a part practice strategy.

acteristic, it would be difficult to perform only one part of a highly organized skill. The jump shot in basketball is a good example of a highly organized skill, because the manner in which a person performs each part will depend on the manner in

---

complexity   the number of parts or components and the amount of information-processing demands that characterize a skill; more complex skills have more component parts and involve more information processing demands than less complex skills.

organization   when applied to a complex motor skill, the relationships among the components of the skill.

which he or she performed the part(s) that preceded it. Although the arm and hand movements involved in the release of the ball could be practiced separately, the spatial location of the arm and hands as well as the timing of the ball release must be related to other parts of the skill, such as the direction and the height of the jump. In contrast, a skill has a *low level of organization* when the spatial-temporal relationships among the component parts of a skill are relatively independent. As a result, it is possible to practice any one component part by itself, because its spatial-temporal performance characteristics do not depend on those of the part that precedes it. Examples here include many dance routines and handwriting certain words.

Skill Characteristics and the Decision to Use Whole or Part Practice

Based on the Naylor and Briggs hypothesis, assessing the levels of complexity and organization of a skill and determining their relationship helps a teacher, coach, or therapist decide whether to use whole or part practice. If the skill is *low in complexity and high in organization,* practice of the whole skill is the better choice. This means that people learn relatively simple skills in which the few component parts are highly related most efficiently using the whole practice method. For example, the skills of buttoning a button, throwing a dart, and putting a golf ball have this combination of characteristics. On the other hand, people learn skills that are *high in complexity and low in organization* most efficiently by the part method. For example, the skills of serving a tennis ball; reaching for, grasping, and drinking from a cup; and shifting gears on a car have these characteristics.

To determine which of these complexity and organization combinations describe a particular skill, it is necessary to first analyze the skill. This analysis needs to focus on identifying the skill's component parts and the extent to which the spatial-temporal performance characteristics of those parts are interdependent. Next, decide which part of the continuum of skill complexity and organization best represents the skill.

By far, most of the motor skills we perform as a part of our daily living activities and sports would be placed closer to the complex than the simple end of a complexity continuum. This means that for most skills, the practitioner must determine the level of organization that characterizes the skill. For skills that we would place on an organization continuum somewhere between the extremes of low and high, an additional task analysis step is required. For these types of skills, it is necessary to determine which component parts are independent of the others and which group together as interdependent. The result of this analysis will determine which parts could be practiced independently. That is, some of the "parts" a person practices would consist of more than one of the component parts that resulted from the initial task analysis. This grouping of parts can be thought of as a "natural unit" within the skill. Because teachers, coaches, and therapists typically work with motor skills that would suggest some sort of practice, we will first consider issues relevant to part practice.

PRACTICING PARTS OF A SKILL

The decision to use a part practice strategy unfortunately solves only part of the problem, because there are several different ways to implement a part practice approach to the practice of a skill. When selecting a part practice strategy, it is important to apply transfer of learning principles, which we discussed in chapter 12. Part practice strategies should involve positive transfer between and among the practiced parts of a task, and between the practiced parts and the whole task.

In their important review of the research literature related to skill training methods, Wightman and Lintern (1985) classified three commonly used part-task strategies. One, called **fractionization,** involves practicing individual limbs first for a skill that involves the asymmetric coordination of the arms or legs. A second method, called **segmentation,** involves separating the skill into parts and then practicing the parts so that after the learner practices one part, he or she then practices that part together with the next part, and so on. Researchers also have called this method the *progressive part method* and the chaining method. A third method of part practice is called **simplification.** This method is actually a variation of a whole practice strategy and involves reducing the difficulty of the whole skill or of different parts of the skill.

Fractionization: Practicing Asymmetric Limb Coordination Skills

Many of the motor skills discussed throughout this text have required people to simultaneously move their arms or legs to achieve a specific spatial and/or temporal goal. Recall from the discussion of coordination in chapter 4 that the coordination tendency is for the arms or legs to move spatially and temporally together. What this means in terms of part versus whole practice is that because of this coordination tendency, a skill that requires symmetric spatial-temporal coordination of the arms (e.g., the butterfly and breaststroke in swimming) or legs (e.g., the flutter kick for a crawl stroke in swimming or the leg movements for cross-country skiing) would be high in organization. As a result, a whole practice approach would be preferable. However, when the task requires the two arms or legs simultaneously to do *different* spatial and/or temporal movements (i.e., asymmetric coordination), the question of the use of a part practice strategy becomes more of an issue.

Because asymmetric coordination of the arms is more characteristic of motor skills than asymmetric coordination of the legs, we will address skills in this section that we referred to in chapter 5 as asymmetric bimanual coordination skills. Consider, for example, the simultaneous arm movements involved in the playing of many musical instruments, such as the violin and accordion. Each requires the person to simultaneously produce distinctly different movement patterns. Other instruments, such as the piano and drums, may require this type of bimanual movement characteristic. Sport skills such as the sidestroke in swimming and the tennis serve also involve this type of bimanual coordination. Is a part practice strategy the best approach for learning these types of skills, or would a whole practice approach be preferable? Some

controversy exists among researchers, and there is evidence to support either approach (see Walter & Swinnen, 1994). If a part practice approach is used, the most appropriate strategy is *fractionization.*

For the asymmetric bimanual skill, the fractionization strategy involves practicing each arm or hand individually before performing the skill bimanually. A relevant question related to the use of this strategy is this: Does it matter which arm or hand practices first? A feature of asymmetric bimanual coordination skills that is important to consider in answering this question is that one arm or hand will sometimes perform a movement, or sequence of movements, that is more difficult or complex than the other. For example, one hand may perform a movement that requires a higher degree of movement accuracy than the other, or one hand may perform a movement that involves more component parts. Research evidence (e.g., Sherwood, 1994) suggests that practice should begin with the hand or arm that must perform the more difficult or complex movement.

Segmentation: The Progressive Part Method

Although practicing individual parts can be helpful in learning a skill, the learner can experience difficulty later, when he or she has to put the part back together with the whole skill. One way to overcome this problem is to use the *progressive part method.* Rather than practicing all parts separately before putting them together as a whole skill, the

---

fractionization   a part-task training method related to asymmetric coordination skills that involves practicing each arm or leg separately before performing with them together.

segmentation   a part-task training method that involves separating the skill into parts and then practicing the parts so that after one part is practiced, it is then practiced together with the next part, and so on; also known as the progressive part method.

simplification   a part-task training method that involves reducing the difficulty of specific parts or features of a skill.

A CLOSER LOOK

An Example of Making the Decision Regarding Use of Whole or Part Practice

Use skill analysis to determine whether to practice juggling three balls as a whole or in parts:

Skill Analysis

Complexity characteristics

1. Hold the three balls in two hands.
2. Toss ball 1 from hand 1.
3. Catch ball 1 in hand 2 while tossing ball 2 with hand 2.
4. Catch ball 2 in hand 1 while tossing ball 3 with hand 2.
5. Catch ball 3 in hand 1 while tossing ball 1 with hand 2.
6. Repeat steps 2 and 5.
7. Between-component timing: critical for performance.

Organization characteristics. Doing any one part without doing the part that precedes or follows it does not allow the learner to experience critical between-component timing aspects.

Conclusion. Three-ball juggling involves several component parts that are highly interdependent. Therefore, juggling three balls is relatively high in complexity and in organization. *Practicing the whole skill* is the predicted appropriate method.

Empirical Evidence Supporting the Whole Practice Prediction

In an experiment that has become a classic, Knapp and Dixon (1952) told university students who had no previous juggling experience to practice until they could make 100 consecutive catches while juggling 3 paddle-tennis balls. Results showed that students who followed a whole practice approach achieved this goal in 65 trials, whereas those who followed a part practice regime needed 77 trials.

---

learner practices the first part as an independent unit, then practices the second part—first separately, and then together with the first part. In this way, each independent part progressively joins a larger part. As practice continues, the learner eventually practices the entire skill as a whole.

A common example of the progressive part method is a frequently used practice scheme for learning the breaststroke in swimming. The breaststroke is easily subdivided into two relatively independent parts, the leg kick and the arm action. Because a difficult aspect of learning the breaststroke is the timing of the coordination of these two parts, it is helpful for the learner to reduce the attention demands of the whole skill by practicing each part independently first. This enables the student to focus his or her attention to just the limb action requirements, because he or she can learn each part without attending to how to coordinate the two parts as a unit. After practicing each part independently, the swimmer can put them together to practice them as a whole unit, with his or her attention

now directed toward the temporal and spatial coordination demands of the arm and leg actions.

Skills that involve learning movement sequences lend themselves particularly well to the progressive part method. Researchers have demonstrated this for both laboratory and real-world skills. For example, Watters (1992) reported that the progressive part method was beneficial for learning to type an eight-key sequence on a computer keyboard. And Ash and Holding (1990) found that people learning a musical score on a piano benefited from a progressive part practice approach. In this experiment, participants learned a musical score of twenty-four quarter notes, grouped into three sets of eight notes. The first two segments were easy and the third segment was difficult. Two types of the progressive part method were better than the whole method for learning to perform this musical score, for which performance was based on errors made, rhythmic accuracy, and rhythmic consistency. Of the two progressive part methods, the one that prescribed an easy-to-difficult progression

A CLOSER LOOK

Whole and Part Practice Conditions That Facilitate the Learning of Bimanual Coordination Skills

Bimanual coordination skills that require each arm to simultaneously perform different movements are difficult to learn because of the tendency for the two arms to spatially and temporally move together. Walter and Swinnen (1994) discussed various training approaches that would facilitate learning to break this "habit" for skills that require different simultaneous arm movements. Their research involved a task that required participants to place each forearm on a lever on a tabletop, and to move them simultaneously so that one arm made a one-direction elbow-flexion movement and the other made a two-direction elbow-flexion-extension movement in a criterion amount of time. Their research demonstrated that the following three techniques accomplished this learning goal. Note that one involved part-task practice and two involved whole-task practice.

- **Fractionization.** The movement patterns were practiced separately for each arm, and then with the two arms moving simultaneously.

- **Speed-based simplification.** Initial practice of the bimanual task was at a slower speed than the criterion; subsequent sets of trials involved the progressive increase of the speed until the criterion speed was practiced.

- **Augmented feedback.** Practice involved the two arms simultaneously moving and augmented feedback provided after each trial as KP (the acceleration-time traces for each limb) or KR (correlation values indicating the degree of between-arm relationship).

---

tended to be better than the one stipulating a difficult-to-easy progression.

A key characteristic of the progressive part method is that it takes advantage of the benefits of both part and whole methods of practice. The part method offers the advantage of reducing the attention demands of performing the whole skill, so that the person can focus attention on specific aspects of a part of the skill. The whole method, on the other hand, has the advantage of requiring important spatial and temporal coordination of the parts to be practiced together. The progressive part method combines both of these qualities. Thus, the attention demands of performing the skill are under control, while the parts are put together progressively so that the learner can practice important spatial and temporal coordination requirements of performing the parts as a whole.

Simplification: Reducing Task Difficulty

For a complex skill, simplification can make either the whole skill or certain parts of the skill less difficult for people to perform. There are several ways

to implement a simplification approach to skill practice. We will discuss six of these here. Each is specific to learning a certain type of skill. All of them involve practicing the whole skill, but simplify certain parts of the skill in various ways.

When a person is learning an object manipulation skill, one way to simplify learning the skill is to *reduce the difficulty of the objects.* For example, someone learning to juggle three balls can practice with scarves or bean bags. This reduces the difficulty of the task by involving objects that move more slowly and are therefore easier to catch. Because these objects move more slowly, the person has more time to make the appropriate movements at the right moments. However, the person still must follow the principles of juggling while learning to juggle the easier objects. We would expect early practice using easier objects to enable the person to learn these juggling principles, and then easily transfer them to juggling with more difficult objects. In fact, research evidence supports this approach to learning to juggle three balls (Hautala, 1988).

LAB LINKS

Lab 17 in the Online Learning Center Lab Manual provides an opportunity for you to develop part practice plans for a person who is learning or relearning a motor skill.

Another way to reduce task difficulty is to *reduce the attention demands of the skill without changing the action goal.* This strategy reduces task difficulty by reducing task complexity. One approach to implementing this strategy is to provide physical assistance devices that allow the person to practice the goal of the skill but at the same time reduce the attention demands of the task. For example, Wulf and her colleagues (Wulf, Shea, & Whitacre, 1998; Wulf & Toole, 1999) found that people who used ski poles while they practiced the slalom ski simulator task learned to perform the task without ski poles better than people who practiced without ski poles. The poles allowed the performers to focus more attention on the movement coordination demands of the task. This was possible because of the reduced attention demands for the dynamic balancing component of the task, which resulted from the poles enabling better body stability. It is also notable that in these experiments, transfer from performing with poles to doing so without the poles led to no appreciable reduction in performance level.

Third, for skills having a distinct rhythmic characteristic, *providing auditory accompaniment* that cues the appropriate rhythm works well to reduce task difficulty and facilitate a person's learning of the activity. This approach is especially interesting because it actually simplifies a task by adding an extra component to it. For example, musical accompaniment has been shown to assist Parkinson's disease patients with gait disorders while they practice walking. An example of research support for this simplification procedure was reported by Thaut et al. (1996). The researchers provided patients with Parkinson's disease with an auditory device that consisted of audiotapes with metronome sounds embedded in instrumental music to desig-nate the rhythmic structure and tempo (i.e., speed) of the music. The patients used the device as part of a three-week home-based gait-training program to pace their steps while walking. Compared to patients who did not use the device, the patients who trained with the auditory accompaniment showed greater improvement in their gait velocity, stride length, and step cadence. In addition, they accurately reproduced the speed of the last training tape without the assistance device.

A fourth simplification method is useful for the learning of complex skills requiring both speed and accuracy. *Reducing the speed* at which a learner first practices a skill can simplify practice. This approach places emphasis on the relative-time relationships among the skill components and on the spatial characteristics of performing the whole skill. Because a characteristic such as relative time is an invariant feature of a well-established coordination pattern and because people can readily vary overall speed, we would expect that a person could learn a relative-time pattern at a variety of overall speeds. By practicing at a slower speed, the learner would establish the essential relative-time characteristics of a coordination pattern.

It is interesting to note that the training strategy of reducing the speed of a task also benefits the learning of asymmetric bimanual coordination tasks in which each arm performs different spatial-temporal patterns but with the same overall duration of time. What makes this interesting is that in the earlier discussion about the fractionization training strategy, that strategy also facilitated the learning of this type of bimanual task.

Evidence for the beneficial effects of the speed-reduction strategy was provided in an experiment by Walter and Swinnen (1992). Participants practiced an asymmetric bimanual coordination task that required them to use one arm to move a horizontal lever in a one-direction elbow flexion movement while at the same time using the other arm to move a lever in a two-direction elbow flexion-extension movement. One group practiced two sets of twenty trials at reduced speeds before practicing the task at the criterion speed. The other group prac-

A CLOSER LOOK

The Simplification Method for Learning Three-Ball Juggling

An experiment reported by Hautala (1988) demonstrated that beginning juggling practice by using easier objects is beneficial for learning to juggle three balls.

The participants were boys and girls ten to twelve years old with no previous juggling experience. All of them practiced 5 min per day for 14 days and then were tested for 1 min with the juggling balls.

The experiment compared four practice conditions:

1. Learners began practice using three "juggling balls" of three different colors.
2. Learners began practice using cube-shaped beanbags.
3. Learners followed a progressive simplification scheme:
   a. scarves of different colors
   b. beanbags
   c. juggling balls
4. Learners began practice using weighted scarves and then switched to the balls.

The results of the three-ball juggling test showed this:

- The beanbags practice condition led to the best test performance.

Note: The ball-juggling score for participants in the beanbag practice group was over 50 percent higher than those for the juggling balls group and the progression group, and over 100 percent higher than that of the group that practiced with weighted scarves and then beanbags before using the balls.

---

ticed all trials at the criterion speed. Transfer test results showed that the reduced-speed training group learned to perform the task more accurately than the group that practiced the criterion speed only.

The fifth strategy is related to the progressive part strategy discussed earlier. It involves the *sequencing of task progressions,* which means that a person practices variations of the skill being learned in a sequence from less to more complex or difficult until the skill being learned is practiced. For example, in the discussion in chapter 1 of Gentile's taxonomy of motor skills, we considered the following task sequence to help young baseball players learn to hit pitches thrown by pitcher: first, hit baseballs off a tee at the same height; next, hit balls off a tee at different heights; then, hit balls thrown by a pitching machine, and finally, hit balls thrown by a pitcher.

The task progression strategy is commonly referred to in the physical education teaching literature (e.g., Rink, 1998). Also included in this strategy is the use of "lead-up games or activities." Although the task progression strategy has not received strong research support, results of an experiment reported by Hebert, Landin, & Solmon (2000) provided evidence that supported the learning benefit for an easy-to-difficult task progression of four distances from the net to practice the tennis serve, with the first distance at the service line, and then progressing back to serving from the baseline. Interestingly, this study included a progressive part training condition for the tennis serve. Although the progressive part condition yielded positive results, an advantage of the task progression strategy was that it led to high success rates for students of low, middle, and high skill levels.

Finally, *simulators and virtual reality environments* are technical devices that provide ways to simplify certain features of a skill to help people learn skills. These devices have several advantages: people can practice skills without concerns about the cost of accidents or performance errors that would characterize practice in real environments; practitioners can control specific aspects of the performance environments more easily than in real environments; and people can often practice for longer periods of time and with more intensity than they could in a real environment.

Simulators are devices that imitate vehicles, machines, or instruments. For example, automobile and truck simulators are commonly used to train people to drive these vehicles. The military uses a variety of simulators, such as those for airplanes, tanks, and submarines, to train personnel who will operate these vehicles. In sports, simulators include devices such as pitching machines in baseball and softball, ball machines in tennis, and rebounders in basketball. Simulators can be used for training purposes by providing practice experiences before operating the actual device, or by providing a practice situation in which certain attention demands are reduced.

Research investigations of the effectiveness of simulators have been more common for their use as training devices to help people learn to drive cars (e.g., Fisher et al., 2002) and to pilot airplanes and helicopters (e.g., Stewart, Dohme, & Nullmeyer, 2002) than for their use in sports contexts. In general, research results support the use of simulators as training devices, especially when they adhere to the similarity principles described in chapter 12 when we discussed theories that explain why transfer occurs. For simulators, these principles concern the degree of similarity between the component parts of the tasks required by the simulator and the real device, between the performance contexts or situations, and between the cognitive processing characteristics.

Virtual reality environments simulate real environments through the use of three-dimensional computer graphics. The virtual environments can be experienced in real time, which provides a realistic experience in that environment without being in the actual environment. You saw an example of the use of a virtual reality training strategy in the experiment by Wilson, Foreman, and Tlaka, which was described in chapter 12 in an A Closer Look discussion. In that experiment, virtual reality training was used to familiarize participants with the spatial layout and objects in three floors of a building. Additional examples of virtual reality training reported in the research literature have involved such diverse fields as physical rehabilitation, surgery, and the military. These have included the following:

- Creating individualized treatment exercises to augment dexterity task performance for post-stroke patients (Merians, et al., 2002);

- Training people to regulate their walking pace so they could walk down a hallway and through doors that were continually opening and closing, at the time the doors were open (Buekers, Montagne, de Rugy, & Laurent, 1999);

- Assessing and training inexperienced powered wheelchair users (Harrison et al., 2002);

- Training surgeons to perform laparoscopic surgery (Gallagher et al. 1999);

- Training submarine officers to perform various ship-handling tasks (Hays & Vincenzi, 2000).

In each of these situations, the use of a virtual reality environment provided an effective means of practice to either prepare people to perform the skills in a real environment, or augment physical practice in a real environment.

A Caution Against Using Miming as a Simplification Method

A common practice in occupational therapy is to have patients mime task performance, or pretend they are performing a task. For example, rather than have a person reach for and grasp a glass of water and drink from it, the therapist asks the person to mime this complete action without the glass present. The problem with this approach is that different patterns of movement characterize the mimed and the real actions.

Mathiowetz and Wade (1995) clearly demonstrated these movement pattern differences for three different tasks for normal adults and adults with multiple sclerosis (MS). The three tasks were eating applesauce from a spoon, drinking from a glass, and turning pages of a book. The authors compared two different types of miming: with and without the object. For both the normal and the MS participants, the kinematic profiles for the three tasks revealed uniquely different characteristics for the real and the mimed situations.

Although this experiment and situation relate specifically to a specific patient population in a physical rehabilitation environment, the results have implications for all skill learning situations. When simplifying the practice of a skill, a therapist, teacher, or coach should have the person perform the natural skill. In each of the simplification methods described in the preceding section, this was always the case.

AN ATTENTION APPROACH TO INVOLVING PART PRACTICE IN WHOLE PRACTICE

Sometimes it is not advisable or practical to separate the parts of a skill physically for practice. This, however, does not mean that a learner cannot practice parts of the whole skill. It is possible to practice the whole skill, but focus attention on specific parts that need work. This approach provides both the advantage of part practice, where emphasis on specific parts of the skill facilitates improvement of these parts, and the advantage of whole practice, in which the emphasis is on how the parts of the skill relate to one another to produce skilled performance.

Both attention theory and research evidence support this attention approach. In Kahneman's model of attention (chapter 8), an important factor in attention allocation policy is called *momentary intentions*. When applied to a performance situation, this factor comes into play when a person focuses his or her attention on a specific aspect of the performance. Because we can manipulate our attention resources in this way, we can direct attention to a specific part of a skill while performing the whole skill.

An example of research evidence supporting the use of this attention-directing strategy for part practice is an experiment by Gopher, Weil, and Siegel (1989). Participants learned a complex computer game, known as the Space Fortress Game,

that requires a person to master perceptual, cognitive, and motor skills as well as to acquire specific knowledge of the rules and game strategy. The player must shoot missiles at and destroy a space fortress. He or she fires the missiles from a movable spaceship, controlling spaceship movement and firing using a joystick and a trigger. To destroy the fortress, the player must overcome several obstacles, such as the fortress's rotating to face the spaceship to defend itself, protection of the fortress by mines that appear on the screen periodically and can destroy the spaceship if it runs into them, and so on (see Mané & Donchin, 1989, for a complete description of this computer game).

In the experiment, three groups received instructions during the first six practice sessions that emphasized a strategy requiring them to direct attention to one specific component of the skill. One group's instructions emphasized focusing attention on controlling the spaceship. The second group's instructions emphasized focusing attention on handling the mines around the fortress. The third group received spaceship control instructions for the first three practice sessions and then mine-handling instructions for the next three sessions. When the researchers compared the performance of these three groups against that of a control group that had not received any strategic instructions, the effectiveness of the attention-directing instructions was evident. As you can see in figure 17.1, the control group improved with practice, but not as much as the three instruction groups did. And the group that received two different strategies outperformed those that received only one.

These results provide evidence that attention-directing instructions can serve to establish a part practice environment while allowing the person to practice the whole skill. And these instructions are more effective than having the person practice the skill without providing such strategies. Neither the motor learning nor the teaching methods literature has addressed this type of part practice with any degree of intensity. It clearly deserves more consideration and investigation.

FIGURE 17.1   Results of the experiment by Gopher, Weil, and Siegel showing the change in performance on the computer game Space Fortress for attention-directing instructions related to specific parts of the skill. [Reprinted from Gopher, D. et al. (1989). Practice under changing priorities: An approach to the training of complex skills. *Acta Psychologica, 71,* 147–177, with kind permission of Elsevier Science-NL, Sara Burgerharstraat 25, 1055 KV Amsterdam, The Netherlands.]

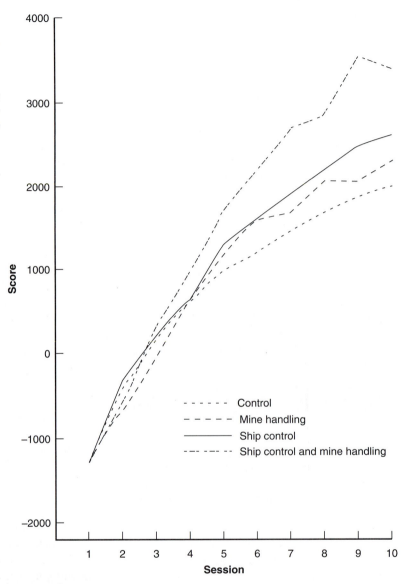

SUMMARY

- Make the initial decision to use a whole or part practice strategy on the basis of the *complexity* and *organization* characteristics of the skill. Use a whole practice strategy when the skill is low in complexity and high in organization; use a part practice when the skill is higher in complexity and is lower in organization.

- Parts of skill that are interdependent in terms of their spatial and temporal performance characteristics should be practiced together as a "natural unit"; parts that are relatively independent in terms of their spatial-temporal relationships can be practiced separately.

- Three methods of part practice were discussed:
  1. *Fractionization* is the practicing of an individual arm or leg of an asymmetric coordi-

nation task involving the arms or legs, and then practicing them together.

2. *Segmentation* is a progressive part method that involves practicing parts in sequence such that the first part is practiced until it can be performed at a certain performance level and then the next part is added and practiced, and so on until the skill is practiced as a whole.

3. *Simplification* involves simplifying parts of the skill, or of the whole skill. We considered several different simplification methods, each of which is specific to certain types of skills or skill characteristics: reducing the difficulty of objects; reducing the attention demands; providing acoustical accompaniment; reducing the performance speed; using task progressions; and using simulators and virtual reality environments.

• An effective whole skill practice strategy is to direct attention focus on a specific part of the skill while performing the whole skill.

RELATED READINGS

Field-Fote, E. C. (2000). Spinal cord control of movement: Implications for locomotor rehabilitation following spinal cord injury. *Physical Therapy, 80,* 477–484

French, K., Rink, J., Rikard, L., Mays, A., Lynn, S., & Werner, P. (1991). The effects of practice progressions on learning two volleyball skills. *Journal of Teaching in Physical Education, 10,* 261–274.

Gray, R. (2002). Behavior of college baseball players in a virtual batting task. *Journal of Experimental Psychology: Human Perception and Performance, 28,* 1131–1148

Klapp, S. T., Nelson, J. M., & Jagacinski, R. J. (1998). Can people tap concurrent bimanual rhythms independently? *Journal of Motor Behavior, 30,* 301–322.

Lee, T. D., Chamberlin, C., & Hodges, N. (2001). Arranging practice conditions and designing instructions. In R. N. Singer, H. Hausenblaus, & C. Janelle, Eds.). *Handbook of sport psychology* (2nd ed., pp. 115–143). New York: John Wiley & Sons. (Read section: "Part versus Whole Task Practice" pp. 121–125.)

Pellett, T. L., & Lox, C. L. (1997). Tennis racquet length comparisons and the effect on beginning college players' playing success and achievement. *Journal of Teaching in Physical Education, 16,* 490–499.

Temple, V. A. (2002, Sept./Oct.). Lacrosse lead-up games. *Strategies,* 25–28.

STUDY QUESTIONS

1. (a) Define the term "organization" as it relates to the relationship among the parts (or components) of a complex motor skill. (b) Give an example of parts of a skill that demonstrate a high degree of organization. Indicate why you consider these parts to be highly organized.

2. (a) How can you decide whether people would learn a skill best if they practiced it as a whole or in parts? (b) Give a motor skill example to show how to apply these rules.

3. Describe examples of how practitioners can apply the part practice methods of fractionization and segmentation to the practice of skills.

4. Describe three ways practitioners can apply the simplification method to the practice of skills.

5. Describe how you could apply an attention allocation policy factor in Kahneman's model of attention to practicing a motor skill as a means of implementing a type of part practice while practicing a whole skill. Give an example

CHAPTER

Mental Practice

*Concept: Mental practice can be effective
for learning and relearning skills,
and for preparing to perform learned skills*

After completing this chapter, you will be able to

- Define *mental practice* and describe the several forms it can take

- Describe two roles for mental practice in the learning and performance of motor skills

- Describe how mental practice can be used to aid skill learning and relearning in various settings

- Describe how mental practice can be used to aid performance preparation in various settings

- Discuss two hypotheses proposed to explain why mental practice is effective

- Discuss the meaning of the term *imagery ability* and how it relates to the effectiveness of mental practice

Application

Situations in which teachers, coaches, and therapists can apply mental practice range from helping a patient employ mental practice to relearn a skill to aiding a world-class athlete perform in a major competitive event. Consider the following three examples.

A gymnast is standing beside the floor exercise mat waiting to begin his routine. Before actually beginning that routine, the gymnast goes through the entire routine mentally, visualizing the performance of each part of the routine, from beginning to end. Following this, the gymnast steps onto the mat and begins the routine.

A stroke patient is having difficulty walking down a flight of stairs. After several failed attempts, the patient is becoming frustrated. The therapist tells the patient to stop practicing and instead to stand on the top step and mentally visualize and feel herself walking down the stairs perfectly ten times in a row. The patient goes through the entire sequence mentally on each practice attempt. Following this procedure, the therapist has the patient go back to physically practicing this skill.

You are playing golf and have just hit a beautiful drive down the middle of the fairway. You would like to hit a few practice drives to try to reproduce and reinforce the swing that produced such a beautiful result. Although you can't do that, you *can* practice that swing mentally as you walk down the fairway to your next shot.

Notice that each of these three situations had a different goal for mental practice. The gymnast used mental practice to prepare for an immediate performance of a well-learned routine. The rehabilitation patient used mental practice to reacquire a skill. Finally, the golfer used a mental practice procedure to reinforce an appropriate action and thereby aid an upcoming performance of that action.

Discussion

In the skill learning and performance literature, the term *mental practice* refers to the cognitive rehearsal of a physical skill in the absence of overt physical movements. We should not confuse this type of mental practice with meditation, which generally connotes an individual's engagement of his or her mind in deep thought in a way that blocks out awareness of what is happening to or around him or her. We can think of meditation as a form of mental practice; in fact, it seems to be a potentially effective means for enhancing physical performance.

In this discussion, we limit the term **mental practice** to mean active cognitive or mental rehearsal of a skill, where a person may think about the cognitive or procedural aspects of a motor skill, or engage in visual or kinesthetic imagery of the performance of a skill or part of a skill. When a person engages in mental practice, an observer would notice no movement related to the skill. Mental practice may occur while a person observes another person live, another person on film or videotape, or himself or herself on film or videotape. Or it may occur without any visual observation at all.

When mental practice involves visual imagery, it can take the form of either internal or external imagery. In *internal imagery,* the individual approximates the real-life situation in such a way that the person actually "imagines being inside his/her body and experiencing those sensations which might be expected in the actual situation" (Mahoney & Avener, 1977, p. 137). During *external*

imagery, on the other hand, the person views himself or herself from the perspective of an observer, as in watching a movie.

Although most discussions of the use of imagery as mental practice involve visual imagery, it is important to note that imagery can take the form of kinesthetic imagery. This form of imagery engages a person in feeling the movements of a skill. Unfortunately, there is very little research that has investigated the use of kinesthetic imagery. But the research available suggests that it can be an effective means of mental practice (e. g., Fery & Morizot, 2000; Hall, Buckolz, & Fishburne, 1992; White & Hardy, 1995). Because of our limited knowledge about kinesthetic imagery, discussions of imagery in this chapter will address visual imagery.

TWO ROLES FOR MENTAL PRACTICE

The study of mental practice as it relates to the learning and performance of motor skills follows two distinct research directions. One concerns the role of mental practice in the *acquisition* of motor skills. Here the critical question is how effective mental practice is for a person in the initial stages of learning or relearning a skill. The other research direction addresses how mental practice can aid in the *performance* of a well-learned skill.

People use mental practice as a performance aid in two ways. You saw the first in the gymnast example in the Application section. The gymnast used mental practice to prepare for the immediately upcoming performance. When used this way, mental practice is *a means of action preparation.* You saw the second approach in the example of yourself

---

mental practice   the cognitive rehearsal of a physical skill in the absence of overt physical movements; it can take the form of thinking about the cognitive or procedural aspects of a motor skill, or of engaging in visual or kinesthetic imagery of the performance of a skill or part of a skill.

as a golfer, mentally imaging a successful swing as you walked down the fairway. Here mental practice combines characteristics of both acquisition and performance situations by providing a person with *a means of facilitating the storage and retrieval from memory* of an appropriate action.

Beginning as early as the 1890s, research literature is replete with mental practice studies. Several excellent reviews of this research literature can be consulted for more specific information than will be discussed here (see Driskell, Copper, & Moran, 1994; Martin, Moritz, & Hall, 1999). These reviews describe the convincing research evidence that supports the concept that mental practice is an effective strategy for aiding both skill acquisition and performance preparation.

MENTAL PRACTICE AIDS SKILL ACQUISITION

Research investigations of the effectiveness of mental practice in motor skill acquisition typically compare mental practice, physical practice, and no practice conditions. In general, results show that physical practice is better than the other conditions. However, mental practice is typically better than no practice. This finding alone is important, because it demonstrates the effectiveness of mental practice in aiding acquisition. Even more impressive is the effect of using *a combination of physical and mental practice.*

One of the more extensive comparisons of combinations of mental and physical practice was an experiment by Hird et al. (1991). The authors compared six different physical and mental practice conditions. At one extreme was 100 percent physical practice, while at the other extreme was 100 percent mental practice. In between were practice routines requiring 75 percent physical and 25 percent mental practice, 50 percent physical and 50 percent mental practice, and 25 percent physical and 75 percent mental practice. The sixth condition required neither physical nor mental practice, but had participants doing a different type of activity during the practice sessions. Participants practiced two tasks. One required them to place as

LAB LINKS

Lab 18 on the Online Learning Center Lab Manual provides an opportunity for you to experience the influence of mental practice on motor skill learning and to compare it to physical practice and to a combination of mental and physical practice.

many round and square pegs in appropriately marked places in the pegboard as they could in 60 sec. The other was a rotary pursuit task in which the target moved in a circular pattern at 45 rpm for 15 sec.

Results of this experiment (figure 18.1) showed three noteworthy effects. First, consistent with other research findings was the result that mental practice alone was better than no practice for both tasks. Second, as the proportion of physical practice increased for both tasks, the level of posttest performance rose. Third, although physical practice alone was better than combinations of mental and physical practice, the differences were small.

The relative similarity in learning effects between physical practice only and combinations of physical and mental practice has been a common finding in research. What is especially notable about this similarity is that the use of a combination of physical and mental practice often involves only half as many physical practice trials as physical practice only.

Why would a combination of mental and physical practice trials lead to learning effects that are as good as physical practice only? We can derive one answer to this question by considering some points discussed throughout this text about the need to engage in effective practice strategies. An important characteristic of effective strategies for optimizing skill acquisition is cognitive problem-solving activity. Physical practice appears not to be the only means of establishing these beneficial conditions. Mental practice can invoke them as well, although not to the same extent. However, the combination of physical and mental practice appears to establish a learning condition that can optimize these important characteristics.

FIGURE 18.1 Results of the experiment by Hird et al. The top graph shows the pre- and posttest results for the different practice conditions for the pegboard task. The bottom graph shows results for the pursuit rotor task. [Reprinted by permission from Hird, J. S., Landers, D. M., Thomas, J. R., & Horan, J. J. (1991). Physical practice is superior to mental practice in enhancing cognitive and motor task performance. *Journal of Sport & Exercise Psychology, 13* (3), p. 288. Human Kinetics, Champaign, IL.]

Mental Practice Benefits in Rehabilitation Settings

In addition to being beneficial for the acquiring of new skills, mental practice can be effective for the relearning of skills, as well as for the improvement of skill performance, in rehabilitation contexts. A research example that demonstrates this is an experiment by Linden et al. (1989). They examined the effects of using mental practice on improving walking balance for women aged 67 to 90 years.

A CLOSER LOOK

Imagery Training as a Posture Development Technique

Two experiments by Fairweather and Sidaway (1993) showed that imagery training can help people diagnosed with postural problems related to abnormal curvature of the spinal column. In one of these experiments, participants were seventeen-year-old males who regularly experienced low back pain and were assessed as having varying degrees of lordosis and kyphosis. The authors compared two different treatments. One involved flexibility and abdominal exercises; the other involved deep muscular relaxation exercises prior to kinesthetic awareness exercises and visualization practice. The visualization technique consisted of creating images of four different action situations involving trunk, buttocks, pelvis, and thighs. For example, participants were told to visualize their buttocks as unbaked loaves of dough and watch them slide downward toward their heels. Results showed that following a three-week training period during which participants engaged in their respective techniques, both techniques led to improved postural form, as measured by spinal angles, and a reduction in back pain.

The task required the women to perform several actions at designated places along an activity course. They began by standing on two footprints and then walked along a simulated balance beam, which was actually a strip of masking tape 4 in. (10.16 cm) wide placed down the center of a carpeted walkway. Then they walked up a ramp that had a 4-degree slope, stepped off the ramp, and walked to a table, where they picked up juice and cookies.

For eight days women in the mental practice group engaged in 6 min of mentally imaging themselves walking along the simulated balance beam. A control group spent the same amount of time sitting and playing word and memory games. The participants performed pretests and posttests for the equilibrium task on the simulated balance beam and for walking the activity course on the day before beginning the mental practice or control activity, and the days after the fourth and eighth days of the mental practice or control activity. Results showed that the mental practice was beneficial for walking balance, as measured by equilibrium and foot placement measures, only when participants carried an object in each hand. Thus, although the mental practice routine was not as successful as the researchers had hoped, it was clinically beneficial.

Mental Practice Benefits for Power Training

A characteristic of many motor skills is the need to generate speed over relatively short distances. Sprint events in running, bicycling, and crew are examples of skills involving this characteristic. An experiment by Van Gyn, Wenger, and Gaul (1990) demonstrated that mental practice can be beneficial for improving power for people learning a 40-m bicycle sprint. After being pretested on a bicycle ergometer (stationary bicycle) to determine peak power for a 40-m sprint, participants began three training sessions each week for six weeks on the bicycle ergometer to improve power performance. This training involved physical practice in which they had to maintain maximum speed for 10 sec.

Two groups imaged themselves performing the sprint eight times. One of these groups did only the mental practice, whereas the other imagery group did imagery practice while they practiced physically. A third group received only the power training. A fourth group served as a control group by receiving neither the imagery nor the power training. The results showed the benefits of combining mental and physical practice. Only the group that received both the imagery and the power training showed an improvement in sprint times at the end of the six-week training period. An interesting result was that only the imagery training group and the imagery and power training group improved their peak power scores between the pre- and posttests.

Mental Practice as a Part of a General Preparation Strategy that Aids Learning

We see an interesting example of incorporating mental practice into a practice routine in some

A CLOSER LOOK

Using Mental Practice in a Physical Therapy Treatment Program

A case study by Page, Levine, Sisto, and Johnson (2001) showed that when mental practice was combined with physical practice, it effectively complemented a physical therapy program for a 56-year-old male with upper-limb hemiparesis due to a subacute stroke five months earlier. The patient's arm function had not improved since he had been discharged from the hospital, where he had received 30 days of inpatient physical therapy. During the study, the patient received the following protocol:

- **Physical therapy:** 3 times per week, in 1-hr segments, for 6 weeks. The exercises in each session involved the arms for 30 min and the legs for 30 min according to the neurodevelopmental treatment (NDT) method.
- **Mental practice:** Two times per week for 10 min in a quiet room 20 min after a physical therapy session; and two times per week at home. Following 2–3 min of relaxation activities, the patient

listened to an audiotape for 5–7 min. The tape included commands for the patient to see himself (external imagery) performing three functional tasks with the affected arm. Each task was mentally practiced for two weeks: reaching for and grasping a cup; turning pages of a large reference book; and reaching for and grasping an item on a high shelf and then bringing the item to himself.

Pretest and posttest comparisons showed the following results:

- Wrist and finger improvements, according to performance on the Fugl-Meyer Scale
- Grip, grasp, and pinch improvements, according to performance on the Action Research Arm Test (ARA)
- Improvements in 6 of the 10 items of the Stroke Rehabilitation Assessment of Movement (STREAM)

---

work from Singer (1986, 1988). He proposed a five-step general learning strategy that involves elements of mental practice in three of the steps. The first step is to get ready physically, mentally, and emotionally. The second step involves mentally imaging performing the action, both visually and kinesthetically. The third step involves concentrating intensely on only one relevant cue related to the action, such as the seams of a tennis ball. The fourth step is to execute the action. Finally, the fifth step is to evaluate the performance outcome.

Several studies have demonstrated the effectiveness of this general strategy for learning a specific skill. For example, Lidor, Tennant, and Singer (1996) compared people who used this strategy with those who didn't to learn a task involving ball-throwing accuracy. Participants sat on a chair 6 m from a target that was standing on the floor behind a badminton net that was 1.32 m high. The task required them to use an overhand motion to throw a ball over the net at the target. Points for each throw were awarded according to where the ball hit the target. However, for the assessment of performance

for research purposes, the actual distance from the center of the target was calculated. The results, which are shown in figure 18.2, indicated that participants who engaged in the five-step general preparation strategy learned to perform the skill more accurately than those who did not use the strategy. It is interesting to note that the transfer test of learning in this study involved the same strategy conditions to perform an underhand throw of a lawn dart from a distance of 3 m from a target mounted on a wall 1.3 m from the floor.

MENTAL PRACTICE AIDS PERFORMANCE PREPARATION

In their review of the research literature related to imagery use in sport, Martin, Moritz, and Hall (1999) described five types of imagery that athletes use for various purposes (see table 18.1). The specific situations in which athletes used imagery were in training periods between competitive events, immediately prior to and during a competitive event, and when they were rehabilitating an injury.

FIGURE 18.2   The results of the experiment by Lidor, Tennant, and Singer that show the comparison of using Singer's five-step strategy and not using the strategy (control) on performance during practice of an overhand ball throw to a target and during a transfer test involving an underhand lawn-dart throw to a target. [*Source:* Modification of figures 3 and 4 in Lidor, Tennant, & Singer (1996). *International Journal of Sport Psychology 27,* 23–36. Modified with permission.]

Because it would be beyond the scope of this textbook to discuss the three motivational types of imagery, only the two cognitive types will be discussed in this chapter (for a more detailed discussion of motivational types of imagery, see Hall, Rodgers, & Barr, 1990; Murphy, 1994). With regard to the types of imagery described in the Martin et al. study, it is important to point out that although the study specifically addressed the use of imagery by athletes, you should not limit the use of imagery in these situations to athletes. The use of imagery can benefit anyone engaged in a situation in which he or she must perform a practiced skill for evaluation purposes.

Surveys and anecdotal evidence indicate that athletes use imagery as part of their preparation strategies for a variety of purposes. Among these are arousal-level regulation, attention focus, and the maintenance of positive and confident feelings. This means that prior to competition, athletes tend to use the motivational types of imagery described in table 18.1. Unfortunately, because of the lack of controlled research investigations on the effectiveness of these imagery strategies, empirically based conclusions are not possible. The primary research problem is that in what would seem to be a simple investigation that compares athletes who use an im-

agery preparation strategy with those who don't, there are no established valid methods for determining if those in the imagery group actually used an imagery strategy, and if they did, what it involved. However, given this limitation, the Martin et al. (1999) review indicates that researchers have reported sufficient evidence to provide "tentative support" (p. 256) for the benefits of the use of imagery as an effective competition preparation strategy.

Swimmers often engage in mental practice before they begin a race.

TABLE 18.1 Five Types of Imagery Related to Motor Skill Performance*

Imagery Type	Description/Example
Motivational	
(a) Specific	Imagery that represents specific goals and goal-orienting behaviors, e.g., *winning a medal for first place; receiving congratulations for a specific accomplishment*
(b) General mastery	Imagery that represents effective coping and mastery of challenging situations, e.g., *being confident; being focused*
(c) General arousal	Imagery that represents feelings of relaxation, stress, arousal, and anxiety in a situation, e.g., *being relaxed prior to an event*
Cognitive	
(a) Specific	Imagery of performing specific skills, e.g., *performing a golf shot; walking down a flight of stairs*
(b) General	Imagery of strategies related to an event, e.g., *strategy to overcome full-court press in basketball; strategy to organize items for cooking a meal*

*Adapted from text of Martin, Moritz, & Hall (1999), p. 250.

WHY IS MENTAL PRACTICE EFFECTIVE?

At present, there are no comprehensive theories that explain why mental practice in the form of imagery is effective (see Martin et al., 1999, for a discussion of proposed explanations). However, there are two generally accepted hypotheses that explain why mental practice benefits the learning and performance of specific motor skills: a neuromuscular hypothesis and a cognitive hypothesis.

A Neuromuscular Hypothesis
We can trace the notion that mental practice of a motor skill has a neuromuscular basis to the work of Jacobson (1931). When he asked people to visualize bending the right arm, Jacobson observed EMG activity in the ocular muscle, but not in the biceps brachii. However, when he asked them to imagine bending the right arm and lifting a 10-lb weight, he noted EMG activity in the biceps brachii on more than 90 percent of the trials. Since Jacobson's early study, many other researchers have provided evidence for this type of electrical activity in the muscles of people asked to imagine movement (e.g., Bakker, Boschker, & Chung, 1996).

The creation of electrical activity in the musculature involved in a movement as a result of the performer's imaging of an action suggests that the appropriate neuromotor pathways involved in the action are activated during mental practice. This activation aids skill learning by helping establish and reinforce the appropriate coordination patterns that are so essential to develop. For someone performing a well-learned skill, this activation tunes, i.e., primes, the neuromotor pathways that will be activated when the person performs the skill. This tuning process increases the likelihood that the person will perform the action appropriately and reduces the demands on the motor control system as it prepares to perform the skill.

A Cognitive Hypothesis
As you studied in chapter 11, researchers generally agree that the first stage of learning a motor skill involves a high degree of cognitive activity. Much of this activity is related to questions about "what to do" with this new task. It should not be surprising, then, that mental practice would be an effective strategy for people acquiring a new skill or relearning an old one. Mental practice can help the person answer many performance-related questions

A CLOSER LOOK

The Use of Mental Imagery by Skilled Athletes

The Martin, Moritz, and Hall (1999) review of research related to athletes' use of imagery included information about the specific uses of imagery in a variety of sports. Listed below is a sampling of these sports and a brief description of the purposes for using imagery in each sport.

- Basketball — Improve free-throw shooting performance
- Football — Rehearse 2-min drill; rehearse specific plays
- Baseball — Rehearse batting strategies (e.g., hitting the ball the opposite way, waiting for specific type of pitch; running past first base and sliding into second base)
- Figure skating — Rehearse routines
- Gymnastics — Rehearse routines
- Wrestling — Rehearse strategies against a specific opponent
- Badminton — Establish confidence and arousal control
- Golf — Develop attention focus and control during putting
- Various sports — Increase or decrease precompetition anxiety
- Sports-related injuries — Use relaxation strategy; increase motivation to adhere to rehab program; manage pain; mentally practice rehab exercises; enhance self-confidence after return to competition

without the pressure that accompanies physical performance of the skill. In the later stages of learning, mental practice can be beneficial in assisting the person to consolidate strategies as well as to correct errors.

MENTAL PRACTICE AND IMAGERY ABILITY

Although researchers have proposed both physiological and psychological reasons for the effectiveness of mental practice for learning and performing motor skills, a related factor also might be operating. There is evidence indicating that the effectiveness of the use of imagery as a form of mental practice is related to a person's **imagery ability,** which is the ability to image an action when requested to do so. Some people have great difficulty imaging a described action, whereas others can image with a high degree of vividness and control.

Evidence demonstrating that imagery ability is an individual-difference variable came from research using the Movement Imagery Questionnaire (MIQ), a test of imagery ability designed specifically to apply to motor skill performance (Hall &

Pongrac, 1983; Hall & Martin, 1997). The MIQ consists of various action situations that a person is asked to physically perform. Then the person is asked to do one of two mental tasks, to either "form as clear and vivid a mental image as possible of the movement just performed" or "attempt to positively feel yourself making the movement just performed without actually doing it." In this test, the first mental task is called "visual imagery," whereas the second mental task is called "kinesthetic imagery." After performing one of these mental tasks, the person rates how easy or difficult it was to do it. A person may be able to do both visual and kinesthetic imagery easily, do one easily and the other with difficulty, or do both with difficulty.

Because imagery ability is an individual–difference variable, Hall proposed that *imagery ability influences the success of mental practice.* People with a high level of imagery ability will benefit more readily from mental practice of motor skills than those with a low level. To test this hypothesis, Goss et al. (1986) selected people who were categorized from their MIQ scores as high visual/high kinesthetic (HH), high visual/low kinesthetic (HL),

A CLOSER LOOK

Examples of Movement Imagery Questionnaire (MIQ) Items

An Item from the Visual Imagery Subscale

Starting position: Stand with your feet slightly apart and your hands at your sides.

Action: Bend down low and then jump straight up in the air as high as possible with both arms extended above your head. Land with your feet apart and lower your arms to your sides.

Mental task: Assume the starting position. Form as clear and vivid a mental image as possible of the movement just performed. Now rate the ease/difficulty with which you were able to do this mental task.

An Item from the Kinesthetic Imagery Subscale

Starting position: Stand with your feet slightly apart and your arms at your sides.

Action: Jump upwards and rotate your entire body to the left such that you land in the same position in which you started. That is, rotate to the left in a complete (360 degree) circle.

Mental task: Assume the standing position. Attempt to feel yourself making the movement just performed without actually doing it. Now rate the ease/difficulty with which you were able to do this mental task.

Imagery Ability Rating Scales Visual Imagery Scale

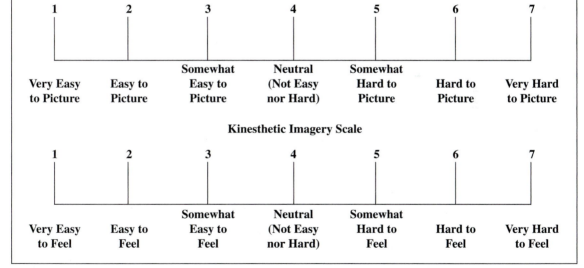

1	2	3	4	5	6	7
Very Easy to Picture	Easy to Picture	Somewhat Easy to Picture	Neutral (Not Easy nor Hard)	Somewhat Hard to Picture	Hard to Picture	Very Hard to Picture

Kinesthetic Imagery Scale

1	2	3	4	5	6	7
Very Easy to Feel	Easy to Feel	Somewhat Easy to Feel	Neutral (Not Easy nor Hard)	Somewhat Hard to Feel	Hard to Feel	Very Hard to Feel

or low visual/low kinesthetic (LL). Before each practice trial of four complex arm movement patterns, participants kinesthetically imaged the movement about which they received instructions. The results supported the hypotheses, as the HH group performed the patterns to criterion in the

imagery ability an individual-difference characteristic that differentiates people who can image an action with a high degree of vividness and control from people who have difficulty imaging an action.

fewest trials, with the HL group next, and the LL group taking the greatest number of trials to achieve criterion. Retention performance showed a similar effect.

Results such as those in the Goss et al. study have led some researchers to question whether the high and low imagery ability effects are due to differences in motivation or the ability to concentrate. An experiment by Lovell and Collins (2002) addressed this question by recording electroencephalograms (EEG) at various brain sites for males who were classified as high or low on movement imagery according to the MIQ. Because of the brainwave activity characteristics recorded during mental imagery across several practice sessions, the authors concluded that their results provided evidence that levels of movement imagery ability are not merely motivation or concentration effects, but relate to distinct neurological processing characteristics associated with the ability to produce mental movement images.

The importance of these experiments is that they support the hypothesis that a relationship exists between imagery ability and the effectiveness of mental practice. In addition, they demonstrate that people with low imagery ability can benefit from mental practice.

SUMMARY

Mental practice involves the cognitive rehearsal of a skill in the absence of overt physical movement.

- Mental practice can take the form of thinking about the cognitive or procedural aspects of a motor skill, or seeing or feeling oneself performing a skill or part of a skill.
- Research evidence shows that mental practice can be effective as a practice strategy to facilitate the learning and relearning of motor skills, and as an action preparation strategy to prepare to perform well-learned skills.
- As a practice strategy, mental practice works best when used in combination with physical practice of the skill being learned or relearned.

- Two hypotheses have been proposed to account for why mental practice is effective:
  1. The neuromuscular hypothesis is based on research evidence showing EMG recordings in muscles that would be involved in the actual physical performance of the imaged skill.
  2. The cognitive hypothesis points to the benefit of mental practice for answering questions concerning "what to do" that are prevalent during the first stage of motor skill learning.

- The ease or difficulty a person may have in using imagery as a form of mental practice is related to a person's imagery ability. However, regardless of a person's level of imagery ability, he or she can benefit from mental practice.

RELATED READINGS

Annett, J. (1995). Motor imagery: Perception or action? *Neuropsychologia, 33,* 1395–1417.

Behrmann, M. (2000). The mind's eye mapped onto the brain's matter. *Current Directions in Psychological Science, 9,* 50–54.

Bohan, M., Pharmer, J. A., & Stokes, A. F. (1999). When does imagery practice enhance performance on a motor task? *Perceptual and Motor Skills, 88,* 651–658.

Boschker, M. S. J., Bakker, F. C., & Michaels, C. F. (2002). Effect of mental imagery on realizing affordances. *Quarterly Journal of Experimental Psychology, 55A,* 775–792.

Gould, D., & Udry, E. (1994). Psychological skills for enhancing performance: Arousal regulation strategies. *Medicine and Science in Sports and Exercise, 26,* 478–485.

Grouios, G., Vakali, M. (2000). The effect of mental practice on the performance of an eye-hand coordination task. *Journal of Human Movement Studies, 38,* 75–92

Kohl, R. M., Ellis, S. D., & Roenker, D. L. (1992). Alternating actual and imagery practice: Preliminary theoretical considerations. *Research Quarterly for Exercise and Sport, 63,* 162–170.

Shanks, D. R., & Cameron, A. (2000). The effect of mental practice on performance in a sequential reaction time task. *Journal of Motor Behavior, 32.* 305–313

Warner, L., & McNeil, M. E. (1988). Mental imagery and its potential for physical therapy. *Physical Therapy, 68,* 516–521.

1. (a) Define *mental practice*. (b) Describe three ways in which a person can engage in mental practice.

2. Describe an example of how you would implement mental practice procedures to aid the learning of a new skill.

3. Describe an example of how you would implement a mental practice strategy to aid your preparation to perform a well-learned skill.

4. What are two reasons researchers have proposed to explain why mental practice aids motor skill learning and performance?

5. (a) Discuss what is meant by the term "imagery ability." (b) How does imagery ability relate to the effectiveness of mental practice?

REFERENCES

Abernethy, B. (1993). Searching for the minimal essential information for skilled perception and action. *Psychological Research, 55,* 131–138.

Abernethy, B. (1999). The Coleman Roberts Griffith Address: Movement expertise: A juncture between psychology theory and practice. *Journal of Applied Sport Psychology, 11,* 126–141.

Abernethy, B., & Burgess-Limerick, R. (1992). Visual information for the timing of skilled movements: A review. In J. J. Summers (Ed.), *Approaches to the study of motor control and learning* (pp. 343–384). Amsterdam: Elsevier.

Abernethy, B., & Russell, D. G. (1987). Expert-novice differences in an applied selective attention task. *Journal of Sport Psychology, 9,* 326–345.

Abernethy, B., & Sparrow, W. A. (1992). The rise and fall of dominant paradigms in motor behavior research. In J. J. Summers (Ed.), *Approaches to the study of motor control and learning* (pp. 3–45). Amsterdam: Elsevier.

Abernethy, B., & Wood, J. M. (2001). Do generalized visual training programmes for sport really work? An experimental investigation. *Journal of Sports Sciences, 19,* 203–222.

Abernethy, B., Wood, J. M., & Parks, S. (1999). Can the anticipatory skills of experts be learned by novices? *Research Quarterly for Exercise and Sport, 70,* 313–318.

Ackerman, P. L. (1988). Determinants of individual differences during skill acquisition: Cognitive abilities and information processing. *Journal of Experimental Psychology: General, 117,* 288–318.

Ackerman, P. L. (1992). Predicting individual differences in complex skill acquisition: Dynamics of ability determinants. *Journal of Applied Psychology, 77,* 598–614.

Acocella, J. (2003, January 6). Second act: Suzanne Farrell returns with a company of her own. *The New Yorker,* pp. 48–61.

Ada, L., O'Dwyer, N. J., & Neilson, P. D. (1993). Improvement in kinematic characteristics and coordination following stroke quantified by linear systems analysis. *Human Movement Science, 12,* 137–153.

Adams, J. A. (1986). Use of the model's knowledge of results to increase the observer's performance. *Journal of Human Movement Studies, 12,* 89–98.

Adams, J. A. (1987). Historical review and appraisal of research on the learning, retention, and transfer of human motor skills. *Psychological Bulletin, 101,* 41–74.

Adams, J. A., & Dijkstra, S. J. (1966). Short-term memory for motor responses. *Journal of Experimental Psychology, 71,* 314–318.

Alcott, A. (1991, December). Winning at golf. *Golf Magazine, 19,* 93.

Allport, D. A. (1980). Attention and performance. In G. Claxton (Ed.), *Cognitive psychology: New directions* (pp. 112–153). London: Routledge & Kegan Paul.

Almasbakk, B., Whiting, H. T. A., Helgerud, J. (2001). The efficient learner. *Biological Cybernetics, 84,* 75–83.

Amazeen, P. G. (2002). Is dynamics the content of a generalized motor program for rhythmic interlimb coordination? *Journal of Motor Behavior, 34,* 233–251.

Amazeen, E. L., Amazeen, P. G., Post, A. A., & Beek, P. J. (1999). Timing the selection of information during rhythmic catching. *Journal of Motor Behavior, 31,* 279–289.

Anderson, D. I., Magill, R. A., & Sekiya, H. (1994). A reconsideration of the trials-delay of knowledge of results paradigm in motor skill learning. *Research Quarterly for Exercise and Sport, 65,* 286–290.

Anderson, D. I., & Sidaway, B. (1994). Coordination changes associated with practice of a soccer kick. *Research Quarterly Exercise and Sport, 65,* 93–99.

Anderson, J. R. (1987). Skill acquisition: Compilation of weak-method problem solutions. *Psychological Review, 94,* 192–210.

Annesi, J. J. (1998). Effects of computer feedback on adherence to exercise. *Perceptual and Motor Skills, 87,* 723–730.

Annett, J. (1959). Learning a pressure under conditions of immediate and delayed knowledge of results. *Quarterly Journal of Experimental Psychology, 11,* 3–15.

Annett, J. (1969). *Feedback and human behavior.* Baltimore, MD: Penguin.

Annett, J. (1970). The role of action feedback in the acquisition of simple motor responses. *Journal of Motor Behavior, 11,* 217–221.

Annett, J., & Piech, J. (1985). The retention of a skill following distributed training. *Programmed Learning and Educational Technology, 22,* 182–186.

Anson, J. G. (1982). Memory drum theory: Alternative tests and explanations for the complexity effects on simple reaction time. *Journal of Motor Behavior, 14,* 228–246.

Ash, D. W., & Holding, D. H. (1990). Backward versus forward chaining in the acquisition of a keyboard skill. *Human Factors, 32,* 139–146.

Assaiante, C., & Amblard, B. (1992). Peripheral vision and age-related differences in dynamic balance. *Human Movement Science, 11,* 533–548.

Assaiante, C., Marchand, A. R., & Amblard, B. (1989). Discrete visual samples may control locomotor equilibrium and foot positioning in man. *Journal of Motor Behavior, 21,* 72–91.

Atkinson, R. C., & Shiffrin, R. M. (1968). Human memory: A proposed system and its control processes. In K. W. Spence & J. T. Spence (Eds.), *The psychology of learning and motivation: Advances in research and theory* (Vol. 2, pp. 89–197). New York: Academic Press.

Baddeley, A. D. (1986). *Working memory.* New York: Oxford University Press.

Baddeley, A. D. (1995). Working memory. In M. S. Gazzaniga (Ed.), *The cognitive neurosciences* (pp. 755–764). Cambridge, MA: MIT Press.

Baddeley, A. D., & Longman, D. J. A. (1978). The influence of length and frequency of training session on the rate of learning to type. *Ergonomics, 21,* 627–635.

Bahill, A. T., & LaRitz, T. (1984). Why can't batters keep their eyes on the ball? *American Scientist, 72,* 249–252.

Bakker, F. C., Boschker, M. S. J., & Chung, T. (1996). Changes in muscular activity while imagining weight lifting using stimulus or response propositions. *Journal of Sport & Exercise Psychology, 18,* 313–324.

Bandura, A. (1986). *Social foundations of thought and action: A social cognitive theory.* Englewood Cliffs, NJ: Prentice Hall.

Bard, C., Fleury, M., & Goulet, C. (1994). Relationship between perceptual strategies and response adequacy in sport situation. *International Journal of Sport Psychology, 25,* 266–281.

Bard, C., Paillard, J., Lajoie, Y., Fleury, M., Teasdale, N., Forget, R., & Lamarre, Y. (1992). Role of afferent information in the timing of motor commands: A comparative study with a deafferented patient. *Neuropsychologia, 30,* 201–206.

Barrow, H. M. (1957). *Motor ability testing for college men.* Minneapolis: Burgess.

Bartlett, F. C. (1932). *Remembering: A study in experimental and social psychology.* Cambridge: Cambridge University Press.

Barton, J. W. (1921). Smaller versus larger units in learning the maze. *Journal of Experimental Psychology, 4,* 414–424.

Battig, W. F. (1979). The flexibility of human memory. In L. S. Cermak & F. I. M. Craik (Eds.), *Levels of processing in human memory* (pp. 23–44). Hillsdale, NJ: Erlbaum.

Bekkering, H., & Neggers, S. F. W. (2002). Visual search is modulated by action intentions. *Psychological Science, 13,* 370–374.

Benedetti, C., & McCullagh, P. (1987). Post-knowledge of results delay: Effects of interpolated activity on learning and performance. *Research Quarterly for Exercise and Sport, 58,* 375–381.

Bennett, S., Davids, K., & Craig, T. (1999). The effect of temporal and informational constraints on one-handed catching performance. *Research Quarterly for Exercise and Sport, 70,* 206–211.

Berg, W. P., Wade, M. G., & Greer, N. L. (1994). Visual regulation of gait in bipedal locomotion: Revisiting Lee, Lishman, & Thomson (1982). *Journal of Experimental Psychology: Human Perception and Performance, 20,* 854–863.

Berger, H. J., van Es, N. J., van Spaendonck, K. P., Teunisse, J. P., Horstink, M. W., van't Hof, M. A., & Cools, A. R. (1999). Relationship between memory strategies and motor symptoms in Parkinson's disease. *Journal of Clinical Experimental Neuropsychology, 21,* 677–684.

Bernstein, N. (1967). *The co-ordination and regulation of movement.* Oxford: Pergamon Press.

Bilodeau, E. A., Bilodeau, I. M., & Schumsky, D. A. (1959). Some effects of introducing and withdrawing knowledge of results early and late in practice. *Journal of Experimental Psychology, 58,* 142–144.

Bilodeau, I. M. (1969). Information feedback. In E. A. Bilodeau (Ed.), *Principles of skill acquisition* (pp. 225–285). New York: Academic Press.

Bizzi, E., & Polit, A. (1979). Processes controlling visually evoked movements. *Neuropsychologia, 17,* 203–213.

Blais, C. (1991). Instructions as constraints on psychomotor performance. *Journal of Human Movement Studies, 21,* 217–231.

Blandin, Y., & Proteau, L. (2000). On the cognitive basis of observational learning: Development of mechanisms for the detection and correction of errors. *Quarterly Journal of Experimental Psychology, 53A,* 846–867.

Blouin, J., Bard, C., Teasdale, N., Paillard, J., Fleury, M., Forget, R., & Lamarre, Y. (1993). Reference systems for coding spatial information in normal subjects and a deafferented patient. *Experimental Brain Research, 93,* 324–331.

Bonnard, M., & Pailhous, J. (1999). Contribution of proprioceptive feedback to preferred versus constrained space-time behavior in rhythmical movements. *Experimental Brain Research, 128,* 568–572.

Bootsma, R. J., Marteniuk, R. G., MacKenzie, C. L., & Zaal, F. T. (1994). The speed-accuracy trade-off in manual prehension: Effects of movement amplitude, object size and object width on kinematic characteristics. *Experimental Brain Research, 98,* 535–541.

Bootsma, R. J., & Peper, C. E. (1992). Predictive visual information sources for the regulation of action with special emphasis on catching and hitting. In L. Proteau & D. Elliott (Eds.), *Vision and motor control* (pp. 285–313). Amsterdam: Elsevier.

Bootsma, R. J., & van Wieringen, P. C. W. (1990). Timing an attacking forehand drive in table tennis. *Journal of Experimental Psychology: Human Perception and Performance, 16,* 21–29.

Boulter, L. R. (1964). Evaluations of mechanisms in delay of knowledge of results. *Canadian Journal of Psychology, 18,* 281–291.

Bouzid, N., & Crawshaw, C. M. (1987). Massed versus distributed wordprocessor training. *Applied Ergonomics, 18,* 220–222.

Boyce, B. A. (1991). The effects of an instructional strategy with two schedules of augmented KP feedback upon skill acquisition of a selected shooting task. *Journal of Teaching in Physical Education, 11,* 47–58.

Brace, D. K. (1927). *Measuring motor ability.* New York: A. S. Barnes and Co.

Brady, F. (1998). A theoretical and empirical review of the contextual interference effect and the learning of motor skills. *Quest, 50,* 266–293.

Brashers-Krug, T., Shadmehr, R., & Bizzi, E. (1996). Consolidation in human motor memory. *Nature, 382,* 252–255.

Brenner, E., & Smeets, J. B. J. (1997). Fast responses of the human hand to changes in target position. *Journal of Motor Behavior, 29,* 297–310.

Bridgeman, B. (1996). Extraretinal signals in visual orientation. In W. Prinz & B. Bridgeman (Eds.), *Handbook of perception and action. Vol. 1: Perception* (pp. 191–223). San Diego, CA: Academic Press.

Brisson, T. A., & Alain, C. (1997). A comparison of two references for using knowledge of performance in learning a motor task. *Journal of Motor Behavior, 29,* 339–350.

Broadbent, D. E. (1958). *Perception and communication.* Oxford: Pergamon Press.

Brown, R. W. (1928). A comparison of the whole, part, and combination methods for learning piano music. *Journal of Experimental Psychology, 11,* 235–247.

Brown, T. G. (1911). The intrinsic factors in the act of progression in the mammal. *Proceedings of the Royal Society of London (Biology), 84,* 308–319.

Brucker, B. S., & Bulaeva, N. V. (1996). Biofeedback effect on electromyographic responses in patients with spinal cord injury. *Archives of Physical Medicine and Rehabilitation, 77,* 133–137.

Bryan, W. L., & Harter, N. (1987). Studies in the physiology and psychology of the telegraphic language. *Psychological Review, 4,* 27–53.

Buekers, M. J. A., & Magill, R. A. (1995). The role of task experience and prior knowledge for detecting invalid augmented feedback while learning a motor skill. *Quarterly Journal of Experimental Psychology, 44A,* 105–117.

Buekers, M. J. A., Magill, R. A., & Hall, K. G. (1992). The effect of erroneous knowledge of results on skill acquisition when augmented information is redundant. *Quarterly Journal of Experimental Psychology, 44A,* 105–117.

Buekers, M. J. A., Magill, R. A., & Sneyers, K. M. (1994). Resolving a conflict between sensory feedback and knowledge of results while learning a motor skill. *Journal of Motor Behavior, 26,* 27–35.

Buekers, M. J., Montagne, G., de Rugy, A., & Laurent, M. (1999). The regulation of externally paced human locomotion in virtual reality. *Neuroscience Letters, 275,* 171–174.

Buekers, M. J., Montagne, G., & Laurent, M. (1999). Is the player in control, or is the control somewhere out of the player? *International Journal of Sport Psychology, 30,* 490–506.

Bullock, D., & Grossberg, S. (1991). Adaptive neural networks for control of movement trajectories invariant under speed and force rescaling. *Human Movement Science, 10,* 3–53.

Butler, D., Andersson, G. B. J., Trafimow, J., Schipplein, O. D., & Andriacchi, T. P. (1993). The influence of load knowledge on lifting technique. *Ergonomics, 36,* 1489–1493.

Butler, M. S., Reeve, T. G., & Fischman, M. G. (1996). Effects of the instructional set in the bandwidth feedback paradigm on motor skill acquisition. *Research Quarterly for Exercise and Sport, 67,* 355–359.

Campbell, K. C., & Proctor, R. W. (1993). Repetition effects with categorizable stimulus and response sets. *Journal of Experimental Psychology: Learning, Memory, and Cognition, 19,* 1345–1362.

Carlton, L. G. (1992). Visual processing time and the control of movement. In L. Proteau & D. Elliott (Eds.), *Vision and motor control* (pp. 3–31). Amsterdam: Elsevier.

Carlton, L. G., Carlton, M. J., & Newell, K. M. (1987). Reaction time and response dynamics. *Quarterly Journal of Experimental Psychology, 39A,* 337–360.

Carroll, W. R., & Bandura, A. (1990). Representational guidance of action production in observational learning: A causal analysis. *Journal of Motor Behavior, 22,* 85–97.

Carron, A. V. (1969). Performance and learning in a discrete motor task under massed vs. distributed practice. *Research Quarterly, 40,* 481–489.

Cauraugh, J. H., Chen, D., & Radlo, S. J. (1993). Effects of traditional and reversed bandwidth knowledge of results on motor learning. *Research Quarterly for Exercise and Sport, 64,* 413–417.

Chapman, P. R., & Underwood, G. (1998). Visual search of driving situations: Danger and experience. *Perception, 27,* 951–964.

Chapman, S. (1968). Catching a baseball. *American Journal of Physics, 36,* 868-870.

Chase, W. G., & Ericcson, K. A. (1982). Skill and working memory. In G.H. Bower (Ed.), *The psychology of learning and motivation* (Vol. 16, pp. 1–58). New York: Academic Press.

Cherry, E. C. (1953). Some experiments on the recognition of speech, with one and two ears. *Journal of the Acoustical Society of America, 25,* 975–979.

Chieffi, S., Allport, D. A., & Woodfin, M. (1999). Hand-centered coding of target location in visuo-spatial working memory. *Neuropsychologia, 37,* 495–502.

Chieffi, S., & Gentilucci, M. (1993). Coordination between the transport and the grasp components during prehension movement. *Experimental Brain Research, 50,* 7–15.

Chiviakowsky, S., & Wulf, G. (2002). Self-controlled feedback: Does it enhance learning because performers get feedback when they need it? *Research Quarterly for Exercise and Sport, 73,* 408–415.

Chollet, D., Micallef, J. P., & Rabischong, P. (1988). Biomechanical signals for external biofeedback to improve swimming techniques. In B. E. Ungerechts, K. Wilke, & K. Reichle (Eds.), *Swimming science V* (pp.389–396). Champaign, IL: Human Kinetics.

Christina, R. W. (1973). Influence of enforced motor and sensory sets on reaction latency and movement speed. *Research Quarterly, 44,* 483–487.

Christina, R. W., Fischman, M. G., Lambert, A. L., & Moore, J. F. (1985). Simple reaction time as a function of response complexity: Christina et al. (1982) revisited. *Research Quarterly for Exercise and Sport, 56,* 316–322.

Christina, R. W., & Rose, D. J. (1985). Premotor and motor response time as a function of response complexity. *Research Quarterly for Exercise and Sport, 56,* 306–315.

Cockrell, D. L., Carnahan, H., & McFayden, B. J. (1995). A preliminary analysis of the coordination of reaching, grasping, and walking. *Perceptual and Motor Skills, 81,* 515–519.

Cole, G., Gellatly, A., & Blurton, B. (2001). Effect of object onset on the distribution of visual attention. *Journal of Experimental Psychology: Human Perception and Performance, 27,* 1356–1368.

Cook, T. W. (1936). Studies in cross education. V. Theoretical. *Psychological Review, 43,* 149–178.

Corbetta D., & Thelen, E. (1996). The developmental origins of bimanual coordination: A dynamic perspective. *Journal of Experimental Psychology: Human Perception and Performance, 22,* 502–522.

Coull, J., Trembley, L. Elliott, D., (2001). Examining the specificity of practice hypothesis: Is learning modality specific? *Research Quarterly for Exercise and Sport, 72,* 345–354.

Coull, J., Trembley, L. Elliott, D., Weir, P. L., & Weeks, D. J. (2000). Monocular and binocular vision in the control of goal-directed movement. *Journal of Motor Behavior, 32,* 347–360.

Craik, R., Herman, R. H., & Finley, F. R. (1976). The human solutions for locomotion: Interlimb coordination. In R. M. Herman, S. Grillner, & P. S. G. Stein (Eds.), *Neural control of locomotion* (pp. 51–63). New York: Plenum.

Crocker, P. R. E., & Dickinson, J. (1984). Incidental psychomotor learning: The effects of number of movements, practice, and rehearsal. *Journal of Motor Behavior, 16,* 61–75.

Cromwell, R. L., Newton, R. A., & Forrest, G. (2002). Influence of vision on head stabilization strategies in older adults during walking. *Journals of Gerontology A-Biological Sciences and Medical Sciences, 57,* M442-448.

Crossman, E. R. F. W. (1959). A theory of the acquisition of speed skill. *Ergonomics, 2,* 153–166.

Crossman, E. R. F. W., & Goodeve, P. J. (1983). Feedback control of hand movements and Fitts' law. *Quarterly Journal of Experimental Psychology, 35A,* 251–278. (Original work published in 1963.)

Cutting, J. E. (1986). *Perception with an eye for motion.* Cambridge, MA: MIT Press.

Cutting, J. E., & Kozlowski, L. T. (1977). Recognizing friends by their walk: Gait perception without familiarity cues. *Bulletin of the Psychonomic Society, 9,* 353–356.

Cutting, J. E., Vishton, P. M., & Braren, P. A. (1995). How we avoid collisions with stationary and moving objects. *Psychological Review, 102,* 627–651.

Cutton, D. M., & Landin, D. (1994). *The effects of two cognitive learning strategies on learning the tennis forehand.* Paper presented at the annual meeting of the Southern District American Alliance for Health, Physical Education, Recreation, and Dance, Nashville, TN.

Czerwinski, M., Lightfoot, N., & Shiffrin, R. A. (1992). Automatization and training in visual search. *American Journal of Psychology, 105,* 271–315.

Daniels, F. S., & Landers, D. M. (1981). Biofeedback and shooting performance: A test of disregulation and systems theory. *Journal of Sport Psychology, 3,* 271–282.

Danion, F., Boyadjian, A., & Marin, L. (2000). Control of locomotion in expert gymnasts in the absence of vision. *Journal of Sports Sciences, 18,* 809–814.

Davids, K. (1988). Developmental differences in the use of peripheral vision during catching performance. *Journal of Motor Behavior, 20,* 39–51.

Davis, R. C. (1942). The pattern of muscular action in simple voluntary movements. *Journal of Experimental Psychology, 31,* 437–466.

den Brinker, B. P. L. M., Stabler, J. R. L. W., Whiting, H. T. A., & van Wieringen, P. C. (1986). The effect of manipulating knowledge of results in the learning of slalom-ski type ski movements. *Ergonomics, 29,* 31–40.

Diedrich, F. J., & Warren, W. H., Jr. (1995). Why change gaits? Dynamics of the walk-run transition. *Journal of Experimental Psychology: Human Perception and Performance, 21,* 183–202.

Diedrich, F. J., & Warren, W. H., Jr. (1998). The dynamics of gait transitions: Effects of grade and load. *Journal of Motor Behavior, 30,* 60–78.

Diewert, G. L. (1975). Retention and coding in motor short-term memory: A comparison of storage codes for distance and location information. *Journal of Motor Behavior, 7,* 183–190.

Diewert, G. L., & Roy, E. A. (1978). Coding strategy for memory of movement extent information. *Journal of Experimental Psychology: Human Learning and Memory, 4,* 666–675.

Dishman, R. K. (1993). Exercise adherence. In R. N. Singer, M. Murphy, & L. K. Tennant (Eds.), *Handbook of research on sport psychology* (pp.779–798). New York: Macmillan.

Donders, F. C. (1969). On the speed of mental processes. Translated and reprinted in *Acta Psychologica, 30,* 412–431. (Original work published in 1868).

Donker, S. F., Beek, P. J., Wagenaar, R. C., & Mulder, T. (2001). Coordination between arm and leg movements during locomotion. *Journal of Motor Behavior, 33,* 86–102

Donovan, J. J., & Radosevich, D. J. (1999). A meta-analytic review of the practice distribution effect: Now you see it, now you don't. *Journal of Applied Psychology, 84,* 795–805.

Doody, S. G., Bird, A. M., & Ross, D. (1985). The effect of auditory and visual models on acquisition of a timing task. *Human Movement Science, 4,* 271–281.

Driskell, J. E., Copper, C., & Moran, A. (1994). Does mental practice enhance performance? *Journal of Applied Psychology, 79,* 481–491.

Driskell, J. E., Willis, R. P., & Copper, C. (1992). Effect of overlearning on retention. *Journal of Applied Psychology, 77,* 615–622.

Drowatzky, J. N., & Zuccato, F. C. (1967). Interrelationships between selected measures of static and dynamic balance. *Research Quarterly, 38,* 509–510.

Durand, M., Geoffroi, V., Varray, A., & Préfaut, C. (1994). Study of the energy correlates in the learning of a complex self-paced cyclical skill. *Human Movement Science, 13,* 785–799.

Eason, R. G., Beardshall, A., & Jaffee, S. (1965). Performance and physiological indicants of activation in a vigilance situation. *Perceptual and Motor Skills, 20,* 3–13.

Edwards, R. V., & Lee, A. M. (1985). The relationship of cognitive style and instructional strategy to learning and transfer of motor skills. *Research Quarterly for Exercise and Sport, 56,* 286–290.

Egeth, H. E., & Yantis, S. (1997). Visual attention: Control, representation, and time course. *Annual Review of Psychology, 48,* 269–297.

Eghan, T. (1988). *The relation of teacher feedback to student achievement.* Unpublished doctoral dissertation. Louisiana State University.

Elliott, D., & Allard, F. (1985). The utilization of visual information and feedback information during rapid pointing movements. *Quarterly Journal of Experimental Psychology, 37A,* 407–425.

Elliott, D., Zuberec, S., & Milgram, P. (1994). The effects of periodic visual occlusion on ball catching. *Journal of Motor Behavior, 26,* 113–122.

Engel, K. C., Flanders, M., & Soechting, J. F. (1997). Anticipatory and sequential motor control in piano playing. *Experimental Brain Research, 113,* 189–199.

Engle, R. W. (2002). Working memory capacity as executive attention. *Current Directions in Psychological Science, 11,* 19–23

Enoka, R. M. (2002). *Neuromechanics of human movement* (3rd ed.). Champaign, IL: Human Kinetics.

Ericsson, K. A., & Kintsch, W. (1995). Long-term working memory. *Psychological Review, 102,* 211–245.

Ericsson, K. A., Krampe, R. T., & Tesch-Romer, C. (1993). The role of deliberate practice in the acquisition of expert performance. *Psychological Review, 100,* 363–406.

Ericsson, K. A., & Smith, J. (1991). Prospects and limits of the empirical study of expertise: An introduction. In K. A. Ericcson & J. Smith (Eds.), *Toward a general theory of expertise: Prospects and limits* (pp. 1–38). Cambridge: Cambridge University Press.

Fairweather, M. M., & Sidaway, B. (1993). Ideokinetic imagery as a postural development technique. *Research Quarterly for Exercise and Sport, 64,* 385–392.

Farrow, D., & Abernethy, B. (2002). Can anticipatory skills be learned through implicit video-based perceptual training? *Journal of Sports Sciences, 20,* 471–485.

Farrow, D., Chivers, P., Hardingham, C., & Sachse, S. (1998). The effect of video-based perceptual training on the tennis return of serve. *International Journal of Sport Psychology, 29,* 36–43.

Feltz, D. L. (1992). Understanding motivation in sport: A self-efficacy perspective. In G. C. Roberts (Ed.), *Motivation in sport and exercise* (pp. 93–127). Champaign, IL: Human Kinetics.

Fery, Y. A., & Morizot, P. (2000). Kinesthetic and visual image in modeling closed motor skills: The example of the tennis serve. *Perceptual and Motor Skills, 90,* 707–722.

Field-Fote, E. C. (2000). Spinal cord control of movement: Implications for locomotor rehabilitation following spinal cord injury. *Physical Therapy, 80,* 477–484.

Fisher, D. L., Laurie, N. E., Glaser, R., Connerney, K., Pollatsek, A., Duffy, S. A., & Brock, J. (2002). Use of a fixed-base driving simulator to evaluate the effects of experience and PC-based risk awareness training on drivers' decisions. *Human Factors, 44,* 287–302.

Fischman, M. G. (1984). Programming time as a function of number of movement parts and changes in movement direction. *Journal of Motor Behavior, 16,* 405–423.

Fischman, M. G., & Schneider, T. (1985). Skill level, vision, and proprioception in simple one-hand catching. *Journal of Motor Behavior, 17,* 219–229.

Fishman, S., & Tobey, C. (1978). Augmented feedback. In W. Anderson & G. Barrette (Eds.), *What's going on in gym: Descriptive studies of physical education classes* (pp. 51–62). *Motor Skills: Theory into Practice,* Monograph 1.

Fitts, P. M., & Posner, M. I. (1967). *Human performance.* Belmont, CA: Brooks/Cole.

Fleishman, E. A. (1967). Performance assessment based on an empirically derived task taxonomy. *Human Factors, 9,* 349–366.

Fleishman, E. A. (1972). On the relationship between abilities, learning, and human performance. *American Psychologist, 27,* 1017–1032.

Fleishman, E. A., & Mumford, M. D. (1989). Abilities as causes of individual differences in skill acquisition. *Human Performance, 2,* 201–223.

Fleishman, E. A., & Quaintance, M. K. (1984). *Taxonomies of human performance.* Orlando, FL: Academic Press.

Fleisig, G. S., Excamilla, R. F., Andrews, J. R., Matsuo, T., Satterwhite, Y., & Barrentine, S. W. (1996). Kinematic and kinetic comparison between baseball pitching and football passing. *Journal of Applied Biomechanics, 12,* 207–224.

Flinn, N. (1995). A task-oriented approach to the treatment of a client with hemiplegia. *American Journal of Occupational Therapy, 49,* 560–569.

Franks, I. M., & Maile, L. J. (1991). The use of video in sport skill acquisition. In P. W. Dowrick (Ed.), *Practical guide to using video in the behavioral sciences* (pp. 105–124). New York: Wiley.

Franks, I. M., & Wilberg, R. B. (1982). The generation of movement patterns during the acquisition of a pursuit tracking task. *Human Movement Science, 1,* 251–272.

Fredenberg, K. B., Lee, A. M., & Solmon, M. L. (2001). The effect of augmented feedback on students' perceptions and performance. *Research Quarterly for Exercise and Sport, 72,* 232–242.

French, K. E., Rink, J. E., & Werner, P. H. (1990). Effects of contextual interference on retention of three volleyball skills. *Perceptual and Motor Skills, 71,* 179–186.

Gabriel, D. A., & Boucher, J. P. (1998). Practice effects on the timing and magnitude of agonist activity during ballistic elbow flexion to a target. *Research Quarterly for Exercise and Sport, 69,* 30–37.

Gallagher, A. G., McClure, N., McGuigan, J., Crothers, I., & Browning, J. (1999). Virtual reality training in laparoscopic surgery: A preliminary assessment of minimally invasive surgical trainer virtual reality (MIST VR). *Endoscopy, 31,* 310–314

Gallagher, J. D., & Thomas, J. R. (1980). Effects of varying post-KR intervals upon children's motor performance. *Journal of Motor Behavior, 12,* 41–46.

Gentile, A. M. (1972). A working model of skill acquisition with application to teaching. *Quest,* Monograph, 17, 3–23.

Gentile, A. M. (1987). Skill acquisition: Action, movement, and neuromotor processes. In J. H. Carr, R. B. Shepherd, J. Gordon, A. M. Gentile, & J. M. Hinds (Eds.), *Movement science: Foundations for physical therapy in rehabilitation* (pp. 93–154). Rockville, MD: Aspen.

Gentile, A. M. (2000). Skill acquisition: Action, movement, and neuromotor processes. In J. H. Carr, & R. B. Shepherd (Eds.), *Movement science: Foundations for physical therapy* (2nd ed., pp. 111–187). Rockville, MD: Aspen.

Gentilucci, M., Chieffi, S., Scarpa, M., & Castiello, U. (1992). Temporal coupling between transport and grasp components during prehension movements: Effect of visual perturbation. *Behavioural Brain Research, 47,* 71–82.

Gibson, J. J. (1966). *The senses considered as perceptual systems.* Boston: Houghton Mifflin.

Gibson, J. J. (1979). *The ecological approach to visual perception.* Boston: Houghton Mifflin.

Gleick, J. (1987). *Chaos: Making a new science.* New York: Viking Penguin.

Glover, S. R., & Dixon, P. (2001). Dynamic illusion effects in a reaching task: Evidence for separate visual representations in the planning and control of reaching. *Journal of Experimental Psychology: Human Perception and Performance, 27,* 560–572.

Goldberger, M., & Gerney, P. (1990). Effects of learner use of practice time on skill acquisition of fifth grade children. *Journal of Teaching in Physical Education, 10,* 84–95.

Goodale, M. A., & Milner, A. D. (1992). Separate visual pathways for perception and action. *Trends in Neurosciences, 15,* 20–25.

Goodale, M. A., & Servos, P. (1996). Visual control of prehension. In H. N. Zelaznik (Ed.), *Advances in motor learning and control* (pp. 87–121). Champaign, IL: Human Kinetics.

Goode, S. L., & Magill, R. A. (1986). The contextual interference effect in learning three badminton serves. *Research Quarterly for Exercise and Sport, 57,* 308–314.

Goodwin, J. E., & Meeuwsen, H. J. (1995). Using bandwidth knowledge of results to alter relative frequencies during motor skill acquisition. *Research Quarterly for Exercise and Sport, 66,* 99–104.

Gopher, D., Weil, M., & Siegel, D. (1989). Practice under changing priorities: An approach to the training of complex skills. *Acta Psychologica, 71,* 147–177.

Goss, S., Hall, C., Buckolz, E., & Fishburne, G. (1986). Imagery ability and the acquisition and retention of motor skills. *Memory and Cognition, 14,* 469–477.

Goulet, C., Bard, C., & Fleury, M. (1989). Expertise differences in preparing to return a tennis serve: A visual information processing approach. *Journal of Sport & Exercise Psychology, 11,* 382–398.

Green, T. D., & Flowers, J. H. (1991). Implicit versus explicit learning processes in a probabilistic, continuous fine-motor catching task. *Journal of Motor Behavior, 23,* 293–300.

Grillner, S. (1981). Control of locomotion in bipeds, tetrapods, and fish. In V.B. Brooks (Ed.), *Handbook of physiology* (Sec. 1, Vol. II, Part 2, pp. 1179–1236). Bethesda, MD: American Physiological Society.

Grillner, S. (1985). Neurobiological bases of rhythmic motor acts in vertebrates. *Science, 228,* 143–148.

Guadagnoli, M. A., Dornier, L. A., & Tandy, R. D. (1996). Optimal length for summary knowledge of results: The influence of task-related experience and complexity. *Research Quarterly for Exercise and Sport, 67,* 239–248.

Guay, M., Salmoni, A., & Lajoie, Y. (1999). The effects of different knowledge of results spacing and summarizing techniques on the acquisition of a ballistic movement. *Research Quarterly for Exercise and Sport, 70,* 24–32.

Hagman, J. D. (1978). Specific-cue effects of interpolated movements on distance and location retention in short-term motor memory. *Memory and Cognition, 6,* 432–437.

Hall, C., Buckolz, E., & Fishburne, G. (1992). Imagery and the acquisition of motor skills. *Canadian Journal of Sport Science, 17,* 19–27.

Hall, C. R., & Martin, K. A. (1997). Measuring movement imagery abilities: A revision of the Movement Imagery Questionnaire. *Journal of Mental Imagery, 21,* 143–154.

Hall, C. R., & Pongrac, J. (1983). *Movement Imagery Questionnaire.* London, Ontario, Canada: University of Western Ontario.

Hall, C. R., Rodgers, W. M., & Barr, K. A. (1990). The use of imagery by athletes in selected sports. *The Sport Psychologist, 4,* 1–10.

Hall, K. G., Domingues, D. A., & Cavazos, R. (1994). Contextual interference effects with skilled baseball players. *Perceptual and Motor Skills, 78,* 835–841.

Hall, K. G., & Magill, R. A. (1995). Variability of practice and contextual interference in motor skill learning. *Journal of Motor Behavior, 27,* 299–309.

Hall, S. J., (2003). *Basic biomechanics* (4th ed.). New York: McGraw-Hill.

Hamilton, W. (1859). *Lectures on metaphysics and logic.* Edinburgh, Scotland: Blackwood.

Hancock, G. R., Butler, M. S., & Fischman, M. G. (1995). On the problem of two-dimensional error scores: Measures and analyses of accuracy, bias, and consistency. *Journal of Motor Behavior, 27,* 241–250.

Hand, J., & Sidaway, B. (1993). Relative frequency of modeling effects on the performance and retention of a motor skill. *Research Quarterly for Exercise and Sport, 64,* 122–126.

Hanlon, R. E. (1996). Motor learning following unilateral stroke. *Archives of Physical Medicine and Rehabilitation, 77,* 811–815.

Harrison, A., Derwent, G., Enticknap, A., Rose, F. D., & Attree, E. A. (2002). The role of virtual reality technology in the assessment and training of inexperienced powered wheelchair users. *Disability and Rehabilitation, 24,* 599–606.

Haskins, M. J. (1965). Development of a response recognition training film in tennis. *Perceptual and Motor Skills, 21,* 207–211.

Hautala, R. M. (1988). Does transfer of training help children learn juggling? *Perceptual and Motor Skills, 67,* 563–567.

Hautala, R. M., & Conn, J. H. (1993). A test of Magill's closed to open continuum for skill development. *Perceptual and Motor Skills, 77,* 219–226.

Hawking, S. (1996). *The illustrated brief history of time.* New York: Bantam Books.

Hayes, R. T., & Vincenzi, D. A. (2000). Fleet assessments of a virtual reality training system. *Military Psychology, 12,* 161–186.

Healy, A. F., & McNamara, D. S. (1996). Verbal learning and memory: Does the modal model still work? *Annual Review of Psychology, 47,* 143–172.

Hebert, E. P., & Landin, D. (1994). Effects of a learning model and augmented feedback on tennis skill acquisition. *Research Quarterly for Exercise and Sport, 65,* 250–257.

Hebert, E., Landin, D., & Menickelli, J. (1998). Videotape feedback: What learners see and how they use it. *Journal of Sport Pedagogy, 4,* 12–28.

Hebert, E. P., Landin, D., & Solmon, M. A. (1996). Practice schedule effects on the performance and learning of low- and high-skilled students: An applied study. *Research Quarterly for Exercise and Sport, 67,* 52–58.

Hebert, E. P., Landin, D., & Solmon, M. A. (2000). The impact of task progressions on students' practice quality and task-related thoughts. *Journal of Teaching in Physical Education, 19,* 338–354.

Heise, G. D. (1995). EMG changes in agonist muscles during practice of a multijoint throwing skill. *Journal of Electromyography and Kinesiology, 5,* 81–94.

Heise, G. D., & Cornwell, A. (1997). Relative contributions to the net joint moment for a planar multijoint throwing skill: Early and late in practice. *Research Quarterly for Exercise and Sport, 68,* 116–124.

Helsen, W. F., Elliott, D., Starkes, J. L., & Ricker, K. L. (1998). Temporal and spatial coupling of point of gaze and hand movements in aiming. *Journal of Motor Behavior, 30,* 249–259.

Helsen, W. F., Elliott, D., Starkes, J. L., & Ricker, K. L. (2000). Coupling of eye, finger, elbow, and shoulder movements during manual aiming. *Journal of Motor Behavior, 32,* 241–248.

Helsen, W., & Pauwels, J. M. (1990). Analysis of visual search activity in solving tactical game problems. In D. Brogan (Ed.), *Visual search* (pp. 177–184). London: Taylor & Francis.

Helsen, W. F., Starkes, J. L., & Buekers, M. J. (1997). Effects of target eccentricity on temporal costs of point of gaze and the hand in aiming. *Motor Control, 1,* 161–177.

Henderson, J. (1996). Visual attention and the attention-action interface. In K. Akins (Ed.), *Perception* (pp. 290–316). New York: Oxford University Press.

Henry, F. M. (1961a). Stimulus complexity, movement complexity, age, and sex in relation to reaction latency and speed in limb movements. *Research Quarterly, 32,* 353–366.

Henry, F. M. (1961b). Reaction time – movement time correlations. *Perceptual and motor skills, 12,* 63–66.

Henry, F. M., & Rogers, D. E. (1960). Increased response latency for complicated movements and the "memory drum" theory of neuromotor reaction. *Research Quarterly, 31,* 448–458.

Heuer, H. (1991). Invariant relative timing in motor-program theory. In J. Fagard & P. H. Wolff (Eds.), *The development of timing control and temporal organization in coordinated action* (pp. 37–68). Amsterdam: Elsevier.

Hick, W. E. (1952). On the rate of gain of information. *Quarterly Journal of Experimental Psychology, 4,* 11–26.

Hicks, R. E., Gualtieri, T. C., & Schroeder, S. R. (1983). Cognitive and motor components of bilateral transfer. *American Journal of Psychology, 96,* 223–228.

Hinds, P. J., Patterson, M., & Pfeffer, J. (2001). Bothered by abstraction: The effect of expertise on knowledge transfer and subsequent novice performance. *Journal of Applied Psychology, 86,* 1232–1243.

Hird, J. S., Landers, D. M., Thomas, J. R., & Horan, J. J. (1991). Physical practice is superior to mental practice in enhancing cognitive and motor task performance. *Journal of Sport & Exercise Psychology, 13,* 281–293.

Hoenkamp, H. (1978). Perceptual cues that determine the labeling of human gait. *Journal of Human Movement Studies, 4,* 59–69.

Holt, K. G., & Jeng, S. F., Ratcliffe, R., & Hamill, J. (1995). Energetic cost and stability during human walking at the preferred stride frequency. *Journal of Motor Behavior, 27,* 164–178.

Holt, K. G., Ratcliffe, R., Jeng, S. (1999). Head stability in walking in children with cerebral palsy and in children and adults without neurological impairment. *Physical Therapy, 79,* 1153–1162.

Horn, R. B., Williams, A. M., & Scott, M. A. (2002). Learning from demonstrations: The role of visual search during observational learning from video and point-light models. *Journal of Sports Sciences, 20,* 253–269.

Hreljac, A. (1993). Preferred and energetically optimal gait transition speeds in human locomotion. *Medicine and Science in Sports and Exercise, 25,* 1158–1162.

Hubbard, A. W., & Seng, C. N. (1954). Visual movements of batters. *Research Quarterly, 25,* 42–57.

Husak, W. S., Cohen, M. J., & Schandler, S. L. (1991). Activation peaking during the acquisition of a motor task under high and low contextual-interference conditions. *Perceptual and Motor Skills, 72,* 1075–1088.

Ille, A., & Cadopi, M. (1999). Memory for movement sequences in gymnastics: Effects of age and skill level. *Journal of Motor Behavior, 31,* 290–300.

Intiso, D., Santilli, V., Grasso, M. G., Rossi, R., & Caruso, I. (1994). Rehabilitation of walking with electromyographic biofeedback in drop-foot after stroke. *Stroke, 25,* 1189–1192.

Ivens, C. J., & Marteniuk, R. G. (1997). Increased sensitivity to changes in visual feedback with practice. *Journal of Motor Behavior, 29,* 326–338.

Ivry, R. B., & Hazeltine, R. E. (1995). Perception and production of temporal intervals across a range of duration: Evidence for a common timing mechanism. *Journal of Experimental Psychology: Human Perception and Performance, 21,* 3–18.

Jackson, G. M., Jackson, S. R., Husain, M., Harvey, M., Kramer, T., & Dow, L. (2000). The coordination of bimanual prehension movements in a centrally deafferented patient. *Brain, 123 (Part 2),* 380–393.

Jacobson, E. (1931). Electrical measurement of neuromuscular states during mental activities: VI. A note on mental activities concerning an amputated limb. *American Journal of Physiology, 43,* 122–125.

Jaegers, S. M. H. J., Peterson, R. F., Dantuma, R., Hillen, B., Geuze, R., & Schellekens, J. (1989). Kinesiologic aspects of motor learning in dart throwing. *Journal of Human Movement Studies, 16,* 161–171.

Jakobson, L. S., & Goodale, M. A. (1991). Factors influencing higher-order movement planning: A kinematic analysis of human prehension. *Experimental Brain Research, 86,* 199–208.

Jambor, E. A., & Weekes, E. M. (1995, February). Videotape feedback: Make it more effective. *Journal of Physical Education, Recreation, and Dance, 66,* 48–50.

James, W. (1890). *Principles of psychology (Vol. 2).* New York: Holt.

Janelle, C. M., Barba, D. A., Frehlich, S. G., Tennant, L. K., & Cauraugh, J. H. (1997). Maximizing performance feedback effectiveness through videotape replay and a self-controlled learning environment. *Research Quarterly for Exercise and Sport, 68,* 269–279.

Janelle, C. M., Kim, J., & Singer, R. N. (1995). Subject-controlled performance feedback and learning of a closed motor skill. *Perceptual and Motor Skills, 81,* 627–634.

Jeannerod, M. (1981). Intersegmental coordination during reaching at natural visual objects. In J. Long & A. Baddeley, (Eds.), *Attention and Performance IX* (pp. 153–168). Hillsdale, NJ: Erlbaum.

Jeannerod, M. (1984). The timing of natural prehension. *Journal of Motor Behavior, 16,* 235–254.

Jeannerod, M., & Marteniuk, R. G. (1992). Fuctional characteristics of prehesion: From data to artificial neural networks. In L. Proteau & D. Elliott (Eds.), *Vision and motor control* (pp. 197–232). Amsterdam: North-Holland.

Jeka, J. J., Ribiero, P., Oie, K., & Lackner, J. R. (1998). The structure of somatosensory information for human postural control. *Motor Control, 2,* 13–33.

Johansson, G. (1973). Visual perception of biological motion and a model for its analysis. *Perception and Psychophysics, 14,* 201–211.

Johnson, S. H. (1998). Cerebral organization of motor imagery: Contralateral control of grip selection in mentally represented prehension. *Psychological Science, 9,* 219–222.

Jongsma, D. M., Elliott, D., & Lee, T. D. (1987). Experience and set in the running sprint start. *Perceptual and Motor Skills, 64,* 547–550.

Kahneman, D. (1973). *Attention and effort.* Englewood Cliffs, NJ: Prentice Hall.

Kamon, E., & Gormley, J. (1968). Muscular activity pattern for skilled performance and during learning of a horizontal bar exercise. *Ergonomics, 11,* 345–357.

Kao, J. C. (2001). *Biomechanical and physiological indicators of the walk-to-run and run-to-walk transitions.* Ph.D. dissertation, Arizona State University.

Kato, T., & Fukuda, T. (2002). Visual search strategies of baseball batters: Eye movements during the preparatory phase of batting. *Perceptual and Motor Skills, 94,* 380–386.

Keele, S. W. (1968). Movement control in skilled motor performance. *Psychological Bulletin, 70,* 387–403.

Keele, S. W., & Posner, M. I. (1968). Processing of visual feedback in rapid movements. *Journal of Experimental Psychology, 77,* 153–158.

Kelso, J. A. S. (1984). Phase transitions and critical behavior in human bimanual coordination. *American Journal of Physiology: Regulatory, Integrative, and Comparative Physiology, 15,* R1000–1004.

Kelso, J. A. S. (1995). *Dynamic patterns: The self-organization of brain and behavior.* Cambridge, MA: MIT Press.

Kelso, J. A. S. (1997). Relative timing in brain and behavior: Some observations about the generalized motor program and self-organized coordination dynamics. *Human Movement Science, 16,* 453–460.

Kelso, J. A. S., & Holt, K. G. (1980). Exploring a vibratory systems analysis of human movement production. *Journal of Neurophysiology, 43,* 1183–1196.

Kelso, J. A. S., Holt, K. G., & Flatt, A. E. (1980). The role of proprioception in the perception and control of human movement: Toward a theoretical reassessment. *Perception and Psychophysics, 28,* 45–52.

Kelso, J. A. S., & Scholz, J. P. (1985). Cooperative phenomena in biological motion. In H. Haken (Ed.), *Complex systems:*

Operational approaches in neurobiology, physical systems, and computers (pp. 124–149). Berlin: Springer-Verlag.

Kelso, J. A. S., Southard, D. L., & Goodman, D. (1979). On the coordination of two-handed movements. *Journal of Experimental Psychology: Human Perception and Performance, 5,* 229–238.

Kelso, J. A. S., & Zanone, P.G. (2002). Coordination dynamics of learning and transfer across different effector systems. *Journal of Experimental Psychology: Human Perception and Performance, 28,* 776–797.

Kernodle, M. W., & Carlton, L. G. (1992). Information feedback and the learning of multiple-degree-of-freedom activities. *Journal of Motor Behavior, 24,* 187–196.

Khan, M. A., Franks, I. M., & Goodman, D. (1998). The effect of practice on the control of rapid aiming movements: Evidence for an interdependency between programming and feedback processing. *Quarterly Journal of Experimental Psychology, 51A,* 425–444.

Knapp, C. G., & Dixon, W. R. (1952). Learning to juggle: II. A study of whole and part methods. *Research Quarterly, 23,* 398–401.

Konczak, J. (1994). Effects of optic flow on the kinematics of human gait: A comparison of young and older adults. *Journal of Motor Behavior, 26,* 225–236.

Kritikos, A., Bennett, K. M. B., Dunai, J., & Castiello, U. (2000). Interface from distractors in reach-to-grasp movements. *Quarterly Journal of Experimental Psychology, 53A,* 131–151.

Laabs, G. J. (1973). Retention characteristics of different reproduction cues in motor short-term memory. *Journal of Experimental Psychology, 100,* 168–177.

Lai, Q., & Shea, C. H. (1999). Bandwidth knowledge of results enhances generalized motor program learning. *Research Quarterly for Exercise and Sport, 70,* 79–83.

Lai, Q., Shea, C. H., Bruechert, L., & Little, M. (2002). Auditory model enhances relative-time learning. *Journal of Motor Behavior, 34,* 299–307.

Landin, D. (1994). The role of verbal cues in skill learning. *Quest, 46,* 299–313.

Landin, D. L., & Hebert, E. P. (1997). A comparison of three practice schedules along the contextual interference continuum. *Research Quarterly for Exercise and Sport, 68,* 357–361.

Landin, D. L., & Hebert, E. P. (1999). The influence of self-talk on the performance of skilled female tennis players. *Journal of Applied Sport Psychology, 11,* 263–282.

Lange, G., Waked, W., Kirshblum, S., & DeLuca, J. (2000). Organizational strategy influence on visual memory performance after stroke: Cortical/subcortical and left/right hemisphere contrasts. *Archives of Physical Medicine and Rehabilitation, 81,* 89–94.

Langley, D. J. (1995). Student cognition in the instructional setting. *Journal of Teaching in Physical Education, 15,* 25–40.

Larish, D. D., & Stelmach, G. E. (1982). Preprogramming, programming, and reprogramming of aimed hand movements as a function of age. *Journal of Motor Behavior, 14,* 322–340.

Lashley, K. S. (1917). The accuracy of movement in the absence of excitation from the moving organ. *American Journal of Physiology, 43,* 169–194.

Lashley, K. S. (1951). The problem of serial order in behavior, In L. A. Jeffress (Ed.), *Cerebral mechanisms in behavior* (pp. 112–136). New York: Wiley.

Laszlo, J. L. (1966). The performance of a single motor task with kinesthetic sense loss. *Quarterly Journal of Experimental Psychology, 18,* 1–8.

Laszlo, J. L. (1967). Training of fast tapping with reduction of kinesthetic, tactile, visual, and auditory sensation. *Quarterly Journal of Experimental Psychology, 19,* 344–349.

Latash, M. L. (1999). Mirror writing: Learning, transfer, and implications for internal inverse models. *Journal of Motor Behavior, 31,* 107–111.

Laugier, C., & Cadopi, M. (1996). Representational guidance of dance performance in adult novices: Effect of concrete vs. abstract movement. *International Journal of Sport Psychology, 27,* 91–108.

Laurent, M., & Thomson, J. A. (1988). The role of visual information in control of a constrained locomotor task. *Journal of Motor Behavior, 20,* 17–38.

Lee, A. M., Keh, N. C., & Magill, R. A. (1993). Instructional effects of teacher feedback in physical education. *Journal of Teaching in Physical Education, 12,* 228–243.

Lee, D. N. (1974). Visual information during locomotion. In R. B. MacLeod & H. Pick (Eds.), *Perception: Essays in honor of J. J. Gibson* (pp. 250–267). Ithaca, NY: Cornell University Press.

Lee, D. N., & Aronson, E. (1974). Visual proprioceptive control of standing in human infants. *Perception and Psychophysics, 15,* 527–532.

Lee, D. N., Lishman, J. R., & Thomson, J. A. (1982). Regulation of gait in long jumping. *Journal of Experimental Psychology: Human Perception and Performance, 8,* 448–459.

Lee, T. D. (1988). Testing for motor learning: A focus on transfer-appropriate processing. In O. G. Meijer & K. Roth (Eds.), *Complex motor behaviour: "The" motor-action controversy* (pp. 210–215). Amsterdam: Elsevier.

Lee, T. D., & Genovese, E. D. (1988). Distribution of practice in motor skill acquisition: Learning and performance effects reconsidered. *Research Quarterly for Exercise and Sport, 59,* 59–67.

Lee, T. D., & Genovese, E. D. (1989). Distribution of practice in motor skill acquisition: Different effects for discrete and continuous tasks. *Research Quarterly for Exercise and Sport, 59,* 277–287.

Lee, T. D., & Hirota, T. T. (1980). Encoding specificity principle in motor short-term memory for movement extent. *Journal of Motor Behavior, 12,* 63–67.

Lee, T. D., & Magill, R. A. (1983). Activity during the post-KR interval: Effects upon performance or learning. *Research Quarterly for Exercise and Sport, 54,* 340–345.

Lee, T. D., & Magill, R. A. (1985). Can forgetting facilitate skill acquisition? In D. Goodman, R. B. Wilberg, & I. M. Franks (Eds.), *Differing perspectives in motor learning, memory and control* (pp. 3–22). Amsterdam: North-Holland.

Lee, T. D., Swinnen, S. P., & Serrien, D. J. (1994). Cognitive effort and motor learning. *Quest, 46,* 328–344.

Lee, T. D., Swinnen, S. P., & Verschueren, S. (1995). Relative phase alterations during bimanual skill acquisition. *Journal of Motor Behavior, 27,* 263–274.

Lee, T. D., White, M. A., & Carnahan, H. (1990). On the role of knowledge of results in motor learning: Exploring the guidance hypothesis. *Journal of Motor Behavior, 22,* 191–208.

Li, Y., & Wright, D. L. (2000). As assessment of the attention demands during random and blocked-practice. *Quarterly Journal of Experimental Psychology, 53A,* 591–606.

Lidor, R., Tennant, K. L., & Singer, R. N. (1996). The generalizability effect of three learning strategies across motor task performances. *International Journal of Sport Psychology, 27,* 23–36.

Lindahl, L. G. (1945). Movement analysis as an industrial training method. *Journal of Applied Psychology, 29,* 420–436.

Linden, C. A., Uhley, J. E., Smith, D., & Bush, M. A. (1989). The effects of mental practice on walking balance in an elderly population. *Occupational Therapy Journal of Research, 9,* 155–169.

Lintern, G. (1991). An informational perspective on skill transfer in human-machine systems. *Human Factors, 33,* 251–266.

Lintern, G., & Roscoe, S. N. (1980). Visual cue augmentation in contact flight simulation. In S. N. Roscoe (Ed.), *Aviation psychology* (pp. 227–238). Ames, IA: Iowa State University Press.

Lintern, G., Roscoe, S. N., & Sivier, J. (1990). Display principles, control dynamics, and environmental factors in pilot training and transfer. *Human Factors, 32,* 299–317.

Little, W. S., & McCullagh, P. M. (1989). Motivation orientation and modeled instruction strategies: The effects on form and accuracy. *Journal of Sport & Exercise Psychology, 11,* 41–53.

Liu, J., & Wrisberg, C. A. (1997). The effect of knowledge of results delay and the subjective estimation of movement form on the acquisition and retention of a motor skill. *Research Quarterly for Exercise and Sport, 68,* 145–151.

Loeb, J. (1890). Untersuchungen uber die Orientirung im Fuhlraum der Hand und im Blickraum. *Pflueger Archives of General Physiology, 46,* 1–46.

Loftus, E. F. (1980). Memory: Surprising new insights into how we remember and why we forget. Reading, MA: Addison-Wesley.

Loftus, E. F., & Loftus, G. R. (1980). On the permanence of stored information in the human brain. American Psychologist, 35, 409–420.

Logan, G. D. (1985). Skill and automaticity: Relations, implications, and future directions. *Canadian Journal of Psychology, 39,* 367–386.

Logan, G. D. (1988). Toward an instance theory of automatization. *Psychological Review, 95,* 492–527.

Logan, G. D. (1998). What is learned during automatization? II. Obligatory encoding of spatial location. *Journal of Experimental Psychology: Human Perception and Performance, 24,* 1720–1736.

Loken, W. J., Thornton, A. E., Otto, R. L., & Long, C. J. (1995). Sustained attention after severe closed head injury. *Neuropsychology, 9,* 592–598.

Lovell, G. & Collins, D. (2002). Electroencephalographic differences between high and low mental imagery ability groups when learning a novel motor skill. *Journal of Human Movement Studies, 43,* 269–295.

Mack, M. G. (2001). Effects of time and movements in the preshot routine on free throw shooting. *Perceptual and Motor Skills, 93,* 567–573.

Mackworth, N. H. (1956). Vigilance. *Nature, 178,* 1375–1377.

Magill, R. A. (1988). Activity during the post-knowledge of results interval can benefit motor skill learning. In O. G. Meijer & K. Roth (Eds.), *Complex motor behavior: "The" motor-action controversy* (pp. 231–246). Amsterdam: Elsevier.

Magill, R. A. (1998). Knowledge is more than we can talk about: Implicit learning in motor skill acquisition. *Research Quarterly for Exercise and Sport, 69,* 104–110.

Magill, R. A., Chamberlin, C. J., & Hall, K. G. (1991). Verbal knowledge of results as redundant information for learning an anticipation timing skill. *Human Movement Science, 10,* 485–507.

Magill, R. A., & Hall, K. G. (1990). A review of the contextual interference effect in motor skill acquisition. *Human Movement Science, 9,* 241–289.

Magill, R. A., & Lee, T. D. (1987). Verbal label effects on response accuracy and organization for learning limb positioning movements. *Journal of Human Movement Studies, 13,* 285–308.

Magill, R. A., & Schoenfelder-Zohdi, B. (1996). A visual model and knowledge of performance as sources of information for learning a rhythmic gymnastics skill. *International Journal of Sport Psychology, 27,* 7–22.

Magill, R. A., & Wood, C. A. (1986). Knowledge of results precision as a learning variable in motor skill acquisition. *Research Quarterly for Exercise and Sport, 57,* 170–173.

Mahoney, M. J., & Avener, A. (1977). Psychology of the elite athlete: An exploratory study. *Cognitive Therapy and Research, 1,* 135–141.

Mané, A., & Donchin, E. (1989). The Space Fortress game. *Acta Psychologica, 71,* 17–22.

Marotta, J. J., Kruyer, A., & Goodale, M. A. (1998). The role of head movement in the control of manual prehension. *Experimental Brain Research, 120,* 134–138.

Marteniuk, R. G. (1986). Information processes in movement learning: Capacity and structural interference. *Journal of Motor Behavior, 5,* 249–259.

Marteniuk, R. G., & Romanow, S. K. E. (1983). Human movement organization and learning as revealed by variability of movement, use of kinematic information and Fourier analysis. In R. A. Magill (Ed.), *Memory and control of action* (pp. 167–197). Amsterdam: North-Holland.

Martin, K. A., Moritz, S. A., & Hall, C. R. (1999). Imagery use in sport: A literature review and applied model. *The Sport Psychologist, 13,* 245–268.

Masser, L. S. (1993). Critical cues help first-grade students' achievement in handstands and forward rolls. *Journal of Teaching in Physical Education, 12,* 301–312.

Mathiowetz, V., & Wade, M. G. (1995). Task constraints and functional motor performance of individuals with and without multiple sclerosis. *Ecological Psychology, 7,* 99–123.

McCloy, C. H. (1934). The measurement of general motor capacity and general motor ability. *Research Quarterly (Supplement), 5,* 46–61.

McCullagh, P., & Meyer, K. N. (1997). Learning versus correct models: Influence of model type on the learning of a free-weight squat lift. *Research Quarterly for Exercise and Sport, 68,* 56–61.

McCullagh, P., Stiehl, J., & Weiss, M. R. (1990). Developmental modeling effects on the quantitative and qualitative aspects of motor performance. *Research Quarterly for Exercise and Sport, 61,* 344–350.

McCullagh, P., & Weiss, M. R. (2001). Modeling: Considerations for motor skill performance and psychological responses. In R. N. Singer, H. A. Hausenblaus, & C. M. Janelle (Eds.), *Handbook of sport psychology* (2nd ed., pp. 205–238). New York: John Wiley & Son.

McDonald, P. V., Oliver, S. K., & Newell, K. M. (1995). Perceptual-motor exploration as a function of biomechanical and task constraints. *Acta Psychologica, 88,* 127–165.

McIntosh, G. C., Brown, S. H., Rice, R. R., & Thaut, M. H. (1997). Rhythmic auditory-motor facilitation of gait patterns in patients with Parkinson's disease. *Journal of Neurology, Neurosurgery, and Psychiatry, 62,* 22–26.

McLeod, P., Driver, J., Dienes, Z., & Crisp, J. (1991). Filtering by movement in visual search. *Journal of Experimental Psychology: Human Perception and Performance, 17,* 55–64.

McLeod, P., Reed, N., & Dienes, Z. (2001). Toward a unified fielder theory: What we do not yet know about how people run to catch a ball. *Journal of Experimental Psychology: Human Perception and Performance, 27,* 1347–1355.

McNevin, N., Magill, R. A., & Buekers, M. J. (1994). The effects of erroneous knowledge of results on transfer of anticipation timing. *Research Quarterly for Exercise and Sport, 65,* 324–329.

McPherson, S. L., & Thomas, J. R. (1989). Relation of knowledge and performance in boy's tennis: Age and expertise. *Journal of Experimental Child Psychology, 48,* 190–211.

Mechsner, F., Kerzel, D., Knoblich, G., & Prinz, W. (2001). Perceptual basis of bimanual coordination. *Nature, 414,* 69–73.

Meeuwsen, H., & Magill, R. A. (1987). The role of vision in gait control during gymnastics vaulting. In T. B. Hoshizaki, J. Salmela, & B. Petiot (Eds.), *Diagnostics, treatment, and analysis of gymnastic talent* (pp. 137–155). Montreal: Sport Psyche Editions.

Melnick, M. J. (1971). Effects of overlearning on the retention of a gross motor skill. *Research Quarterly, 42,* 60–69.

Mercer, V. S. & Sahrmann, S. A. (1999). Postural synergies associated with a stepping task. *Physical Therapy, 79,* 1142–1152.

Merians, A. S., Jack, D., Boian, R., Tremaine, M., Burdea, G. C., Adamovich, S. V., Reece, M., & Poizner, H. (2002). Virtual reality-augmented rehabilitation for patients following stroke. *Physical Therapy, 82,* 898–915.

Meyer, D. E., Abrams, R. A., Kornblum, S., Wright, C. E., & Smith, J. E. K. (1988). Optimality in human motor performance: Ideal control of rapid aimed movements. *Psychological Review, 95,* 340–370.

Meyer, D. E., Smith, J. E. K., Kornblum, S., Abrams, R. A., & Wright, C. E. (1990). Speed-accuracy trade-offs in aimed movements: Toward a theory of rapid voluntary action. In M. Jeannerod (Ed.), *Attention and performance XIII* (pp. 173–226). Hillsdale, NJ: Erlbaum.

Miller, G. A. (1956). The magical number seven plus or minus two: Some limits on our capacity for processing information. *Psychological Review, 63,* 81–97.

Miller, G. A., Galanter, E., & Pribram, K. H. (1960). *Plans and the structure of behavior.* New York: Holt, Rinehart, and Winston.

Millslagle, D. G. (2002). Recognition accuracy by experienced men and women players of basketball. *Perceptual and Motor Skills, 95,* 163–172.

Montagne, G., Cornus, S., Glize, D., Quaine, F., & Laurent, M. (2000). A perception-action coupling type of control in long jumping. *Journal of Motor Behavior, 32,* 37–43.

Moore, S. P., & Marteniuk, R. G. (1986). Kinematic and electromyographic changes that occur as a function of learning a time-constrained aiming task. *Journal of Motor Behavior, 18,* 397–426.

Moreland, J., & Thomson, M. A. (1994). Efficacy of electromyographic biofeedback compared with conventional physical therapy for upper-extremity function in patients following stroke: A research overview and meta-analysis. *Physical Therapy, 74,* 534–546.

Moreland, J. D., Thomson, M. A., & Fuoco, A. R. (1998). Electromyographic biofeedback to improve lower extremity function after stroke: A meta-analysis. *Archives of Physical Medicine and Rehabilitation, 79,* 134–140.

Morris, M. E., Iansek, R., Matyas, T. A., & Summers, J. J. (1994). Ability to modulate walking cadence remains intact in Parkinson's disease. *Journal of Neurology, Neurosurgery, and Psychiatry, 57,* 1532–1534.

Mourant, R. R., & Rockwell, T. H. (1972). Strategies of visual search by novice and experienced drivers. *Human Factors, 14,* 325–335.

Murphy, S. M. (1994). Imagery interventions in sport. *Medicine and Science in Sports and Exercise, 26,* 486–494.

Nagel, M. J., & Rice, M. S. (2001). Cross-transfer effects in the upper extremity during an occupationally embedded exercise. *American Journal of Occupational Therapy, 55,* 317–323.

Navon, D., & Gopher, D. (1979). On the economy of the human processing system. *Psychological Review, 86,* 214–255.

Naylor, J., & Briggs, G. (1963). Effects of task complexity and task organization on the relative efficiency of part and whole training methods. *Journal of Experimental Psychology, 65,* 217–244.

Neumann, O. (1996). Theories of attention. In O. Neumann & A. F. Sanders (Eds.), *Handbook of perception and action. Vol. 3: Attention* (pp. 389–446). San Diego, CA: Academic Press.

Newell, K. M. (1986). Constraints on the development of coordination. In M. G. Wade & H. T. A. Whiting (Eds.), *Motor development in children: Aspects of coordination and control* (pp. 341–360). The Hague, The Netherlands: Nijhoff.

Newell, K. M., & Cesari, P. (1999). On taking the grasping out of prehension. *Motor Control, 3,* 285–288.

Newell, K. M., & van Emmerik, R. E. A. (1989). The acquisition of coordination: Preliminary analysis of learning to write. *Human Movement Science, 8,* 17–32.

Nideffer, R. M. (1993). Attention control training. In R. N. Singer, M. Murphey, & L. K. Tennant (Eds.), *Handbook of research on sport psychology* (pp. 542–556). New York: Macmillan.

Norman, D. A. (1968). Toward a theory of memory and attention. *Psychological Review, 75,* 522–536.

O'Shea, S., Morris, M.E., & Iansek, R. (2002). Dual task interference during gait in people with Parkinson's disease: Effects of motor versus cognitive secondary tasks. *Physical Therapy, 82,* 888–897.

Oudejans, R. R. D., van de Langenberg, R. W., & Hunter R. I. (2002). Aiming at a far target under different viewing conditions: Visual control in basketball jump shooting. *Human Movement Science, 21,* 457–480.

Patla, A. E., Rietdyk, S., Martin, C., & Prentice, S. (1996). Locomotor patterns of the leading and trailing limbs as solid and fragile obstacles are stepped over: Some insights into the role of vision during locomotion. *Journal of Motor Behavior, 28,* 35–47.

Page, S. J., Levine, P., Sisto, S. A., & Johnston, M. V. (2001). Mental practice combined with physical practice for upper-limb motor deficit in subacute stroke. *Physical Therapy, 81,* 1455–1462.

Paillard, J. (1980). The multichanneling of visual cues for the processing of spatial relationship. In G. E. Stelmach & J. Requin (Eds.), *Tutorials in motor behavior* (pp. 259–279). Amsterdam: North-Holland.

Pashler H., & Harris C. R. (2001). Spontaneous allocation of visual attention: Dominant role of uniqueness. *Psychonomic Bulletin & Review, 8,* 747–752.

Peterson, L. R., & Peterson, M. J. (1959). Short-term retention of individual verbal items. *Journal of Experimental Psychology, 58,* 193–198.

Polit, A., & Bizzi, E. (1978). Processes controlling arm movements in monkeys. *Science, 201,* 1235–1237.

Pollock, B. J., & Lee, T. D. (1992). Effects of the model's skill level on observational learning. *Research Quarterly for Exercise and Sport, 63,* 25–29.

Prinz, W. (1997). Perception and action planning. *European Journal of Cognitive Psychology, 9,* 129–154.

Proctor, R., & Reeve, T. G. (Eds.). (1990). *Stimulus-response compatibility: An integrated perspective.* Amsterdam: North-Holland.

Proteau, L., & Marteniuk, R. G. (1993). Static visual information and the learning and control of a manual aiming movement. *Human Movement Science, 12,* 515–536.

Proteau L., Tremblay, L., & DeJaeger, D. (1998). Practice does not diminish the role of visual information in on-line control of a precision walking task: Support for a specificity of practice hypothesis. *Journal of Motor Behavior, 30,* 143–150.

Raynor, A. J. (1998). Fractionated reflex and reaction times in children with developmental coordination disorder. *Motor Control, 2,* 114–124.

Redelmeier, D. A., & Tibshirani, R. J. (1997). Association between cellular-telephone calls and motor vehicle collisions. *New England Journal of Medicine, 336,* 453–458.

Rice, M. S. (1998). Purposefulness and cross transfer in a forearm supination and pronation task. *Scandinavian Journal of Occupational Therapy, 5,* 31–37.

Rijntjes, M., Dettmers, C., Büchel, C., Kiebel, S., Frackowiak, R. S. J., & Weiller, C. (1999). A blueprint for movement: Functional and anatomical representations in the human motor system. *Journal of Neuroscience, 19,* 8043–8048.

Rink, J. E. 91998). *Teaching physical education for learning* (3rd ed.). St Louis, MO: Mosby.

Robertson, S., Collins, J., Elliott, D., & Starkes, J. (1994). The influence of skill and intermittent vision on dynamic balance. *Journal of Motor Behavior, 26,* 333–339.

Robertson, S., & Elliott, D. (1996). The influence of skill in gymnastics and vision on dynamic balance. *International Journal of Sport Psychology, 27,* 361–368

Rogers, C. A. (1974). Feedback precision and postfeedback interval duration. *Journal of Experimental Psychology, 102,* 604–608.

Rose, J., Wolff, D. R., Jones, V. K., Bloch, D. A., Oehlert, J. W., & Gamble, J. G. (2002). Postural balance in children with cerebral palsy. *Developmental Medicine and Child Neurology, 44,* 58–63.

Rosenbaum, D. A. (1980). Human movement initiation: Specification of arm, direction, and extent. *Journal of Experimental Psychology: General, 109,* 444–474.

Rosenbaum, D. A. (1983). The movement precuing technique: Assumptions, applications, and extensions. In R. A. Magill (Ed.), *Memory and control of action* (pp. 251–274). Amsterdam: North-Holland.

Rosenbaum, D. A. (1991). *Human motor control.* San Diego, CA: Academic.

Rosenbaum, D. A., & Jorgensen, M. J. (1992). Planning macroscopic aspects of manual control. *Human Movement Science, 11,* 61–69.

Rosenbaum, D. A., van Heutgen, C. M., & Caldwell, C. E. (1996). From cognition to biomechanics and back: The end-state comfort effect and the middle is faster effect. *Acta Psychologica, 94,* 59–85.

Rothstein, A. L., & Arnold, R. K. (1976). Bridging the gap: Application of research on videotape feedback and bowling. *Motor Skills: Theory into Practice, 1,* 36–61.

Rothwell, J. (1995). *Control of human voluntary movement.* London: Chapman & Hall.

Roy, E. A., & Davenport, W. G. (1972). Factors in motor short-term memory: The interference effect of interpolated activity. *Journal of Experimental Psychology, 96,* 134–137.

Saling, M., Alberts, J., Stelmach, G. E., & Bloedel, J. R. (1998). Reach-to-grasp movements during obstacle avoidance. *Experimental Brain Research, 118,* 251–258.

Salmoni, A. W., Schmidt, R. A., & Walter, C. B. (1984). Knowledge of results and motor learning: A review and reappraisal. *Psychological Bulletin, 95,* 355–386.

Savelsbergh, G. J. P., Whiting, H. T. A., Pijpers, J. R., & van Santvoord, A. A. M. (1993). The visual guidance of catching. *Experimental Brain Research, 93,* 148–156.

Savelsbergh, G. J. P., Williams, A. M., van der Kamp, J., & Ward, P. (2002). Visual search, anticipation and expertise in soccer goal keepers. *Journal of Sports Sciences, 200,* 279–287.

Schendel, J. D., & Hagman, J. D. (1982). On sustaining procedural skills over a prolonged retention interval. *Journal of Applied Psychology, 67,* 605–610.

Schmidt, R. A. (1975). A schema theory of discrete motor skill learning theory. *Psychological Review, 82,* 225–260.

Schmidt, R. A. (1985). The search for invariance in skilled movement behavior. *Research Quarterly for Exercise and Sport, 56,* 188–200.

Schmidt, R. A. (1988). Motor and action perspectives on motor behavior. In O. G. Meijer & K. Roth (Eds.), *Complex motor behaviour: "The" motor-action controversy* (pp. 3–44). Amsterdam: Elsevier.

Schmidt, R. A., Lange, C., & Young, D. E. (1990). Optimizing summary knowledge of results for skill learning. *Human Movement Science, 9,* 325–348.

Schmidt, R. A., & Lee, T. D. (1999). *Motor control and learning: A behaviorial emphasis* (3rd ed.). Champaign, IL: Human Kinetics.

Schmidt, R. A., & Young, D. E. (1987). Transfer of movement control in motor skill learning. In S. M. Cormier & J. D. Hagman (Eds.), *Transfer of learning* (pp. 47–79). Orlando, FL: Academic Press.

Schmidt, R. A., Young, D. E., Swinnen, S., & Shapiro, D. C. (1989). Summary knowledge of results for skill acquisition: Support for the guidance hypothesis. *Journal of Experimental Psychology: Learning, Memory, and Cognition, 15,* 352–359.

Schmidt, R. A., Zelaznik, H. N., Hawkins, B., Frank, J. S., & Quinn, J. T. Jr. (1979). Motor output variability: A theory for the accuracy of rapid motor acts. *Psychological Review, 86,* 415–451.

Schneider, K., Zernicke, R. F., Schmidt, R. A., & Hart, T. J. (1989). Changes in limb dynamics during the practice of rapid arm movement. *Journal of Biomechanics, 22,* 805–817.

Schoenfelder-Zohdi, B. G. (1992). *Investigating the informational nature of a modeled visual demonstration.* Ph.D. dissertation, Louisiana State University.

Schoenfelt, E. L., Snyder, L. A., Maue, A. E., McDowell, C. P., & Woolard, C. D. (2002). Comparison of constant and variable practice conditions on free-throw shooting. *Perceptual and Motor Skills, 94,* 1113–1123.

Scholz, J. P. (1990). Dynamic pattern theory: Some implications for therapeutics. *Physical Therapy, 70,* 827–843.

Scully, D. M., & Newell, K. M. (1985). Observational learning and the acquisition of motor skills: Toward a visual perception perspective. *Journal of Human Movement Studies, 11,* 169–186.

Sekiya, H., & Magill, R. A. (2000). The contextual interference effect in learning force and timing parameters of the same generalized motor program. *Journal of Human Movement Studies, 39,* 45–71.

Sekiya, H. Magill, R. A., Sidaway, B., & Anderson, D. I. (1994). The contextual interference effect for skill variations from the same and different generalized motor programs. *Research Quarterly for Exercise and Sport, 65,* 330–338.

Selder, D. J., & Del Rolan, N. (1979). Knowledge of performance, skill level and performance on the balance beam. *Canadian Journal of Applied Sport Sciences, 4,* 226–229.

Servos, P. (2000). Distance estimation in the visual and visuomotor systems. *Experimental Brain Research, 130,* 35–47.

Shadmehr, R., & Brashers-Krug, T. (1997). Functional stages in the formulation of human long-term motor memory. *Journal of Neuroscience, 17,* 409–419.

Shank, M. D., & Haywood, K. M. (1987). Eye movements while viewing a baseball pitch. *Perceptual and Motor Skills, 64,* 1191–1197.

Shapiro, D. C., Zernicke, R. F., Gregor, R. J., & Diestel, J. D. (1981). Evidence for generalized motor programs using gait-pattern analysis. *Journal of Motor Behavior, 13,* 33–47.

Shea, C. H., & Kohl, R. M. (1990). Specificity and variability of practice. *Research Quarterly for Exercise and Sport, 61,* 169–177.

Shea, C. H., & Kohl, R. M. (1991). Composition of practice: Influence on the retention of motor skills. *Research Quarterly for Exercise and Sport, 62,* 187–195.

Shea, C. H., Kohl, R., & Indermill, C. (1990). Contextual interference contributions of practice. *Acta Psychologica, 73,* 145–157.

Shea, C. H., Lai, Q., Black, C., & Park, J. C. (2000). Spacing practice sessions across days benefits the learning of motor skills. *Human Movement Science, 19,* 737–760.

Shea, J. B. (1977). Effects of labeling on motor short-term memory. *Journal of Experimental Psychology: Human Learning and Memory, 3,* 92–99.

Shea, J. B., & Morgan, R. L. (1979). Contextual interference effects on the acquisition, retention, and transfer of a motor skill. *Journal of Experimental Psychology: Human Learning and Memory, 5,* 179–187.

Shea, J. B., & Zimny, S. T. (1983). Context effects in memory and learning in movement information. In R. A. Magill (Ed.), *Memory and control of action* (pp. 345–366). Amsterdam: North-Holland.

Shepherd, R. B., & Gentile, A. M. (1994). Sit-to-stand: Functional relationship between upper and lower body limb segments. *Human Movement Science, 13,* 817–840.

Sheridan, M. R. (1984). Response programming, response production, and fractionated reaction time. *Psychological Research, 46,* 33–47.

Sherrington, C. S. (1906). *Integrative action of the nervous system.* New York: Scribner.

Sherwood, D. E. (1988). Effect of bandwidth knowledge of results on movement consistency. *Perceptual and Motor Skills, 66,* 535–542.

Sherwood, D. E. (1994). Hand preference, practice order, and spatial assimilation in rapid bimanual movement. *Journal of Motor Behavior, 26,* 123–134.

Shinar, D., Meir, M., & Ben-Shoham, I. (1998). How automatic is manual gear shifting? *Human Factors, 40,* 647–654.

Short, M. W., & Cauraugh, J. H. (1999). Precision hypothesis and the end-state comfort effect. *Acta Psychologica, 100,* 243–252.

Sidaway, B., Heise, G., & Schoenfelder-Zohdi, B. (1995). Quantifying the variability of angle-angle plots. *Journal of Human Movement Studies, 29,* 181–197.

Sidaway, B., McNitt-Gray, J., & Davis, G. (1989). Visual timing of muscle preactivation in preparation for landing. *Ecological Psychology, 1,* 253–264.

Sidaway, B., Moore, B., & Schoenfelder-Zohdi, B. (1991). Summary and frequency of KR presentation effects on retention of a motor skill. *Research Quarterly for Exercise and Sport, 62,* 27–32.

Sidaway, B., Sekiya, H., & Fairweather, M. (1995). Movement variability as a function of accuracy demands in programmed aiming responses. *Journal of Motor Behavior, 27,* 67–76.

Siegel, D. (1986). Movement duration, fractionated reaction time, and response programming. *Research Quarterly for Exercise and Sport, 57,* 128–131.

Silverman, S., Tyson, L. A., & Krampitz, J. (1991). *Teacher feedback and achievement in physical education: Interaction with student practice.* Paper presented at the annual meeting of the American Educational Research Association, Chicago, Illinois.

Silverman, S., Woods, A. M., & Subramaniam, P. R. (1998). Task structures, feedback to individual students, and student skill level in physical education. *Research Quarterly for Exercise and Sport, 69,* 420–424.

Silverman, S., Woods, A. M., & Subramaniam, P. R. (1999). Feedback and practice in physical education: Interrelationships with task structures and student skill level. *Journal of Human Movement Studies, 36,* 203–224.

Simmons, R. W., Smith, K., Erez, E., Burke, J. P., & Pozos, R. E. (1998). Balance retraining in a hemiparetic patient using center of gravity biofeedback: A single-case study. *Perceptual and Motor Skills, 87,* 603–609.

Simon, D. A., & Bjork, R. A. (2001). Metacognition in motor learning. *Journal of Experimental Psychology: Learning, Memory, and Cognition, 27,* 907–912.

Singer, R. N. (1986). Sports performance: A five-step mental approach. *Journal of Physical Education and Recreation, 57,* 82–84.

Singer, R. N. (1988). Strategies and metastrategies in learning and performing self-paced athletic skills. *The Sport Psychologist, 2,* 49–68.

Singer, R. N., Cauraugh, J. H., Chen, D., Steinberg, G. M., Frehlich, S. G., & Wang, L. (1994). Training mental quickness in beginning/intermediate tennis players. *The Sport Psychologist, 8,* 305–318.

Singer, R. N., Cauraugh, J., Tennant, L. K., Murphey, M., Chen, R., & Lidor, R. (1991). Attention and distractors: Considerations for enhancing sport performances. *International Journal of Sport Psychology, 22,* 95–114.

Singer, R. N., Williams, A. M., Frehlich, S. G, Janelle, C. M., Radlo, S. J., Barba, D. A., & Bouchard, L. J. (1998). New frontiers in visual search: An exploratory study in live tennis situations. *Research Quarterly for Exercise and Sport, 69,* 290–296.

Sivak, B., & MacKenzie, C. L. (1990). Integration of visual information and motor output in reaching and grasping: The contributions of peripheral and central vision. *Neuropsychologia, 28,* 1095–1116.

Smith, E. E. (2000). Neural bases of human working memory. *Current Directions in Psychological Science, 9,* 45–49.

Smith, W. M., & Bowen, K. F. (1980). The effects of delayed and displaced visual feedback on motor control. *Journal of Motor Behavior, 12,* 91–101.

Smyth, M. M., & Marriott, A. M. (1982). Vision and proprioception in simple catching. *Journal of Motor Behavior, 14,* 143–152.

Smyth, M. M., & Pendleton, L. R. (1990). Space and movement in working memory. *Quarterly Journal of Experimental Psychology, 42A,* 291–304.

Smyth, M. M., & Silvers, G. (1987). Functions of vision in the control of handwriting. *Acta Psychologica, 65,* 47–64.

Snoddy, G. S. (1926). Learning and stability: A psychophysical analysis of a case of motor learning with clinical applications. *Journal of Applied Psychology, 10,* 1–36.

Soechting, J. F., & Flanders, M. (1992). Organization of sequential typing movements. *Journal of Neurophysiology, 67,* 1275–1290.

Solmon, M. A., & Boone, J. (1993). The impact of student goal orientation in physical education classes. *Research Quarterly for Exercise and Sport, 64,* 418–424.

Solmon, M. A., & Lee, A. M. (1996). Entry characteristics, practice variables, and cognition: Student mediation of instruction. *Journal of Teaching in Physical Education, 15,* 136–150.

Solomons, L. M., & Stein, G. (1896). Normal motor automatism. *Psychological Review, 3,* 492–512.

Southard, D., & Amos, B. (1996). Rhythmicity and preperformance ritual: Stablizing a flexible system. *Research Quarterly for Exercise and Sport, 67,* 288–296.

Southard, D., & Higgins, T. (1987). Changing movement patterns: Effects of demonstration and practice. *Research Quarterly for Exercise and Sport, 58,* 77–80.

Southard, D., & Miracle, A. (1993). Rhythmicity, ritual, and motor performance: A study of free-throw shooting in basketball. *Research Quarterly for Exercise and Sport, 64,* 284–290.

Sparrow, W. A., Donovan, E., van Emmerik, R. E. A., & Barry, E. B. (1987). Using relative motion plots to measure changes in intra-limb and inter-limb coordination. *Journal of Motor Behavior, 19,* 115–119.

Sparrow, W. A., Hughes, K. M., Russell, A. P., & Le Rossingnol, P. F. (1999). Effects of practice and preferred rate on perceived exertion, metabolic variables, and movement control. *Human Movement Science, 18,* 137–153.

Sparrow, W. A., & Irizarry-Lopez, V. W. (1987). Mechanical efficiency and metabolic cost as measures of learning a novel gross motor task. *Journal of Motor Behavior, 19,* 240–264.

Sparrow, W. A., & Newell, K. M. (1994). Energy expenditure and motor performance relationships in humans learning a motor task. *Psychophysiology, 31,* 338–346.

Spijkers, W. A. C., & Lochner, P. (1994). Partial visual feedback and spatial end-point accuracy of visual aiming movements. *Journal of Motor Behavior, 26,* 283–295.

Starek, J., & McCullagh, P. (1999). The effect of self-modeling on the performance of beginning swimmers. *The Sport Psychologist, 13,* 269–287.

Starkes, J. L., Deakin, J. M., Lindley, S., & Crisp, F. (1987). Motor versus verbal recall of ballet sequences by young expert dancers. *Journal of Sport Psychology, 9,* 222–230.

Steenbergen, B., Marteniuk, R. G., & Kalbfleisch, L. E. (1995). Achieving coordination in prehension: Joint freezing and postural contributions. *Journal of Motor Behavior, 27,* 333–348.

Ste.-Marie, D. M. (2000). Motor learning through observation: Contributions of attention and retention process. *Journal of Human Movement Studies, 38,* 323–349.

Ste.-Marie, D. M., & Lee, T. D. (1991). Prior processing effects on gymnastic judging. *Journal of Experimental Psychology: Learning, Memory, and Cognition, 17,* 126–136.

Ste.-Marie, D. M., & Valiquette, S. (1996). Enduring memory-influenced biases in gymnastic judging. *Journal of Experimental Psychology: Learning, Memory, and Cognition, 22,* 1498–1502.

Ste.-Marie, D. M., & Valiquette, S. M., & Taylor, G. (2001). Memory-influenced biases in gymnastic judging occur across different prior processing conditions. *Research Quarterly for Exercise and Sport, 72,* 420–426.

Stelmach, G. E. (1969). Prior positioning responses as a factor in short-term retention of a simple motor response. *Journal of Experimental Psychology, 81,* 523–526.

Stewart, J. E., Dohme, J. A., & Nullmeyer, R. T. (2002). U.S. Army initial entry rotary-wing transfer of training research. *International Journal of Aviation Psychology, 12,* 359–375.

Strayer, D. L., & Johnston, W. A. (2001). Driven to distraction: Dual-task studies of simulated driving and conversing on a cellular telephone. *Psychological Science, 12,* 462–466

Summers, J. J. (1975). The role of timing in motor program representation. *Journal of Motor Behavior, 7,* 229–242.

Swinnen, S. P., (1990). Interpolated activities during the knowledge of results delay and postknowledge of results interval: Effects of performance and learning. *Journal of Experimental Psychology: Learning, Memory, and Cognition, 16,* 692–705.

Swinnen, S. P., Schmidt, R. A., Nicholson, D. E., & Shapiro, D. C. (1990). Information feedback for skill acquisition: Instantaneous knowledge of results degrades learning. *Journal of Experimental Psychology: Learning, Memory, and Cognition, 16,* 706–716.

Swinnen, S. P., Walter, C. B., Lee, T. D., & Serrien, D. J. (1993). Acquiring bimanual skills: Contrasting forms of information feedback for interlimb decoupling. *Journal of Experimental Psychology: Learning, Memory, and Cognition, 19,* 1321–1344.

Taub, E., & Berman, A. J. (1963). Avoidance conditioning in the absence of relevant proprioceptive and exteroceptive feedback. *Journal of Comparative and Physiological Psychology, 56,* 1012–1016.

Taub, E., & Berman, A. J. (1968). Movement and learning in the absence of sensory feedback. In S. J. Freedman (Ed.), *The neuropsychology of spatially oriented behavior* (pp. 173–192). Homewood, IL: Dorsey Press.

Teichner, W. H. (1954). Recent studies of simple reaction time. *Psychological Bulletin, 51,* 128–149.

Thaut, M. H., McIntosh, G. C., Rice, R. R., Miller, R. A., Rathburn, J., & Brault, J. M. (1996). Rhythmic auditory stimulation in gait training for Parkinson's disease patients. *Movement Disorders, 11,* 193–200.

Thomas, J. R., & Halliwell, W. (1976). Individual differences in motor skill acquisition. *Journal of Motor Behavior, 8,* 89–100.

Thorndike, E. L. (1914). *Educational psychology: Briefer course.* New York: Columbia University Press.

Travlos, A. K. (1999). More practice does not necessarily enhance transfer of learning: Evidence and interpretations. *Perceptual and Motor Skills, 89,* 1161–1175.

Treisman, A. (1988). Features and objects: The fourteenth Bartlett Memorial Lecture. *Quarterly Journal of Experimental Psychology, 40A,* 201–237.

Treisman, A., & Gelade, G. (1980). A feature integration theory of attention. *Cognitive Psychology, 12,* 97–136.

Tremblay, L., & Proteau, L. (1998). Specificity of practice: The case of powerlifting. *Research Quarterly for Exercise and Sport, 69,* 284–289.

Trevarthen, C. B. (1968). Two mechanisms of vision in primates. *Psychological Research, 31,* 299–337.

Trinity, J., & Annesi, J. J. (1996, August). Coaching with video. *Strategies, 9,* 23–25.

Trowbridge, M. H., & Cason, H. (1932). An experimental study of Thorndike's theory of learning. *Journal of General Psychology, 7,* 245–258.

Trussell, E. (1965). Prediction of success in a motor skill on the basis of early learning achievement. *Research Quarterly, 36,* 342–347.

Tseng, M. H., & Chow, S. M. K. (2000). Perceptual-motor function of school-age children with slow handwriting speed. *American Journal of Occupational Therapy, 54,* 83–88.

Tsiglis, N., Zachopoulou, E., & Mavridis, T. (2001). Evaluation of the specificity of selected dynamic balance tests. *Perceptual and Motor Skills, 90,* 827–833.

Tulving, E. (1985). How many memory systems are there? *American Psychologist, 40,* 385–398.

Tulving, E., & Thomson, D. M. (1973). Encoding specificity and retrieval processes in episodic memory. *Psychological Review, 80,* 352–373.

Turvey, M. T. (1990). Coordination. *American Psychologist, 45,* 938–953.

Turvey, M. T., Holt, K. G., LaFiandra, M. E., & Fonseca, S. T. (1999). Can the transitions to and from running and the metabolic cost of running be determined from the kinetic energy of running? *Journal of Motor Behavior, 31,* 265–278.

Twitmeyer, E. M. (1931). Visual guidance in motor learning. *American Journal of Psychology, 43,* 165–187.

van Emmerik, R. E. A., & Wagenaar, R. C. (1996). Effect of walking velocity on relative phase dynamics in the trunk in human walking. *Journal of Biomechanics, 29,* 1175–1184.

Van Gyn, G. H., Wenger, H. A., & Gaul, C. A. (1990). Imagery as a method of enhancing transfer from training to performance. *Journal of Sport & Exercise Psychology, 12,* 366–375.

Vander Linden, D. W., Cauraugh, J. H., & Greene, T. A. (1993). The effect of frequency of kinetic feedback on learning an isometric force production task in nondisabled subjects. *Physical Therapy, 73,* 79–87.

van Rossum, J. H. A (1990). Schmidt's schema theory: The empirical base of the variability of practice hypothesis. *Human Movement Science, 9,* 387–435.

van Wieringen, P. C. W. (1996). Ecological and dynamical approaches to rehabilitation: An epilogue. *Human Movement Science, 15,* 315–323.

Vereijken, B., van Emmerik, R. E. A., Whiting, H. T. A., & Newell, K. M. (1992). Free(z)ing degrees of freedom in skill acquisition. *Journal of Motor Behavior, 24,* 133–142.

Vereijken, B., & Whiting, H. T. A. (1990). In defence of discovery learning. *Canadian Journal of Sport Science, 15,* 99–106.

Verschueren, S. M. P., Swinnen, S. P., Cordo, P. J., & Dounskaia, N. V. (1999a). Proprioceptive control of multijoint movement: Bimanual circle drawing. *Experimental Brain Research, 127,* 182–192.

Verschueren, S. M. P., Swinnen, S. P., Cordo, P. J., & Dounskaia, N. V. (1999b). Proprioceptive control of multijoint movement: Unimanual circle drawing. *Experimental Brain Research, 127,* 171–181.

Verschueren, S. M. P., Swinnen, S. P., Dom, R., & DeWeerdt, W. (1997). Interlimb coordination in patients with Parkinson's disease: Motor learning deficits and the importance of augmented information feedback. *Experimental Brain Research, 113,* 497–508.

Vickers, J. N. (1992). Gaze control in putting. *Perception, 21,* 117–132.

Vickers, J. N. (1996). Visual control when aiming at a far target. *Journal of Experimental Psychology: Human Perception and Performance, 22,* 342–354.

Vishton, P. M., & Cutting, J. E. (1995). Wayfinding, displacements, and mental maps: Velocity fields are not typically used to determine one's aimpoint. *Journal of Experimental Psychology: Human Perception and Performance, 21,* 978–995.

Vorro, J., Wilson, F. R., & Dainis, A. (1978). Multivariate analysis of biomechanical profiles for the coracobrachialis and biceps brachii (caput breve) muscles in humans. *Ergonomics, 21,* 407–418.

Wagenaar, R. C., & Beek, W. J. (1992). Hemiplegic gait: A kinematic analysis using walking speed as a basis. *Journal of Biomechanics, 25,* 1007–1015.

Wagenaar, R. C., & van Emmerik, R. E. A. (1994). Dynamics of pathological gait. *Human Movement Science, 13,* 441–471.

Wallace, S. A., & Hagler, R. W. (1979). Knowledge of performance and the learning of a closed motor skill. *Research Quarterly, 50,* 265–271.

Walter, C. B. (1998). An alternative view of dynamical systems concepts in motor control and learning. *Research Quarterly for Exercise and Sport, 69,* 326–333.

Walter, C. B., & Swinnen, S. P. (1992). Adaptive tuning of interlimb attraction to facilitate bimanual coupling. *Journal of Motor Behavior, 24,* 95–104.

Walter, C. B., & Swinnen, S. P. (1994). The formulation and dissolution of "bad habits" during the acquisition of coordination skills. In S. Swinnen, H. Heuer, J. Maisson, & P. Casaer (Eds.), *Interlimb coordination: Neural, dynamical, and cognitive constraints* (pp. 491–513). San Diego, CA: Academic Press.

Wann, J. P., & Nimmo-Smith, I. (1991). The control of pen pressure in handwriting: A subtle point. *Human Movement Science, 10,* 223–246.

Warren, W. H. (1984). Perceiving affordances: Visual guidance of stair climbing. *Journal of Experimental Psychology: Human Perception and Performance, 10,* 683–703.

Warren, W. H., & Whang, S. (1987). Visual guidance of walking through apertures: Body-scaled information for affordances. *Journal of Experimental Psychology: Human Perception and Performance, 13,* 371–383.

Warren, W. H., Jr., Young, D. S., & Lee, D. N. (1986). Visual control of step length during running over irregular terrain. *Journal of Experimental Psychology: Human Perception and Performance, 12,* 259–266.

Watters, R. G. (1992). Retention of human sequenced behavior following forward chaining, backward chaining, and whole task training procedures. *Journal of Human Movement Studies, 22,* 117–129.

Weeks, D. J., & Proctor, R. W. (1990). Salient-features coding in the translation between orthogonal stimulus and response dimensions. *Journal of Experimental Psychology: General, 119,* 355–366.

Weeks, D. L., & Kordus, R. N. (1998). Relative frequency of knowledge of performance and motor skill learning. *Research Quarterly for Exercise and Sport, 68,* 224–230.

Weeks, D. L., & Sherwood, D. E. (1994). A comparison of knowledge of results scheduling methods for promoting motor skill acquisition and retention. *Research Quarterly for Exercise and Sport, 65,* 136–142.

Weeks, D. L., & Wallace, S. A. (1992). Premovement posture and focal movement velocity effects on postural responses accompanying rapid arm movement. *Human Movement Science, 11,* 717–734.

Weinberg, D. R., Guy, D. E., & Tupper, R. W. (1964). Variations of post-feedback interval in simple motor learning. *Journal of Experimental Psychology, 67,* 98–99.

Weir, P. L., & Leavitt, J. L. (1990). The effects of model's skill level and model's knowledge of results on the acquisition of an aiming task. *Human Movement Science, 9,* 369–383.

Welford, A. T. (1952). The psychological refractory period and the timing of high-speed performance—A review and a theory. *British Journal of Psychology, 43,* 2–19.

Welford, A. T. (1967). Single channel operations in the brain. *Acta Psychologica, 27,* 5–22.

Whiting, H. T. A. (Ed.). (1984). *Human movement actions: Bernstein reassessed.* Amsterdam: North-Holland.

Whiting, H. T. A. (1988). Imitation and the learning of complex cyclical actions. In O. G. Meijer & K. Roth (Eds.), *Complex motor behaviour: "The" motor-action controversy* (pp. 381–401). Amsterdam: North-Holland.

Whiting, H. T. A., Gill, E. B., & Stephenson, J. M. (1970). Critical time intervals for taking in-flight information in a ball-catching task. *Ergonomics, 13,* 265–272.

Wickens, C. D. (1980). The structure of processing resources. In R. Nickerson (Ed.), *Attention and performance VII* (pp. 239–257). Hillsdale, NJ: Erlbaum.

Wickens, C. D. (1992). *Engineering psychology and human performance* (2nd ed.). New York: HarperCollins.

Wickstrom, R. L. (1958). Comparative study of methodologies for teaching gymnastics and tumbling stunts. *Research Quarterly, 29,* 109–115.

Wiese-Bjornstal, D. M., & Weiss, M. R. (1992). Modeling effects on children's form kinematics, performance outcome, and cognitive recognition of a sport skill. *Research Quarterly for Exercise and Sport, 63,* 67–75.

Wightman, D. C., & Lintern, G. (1985). Part-task training strategies for tracking and manual control. *Human Factors, 27,* 267–283.

Wilberg, R. B., & Salmela, J. (1973). Information load and response consistency in sequential short-term memory. *Perceptual and Motor Skills, 37,* 23–29.

Williams, A. M., Davids, K., Burwitz, L., & Williams, J. G. (1994). Visual search strategies in experienced and inexperienced soccer players. *Research Quarterly for Exercise and Sport, 65,* 127–135.

Williams, J. G. (1988). Perception of a throwing action from point-light demonstrations. *Perceptual and Motor Skills, 67,* 273–274.

Williams, J. G., &. McCririe, N. (1988). Control of arm and fingers during ball catching. *Journal of Human Movement Studies, 14,* 241–247.

Wilson, P. N., Foreman, N., & Tlauka, M. (1997). Transfer of spatial information from a virtual to a real environment. *Human Factors, 39,* 526–531.

Winstein, C. J., Pohl, P. S., Cardinale, C., Green, A., Scholtz, L., Waters, C. S. (1996). Learning a partial-weight-bearing skill: Effectiveness of two forms of feedback. *Physical Therapy, 76,* 985–993.

Winstein, C. J., & Schmidt, R. A. (1990). Reduced frequency of knowledge of results enhances motor skill learning. *Journal of Experimental Psychology: Learning, Memory, and Cognition, 16,* 677–691.

Winther, K. T., & Thomas, J. R. (1981). Developmental differences in children's labeling of movement. *Journal of Motor Behavior, 13,* 77–90.

Wood, C. A., Gallagher, J. D., Martino, P. V., & Ross, M. (1992). Alternate forms of knowledge of results: Interaction of augmented feedback modality on learning. *Journal of Human Movement Studies, 22,* 213–230.

Wood, C. A., & Ging, C. A. (1991). The role of interference and task similarity on the acquisition, retention, and transfer of simple motor skills. *Research Quarterly for Exercise and Sport, 62,* 18–26.

Wood, J. M., & Abernethy, B. (1997). As assessment of the efficacy of sports vision training programs. *Optometry and Vision Science, 74,* 646–659.

Woodworth, R. S. (1899). The accuracy of voluntary movement. *Psychological Review Monographs, 3* (Whole No. 302).

Wright, C. E. (1990). Generalized motor programs: Reexamining claims of effector independence in writing. In M. Jeannerod (Ed.). *Attention and Performance XII: Motor Representation and Control* (pp. 294–320). Hillsdale, NJ: Erlbaum.

Wright, D. L., & Shea, C. H. (1994). Cognition and motor acquisition: Contextual dependencies. In C. R. Reynolds (Ed.), *Cognitive assessment: A multidisciplinary perspective* (pp. 89–106). New York: Plenum.

Wright, D. L., Snowden, S., & Willoughby, D. (1990). Summary KR: How much information is used from the summary? *Journal of Human Movement Studies, 19,* 119–128.

Wrisberg, C. A., & Liu, Z. (1991). The effect of contextual variety on the practice, retention, and transfer of an applied motor skill. *Research Quarterly for Exercise and Sport, 62,* 406–412.

Wrisberg, C. A., & Pein, R. L. (1992). The preshot interval and free-throw shooting accuracy: An exploratory investigation. *The Sport Psychologist, 6,* 14–23.

Wu, C., Trombly, C. A., Lin, K., & Tickle-Degnen, L. (1998). Effects of object affordances on reaching performance in persons with and without cerebrovascular accident. *American Journal of Occupational Therapy, 52,* 447–456.

Wulf, G., Lauterbach, B., & Toole, T. (1999). The learning advantages of an external focus of attention in golf. *Research Quarterly for Exercise and Sport, 70,* 120–126.

Wulf, G., & Lee, T. D. (1993). Contextual interference in movements of the same class: Differential effects on program and parameter learning. *Journal of Motor Behavior, 25,* 254–263.

Wulf, G., McNevin, N., & Shea, C. H. (2001). The automaticity of complex motor skill learning as a function of attentional focus. *Quarterly Journal of Experimental Psychology, 54A,* 1143–1154.

Wulf, G., & Prinz, W. (2001). Directing attention to movement effects enhances learning: A review. *Psychonomic Bulletin & Review, 8,* 648–660.

Wulf, G., & Schmidt, R. A. (1996). Average KR degrades parameter learning. *Journal of Motor Behavior, 28,* 371–381.

Wulf, G., Shea, C. H., & Whitacre, C. A. (1998). Physical guidance benefits in learning a complex motor skill. *Journal of Motor Behavior, 30,* 367–380.

Wulf, G., & Toole, T. (1999). Physical assistance devices in complex motor skill learning: Benefits of a self-controlled practice schedule. *Research Quarterly for Exercise and Sport, 70,* 265–272.

Wuyts, I. J., & Buekers, M. J. (1995). The effects of visual and auditory models on the learning of a rhythmical synchronization dance skill. *Research Quarterly for Exercise and Sport, 66,* 105–115.

Yao, W. X., & Fischman, M. G. (1999). Kinematic characteristics of aiming movements as a function of temporal and spatial constraints. *Motor Control, 3,* 424–435.

Yao, W. X., Fischman, M. G., & Wang, Y. T. (1994). Motor skill acquisition and retention as a function of average feedback, summary feedback, and performance variability. *Journal of Motor Behavior, 26,* 273–282.

Young, D. E., & Schmidt, R. A. (1992). Augmented kinematic feedback for motor learning. *Journal of Motor Behavior, 24,* 261–273.

Zanone, P. G., & Kelso, J. A. S. (1994). The coordination dynamics of learning: Theoretical structure and experimental agenda. In S. Swinnen, H. Heuer, J. Massion, & P. Casaer (Eds.), *Interlimb coordination: Neural, dynamical, and cognitive constraints* (pp. 461–490). San Diego: Academic Press.

Zelaznik, H. N., & Franz, E. (1990). Stimulus-response compatibility and the programming of motor activity: Pitfalls and possible new directions. In R. Proctor & T. G. Reeve (Eds.), *Stimulus-response compatibility: An integrated perspective* (pp. 279–295). Amsterdam: North-Holland.

Zelaznik, H. N., Hawkins, B., & Kisselburgh, L. (1983). Rapid visual feedback processing in single-aiming movements. *Journal of Motor Behavior, 15,* 217–236.

Zelaznik, H. N., Spencer, R. M., & Doffin, J. G. (2000). Temporal precision in tapping and circle drawing movements at preferred rates is not correlated: Further evidence against timing as a general-purpose ability. *Journal of Motor Behavior, 32,* 193–199.

Zelinsky, G. J., Rao, R. P. N., Hayhoe, M. M., & Ballard, D. H. (1997). Eye movements reveal the spatiotemporal dynamics of visual search. *Psychological Science, 8,* 448–453.

Zetou, E., Tzetzis, G., Vernadakis, N, & Kioumourtzoglou, E. (2002). Modeling in learning two volleyball skills. *Perceptual and Motor Skills, 94,* 1131–1142.

Zubiaur, M., Oña, A., & Delgado, J. (1999). Learning volleyball serves: A preliminary study of the effects of knowledge of performance and results, *Perceptual and Motor Skills, 89,* 223–232.

GLOSSARY

Ability   A general trait or capacity of an individual that is a determinant of a person's achievement potential for the performance of specific skills.

Absolute error (AE)   The unsigned deviation from the target or criterion, representing amount of error. A measure of the magnitude of an error without regard to the direction of the deviation.

Action   A goal-directed activity that consists of body and/or limb movements.

Action effect hypothesis   The proposition that actions are best planned and controlled by their intended effects. When related to attention focus, this hypothesis proposes that the learning and performance of skills are optimized when the performer's attention is directed to the intended outcome of the action rather than on the movements themselves.

Action preparation   The activity that occurs between the intention to perform and the initiation of an action. Sometimes, the term *motor programming* is used to refer to this activity.

Arousal   The general state of excitability of a person, involving physiological, emotional, and mental systems.

Associative stage   The second stage of learning in the Fitts and Posner model. An intermediate stage on the learning stages continuum.

Asymmetric transfer   Bilateral transfer in which there is a greater amount of transfer from one limb than from the other limb.

Attention   In human performance, conscious or nonconscious engagement in perceptual, cognitive, and/or motor activities before, during, and after performing skills. The human information-processing system includes limitations to the number of these activities that can be performed simultaneously.

Attentional focus   The directing of attention to specific characteristics in a performance environment, or to action preparation activities.

Attractors   The stable behavioral steady states of systems. In terms of human coordinated movement, attractors characterize preferred behavioral states, such as the in-phase and out-of-phase states for rhythmic bimanual finger movements.

Augmented feedback   A generic term used to describe information about performing a skill that is added to sensory feedback and comes from a source external to the person performing the skill. It is sometimes referred to as extrinsic or external feedback.

Automaticity   The term used to indicate that a person performs a skill, or engages in certain information-processing activities, without requiring attention resources.

Autonomous stage   The third stage of learning in the Fitts and Posner model. The final stage on the learning continuum. Also called the *automatic stage*.

■

Bilateral transfer   Transfer of learning that occurs between two limbs.

Bimanual coordination   A motor skill that requires the simultaneous use of the two arms. The skill may require the two arms to move with the same or different spatial and/or temporal characteristics.

Biofeedback   A type of augmented feedback that provides information about physiological processes through the use of instrumentation (e.g., EMG biofeedback).

■

Central-resource theories   Attention-capacity theories that propose one central source of attention resources for which all activities requiring attention compete.

Choice RT   The reaction time when the situation involves more than one signal and each signal requires its own specified response.

Closed-loop control system   A system of control in which during the course of an action, feedback is compared against a standard or reference to enable an action to be carried out as planned.

Closed motor skill   A motor skill performed in a stable or predictable environment where the performer determines when to begin the action.

Cognitive mediation theory   A theory for explaining the benefit of a demonstration proposing that when a person observes a skilled model, the person translates the observed movement information into a cognitive code that the person stores in memory and uses when the observer performs the skill.

Cognitive stage   The first stage of learning in the Fitts and Posner model. The beginning or initial stage on the learning continuum.

Complexity   The number of parts or components and the amount of information-processing demands that characterize a skill. More complex skills have more component parts and involve more information processing demands than less complex skills.

Concurrent augmented feedback   Augmented feedback that is provided while a person is performing a skill or making a movement.

Constant error(CE)   The signed (+/−) deviation from the target or criterion. It represents amount and direction of error and serves as a measure of performance bias.

Contextual interference   The interference that results from performing variations of a skill within the context of practice.

Contextual interference effect   The learning benefit resulting from performing multiple skills in a high contextual interference practice schedule (e.g., random practice), rather than practicing the skills in a low contextual interference schedule (e.g., blocked practice).

Continuous motor skill   A motor skill with arbitrary beginning and end points. These skills usually involve repetitive movements.

Control parameters   Coordinated movement control variables (e.g., tempo, or speed, and force) that freely change according to the characteristics of an action situation. According to the dynamic pattern view of motor control, when a control parameter is systematically varied (e.g., speed is increased from slow to fast), an order parameter may remain stable or change its stable state characteristic at a certain level of change of the control parameter.

Coordination   The patterning of body and limb motions relative to the patterning of environmental objects and events.

Coordinative structures   Functionally specific collectives of muscles and joints that are constrained by the nervous system to act cooperatively to produce an action.

Cost-benefit trade-off   The cost (in terms of slower RT) and benefit (in terms of faster RT) that occur as a result of biasing the preparation of an action in favor of one of several possible actions (as opposed to preparing as if each possible action were equally probable).

■

Deafferentation   A procedure that researchers use to make proprioceptive feedback unavailable (through surgically severing or removing afferent neural pathways involved in the movement). It also can result from injury or surgery to afferent neural pathways involved in proprioception.

Declarative knowledge   Knowledge about "what to do" in a situation; this knowledge typically is verbalizable.

Degrees of freedom   The number of independent elements or components in a control system and the number of ways each component can act.

Degrees of freedom problem   A control problem that occurs in the designing of a complex system that must produce a specific result. The design problem involves determining how to constrain the system's many degrees of freedom so that it can produce the specific result.

Descriptive KP   A verbal knowledge of performance (KP) statement that only describes the error a person has made during the performance of a skill.

Discrete motor skill   A motor skill with clearly defined beginning and end points, usually requiring a simple movement.

Discrimination RT   The reaction time when the situation involves more than one signal but only one response, which is to only one of the signals; the other signals require no response.

Distributed practice   A practice schedule in which the amount of rest between practice sessions or trials is relatively long.

Dual-task procedure   An experimental procedure used in the study of attention to determine the amount of attention required to perform an action, or a part of an action. The procedure involves assessing the degree of interference caused by one task when a person is simultaneously performing another task.

Dynamic pattern theory   An approach to describing and explaining the control of coordinated movement that emphasizes the role of information in the environment and the dynamic properties of the body and limbs. It is also known as the dynamical systems theory.

Dynamic view of modeling   A theoretical view explaining the benefit of observing a skilled model demonstrate a skill. It proposes that the visual system is capable of automatically processing the observed movement in a way that constrains the motor control system to act accordingly, so that the person does not need to engage in cognitive mediation.

■

Encoding   A memory process involving the transformation of information to be remembered into a form that can be stored in memory.

Encoding specificity principle   A memory principle that indicates the close relationship between encoding and retrieval memory processes. It states that memory test performance is directly related to the amount of similarity between the practice and the test contexts, i.e., the more similarity, the better the test performance will be.

■

Feedback   Information from the sensory system that indicates the status of a movement to the central nervous system. In a closed-loop system, feedback is used to make corrections to an ongoing movement.

Fine motor skill   A motor skill that requires control of small muscles to achieve the goal of the skill; typically involves eye-hand coordination and requires a high degree of precision of hand and finger movement.

Fitts' law   A human performance law specifying the movement time for an aiming action when the distance to move and the target size are known. It is quantified as $MT = a + b \log_2(2 \, D/W)$, where a and b are constants and W = target width, and D = distance from the starting point to the target.

Fixation/diversification   The learner's goals in the second stage of learning in Gentile's model. *Fixation* refers to the goal for learning closed skills in which learners refine movement patterns so that they can produce them correctly, consistently, and efficiently from trial to trial. *Diversification* refers to the goal for learning open skills in which learners acquire the capability to modify the movement pattern according to environmental context characteristics.

Foreperiod   In a reaction time paradigm, the time interval between a warning signal and the go signal, or stimulus.

Fractionization   A part-task training method related to asymmetric coordination skills that involves practicing each arm or leg separately before performing with them together.

Freezing the degrees of freedom   A common initial strategy of beginning learners to control the many degrees of freedom associated with the coordination demands of a motor skill (e.g., the person holds some arm joints rigid, i.e., "freezes" them, while performing the skill).

■

General motor ability hypothesis   A hypothesis that maintains that the many different motor abilities that exist in an individual are highly related and can be characterized in terms of a singular, global motor ability.

Generalized motor program   The general memory representation of a class of actions that share common invariant characteristics. It provides the basis for controlling a specific action within the class of actions.

Gross motor skill   A motor skill that requires the use of large musculature to achieve the goal of the skill.

Guidance hypothesis   A hypothesis indicating that the role of augmented feedback in learning is to guide performance to be correct during practice. However, if it is provided too frequently, it can cause the learner to develop a dependency on its availability and therefore to perform poorly when it is not available.

■

Hick's law   A law of human performance stating that RT will increase logarithmically as the number of stimulus-response choices increases.

■

Identical elements theory   An explanation of positive transfer proposing that transfer is due to the degree of similarity between the component parts or characteristics of two skills or two performance contexts.

Imagery ability   An individual-difference characteristic that differentiates people who can image an action with a high degree of vividness and control from people who have difficulty imaging an action.

Index of difficulty (ID)   According to Fitts' law, a quantitative measure of the difficulty of performing a skill involving both speed and accuracy requirements. It is calculated as the $\log_2 (2\,D/W)$, where W = target width, and D = distance from the starting point to the target.

Intertrial variability   An environmental context characteristic in Gentile's taxonomy of motor skills. The term refers to whether the regulatory conditions that exist for the performance of a skill in one situation or for one trial are present or absent in the next situation or trial.

Invariant features   A unique set of characteristics that defines a generalized motor program and does not vary from one performance of the action to another.

■

Knowledge of performance (KP)   A category of augmented feedback that gives information about the movement characteristics that led to a performance outcome.

Knowledge of results (KR)   A category of augmented feedback that gives information about the outcome of performing a skill or about achieving the goal of the performance.

KR-delay interval   The interval of time between the completion of a movement and the presentation of augmented feedback.

■

Learning   A change in the capability of a person to perform a skill. It must be inferred from a relatively permanent improvement in performance as a result of practice or experience.

Long-term memory   A component of the structure of memory that serves as a relatively permanent storage repository for information.

■

Massed practice   A practice schedule in which the amount of rest between practice sessions or trials is very short.

Mental practice   The cognitive rehearsal of a physical skill in the absence of overt physical movements; it can take the form of thinking about the cognitive or procedural aspects of a motor skill, or of engaging in visual or kinesthetic imagery of the performance of a skill or part of a skill.

Modeling   The use of demonstration as a means of conveying information about how to perform a skill.

Motor ability   An ability that is specifically related to the performance of a motor skill.

Motor equivalence   The capability of the motor control system to enable a person to achieve an action goal in a variety of situations and conditions (e.g., writing your signature with either hand).

Motor program   A memory representation that stores information needed to perform an action.

Motor skill A skill that requires voluntary body and/or limb movement to achieve its goal.

Movements Behavioral characteristics of specific limbs or a combination of limbs that are component parts of an action or motor skill.

Movement time (MT) The interval of time between the initiation of a movement and the completion of the movement.

Multiple-resource theories Theories of attention proposing that there are several attention resource mechanisms, each of which is related to a specific information-processing activity, and is limited in how much information it can process simultaneously.

■

Negative transfer The negative effect of prior experience on performance of a skill, so a person performs the skill less well than he or she would have without prior experience.

Nonlinear behavior A behavior that changes in abrupt, nonlinear ways in response to systematic linear increases in the value of a specific variable (e.g., the change from smooth to turbulent water flow in a tube at a specific increase in water velocity; the change from a walking to a running gait at a specific increase in gait velocity).

Nonregulatory conditions Characteristics of the performance environment that do *not* influence the movement characteristics required to achieve an action goal.

■

Observational learning Learning a skill by observing a person performing the skill. Also known as *modeling.*

Open-loop control system A control system in which all the information needed to initiate and carry out an action as planned is contained in the initial instructions to the effectors.

Open motor skill A motor skill that involves a nonstable unpredictable environment where an object or environmental context is in motion and determines when to begin the action.

Optical flow The patterns of rays of light that strike the retina of the eye that emanate from and are specific to objects and features in the environment.

Order parameters Functionally specific variables that define the overall behavior of a system. They enable a coordinated pattern of movement to be reproduced and distinguished from other patterns (e.g., relative phase). Known also as collective variables.

Organization When applied to a complex motor skill, the relationships among the components of the skill.

Overlearning Practice that continues beyond the amount needed to achieve a certain performance criterion.

■

Parameters Features of the generalized motor program that can be varied from one performance of a skill to another. The features of a skill that must be added to the invariant features of a generalized motor program before a person can perform a skill to meet the specific demands of a situation.

Perception-action coupling The interaction between perceptual and movement variables that results in specific movement dynamics of an action in accordance with specific characteristics of the perceptual variable (e.g., the stride-length adjustments of long jumpers during the end of the run-up according to the time to contact with the take-off board, which is specified by the perceptual variable *tau;* the specific kinematic characteristics of a reach-and-grasp action associated with specific object characteristics).

Performance The behavioral act of executing a skill at a specific time and in a specific situation.

Performance bandwidth In the context of providing augmented feedback, a range of acceptable performance error. Augmented feedback is given only when the amount of error is greater than this tolerance limit.

Performance curve A line graph describing performance in which the level of achievement of a performance measure is plotted for a specific sequence of time (e.g., sec, min, days) or trials. The units of the performance measure are on the Y-axis (vertical axis) and the time units or trials are on the X-axis (horizontal axis).

Performance outcome measures A category of motor skill performance measures that indicate the outcome or result of performing a motor skill (e.g., how far a person walked, how fast a person ran a certain distance, or how many degrees a person flexed a knee).

Performance plateau While learning a skill, a period of time in which the learner experiences no improvement after having experienced consistent improvement. Typically, the learner then experiences further improvement with continued practice.

Performance production measures A category of motor skill performance measures that indicate the performance of specific aspects of the motor control system during the performance of an action (e.g., limb kinematics, force, EEG, EMG, etc.).

Point-light technique A research procedure used to determine the relative information people use to perceive and identify coordinated human actions. It involves placing LEDs or light-reflecting material on certain joints of a person, then filming or videotaping the person performing an action. When an observer views the film or video, he or she sees only the joints in action.

Positive transfer The beneficial effect of previous experience on the learning or performance of a new skill, or on the performance of a skill in a new context.

Post-KR interval The interval of time between the presentation of augmented feedback and the beginning of the next trial.

Power law of practice A mathematical law describing the change in rate of performance improvement during skill learning. Large amounts of improvement occur during early practice, but smaller improvement rates characterize further practice.

Practice variability The variety of movement and context characteristics a person experiences while practicing a skill.

Prehension The action of reaching for and grasping an object that may be stationary or moving.

Prescriptive KP A verbal knowledge of performance (KP) statement that describes errors made during the performance of a skill and states (i.e., prescribes) what needs to be done to correct them.

Proactive interference A cause of forgetting due to activity that occurs prior to the presentation of information to be remembered.

Procedural knowledge Knowledge that enables a person to know "how to do" a skill; this knowledge typically is difficult to verbalize, or is not verbalizable.

Proprioception The perception of limb, body, and head movement characteristics. Afferent neural pathways send to the central nervous system proprioceptive information about characteristics such as limb movement direction, location in space, and velocity.

Psychological refractory period (PRP) A delay period during which a person seems to put planned action "on hold" while executing a previously initiated action.

■

Qualitative augmented feedback Augmented feedback that is descriptive in nature (e.g., using such terms as *good, long*), and indicates the quality of performance.

Quantitative augmented feedback Augmented feedback that includes a numeric value related to the magnitude of a performance characteristic (e.g., the speed of a pitched baseball).

■

Reaction time (RT) The interval of time between the onset of a signal (stimulus) and the initiation of a response.

Recall test An explicit memory test that requires a person to produce a required response with few, if any, available cues or aids.

Recognition test An explicit memory test that requires a person to select a correct response from several alternative responses.

Regulatory conditions Characteristics of the environmental context that determine (i.e., "regulate") the required movement characteristics needed to perform an action.

Relative time The proportion of the total amount of time required by each of the various components of a skill during the performance of that skill.

Response time The time interval involving both reaction time and movement time; that is, the time from the onset of a signal (stimulus) to the completion of a response.

Retention test A test of a practiced skill that a learner performs following an interval of time after practice has ceased.

Retrieval A memory process involving the search through long-term memory for information needed to perform the task at hand.

Retroactive interference A cause of forgetting due to activity occurring during the retention interval.

Root-mean-squared error (RMSE)   An error measure used for continuous skills to indicate the amount of error between the performance curve produced and the criterion performance curve for a specific amount of time during which performance is sampled.

■

Schema   A rule or set of rules that serves to provide the basis for a decision. In Schmidt's schema theory, an abstract representation of rules governing movement.

Segmentation   A part-task training method that involves separating the skill into parts and then practicing the parts so that after one part is practiced, it is then practiced together with the next part, and so on. Also known as the progressive part method.

Self-organization   The emergence of a specific stable pattern of behavior due to certain conditions characterizing a situation rather than to a specific control mechanism organizing the behavior; e.g., in the physical world hurricanes self-organize when certain wind and water temperature conditions exist.

Serial motor skill   A motor skill involving a series of discrete skills.

Simple RT   The reaction time when the situation involves only one signal (stimulus) that requires only one response.

Simplification   A part-task training method that involves reducing the difficulty of specific parts or features of a skill.

Skill   (a) An action or task that has a specific goal to achieve. (b) An indicator of quality of performance.

Specificity of motor abilities hypothesis   A hypothesis that maintains that the many motor abilities in an individual are relatively independent.

Speed-accuracy trade-off   A characteristic of motor skill performance in which the speed at which a skill is performed is influenced by movement accuracy demands. The trade-off is that increasing speed yields decreasing accuracy, and vice versa.

Stability   A behavioral steady state of a system that represents a preferred behavioral state and incorporates the notion of invariance by noting that a stable system will spontaneously return to a stable state after it is slightly perturbed.

Stimulus-response compatibility   A characteristic of the spatial arrangement relationship between a stimulus and a response. This relationship will influence the amount of preparation time in a reaction time task involving stimulus and response choices.

Superdiagonal form   A term describing the way the trial-to-trial correlations appear in a correlation matrix where all trials are correlated with each other. Trials that are closer to each other have scores more highly correlated. The correlation decreases as trials become farther apart.

Symmetric transfer   Bilateral transfer in which the amount of transfer is similar from one limb to another, no matter which limb is used first.

■

Task-intrinsic feedback   The sensory feedback that is naturally available while performing a skill.

Taxonomy   A classification system organized according to relationships among the component characteristics of the group of items or objects being classified.

Terminal augmented feedback   Augmented feedback that is provided after a person has completed the performance of a skill or the making of a movement.

Transfer-appropriate processing theory   An explanation of positive transfer proposing that transfer is due to the similarity in the cognitive processing characteristics required by the two skills or two performance situations.

Transfer of learning   The influence of having previously practiced or performed a skill or skills on the learning of a new skill.

Transfer test   A test in which a person performs a skill that is different from the skill that he or she practiced, or performs the practiced skill in a context or situation different from the practice context or situation.

■

Variable error (VE)   An error score representing the variability (or conversely, the consistency) of performance.

Verbal cues   Short, concise phrases that direct a performer's attention to important environmental regulatory characteristics or that prompt the person to perform key movement components of skills.

Vigilance   Maintaining attention in a performance situation in which stimuli requiring a response occur infrequently.

Visual search The process of directing visual attention to locate relevant information in the environment that will enable a person to determine how to perform a skill in a specific situation.

Visual selective attention The process of engaging vision in directing attention to specific environmental information (i.e., cues) that influence the preparation and/or performance of an action. It is selective because the specific cues attended to must be chosen from among other possible cues in the performance environment. The selective attention process may be active or passive.

■

Working memory A functional component of the structure of memory that operates to temporarily store and use recently presented information; it also serves as a temporary work space to integrate recently presented information with information retrieved from long-term memory to carry out problem-solving, decision-making, and action-preparation activities.

NAME INDEX

SUBJECT INDEX